Spring in Practice

Spring in Practice

WILLIE WHEELER
with JOSHUA WHITE

MANNING
Shelter Island

For online information and ordering of this and other Manning books, please visit
www.manning.com. The publisher offers discounts on this book when ordered in quantity.
For more information, please contact

Special Sales Department
Manning Publications Co.
20 Baldwin Road
PO Box 261
Shelter Island, NY 11964
Email: orders@manning.com

Manning Publications Co.　　　　Development editor:　Cynthia Kane
20 Baldwin Road　　　　　　　　Technical editor:　Doug Warren
PO Box 261　　　　　　　　　　　Copyeditor:　Tiffany Taylor
Shelter Island, NY 11964　　　　　Proofreader:　Elizabeth Martin
　　　　　　　　　　　　　　　　　Typesetter:　Gordan Salinovic
　　　　　　　　　　　　　　Cover designer:　Marija Tudor

ISBN 9781935182054
Printed in the United States of America
2 3 4 5 6 7 8 9 10 – MAL – 18 17 16 15 14 13

brief contents

v

contents

preface

I started using Spring in 2004 after having used Enterprise JavaBeans 2 (EJB) for a couple of years. Unlike many who made the jump in those early days, I don't have any EJB horror stories to recount. My EJB project was too small to have had any serious technology issues—pretty much any technology would have worked. Although I never fell in love with EJB, my team was able to make it work, so we didn't have any major complaints.

In 2004 I took a job with a new employer where everybody was using Spring. It was immediately clear to me that Spring's POJO- and injection-based approach was simpler to use than EJB and that it resulted in cleaner code. Moreover, our Spring apps were supporting thousands of concurrent users without issue. Contrary to the orthodoxy of the day, Spring was certainly ready to take on enterprise demands without EJBs and heavyweight app servers.

My teams and I built a number of Spring apps. Even as a manager, I did quite a bit of hands-on development, and that's how I learned the framework. After a while, though, my management responsibilities made it harder to do as much development as I wanted to do. I started blogging about Spring (springinpractice.com) to maintain and expand my knowledge of the framework. Eventually, Manning came across my blog and asked me to write this book.

Nowadays I again do hands-on development, and to this day I use Spring for almost all of my Java development. It's a fantastic framework that makes development enjoyable and productive.

WILLIE WHEELER

Early in my career, I worked on several large enterprise projects that used EJB 1.0. It quickly became evident to me that enterprise Java development was painful. Solutions were often complex, tedious, time-consuming, and error-prone. By the time Rod Johnson's book *Expert One-on-One J2EE Design and Development* came out in 2002, I was more than ready for a change. The ideas that Rod expressed in his book, and later incorporated into the Spring Framework, struck a chord not only with me but with the Java development community at large. Because the framework handled the infrastructure code for me, my code was cleaner, simpler, and less error-prone. It became clear that with Spring, I was more productive and enjoying development again. I have been an evangelist of the Spring Framework ever since.

As Spring grew, my thirst for knowledge about the framework, its surrounding technologies, and its ecosystem grew as well. Over the years, I had become an avid technical reader and soon found myself reviewing and providing technical input for other authors' books. It wasn't until Manning provided me with the opportunity to team up with Willie and coauthor this book that I was able to experience being on the other side of the fence.

JOSHUA WHITE

acknowledgments

Willie here. As a longtime acknowledgments reader, I'm familiar with the typical expressions of gratitude aimed toward one's significant other, children, and other inconvenienced parties. But sitting now in the writer's seat, I more fully appreciate how inadequate even the more vigorous of these expressions are.

I owe my first and largest debt to my wife, Raylene, who supported my efforts far beyond what was fair to ask or expect. Personal shame prevents me from describing the many sacrifices she made on my behalf, but, suffice it to say that she's eagerly looking forward to receiving her copy of the book so she can set it aflame. Thank you, Raylene, for making this book possible—your name belongs on the cover of this book every bit as much as mine does.

Next, I thank our children, Max, Jude, Lucy, and Ben, two of whom have never known life without "the book." They, like their mom, have been nothing but patient and supportive during the entire process, and I am deeply grateful.

Thanks to my in-laws, Ray, Jane, Renee, Rana, and Raymond, for making their home available to my family for many weekend getaways.

And, of course, big thanks to my coauthor, Josh, for helping get the book across the finish line.

Both Josh and I would like to thank the team at Manning: Marjan Bace, Cynthia Kane, Elizabeth Martin, Mary Piergies, Maureen Spencer, Tiffany Taylor, and Megan Yockey. A special and heartfelt thanks to our development editor, Cynthia Kane. Besides providing outstanding support on the editorial side, Cynthia was a driving force in seeing this project through to its successful completion. Thank you, Cynthia, for your expertise, patience, and support.

Thanks are due both to the technical reviewers and to the MEAP customers for their invaluable questions and feedback during the development process. Their efforts have made this a much better book. We would especially like to acknowedge Al Scherer, Brian O'Shea, Carol McDonald, Craig Walls, Daniel Alford, Deepak Vohra, Dmitry Sklyut, Erwin Vervaet, George Franciscus, Gordon Dickens, Jeremy Flowers, Jeroen Nouws, John Guthrie, John Ryan, John Tyler, Kenneth Kousen, Kenrick Chien, Mario Arias, Patrick Steger, Prasad A Chodavarapu, Rama Kanneganti, Ricardo Lima, Rizwan Lodhi, Robby O'Connor, Robert Casazza, Robert Hanson, Ryan Stephens, Srikanth Balusani, and Willem Jiang.

And, finally, a special thanks to our technical editor, Doug Warren, whose tireless efforts and attention to detail resulted in many improvements throughout the book. We could not have done it without you!

about Spring

Spring was originally conceived as a way to simplify Java Enterprise Edition (JEE) development, but it's not exactly a simple framework. It's huge. The core framework is large, and dozens of portfolio projects extend that core, covering things like security, web flow, SOAP web services (REST web services are part of the core), enterprise integration, batch processing, mobile, various flavors of social (Facebook, LinkedIn, Twitter, GitHub, and so on), various flavors of NoSQL (MongoDB, Neo4j, Riak, and so on), BlazeDS/Flex, AMQP/Rabbit, and many more. If "simple" means something with few parts, then Spring isn't simple.

Yet Spring does simplify Java development. As a general rule, it does so by isolating infrastructural concerns (such as persistence management and transaction management) from domain concerns. The framework handles the former so app developers can focus on the latter. In this respect, Spring is like JEE and even its earlier J2EE incarnation. Spring's approach—based on POJOs, dependency injection, and support for a wide variety of third-party libraries—proved to be more effective than J2EE with EJB. JEE closed the gap by adopting key elements of that approach.

That Spring simplifies development without itself being simple isn't paradoxical. Tools that simplify work don't themselves have to be simple to learn. IDEs are a case in point.

The good news is that Spring keeps the learning curve reasonable in several ways:

- There's a distinction between the framework's core and its various "portfolio" projects. The core framework addresses general development needs, such as database development, object/relational mapping, transactions, web development, and so on. The portfolio projects are more special-purpose. One good way to learn Spring is to learn the basics of the core framework first and then move on to portfolio projects.

- Certain approaches and patterns, such as POJOs, dependency injection, templates, AOP-based auto proxying, and so forth, recur throughout the framework. Learning Spring is a matter of learning a reasonably constrained set of core approaches.

- One of the original approaches was XML-based configuration. Over time, some developers became grumpy about this: it requires a lot of explicit bean wiring, and XML compares unfavorably to terser formats like JSON, YAML, and perhaps even Java. Spring addressed this by adding a number of simpler configuration options, including namespace-based, annotation-based, and Java-based.

- Spring's development team pays attention to what's happening outside the Java world and freely adopts ideas that offer simplifications. Ruby on Rails has been a particularly rich source of such ideas—Spring Roo and Grails are essentially Rails clones, bringing Rails-like development to Java and Groovy, respectively. (SpringSource leads the development of the Groovy language and the Grails framework.)

- Spring has strong IDE support in the form of the Spring Tool Suite (STS), which is a branded and extended version of Eclipse. This support makes it easier to visualize bean dependencies, to understand where aspect-oriented programming (AOP) advice is being applied, and so on. Some of the portfolio projects have additional IDE integration, such as Spring Integration with integration visualizations.

This isn't a complete list, but it gives the basic idea.

Our hope in writing this book is to make the learning curve gentler. We do this by presenting a reasonably wide range of problems you're likely to encounter at some point (if you haven't already) and showing how Spring can help you solve them. The core framework appears throughout, so you'll get plenty of practice with that. But we also pull in several portfolio projects, mostly because they're appropriate to the problem at hand, but also because seeing them will help you develop a sense for the recurring themes.

By the end of this book, you'll have a broad understanding of the core framework and many of the portfolio projects. You'll also have sufficient practical knowledge to do real work with Spring. We won't make you an expert, but you'll understand enough of the nuts and bolts to know roughly what the answers look like and where to find them.

about this book

Spring in Practice is a practice-oriented book. The first three chapters are background, but are still quite substantial, and we expect most readers will find some new information in them. Chapter 2 and the final 11 chapters use a cookbook format to tackle a given problem with incremental recipe-by-recipe, or technique-by-technique, solutions. There are 66 techniques covered in this book.

Roadmap

As noted, chapters 1 through 3 provide background material that we use throughout the rest of the book:

- Chapter 1 explains the Spring inversion of control lightweight container.
- Chapter 2 shows how to work with data access, ORM, and transactions. Although we pursue the more traditional approach of implementing a generic DAO, we also show how to take advantage of Spring Data JPA's powerful capabilities.
- Chapter 3 presents an overview of Spring Web MVC, a rich framework for implementing web applications. Chapter 3 also presents Spring Mobile, which extends Spring Web MVC to provide support for mobile application development. Although Spring Mobile doesn't count as background material, it fit fairly naturally with chapter 3, so we went with it.

Chapters 4 and 5 present two different approaches to implementing registration forms; the material is easy to generalize to other problem domains:

- Chapter 4 shows how to implement a single-page, web-based registration form using Spring Web MVC. The techniques apply to single-page form development in general.
- Chapter 5 uses Spring Web Flow to implement a more sophisticated, multipage registration process. Here the techniques apply to flow-based interactions generally, such as application processes, checkout processes, and so forth.

In chapters 6 and 7 we switch gears, treating two important aspects of security:

- Chapter 6 uses Spring Security to implement a login process.
- Chapter 7 continues with Spring Security by showing how to add authorization to a web forum application. We consider both role-based and ACL-based authorization.

Chapters 8 and 9 explore another common concern in application development—communicating with users and making it possible for them to communicate with one another.

- Chapter 8 covers web-based Contact Us forms, email responses, as well as notifications, mailing lists, and RSS feeds.
- Chapter 9 shows how to implement a rich-text comment engine using the Page-Down editor, which is the same one that StackOverflow uses.

The remaining chapters mostly stand alone:

- Chapter 10 illustrates the use of the Spring TestContext Framework when implementing integration tests.
- Chapter 11 presents a configuration management database (CMDB) based on Neo4j, Spring Data Neo4j, Spring Social, and more.
- Chapter 12 shows how to build an article delivery engine against both Java Content Repository (JCR) and MongoDB.
- Chapter 13 covers building a Spring-based help desk system on the inbound and the outbound side. Our focus is on building a basic structure.
- Chapter 14 demonstrates techniques for building your own Spring-based frameworks, with support for namespace-based configuration, AOP, annotations, and more. Our example is a framework for site resiliency.

The appendix explains how we've organized the book's source code, as well as how to build, configure, and run it.

Who should read this book?

As its title suggests, *Spring in Practice* aims to help you put the Spring Framework to practical use. Although we do explain the occasional concept (such as dependency injection) or principle (like preferring whitelisting to blacklisting), there's comparatively little of that. Most of the time, we're showing *how* to do things.

Accordingly we assume that you come to the book with enough experience to understand what you're trying to accomplish and why. This isn't a first book on

Spring. We think it makes a nice complement to books that expand more upon the foundations, such as *Spring in Action, Third Edition* by Craig Walls (Manning, 2011).

Nearly all of the recipes deal with web application development in some way. This reflects the ongoing importance of web application development, as well as the background of your lead author. We assume that you know the basics of Java web application development, including HTTP, servlets, JSPs, and tag libraries.

Many of the recipes involve various Java enterprise APIs, such as JNDI, JPA, JavaMail, and JMX. We use Hibernate quite a bit, too. In addition, more recent trends such as mobile, social, and NoSQL are now commonplace in both corporate and noncorporate settings, and some of the recipes in the book treat topics such as GitHub, OAuth, MongoDB, and Neo4j as well. In general, we assume that you have enough experience to set those up on your own (even if you have to read about them elsewhere), and we focus on the Spring part.

This isn't a book for absolute beginners; most developers who have been doing Java development for the past few years should find the book useful for expanding their knowledge of Spring.

Code conventions and downloads

You can find the source code for all of the examples in the book at www.manning.com/SpringinPractice or at https://github.com/springinpractice. The repositories for the book are sip02, sip03, sip04, and so forth. The appendix contains more information about how to build, configure, and run the code.

The following conventions are used throughout the book:

- *Italic* typeface is used to introduce new terms.
- Courier typeface is used to denote code samples, as well as elements and attributes, method names, classes, interfaces, and other identifiers.
- Code annotations accompany many segments of code. Certain annotations are marked with numbered bullets. These annotations have further explanations that follow the code.
- Code line continuations use the ➥ symbol.

Author Online

The purchase of *Spring in Practice* includes free access to a private web forum run by Manning Publications, where you can make comments about the book, ask technical questions, and receive help from the authors and from other users. To access the forum and subscribe to it, point your web browser to www.manning.com/SpringinPractice. This page provides information on how to get on the forum once you are registered, what kind of help is available, and the rules of conduct on the forum.

Manning's commitment to our readers is to provide a venue where a meaningful dialogue between individual readers and between readers and the authors can take place. It is not a commitment to any specific amount of participation on the part of the authors, whose contribution to the forum remains voluntary (and unpaid).

We suggest you try asking the authors some challenging questions lest their interest stray!

The Author Online forum and the archives of previous discussions will be accessible from the publisher's web site as long as the book is in print.

About the authors

WILLIE WHEELER currently serves as a principal applications engineer at Expedia, with a focus on continuous delivery and web operations. He has been working with Java since 1997 and with Spring since 2005. If you like this book, you can find more of the same at Willie's Spring blog, springinpractice.com. He also runs a devops blog at zkybase.org/blog. Willie lives in Sammamish, Washington, with his wife Raylene and their four children Max, Jude, Lucy, and Ben.

JOSHUA WHITE is currently director of software engineering and innovation at Cigna and has more than 12 years of experience developing and architecting complex software systems for a number of financial and health services organizations. He has worked with and evangelized the use of the Spring Framework since its inception in 2002. Joshua lives in Farmington, Connecticut.

about the cover illustration

The figure on the cover of *Spring in Practice* is an "Officer of the Grand Signior," the elite guard that surrounded the Sultan. The illustration is taken from a collection of costumes of the Ottoman Empire published on January 1, 1802, by William Miller of Old Bond Street, London. The title page is missing from the collection and we have been unable to track it down to date. The book's table of contents identifies the figures in both English and French, and each illustration bears the names of two artists who worked on it, both of whom would no doubt be surprised to find their art gracing the front cover of a computer programming book...a bit more than two hundred years.

The collection was purchased by a Manning editor at an antiquarian flea market in the "Garage" on West 26th Street in Manhattan. The seller was an American based in Ankara, Turkey, and the transaction took place just as he was packing up his stand for the day. The Manning editor did not have on his person the substantial amount of cash that was required for the purchase and a credit card and check were both politely turned down. With the seller flying back to Ankara that evening the situation was getting hopeless. What was the solution? It turned out to be nothing more than an old-fashioned verbal agreement sealed with a handshake. The seller simply proposed that the money be transferred to him by wire and the editor walked out with the bank information on a piece of paper and the portfolio of images under his arm. Needless to say, we transferred the funds the next day, and we remain grateful and impressed by this unknown person's trust in one of us. It recalls something that might have happened a long time ago.

The pictures from the Ottoman collection, like the other illustrations that appear on our covers, bring to life the richness and variety of dress customs of two centuries ago. They recall the sense of isolation and distance of that period—and of every other historic period except our own hyperkinetic present. Dress codes have changed since then and the diversity by region, so rich at the time, has faded away. It is now often hard to tell the inhabitant of one continent from another. Perhaps, trying to view it optimistically, we have traded a cultural and visual diversity for a more varied personal life. Or a more varied and interesting intellectual and technical life.

We at Manning celebrate the inventiveness, the initiative, and, yes, the fun of the computer business with book covers based on the rich diversity of regional life of two centuries ago, brought back to life by the pictures from this collection.

Introducing Spring: the dependency injection container

This chapter covers

- Major functional areas of the Spring Framework
- Flexible configuration using dependency injection
- Wiring beans using XML
- Autowiring and component scanning using annotations

In this chapter, we'll provide a brief overview of the Spring Framework, beginning with a discussion of what Spring is and giving an overview of its major pieces. Then we'll delve into the underlying principles behind the Spring Framework, and talk about inversion of control and how it relates to dependency injection. Finally, we'll dive into a small example that shows how to use the Spring Core Container hands-on. Let's get started.

1.1   *What is Spring, and why use it?*

The Spring Framework is an open source application framework created to simplify the development of enterprise Java software. The framework achieves this goal by providing developers with a component model and a set of simplified and consistent APIs that effectively insulate developers from the complexity and error-prone boilerplate code required to create complex applications.

Over the last nine years, the breadth and depth of the framework has increased significantly, yet it has remained simple to learn and easy to use. The framework has evolved into roughly 20 modules that can be grouped into 6 basic functional areas. As shown in figure 1.1, these functional areas are Data Access/Integration, Web, Aspect-Oriented Programming (AOP), Instrumentation, the Core Container, and Test.

This modularity gives developers the freedom to choose which parts of the framework to use in their applications without the need to include the entire framework. Let's begin our tour by looking at each of these functional areas.

1.1.1   *The major pieces of the framework*

In the paragraphs that follow, we'll give you a brief introduction to each of Spring's six basic functional areas. We'll take a deeper dive into each of these topics as we work through individual recipes later in the book.

THE CORE SPRING CONTAINER

We'll further dissect what dependency injection (DI) is in section 1.2. For now, it's enough to know that the DI container is at the core of the Spring Framework and provides the fundamental capabilities on which all the other modules are built. The

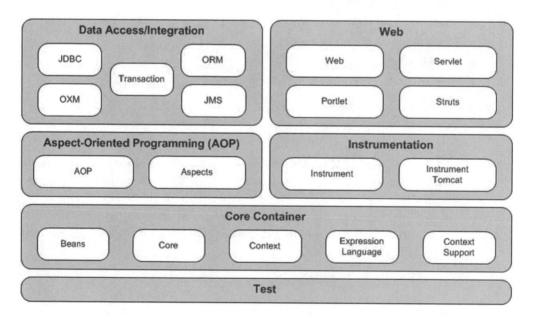

Figure 1.1   A high-level block diagram illustrating Spring's six basic functional areas

container provides the facility for decoupling the creation, configuration, and management of beans (discussed later) from your application code.

ASPECT-ORIENTED PROGRAMMING (AOP)

The Spring Framework also supports aspect-oriented programming with both a simpler approach called Spring AOP and the more powerful AspectJ approach. AOP, which is covered in more detail later, aims to encapsulate cross-cutting concerns (security, logging, transaction management, and so on) into aspects to retain modularity and reusability. These concerns often can't be cleanly decomposed from the rest of the system and can result in code duplication, significant dependencies between systems, or both. Like the DI container, AOP support is both independently useful to developers and used to implement different parts of framework functionality. For example, Spring implements its support for declarative transaction management through AOP because transactions are a cross-cutting concern.

DATA ACCESS/INTEGRATION

The Data Access/Integration module provides support for the Java Database Connectivity API (JDBC), object-relational mapping (ORM), Object/XML mapping (OXM), Java Message Service (JMS), and transactional support.

The JDBC module provides an abstraction layer that relieves developers from having to write tedious and error-prone boilerplate code by automatically managing database connections and connection pools, and by mapping vendor-specific errors into a uniform exception hierarchy. It also makes it easy to map `java.sql.ResultSets` to lists of domain objects and execute stored procedures.

If you prefer to use ORM instead of straight JDBC for database access code, you're in luck. The ORM module supports the best and most popular ORMs available, including Hibernate, iBATIS, Java Data Objects (JDO), and the Java Persistence API (JPA).

> ### A quick note about iBATIS
> Apache iBATIS was retired in 2010 and has been superseded by MyBatis (mybatis.org). Although iBATIS 2 has been supported since Spring 2, due to release timing issues, Spring 3 doesn't yet include official support for it. See the MyBatis-Spring module at www.mybatis.org/spring.

The OXM module provides an abstraction layer that offers simplified and consistent support for popular Object/XML mapping tools such as Castor, the Java Architecture for XML Binding (JAXB), JiBX, XMLBeans, and XStream.

The JMS module provides simplified APIs for producing and consuming messages. Finally, the Transaction module provides support for both programmatic and declarative transaction management.

WEB

Spring's Web module provides common web infrastructure code for integrating Spring into web applications, multipart file upload, and web-based remoting capabilities. In addition to providing its own servlet- or portlet-based Model-View-Controller (MVC) framework, this module integrates with popular web-development frameworks and technologies like Struts, JavaServer Faces (JSF), Velocity, FreeMarker, and JavaServer Pages (JSP).

TEST

Last but not least in the framework stack is Spring's testing support. This module provides support for using both the JUnit and TestNG frameworks.

Now that we've provided a high-level overview of the Spring Framework, let's discuss the benefits of using the framework.

1.1.2   Why use it?

You may have worked with or even developed other frameworks or APIs that handle one or more of the Spring Framework's concerns. Why would you stop to learn something that requires a fairly substantial time investment? In addition to providing you with a component model and a simplified and consistent set of APIs that effectively insulate developers from complexity and error-prone boilerplate code, here are other reasons:

- *Quality*—From the overall design of the modules, packages, class structures, and APIs to the implementation and test coverage of the source code, the Spring Framework is a great example of high-quality open source software.
- *Modularity*—As we mentioned earlier, the framework has evolved into roughly 20 modules, giving developers the freedom to choose which parts of the framework to use in their applications without the need to include the entire framework.
- *Promotes best practices*—Spring's plain old Java object (POJO)-based programming model promotes decoupled component models, unit testing, and other best practices.
- *Modest learning curve*—Due to the consistency and simplicity of the APIs, Spring isn't hard to learn. As we make our way through the framework, you'll see that common patterns emerge. Plus, hundreds of resources online and in print are at your disposal, including message boards where the core developers often participate.
- *Popularity*—As evidenced by myriad publications, websites, and job postings, the Spring Framework is almost ubiquitous.

For an excellent print reference that will certainly be of aid during your journey with this book, check out Craig Walls' *Spring in Action*, 3rd Edition (Manning Publications, 2011).

Spring offers a lot, and it takes time to understand and appreciate the landscape. But rest assured that the effort is well worth it. By learning Spring and using it to solve problems, you'll see how to bring together disparate technologies and incorporate them into cohesive applications. You'll keep hardcoded configuration parameters out of your classes and centralized in standard locations. You'll design interface-based dependencies between classes and better support changing requirements. And ultimately, you'll get more done with less effort and in less time because the Spring Framework handles the plumbing while you focus on writing code to solve business problems.

Figure 1.2 The Core Container

Now that you have a general idea of what the framework offers, let's take a deeper dive into the capabilities of the Core Container shown in figure 1.2. Spring's Core Container provides the inversion of control (IoC) and DI capabilities on which all the other modules are built.

1.2 Flexible configuration via dependency injection

IoC became popular some years back through DI containers like Spring. Although that might be eons ago in internet time, it's still a relatively new and unfamiliar concept for many developers. In this section, we'll explain what IoC is and examine the forces that produced it. You'll even get your hands a little dirty and see how to configure Spring's container.

1.2.1 Configuring dependencies the old way

Consider the relationship between a data access object (DAO) and the DataSource it relies on in the following code sample. For the DAO to work with the DataSource, you need to create and initialize the DataSource with various connection parameters within the JdbcAccountDao class:

```
// Source project: sip01, branch: 01 (Maven Project)
package com.springinpractice.ch01.dao.jdbc;

import org.apache.commons.dbcp.BasicDataSource;
import com.springinpractice.ch01.dao.AccountDao;

public class JdbcAccountDao implements AccountDao {
    private BasicDataSource dataSource;

    public JdbcAccountDao() {
        dataSource = new BasicDataSource();
        dataSource.setDriverClassName("com.mysql.jdbc.Driver");
        dataSource.setUrl("jdbc:mysql://localhost:3306/springbook" +
            "?autoReconnect=true");
        dataSource.setUsername("root");
        dataSource.setPassword("");
    }

}
```

In this code sample, JdbcAccountDao specifies a *dependency* on a JDBC DataSource. Coding to interfaces is certainly a best practice. As shown in figure 1.3, the code also specifically creates a dependency on a BasicDataSource, a specific DataSource implementation from the Apache Commons Database Connection Pool (DBCP) project.

Figure 1.3 `JdbcAccountDao` **specifies a dependency on Apache DBCP's** `BasicDataSource`, **which is a concrete** `DataSource` **implementation.**

An obvious problem here is that the `JdbcAccountDao` class is intimately aware of the DataSource's implementation, creation, and configuration. Another potential problem is that it's likely that many DAOs may need to share this connection information. As a result of the current design, changing the `DataSource`'s implementation or configuration may involve multiple code changes, recompilations, and redeployments every time the `DataSource` implementation or configuration changes.

You could externalize the connection parameters with `java.util.Properties`, and that would certainly be an improvement. But a more subtle problem would remain. In the previous code sample, the class is specifying and driving the dependencies. Let's look at how you can invert this control by injecting your dependencies instead.

1.2.2 *Dependency injection*

One way to eliminate the concrete dependency on `BasicDataSource` would be to specify the dependency externally and have that dependency injected into the `JdbcAccountDao` as a `DataSource`. This gives you a lot of flexibility because you can easily change the configuration in one place. If you want to proxy the `DataSource` before injecting it, you can do that. In unit-testing scenarios, if you want to replace the `DataSource` with a mock, you can do that too. Again, DI provides a lot of flexibility that you don't have when the dependency's construction is hardwired into the components relying on the dependency.

To make DI work, you need to create the `DataSource` externally and then either construct the DAO with it or set it on the DAO with a setter method, as shown here:

```
// Source project: sip01, branch: 02 (Maven Project)
package com.springinpractice.ch01.dao.jdbc;

import javax.sql.DataSource;
import com.springinpractice.ch01.dao.AccountDao;

public class JdbcAccountDao implements AccountDao {

    private DataSource dataSource;

    public JdbcAccountDao() {}

    public void setDataSource(DataSource dataSource) {
        this.dataSource = dataSource;
    }

}
```

Notice that the DAO no longer has a hardwired dependency on `BasicDatasource`. As a result, you'll notice that the `BasicDataSource` import has been removed. Because the dependency is provided via a setter, it's no longer necessary to provide a constructor to initialize the DataSource explicitly. Another approach to refactoring this class would have been to provide a DataSource implementation as a constructor argument instead of using a setter. Either approach represents an improvement. But you might argue reasonably that you've succeeded only in pushing the construction of this dependency elsewhere in the code. Look at the service that creates the DAO:

```
//Source project: sip01, branch: 02 (Maven Project)
package com.springinpractice.ch01.service;
import java.util.Properties;
import java.io.InputStream;
import org.apache.commons.dbcp.BasicDataSource;
import com.springinpractice.ch01.dao.jdbc.JdbcAccountDao;

public class AccountService {
    private JdbcAccountDao accountDao;

    public AccountService() {
        try {
            Properties props = new Properties();
            InputStream inputStream = this.getClass().getClassLoader()
                .getResourceAsStream("dataSource.properties");
            props.load(inputStream);

            BasicDataSource dataSource = new BasicDataSource();
            dataSource.setDriverClassName(
                    props.getProperty("driverClassName"));
            dataSource.setUrl(props.getProperty("url"));
            dataSource.setUsername(props.getProperty("username"));
            dataSource.setPassword(props.getProperty("password"));

            accountDao = new JdbcAccountDao();
            accountDao.setDataSource(dataSource);
        } catch (Exception e) {
            throw new RuntimeException(e);
        }
    }
}
```

In one respect, you've made things worse: you've introduced dependencies between AccountService and BasicDataSource—a relationship that is clearly undesirable. You also have a dependency between AccountService and JdbcAccountDao (a concrete class), so you're still in the same boat you started in (see figure 1.4)! It's easy to see how the entire dependency graph for a particular system could become complicated and inflexible with nodes that are hard to swap out.

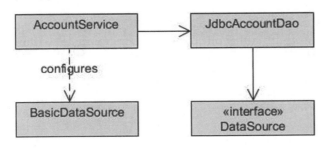

Figure 1.4　Now `JdbcAccountDao` **has the desired interface dependency on** `DataSource`, **but** `AccountService` **has dependencies on two concrete classes.**

That doesn't mean DI was a failed experiment. It's taking you in the right direction. To clean things up, you need to revise *what* is doing the injecting.

1.2.3 *Inversion of control*

You can move the DI away from client code and over to Spring. In this scenario, client code doesn't request or look up an `AccountService`. Instead, the `AccountService` is transparently injected into client code when the client code is initialized. The following code shows `AccountService` with a strict interface dependency on `AccountDao`:

```
//Source project: sip01, branch: 03 (Maven Project)
package com.springinpractice.ch01.service;
import com.springinpractice.ch01.dao.AccountDao;

public class AccountService {
    private AccountDao accountDao;

    public AccountService() {}

    public void setAccountDao(AccountDao accountDao) {
        this.accountDao = accountDao;
    }

}
```

How do you specify the dependency chain? With Spring, one option is to use XML to assemble it declaratively, as in the following listing.

Listing 1.1   Spring configuration file that specifies object relationships

```
<?xml version="1.0" encoding="UTF-8"?>
<!-- Source project: sip01, branch: 03 (Maven Project) -->

<beans xmlns="http://www.springframework.org/schema/beans"
    xmlns:xsi="http://www.w3.org/2001/XMLSchema-instance"
    xsi:schemaLocation="http://www.springframework.org/schema/beans
        http://www.springframework.org/schema/beans/spring-beans-3.1.xsd">

    <bean id="dataSource" class="org.apache.commons.dbcp.BasicDataSource"
        destroy-method="close">
        <property name="driverClassName" value="com.mysql.jdbc.Driver"/>
        <property name="url"
        value="jdbc:mysql://localhost:3306/springbook?autoReconnect=true"/>
        <property name="username" value="someusername"/>
        <property name="password" value="somepassword"/>
    </bean>

    <bean id="accountDao"
        class="com.springinpractice.ch01.dao.jdbc.JdbcAccountDao">
        <property name="dataSource" ref="dataSource"/>
    </bean>

    <bean id="accountService"
        class="com.springinpractice.ch01.service.AccountService">
        <property name="accountDao" ref="accountDao"/>
    </bean>
</beans>
```

DataSource configured with parameters ❶

DataSource injected into JdbcAccountDao ❷

JdbcAccountDao injected into AccountService ❸

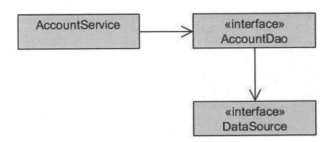

Figure 1.5 Now the dependencies are interface-based and the concrete classes are configured transparently through Spring.

If you're new to Spring, this configuration might be unfamiliar, but its meaning should be clear enough. At ❶ you declare the DataSource and set it up with its configuration parameters. At ❷ you declare the JdbcAccountDao and inject it with the DataSource. Similarly, you inject the JdbcAccountDao into the AccountService at ❸. The end result is that the service now carries the entire dependency chain, and the configuration is entirely transparent to the service. The cleaned up, new relationship is shown in the class diagram in figure 1.5.

As you can see, the class structure has taken on more of a layered approach. In contrast to figure 1.4, notice that the layers above are dependent only on the layers below, and all the dependencies are expressed as interfaces. This simplifies the dependency graph and makes it easier to swap out individual nodes. In the next section, we'll use an example to illustrate how you can use Spring to manage and inject the concrete implementations of your dependencies.

1.3 A simple bean configuration example

With the *what* and the *why* past you, you'll get your hands dirty and try Spring Framework DI with a small sample application. The application won't be anything serious—just enough to learn the basics of expressing and managing dependencies using Spring. You'll build a domain object, a DAO that reads from a CSV file, and a service, and then you'll wire everything up.

The code will get a list of delinquent accounts for an imaginary utility company. You'll define a delinquent account as one with an unpaid balance that hasn't been credited for 30 days or more. The service will have the responsibility of finding out which accounts are delinquent, but it will need to delegate to the DAO to get a list of candidate accounts. Before you create the DAO, you'll create the domain object it works with.

1.3.1 Creating the account domain object

The toy Account domain object in the following listing has only the fields and methods you need to demonstrate DI through other parts of the sample application.

Listing 1.2 Basic account bean, Account.java

```
// Source project: sip01, branch: 04 (Maven Project)
package com.springinpractice.ch01.model;
```

```
import java.math.BigDecimal;
import java.util.Date;

public class Account {

    private String accountNo;
    private BigDecimal balance;
    private Date lastPaidOn;

    public Account(String accountNo, BigDecimal balance, Date lastPaidOn) {
        this.accountNo = accountNo;
        this.balance = balance;
        this.lastPaidOn = lastPaidOn;
    }

    public String getAccountNo() {
        return accountNo;
    }

    public BigDecimal getBalance() {
        return balance;
    }

    public Date getLastPaidOn() {
        return lastPaidOn;
    }
}
```

In a real application, accounts wouldn't appear out of thin air. You'd have databases, files, and other systems that you'd store and read them from. For the example, you'll create a DAO that parses a comma-separated values (CSV) file with data like this:

```
100,0,09012008
200,100,08012008
300,-100,09012008
```

In the CSV file, accounts.csv, the first field is the account number, the second is the balance (positive or negative), and the third is the date the account was last credited in MMDDYYYY format. As mentioned in section 1.2, interface-based dependencies keep things flexible by allowing pluggable, varying implementations. Before you create the DAO responsible for consuming this file, let's create an interface for it.

1.3.2 Creating the account DAO interface and implementation

The following interface has only a single read operation to get all accounts from whatever back-end store a particular implementation would read against. We're leaving out the rest of the CRUD operations because you don't need them for this example:

```
// Source project: sip01, branch: 04 (Maven Project)
package com.springinpractice.ch01.dao;

import java.util.List;

import com.springinpractice.ch01.model.Account;

public interface AccountDao {

    List<Account> findAll() throws Exception;

}
```

Now you'll create the concrete `AccountDao` implementation that reads `Accounts` from a CSV file. Assume that the name of the CSV file might change over time; therefore, you won't hardcode it. It would be perfectly legitimate to externalize it in a properties file and use `java.util.Properties` to read it in; but instead of doing that, you'll configure it with Spring. Here's the code.

Listing 1.3 Reading accounts from a CSV file, CsvAccountDao.java

```java
// Source project: sip01, branch: 04 (Maven Project)
package com.springinpractice.ch01.dao.csv;

import java.io.BufferedReader;
import java.io.FileReader;
import java.math.BigDecimal;
import java.text.DateFormat;
import java.text.SimpleDateFormat;
import java.util.ArrayList;
import java.util.Date;
import java.util.List;
import org.springframework.core.io.Resource;
import com.springinpractice.ch01.dao.AccountDao;
import com.springinpractice.ch01.model.Account;

public class CsvAccountDao implements AccountDao {           ❶ CSV file path Spring
                                                               will configure
    private Resource csvResource;

    public void setCsvResource(Resource csvFile) {           Required for
        this.csvResource = csvFile;                        ❷ setter injection
    }

    public List<Account> findAll() throws Exception {          Implements
        List<Account> results = new ArrayList<Account>();      AccountDao
                                                             ❸ interface
        DateFormat fmt = new SimpleDateFormat("MMddyyyy");
        BufferedReader br = new BufferedReader(
                new FileReader(csvResource.getFile()));
        String line;
        while ((line = br.readLine()) != null) {
            String[] fields = line.split(",");

            String accountNo = fields[0];
            BigDecimal balance = new BigDecimal(fields[1]);
            Date lastPaidOn = fmt.parse(fields[2]);
            Account account =
                new Account(accountNo, balance, lastPaidOn);
            results.add(account);
        }
        br.close();
        return results;
    }
}
```

The `CsvAccountDao` declares a `csvFile` field where Spring populates ❶. For Spring to set it for you, you define the required public setter at ❷. The implementation of `findAll()` at ❸ rolls through the lines in a file, tokenizing and parsing them into your `Account` domain objects, which are collected in an `ArrayList` and returned to calling code.[1]

Omission of error checking and assertions

To keep the examples clear, we've omitted error checking that you would expect to see in production-ready code. For example, in the previous sample, production-ready code would assert that the `String` passed in for the location of the `csvFile` was not null and that the file existed at the path specified.

1.3.3   *Configuring CsvAccountDao with Spring*

You have enough code in place to bring Spring into the picture. There are different ways to configure objects and their dependencies with Spring, and the most popular are XML and annotations. You'll use XML in this section; we'll build on these concepts when we introduce annotation-style configuration in section 1.5. The XML file in the following listing shows how to define and configure a bean using Spring.

Listing 1.4   Spring configuration file, applicationContext.xml

```xml
<?xml version="1.0" encoding="UTF-8"?>
<!-- Source project: sip01, branch: 04 (Maven Project) -->

<beans xmlns="http://www.springframework.org/schema/beans"          ❶ Spring beans
    xmlns:xsi="http://www.w3.org/2001/XMLSchema-instance"              schema
    xsi:schemaLocation="http://www.springframework.org/schema/beans
        http://www.springframework.org/schema/beans/spring-beans-3.1.xsd">

    <bean id="accountDao"
       class="com.springinpractice.ch01.dao.csv.CsvAccountDao">      ❷ CsvAccountDao
         <property name="csvResource" value="accounts.csv"/>            bean definition
    </bean>
                                                                    ❸ Configured
    <bean id="accountService"                                          csvResource property
       class="com.springinpractice.ch01.service.AccountService">
         <property name="accountDao" ref="accountDao"/>
    </bean>
</beans>
```

By convention, developers usually name the Spring configuration file `application-Context.xml`, but it can be named anything. In real-world applications, it usually makes sense to break out the Spring configuration across multiple files, especially when the applications are large with many bean definitions. When you do that, the configuration is often broken out by architectural, rather than functional, slice. You might create configuration files dedicated to DAOs, services, servlets, and security. As

---

[1]   The method of configuration used here is called *setter injection*. Spring provides other ways to configure beans and wire dependencies, including *constructor injection* and *factory-method injection*. In this book, we mostly use setter injection because it's the most popular approach. For the pros and cons of the different injection strategies, see the "Constructor versus Setter Injection" section of Martin Fowler's "Inversion of Control Containers and the Dependency Injection pattern," January 2004, http://mng.bz/xvk5.

you progress through this book, you'll indeed do this. Because your needs are minimal to start, a single file will suffice.

Spring ships with different schemas for configuring its different pieces of functionality, such as AOP and transaction management. For now, you declare the beans schema at ❶, which is the most fundamental of the schemas in that the functionality that the other schemas provide is generally expressible (albeit in a more verbose fashion) as explicit bean definitions. The beans schema provides everything you need to define beans of all sorts, configure them, and wire them together.

You define your first bean at ❷. The bean element has two attributes: id and class. You use the ID to support dependencies between beans. The class attribute is set to the fully qualified name of the CsvAccountDao. Spring uses reflection to instantiate the class as you request it through the container (or request other classes that depend on it). At ❸, you declare a property element for the csvResource property. Again, Spring uses reflection to set this to the value in the value attribute. If you're following the code examples, you'll find this file in the src/main/resources directory. Spring relies on the JavaBeans programming model in order to set the property, so that's why you declare the setter in the Account domain object.

1.3.4 Creating the account service that finds delinquent accounts

With the domain object and DAO out of the way, you can build the service that has the responsibility of scanning all accounts and finding delinquent ones. The logic in the next listing is fairly straightforward.

Listing 1.5 AccountService.java: a service responsible for finding delinquent accounts

```java
//Source project: sip01, branch: 04 (Maven Project)
package com.springinpractice.ch01.service;
import java.math.BigDecimal;
import java.util.ArrayList;
import java.util.Calendar;
import java.util.Date;
import java.util.GregorianCalendar;
import java.util.List;

import com.springinpractice.ch01.dao.AccountDao;
import com.springinpractice.ch01.model.Account;

public class AccountService {
    private AccountDao accountDao;              ❶ AccountDao that Spring will resolve

    public AccountService() {}

    public void setAccountDao(AccountDao accountDao) {   ❷ Setter Spring needs for injection
        this.accountDao = accountDao;
    }

    public List<Account> findDeliquentAccounts() throws Exception {
        List<Account> delinquentAccounts = new ArrayList<Account>();
        List<Account> accounts = accountDao.findAll();

        Date thirtyDaysAgo = daysAgo(30);          ❸ Finds delinquent accounts
```

```
        for (Account account : accounts) {
            boolean owesMoney = account.getBalance()
                .compareTo(BigDecimal.ZERO) > 0;
            boolean thirtyDaysLate = account.getLastPaidOn()
                .compareTo(thirtyDaysAgo) <= 0;

            if (owesMoney && thirtyDaysLate) {
                delinquentAccounts.add(account);
            }
        }
        return delinquentAccounts;
    }

    private static Date daysAgo(int days) {
        GregorianCalendar gc = new GregorianCalendar();
        gc.add(Calendar.DATE, -days);
        return gc.getTime();
    }
}
```

The AccountDao dependency is declared by interface at ❶. The required setter method is at ❷. At ❸, you iterate through all the Accounts that the DAO returns and test whether they're delinquent. If they are, you add them to a list and return them.

1.3.5 *Wiring up the AccountService to CsvAccountDao*

Now, let's wire up the AccountService with CsvAccountDao. All you need to do is add a simple bean definition to the applicationContext.xml configuration file as shown next.

Listing 1.6   Completed Spring configuration file

```
<?xml version="1.0" encoding="UTF-8"?>
<!-- Source project: sip01, branch: 04 (Maven Project) -->

<beans xmlns="http://www.springframework.org/schema/beans"
    xmlns:xsi="http://www.w3.org/2001/XMLSchema-instance"
    xsi:schemaLocation="http://www.springframework.org/schema/beans
        http://www.springframework.org/schema/beans/spring-beans-3.1.xsd">

    <bean id="accountDao"
       class="com.springinpractice.ch01.dao.csv.CsvAccountDao">
        <property name="csvResource" value="accounts.csv"/>
    </bean>
    <bean id="accountService"                                ◁────┐ AccountService
       class="com.springinpractice.ch01.service.AccountService">   bean definition
        <property name="accountDao" ref="accountDao"/>       ◁──┐
    </bean>                                                        Injection of
</beans>                                                          AccountDao
```

Like the CsvAccountDao you defined in listing 1.4, you give the AccountService bean definition id and class attributes. The subtle but important difference is the way you're injecting the AccountDao into the service. Here, you're using the ref instead of the value attribute. The ref attribute is used for injecting other beans you've defined

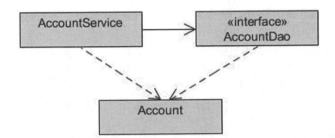

Figure 1.6 `AccountService` **has an interface-based association with** `AccountDao`, **and both depend on** `Account`.

with Spring. The `value` attribute injects simple primitive and value object properties. Figure 1.6 shows the class diagram for the objects.

All you need to do is create a console application to run the code. Based on the three accounts you've defined, the only one that is delinquent is 200. The following code prints the delinquent account number.

Listing 1.7   ConsoleApp.java, which retrieves the `AccountService` from Spring

```
// Source project: sip01, branch: 04 (Maven Project)
package com.springinpractice.ch01;

import java.util.List;

import org.springframework.context.ApplicationContext;
import org.springframework.context.support.ClassPathXmlApplicationContext;

import com.springinpractice.ch01.model.Account;
import com.springinpractice.ch01.service.AccountService;

public class ConsoleApp {
    public static void main(String[] args) throws Exception {
        ApplicationContext appCtx =
            new ClassPathXmlApplicationContext("applicationContext.xml");
        AccountService accountService =
            (AccountService)appCtx.getBean("accountService");
        List<Account> delinquentAccounts = accountService
            .findDeliquentAccounts();

        for (Account a : delinquentAccounts) {
            System.out.println(a.getAccountNo());
        }
    }
}
```

❶ **Dependency injection container**

❷ **Retrieves AccountService from container**

You create an instance of `ClassPathXmlApplicationContext` at ❶ and pass in the classpath-relative location of the configuration file. With this class, you can get a reference to any bean you define in the Spring configuration file by the ID you defined in the bean's definition. The `ApplicationContext` interface and its implementations are the gateway into the beans through Spring. They essentially make up a sophisticated implementation of the factory pattern. In order for the factory to instantiate beans, the beans must have a no-argument constructor. (The implicit, default no-argument constructor is fine.) Spring provides support for instantiating beans with constructor arguments, which we'll talk about in the next section. At ❷, you get a reference to the `AccountService` you've defined along with its `AccountDao` dependency and the `AccountDao`'s configured `csvFile` property in one fell swoop.

In this section, you built a simple application with the Spring Framework. It's easy to see that a full-blown application with many DAOs, services, and other components configured and wired together through Spring would be more cleanly separated and easier to manage than one that wasn't.

Now that we've piqued your interest with the basics, in the next section we'll take a more detailed look at the framework's DI capabilities. After examining the `beans` namespace, we'll look at different ways of injecting dependencies, configuring and externalizing bean properties, bean scopes, and a little syntax sugar to make your configuration more clear and concise.

1.4 *Wiring beans using XML*

As you've seen, a Spring bean represents a POJO component. Because the other five functional areas of the Spring Framework (Data Access/Integration, Web, AOP, Instrumentation, and Test) build on the capabilities offered by the Core Container, learning how to wire beans is paramount to understanding and using the Spring Framework. In this section, we'll look at using XML to configure Spring. In the following sections, we'll discuss two of Spring's XML namespaces that we'll be using throughout this book: the core beans namespace and the handy p namespace.

1.4.1 *An overview of the beans namespace*

The beans namespace is the most fundamental and deals with DI; it provides a way to define beans and wire dependency relationships between them. To create a configuration file that uses the beans namespace, you create an XML document and reference the schema:

```
<?xml version="1.0" encoding="UTF-8"?>

<beans xmlns="http://www.springframework.org/schema/beans"
    xmlns:xsi="http://www.w3.org/2001/XMLSchema-instance"
    xsi:schemaLocation="http://www.springframework.org/schema/beans
        http://www.springframework.org/schema/beans/spring-beans-3.1.xsd">
</beans>
```

At this point, all you have is an empty configuration. You can add object definitions with the inner bean element:

```
<beans xmlns="http://www.springframework.org/schema/beans"
    xmlns:xsi="http://www.w3.org/2001/XMLSchema-instance"
    xsi:schemaLocation="http://www.springframework.org/schema/beans
        http://www.springframework.org/schema/beans/spring-beans-3.1.xsd">

    <bean id="accountService"
        class="com.springinpractice.ch01.service.AccountService"/>
</beans>
```

Here you define an `AccountService` by creating a bean element with `id` and `class` attributes. The `id` is a convenient handle to the bean. As described in section 1.3, Spring uses reflection to create a new instance of the class specified as you fetch instances by ID programmatically through the `ApplicationContext` interface.

WIRING BEANS TOGETHER

You could have constructed the `AccountService` using the `new` keyword, but the creation of service layer objects is rarely so straightforward. They often depend on DAOs, mail senders, SOAP proxies, and whatnot. You could instantiate each of those dependencies programmatically in the `AccountService` constructor (or through static initialization), but that leads to hard dependencies and cascading changes as they're swapped out. Additionally, you could create dependencies externally and set them on the `AccountService` via setter methods or constructor arguments. Doing so would eliminate the hard internal dependencies (as long as they were declared in the `AccountService` by interface), but you'd have duplicated initialization code everywhere. Here's how you create a DAO and wire it up to your `AccountService` the Spring way:

```
<bean id="accountDao"
    class="com.springinpractice.ch01.dao.jdbc.JdbcAccountDao"/>

<bean id="accountService"
    class="com.springinpractice.ch01.service.AccountService">
    <property name="accountDao" ref="accountDao"/>
</bean>
```

You've injected the `AccountService` with a `JdbcAccountDao` by declaring a `property` element for the dependency. The `property` element has a `name` attribute, which is the name of the property you want to set; and it has a `ref` attribute that's set to the `id` of the bean you want to inject.

Other services and classes can depend on the `accountDao` bean. If its implementation changes, say from a JDBC one to a Hibernate one, you just need to update the `class` attribute in its configuration instead of going to each class with the dependency and swapping it out manually. Spring supports this type of wiring and can easily work with complex object graphs that are multiple levels deep.

CONSTRUCTOR AND SETTER INJECTION

Just as `AccountService` needs a no-argument constructor so Spring can use reflection to instantiate it, it also needs to have a `setAccountDao()` setter method that corresponds to the `accountDao` property:

```
public class AccountService {

    private AccountDao accountDao;

    public void setAccountDao(AccountDao accountDao) {
        this.accountDao = accountDao;
    }
    //...
}
```

This type of injection is called *setter injection*. But, as mentioned previously, Spring lets you instantiate objects with constructor arguments, too. You can nix the setter method and declare a constructor instead:

```
public AccountService(AccountDao accountDao) {
    this.accountDao = accountDao;
}
```

In Spring, you resolve the dependency like this:

```
<bean id="accountService"
    class="com.springinpractice.ch01.service.AccountService">
    <constructor-arg ref="accountDao"/>
</bean>
```

As you've probably guessed, this is called *constructor injection*. We mostly use setter injection in this book.

CONFIGURING SIMPLE BEAN PROPERTIES

The JdbcAccountDao you configured is likely to have additional initialization requirements. In the example, you'll register a JDBC driver and set up additional connection information. In the following code sample, you configure a BasicDataSource with simple properties using the property element instead of the ref attribute:

```
<bean id="dataSource" class="org.apache.commons.dbcp.BasicDataSource"
    destroy-method="close">
    <property name="driverClassName" value="com.mysql.jdbc.Driver"/>
    <property name="url"
    value="jdbc:mysql://localhost:3306/springbook?autoReconnect=true"/>
    <property name="username" value="someusername"/>
    <property name="password" value="somepassword"/>
</bean>

<bean id="accountDao"
    class="com.springinpractice.ch01.dao.jdbc.JdbcAccountDao">
    <property name="dataSource" ref="dataSource"/>
</bean>
```

Of course, in a production system, you'd likely use a javax.sql.DataSource with connection pooling. (We'll show you how to do that in chapter 2.) Here you're setting simple String properties on the BasicDataSource. But what if the properties were numeric or java.util.Date properties? In that case, Spring would attempt to convert the String specified in the value attribute to its appropriate type with a java.beans.PropertyEditor implementation. Spring ships with quite a few of such implementations and allows you to define your own if you need to.[2]

EXTERNALIZING SIMPLE PROPERTIES WITH A PROPERTYPLACEHOLDERCONFIGURER

In one sense, you could say you've done a good thing by configuring the JdbcAccount-Dao properties externally to the class. Changing configuration parameters won't require any recompiling of code; you can just update the XML. Also, having a centralized configuration makes it easy to change things in one place (or a few logically related places

---

[2] You can read more about the built-in PropertyEditors at http://mng.bz/7CO9.

if you're using multiple configuration files). But in most environments, you don't hook straight up to a production database server and start cranking out and running untested code. You have one or more QA environments. Luckily, Spring allows you to handle scenarios like this with an API class: `PropertyPlaceholderConfigurer`.

In order to use `PropertyPlaceholderConfigurer`, you first create a properties file (call it springbook.properties):

```
dataSource.driverClassName=com.mysql.jdbc.Driver
dataSource.url=jdbc:mysql://localhost:3306/springbook?autoReconnect=true
dataSource.username=root
dataSource.password=secret
```

Then, you define the `PropertyPlaceholderConfigurer` bean in the Spring configuration. Finally, as you define beans, you use the placeholder constructs ${} when specifying their property values, so the container can resolve them at runtime.

Listing 1.8 Declaring a `PropertyPlaceholderConfigurer` to substitute properties

```xml
<?xml version="1.0" encoding="UTF-8"?>
<!-- Source project: sip01, branch: 05 (Maven Project) -->

<beans xmlns="http://www.springframework.org/schema/beans"
    xmlns:xsi="http://www.w3.org/2001/XMLSchema-instance"
    xsi:schemaLocation="http://www.springframework.org/schema/beans
        http://www.springframework.org/schema/beans/spring-beans-3.1.xsd">

    <bean class="org.springframework.beans.factory.config.
        PropertyPlaceholderConfigurer">                            ❶ Declare Property-
        <property name="location" value="springbook.properties"/>    PlaceholderConfigurer
    </bean>
                                          location uses Java system
    <bean id="accountService"                environment variable  ❷
       class="com.springinpractice.ch01.service.AccountService">
        <property name="accountDao" ref="accountDao"/>
    </bean>

    <bean id="accountDao"
       class="com.springinpractice.ch01.dao.jdbc.JdbcAccountDao">
        <property name="dataSource" ref="dataSource"/>
    </bean>

    <bean id="dataSource"
      class="org.apache.commons.dbcp.BasicDataSource"
      destroy-method="close">                        Placeholders substituted ❸
        <property name="driverClassName"                 at runtime
          value="${dataSource.driverClassName}"/>
        <property name="url" value="${dataSource.url}"/>
        <property name="username" value="${dataSource.username}"/>
        <property name="password" value="${dataSource.password}"/>
    </bean>

</beans>
```

The `PropertyPlaceholderConfigurer` ❶ doesn't have an id attribute. That's because the Spring container detects its presence automatically and enables its functionality

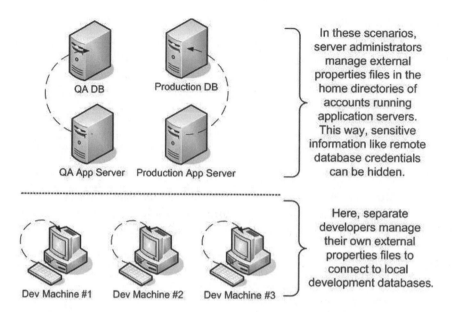

In these scenarios, server administrators manage external properties files in the home directories of accounts running application servers. This way, sensitive information like remote database credentials can be hidden.

Here, separate developers manage their own external properties files to connect to local development databases.

Figure 1.7   Using external properties files to manage configuration for separate environments

for you. In the `location` property ❷ of the `PropertyPlaceholderConfigurer`, the file is located in the root of your classpath. If you're following the code examples, the springbook.properties file is located in the src/main/resources directory, which is included in your classpath. You could also change the configuration at ❷ to

```
<property name="location" value="file:${user.home}/springbook.properties"/>
```

In the previous configuration, you point to a file located in the home directory of whatever computer account is running your application through a Java system environment variable. (Spring will attempt to substitute Java system environment variables in the placeholders if they aren't found in the properties files.) This is handy because server admins can store sensitive information in these files, which developers may not need to access. Also, this makes it easy for multiple developers to work on a project while pointing to their own databases. Figure 1.7 shows these scenarios in action. At ❸, you change the hardcoded values over to substitution placeholders.

At this point, you're beginning to get a solid picture of how beans are configured cleanly in Spring. Although there's more than we can possibly hope to cover here, let's spend a little time going into depth about the important concept of bean scopes.

1.4.2   *Bean scopes*

When defining a bean with Spring, you can specify how you want instances created and managed as they're retrieved from the container. This is called the *bean scope*. There are five such scopes: singleton, prototype, request, session, and global session. Scope is configured with the `scope` attribute:

```
<bean id="accountDao"
    class="com.springinpractice.ch01.dao.jdbc.JdbcAccountDao"
    scope="singleton|prototype|request|session|globalSession"/>
```

SINGLETON SCOPE

Singleton scope is the default scope for beans declared in Spring. These singletons are different than Java classes that implement the singleton design pattern. Declaring a singleton bean in Spring ensures that only one instance exists on a per-container basis, whereas an instance of a class that implements the singleton design pattern will be the only one available on a per-classloader basis.

As you request singleton beans from the container, Spring will create instances and cache them if they haven't been created (see figure 1.8); otherwise, Spring will return already-existing instances from its cache. Therefore, singleton beans in Spring often don't maintain state because they're usually shared among multiple threads (such as in servlet environments). For example, singleton services often have references to singleton DAOs, and the DAOs might have references to Hibernate `SessionFactory`s, which are thread-safe. As long as resources are thread-safe—meaning they're synchronized, immutable, have no state, or have fields where any of the previous criteria are strictly met—you can safely declare them with singleton scope to eliminate the overhead of creating them each time they're requested.

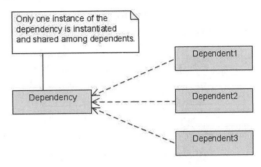

Figure 1.8 Singleton-scoped beans are shared among dependent class instances.

PROTOTYPE SCOPE

Prototype-scoped beans are created every time they're requested via `ApplicationContext`'s `getBean()` method, or each time they're injected into other beans. Let's consider the second case. The following code injects a bean with prototype scope into another bean with default singleton scope. (Note that you generally wouldn't declare a DAO with prototype scope because you design them for thread-safety. We're using a DAO to maintain consistency with previous examples.)

```
<bean id="accountDao"
    class="com.springinpractice.ch01.dao.jdbc.JdbcAccountDao"
    scope="prototype"/>

<bean id="accountService"
    class="com.springinpractice.ch01.service.AccountService">
    <property name="accountDao" ref="accountDao"/>
</bean>
```

In this scenario, `AccountService` is created once and cached. During that time, `JdbcAccountDao` is created and injected, but never cached. Subsequent requests for `accountService`, by way of `ApplicationContext`'s `getBean()` method or through injection, will yield the sole, cached `AccountService` instance along with its `Jdbc-AccountDao` reference. A singleton referencing a prototype makes the prototype effectively singleton in scope. But if you were to simultaneously inject `JdbcAccountDao` into another bean with singleton scope, that bean would maintain a reference to a separate instance. Figure 1.9 illustrates prototype scope.

Prototype-scoped beans have different lifecycle semantics than singleton-scoped beans. Spring can manage the complete lifecycle including creation and destruction of singleton-scoped beans, but it can only manage the creation (instantiation, configuration, and decoration through dynamic proxying) of prototype-scoped beans. It's up to the client code to clean up, release resources, and otherwise manage the lifecycle of prototype-scoped beans. In this way, prototype beans are similar to classes created with the new keyword in Java, although it would be irregular to substitute the former for the latter unless there are complex initialization requirements for stateful beans that Spring will make easier to manage.

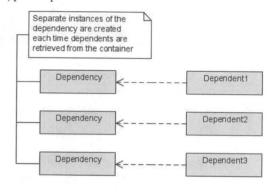

Figure 1.9   **Prototype-scoped beans are instantiated every time one of their dependent classes is retrieved from the container. But if the dependent class is singleton-scoped, subsequent retrievals of it will return already-cached instances where the prototype-scoped dependency is effectively cached as well (it isn't reinstantiated).**

REQUEST, SESSION, AND GLOBAL SESSION SCOPE

The last three scopes—request, session and global session—are useful only in the context of web applications. It doesn't matter what web framework you're using; they function identically across all of them.

Request-scoped beans are created each time an HTTP request makes its way into a servlet resource that is injected with one. Similar to request-scoped variables in servlets, these beans are safe to change and work with because the servlet specification dictates one thread per HTTP request.

Session-scoped beans are confined to the scope of standard session-scoped variables. These, like request-scoped beans, are safe to modify and work with because although their access isn't restricted to the same, single thread, it's restricted to one thread at a time, which is tied to the current session of the client making the requests.

Global session–scoped beans are applicable only in the context of portlet applications. Like session-scoped beans, they exist throughout an entire session, but they're shared among all the portlets in a complete portlet web application, whereas session-scoped beans are created and managed for each individual portlet.

There are a few prerequisites to employing beans with these scopes. First, if you're using a framework other than Spring Web MVC, you have to register a `Request-ContextListener` in the servlet deployment descriptor (web.xml):

```
<web-app>
    ...
    <listener>
        <listener-class>
            org.springframework.web.context.request.RequestContextListener
        </listener-class>
    </listener>
    ...
</web-app>
```

You can use `RequestContextListener` in Servlet containers that implement version 2.4 of the Servlet specification or greater. For 2.3 containers, a corresponding `Request-ContextFilter` implementation is available. These listeners and filters enable the required integration between Spring and whatever servlet container you're using. Basically, Spring can intercept requests and decorate them with this scoping functionality.

If you're fetching beans with these scopes from an `ApplicationContext`, the `ApplicationContext` implementation must be a web-aware one such as `XmlWebApplicationContext`. Otherwise you'll get an `IllegalStateException` complaining about unknown bean scopes.

We've spent a lot of time with the `beans` namespace. As indicated at the outset, this chapter's treatment isn't comprehensive, and there's quite a bit more to learn if you decide to pursue a more in-depth study. At this point, let's turn our attention to the `p` namespace, whose mission is to make your XML configuration a little cleaner than you can make it with the `beans` namespace alone.

1.4.3   The p namespace

The `p` namespace extends the `beans` namespace by providing an alternate property-declaration syntax. Instead of configuring properties as XML elements as you do with `JdbcAccountDao`, you can declare them as attributes on the bean element. As shown in the following listing, properties are specified as attributes using the format `p:[prop-ertyName]="someValue"`.

Listing 1.9   Declaring a `PropertyPlaceholderConfigurer` to substitute properties

```
<?xml version="1.0" encoding="UTF-8"?>
<!-- Source project: sip01, branch: 06 (Maven Project) -->

<beans xmlns="http://www.springframework.org/schema/beans"          ❶ Declare p
    xmlns:xsi="http://www.w3.org/2001/XMLSchema-instance"               namespace
    xmlns:p="http://www.springframework.org/schema/p"
    xsi:schemaLocation="http://www.springframework.org/schema/beans
    http://www.springframework.org/schema/beans/spring-beans-3.1.xsd">

    ...

    <bean id="dataSource"
        class="org.apache.commons.dbcp.BasicDataSource"
        destroy-method="close"                                       ❷ Declare properties
          p:driverClassName="${dataSource.driverClassName}"             as bean element
        p:url="${dataSource.url}"                                       attributes
```

```
        p:username="${dataSource.username}"
        p:password="${dataSource.password}"/>
```

2 Declare properties as bean element attributes

```
     ...
</beans>
```

The p namespace provides you with XML syntax sugar and makes the configuration more concise. You declare the namespace at **1** but don't put a corresponding schema location. It's easy to see why, when you look at the namespace usage at **2**. It doesn't define any elements or attributes. The p namespace isn't defined in an XSD file like the beans namespace. Instead, this functionality is implemented in Spring. In addition to specifying simple properties, you can also inject full-blown beans:

```
<bean
     id="accountService"
     class="com.springinpractice.ch01.service.AccountService"
     p:accountDao-ref="accountDao"/>
```

The only difference between this attribute declaration and the ones for simple properties is that you append -ref onto the end of this attribute.

In the next section, we'll introduce annotation-based configuration. In general, we tend to favor the convenience and clarity of using annotations for configuring many cross-cutting concerns (validation, persistence, transactions, security, web services, request mappings, and so on), so we'll use them quite a bit. (Subsection 1.5.4 discusses some of the debate regarding XML versus annotation-based configuration.) The foregoing techniques are still useful for a couple of reasons: not everything that Spring offers can be configured solely with annotations, and you may prefer to keep your POJOs insulated from configuration concerns, which arguably is the whole point.

1.4.4   *The c namespace*

Spring 3.1 introduced the c namespace with two goals in mind. The first was to improve on the existing constructor-injection syntax and clarify which constructor arguments are being set. The second goal was to provide similar XML syntax sugar for those who prefer constructor-based injection. It's no longer necessary to provide a number of constructor-arg elements for constructor injection.

Let's start with a very simple example. Look at the following fictional Person class. Notice the two String arguments in its constructor:

```
public Person(String firstName, String lastName) {
    this.firstName = firstName;
    this.lastName = lastName;
}
```

Prior to Spring 3.1, you had to configure this bean as follows:

```
<beans xmlns="http://www.springframework.org/schema/beans"
    xmlns:xsi="http://www.w3.org/2001/XMLSchema-instance"
    xsi:schemaLocation="http://www.springframework.org/schema/beans
        http://www.springframework.org/schema/beans/spring-beans-3.1.xsd">
```

```
    <bean id="joshAsPerson" class="foo.Person">
        <constructor-arg value="Joshua"/>
        <constructor-arg value="White"/>
    </bean>

</beans>
```

Using Spring 3.1, you now have two options. Each is illustrated here:

```
<beans xmlns="http://www.springframework.org/schema/beans"        ❶ Declare c
    xmlns:c="http://www.springframework.org/schema/c"                namespace
    xmlns:xsi="http://www.w3.org/2001/XMLSchema-instance"
    xsi:schemaLocation="http://www.springframework.org/schema/beans
        http://www.springframework.org/schema/beans/spring-beans-3.1.xsd">

    <bean id="joshAsPerson" class="foo.Person"
        c:firstName="Joshua"                        ❷ Declare constructor arguments
        c:lastName="White"/>                           using variable names

    <bean id="willieAsPerson" class="foo.Person"
        c:_0="Willie"                               ❸ Declare constructor arguments
        c:_1="Wheeler"/>                               using variable order
</beans>
```

Similar to the p namespace, the c namespace provides XML syntax sugar and makes the configuration clearer and more concise. You declare the required namespace at ❶ in the example configuration. Again, you don't specify a corresponding schema location. Just like the p namespace, the c namespace isn't defined in an XSD file. The functionality is implemented in Spring.

At ❷ you begin to see the benefit of the new syntax. Using the format c:[variable-Name]="someValue", it becomes clear which value is being associated with which constructor argument. The ability to match names in the XML with the names of constructor arguments is dependent on the code being compiled with debugging information. If you're using a third-party library where this may not be in your control, you can use the format c:_[variableIndex]="someValue" shown at ❸. Instead of depending on the presence of variable names in the bytecode, this configuration style lets you specify the index of each constructor argument. Just as with the p namespace, you can append the same -ref suffix to reference other beans.

In this section, we took a closer look at how to wire beans using XML and covered a significant amount of ground. We examined the beans namespace and wiring beans together. Then we looked at constructor and setter injection as well as configuring and externalizing bean properties. Finally, we introduced bean scopes and demonstrated how you can use the p and c namespaces. In the next section, you'll see how you can use Java annotations to define Spring components and their dependencies without using XML.

1.5   *Autowiring and component scanning using annotations*

Now that we've shown you the basics of wiring beans together, we'll introduce the annotation-based configuration that was introduced in Spring 2.0 and further enhanced in

Spring 2.5. The `@Autowired` annotation can be applied to constructors or fields and allows you to wire relationships by type, without having to explicitly set them up in the XML configuration. After that, we'll explore the stereotype annotations that come with the framework: `@Component`, `@Repository`, `@Service`, and `@Controller`. With `@Autowired` and the stereotype annotations, you can enable component scanning for dependencies using annotations and minimal XML configuration. We use autowiring and component scanning often in this book because they're much more compact (although less explicit).[3]

1.5.1 @Autowired

In the previous section, you injected a DAO into a service using regular `bean` declarations along with the p namespace:

```
<bean id="accountDao"
    class="com.springinpractice.ch01.dao.jdbc.JdbcAccountDao"/>

<bean id="accountService"
    class="com.springinpractice.ch01.service.AccountService"
    p:accountDao-ref="accountDao"/>
```

With the `@Autowired` annotation, you can eliminate the `p:accountDao-ref` attribute. First let's look at the annotation, and then you'll modify the XML configuration to support it:

```
import org.springframework.beans.factory.annotation.Autowired;

... other imports omitted ...

public class AccountService {

    @Autowired
    private AccountDao accountDao;

    ...

}
```

THE CONTEXT NAMESPACE

The `@Autowired` annotation won't do you any good until you modify the XML configuration to use it. You have to reference the `context` schema in your configuration and declare the `annotation-config` element as shown in the next listing. You've also removed the setters from the `accountDao` and `accountService` beans.

> **Listing 1.10   Spring configuration modified to support annotations**

```
<?xml version="1.0" encoding="UTF-8"?>
<!-- Source project: sip01, branch: 07 (Maven Project) -->

<beans xmlns="http://www.springframework.org/schema/beans"
    xmlns:xsi="http://www.w3.org/2001/XMLSchema-instance"
```

---

[3] There is a tradeoff between using autowiring and not using it. Autowiring cleans up your configuration but makes the dependencies between components less clear—some might say "magical." The more complex your configuration is, the less sense it makes to autowire components, although this point is certainly debatable.

```
xmlns:p="http://www.springframework.org/schema/p"
xmlns:context="http://www.springframework.org/schema/context"
xsi:schemaLocation="
    http://www.springframework.org/schema/beans
    http://www.springframework.org/schema/beans/spring-beans-3.1.xsd
    http://www.springframework.org/schema/context
    http://www.springframework.org/schema/context/spring-context-
3.1.xsd">

    <context:annotation-config/>

    <bean
        class="org.springframework.beans.factory.config.
        PropertyPlaceholderConfigurer"
        p:location="springbook.properties"/>

    <bean
        id="accountService"
        class="com.springinpractice.ch01.service.AccountService"/>

    <bean
        id="accountDao"
        class="com.springinpractice.ch01.dao.jdbc.JdbcAccountDao"/>

    <bean id="dataSource"
      class="org.apache.commons.dbcp.BasicDataSource"
      destroy-method="close"
      p:driverClassName="${dataSource.driverClassName}"
      p:url="${dataSource.url}"
      p:username="${dataSource.username}"
      p:password="${dataSource.password}"/>

</beans>
```

Context schema reference ❶

Enables annotation-based configuration ❷

Explicit injection no longer required ❸

String-based configuration parameters still used ❹

The context namespace elements deal with configuration issues. One of those is whether the container should enable annotation-based configuration. You declare the context schema at ❶. After that, turning on annotations is a simple matter of declaring the annotation-config element ❷. You can see at ❸ that the p:accountDao-ref attribute is no longer necessary. Notice that you also split out the DataSource configuration ❹ into its own bean. As we'll discuss in the next chapter, notice that the simple String-based configuration parameters are still used to configure the properties of this bean.

If you were to run an application that used these beans and this configuration, you'd see that Spring would inject the AccountService with the JdbcAccountDao. When a field is @Autowired, Spring looks through the container for beans with a matching type to inject. Because JdbcAccountDao implements the AccountDao interface and AccountService declares an AccountDao field, Spring automatically wires the dependency. What happens when there's more than one bean with a matching type?

```
...
<bean id="jdbcAccountDao"
    class="com.springinpractice.ch01.dao.jdbc.JdbcAccountDao"/>
<bean id="hibernateAccountDao"
```

```
          class="com.springinpractice.ch01.dao.hibernate.HibernateAccountDao"/
<bean id="accountService"
      class="com.springinpractice.ch01.service.AccountService"/>
```

`...`

Spring complains with a `BeanCreationException`:

```
Exception in thread "main"
org.springframework.beans.factory.BeanCreationException: Error creating
bean with name 'accountService': Autowiring of fields failed; nested
exception is org.springframework.beans.factory.BeanCreationException: Could
not autowire field: private springinpractice.ch01.dao.AccountDao
springinpractice.ch01.service.AccountService.accountDao; nested exception
is org.springframework.beans.factory.NoSuchBeanDefinitionException: No
unique bean of type [springinpractice.ch01.dao.AccountDao] is defined:
expected single matching bean but found 2: [jdbcAccountDao,
hibernateAccountDao]
```

As an aside, if you declared the field as an `AccountDao` array or an `AccountDao`-typed collection, Spring would populate the array or collection with both DAOs:

```
@Autowired
private AccountDao[] accountDaos;
```

Obviously, it wouldn't make much sense to have an array of DAOs in most cases, but it's fairly common to have multiple implementations of an interface and a need to specify one at a time. Fortunately, `@Autowired` permits you to specify the bean you want:

```
import org.springframework.beans.factory.annotation.Autowired;
import org.springframework.beans.factory.annotation.Qualifier;

public class AccountService {

    @Autowired
    @Qualifier("hibernateAccountDao")
    private AccountDao accountDao;
}
```

You qualify by the `id` attribute of the bean declaration. This isn't the only way to do it; the `context` namespace supplies a `qualifier` element you could nest in the `Account-Dao` declarations. The `qualifier` element would come in handy if you needed to keep the `id` attributes as they are (maybe because you had a convention in place) and also needed different qualification rules. For example, you could distinguish a regular Hibernate-based DAO from a high-octane straight-JDBC DAO with hand-crafted SQL that a DBA spent hours tuning for performance.

1.5.2   *Stereotype annotations*

So far, we've shown how to wire beans using `@Autowired`. But using `@Autowired` alone handles only wiring. You still have to define the beans themselves so the container is aware of them and can inject them for you. But with Spring's stereotype annotations, you can annotate classes and enable component scanning (which we'll talk about shortly), and Spring will automatically import the beans into the container so you don't have to define them explicitly with XML. There are currently four core stereo-type annotations: @Component, @Repository, @Service, and @Controller.

The @Component annotation flags a bean so the component-scanning mechanism can pick it up and pull it into the application context. If you wanted to get rid of the JdbcAccountDao in the XML configuration, all you'd have to do is place @Component above the class declaration:

```
import org.springframework.stereotype.Component;

@Component
public class JdbcAccountDao implements AccountDao {
    ...
}
```

Now you could completely wipe out the XML bean declaration, and the @Autowired accountDao field in AccountService would be automatically populated with a Jdbc-AccountDao instance. Although this is all well and good, there is another, more suit-able annotation that provides additional benefits specifically for DAOs.

The @Repository annotation is a specialization of the @Component annotation. It not only imports the DAOs into the DI container, but it also makes the unchecked exceptions that they throw eligible for translation into Spring DataAccessExceptions (also unchecked).

The @Service annotation is also a specialization of the component annotation. It doesn't currently provide any additional behavior over the @Component annotation, but it's a good idea to use @Service over @Component in service-layer classes because it specifies intent better. Additionally, tool support and additional behavior might rely on it in the future.

Finally, the @Controller annotation marks a class as a Spring Web MVC controller. It too is a @Component specialization, so beans marked with it are automatically imported into the DI container. We haven't talked much about Spring Web MVC yet, but we'll be using it heavily throughout this book. Basically, when you add the @Controller anno-tation to a class, you can use another annotation, @RequestMapping, to map URLs to instance methods of a class. That is, you can tell Spring that you want a certain method invoked when a user agent requests one of your application's URLs. We'll get more into that later.

1.5.3 Component scanning

Just as you need to declare context:annotation-config to turn on autowiring, you need to declare context:component-scan to enable the importing of classes that are annotated with the stereotypes. The following listing shows how this is done.

> **Listing 1.11 Spring configuration modified to support component scanning**

```
<?xml version="1.0" encoding="UTF-8"?>
<!-- Source project: sip01, branch: 08 (Maven Project) -->

<beans xmlns="http://www.springframework.org/schema/beans"
```

```
     xmlns:xsi="http://www.w3.org/2001/XMLSchema-instance"
     xmlns:p="http://www.springframework.org/schema/p"
     xmlns:context="http://www.springframework.org/schema/context"
     xsi:schemaLocation="
         http://www.springframework.org/schema/beans
         http://www.springframework.org/schema/beans/spring-beans-3.1.xsd
         http://www.springframework.org/schema/context
         http://www.springframework.org/schema/context/
     spring-context-3.1.xsd">

     <context:component-scan base-package="com.springinpractice.ch01"/>

     ...

</beans>
```

The `context:component-scan` element requires a `base-package` attribute, which, as its name suggests, specifies a starting point for a recursive component search. Here you set it to `com.springinpractice.ch01`. Also, the `component-scan` element can be declared multiple times and pointed to multiple packages. It's common to lay out package structures by application layer (which is the convention we follow for the recipes in this book), so you might have packages for DAOs, services, and controllers. In that case, you'd declare three `component-scan` elements, each with a `base-package` attribute pointing to a different package.

Also, when `component-scan` is declared, you no longer need to declare `context:annotation-config`, because autowiring is implicitly enabled when component scanning is enabled.

Finally, you no longer need to declare the flagged beans in your configuration. When component scanning kicks in at application startup, Spring will recurse over all the packages you've specified, look for stereotype-annotated classes, and import them into the container. Their default bean names are their uncapitalized, nonqualified classnames.[4] For example, `springinpractice.ch01.dao.jdbc.JdbcAccountDao` resolves to `jdbcAccountDao`. The resulting configuration file looks like this.

Listing 1.12 Final Spring configuration using component scanning

```
<?xml version="1.0" encoding="UTF-8"?>
<!-- Source project: sip01, branch: 08 (Maven Project) -->

<beans xmlns="http://www.springframework.org/schema/beans"
     xmlns:xsi="http://www.w3.org/2001/XMLSchema-instance"
     xmlns:p="http://www.springframework.org/schema/p"
     xmlns:context="http://www.springframework.org/schema/context"
     xsi:schemaLocation="
         http://www.springframework.org/schema/beans
         http://www.springframework.org/schema/beans/spring-beans-3.1.xsd
```

---

[4] If the default bean names aren't suitable for your purposes, you can implement Spring's `BeanNameGenerator` interface to customize the naming strategy. Then, when declaring the `component-scan` element, tack on the `name-generator` attribute and point it to the name of your custom `BeanNameGenerator`. See Rod Johnson et al, "Naming autodetected components," The Spring Framework Reference Documentation, SpringSource, http://mng.bz/23kk.

```
          http://www.springframework.org/schema/context
          http://www.springframework.org/schema/context/
➡️   spring-context-3.1.xsd">

     <context:component-scan base-package="com.springinpractice.ch01"/>

     <bean
          class="org.springframework.beans.factory.config.
               PropertyPlaceholderConfigurer"
➡️        p:location="springbook.properties"/>

     <bean id="dataSource"
        class="org.apache.commons.dbcp.BasicDataSource"
        destroy-method="close"
        p:driverClassName="${dataSource.driverClassName}"
        p:url="${dataSource.url}"
        p:username="${dataSource.username}"
        p:password="${dataSource.password}"/>

</beans>
```

Because you enable component scanning and use the `@Service` annotation in the `accountService` and `@Repository` annotation in the `accountDao`, you no longer need to specify their configuration in XML. Because you're using a compiled class from a third-party library (`BasicDataSource`), you're unable to decorate its code with annotations. As a result, you must still specify its configuration here.

1.5.4   *XML vs. annotations: which is better?*

Throughout the book, we'll use annotation-based configuration liberally. Many of the recipes use Hibernate, JPA, and Hibernate Validator annotations as well. This in part reflects the general direction in which the Spring team is steering, and in part reflects the fact that annotations are more convenient and usable in a wide variety of situations.

The choice of whether to use XML or annotations for configuration is the subject of much community debate. With XML the configuration is centralized into a set of files, and each file is typically dedicated to a particular architectural concern or slice. For example, if you had a Spring configuration file for DAOs and another for services and you wanted to change something, you'd pull up the appropriate file, scan through it, and make the change. It's easy to locate the file, but depending how large it is, it could be difficult to scan through. Additionally, keeping configuration in the XML keeps POJOs clean, which is a big part of the argument for using Spring in the first place. Distributing configuration makes it more challenging to replace one piece of infrastructure technology with another.

On the other hand, if you use annotations, your configuration is consolidated according to application verticals. We prefer this because feature changes are likely to span architectural slices, and it's nice to be able to change things in one place. For instance, if you needed to add a field to a domain class, you'd open the class in your IDE, add the field, and add JPA and Bean Validation Framework annotations to it at the same time. This is easier than opening each respective XML configuration file, scanning through it, and making the necessary changes. Another benefit of using annotations is that it's easy to get a 360-degree view of individual domain services and objects.

Some XML configuration will still be necessary. You need to enable component scanning in XML, and Spring ships with several classes that can only be configured with XML.

1.6   *Summary*

This chapter has provided a brief overview of the Spring Framework, its major pieces, and its underlying principles, including inversion of control and how it relates to dependency injection. Through several examples, we've demonstrated the benefits of using Spring to manage an application's dependencies and described how to define these dependencies using both XML and Java annotations.

In the next chapter, we'll move away from the container and explore some of the (very) useful components that Spring provides around persistence, object-relational mapping, and transaction management. In many cases, you can incorporate these components into your application in a transparent fashion.

Data persistence, ORM, and transactions

2

This chapter covers

- Understanding Spring JDBC data-persistence templates
- Exploiting ORM using Hibernate and JPA
- Learning how transactions manage database concurrency

This chapter assembles the data persistence, ORM, DAO, and transaction-management infrastructure you'll be using throughout the rest of the book. Although there are cases where it's useful to work directly with JDBC, the ORM approach confers major benefits in terms of simplifying the codebase. Most of the persistence examples throughout the book are ORM-based—specifically Hibernate-based—and so a large part of what we'll do here is explain not only how ORM fits into the scheme of things, but also how to perform common tasks with Hibernate specifically. We don't pretend to offer an exhaustive treatment of

Hibernate, but we hope that it's sufficient to allow you to make sense of the code examples and get started with Hibernate if you aren't already using it.[1]

Here's an overview of what we'll be doing in this chapter:

- Recipe 2.1 shows how Spring simplifies JDBC-based access to the database using the `JdbcTemplate`.
- Recipe 2.2 shows how to acquire a JDBC `DataSource` using the Java Naming and Directory Interface (JNDI).
- In recipe 2.3, you'll replace your JDBC-based approach with ORM via Hibernate. We'll also look at transactions.
- Recipe 2.4 shows how to create a data access layer that presents the app with a clean persistence API that hides the mapping details.
- (Optional) Recipe 2.5 shows how to use the JPA instead of use Hibernate directly. Although the rest of the book uses Hibernate directly, it's useful to see how to do things with JPA.
- (Optional) Recipe 2.6 presents the recent Spring Data JPA project, which simplifies data access even further. You don't use it in the following chapters—primarily because it came out after most of the book was already written—but it's good to see what it is and how to use it.

Figure 2.1 presents a visual lay of the land, illustrating the layering in a typical Java-based persistence architecture.

You'll begin by learning how to use Spring to simplify JDBC-based database access. In the following recipe and throughout the chapter, you'll work with a simple contact management application. The complete code is available from the GitHub master at https://github.com/springinpractice/sip02/. There is also a

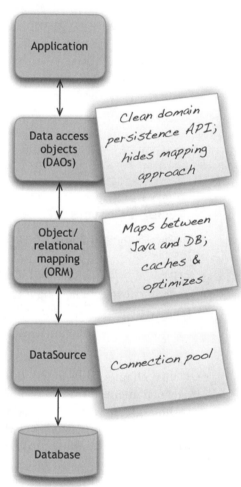

Figure 2.1   The layers involved when implementing a typical Java-based persistence architecture

---

[1]   For the definitive reference on Hibernate, see *Java Persistence with Hibernate* by Christian Bauer and Gavin King (Manning 2006), http://manning.com/bauer2/.

GitHub branch (01-06) available that corresponds to each of the recipes in this chapter. Don't worry if there are parts (even lots of parts) you don't fully understand, because that's what the rest of the book is for.

2.1 Data access using JDBC

PREREQUISITES
None. Assumes familiarity with SQL and JDBC.

KEY TECHNOLOGIES
SQL, JDBC, Spring JDBC

Background

The JDBC API is a useful and well-known approach to accessing data in a relational database. But it can be somewhat cumbersome to use, because it involves a lot of boilerplate code that acquires connections, creates statements, executes queries, and then closes all those things in the reverse order. This recipe shows how Spring simplifies JDBC-based data access.

Problem

Issue queries and updates against a relational database.

Solution

As noted, you'll use JDBC to talk with the database, but you'll see how that looks using Spring's `NamedParameterJdbcOperations` and `RowMapper` abstractions. The following listing shows how to do it.

Listing 2.1 ContactServiceImpl.java, with JDBC access code

```
package com.springinpractice.ch02.service.impl;

import java.util.HashMap;
import java.util.List;
import javax.inject.Inject;
import org.springframework.jdbc.core.namedparam.MapSqlParameterSource;
import org.springframework.jdbc.core.namedparam.
        NamedParameterJdbcOperations;
import org.springframework.jdbc.core.namedparam.SqlParameterSource;
import org.springframework.jdbc.support.GeneratedKeyHolder;
import org.springframework.jdbc.support.KeyHolder;
import org.springframework.stereotype.Service;
import com.springinpractice.ch02.model.Contact;
import com.springinpractice.ch02.service.ContactService;

@Service
public class ContactServiceImpl implements ContactService {          ❶ SQL update with
    private static final String CREATE_SQL =                           named params
        "insert into contact (last_name, first_name, mi, email) " +
        "values (:lastName, :firstName, :mi, :email)";
    private static final String FIND_ALL_SQL =
```

```
            "select id, last_name, first_name, mi, email from contact";
    private static final String FIND_ALL_BY_EMAIL_LIKE_SQL =
        "select id, last_name, first_name, mi, email from contact " +
        "where email like :email";
    private static final String FIND_ONE_SQL =
        "select id, last_name, first_name, mi, email from contact " +
        "where id = :id";
    private static final String UPDATE_SQL =
        "update contact set last_name = :lastName, " +
        "first_name = :firstName, mi = :mi, email = :email " +
        "where id = :id";
    private static final String DELETE_SQL =
        "delete from contact where id = :id";

    @Inject private NamedParameterJdbcOperations jdbcTemplate;
    @Inject private ContactRowMapper contactRowMapper;

    public void createContact(Contact contact) {
        SqlParameterSource params = new MapSqlParameterSource()
            .addValue("lastName", contact.getLastName())
            .addValue("firstName", contact.getFirstName())
            .addValue("mi", contact.getMiddleInitial())
            .addValue("email", contact.getEmail());
        KeyHolder keyHolder = new GeneratedKeyHolder();
        jdbcTemplate.update(CREATE_SQL, params, keyHolder);
        contact.setId(keyHolder.getKey().longValue());
    }

    public List<Contact> getContacts() {
        return jdbcTemplate.query(
            FIND_ALL_SQL, new HashMap<String, Object>(), contactRowMapper);
    }

    public List<Contact> getContactsByEmail(String email) {
        SqlParameterSource params =
            new MapSqlParameterSource("email", "%" + email + "%");
        return jdbcTemplate.query(
            FIND_ALL_BY_EMAIL_LIKE_SQL, params, contactRowMapper);
    }

    public Contact getContact(Long id) {
        SqlParameterSource params =
            new MapSqlParameterSource("id", id);
        return jdbcTemplate.queryForObject(
            FIND_ONE_SQL, params, contactRowMapper);
    }

    public void updateContact(Contact contact) {
        SqlParameterSource params = new MapSqlParameterSource()
            .addValue("id", contact.getId())
            .addValue("lastName", contact.getLastName())
            .addValue("firstName", contact.getFirstName())
            .addValue("mi", contact.getMiddleInitial())
            .addValue("email", contact.getEmail());
        jdbcTemplate.update(UPDATE_SQL, params);
    }

    public void deleteContact(Long id) {
```

2 SQL query with named param

3 JDBC operations

4 Row mapper

5 Executes update

6 Executes query

```
        jdbcTemplate.update(DELETE_SQL,
            new MapSqlParameterSource("id", id));
    }
}
```

At ❶ and ❷ you create an SQL update and query with named parameters, respectively. You prefix each named parameter with a colon. Then at ❸ you have the JDBC operations object, against which you execute your queries and updates. You use the row mapper at ❹ to map JDBC result sets to object lists, which is useful for queries that return multiple rows. You'll see the row mapper in detail in a minute.

❺ is an example of an update operation, which here is an insert. Note that you use `MapSqlParameterSource.addValue()` to specify the parameters that you want to substitute into the query. In this case, the insert involves an autogenerated key, so you create a `GeneratedKeyHolder` as well. You execute the update by calling `update()` on the JDBC operations object, and then you use the key holder to update the ID on the entity.

You also have a query example at ❻. In this case, there is only a single parameter, so you take advantage of the corresponding constructor. (The flanking `%` characters are SQL wildcards indicating zero or more characters, which is useful for text searches.) Here you call `query()` to get the results.

Notice that in making the query, you pass in the `contactRowMapper`. This is what lets you map a JDBC result set to a list of contacts. The next listing shows how to implement the `RowMapper` interface to achieve this result.

Listing 2.2   ContactRowMapper.java

```java
package com.springinpractice.ch02.service.impl;

import java.sql.ResultSet;
import java.sql.SQLException;
import org.springframework.jdbc.core.RowMapper;
import org.springframework.stereotype.Component;
import com.springinpractice.ch02.model.Contact;

@Component                                                          ❶ Implements
public class ContactRowMapper implements RowMapper<Contact> {  ←      RowMapper

    public Contact mapRow(ResultSet resultSet, int rowNum)   ←    ❷ Implements
        throws SQLException {                                        mapRow()

        Contact contact = new Contact();
        contact.setId(resultSet.getLong(1));
        contact.setLastName(resultSet.getString(2));
        contact.setFirstName(resultSet.getString(3));
        contact.setMiddleInitial(resultSet.getString(4));
        contact.setEmail(resultSet.getString(5));
        return contact;
    }
}
```

It should be easy to follow what's happening in listing 2.2 because you've no doubt written similar code before. At ❶ you implement the `RowMapper` interface so Spring can use it. At ❷ you perform a standard mapping to extract a `Contact` from a

`ResultSet`. Spring handles the iteration for you, so all you need to do is perform the row-level mapping.

That's all you need to do as far as actual code goes. You still need to configure the app. In the next section, we'll show how to do that.

The `NamedParameterJdbcOperations` abstraction does a nice job of hiding any configuration messiness. Once you have the operations object, you're good to go. But of course you need to create that object somewhere, and so that's what you'll do now.

Listing 2.3 beans-service.xml configuration

```xml
<?xml version="1.0" encoding="UTF-8"?>
<beans xmlns="http://www.springframework.org/schema/beans"
    xmlns:c="http://www.springframework.org/schema/c"
    xmlns:context="http://www.springframework.org/schema/context"
    xmlns:p="http://www.springframework.org/schema/p"
    xmlns:xsi="http://www.w3.org/2001/XMLSchema-instance"
    xsi:schemaLocation="
        http://www.springframework.org/schema/beans
        http://www.springframework.org/schema/beans/spring-beans-3.1.xsd
        http://www.springframework.org/schema/context
        http://www.springframework.org/schema/context/
                spring-context-3.1.xsd">

    <context:property-placeholder
        location="classpath:/spring/environment.properties" />     ❶ Source config properties

    <bean id="dataSource"
        class="org.apache.commons.dbcp.BasicDataSource"            ❷ Configures DataSource
        destroy-method="close"
        p:driverClassName="${dataSource.driverClassName}"
        p:url="${dataSource.url}"
        p:username="${dataSource.username}"
        p:password="${dataSource.password}" />

    <bean class="org.springframework.jdbc.core.namedparam.
            NamedParameterJdbcTemplate"                            ❸ Creates JDBC template
        c:dataSource-ref="dataSource" />

    <context:component-scan
        base-package="com.springinpractice.ch02.service" />
</beans>
```

At ❶ you source externalized configuration properties, as described in chapter 1. This allows you to avoid hard-coding environment-specific information into your app.

You configure a JDBC `DataSource` at ❷. A `DataSource` is essentially a factory for database connections. As such, `DataSource`s are an important part of most web and enterprise applications. Here you're using the Apache Commons Database Connection Pool (DBCP) implementation, `BasicDataSource`, which pools connections. You specify a bean ID and class, as usual. The optional `destroy-method` attribute tells Spring to call `DataSource.close()` upon shutting down the Spring container, which releases all pooled `Connection`s. Finally, you have the standard `driverClassName`, `url`, `username`, and `password` attributes.

Note that in this configuration, you create and manage the `DataSource` from the app itself, rather than looking up a container-managed `DataSource`.[2] See figure 2.2.

Now that you have a `DataSource`, you can create the JDBC operations object. The specific implementation is `NamedParameter-JdbcTemplate` ❸. You pass the `DataSource` into the constructor using Spring's constructor namespace.

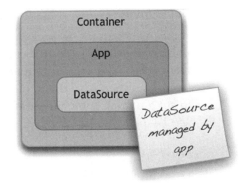

That's all there is to it. Set up your database using the SQL scripts at /src/main/sql, and create the externalized environment .properties file as described in appendix A. Run the app using

Figure 2.2   An app-managed `DataSource`

```
mvn -e clean jetty:run
```

and aim your browser at http://localhost:8080/sip/.

Click the Contacts link in the navigation bar. You should be able to view the contact list and search for contacts by email address. You should also be able to view, edit, and delete individual contacts. Try it out.

Discussion

In this recipe, you configured the `DataSource` as part of the application configuration. Although this is an option, it has drawbacks:

- Without proper configuration externalization (for example, moving URLs and credentials out of the main configuration), you end up tying the app to a particular environment.
- If multiple apps in the same container want to use the same `DataSource`, you have to repeat the configuration for all of them.
- This approach doesn't allow different apps to share a connection pool, which can lead to an inefficient use of system resources.

In the next recipe, we look at a more centralized alternative to managing `DataSources`. This alternative addresses these issues.

2.2   Looking up a DataSource with JNDI

PREREQUISITES
Recipe 2.1, "Data access using JDBC"

KEY TECHNOLOGIES
JDBC, JNDI

---

[2]   You'll learn how to use a container-managed `DataSource` in recipe 2.2.

Background

You can address the issues we raised in the discussion of recipe 2.1 by adopting a centralized approach to configuring the DataSource. Instead of having each application manage its database configuration, you can configure the DataSource inside the container and then have the applications point to that shared configuration. In addition to streamlining the configuration, this allows you to share a single connection pool across applications.

Problem

Configure the DataSource centrally to simplify configuration management and share a connection pool.

Solution

In this configuration, the application container manages the DataSource, and the app makes a JNDI call to get a reference to it. See figure 2.3.

We assume that you've already configured your application server to expose your DataSource through JNDI. If not, please consult the documentation for your app server for more information. The sample code for most of the chapters in the book includes a /sample_conf/jetty-env.xml file that shows how to do it for Jetty.

To do a namespace-based JNDI Data-Source lookup, you need to declare the jee namespace[3] in your app context and include the jee:jndi-lookup element. The following listing shows how to do this.

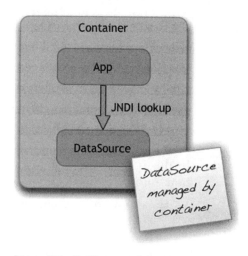

Figure 2.3 Getting a container-managed DataSource via JNDI lookup

---

Listing 2.4 beans-service.xml, with JNDI-based DataSource lookup

```xml
<?xml version="1.0" encoding="UTF-8"?>
<beans xmlns="http://www.springframework.org/schema/beans"
    xmlns:jee="http://www.springframework.org/schema/jee"
    xmlns:xsi="http://www.w3.org/2001/XMLSchema-instance"
    xsi:schemaLocation="http://www.springframework.org/schema/beans
        http://www.springframework.org/schema/beans/spring-beans-3.1.xsd
        http://www.springframework.org/schema/jee
        http://www.springframework.org/schema/jee/spring-jee-3.1.xsd">

    <jee:jndi-lookup id="dataSource"
```

❶ Declares namespace

Specifies schema location ❷

---

[3] Spring's context JAR supports the jee namespace.

```
    jndi-name="jdbc/Sip02DS"
    resource-ref="true" />                          ◁─┐    Performs
                                                     ❸  JNDI lookup
    . . .

</beans>
```

In the namespace part, you declare the `jee` namespace ❶, which gives you access to some elements related to JNDI and stateless session beans. Here you care about JNDI. You specify the schema location ❷ as well. (Note that the code download includes other namespaces that we've suppressed here because you don't need them for this recipe.)

Finally, you perform the lookup ❸. The `id` attribute specifies the ID under which the `DataSource` bean will be exposed; in this case you're being unimaginative and calling it `dataSource`. The `jndi-name` attribute gives the `DataSource`'s configured JNDI name (whatever you or your app server admin picked), and `resource-ref="true"` indicates that the target object is a *resource*—an object that the app server makes available as part of the general environment instead of an application-specific object. (Other common resources come from JMS, JavaMail, and JCA.) Because you've set this to `true`, Spring will automatically prepend the JNDI name you specified with the standard `java:comp/env/` prefix. The full name is therefore `java:comp/env/jdbc/Sip02DS`.

All you've really done is replace the app-specific `DataSource` configuration with a JNDI lookup. This change doesn't affect the app itself. Try the app again to confirm.

Discussion

In this recipe and the last, we explored a couple of different ways to set up a `Data-Source` in Spring:

- Configure the `DataSource` directly in your Spring application context using an implementation like the `BasicDataSource` class from the Apache Commons DBCP library.
- Configure your `DataSource` in your app server and expose it through JNDI, as you just saw.

The former approach is probably more straightforward to set up, because it doesn't require you to configure anything in the container. In addition, the DataSource configuration is more portable across containers. Finally, it's useful when you want apps to have isolated connection pools so as to ensure that a greedy app doesn't prevent other apps from getting connections.

The centralized JNDI approach is useful when you want to configure your `Data-Source` one time and share a connection pool across applications. It also provides a nice way to push sensitive database credentials out of your application sources, although there are other ways to do that as well: for instance, with `PropertyPlace-holderConfiguraton`, as we showed in recipe 2.1.

That concludes our treatment of `DataSource`s and JDBC-based access. Next we'll look at a different model for database interaction: ORM. This approach makes database access more object-oriented in nature. We'll explore the very popular Hibernate ORM framework.

2.3   *Object-relational mapping and transactions via Hibernate*

PREREQUISITES

Recipe 2.1, "Data access using JDBC"

KEY TECHNOLOGIES

Hibernate, transactions

Background

In addition to code examples, this recipe offers a high-level overview of ORM with Hibernate. A full discussion would take a whole book—indeed, the book exists: *Java Persistence with Hibernate* by Christian Bauer and Gavin King (Manning, 2006)—so we won't attempt it here. But this overview should equip newbies to understand what's happening in the code examples in the rest of the book.

Problem

Simplify and streamline data access, as compared to JDBC.

Solution

You'll use the Hibernate ORM framework to establish a simpler, more object-oriented interface for working with the database. We need to investigate multiple elements of the framework:

- *Mapping*—You'll learn how Hibernate makes it easier to work with entities, relationships, and SQL queries by exposing corresponding POJOs and an object-oriented query language.
- *Querying and updating*—You'll see how Hibernate's Session API allows you to execute queries and updates against the database.
- *Transactions*—You'll learn how to use Spring and Hibernate together for transaction management.

Let's start at the beginning with the mapping itself.

PERFORMING THE MAPPING

The primary function of ORM is to resolve the so-called *impedance mismatch* between working with Java objects and working with databases. The idea is that although there are some correspondences (classes versus tables, properties versus columns, instances versus rows, and so on), there are also key differences (inheritance in Java has no natural counterpart in databases; Java has collections but databases don't). ORM attempts to make database development simpler and cleaner for software developers by facilitating the mapping between the two worlds.

The first thing ORM helps with is translating Java objects back and forth into database entities, and mapping associations between objects back and forth into database relationships. As noted, classes correspond to tables, properties to columns, and instances to rows. With associations, things are quite a bit more involved, because you have to

**Java objects and
associations**

**Database entities
and relationships**

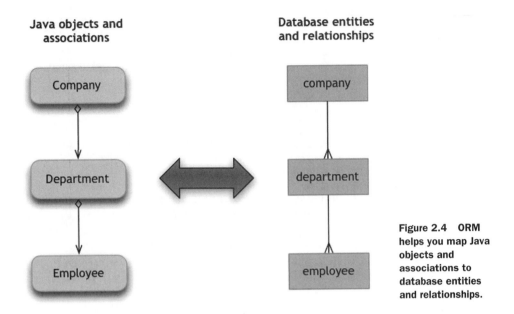

Figure 2.4 **ORM
helps you map Java
objects and
associations to
database entities
and relationships.**

account for various concerns (multiplicity, directionality, whether the associated objects have dependent or independent lifecycles, and so on). We won't get too deep into the weeds here, but see figure 2.4 for the basic concept.

Once you have the basic framework of mapping objects and relationships, it's not a huge leap to map queries. ORM frameworks typically provide an object-oriented query language that they translate behind the scenes into SQL. These object-oriented query languages, as you might guess, involve queries on objects and their properties. Figure 2.5 shows an example of how the Java Persistence Query Language (JPQL)— used for JPA queries—maps to standard SQL.

In most cases, object-oriented queries (such as JPQL) are more concise than their SQL counterparts. They also tend to be more natural to developers, who are in many cases more comfortable working with Java objects than with database constructs.

Now let's look at the code. The first order of business is to perform the mapping itself. The following listing shows how to perform both entity and query mapping.

JPA queries:

```
from
    Employee e
where
    e.department.company.name
        = 'Acme, Inc.'
```

SQL queries:

```
select
    *
from
    employee e, department d, company c
where
    e.department_id = d.id and
    d.company_id = c.id and
    c.name = 'Acme, Inc.'
```

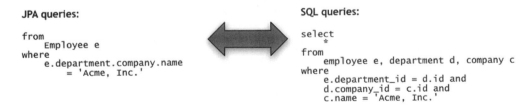

Figure 2.5 **Mapping JPA queries to SQL queries**

Listing 2.5   Contact.java, illustrating how to map between Java and the database

```
package com.springinpractice.ch02.model;

import javax.persistence.Column;                              ◄——— ❶ JPA annotations
import javax.persistence.Entity;
import javax.persistence.GeneratedValue;
import javax.persistence.GenerationType;
import javax.persistence.Id;
import javax.persistence.NamedQuery;
import javax.persistence.Table;
import javax.persistence.Transient;
import javax.validation.constraints.NotNull;
import org.hibernate.validator.constraints.Email;
import org.hibernate.validator.constraints.Length;
import com.springinpractice.util.StringUtils;
                                                              ❷ Identify
@Entity                                                    ◄—    as entity
@Table(name = "contact")              ◄——— ❸ Maps to table
@NamedQuery(                                                   ❹ JPQL
    name = "findContactsByEmail",                          ◄—    query
    query = "from Contact where email like :email")
public class Contact {
    private Long id;
    private String lastName;
    private String firstName;
    private String middleInitial;
    private String email;                      ❺ Identify as
                                                  primary key
    @Id                                       ◄—
    @GeneratedValue(strategy = GenerationType.AUTO)    ◄——— ❻ PK generation strategy
    @Column                                          ◄—
    public Long getId() { return id; }            ❼ Maps
                                                     to column
    public void setId(Long id) { this.id = id; }

    @NotNull
    @Length(min = 1, max = 40)
    @Column(name = "last_name")
    public String getLastName() { return lastName; }

    public void setLastName(String lastName) {
        this.lastName = StringUtils.cleanup(lastName);
    }

    @NotNull
    @Length(min = 1, max = 40)
    @Column(name = "first_name")
    public String getFirstName() { return firstName; }

    public void setFirstName(String firstName) {
        this.firstName = StringUtils.cleanup(firstName);
    }

    @Length(max = 1)
    @Column(name = "mi")
    public String getMiddleInitial() { return middleInitial; }

    public void setMiddleInitial(String mi) {
```

```
        this.middleInitial = StringUtils.cleanup(mi);
    }

    @Email
    @Column
    public String getEmail() { return email; }

    public void setEmail(String email) {
        this.email = StringUtils.cleanup(email);
    }

    @Transient
    public String getFullName() {
        String fullName = lastName + ", " + firstName;
        if (! (middleInitial == null || "".equals(middleInitial.trim()))) {
            fullName += " " + middleInitial + ".";
        }
        return fullName;
    }

    public String toString() {
        return "[Contact: id=" + id
            + ", firstName=" + firstName
            + ", middleInitial=" + middleInitial
            + ", lastName=" + lastName
            + ", email=" + email
            + "]";
    }
}
```

8 Marks as transient

The Contact class shows how JPA annotations work. There are many such annotations in the javax.persistence package (many more than we're using here), and you use them to perform the mapping. You import the annotations you're using at ❶.

The first part of the mapping identifies the Contact class as an entity ❷ and maps it to a table ❸. The @Entity annotation supports package scanning.

At ❹ you use the @NamedQuery annotation to build a JPQL query based on the entity. This example is close to the simplest possible query, but it will do for now. You'll see more interesting queries over the course of the book. Please consult *Java Persistence with Hibernate* for more information.

You use @Id ❺ to identify your contact's primary key and @GenerationStrategy ❻ to pick out a primary key generation strategy (in this case, the IDs are autogenerated). Then you have an @Column ❼ annotation to map the bean property to a database column. By default, the column name is the same as the property name, although you can use the name attribute to specify the column name explicitly. Finally, at ❽ you mark getFullName() as @Transient, which means you're not mapping it to a column in the database.

Although you don't use them here, JPA includes annotations for mapping associations: one-one, one-many, many-one, and many-many. You'll see plenty of examples in subsequent chapters. See *Java Persistence with Hibernate* for more information on the intricacies of association mapping.

That's it for ORM. Next you'll execute queries and updates based on this mapping.

EXECUTING QUERIES AND UPDATES

In the foregoing discussion, we've focused on what Bauer and King describe as the *structural mismatch problem* (p. 384). This is where you map structures in the Java domain to structures in the database domain.

But in addition to structural mappings, you need to deal with the *behavioral mismatch*. Lookups and other dynamic behavior based on Java collections and the like are different than database queries and updates, and you need a way to ensure that your database queries end up meeting whatever performance requirements you have.

Hibernate's Session API is the key piece of the behavioral strategy. It provides an interface against which to perform persistence operations (basic Create, Read, Update, and Delete [CRUD] queries and updates, transaction control, and context management), and it does so against an internal persistence context, supporting optimizations such as automatic dirty checking (don't flush to the database unless something changed), transactional write-behind (flush as late as possible to minimize database lock times), and caching (support repeatable reads for free, avoid database hits when nothing has changed, and so on).

More generally, the Session API allows you to transition objects through the persistence lifecycle. In Hibernate, objects have one of four states—transient, persistent, removed, and detached—and the various Session API methods amount to ways to effect state transitions on individual objects. For example, `Session.save()` moves an object from the transient state (meaning Hibernate isn't managing it) to the persistent state (meaning Hibernate *is* managing it).

In the next listing you reimplement `ContactServiceImpl`, this time using Hibernate's Session API instead of `NamedParameterJdbcOperations`. Compare this with listing 2.1.

Listing 2.6   ContactServiceImpl.java revisited: Hibernate-based implementation

```
package com.springinpractice.ch02.service.impl;

import java.util.List;
import javax.inject.Inject;
import org.hibernate.Session;
import org.hibernate.SessionFactory;
import org.springframework.stereotype.Service;
import org.springframework.transaction.annotation.Transactional;
import com.springinpractice.ch02.model.Contact;
import com.springinpractice.ch02.service.ContactService;

@Service
@Transactional                                               ❶ Marks as
public class ContactServiceImpl implements ContactService {     transactional
    @Inject private SessionFactory sessionFactory;           ❷ Injects
                                                                SessionFactory
    public void createContact(Contact contact) {
        getSession().save(contact);                          ❸ Saves
    }                                                           contact

    @SuppressWarnings("unchecked")
```

```
public List<Contact> getContacts() {
    return getSession()
        .createQuery("from Contact")            ④ Creates
        .list();                                   query
}

public List<Contact> getContactsByEmail(String email) {
    return getSession()                         ⑤ Gets named
        .getNamedQuery("findContactsByEmail")      query
        .setString("email", "%" + email + "%")
        .list();
}

public Contact getContact(Long id) {            ⑥ Gets single
    return (Contact) getSession().get(Contact.class, id);   contact
}

public void updateContact(Contact contact) {
    getSession().update(contact);
}

public void deleteContact(Long id) {            ⑦ Deletes
    getSession().delete(getContact(id));           contact
}

private Session getSession() {
    return sessionFactory.getCurrentSession();     Gets current
}                                               ⑧ session
}
```

You mark the class as @Transactional at ❶. This indicates that all public methods are transactional. You can also do method-level overrides, although you don't do that here. The crucial point is that this is the extent of your explicit treatment of transactions: the @Transactional annotation allows you to avoid explicit transaction-management code against the Hibernate Session, which keeps your code clean. We'll look more carefully at transaction management in the next section.

Everything else deals with various persistence operations against the Session. At ❷ you inject a SessionFactory so you have a way to get the current session (the session bound to the request thread) via getCurrentSession() ❽. The persistence operations save a contact ❸, find all contacts by creating a JPQL query ❹, find all contacts with a matching email address by looking up a named JPQL query ❺, return a single contact ❻, and delete a contact ❼.

We've touched on both structural and behavioral mapping. The third topic is transaction management.

TRANSACTION MANAGEMENT

DAOs provide a way to perform persistence operations on entities, but they aren't themselves domain logic—they're pure mechanism. Instead, domain logic lives in the service layer that sits above the data access layer.

Any given service method might invoke a number of persistence methods, and these might involve multiple operations on multiple entities. In most cases, you want a service method to operate as a transaction with the standard ACID semantics. If the service

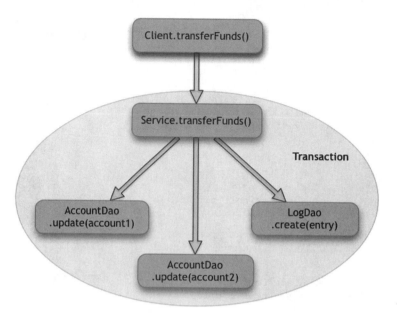

Figure 2.6 **A single transaction spanning multiple updates to the database**

method makes multiple persistence calls against one or more DAOs, you generally (or at least often) want those calls to operate as part of a single transaction. Figure 2.6 shows an example.

To handle this, your service layer needs a way to embed its database calls within the context of a transaction.[4] When a client calls a service method, you want to see something like the following flow:

1 Start a transaction.
2 Create a Hibernate session, and bind it to the transaction.
3 Execute the service method, including any DAO calls.
4 Flush the Hibernate session to the database.
5 Commit (or roll back) the transaction.
6 Clean up (unbind resources, close the Hibernate session).

Notice that step 3 is the only one that's interesting from an application development standpoint. The other steps are pure infrastructural boilerplate. Spring's transaction framework essentially does the boilerplate so developers can focus on the domain logic.

Because the framework handles the actual logic, all you need to do is tell the transaction infrastructure where the transactional boundaries are and which transactional semantics to apply in terms of propagation, isolation, rollback behavior, and so forth. You use Spring's `@Transactional` annotation to do this. Basically, you attach the annotation to methods that you want to run within a transaction. You can define specifics

---

[4] Although the service layer doesn't typically make direct database calls, the DAO calls that it does make pass through ORM, and these in turn ultimately go to the database. You usually want these to be part of a single transaction.

around the transaction (such as propagation behavior and isolation level) using the same annotation. Table 2.1 lists the options.

Table 2.1 Defining transactions with @Transactional elements

Element	Description	Possible values	Default
propagation	Transaction-propagation behavior.	MANDATORY, NESTED, NEVER, NOT_SUPPORTED, REQUIRED, REQUIRES_NEW, SUPPORTS	REQUIRED
isolation	Transaction isolation level.	DEFAULT, READ_COMMITTED, READ_UNCOMMITTED, REPEATABLE_READ, SERIALIZABLE	DEFAULT
timeout	Transaction timeout in seconds.	Integer	-1 (no timeout)
readOnly	Indicates whether the transaction is read-only.	true, false	false
rollbackFor	Zero or more Throwables that trigger a rollback.		{}
rollbackFor ClassName	Like rollbackFor, but with class names. Can be a substring.		{}
noRollbackFor	Zero or more Throwables that do *not* trigger a rollback.		{}
noRollbackFor ClassName	Like noRollbackFor, but with class names. Can be a substring.		{}

This way of specifying transactions is called *declarative* transaction management, because you attach @Transactional to a method when you want it to be transactional. It's the best-practice approach to building transactional Spring applications.

Declarative transaction management stands in contrast to *programmatic* transaction management, where you code up all the logic to create new transactions, bind sessions and connections to them, write if/else logic to decide which exceptions trigger rollbacks, commit the transaction, clean everything up, and so forth. This is in general *not* what you want to do as an application developer.

You saw in listing 2.6 that all you had to do was affix a class-level @Transactional annotation to your service bean. You could have specified additional transactional semantics, such as read-only transactions, but you didn't do that. Again, you can apply @Transactional to individual methods; these override any class-level definition that might exist.

TIP   An overriding method-level @Transactional completely overrides the class-level @Transactional rather than augmenting it in an additive way. If, for example, a class-level @Transactional specifies SERIALIZABLE isolation and a method-level @Transactional doesn't explicitly specify anything, the method's isolation level will be DEFAULT, not SERIALIZABLE.

The only thing remaining to see is the configuration.

Listing 2.7   beans-service.xml, with Hibernate configuration

```xml
<?xml version="1.0" encoding="UTF-8"?>
<beans xmlns="http://www.springframework.org/schema/beans"
    xmlns:c="http://www.springframework.org/schema/c"
    xmlns:context="http://www.springframework.org/schema/context"
    xmlns:jee="http://www.springframework.org/schema/jee"
    xmlns:p="http://www.springframework.org/schema/p"
    xmlns:tx="http://www.springframework.org/schema/tx"
    xmlns:util="http://www.springframework.org/schema/util"
    xmlns:xsi="http://www.w3.org/2001/XMLSchema-instance"
    xsi:schemaLocation="
        http://www.springframework.org/schema/beans
        http://www.springframework.org/schema/beans/spring-beans-3.1.xsd
        http://www.springframework.org/schema/context
        http://www.springframework.org/schema/context/
            spring-context-3.1.xsd
        http://www.springframework.org/schema/jee
        http://www.springframework.org/schema/jee/spring-jee-3.1.xsd
        http://www.springframework.org/schema/tx
        http://www.springframework.org/schema/tx/spring-tx-3.1.xsd
        http://www.springframework.org/schema/util
        http://www.springframework.org/schema/util/spring-util-3.1.xsd">

    <jee:jndi-lookup id="dataSource" jndi-name="jdbc/Sip02DS"
        resource-ref="true" />                                     ❶ Hibernate
                                                                     properties
    <util:properties id="hibernateProperties">
        <prop key="hibernate.dialect">
            org.hibernate.dialect.MySQL5InnoDBDialect
        </prop>
        <prop key="hibernate.show_sql">false</prop>
    </util:properties>
                                                                   ❷ Session
    <bean id="sessionFactory"                                        factory
        class="org.springframework.orm.hibernate3.annotation.
            AnnotationSessionFactoryBean"
        p:dataSource-ref="dataSource"
        p:packagesToScan="com.springinpractice.ch02.model"
        p:hibernateProperties-ref="hibernateProperties" />
                                                                   ❸ Transaction
    <bean id="transactionManager"                                    manager
        class="org.springframework.orm.hibernate3.
            HibernateTransactionManager"
        p:sessionFactory-ref="sessionFactory" />
                                                                   ❹ Activates
    <tx:annotation-driven />                                          @Transactional
```

```
    <context:component-scan
        base-package="com.springinpractice.ch02.service.impl" />
</beans>
```

You set Hibernate configuration properties using the `util` namespace at ❶. Then you use them to define an `AnnotationSessionFactoryBean` at ❷, which is a factory that produces a `SessionFactory`. The `SessionFactory` knows how to read the Hibernate and JPA mapping annotations that you place on entity classes, as you did with `Contact` in listing 2.5. You inject the `DataSource` into the `AnnotationSessionFactoryBean` because your `Sessions` ultimately need to read from and write to the `DataSource`. You also tell the `AnnotationSessionFactoryBean` which package(s) to scan for entities. Here you have only one package, but you can also use multiple comma-separated packages. Figure 2.7 shows how this all fits together.

At ❸ you define a `Hibernate-TransactionManager`. This handles the complicated transaction-management logic that you'd rather not have to deal with. Behind the scenes, the transaction manager invokes transaction-management methods on the underlying `SessionFactory`.

The `<tx:annotation-driven/>` at ❹ activates the transaction manager by wrapping beans (usually service beans) annotated with `@Transactional` with transactional proxies.[5] Each proxy has a reference to the transaction manager, which by default has the ID `transactionManager`. (That's why you used this ID when you defined the transaction manager.) The proxy uses the transaction manager to manage transactions on behalf of the proxy's target bean. This is entirely transparent to clients of the target bean, which work with the proxy and are none the wiser.

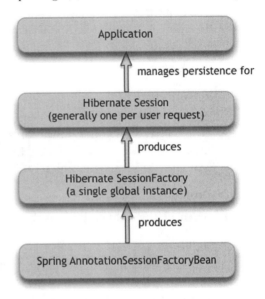

Figure 2.7 How applications get access to sessions

Declarative, transparent transaction management is arguably one of the most useful features of the entire Spring framework.

With that, you've established the data access and transaction background necessary to make sense of what you do in the rest of the book. Note that Spring's transaction framework is rich, and there's much that we couldn't cover here. Consult the Spring reference manual for more information.

As with recipe 2.2, the changes you've made don't affect the behavior of the app. Try running the application again to make sure everything is still working.

---

[5] It's also possible to weave these with AspectJ, although you aren't doing that here.

Discussion

This recipe showed how to clean up your persistence code using Hibernate ORM. You can see that there's a big difference between the JDBC-based code in listing 2.1 and the ORM-based code in listing 2.6.

But there is another improvement to be had. Ideally, your service tier doesn't have to involve itself in the mechanics of persistence management. Instead, the service tier should focus on domain logic and delegate persistence concerns to something else. That "something else" is the topic of the next recipe.

2.4 Creating a data access layer

PREREQUISITES

Recipe 2.3, "Object-relational mapping and transactions via Hibernate"

KEY TECHNOLOGIES

Hibernate

Background

Persistence is a fairly low-level concern; it's not part of the domain logic that forms the core concern for your application's service tier. Unfortunately, so far your service bean focuses squarely on persistence. In this recipe, you'll learn how to isolate domain logic from persistence logic, which creates a cleaner architecture.

Problem

Separate the domain logic and persistence logic concerns.

Solution

The classical solution to separating the domain logic and persistence logic concerns is called the *data access object (DAO) pattern*.[6] The basic idea is to consolidate persistence-related code in a dedicated architectural tier that sits above the database, and have the service tier (which handles domain logic) defer persistence-related concerns to this persistence-centric tier.

The approach to implementing DAOs is simple: inject the Hibernate `SessionFactory` into each DAO, and then implement persistence methods backed by the sessions you grab from the factory. Because a lot of the persistence operations are common, it's useful to define a general DAO interface and an abstract base DAO, and then derive corresponding entity-specific interfaces and classes as shown in figure 2.8.

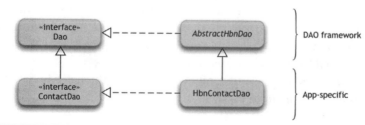

Figure 2.8 Class diagram illustrating the relationship between generic framework classes and app-specific implementations

---

6   Core J2EE Patterns—Data Access Object, Oracle, http://mng.bz/0PSy.

The following listing presents the generic DAO interface that you'll use throughout the book.

Listing 2.8 Dao.java, a generic DAO interface

```
package com.springinpractice.dao;                    ◁─┐   Common DAO
                                                     ❶   package
import java.io.Serializable;
import java.util.List;

public interface Dao<T extends Object> {             ◁─┐   Generic type
                                                     ❷   parameter
    void create(T t);                  ◁──❸  CRUD operation

    T get(Serializable id);

    T load(Serializable id);

    List<T> getAll();                            ◁──❹  A query

    void update(T t);

    void delete(T t);

    void deleteById(Serializable id);

    void deleteAll();

    long count();

    boolean exists(Serializable id);
}
```

There's not a single way to implement a generic DAO interface, but this one meets the needs for this book. Let's take a look.

First, note that this interface is in the `com.springinpractice.dao` package ❶. We put it there instead of in `com.springinpractice.ch02` because you'll use this interface throughout the book. To get the sample DAO code, grab the download at https://github.com/springinpractice/sip-top/.

A key feature is the use of a generic type parameter ❷. This allows you to adapt derived interfaces to specific domain classes, making them friendlier to use. You include the various CRUD methods such as `create()` ❸. You can also include general-purpose queries; here you use a `getAll()` finder method ❹ that finds all instances of the relevant type.

Deriving a subinterface is easy. You can add entity-specific methods as you please, as shown in the next listing.

Listing 2.9 ContactDao.java: a contact DAO interface

```
package com.springinpractice.ch02.dao;

import java.util.List;
import com.springinpractice.ch02.model.Contact;
import com.springinpractice.dao.Dao;

public interface ContactDao extends Dao<Contact> {

    List<Contact> findByEmail(String email);
}
```

You now have a base DAO interface, and you know how to derive entity-specific interfaces from it. You're going to do the same thing on the implementation side, defining a generic base DAO class, then subclassing it on a per-entity basis. The implementation is based on Hibernate.

Listing 2.10   AbstractHbnDao.java: a generic base class for implementing DAOs

```java
package com.springinpractice.dao.hibernate;

import java.io.Serializable;
import java.lang.reflect.Method;
import java.lang.reflect.ParameterizedType;
import java.util.Date;
import java.util.List;
import javax.inject.Inject;
import org.hibernate.Session;
import org.hibernate.SessionFactory;
import org.springframework.util.ReflectionUtils;
import com.springinpractice.dao.Dao;

public abstract class AbstractHbnDao<T extends Object>          ❶ Uses generics
        implements Dao<T> {

    @Inject private SessionFactory sessionFactory;             ❷ Injects
    private Class<T> domainClass;                                  SessionFactory

    protected Session getSession() {
        return sessionFactory.getCurrentSession();             ❸ Returns current
    }                                                             session

    @SuppressWarnings("unchecked")
    private Class<T> getDomainClass() {                         ❹ Returns domain
        if (domainClass == null) {                                class
            ParameterizedType thisType =
                (ParameterizedType) getClass().getGenericSuperclass();
            this.domainClass =
                (Class<T>) thisType.getActualTypeArguments()[0];
        }
        return domainClass;
    }

    private String getDomainClassName() {
        return getDomainClass().getName();
    }

    public void create(T t) {                                  ❺ CRUD method
        Method method = ReflectionUtils.findMethod(
            getDomainClass(), "setDateCreated",
            new Class[] { Date.class });
        if (method != null) {
            try {
                method.invoke(t, new Date());
            } catch (Exception e) { /* Ignore */ }
        }

        getSession().save(t);
    }
```

```
@SuppressWarnings("unchecked")
public T get(Serializable id) {
    return (T) getSession().get(getDomainClass(), id);
}

@SuppressWarnings("unchecked")
public T load(Serializable id) {
    return (T) getSession().load(getDomainClass(), id);
}

@SuppressWarnings("unchecked")
public List<T> getAll() {
    return getSession()
        .createQuery("from " + getDomainClassName())
        .list();
}

public void update(T t) { getSession().update(t); }

public void delete(T t) { getSession().delete(t); }

public void deleteById(Serializable id) { delete(load(id)); }

public void deleteAll() {
    getSession()
        .createQuery("delete " + getDomainClassName())
        .executeUpdate();
}

public long count() {                                    ◁── ⑥ Query
    return (Long) getSession()
        .createQuery("select count(*) from " + getDomainClassName())
        .uniqueResult();
}

public boolean exists(Serializable id) { return (get(id) != null); }
}
```

In line with the Dao interface, the base class uses generics ❶. You inject the Hibernate SessionFactory ❷ and then offer a protected getSession() method ❸, allowing subclasses to perform persistent operations against the Hibernate Session.

Implementing general versions of your CRUD operations and queries requires a reference to the actual domain class. You use reflection to discover and return it ❹.

The various methods are implementations of Dao methods. You have, for example, a CRUD method ❺ and a query ❻. The create() method sets the dateCreated property if it exists.

The following listing shows how to extend AbstractHbnDao to create an entity-specific DAO.

Listing 2.11   HbnContactDao.java: Hibernate-based DAO for contacts

```
package com.springinpractice.ch02.dao.hbn;

import java.util.List;
import org.springframework.stereotype.Repository;
import com.springinpractice.ch02.dao.ContactDao;
```

```
import com.springinpractice.ch02.model.Contact;
import com.springinpractice.dao.hibernate.AbstractHbnDao;

@Repository
public class HbnContactDao extends AbstractHbnDao<Contact>
        implements ContactDao {

    @SuppressWarnings("unchecked")
    public List<Contact> findByEmail(String email) {
        return getSession()
            .getNamedQuery("findContactsByEmail")
            .setString("email", "%" + email + "%")
            .list();
    }
}
```

Clearly, `AbstractHbnDao` makes life much simpler. You don't have to implement the core persistence methods, because they're available in `AbstractHbnDao`. Instead, you can focus on entity-specific extensions such as `findByEmail()`. Note the use of the fluent `Query` interface in this implementation of the `findByEmail()` method.

Also note the use of the `@Repository` annotation. This allows Spring to component-scan the bean, among other things.

The next listing shows the effect of your refactoring on the `ContactServiceImpl` bean.

Listing 2.12 ContactServiceImpl.java without persistence code

```
package com.springinpractice.ch02.service.impl;

import java.util.List;
import javax.inject.Inject;
import org.springframework.stereotype.Service;
import org.springframework.transaction.annotation.Transactional;
import com.springinpractice.ch02.dao.ContactDao;
import com.springinpractice.ch02.model.Contact;
import com.springinpractice.ch02.service.ContactService;

@Service
@Transactional
public class ContactServiceImpl implements ContactService {
    @Inject private ContactDao contactDao;

    public void createContact(Contact contact) {
        contactDao.create(contact);
    }

    public List<Contact> getContacts() {
        return contactDao.getAll();
    }

    public List<Contact> getContactsByEmail(String email) {
        return contactDao.findByEmail(email);
    }

    public Contact getContact(Long id) {
        return contactDao.get(id);
    }
```

```
    public void updateContact(Contact contact) {
        contactDao.update(contact);
    }
    public void deleteContact(Long id) {
        contactDao.deleteById(id);
    }
}
```

As you can see, this "service" is a pass-through layer to the DAO. In a more realistic application, you'd expect to see service beans include more domain logic. Sometimes this is domain logic proper, and sometimes it's other non-domain logic that for whatever reason hasn't been externalized. Examples are validation, security, messaging, and workflow. In any event, you've successfully moved the persistence concern out of the service bean into a dedicated tier.

This recipe was just a refactoring; rerun the application to ensure that it still functions before continuing on to the next recipe. Don't forget to add

```
<context:component-scan
    base-package="com.springinpractice.ch02.dao.hbn" />
```

to beans-service.xml so Spring can find the HbnContactDao you created.

Discussion

You've defined general persistence operations in the Dao interface. AbstractHbnDao implements this interface using Hibernate's Session API. You create entity-specific interfaces by extending Dao, and you create entity-specific implementations by extending AbstractHbnDao.

The next two recipes are optional because they present material that you don't use elsewhere in the book. But we strongly recommend that you review them, because they present an official framework for building DAOs, similar to the earlier ones, based on JPA and Spring Data JPA. Spring Data JPA is a fairly recent addition to the Spring portfolio, and we didn't have time to rework all the examples in the book to use JPA and Spring Data JPA instead of Hibernate and custom DAOs. But we would have liked to have done so. Look at the next two recipes, and consider using the approach described in your own projects.

2.5   *Working with JPA (optional)*

PREREQUISITES
Recipe 2.4, "Creating a data access layer"

KEY TECHNOLOGIES
JPA, Hibernate

Background

Hibernate was a pioneer in Java-based ORM. Eventually the idea caught on, and Sun created the Java Persistence API (JPA) standard around ORM, based in large part on Hibernate. Although you can use Hibernate in a standalone fashion, it's a compliant

JPA implementation. So you also have the option of using JPA and treating Hibernate as a persistence provider. This allows you to use JPA-based frameworks like Spring Data JPA, which you'll pursue in the following recipe.

Problem

Use the standard JPA API instead of using Hibernate's proprietary persistence API.

Solution

So far, we've described a configuration in which applications (the DAO part of apps, anyway) work directly with the Hibernate API. Although you do use standardized JPA annotations to declare the mappings on the entities (Hibernate understands them), you've been using Hibernate's `SessionFactory`, `Session`, `Query`, and so forth to implement the DAOs (see figure 2.9).

There's little danger in doing this because you've isolated all such code in the data access layer, and this is the approach used throughout the book. It's a more or less straightforward configuration, and it's nice for developers who are already familiar with the well-known Hibernate API.

But you may prefer to use standardized JPA interfaces such as `EntityManagerFactory` and `EntityManager` when you implement your DAOs. This approach offers additional flexibility with respect to choosing a persistence provider. You can, of course, continue to use Hibernate, because it's a mature JPA implementation. But you have other options, such as EclipseLink and OpenJPA. Figure 2.10 shows the JPA-based configuration.

The following listing shows how to reimplement `ContactDao` using JPA.

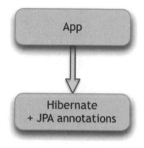

Figure 2.9   DAOs call the Hibernate API directly.

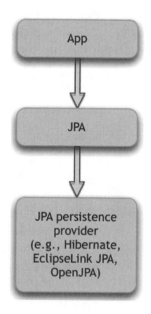

Figure 2.10   DAOs call JPA interfaces. You can bind an arbitrary persistence provider to the interface (EclipseLink JPA, OpenJPA, Hibernate, and so on).

Listing 2.13   JpaContactDao.java: a JPA-based DAO

```
package com.springinpractice.ch02.dao.jpa;

import java.io.Serializable;
import java.util.List;
import javax.persistence.EntityManager;
import javax.persistence.PersistenceContext;
import org.springframework.stereotype.Repository;
import com.springinpractice.ch02.dao.ContactDao;
```

```
import com.springinpractice.ch02.model.Contact;

@Repository
public class JpaContactDao implements ContactDao {
    @PersistenceContext private EntityManager entityManager;
```

1 EntityManager

```
    public void create(Contact contact) {
        entityManager.persist(contact);
    }
```

2 Persistence method

```
    public Contact get(Serializable id) {
        return entityManager.find(Contact.class, id);
    }

    public List<Contact> getAll() {
        return (List<Contact>) entityManager
            .createQuery("from Contact")
            .getResultList();
    }

    ... other persistence methods ...
}
```

This implementation is similar to what you did with Hibernate in listings 2.10 and 2.11. You begin by using the JPA @PersistenceContext annotation to inject not an Entity-ManagerFactory (the analog to Hibernate's SessionFactory) but a shared, thread-safe EntityManager ❶. This is analogous to injecting a Hibernate Session, which you can do with JPA.

You also have standard persistence methods, this time implemented against the EntityManager instead of against a Hibernate Session ❷.

The other piece relevant to Spring/JPA integration is the application context configuration.

Listing 2.14   beans-service.xml with a JPA-based persistence configuration

```
<?xml version="1.0" encoding="UTF-8"?>
<beans xmlns="http://www.springframework.org/schema/beans"
    xmlns:c="http://www.springframework.org/schema/c"
    xmlns:context="http://www.springframework.org/schema/context"
    xmlns:jee="http://www.springframework.org/schema/jee"
    xmlns:p="http://www.springframework.org/schema/p"
    xmlns:tx="http://www.springframework.org/schema/tx"
    xmlns:xsi="http://www.w3.org/2001/XMLSchema-instance"
    xsi:schemaLocation="
        http://www.springframework.org/schema/beans
        http://www.springframework.org/schema/beans/spring-beans-3.1.xsd
        http://www.springframework.org/schema/context
        http://www.springframework.org/schema/context/
            spring-context-3.1.xsd
        http://www.springframework.org/schema/jee
        http://www.springframework.org/schema/jee/spring-jee-3.1.xsd
        http://www.springframework.org/schema/tx
        http://www.springframework.org/schema/tx/spring-tx-3.1.xsd">

    <jee:jndi-lookup id="dataSource" jndi-name="jdbc/Sip02DS"
```

```
                 resource-ref="true" />
      <bean id="entityManagerFactory"                        ◄——❶ EntityManagerFactory
          class="org.springframework.orm.jpa.
                   LocalContainerEntityManagerFactoryBean"
          p:dataSource-ref="dataSource"
          p:packagesToScan="com.springinpractice.ch02.model">

          <property name="persistenceProvider">
              <bean class="org.hibernate.ejb.HibernatePersistence" />
          </property>
          <property name="jpaProperties">
              <props>
                  <prop key="hibernate.dialect">
                      org.hibernate.dialect.MySQL5Dialect
                  </prop>
                  <prop key="hibernate.show_sql">false</prop>
              </props>
          </property>
      </bean>
                                                       ❷  TransactionManager
      <bean id="transactionManager"                        ◄—
          class="org.springframework.orm.jpa.JpaTransactionManager"
          p:entityManagerFactory-ref="entityManagerFactory" />

      <tx:annotation-driven />

      <context:component-scan
          base-package="com.springinpractice.ch02.dao.jpa" />
      <context:component-scan
          base-package="com.springinpractice.ch02.service.impl" />
 </beans>
```

As with the DAO, the JPA version of bean-service.xml is similar to its Hibernate counterpart. You create a LocalContainerEntityManagerFactoryBean (analogous to the
AnnotatedSessionFactoryBean) at ❶. There are other options, depending in part
on what sort of container you want to use, but this is the one that makes sense for web
containers such as Tomcat and Jetty. (See the Spring reference documentation for
more information.) You don't have to provide an explicit persistence.xml JPA configuration because you specify the DataSource, provider, and provider-specific properties
right here in the Spring configuration. You create a JpaTransactionManager at ❷,
which takes the place of the HibernateTransactionManager you used formerly.

You've completely decoupled the app from Hibernate. You can still use Hibernate
as a JPA persistence provider, or you can use EclipseLink JPA, OpenJPA, or any other
JPA provider.

As with previous recipes, verify that the contact-management app still works before
continuing to the final recipe in this chapter.

Discussion

The next recipe builds on what you've done here with JPA. It presents the Spring Data
JPA project, which allows you to simplify your already simple DAO layer even further.

2.6   *Spring Data JPA overview (optional)*

PREREQUISITES
Recipe 2.5, "Working with JPA"

KEY TECHNOLOGIES
JPA, Spring Data JPA

Background

Until recently, it has been up to developers to implement their own DAO framework, as we showed how to do in recipe 2.4. With Spring Data JPA, that has changed. Spring Data JPA provides an official DAO framework as part of Spring itself—one that includes several useful characteristics and features:

- The generic DAO interface is comprehensive. It includes support for paging, sorting, and batch operations.
- Another nice touch is that in addition to the entity class, the ID class is a type parameter. That way you can use `Long`, `String`, or any other `Serializable` type in a typesafe way.
- Spring Data JPA automatically generates concrete DAO classes using dynamic proxies.
- It automatically generates query method implementations based on the name of the query method.
- It automatically translates exceptions to Spring's `DataAccessException` hierarchy.

Once you've updated your app to use JPA instead of using Hibernate directly, you can take advantage of Spring Data JPA. This recipe shows how.

Problem

Replace your custom DAO framework with the simpler and more powerful Spring Data JPA.

Solution

Spring Data JPA provides a generic DAO interface called `JpaRepository` that serves the same function your `Dao` interface does, although in a more comprehensive way. Let's begin by creating a `ContactDao` interface based on `JpaRepository`.

Listing 2.15   ContactDao.java, revised to use Spring Data JPA

```
package com.springinpractice.ch02.dao;

import java.io.Serializable;
import java.util.List;

import org.springframework.data.jpa.repository.JpaRepository;
import com.springinpractice.ch02.model.Contact;
```

```
public interface ContactDao extends JpaRepository<Contact, Long> {

    List<Contact> findByEmailLike(String email);
}
```

❶ Extends JpaRepository

Finder method ❷ for search

To support contacts, you pass the Contact and Long type parameters into JpaRepository ❶. Those are the domain class and the ID class, respectively.

You also declare a finder method to support email search at ❷. The method name is significant because it's what allows Spring Data JPA to figure out how to build the corresponding query dynamically. See the Spring Data JPA reference documentation for more information on how Spring Data JPA maps method names to queries.

Now let's look at the revised beans-service.xml configuration.

Listing 2.16   beans-service.xml, revised to use Spring Data JPA

```xml
<?xml version="1.0" encoding="UTF-8"?>
<beans xmlns="http://www.springframework.org/schema/beans"
    xmlns:c="http://www.springframework.org/schema/c"
    xmlns:context="http://www.springframework.org/schema/context"
    xmlns:jee="http://www.springframework.org/schema/jee"
    xmlns:jpa="http://www.springframework.org/schema/data/jpa"
    xmlns:p="http://www.springframework.org/schema/p"
    xmlns:tx="http://www.springframework.org/schema/tx"
    xmlns:xsi="http://www.w3.org/2001/XMLSchema-instance"
    xsi:schemaLocation="
        http://www.springframework.org/schema/beans
        http://www.springframework.org/schema/beans/spring-beans-3.1.xsd
        http://www.springframework.org/schema/context
        http://www.springframework.org/schema/context/
            spring-context-3.1.xsd
        http://www.springframework.org/schema/data/jpa
        http://www.springframework.org/schema/data/jpa/spring-jpa-1.1.xsd
        http://www.springframework.org/schema/jee
        http://www.springframework.org/schema/jee/spring-jee-3.1.xsd
        http://www.springframework.org/schema/tx
        http://www.springframework.org/schema/tx/spring-tx-3.1.xsd">

    <jee:jndi-lookup id="dataSource" jndi-name="jdbc/Sip02DS"
        resource-ref="true" />

    <bean id="entityManagerFactory"
        class="org.springframework.orm.jpa.
            LocalContainerEntityManagerFactoryBean"
        p:dataSource-ref="dataSource"
        p:packagesToScan="com.springinpractice.ch02.model">

        <property name="persistenceProvider">
            <bean class="org.hibernate.ejb.HibernatePersistence" />
        </property>
        <property name="jpaProperties">
            <props>
                <prop key="hibernate.dialect">
                    org.hibernate.dialect.MySQL5Dialect
                </prop>
```

Declares JPA ❶ namespace

```
                <prop key="hibernate.show_sql">false</prop>
            </props>
        </property>
    </bean>

    <bean id="transactionManager"
        class="org.springframework.orm.jpa.JpaTransactionManager"
        p:entityManagerFactory-ref="entityManagerFactory" />

    <tx:annotation-driven />                           Discovers DAOs ❷

    <jpa:repositories base-package="com.springinpractice.ch02.dao" />  ◁┘
    <context:component-scan
        base-package="com.springinpractice.ch02.service.impl" />
</beans>
```

We've bolded the few parts that have changed from listing 2.14. You add the jpa namespace (and its schema location) to the configuration ❶. And you replace the DAO component scan with a `<jpa:repositories>` definition ❷, which is almost like a component scan, except that it discovers the DAO interfaces and then automatically provides dynamic proxy implementations for you. *That's right: you don't have to write the DAO implementations.* Nor do you need to mark up the interface with @Repository or @Component, because `<jpa:repositories>` can determine which interfaces implement JpaRepository.

Your data access tier has come a long way, when you think back to recipe 2.1. What started out as a bunch of SQL with named parameter substitutions and row mappings is now effectively a single findByEmailLike() method declaration.

Run the app to confirm that it functions as expected with the new Spring Data JPA data access tier in place.

Discussion

This recipe provides only a flavor of what Spring Data JPA is all about. But even with this small taste, it's clear that Spring Data JPA provides a powerful and streamlined approach to building out a data access tier. For more information on Spring Data JPA, visit the project home page at www.springsource.org/spring-data/jpa.

2.7 Summary

In this chapter, you learned how to put together a persistence and transaction infrastructure using a DataSource, Hibernate, the data access object design pattern, and declarative transactions. This popular combination makes for a powerful back end because it cleanly separates the infrastructure from the domain logic.

We also explored building DAOs against JPA rather than coding directly against Hibernate. Even though this book uses Hibernate directly, it's useful to see how the JPA-based approach works and how Spring makes it simple to move from one to the other.

Finally, we took a brief glimpse at Spring Data JPA, one of the projects under the Spring Data umbrella. Spring Data JPA simplifies the development of JPA-based DAOs.

In addition to JPA support, Spring Data has projects for several nonrelational data stores, including Hadoop, GemFire, Redis, Riak, MongoDB, Neo4j, and Amazon S3.

In chapter 3, we'll move up the stack to the web tier, where you'll see how to develop web-based model-view-controller (MVC) apps using Spring Web MVC.

Building web applications
with Spring Web MVC

This chapter covers

- Creating your first Spring Web MVC application
- Serving and processing forms
- Configuring Spring Web MVC
- Spring Mobile technology preview

This book is mostly about web application development, partly because that's where the bulk of your authors' experience lies, and partly because there's enough interesting material to support an entire book. (Actually, there's enough to support a lot of books, as any visit to your local bookstore will reveal.) Therefore most of the recipes involve some amount of web-related code and configuration, and you'll find that many of the same ideas and techniques recur throughout. Instead of repeating those over and over, we'll take a moment to discuss the basics here. This way, you can easily refer back to this material for review as you work through the recipes ahead.

Despite the large number of Java web frameworks, we're going to concentrate our efforts around using and understanding Spring Web MVC, which is the web framework that ships with Spring. We're more concerned with covering a variety of business problems using core Spring technologies and less concerned with covering every available technical option. No doubt the technical alternatives are interesting in their own right, but given our limited space we'll leave that treatment for reference manuals.

We'll begin by laying out background material, including a quick overview of the model-view-controller (MVC) pattern, Spring's approach to MVC, and its architectural underpinnings. Next you'll try your hand at writing some Spring Web MVC code, with your goal being to get an intuitive feel for how things work in Spring Web MVC. The rest of the chapter offers a more systematic treatment of writing controllers and configuring web applications to use them.

First things first: let's go over some important background information.

3.1   Spring Web MVC background

To understand Spring Web MVC, it will be useful to understand web-based MVC frameworks in general, Spring's version of web MVC, and the highlights of Spring Web MVC architecture, including the key components and control flow through those components. We'll cover each of those topics now.

3.1.1   A review of the model-view-controller (MVC) pattern

Model-view-controller (MVC) refers to the architectural pattern in which you separate your business services and domain objects (the *model*) from the UI (the *view*) and mediate their interaction through one or more *controllers*. You'd like to be able to modify your UI without having to change your business logic and domain objects, and separating the model and view makes it easier to do just that. It's a simple but proven concept.

Java web applications typically realize MVC in roughly the following way: the model encompasses business-tier code (service beans, POJOs, Enterprise JavaBeans [EJBs], and so forth), the view involves JSPs or similar technologies, and the controller is usually servlet-based. HTTP requests come into the servlet, which routes the request to a handler component (sometimes called an *action*, sometimes called a *controller*) that in turn processes the request. The handler makes any necessary calls against the service tier and grabs any domain objects[1] it needs to populate the view. Finally, the handler figures out which view to deliver and forwards processing to that view. Figure 3.1 shows the typical flow.

The flow works like this. As shown in figure in 3.1, an HTTP request comes into the controller ❶. The controller accesses the model ❷, possibly getting data ❸, possibly updating the model, and possibly both. The controller then uses the view ❹ to generate a response ❺, passing any relevant data it pulled out of the model. The client receives the generated response ❻, and service is complete.

---

[1] It's not always desirable to use domain objects in the presentation layer. See section 3.3.1 for a more detailed discussion of this topic.

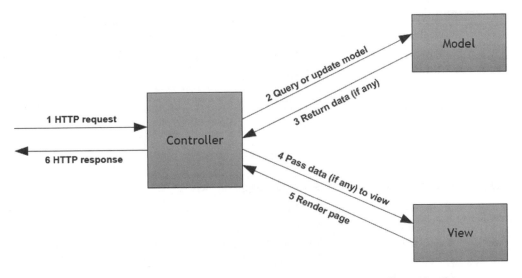

Figure 3.1   A conceptual view of control flow in web-based model-view-controller applications

The separation of concerns is clear. The model is insulated from changes to the view, and the view is insulated from at least certain changes to the model. Of course, because the view renders model data, the view isn't completely insulated from model changes. But in general, separating the model and view into separate components means it's easier to update one without breaking the other.

We'll begin by exploring what Spring Web MVC is and how it helps us build web applications.

3.1.2   *What is Spring Web MVC?*

Spring Web MVC, as you might guess, is Spring's web-centric MVC framework. Its primary job is to support the MVC way of dividing application functionality, so it provides explicit support for organizing the web layer into models, views, and controllers. Separation between the three concerns is clean; for example, when a controller selects a view, it does so by selecting only a view name (not a `View` object, not a hardcoded path), and dependency injection makes it possible to treat even view names as injected values.

Besides a clean separation of concerns, another major design goal for Spring Web MVC is flexibility. There are many ways for you to customize the way it works. If you want to use POJO controllers, you can do that. If you prefer defining an interface for controllers, you can do that too. You can control how requests map to controllers, how view names are generated, and how view names are resolved to views. You can define interceptor chains and exception handling for your controllers, and you can choose from different strategies for resolving locales, UI themes, multipart resolvers, and more.

> **NOTE**   Spring 3 deprecates the `org.springframework.web.servlet.mvc` `.Controller` hierarchy, so we will not cover these interfaces and classes here. Spring 3 controllers are generally POJOs.

Speaking of flexibility, one of our favorite things about Spring Web MVC is the tremendous flexibility it provides around handler[2] method parameters and return values: if you want to expose an `HttpServletRequest` to a handler method, just declare the parameter, and it's automatically provided to the method. If you don't want it, leave it out. You can do the same thing with a whole host of parameters, as you'll see.

Don't worry if that sounds like mumbo-jumbo at this point. We'll look at this in detail over the course of the chapter. Suffice it to say that Spring Web MVC is flexible and capable.

Let's see some highlights of the Spring Web MVC architecture.

3.1.3   *An architectural overview of Spring Web MVC*

The center of the Spring Web MVC universe is the `DispatcherServlet`, a front controller[3] that dispatches requests to registered request handlers. The handlers can be UI controllers or endpoints for HTTP-based remote services. Each handler performs a service and then specifies a view to which the `DispatcherServlet` passes the request. See figure 3.2.

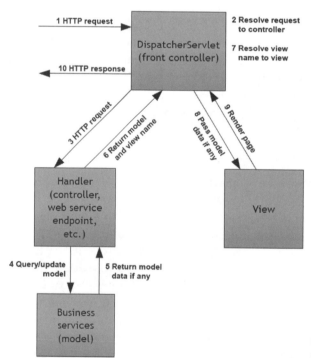

Figure 3.2   **A conceptual view of control flow in Spring Web MVC**

---

[2] In Spring Web MVC, *handler* is a more general way of referring to a UI controller. The idea is the same, but handlers include HTTP-based remote service endpoints, which wouldn't normally be considered UI controllers even though in reality they're doing roughly the same thing: grabbing data and exporting it in a desired format. We'll mostly use *handler* and *controller* interchangeably.

[3] A front controller is a top-level controller. It often manages other controllers. See Core J2EE Patterns—Front Controller, Oracle, http://mng.bz/AB9X for more information.

We're still dealing with the conceptual here, so don't take figure 3.2 too literally, but here's how it works. The request comes into the `DispatcherServlet` ❶. Based on the request path, the `DispatcherServlet` figures out which of its registered handlers is the right one to service the request ❷. It then passes the HTTP request (or, more abstractly, the user command or form data that the request represents) to a handler for processing ❸. The handler queries or updates the model (or both) ❹, and if appropriate the model returns the requested data ❺. The handler then returns both the data and a logical view name back to the `DispatcherServlet` ❻. The `DispatcherServlet` resolves the view name into an actual view ❼ and then passes the model data (if any) along to that view ❽ so it can be used in generating a response ❾. Processing is complete, and the `DispatcherServlet` has serviced the request ❿.

We've suppressed a lot of details, but now you have a basic understanding of how Spring Web MVC works. Let's get right to the good stuff: writing your first Spring Web MVC application (a toy app) and seeing it in action.

3.2 Creating your first Spring Web MVC application

Let's build a simple application (in the broadest sense of the term) to manage a roster of some sort. We're going to present this without tons of detailed explanation; our goal is to give you an intuition for how things work in Spring Web MVC, rather than exhaustively cover all the bases. This leisurely stroll will give you a context against which to understand a more detailed discussion afterward. You'll begin with the app configuration.

3.2.1 Configuring the application

The following listing shows a bare-bones web.xml configuration, but it will work just fine.

Listing 3.1   Simple `DispatcherServlet` configuration in web.xml

```xml
<?xml version="1.0" encoding="UTF-8"?>
<!-- Source project: sip03, branch: 01 (Maven Project) -->

<web-app xmlns="http://java.sun.com/xml/ns/javaee"
    xmlns:xsi="http://www.w3.org/2001/XMLSchema-instance"
    xsi:schemaLocation="http://java.sun.com/xml/ns/javaee
        http://java.sun.com/xml/ns/javaee/web-app_2_5.xsd"
    version="2.5">

    <servlet>
        <servlet-name>main</servlet-name>
        <servlet-class>
            org.springframework.web.servlet.DispatcherServlet        ❶ Declares
        </servlet-class>                                                DispatcherServlet
    </servlet>
    <servlet-mapping>
        <servlet-name>main</servlet-name>
        <url-pattern>/main/*</url-pattern>                           ❷ Maps requests
    </servlet-mapping>                                                  to it
</web-app>
```

As promised, this is as simple as they come. You've defined a minimal `Dispatch-erServlet` ❶, which again is Spring Web MVC's front controller, and you've indicated that you want to send `/main/*` requests to it ❷. You're not tied to that particular mapping; that's just what you happen to have chosen.

Now let's see the application context. You didn't define a `ContextLoaderListener` in web.xml, so you might be wondering where the app context comes from. The answer is that each `DispatcherServlet` instance creates its own local app context using an XML configuration we provide, so here's that configuration.

> **Listing 3.2   /WEB-INF/main-servlet.xml, the `DispatcherServlet`'s local app context**

```xml
<?xml version="1.0" encoding="UTF-8"?>
<!-- Source project: sip03, branch: 01 (Maven Project) -->

<beans xmlns="http://www.springframework.org/schema/beans"
    xmlns:p="http://www.springframework.org/schema/p"
    xmlns:xsi="http://www.w3.org/2001/XMLSchema-instance"
    xsi:schemaLocation="http://www.springframework.org/schema/beans
        http://www.springframework.org/schema/beans/spring-beans-3.1.xsd">

    <bean name="/roster/*"
        class="com.springinpractice.ch03.web.RosterController"/>      ◁── ❶ Controller bean

    <bean class="org.springframework.web.servlet.view.
            InternalResourceViewResolver"
        p:prefix="/WEB-INF/jsp/"                                       ❷ Maps view names to views
        p:suffix=".jsp"/>                                             ◁──
</beans>
```

`DispatcherServlet` knows where to find this file by using a convention you can probably guess.[4] You can configure the location, but we won't worry about that right now.

First you define the controller, `RosterController` ❶. The controller name specifies the requests that the `RosterController` services.

You also define a `ViewResolver` ❷, which allows you to convert logical view names to views. For now it's enough to know that a logical view name such as `foo` is converted to `/WEB-INF/jsp/foo.jsp` given the definition here. When dealing with JSP views in particular, it's a good practice to place them somewhere inside the WEB-INF folder (WEB-INF/jsp is the official recommendation) so clients can't access them directly. That's what you do here.

That does it for configuration. You'll create a controller in a few minutes, but in preparation for that, let's create a domain object to represent a member of your roster.

3.2.2   A simple domain object

The following listing shows Member.java, a simple domain object you'll use in your controller.

---

[4] The location convention is /WEB-INF/[servlet-name]-servlet.xml, if you're feeling lazy.

Listing 3.3   Member.java

```
// Source project: sip03, branch: 01 (Maven Project)
package com.springinpractice.ch03.model;

public class Member {
    private String firstName;
    private String lastName;

    public Member() { }

    public Member(String firstName, String lastName) {
        this.firstName = firstName;
        this.lastName = lastName;
    }

    public String getFirstName() { return firstName; }

    public void setFirstName(String firstName) {
        this.firstName = firstName;
    }

    public String getLastName() { return lastName; }

    public void setLastName(String lastName) {
        this.lastName = lastName;
    }

    public String toString() {
        return firstName + " " + lastName;
    }
}
```

There isn't anything too special here. You include two constructors because you'll eventually use both of them.

Now let's get to the controller, which is more interesting.

3.2.3   *Writing a basic controller*

The next listing shows the RosterController. To keep things simple, you'll hard-code some fake roster data directly in the controller. In a real application, the controller would typically delegate to either a service or a DAO to obtain this data on the controller's behalf. This is a pattern we'll demonstrate in chapter 4.

Listing 3.4   RosterController.java, the simple controller

```
// Source project: sip03, branch: 01 (Maven Project)
package com.springinpractice.ch03.web;

import java.util.*;
import org.springframework.stereotype.Controller;
import org.springframework.ui.Model;
import org.springframework.web.bind.annotation.RequestMapping;
import org.springframework.web.bind.annotation.RequestParam;
import com.springinpractice.ch03.model.Member;                    ❶ @Controller for
                                                                     controllers
@Controller
public final class RosterController {          ◁── ❷ Just a POJO
```

```
        private List<Member> members = new ArrayList<Member>();

        public RosterController() {
            members.add(new Member("John", "Lennon"));
            members.add(new Member("Paul", "McCartney"));
            members.add(new Member("George", "Harrison"));
            members.add(new Member("Ringo", "Starr"));
        }

        @RequestMapping
        public void list(Model model) {
            model.addAttribute(members);
        }

        @RequestMapping
        public void member(@RequestParam("id") Integer id, Model model) {
            model.addAttribute(members.get(id));
        }
    }
```

❸ Maps requests to method

❹ Model provided

❺ Passes data to view

Accepts request param ❻

There's a lot packed into this small controller class, and you're relying heavily on conventions. Don't feel bad if you're not seeing the details of how everything is wired up; you'll have plenty of time to get to that in the pages ahead.

Because the controller is a POJO, it's useful for certain purposes (for example, for request mapping purposes) to have an alternative way to flag it as a controller. That's what the @Controller annotation is doing ❶. You're not extending any other classes or implementing any interfaces ❷; you're effectively defining the contract for this controller.

> **WARNING** It should be obvious that you've hardcoded the member list into the controller. In a real application, you'd likely grab that from a service bean. But here you're trying to see how the MVC part works, so you're faking the member list.

You attach an @RequestMapping attribute to the list() and member() methods ❸. This identifies them as request-servicing methods. The actual paths involved are specified by conventions you'll see soon; here the paths are /roster/list[.*] and /roster/member[.*] respectively, where * is any extension. For example, /roster/list, /roster/list.do, and /roster/list.html all map to the list() method.

The signature of the list() method is largely up to you. You declare whatever you'd like to have, within certain bounds of course. (This is the part we were saying earlier that we like about Spring Web MVC.) You declare a Model parameter ❹, which means Spring will automatically pass you a Model object (essentially it functions as a Map, even though it doesn't implement that interface). Anything you put on the Model will be available to the JSP as a JSP expression language (EL) variable. Here, you've placed the list of members on the Model ❺. When you place objects on the model, they're stored as name/value pairs. Here, you haven't explicitly assigned a name to the attribute, so Spring will automatically generate the name by convention. Here, because the type is List<Member>, the generated name is memberList. You'll be able to access it from your JSP using ${memberList}.

At ❻ you can see another example of the flexible method signatures in action. This time you declare that you want to accept an HTTP parameter called id, and you want it to be automatically parsed into an Integer. That's exactly what happens here. (We told you it was cool.) And again, with the model you haven't provided an explicit attribute name, so the name will be autogenerated based on the attribute type. In this case the name will be member, and it will be available to the JSP using ${member}.

You may have noticed that you haven't explicitly specified any view names. How does DispatcherServlet know which view gets the request after a given handler method is finished with it. The answer is that you're using a convention that automatically translates the request URL to a logical view name. Because the request URL for the list() method is /roster/list[.*], the view name according to the convention will be list. Similarly, because the request URL for the member() method is /roster/member[.*], the view name will be member. You'll see more about this convention later when we discuss the DefaultRequestToViewNameTranslator.

Another thing to note is that you define a couple of different actions. You can define as many as you like, but for now you're keeping it simple. Normally you would put closely related functionality together in a single controller as you do here.

Now let's peek at the master and details JSPs.

3.2.4 *Implementing the master and details views*

The following listing shows list.jsp, which displays the entire roster.

Listing 3.5 /WEB-INF/jsp/roster/list.jsp, a roster master page

```
<%-- Source project: sip03, branch: 01 (Maven Project) --%>
<%@ taglib prefix="c" uri="http://java.sun.com/jsp/jstl/core" %>

<html>
    <head>
        <title>Roster</title>
    </head>
    <body>
        <h1>Roster</h1>
        <ul>
            <c:forEach var="member" items="${memberList}"        ❶ Member list exposed
                varStatus="status">                                  as ${memberList}
                <li>
                    <a href="member.do?id=${status.index}">       ❷ Passes id
                        <c:out value="${member}"></c:out>            param
                    </a>
                </li>
            </c:forEach>
        </ul>
    </body>
</html>
```

In this listing you reference the memberList attribute you set in the controller through a JSP EL variable ❶. You list the members ❷, with their names being links to details pages. You also pass an id parameter along, which the member() method expects as you saw in listing 3.4.

Next, here's the details page, member.jsp.

Listing 3.6   /WEB-INF/jsp/roster/member.jsp, a member details page

```
<%-- Source project: sip03, branch: 01 (Maven Project) --%>
<%@ taglib prefix="c" uri="http://java.sun.com/jsp/jstl/core" %>

<html>
    <head>
        <title>Member: ${member}</title>
    </head>
    <body>
        <h1>Member: ${member}</h1>
        <p><a href="list.do">Back</a></p>
    </body>
</html>
```

❶ Member exposed as ${member}

Nothing much happening here. It's another example of grabbing data from the Model and displaying it in the JSP ❶. Let's stop at this point to admire the beauty of your work so far. Point your browser to http://localhost:8080/sip/main/roster/list.do. It won't win any design awards, but it works.

Let's try adding a form.

3.3   Serving and processing forms

Now that you've seen how to create a simple POJO controller, it's time to get a little more adventurous and implement form serving and processing functionality. Let's pretend you create a form to allow the user to nominate a member for an award. (Yeah, we're making this example up as we go.) Although it's entirely possible to mix and match form methods with non-form methods on a single controller, let's create a new controller because showing rosters and roster members isn't closely related to nominating members for awards.

A best practice for controllers

With Spring Web MVC before Spring 2.5, the way you bundled controller methods together was dictated more by the classes in the Controller hierarchy than it was by which methods were closely related. With POJO controllers that's no longer the case. A best practice is to bundle closely related methods together in a single controller, and to put unrelated methods on other controllers.

Before creating your new controller, you'll need a form bean. One of the nice features of Spring Web MVC is that if it makes sense to do so, you can use your domain objects as form beans. Let's see what's involved with that.

3.3.1   Using domain objects as form beans

To add a form, the first thing you need to do is create a bean to store the form data. This is called a *form bean* or *form-backing bean*. There are a couple of different approaches to doing this, and they aren't mutually exclusive.

One approach is to use your domain objects as your form beans. This works well when there's a close match between the fields you require on the form and the properties your domain model has, as is often the case. The advantage of this approach is that you can avoid creating separate but parallel sets of classes for your domain objects and your form beans, which keeps the clutter down. (With Struts 1, for instance, it was common to have parallel sets of classes like this.)

Another approach is to implement your form bean separately from your domain model. This can make sense when the domain model has properties for which there aren't corresponding form fields, when the form has fields for which there aren't corresponding domain object properties, or both. A good example (which you'll see in chapter 4, even though there you use the domain object as a form bean after all) is a user registration form. Most registration forms have a "confirm password" field, and many have CAPTCHA fields, but neither of those is properly part of the domain model. Similarly, the domain model often has properties such as confirmed, enabled, and so forth. Obviously you wouldn't include those as form fields.

When using this second approach, you have to pay attention to how you handle the extra fields on both sides. If the form has extra fields, like a "confirm password" field, you can declare those as separate @RequestParam parameters as you did in listing 3.4. If the domain model has extra properties, such as confirmed or enabled, you'll need to make sure users can't bind extraneous HTTP parameters to those properties. That involves creating a form-binding whitelist. See section 3.3.6 for more information.

> ### Is it really OK to use domain objects as form beans?
>
> Even in cases where there's not an exact match between form beans and domain objects, it's a judgment call and a matter of architectural sensibilities whether you reuse your domain objects for your form.
>
> Some prefer not to do it because they (reasonably) draw a strong architectural distinction between form beans and domain objects. Struts 1, for instance, works like this: the framework enforces a clean separation between domain objects and form models.
>
> Others, your authors included, don't mind a little architectural impurity if we can avoid having two parallel sets of strongly similar classes (which carries its own costs). If our domain objects and form beans mostly overlap, we're willing to accept (for instance) JPA annotations in our form bean as the cost of having a single class.
>
> Spring Web MVC provides this option by design. Reasonable minds will differ as to its architectural merits. In practice we find the option useful and not confusing.

Again, the approaches aren't mutually exclusive, meaning you can use domain objects to back forms in certain cases and dedicated form beans in other cases.

That's enough philosophizing for now. In this case, the Member class is exactly what you'd want from a form bean, so you'll use it as a form bean.

Let's build the new controller.

3.3.2   *Adding a controller*

The new form will allow the user to nominate a member for an award. The controller won't *do* anything other than show some log output and forward to a "thanks" page. You just want to see how to set up a form. The following listing contains the new form controller.

Listing 3.7   NomineeController.java, a simple form controller

```java
// Source project: sip03, branch: 02 (Maven Project)
package com.springinpractice.ch03.web;

import org.apache.log4j.Logger;
import org.springframework.stereotype.Controller;
import org.springframework.ui.Model;
import org.springframework.web.bind.annotation.RequestMapping;
import org.springframework.web.bind.annotation.RequestMethod;

import com.springinpractice.ch03.model.Member;

@Controller
public final class NomineeController {
    private static final Logger log =
        Logger.getLogger(NomineeController.class);

    private String thanksViewName;

    public void setThanksViewName(String thanksViewName) {          ❶ Injects view name
        this.thanksViewName = thanksViewName;
    }
                                                                     ❷ Handles GET requests
    @RequestMapping(method = RequestMethod.GET)
    public Member form() { return new Member();}                    ❸ Serves empty form

    @RequestMapping(method = RequestMethod.POST)                    ❹ Handles POST requests
    public String processFormData(Member member) {
        log.info("Processing nominee: " + member);
        return thanksViewName;                                      ❺ Gets form data as bean
    }
}                                                                   ❻ Returns view name
```

The new controller is dedicated to serving and processing a form. You define a setter so you can inject a logical view name for a "thanks" page after the user submits a nomination ❶. It's probably obvious why you don't want to return something like /WEB-INF/jsp/nominee/thanks.jsp: that doesn't give you a good separation between the controller and the view. But it may be less obvious why you don't return a logical view name, say thanks. You'll see the answer to that when we discuss the redirect-after-post pattern, but for now take it on faith that even with the view name it often makes sense to keep the controller and view separate.

You have two methods. One is marked as handling GET requests and the other as handling POSTs. In the GET handler ❷, you return an empty form bean so the HTML form fields have something to bind to. In this case you aren't prepopulating the Member form bean, but sometimes it's useful to do that kind of thing.

> **Prepopulating form beans**
>
> The most common case of prepopulating form beans arises in validation scenarios:
> when the user enters invalid form data, you usually want to re-present that invalid
> data in the form so the user can correct it, rather than making them reenter the data
> from scratch. There are other examples too. You might prepopulate a request for in-
> formation (RFI) form bean with location data based on the user's IP address.

Whether or not you prepopulate the form bean with data, by returning it from the
method you're placing it on the Model under the generated attribute name member ❸.
If you wanted to use another attribute name, such as nominee, you would do something
like this:

```
@RequestMapping(method = RequestMethod.GET)
public void form(Model model) {
    model.addAttribute("nominee", new Member());
}
```

The result is the same, except that the form bean's attribute name is nominee instead
of member.

At any rate, let's be happy with the attribute name member and return a Member. But
the choice is yours. This is yet another example of how flexible Spring Web MVC is.

Now let's look at the POST handler. You include an annotation marking it as such ❹,
and then you have a method signature that takes a Member and returns a String ❺. Once
again, the signature you use is dependent on your need. By taking a Member parameter,
the submitted form data will be automatically bound to a Member bean, the bean will be
placed on the model as an attribute under its generated name (member), and the bean
will be passed into the method itself. But as with return types, you aren't forced to use
the generated name here: you can use the @ModelAttribute annotation[5] to select a different name. Play around with the following, adding and removing the @ModelAttrib-
ute annotation, to see how it works:

```
@RequestMapping(method = RequestMethod.POST)
public String processFormData(
    @ModelAttribute("nominee") Member member, Model model) {

    log.info("Processing nominee: " + member);
    Map map = model.asMap();
    log.info("model[member]=" + map.get("member"));
    log.info("model[nominee]=" + map.get("nominee"));
    return thanksViewName;
}
```

For the following discussion, assume that you're using the code from listing 3.8
rather than the modified version. We wanted to give you a nice way to understand
what's going on with the form bean parameter, as well as exposure to the @ModelAt-
tribute annotation.

---

[5] The fully qualified class name is org.springframework.web.bind.annotation.ModelAttribute.

At ❻ you return the view name. Any time the return type is a `String`, `Dispatch-erServlet` assumes that the return value represents a logical view name.

You'll need a couple more JSPs: one to display the form and one to thank the user for submitting the form.

3.3.3 *Adding a form JSP and a "thanks" JSP*

The following listing shows the form.

> **Listing 3.8 /WEB-INF/jsp/nominee/form.jsp**

```
<%-- Source project: sip03, branch: 02 (Maven Project) --%>
<%@ taglib prefix="form"
    uri="http://www.springframework.org/tags/form" %>          ◁─┐  Declares form
<html>                                                         ❶  tag library
    <head>
        <title>Nominate a member for the award</title>
    </head>
    <body>
        <h1>Nominate a member for the award</h1>        ❷  Defines form
        <form:form modelAttribute="member">        ◁─┘
                                                             ❸  Binding
            <div>First name: <form:input path="firstName"/></div>  ◁─┘  input
            <div>Last name: <form:input path="lastName"/></div>
            <div><input type="submit" value="Submit"></input></div>  ◁─┐
        </form:form>
    </body>                                        No special
</html>                                            submit tag  ❹
```

The form is modest and looks a lot like a normal HTML form. The main difference is that you declare the Spring form tag library ❶, and you're using that to represent the form and its inputs. The primary advantage of using the form tag library is that it provides binding form inputs. If you were to prepopulate the `Member` bean with data, that data would automatically be rendered in the corresponding text field. (Try it out if you like.)

At ❷ you bind the form to the `member` attribute that the controller placed on the `Model`. This gives you a way to interpret input paths (discussed in a moment) as bean properties. If you don't specify an explicit value for `modelAttribute`, the default form bean attribute name is `command`, which isn't descriptive. You should probably always set a `modelAttribute` explicitly.

At ❸ you have a text field that binds to `member.firstName`. There's one for the last name too. The form tag library has tags for all the standard HTML input controls, although you're using only text fields here.

Finally you have a submit button ❹. There's no tag from the tag library for this because there isn't anything for the submit button to bind to; that is, the submit button doesn't have a corresponding bean property. So you use a normal HTML submit button.

The next listing shows a basic "thanks" page.

Listing 3.9   /WEB-INF/jsp/nominee/thanks.jsp

```
<%-- Source project: sip03, branch: 02 (Maven Project) --%>
<html>
    <head>
        <title>Thanks</title>
    </head>
    <body>
        <h1>Thanks</h1>
        <p>Thanks for nominating ${member}.</p>
    </body>
</html>
```

The only reason we're looking at this is that it shows you that the Member form bean passed into processFormData() lives on the Model under the member attribute name.

As you can see, adding a form is more involved than actions that grab data and display it. And we haven't yet touched whitelisting and validation. But all things considered, it's still fairly straightforward. The framework handles form/bean binding automatically, and you define the controller methods to use just what you need and nothing else.

Let's finish the form (for the moment) by updating the application context.

3.3.4   *Updating the application context*

You need to make only one change to the main-servlet.xml application context file. Add the following bean, and you're set:

```
<bean name="/nominee/*"
    class="com.springinpractice.ch03.web.NomineeController"
    p:thanksViewName="nominee/thanks"/>
```

It's time to try the new form. Point your browser to http://localhost:8080/sip/main/ nominee/form.do. You should get the nomination form. When you complete the form and submit it, you should get the "thank you" message, complete with the nominee's name.

The form basically works, but it's not done yet. You need to address important usability and security issues. Let's look at those.

3.3.5   *Adding redirect-after-post behavior*

One common pattern to use with web-based forms is called *redirect-after-post*. The idea is that when a user submits a form via HTTP POST, it's nice to force a redirect to minimize the likelihood of a double submit, to avoid browser warnings when the user clicks the back button, to make the resulting page easier to bookmark, and so forth. To do this, prepend redirect: to the logical view name. This will cause RedirectView to kick in, and the browser will request whatever page you tell it to request.

This illustrates a good reason for using dependency injection to set logical view names. Presumably controllers shouldn't know whether they're issuing forwards or redirects. By keeping the view names configurable, you achieve controller/view separation.

Now let's look at a security issue you need to address when working with forms.

3.3.6 *Adding form-binding whitelisting*

In July 2008, Ounce Labs[6] discovered a security vulnerability in Spring Web MVC related to automatic form binding. Because Spring automatically binds HTTP parameters to form bean properties, an attacker could conceivably bind to properties that weren't intended for binding by providing suitably named HTTP parameters. This might be a real problem in cases where a domain object is serving as the form-backing bean, because domain objects often have fields that are suppressed when used in form-backing scenarios, as we discussed in section 3.3.1.

To address this problem, you can define explicit whitelists in your controllers. You can do this using so-called @InitBinder methods. You'll need one for each form. (If your controller has two forms, it needs two separate @InitBinder methods.)

Here's an example you'll see later in the book. You have a controller that handles two forms: one to allow users to subscribe to a mailing list using a form called sub-scriber, and one to allow them to unsubscribe using a form called unsubscriber. You use these @InitBinder methods to whitelist the form fields:

```
@InitBinder("subscriber")
public void initSubscriberBinder(WebDataBinder binder) {
    binder.setAllowedFields(new String[] {
        "firstName", "lastName", "email"
    });
}

@InitBinder("unsubscriber")
public void initUnsubscriberBinder(WebDataBinder binder) {
    binder.setAllowedFields(new String[] { "email" });
}
```

If there's only one form, you don't need to provide an explicit annotation value. But because you have two forms, you need to specify subscriber or unsubscriber to let Spring know which binder to initialize.

Even after initializing the binders, you aren't finished. You have to verify that the whitelist has been respected each time the user submits a form. One simple way to do this is to define a helper class with a static verification method and call that from your form-processing methods. Here's a sample implementation:

```
public static void verifyBinding(BindingResult result) {
    String[] suppressedFields = result.getSuppressedFields();
    if (suppressedFields.length > 0) {
        throw new RuntimeException(
            "Attempting to bind suppressed fields: " +
            StringUtils.arrayToCommaDelimitedString(suppressedFields));
    }
}
```

---

[6] Ounce Labs was acquired by IBM in 2009.

A more sophisticated way to do this might be to define an aspect that automatically applies the verification to all form-processing methods, although you don't do that here.

See recipe 4.1 for more information on whitelisting form bindings.

3.3.7 Adding form validation

When users submit form data, you typically want to validate it before accepting it for processing. For example, in the present case you'd want to make sure that the fields aren't empty, that they aren't too long, that the e-mail field looks like a real e-mail address, and so forth. The preferred approach will eventually be to use JSR 303 (Bean Validation) to define annotation-based validation semantics on objects requiring validation. But JSR 303 isn't ready at the time of this writing, so the preferred approach until then is to use Hibernate Validator. Please see recipe 4.2 for a detailed example of how to perform annotation-based form validation in Spring.

Now that you've toured some of the capabilities Spring provides for implementing web-based MVC applications, let's look more carefully at configuration.

3.4 Configuring Spring Web MVC: web.xml

In sections 3.2 and 3.3 you created a toy application, and then we discussed in some detail how it works. We focused on the programming model rather than the configuration model, but now it's time to address configuration. Understanding Spring Web MVC configuration amounts to understanding how to configure the `DispatcherServlet`.

There are two levels of `DispatcherServlet` configuration. First, because it's a servlet, you declare one or more `DispatcherServlet` instances and their corresponding servlet mappings inside web.xml. Second, each `DispatcherServlet` instance has its own application context, and by configuring that you configure the `DispatcherServlet` itself. In this section we'll look at web.xml; in the following sections we'll look at the much more involved matter of configuring the servlet's application context.

`DispatcherServlet` is only a servlet, so at a certain level of abstraction there's no difference between configuring `DispatcherServlet` and configuring other servlets. The following listing shows a perfectly simple and valid `DispatcherServlet` configuration.

Listing 3.10 Simple `DispatcherServlet` configuration in web.xml

```xml
<?xml version="1.0" encoding="UTF-8"?>

<web-app xmlns="http://java.sun.com/xml/ns/javaee"
    xmlns:xsi="http://www.w3.org/2001/XMLSchema-instance"
    xsi:schemaLocation="http://java.sun.com/xml/ns/javaee
        http://java.sun.com/xml/ns/javaee/web-app_2_5.xsd"
    version="2.5">

    <listener>                                              Loads root ❶
        <listener-class>                                    app context
            org.springframework.web.context.ContextLoaderListener  ⟵
        </listener-class>
```

```
    </listener>
    <servlet>
        <servlet-name>main</servlet-name>
        <servlet-class>
            org.springframework.web.servlet.DispatcherServlet
        </servlet-class>
    </servlet>
    <servlet-mapping>
        <servlet-name>main</servlet-name>
        <url-pattern>/main/*</url-pattern>
    </servlet-mapping>
</web-app>
```

❷ Creates DispatcherServlet

❸ Maps requests

This is a minimal `DispatcherServlet` configuration. You load a root application context from the default location, /WEB-INF/applicationContext.xml ❶. Then you create the `DispatcherServlet` ❷. Because you haven't specified a location for the servlet's dedicated application context configuration, `DispatcherServlet` assumes that it exists at /WEB-INF/main-servlet.xml; the general pattern for the default location is /WEB-INF/[servlet-name]-servlet.xml. Finally, you specify the requests that you want the `DispatcherServlet` to service ❸.

When `DispatcherServlet` creates its application context, it uses the root app context as a parent context. But note that it isn't necessary to create a root app context. In that case, `DispatcherServlet`'s app context will be free-standing (no parent).

The servlet's application context can "see" beans in the root context, but not the other way around. Thus a nice way to use the servlet's app context is to put Spring Web MVC stuff in it rather than in the root context. That way your root context stays nice and tidy.

`DispatcherServlet` supports several configuration options. We'll mostly ignore them because they're fairly esoteric, but one that's worth knowing is `contextConfigLocation`. This works exactly like the same parameter for the root context (see chapter 1), but here it's a servlet `init-param` instead of an application `context-param`. If you wanted to move the XML file into a WEB-INF/conf directory, you would do something like this:

```
<servlet>
    <servlet-name>dispatcher</servlet-name>
    <servlet-class>
        org.springframework.web.servlet.DispatcherServlet
    </servlet-class>
    <init-param>
        <param-name>contextConfigLocation</param-name>
        <param-value>/WEB-INF/conf/main-servlet.xml</param-value>
    </init-param>
</servlet>
```

As with the root application context, you can specify multiple whitespace- or comma-delimited locations in the `param-value`. The resulting application context will include the beans from all files, with beans defined later in the list taking priority over those defined earlier in the case of naming conflicts.

> **NOTE** If you're interested in the other configuration parameters, look at the `DispatcherServlet` Javadocs. It turns out that its various JavaBean properties (such as `contextConfigLocation`, `contextAttribute`, `contextClass`, `dispatchOptionsRequest`, `detectAllHandlerMappings`, and so on) are all settable via the `init-param` mechanism. Pretty cool, right? Servlets don't usually work that way, but `DispatcherServlet` descends from `HttpServletBean`, which provides this special behavior.

That's about all you need to know about the web.xml configuration. But the core servlet configuration lives in the servlet's application context, and we'll visit that large topic right now.

3.5　*Configuring Spring Web MVC: the application context*

We're now going to look at the various `DispatcherServlet` configuration options at your fingertips. In calling these `DispatcherServlet` configuration options, note that we're talking about Spring Web MVC configuration generally, because `DispatcherServlet` does play that large a role in Spring Web MVC.

Fundamentally, `DispatcherServlet` provides a central place for registering controllers you write and an infrastructure for using the controllers to service requests. The configuration of that infrastructure is strategy-based, meaning Spring Web MVC defines a number of interfaces corresponding to the properties that need to be configured. Your job as application developers is to select or create appropriate implementations (*strategies*, in design pattern lingo) for those interfaces. Spring Web MVC provides several default strategy implementations, and normally you could use them as opposed to being forced to write your own. But the possibility of writing your own is certainly there, which speaks to the aforementioned flexibility of the design.

Before jumping into the specifics of controllers and `DispatcherServlet` configuration, we'll summarize the strategies and their default implementations in table 3.1.

Table 3.1 `DispatcherServlet` **strategy interfaces and default implemetations**

Strategy interface	#	Default implementation(s)
HandlerMapping	1–n	BeanNameUrlHandlerMapping, DefaultAnnotationHandlerMapping (Java 5+ only)
HandlerAdapter	1–n	HttpRequestHandlerAdapter, SimpleControllerHandlerAdapter, ThrowawayControllerHandlerAdapter, AnnotationMethodHandlerAdapter (Java 5+ only)
HandlerExceptionResolver	0–n	None
ViewResolver	1–n	InternalResourceViewResolver

Table 3.1 `DispatcherServlet` **strategy interfaces and default implemetations** *(continued)*

Strategy interface	#	Default implementation(s)
`RequestToViewNameTranslator` (bean ID: `viewNameTranslator`)	1	`DefaultRequestToViewNameTranslator`
`MultipartResolver` (bean ID: `multipartResolver`)	0–1	None
`LocaleResolver` (bean ID: `localeResolver`)	1	`AcceptHeaderLocaleResolver`
`ThemeResolver` (bean ID: `themeResolver`)	1	`FixedThemeResolver`

The table contains the major `DispatcherServlet` configuration options. Each option requires a given number of implementing beans, as described. For example, you can have as many `HandlerMapping` beans as you like, as long as you have at least one. If you don't specify any, then `DispatcherServlet` chooses defaults. (The annotation-based handler mapping and adapter are created only for Java 5+.)

Some of the beans are discovered by type, and some require the use of well-known names. In the case of `DispatcherServlet`, strategy interfaces allowing *n* implementations do type-based discovery, and interfaces allowing at most one implementation all require the use of well-known names if you want the `DispatcherServlet` to find your beans.

Now that you have some hint as to how `DispatcherServlet` configuration works in the application context, let's consider each strategy interface individually.

3.5.1 *Configuring HandlerMappings*

We'll begin with the `HandlerMapping` interface. Here's the idea behind handler mappings. Whenever `DispatcherServlet` receives a new HTTP request, it needs to find a handler (controller) to service that request. To this end `DispatcherServlet` maintains an ordered list of 1–*n* HandlerMappings.[7] When it receives a request, it checks each of its registered `HandlerMappings`, in order, to see whether it's able to generate a handler for the given request. If so, then that's the selected handler. If the process bottoms out without a handler being selected, then `DispatcherServlet` generates an HTTP 404.

There's more we can say about how `HandlerMappings` work, but let's pause to digest what you've learned so far. Table 3.2 shows the different `HandlerMapping` implementations available (and again, you can always write your own).[8] Each mapping scheme describes a way to match a request to a handler bean.

---

[7] We know that all lists are ordered. We're emphasizing the list order because it matters here.

[8] As of Spring 3.0, `CommonsPathMapHandlerMapping` no longer exists. Use annotation-based request mapping as a replacement.

Table 3.2   HandlerMapping implementations

Implementation	Mapping scheme
`BeanNameUrlHandlerMapping`	Match the request URL with a handler bean name, which must be URL-like and begin with a slash (`/`): for example, `/contact.do`. Wildcards are OK. This mapping is activated by default if (and only if) you don't specify mappings explicitly.
`ControllerBeanNameHandlerMapping`	Match the request URL with a plain handler bean name, which is converted into a URL by prepending an optional prefix, appending an optional suffix, and prepending a slash.
`ControllerClassNameHandlerMapping`	Match the request URL with a handler class name, which is converted into a base URL using a certain convention.
`DefaultAnnotationHandlerMapping`	Match based on the presence of the `@RequestMapping` annotation at the handler-type level or the existence of `@Controller` at the handler-type level and `@RequestMapping` at the handler-method level.
`SimpleUrlHandlerMapping`	Match according to a map whose keys are URL paths (possibly wildcarded) and whose values are bean IDs or names.

Let's see how (most of) the individual `HandlerMapping` implementations work.

BEANNAMEURLHANDLERMAPPING

As indicated, `BeanNameUrlHandlerMapping` is one of the defaults you get if you don't specify some other mapping. (If you do specify another mapping, then if you want the `BeanNameUrlHandlerMapping` you have to define it explicitly, because explicit handler mapping definitions displace the defaults.) It's very simple. You use the controller bean's name to specify the handler URLs that map to the controller. Here's how it works:

```
<bean name="/contact/*" class="mypackage.MyController"/>
```

The URL is relative to the servlet path. This approach is nice for its simplicity, but it can be verbose if you have a lot of controllers. Let's see another handler mapping—one that's concise.

CONTROLLERCLASSNAMEHANDLERMAPPING

`ControllerClassNameHandlerMapping` allows you to use the name of the controller to implicitly define the URLs that map to the controller. All you need to do is place the handler-mapping bean on the application context, and it's activated. The mapping works for controllers defined using the old `Controller` hierarchy as well as for those defined using the newer `@Controller` annotation.

Here's how to put it on the app context:

```
<bean class="org.springframework.web.servlet.mvc.support.
      ControllerClassNameHandlerMapping"/>
```

Once you do that, URLs will map to controllers based on controller names. If you have a controller called `ContactController`, for example, requests like `/contact` and `/contact/*` will map to the `ContactController`. The exact mappings depend on the type of controller; the mappings we just described apply to `MultiActionControllers` and `@Controller` beans. For more information please consult the Javadocs for `ControllerClassNameHandlerMapping`.

DEFAULTANNOTATIONHANDLERMAPPING

This is the second default handler mapping that's available, although only under Java 5. If you define another handler mapping explicitly, `DefaultAnnotationHandlerMapping` will be displaced and you'll need to define it explicitly if you want it.

This handler mapping works by inspecting method-level `@RequestMapping` annotations. Under this handler mapping, any annotations discovered on the methods automatically generate mappings to the handler itself.

`DefaultAnnotationHandlerMapping` typically depends on a type-level `@Controller` annotation to determine whether a given bean generates mappings, but this isn't strictly required. The other alternative is to have a type-level `@RequestMapping` annotation. One of the two type-level annotations must be present.

SIMPLEURLHANDLERMAPPING

This handler mapping is similar to `BeanNameUrlHandlerMapping` in the sense that it involves defining explicit URL/handler pairs in the application context file; but `SimpleUrlHandlerMapping` allows you to define multiple mapping patterns with a single bean; `BeanNameUrlHandlerMapping` allows only one mapping pattern per bean. Here's an example of how it works:

```
<bean class="org.springframework.web.servlet.handler.
      SimpleUrlHandlerMapping">
   <property name="mappings">
      <props>
         <prop key="/index.html">coreController</prop>
         <prop key="/about.html">coreController</prop>
         <prop key="/contact/*">contactController</prop>
         <prop key="/forums/*">forumsController</prop>
      </props>
   </property>
</bean>
```

As with the `BeanNameUrlHandlerMapping`, the URLs are relative to the servlet path. This handler mapping provides a nice way to combine several mappings in a single bean definition.

USING MULTIPLE HANDLER MAPPINGS AT ONCE

You may find yourself needing to use multiple handler mappings in a single `DispatcherServlet`. Maybe you want to use `ControllerClassNameHandlerMapping` as your main handler mapping strategy, but you want to use `SimpleUrlHandlerMapping` to cover some cases where your URLs don't match the controller class name in the way that would be required for the `ControllerClassNameHandlerMapping` to work. What to do, what to do?

You can accomplish this by placing any desired handler mappings on the context and defining an order. `DispatcherServlet` will find all of your handler mappings, and it will determine handler-mapping priority based on the handler mapping's `order` property, which all `AbstractHandlerMappings` have by virtue of implementing the `Order` interface. Here, the lower the number (with `Integer.MIN_VALUE` being the lowest possibility), the higher the precedence. When routing a request, `DispatcherServlet` iterates over its registered handler mappings starting with the highest-priority mapping, trying at each step to generate a handler match. Once a match is found, request processing continues with the matched handler. If there's no match, `DispatcherServlet` generates an HTTP 404.

Here's how it looks in code:

```
<bean class="org.springframework.web.servlet.handler.
➡        SimpleUrlHandlerMapping"
    p:order="0">
    <property name="mappings">
        <props>
            <prop key="/index.html">coreController</prop>
            <prop key="/about.html">coreController</prop>
            <prop key="/contact/*">contactController</prop>
            <prop key="/forums/*">forumsController</prop>
        </props>
    </property>
</bean>

<bean class="org.springframework.web.servlet.mvc.support.
➡        ControllerClassNameHandlerMapping"
    p:order="1"/>
```

Now let's look at what happens when the routing actually occurs. Although in most cases the request goes directly to a controller, that's not the only way it works. You can define interceptors around the controller to modify processing both coming in and going out.

HANDLERINTERCEPTORS

Any `HandlerMapping` implementation extending from `AbstractHandlerMapping` (and that would include all of the `HandlerMapping` implementations provided out of the box) allows you to specify an array of interceptors—implementing the `HandlerInterceptor` interface—which wrap handler requests in the same way that servlet filters wrap servlet requests. Figure 3.3 shows how this works.

Spring comes with several out-of-the-box `HandlerInterceptor` implementations. One example is `WebContentInterceptor`, which supports request checks such as checking whether the HTTP method is permissible and whether a session exists (if sessions are required). You can apply interceptors by injecting them into handler mappings, as shown next.

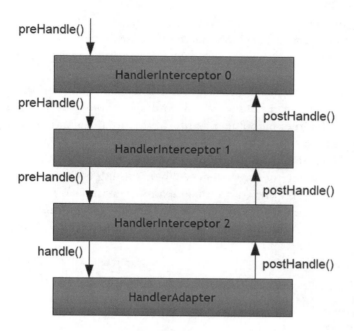

Figure 3.3   Control flow in a HandlerExecutionChain

Listing 3.11   How to intercept controllers with `HandlerInterceptors`

```
...
                                                           Defines interceptor  ❶
<bean id="webContentInterceptor"
    class="org.springframework.web.servlet.mvc.WebContentInterceptor">
    <property name="supportedMethods">
                                                           ❷  Configures it
        <list>
            <value>GET</value>
            <value>POST</value>
        </list>
    </property>
</bean>

<bean class="org.springframework.web.servlet.mvc.support.        ❸  Defines handler
        ControllerClassNameHandlerMapping">                          mapping
    <property name="interceptors">
        <list>                                          ❹  Injects
            <ref bean="webContentInterceptor"/>             interceptors
        </list>
    </property>                                          ❺  References defined
</bean>                                                      interceptor

...
```

In listing 3.7, you begin by defining an interceptor ❶. Here you're using one of the ready-made interceptors; you'll use it to block any HTTP request that isn't a GET or a POST. You accomplish this by configuring the `supportedMethods` property ❷, which is of course specific to this particular interceptor class. Although the property type is a `String[]`, Spring knows how to convert your list into an array.

Next is the handler-mapping definition ❸. Because this particular handler mapping extends `AbstractHandlerMapping`, you can define an `interceptors` property and pass along the list of interceptors ❹. Here there's only one. As previously mentioned, the `interceptors` property expects an array, but Spring knows how to convert the list to an array. You pass in the single `WebContentInterceptor` you created ❺. The result will be that for any request coming through that handler mapping, if it isn't either a `GET` or a `POST`, it will be blocked. For more information on interceptors, please see the `HandlerInterceptor` Javadocs.

Now let's move on to handler adapters, which allow Spring to be flexible with respect to the type of controllers it permits.

3.5.2 *Configuring HandlerAdapters*

Recall from our earlier discussion that one of the design goals behind Spring Web MVC is to be flexible. One expression of this flexibility lies in the fact that controllers don't have to implement any particular interface, at least as far as the app developer is concerned. Developers can implement interfaces in the `Controller` hierarchy, or they can add `@Controller` to their POJOs.

Ultimately, of course, `DispatcherServlet` needs to have some way to invoke the handlers, and it accomplishes this through the `HandlerAdapter` interface. The idea is that as long as there's a `HandlerAdapter` implementation that knows how to deal with your specific type of controller, `DispatcherServlet` is happy and can work with your controller. `HandlerAdapter` is therefore more a service provider interface (SPI) that you would implement only if you needed to support a new handler type; you wouldn't normally make calls against it yourself. Only `DispatcherServlet` needs to call it.[9]

3.5.3 *Configuring HandlerExceptionResolvers*

We've been discussing handler execution chains, which consist of a handler and its interceptors. Sometimes you want to define special exception handlers for the handler execution chains, and for that you turn to `HandlerExceptionResolvers`. By default `DispatcherServlet` doesn't have any, but if you decide you want one or more, it's easy to do. You place the desired `HandlerExceptionResolver` beans in the app context, using the `order` property to set precedence if you have more than one. If any given resolver is able to determine an appropriate landing page for the exception, it provides the page; otherwise, it returns null and the next resolver in the chain takes a crack at it. If all resolvers return null, then normal processing occurs (that is, whatever happens when there's an exception and no `HandlerExceptionResolvers` to handle it).

3.5.4 *Configuring ViewResolvers*

When a controller is done processing a request, it generally returns a logical view name to `DispatcherServlet`. The view name serves as a basis for view resolution.

---

[9] Probably `HandlerAdapter` is a misleading name for the interface. With the adapter design pattern, *adapter* refers to the implementation code that bridges the two interfaces. The outer interface itself isn't an adapter. No biggie, especially because nothing sees `HandlerAdapter` except `DispatcherServlet`.

(The controller can also return a null view name to indicate that it has itself handled processing.) When `DispatcherServlet` receives the view name, it grabs its list of `ViewResolvers` and iterates over them until it finds one that's able to generate a `View` from the view name.

We'll look at this chaining behavior in a few moments, but first let's examine the default view resolver, which is `InternalResourceViewResolver`.

INTERNALRESOURCEVIEWRESOLVER, THE DEFAULT VIEW RESOLUTION STRATEGY

The default strategy for view resolution is `InternalResourceViewResolver`. This allows you to map view names to `InternalResourceViews`, which represent servlet-based view technologies such as servlets, JSPs, JSTL-based JSPs, and Tiles pages.

`InternalResourceViewResolver` converts the logical view name to a physical path by taking the logical view name, prepending a configurable prefix, and appending a configurable suffix. By default, the prefix and suffix are empty, which means you have to specify full view paths instead of logical view names to use. Because you don't usually want to specify full view paths from your controllers—that ties the controller too closely to the view—you'll generally want to define your own `InternalResourceView-Resolver`. Here's a typical configuration:

```
<bean class="org.springframework.web.servlet.view.
      InternalResourceViewResolver"
    p:prefix="/WEB-INF/jsp/"
    p:suffix=".jsp"/>
```

If this resolver receives the logical view name `contact`, for example, it converts that to /WEB-INF/jsp/contact.jsp and then builds a corresponding view. The view is an `InternalResourceView` if JavaServer Pages Standard Tag Library (JSTL) isn't on the classpath or else a `JstlView` if JSTL is present. `InternalResourceViewResolver` automatically detects the presence or absence of JSTL and selects the correct view type accordingly.

> #### Best practice: place JSPs in /WEB-INF/jsp or /WEB-INF/views
> In MVC applications, controllers mediate access to views, and you don't usually want users hitting JSP pages directly. A best practice is to place the JSPs under the /WEB-INF folder where users can't get to them. Most applications place the JSPs under /WEB-INF/jsp or /WEB-INF/views. By configuring `InternalResourceViewResolver` with the /WEB-INF/jsp/ or /WEB-INF/views/ prefix, you can ensure that logical view names resolve to JSPs inside /WEB-INF/jsp or /WEB-INF/views, respectively.

Let's look at a couple of special view names that `InternalResourceViewResolver` knows how to handle.

REDIRECT: AND FORWARD:

`InternalResourceViewResolver` inherits from its `UrlBasedViewResolver` superclass an awareness of two special view name prefixes, `redirect:` and `forward:`. When

`InternalResourceViewResolver` sees a view name that begins with either of these, it short-circuits standard view resolution and instead returns a special view, either a `RedirectView` or an `InternalResourceView` according to whether the prefix is the redirect prefix or the forward prefix.

> ### Does forward: do anything?
>
> Once the view name reaches `InternalResourceViewResolver`, using `forward:` is almost—but not exactly—the same as using the logical view name. The difference is that with an unprefixed view name, the returned `View` is either an `InternalResourceView` or a `JstlView` depending on whether JSTL is present. With `forward:` the view is always an `InternalResourceView`. Because `JstlView` provides a superset of the functionality that `InternalResourceView` provides, there isn't a good reason to use `forward:`.
>
> One possible way of using `forward:` might be to prevent a view name from being handled by some other view resolver (other than `InternalResourceViewResolver`) in view resolver chaining scenarios. We're a little skeptical of this idea, but it might be useful in some cases.

Redirecting is especially helpful after processing form requests, as you saw in section 3.3.5. It does, of course, have other applications.

Let's look at some other view resolvers you can use.

BEANNAMEVIEWRESOLVER

One of the simpler view resolvers is `BeanNameViewResolver`. When it receives a candidate view name, it checks the application context for a bean with a matching name or ID. If it finds one, it assumes the bean is the desired `View` and returns it. Otherwise it returns null, which means the `DispatcherServlet` will move to the next resolver in the chain.

`BeanNameViewResolver` is nice for simple applications, but as the number of views grows, `XmlViewResolver` becomes more helpful.

XMLVIEWRESOLVER

`XmlViewResolver` is conceptually similar to `BeanNameViewResolver` in that it uses named `View` beans to resolve view names to views. The difference is that `BeanNameViewResolver` assumes that the `View` beans are defined in the application context, whereas `XmlViewResolver` assumes that they're defined in a separate file, using the same Spring beans schema. By default the file is /WEB-INF/views.xml.

OTHER VIEWRESOLVERS AND VIEWS

Spring includes several `ViewResolver` and `View` implementations, including those for handling FreeMarker views, Velocity views, and XSLT views.[10] Spring 3 introduces new

---

[10] Please see the new Thymeleaf template engine at www.thymeleaf.org. It directly supports integration with Spring 3.

views for generating RSS and Atom feeds; we show how to generate an RSS feed using the BeanNameViewResolver and AbstractRssFeedView in chapter 8.

CHAINING VIEWRESOLVERS

We've alluded several times to the fact that you can chain view resolvers. The usual scenario is that you want a standard InternalResourceViewResolver to handle most of your view resolution needs, but sometimes you want other view resolvers, such as BeanNameViewResolver or XmlViewResolver, to handle special cases. Here's a simple example. Maybe most of your views are JSPs but you also publish an RSS feed. To handle that, you'd have an InternalResourceViewResolver to handle the JSPs, and you'd probably include a single BeanNameViewResolver for the RSS feed.

To configure multiple view resolvers, you add them to the application context as beans. The ViewResolver implementations implement the Ordered interface, so you can define a processing order using the resolver's order property if you like. (The numerically lower the order, the higher the precedence.) If you don't define an explicit processing order, the InternalResourceViewResolver is automatically assumed to be the last resolver in the chain, because it never returns null (and hence never passes processing along to the next processor in the chain).

3.5.5   *Configuring a RequestToViewNameTranslator*

We've noted that controllers return a logical view name once they're done processing, and that DispatcherServlet hands that view name over to a chain of view resolvers to generate a corresponding view. But in many cases it's easy to automate the generation of logical view names such that controllers don't have to provide them explicitly.

That's where RequestToViewNameTranslator comes in. Its job is to map requests to logical view names. The controller can always override the generated view name by providing its own explicit view name; otherwise, the controller can let Request-ToViewNameTranslator do all the hard work.

The default strategy is DefaultRequestToViewNameTranslator. It maps request URLs to logical view names in a configurable way: you can configure a prefix and a suffix for the generated view names, and you can configure slash- and extension-stripping behavior. Here are some translation examples:

```
http://localhost:8080/app/home.html -> home
http://localhost:8080/app/aboutUs.html -> aboutUs
http://localhost:8080/app/admin/index.html -> admin/index
```

You can define your own RequestToViewNameTranslator strategy by creating a bean with the well-known name viewNameTranslator.

Effective use of RequestToViewNameTranslator can be a nice way to adopt convention over configuration practices. In some cases you won't be able to use it. This happens, for instance, when your controller method returns a different view name depending on the outcome of processing (for example, returning either a success or a failure page following an attempt to process form data). In cases where you can use it, it makes your code cleaner. We'll use request-to-view-name translation liberally throughout the book.

3.5.6 *Configuring other resolvers*

`DispatcherServlet` uses a few other resolvers as well: `MultipartResolver` (for supporting file uploads), `LocaleResolver` (for supporting internationalization), and `ThemeResolver` (for supporting skinnable UIs). We'll treat each of these in separate recipes later in the book:

- `MultipartResolver` is tackled in chapter 11 when you upload product photos to a product catalog.
- `LocaleResolver` and `ThemeResolver` appear in chapter 7, where we present general UI recipes.

With that, we've completed our examination of the Spring Web MVC configuration. As you have seen, Spring MVC is a flexible and capable framework. To show you how easy it is to extend and use this framework, we'll provide a technology preview of Spring Mobile, a relatively simple but powerful extension of Spring MVC.

3.6 *Spring Mobile technology preview*

Up to this point, we've focused on using Spring MVC to create normal web applications. But what if you were asked to extend the capabilities of an existing Spring MVC application to provide a more customized user experience for mobile users or to create a completely new application that specifically targets mobile devices? In addition to detecting mobile devices, one of the most concerning problems that mobile web applications face is that both the screen size and capabilities of the each web browser vary significantly among today's smartphone, PDA, tablet, and other mobile devices.

The Spring Mobile project provides extensions to Spring MVC for developing mobile web applications and offers server-side device detection, site preference management, and site-switcher functionality out of the box. This gives you all the foundational tools necessary to enhance an existing web application or create a web application that provides a more customized user experience that mobile visitors will find more enjoyable and intuitive to use.

The Spring Mobile project provides two approaches for handling mobile devices:

- Determine the type of device that initiated a web request. Provide the information to a web application's runtime that would provide the opportunity to customize its user experience. For example, you could customize the layout, Cascading Style Sheets (CSS), and JavaScript based on this information.
- Determine the type of device that initiated a web request. Redirect the user to a separate site that caters specifically to mobile devices. A common pattern is to redirect users of mysite.com to domains such as m.mysite.com or mysite.mobi where the content is designed specifically for mobile devices.

The ability to detect a mobile device is something that is common to both approaches. We'll take a deeper dive into the anatomy of an HTTP request in the next section. In the pages that follow, you'll create a trivial Contact List sample application that will demonstrate the first approach to handling mobile devices. At its core, this application is similar to the Spring MVC Roster sample application covered in section 3.2. As such, the process of constructing master/detail views in Spring MVC should already be familiar. You should focus on how easy it is to use Spring Mobile and a JavaScript library to create an interface that will be recognizable to existing smartphone users. Instead of building a full-blown application, we'll focus on building out the pieces that illustrate detecting a mobile device as well as managing site preferences (full versus mobile). Before we conclude our preview of Spring Mobile, we'll show you the configuration required to implement the second approach to handling mobile devices.

As of this writing, Spring Mobile version 1.0.0.RC1 has been released. A word of warning: although the changes to the API have slowed considerably, additional changes may still occur before Spring Mobile finally becomes generally available. You can download the source code for this working application here: https://github.com/springinpractice/sip03, branch 03. Let's get started by talking about how mobile devices are detected on the server side using Spring Mobile.

3.6.1 *A brief anatomy of an HTTP request*

Spring Mobile's `DeviceResolvers` use information present in an HTTP request to sniff out the presence of a mobile device. To give you an idea of how this works and what this information looks like, let's look at how a typical HTTP request is made.

HTTP, like most network protocols, uses a client-server communication model. An HTTP client opens a connection and sends a request message to an HTTP server. The server then returns a response message that normally contains the resource that was originally requested. After the response is completed, the server closes the connection.

If you were to open your browser and type in http://www.google.com and press Enter, your browser would create a request message that looks something like this:

```
GET / HTTP/1.1
Host: www.google.com
User-Agent: Mozilla/5.0 (Windows NT 5.1; rv:6.0.2) Gecko/20100101 Firefox/
    6.0.2
Accept: text/html,application/xhtml+xml,application/xml;q=0.9,*/*;q=0.8
Accept-Language: en-us,en;q=0.5
Accept-Encoding: gzip, deflate
Accept-Charset: ISO-8859-1,utf-8;q=0.7,*;q=0.7
Connection: keep-alive
```

In the first line of this message, you define that you're using the `GET HTTP` method to obtain the resource at / and that you're using HTTP 1.1. Following this initial request line is a list of header lines. Each line defines a header in the format `Header-Name:` `value`. Note that in some cases, a header can have multiple values and span multiple lines. In addition, when using HTTP 1.1, only the `Host` header is required. This means all the other headers are optional.

The important header to focus on here is `User-Agent`. It identifies the program that is making the request. In the example, we used Firefox version 6.0.2 on Windows

NT 5.1 (Windows XP). If we were to make the same request using an iPhone, the User-Agent header might look like this:

```
User-Agent: Mozilla/5.0 (iPhone; U; CPU iPhone OS 4_2_10 like Mac OS X;
en-us) AppleWebKit/533.17.9 (KHTML, like Gecko) Version/5.0.2
Mobile/8E600 Safari/6533.18.5
```

In the sample User-Agent header, you can now tell that the platform has changed from Windows NT 5.1 to iPhone. Each device leaves its own request fingerprint that may consist of information from only the User-Agent header or from a combination of information in the HTTP request. As you'll see next, you don't necessarily need to own or have access to these devices to get started developing mobile web applications.

SIMULATING A MOBILE DEVICE

Several browser-based plug-ins/extensions provide the ability to switch the User-Agent header that is supplied by the browser. For example, User Agent Switcher, a Firefox extension, provides a menu and toolbar button to switch the user agent of a browser to any number of values simulating mobile devices. This is useful for development and testing. If you'll only be deploying the sample Contact List application to your desktop, you'll need this or a similar plug-in for testing.

Now that you have an idea of the information available in an HTTP request and a mechanism to manipulate it, let's see how Spring Mobile detects a mobile device.

3.6.2 *Detecting a mobile device with Spring Mobile*

Spring Mobile's server-side device resolution functionality is based primarily on two interfaces, DeviceResolver and Device. The DeviceResolver interface attempts to determine which device created the current web request. We have omitted the comments in the code sample for brevity.

```
public interface DeviceResolver {

    Device resolveDevice(HttpServletRequest request);

}
```

The default implementation of the DeviceResolver interface is the LiteDevice-Resolver, which attempts to detect the presence of a mobile device based on information in the request headers. LiteDeviceResolver looks for clues such as the use of the Wireless Access Protocol (WAP) or by comparing the contents of the User-Agent header to a list of 90 or so keywords or prefixes. For example, LiteDeviceResolver would find the keyword *phone* in the iPhone User-Agent string (case-insensitive) we discussed earlier. Just as the name implies, LiteDeviceResolver only aims to determine if the device that created the current request is a mobile device. LiteDeviceResolver returns an instance of LiteDevice, which implements the Device interface:

```
public interface Device {

    boolean isMobile();

}
```

For more information, look at the `WurflDeviceResolver`. WURFL stands for *Wireless Universal Resource FiLe* and is a community effort focused on mobile device detection. This `DeviceResolver` implementation provides specific device and feature information (screen size and other device specific capabilities).

A quick note about WurflDeviceResolver

`WurflDeviceResolver` was originally part of the Spring Mobile project. It was removed after WURFL, which used to be free and open source software (FOSS), was changed to an AGPL license as of version 2.2. The original support for WURFL has been factored out of the Spring Mobile distribution and placed here: https://github.com/kdonald/wurfl-spring. The team is currently looking to contribute this integration to the official WURFL project.

Now that we've talked about Spring Mobile's server-side device-resolution functionality, let's get started building an example application.

3.6.3   *Configuring Spring Mobile*

Because Spring Mobile is an extension of Spring MVC, configuring the Contact List application will be a breeze. You start by configuring the Spring MVC DispatcherServlet in the web.xml file.

Listing 3.12   web.xml

```xml
<?xml version="1.0" encoding="UTF-8"?>
<!-- Source project: sip03, branch: 03 (Maven Project) -->
<web-app
    xmlns:xsi="http://www.w3.org/2001/XMLSchema-instance"
    xmlns="http://java.sun.com/xml/ns/javaee"
    xmlns:web="http://java.sun.com/xml/ns/javaee/web-app_2_5.xsd"
    xsi:schemaLocation="http://java.sun.com/xml/ns/javaee
    http://java.sun.com/xml/ns/javaee/web-app_2_5.xsd" version="2.5">
  <servlet>
    <servlet-name>main</servlet-name>                              Configures
    <servlet-class>                                             ❶ DispatcherServlet
      org.springframework.web.servlet.DispatcherServlet
    </servlet-class>
  </servlet>
  <servlet-mapping>
    <servlet-name>main</servlet-name>
    <url-pattern>/main/*</url-pattern>
  </servlet-mapping>
</web-app>
```

As we talked about earlier, when configuring `DispatcherServlet`, Spring looks for a file in the WEB-INF directory of the web application by the name of main-servlet.xml ❶, unless a different name and location are explicitly configured. Let's look at this file now.

Listing 3.13   main-servlet.xml

```xml
<?xml version="1.0" encoding="UTF-8"?>
<!-- Source project: sip03, branch: 03 (Maven Project) -->

<beans:beans xmlns="http://www.springframework.org/schema/mvc"
  xmlns:xsi="http://www.w3.org/2001/XMLSchema-instance"
  xmlns:beans="http://www.springframework.org/schema/beans"
  xmlns:p="http://www.springframework.org/schema/p"
  xmlns:context="http://www.springframework.org/schema/context"
  xsi:schemaLocation="
    http://www.springframework.org/schema/mvc
    http://www.springframework.org/schema/mvc/spring-mvc-3.1.xsd
    http://www.springframework.org/schema/beans
    http://www.springframework.org/schema/beans/spring-beans-3.1.xsd
    http://www.springframework.org/schema/beans
    http://www.springframework.org/schema/beans/spring-beans-3.1.xsd
    http://www.springframework.org/schema/context
    http://www.springframework.org/schema/context/spring-context-3.1.xsd">

  <interceptors>
    <beans:bean class="org.springframework.mobile.device.      ◀──┐
    DeviceResolverHandlerInterceptor" />          Configures      │
  </interceptors>                    DeviceResolverHandlerInterceptor ❶

  <resources mapping="/resources/**" location="/resources/" />

  <beans:bean class="org.springframework.web.servlet.view.       ◀──┐
  InternalResourceViewResolver">                  Configures        │
    <beans:property name="viewClass"     InternalResourceViewResolver ┘
      value="org.springframework.web.servlet.view.JstlView"
    />
    <beans:property name="prefix" value="/WEB-INF/jsp/" />
    <beans:property name="suffix" value=".jsp" />
  </beans:bean>

  <context:component-scan base-package="com.springinpractice.ch03" />

</beans:beans>
```

The thing added in the Contact List application above and beyond a vanilla Spring
MVC configuration is the DeviceResolverHandlerInterceptor at ❶. We talked about
HandlerInterceptors in section 3.5.1. In short, HandlerInterceptors behave much
like servlet filters. In this case, the preHandle() method of DeviceResolverHandler-
Interceptor delegates to a DeviceResolver to resolve the device that originated the
current request.

By default, DeviceResolverHandlerInterceptor delegates to a LiteDevice-
Resolver that resolves the device to a LiteDevice. If you wanted to use the Wurfl-
DeviceResolver we talked about earlier, you would inject this device resolver's
implementation into the HandlerInterceptor via constructor injection.

Based on this configuration alone, you can now detect when a mobile device is
requesting a resource from the Contact List application. In the code, you can obtain a
reference to the current device by using the DeviceUtils class:

```
Device device = DeviceUtils.getRequiredCurrentDevice(servletRequest);

if (device.isMobile()) {
//Do something
}
```

If you want to have the `Device` passed in as an argument to one of your `@Controller` methods, you can configure a `WebArgumentResolver`. This is a Spring MVC feature that is new in version 3.1. You can do this by adding the following to the main-servlet.xml file.

Listing 3.14   Configuring `WebArgumentResolvers`

```
<annotation-driven>                                                    ❶ Configures
  <argument-resolvers>                                                   DeviceWeb-
    <beans:bean class="org.springframework.mobile.device.              ArgumentResolver
➥   DeviceWebArgumentResolver" />
    <beans:bean class="org.springframework.mobile.device.site.
➥   SitePreferenceWebArgumentResolver" />                             Configures
  </argument-resolvers>                               SitePreferenceWebArgumentResolver ❷
</annotation-driven>
```

You configure two different `WebArgumentResolvers`. The `DeviceWebArgument-Resolver` ❶ allows you to pass in the current device in your `@Controller` method like this:

```
@Controller
@RequestMapping("/contact")
public final class ContactController {

  ...

  @RequestMapping("/list")
  public void list(Model model, Device device) {
    if (device.isMobile()) {
      //Do something
    }
  }
}

...
```

We'll talk more about the `SitePreferenceArgumentResolver` ❷ in the next section.

Now that you have the ability to detect mobile devices in the Contact List application using Spring Mobile's server-side device detection, you can control the user experience based on this knowledge. For example, to optimize a user's mobile experience, it's possible to redirect the user to a mobile-specific version of the site. In most cases, this site may be a thinned-down version of the original site to accommodate a device's smaller screen size. But what if the end user wants to visit the normal site?

3.6.4   *Handling site preferences*

The Spring Mobile team has provided a facility to handle user site preference management as well. The code uses a pattern similar to the server-side device-detection code we talked about earlier. This time, instead of talking about `DeviceResolverHandlerInterceptor`, `DeviceResolver`, and `Device`, we're talking about `SitePreferenceHandlerInterceptor`, `SitePreferenceHandler`, and `SitePreference`.

The `SitePreferenceHandlerInterceptor` is added to your configuration after the `DeviceResolverHandlerInterceptor` at ❶ in listing 3.13. This interceptor delegates to an instance of `SitePreferenceHandler`. The default implementation, `StandardSitePreferenceHandler`, checks to see if a user specified a `SitePreference`. If not, its value defaults to `MOBILE` if a mobile device has been detected or `NORMAL` if not. By default, this value is stored using the `CookieSitePreferenceRepository`, which is the default implementation of `SitePreferenceRepository`.

`StandardSitePreferenceHandler` supports query-parameter-based site-preference switching. For example, the following code can be used to set a user's site preference:

```
<c:if test="${currentDevice.mobile}">
 <c:choose>
    <c:when test="${currentSitePreference.mobile}">
     <a href="${currentUrl}?site_preference=normal">
      Switch To: Normal Site
     </a>
    </c:when>
    <c:otherwise>
     <a href="${currentUrl}?site_preference=mobile">
      Switch To: Mobile Site
     </a>
    </c:otherwise>
  </c:choose>
</c:if>
```

Configuring site preference management is similar to configuring Spring Mobile's server-side device detection. To configure the site-preference management in the Contact List application, you need to add the `SitePreferenceHandlerInterceptor` right after the `DeviceResolverHandlerInterceptor` in your main-servlet.xml file:

```
<interceptors>
  <beans:bean
      class="org.springframework.mobile.device.
➡   DeviceResolverHandlerInterceptor" />
  <beans:bean
    class="org.springframework.mobile.device.site.
➡   SitePreferenceHandlerInterceptor" />
</interceptors>
```

Based on this single configuration change, you can now detect an end-user's explicit or default site preference when a resource is requested from your application. In your code, you can obtain a reference to the current device by using the `SitePreferenceUtils` class:

```
SitePreference sitePreference = SitePreferenceUtils
➡     .getCurrentSitePreference(servletRequest);

if (SitePreference.MOBILE == sitePreference) {
  //Do something
}
```

Similar to how you handled the Device earlier, if you want the SitePreference passed in as an argument to one of your @Controller methods, you can configure an additional WebArgumentResolver as seen at ❷ in listing 3.14 to the main-servlet.xml file. The SitePreferenceWebArgumentResolver allows you to pass in the current device in your @Controller method like this:

```
@Controller
@RequestMapping("/contact")
public final class ContactController {

  ...

  @RequestMapping("/list")
  public void list(Model model, SitePreference sitePreference) {
    if (SitePreference.MOBILE == sitePreference) {
      //Do something
    }
  }
}
  ...
```

The Contact List application is taking shape. You can now detect if a mobile device is accessing your site, and a mechanism lets users manage their own site preference (full versus mobile). This gives you the information you need to make decisions about how you might want to customize your site to provide a more enjoyable and intuitive user experience for your mobile visitors. In the next section, we'll look at how you can use a JavaScript framework to do just this.

3.6.5 *Using JavaScript frameworks for enhanced look and feel*

The beauty of mobile JavaScript frameworks is that they let you use the HTML 5, CSS3, and JavaScript skills you already have. These frameworks offer an abstraction layer that simplifies mobile web development by providing a collection of cross-browser UI elements/widgets that often mimic the native device's look and feel as well as a unified way to access native mobile OS features.

In the Contact List sample application, we chose to use jQuery Mobile (http://jquerymobile.com/). jQuery Mobile is a touch-optimized web framework for smartphones and tablets that is built on top of jQuery and jQuery UI. Measuring in at 12 KB, the framework is relatively lightweight, a feature that is important for devices that may have limited bandwidth. Based on figures 3.4 and 3.5, you can see how you can turn normal HTML 5 into something that closely resembles a mobile devices look and feel.

To experiment with this trivial sample application and see all the items we talk about in action, download and

All Contacts

A
- Cheryl Albro
- Marvin Aylward

B
- Michael Bartow
- Yong Blythe
- Kim Boozer
- Leon Bowling
- Jayne Bradburn
- Daniel Bridges
- Dawn Brown
- Kathleen Butler

C
- Rachel Campos
- Carin Caufield
- Wendell Chambers
- Edward Chang
- Ora Churchill
- Lisa Craig
- Thomas Crook

Figure 3.4   The Contact List sample application when viewed by a normal browser

run the source code for this chapter and point your browser to http://local-host:8080/sip/main/contact/list. As shown in figure 3.4, in a normal browser you see a rather vanilla-looking list of contacts.

When you view the same address using a mobile device browser or normal browser with a user-agent switcher to mimic a mobile device, you'll see the view shown in figure 3.5.

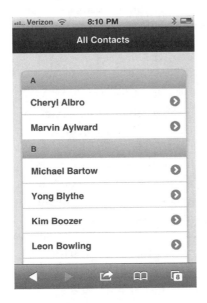

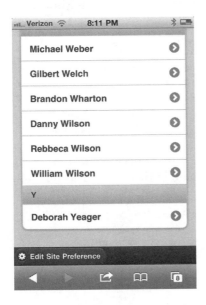

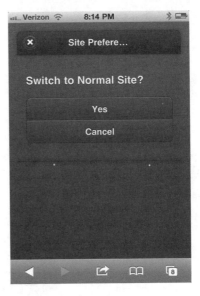

Figure 3.4   The Contact List sample application when viewed by a mobile device

As we mentioned at the beginning of section 3.6, Spring Mobile provides two different approaches to handling mobile devices. Although trivial, the Contact List sample application you just finished demonstrates how Spring Mobile can provide the information necessary to a web application's runtime that can allow you to customize the layout, CSS, and JavaScript based on the type of device accessing the site. Before we conclude our Spring Mobile preview, let's look at the out-of-the-box site-switching functionality that Spring Mobile provides. This secondary approach can be useful when you would like to detect mobile users and redirect them to an entire site that might be designed specifically to cater to the needs of mobile users. Let's look at this additional approach next.

3.6.6 *Switching to a separate mobile site*

As opposed to using `SitePreferenceHandlerInterceptor` to manage preferences within the same site, you can use `SiteSwitcherHandlerInterceptor` to redirect mobile users to a separate site.

`SiteSwitcherHandlerInterceptor` provides convenient factory methods out of the box to handle redirecting users to either a site with an "m." subdomain (such as m.yourdomain.com) or a ".mobi" top-level domain (TLD) (yourdomain.mobi). An example of each is provided in the following sections. Keep in mind that `SiteSwitcherHandlerInterceptor` delegates to a `SitePreferenceHandler` internally so there is no need to configure a `SitePreferenceHandlerInterceptor` explicitly.

MDOT SITESWITCHER

You can use the `mDot` factory method to create an instance of the `SiteSwitcherHandlerInterceptor` that redirects users to a domain in the format m.yourdomain.com:

```
<interceptors>
  <beans:bean class="org.springframework.mobile.device.
➥    DeviceResolverHandlerInterceptor"/>
  <beans:bean class="org.springframework.mobile.device.switcher.
➥    SiteSwitcherHandlerInterceptor" factory-method="mDot">
    <beans:constructor-arg value="yourdomain.com"/>
  </beans:bean>
</interceptors>
```

DOTMOBI SITESWITCHER

You can use the `dotMobi` factory method to create an instance of `SiteSwitcherHandlerInterceptor` that redirects users to a domain in the format yourdomain.mobi:

```
<interceptors>
  <beans:bean class="org.springframework.mobile.device.
➥    DeviceResolverHandlerInterceptor"/>
  <beans:bean class="org.springframework.mobile.device.switcher.
➥    SiteSwitcherHandlerInterceptor" factory-method="dotMobi">
    <beans:constructor-arg value="yourdomain.com"/>
  </beans:bean>
</interceptors>
```

This concludes our technology preview of the Spring Mobile project. Over the last several pages, we have discussed how this project provides extensions to Spring MVC for developing mobile web applications and offers server-side device detection, site-preference management, and site-switcher functionality out of the box. We also talked about how you can use Spring Mobile to detect and customize a single site for both mobile and nonmobile devices or redirect mobile users to a different site. Spring Mobile provides all the foundational tools necessary to enhance an existing web application or create a web application that provides a more customized user experience that mobile visitors will find more enjoyable and intuitive to use.

3.7 Related technologies

Spring Web MVC is closely related to other technologies in the Spring stack. We'll mention them briefly here so that if you're interested, you can do some follow-up study.

3.7.1 Spring Web Flow

Spring Web Flow (SWF) brings web-based conversations to Spring Web MVC. The idea is that there are use cases in which it's necessary to treat a series of user interactions as a single transaction. Examples include checkout processes (for example, buying a plane ticket, booking a hotel, and buying something from an e-commerce site), multipage user registration and application processes, and product-configuration wizards.

In SWF, you model each process with *flows* (see chapter 5 for more details). Flows are essentially state-transition graphs, and they have a hierarchical structure so you can reuse finer-grained flows inside coarser-grained flows. You might have a user-registration flow and a login flow, and you might incorporate those into a larger checkout flow such that at the end of a checkout process the user is given the option of creating an account or logging in. SWF defines flows using an intuitive XML grammar.

3.7.2 Spring JavaScript

Spring JavaScript provides a client-side abstraction over JavaScript toolkits, with an emphasis on progressive enhancement, widgets, and AJAX support. It began life as part of Spring Web Flow, but eventually it became its own project because it's not inherently tied to SWF. Currently Spring JavaScript has a Dojo implementation. In the future it will likely have other implementations.

3.7.3 Spring Faces

The Spring Faces project provides for integration between Spring and JavaServer Faces. Like Spring JavaScript, it originated in the Spring Web Flow project, but became a separate project because it's not specifically tied to SWF.

3.7.4   *Spring Security*

Although Spring Security (née Acegi) isn't inherently tied to Spring Web MVC, it's worth mentioning here because it includes a great deal of support for securing web applications. Spring Security isn't limited to web apps, but it does provide strong support for securing them.

Spring Security primarily addresses two major areas of security: authentication and authorization.[11] Concerning web authentication, it provides a built-in username/password login form with optional remember-me functionality, support for CAS-based SSO, OpenID authentication, and others. Concerning authorization, Spring Security supports both role- and ACL-based authorization at multiple application tiers. You can selectively display and hide JSP page content using tag libraries. You can authorize web requests using servlet filters. And you can authorize methods (in any application tier—especially the web and service tiers) using aspects.

Chapters 4–6 present recipes that draw heavily from the Spring Security framework.

3.7.5   *RESTful web services*

Beginning with Spring 3.0, RESTful web services live in the world of Spring Web MVC. The `@RequestMapping` annotation with its `method` element—accepting values from the `RequestMethod` enum, such as `GET`, `POST`, `PUT`, and `DELETE`—was apparently too good a REST-match not to explicitly provide REST support, so that's what happened. We won't cover Spring MVC's REST support in this book. But if you want more information on how to use Spring MVC to support REST, have a look at *Spring in Action,* 3rd edition, by Craig Walls (Manning, 2011).

3.8   *Summary*

This has been a whirlwind tour through Spring Web MVC. We've covered a great deal of what the framework provides, so if you understand the material in this chapter, you should be in a good place to understand the recipes in the chapters that follow.

Unlike the recipe chapters, chapters 1 and 3 are intended to be reference-like in nature. Please refer to them as you work through the recipes any time you need to review the material.

---

[11] Spring Security addresses other areas too, such as privacy (for example, encryption and SSL, hashing, and salting passwords), but most of the focus is on authentication and authorization.

Basic web forms

Web forms provide a means by which we can collect data from end users. As such, they're a key aspect of any nontrivial web application. This chapter shows how to use Spring Web MVC and related technologies to build a simple user registration form with standard features such as redirect-after-post, externalized strings, form data validation, and persistence.

Our approach is hands-on and practical. See *Spring in Action*, 3rd edition by Craig Walls (Manning, 2011) for additional material on Spring Web MVC.

4.1 Displaying a web form

PREREQUISITES

None

KEY TECHNOLOGIES

Spring Web MVC, Spring form tag library

Background

Users establish a relationship with a website or an organization by registering. The resulting user account allows logins, order placement, community participation, and so on. The first step in supporting a user registration process is to display a registration form.

Problem

Create a web-based form.

Solution

In this recipe you'll use Spring Web MVC to display a user registration form. You'll build a user account form bean, a web controller, a registration form, and a confirmation page.

It won't hurt to have a visual on the UI you're planning to create in this recipe. Figure 4.1 shows what you're aiming for.

Let's begin by creating a form bean for your user accounts.

CREATING AN ACCOUNT FORM BEAN

You use a form bean to store form data, as shown in the following listing.

Listing 4.1   AccountForm.java, a form bean for user accounts

```java
package com.springinpractice.ch04.web;

import org.apache.commons.lang3.builder.ToStringBuilder;
import org.apache.commons.lang3.builder.ToStringStyle;

public class AccountForm {
    private String username, password, confirmPassword, firstName,
        lastName, email;
    private boolean marketingOk = true;
    private boolean acceptTerms = false;

    public String getUsername() { return username; }

    public void setUsername(String username) { this.username = username; }

    ... other getter/setter pairs ...

    public String toString() {
        return new ToStringBuilder(this, ToStringStyle.SHORT_PREFIX_STYLE)
            .append("username", username)
            .append("firstName", firstName)
            .append("lastName", lastName)
            .append("email", email)
            .append("marketingOk", marketingOk)
            .append("acceptTerms", acceptTerms)
            .toString();
    }
}
```

① Demographic data

② Marketing preference

③ Legal confirmation

④ toString() implementation

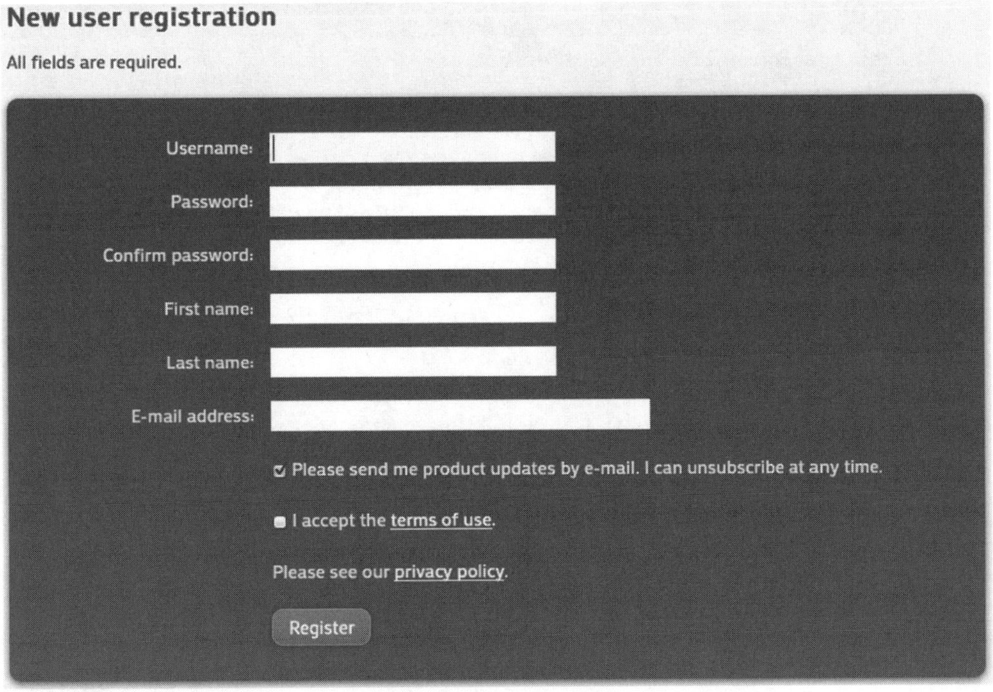

New user registration

All fields are required.

Username:

Password:

Confirm password:

First name:

Last name:

E-mail address:

☑ Please send me product updates by e-mail. I can unsubscribe at any time.

☐ I accept the terms of use.

Please see our privacy policy.

Register

Figure 4.1   The simple web-based registration form that you'll build in this recipe

AccountForm is a POJO.[1] It has properties for personal ❶, marketing ❷, and legal ❸ data. These are typical concerns when modeling user accounts. You also include a descriptive toString() method ❹, based on the Commons Lang library, so you can observe the form-binding later in the recipe. By design, you suppress the password here to avoid accidentally revealing it.

You default the marketingOk property to true because you'd like to market to your users unless they explicitly opt out. On the other hand, you default acceptTerms to false because you want the user's acceptance of the terms of use to be active rather than passive. Presumably this gives you a stronger legal leg to stand on in the event of a disagreement with the user.[2]

You have a form bean, but without a web controller, it's inert. Let's take care of that.

CREATING A WEB CONTROLLER

Your account controller, which appears in the following listing, handles form delivery and processing.

---

[1] See http://en.wikipedia.org/wiki/Plain_Old_Java_Object.
[2] Disclaimer: We aren't lawyers! Consult a qualified legal expert if necessary.

Listing 4.2   AccountController.java to handle user registrations

```
package com.springinpractice.ch04.web;

import org.slf4j.Logger;
import org.slf4j.LoggerFactory;
import org.springframework.stereotype.Controller;
import org.springframework.ui.Model;
import org.springframework.web.bind.annotation.RequestMapping;
import org.springframework.web.bind.annotation.RequestMethod;

@Controller
@RequestMapping("/users")
public class AccountController {
    private static final Logger log =
        LoggerFactory.getLogger(AccountController.class);

    @RequestMapping(value = "new", method = RequestMethod.GET)
    public String getRegistrationForm(Model model) {
        model.addAttribute("account", new AccountForm());
        return "users/registrationForm";
    }

    @RequestMapping(value = "", method = RequestMethod.POST)
    public String postRegistrationForm(AccountForm form) {
        log.info("Created registration: {}", form);
        return "redirect:registration_ok";
    }
}
```

❶ **Declares @Controller**

❷ **Base controller path**

❸ **No special interface**

❹ **Serves form**

❺ **Accepts form submission**

❻ **Redirects to another page**

At ❶ the @Controller annotation tells Spring that this is a web controller. You establish a base path for request mapping using the @RequestMapping annotation ❷. This path contextualizes paths declared at the method level. At ❸ you're not implementing any special interfaces or extending special classes.

You serve the empty form bean at ❹. The associated request mapping is /users/new, which you obtain by combining the class-level /users base path with the method-level new mapping. (To override a class-level mapping rather than refine it, place a slash in front of the method-level mapping.) The method itself places a new Account-Form instance on the model under the key account and returns the view name.

You process form submissions at ❺, specifying the POST request method. The request mapping is just /users because that's the result of combining the base path with the empty string. For now, when users post form data, you log it and redirect them to a view that thanks them for registering ❻. We'll discuss the redirection in more detail later in the recipe.

Let's move on to the two view pages. First you'll create the view for the registration form, and after that you'll create the "thanks" page for successful form submissions.

CREATING THE VIEW PAGES

The next listing shows how to implement the registration form from figure 4.1. Note that we've suppressed the layout and CSS code; see the code download (src/main/webapp/WEB-INF/jsp/users/registrationForm.jsp) for the full version.

Listing 4.3   registrationForm.jsp: view to display your registration form

```
<%@ taglib prefix="form" uri="http://www.springframework.org/tags/form" %>
<html>
    <head><title>New User Registration</title></head>
    <body>
        <form:form action="." modelAttribute="account">      ❶ Renders
                                                                HTML form
<h1>New User Registration</h1>
<div>Username: <form:input path="username" /></div>          ❷ HTML text field
<div>Password: <form:password path="password" /></div>
<div>Confirm password: <form:password path="confirmPassword" /></div>    HTML
<div>E-mail address: <form:input path="email" /></div>       password
<div>First name: <form:input path="firstName" /></div>       ❸ field
<div>Last name: <form:input path="lastName" /></div>
<div><form:checkbox id="marketingOk" path="marketingOk" />    HTML
    Please send me product updates by e-mail.</div>          ❹ check box
<div><form:checkbox id="acceptTerms" path="acceptTerms" />
    I accept the <a href="#">terms of use</a>.</div>
<div><input type="submit" value="Register" /></div>          No special
        </form:form>                                         ❺ submit tag
    </body>
</html>
```

The registration page uses the form ❶ tag to create an HTML form. You use action="." to post the form submission to /main/users/. The modelAttribute attribute references the model object to be used as the form-backing bean. The HTML form elements are bound to the form bean's properties in both directions:

- *Inbound*—The form bean is populated with the HTML form element values when the form is submitted and passed to the controller for validation and processing.
- *Outbound*—The form elements are prepopulated with the form bean's values. You use this, for example, to set the default value of the marketingOk check box to true and acceptTerms to false. Form elements are also prepopulated before representing a form to a user for remediating invalid form data; you'll see this in recipe 4.3.

Figure 4.2 presents a high-level view of form binding.

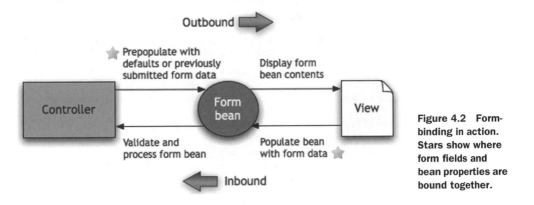

Figure 4.2   Form-binding in action. Stars show where form fields and bean properties are bound together.

You use input ❷, password ❸, and checkbox ❹ tags from the Spring form tag library to render HTML form elements. These are essentially form-binding versions of the corresponding HTML elements. The tag library doesn't provide anything for submit buttons (there's nothing to bind to here), so you use standard HTML ❺.

After the user successfully submits a registration, you need a page to let the user know that the registration succeeded. Here's a minimalistic registrationOk.jsp file:

```
<html>
    <head><title>Registration Confirmed</title></head>
    <body><p>Thank you for registering.</p></body>
</html>
```

In this case, the page doesn't even need to be a JSP, although you'll leave it as is because it's always possible that you'll want to present dynamic information through the page.

You're done with your form bean, controller, and views. All that remains is configuration.

CONFIGURING THE APP

The key part of your web.xml configuration is the following:

```
<servlet>
    <servlet-name>spring</servlet-name>
    <servlet-class>
        org.springframework.web.servlet.DispatcherServlet
    </servlet-class>
    <init-param>
        <param-name>contextConfigLocation</param-name>
        <param-value>classpath:/spring/beans-web.xml</param-value>
    </init-param>
</servlet>
<servlet-mapping>
    <servlet-name>spring</servlet-name>
    <url-pattern>/</url-pattern>
</servlet-mapping>
```

This web.xml configuration references a single Spring configuration, called beans-web.xml, associated with the DispatcherServlet. It goes in src/main/resources/spring so it will be on the classpath when you package and deploy the app.

Listing 4.4   beans-web.xml: web tier configuration

```
<?xml version="1.0" encoding="UTF-8"?>
<beans xmlns="http://www.springframework.org/schema/beans"
    xmlns:context="http://www.springframework.org/schema/context"
    xmlns:p="http://www.springframework.org/schema/p"
    xmlns:xsi="http://www.w3.org/2001/XMLSchema-instance"
    xmlns:mvc="http://www.springframework.org/schema/mvc"
    xsi:schemaLocation="http://www.springframework.org/schema/mvc
        http://www.springframework.org/schema/mvc/spring-mvc-3.1.xsd
        http://www.springframework.org/schema/beans
```

```
          http://www.springframework.org/schema/beans/spring-beans-3.1.xsd
          http://www.springframework.org/schema/context
          http://www.springframework.org/schema/context/
                 spring-context-3.1.xsd">

    <context:component-scan                                    ❶  Discovers
        base-package="com.springinpractice.ch04.web" />           @Controller

    <mvc:annotation-driven />                    ❷  Activates annotations

    <mvc:view-controller path="/users/registration_ok"  ❸  Creates
        view-name="users/registrationOk" />                 controller

    <bean class="org.springframework.web.servlet.view.      ❹  View resolver
           InternalResourceViewResolver"
        p:viewClass="org.springframework.web.servlet.view.JstlView"
        p:prefix="/WEB-INF/jsp/" p:suffix=".jsp" />
</beans>
```

The listing ties everything together. You use component scanning to discover the AccountController ❶ based on its @Controller annotation.

Spring 3 introduces the mvc namespace. You use <mvc:annotation-driven> at ❷ to activate annotation-based configuration inside the DispatcherServlet explicitly.

At ❸ you use <mvc:view-controller> to configure a new controller for the registration success page. Recall from listing 4.2 that you redirected the request to a success page, but you never specified a controller to display the success page. That's what <mvc:view-controller> does. It creates a ParameterizableViewController instance whose job is to accept requests for /users/registration_ok and serve up the logical view name users/registrationOk for view resolution.

You redirect rather than forward to the success page because you want to apply the redirect-after-post pattern to your form submission. With this pattern, a successful form submission issues an HTTP redirect to avoid resubmissions if the user reloads or bookmarks the page, as illustrated by the sequence diagram in figure 4.3.

The figure suppresses the ViewResolver, but the DispatcherServlet uses the instance you created for both view resolutions depicted. The DispatcherServlet uses the ViewResolver ❹ to convert logical view names into views.

Why do you need <mvc:annotation-driven>?

You might wonder why you need to declare <mvc:annotation-driven> explicitly. After all, the DispatcherServlet default configuration already has an internal DefaultAnnotationHandlerMapping instance to handle @RequestMapping annotations. The reason: behind the scenes, <mvc:view-controller> creates a SimpleUrlHandlerMapping to map the ParameterizableViewController to the specified path, and this replaces the DefaultAnnotationHandlerMapping that would otherwise have been created. You use <mvc:annotation-driven> to indicate that you want the DefaultAnnotationHandlerMapping as well.

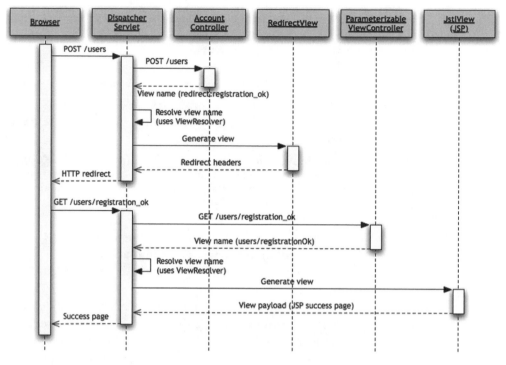

Figure 4.3   The redirect-after-post implementation for successful registrations

That almost wraps it up for the configuration. You'll also need a WEB-INF/decorators.xml file for SiteMesh; see the code download for that. To run the app, run Maven with the `jetty:run` goal. On the command line, it looks like this:

```
mvn -e clean jetty:run
```

Then go to http://localhost:8080/sip/users/new.html. You should see a registration page that looks like the one from figure 4.1.

Discussion

What you've done so far isn't tied to registration forms; this recipe is a blueprint for displaying web forms in general. As you move forward in the chapter, you'll continue to target registration forms, but the discussion and techniques are broadly applicable.

In the next recipe, you'll make your view pages more flexible by externalizing the strings that appear in the JSPs.

4.2   *Externalizing strings in the view*

PREREQUISITE
Recipe 4.1 Displaying a web form

KEY TECHNOLOGIES
Java resource bundles, Spring tag library

Background

It's often desirable to decouple a view from the specific bits of text rendered in the view. Reasons include internationalization and centralized management. This recipe shows how.

Problem

Externalize the strings that appear in the registration JSPs so they can be managed centrally.

Solution

The solution involves three steps:

1 Create a resource bundle that contains the externalized strings, or *messages* in the Spring vernacular.
2 Add a `ReloadableResourceBundleMessageSource` to the configuration.
3 Replace the hardcoded strings in the JSPs with references to the externalized strings in the resource bundle.

First up is the resource bundle, which contains your messages.

CREATING A RESOURCE BUNDLE FOR THE MESSAGES

The following listing shows how to create a resource bundle for your messages. This file goes in src/main/resources because you want it to appear at the root of the classpath on deployment.

Listing 4.5 messages.properties: resource bundle for externalized strings

```
common.message.unimplemented=Not implemented          ←—① Common messages

newUserRegistration.pageTitle=New User Registration    ←—② Reg form messages
newUserRegistration.message.allFieldsRequired=All fields are required.
newUserRegistration.label.username=Username:
newUserRegistration.label.firstName=First name:
newUserRegistration.label.lastName=Last name:
newUserRegistration.label.email=E-mail address:
newUserRegistration.label.password=Password:
newUserRegistration.label.confirmPassword=Confirm password:
newUserRegistration.label.marketingOk=Please send me product updates by
       e-mail. I can unsubscribe at any time.
newUserRegistration.label.acceptTerms=I accept the <a class="unimplemented"
       href="#" title="Not implemented"> terms of use</a>.
newUserRegistration.label.privacyPolicy=Please see your <a
       class="unimplemented" href="#" title="Not implemented" >privacy
       policy</a>.
newUserRegistration.label.register=Register               ③ Success page
                                                              messages
registrationOk.pageTitle=Registration Confirmed
registrationOk.message.thanks=Thank you for registering.
registrationOk.label.continue=Continue &raquo;
```

You can organize these messages as you like. In this case, you have three sections: one for messages that are common to both pages ❶, another for registration form messages ❷, and a third for messages that appear on the success page ❸. The key names reflect this organization.

Next you add a single bean to the beans-web.xml configuration.

ADDING A MESSAGE SOURCE TO BEANS-WEB.XML

Add the following code snippet to beans-web.xml:

```
<bean id="messageSource"
    class="org.springframework.context.support.
          ReloadableResourceBundleMessageSource"
    p:basename="classpath:messages" />
```

This creates a message source, backed by the resource bundle, that you can use to drive dereferencing in the JSP. The ID messageSource is required.

The third and final step is to replace the hardcoded strings in the JSP with references.

REPLACING THE HARDCODED STRINGS WITH REFERENCES

The next listing shows how to convert hardcoded strings into references using the <spring:message> tag.

Listing 4.6   Updating registrationForm.jsp to use external messages

Declares tag library ❶

```
<%@ taglib prefix="form" uri="http://www.springframework.org/tags/form" %>
<%@ taglib prefix="spring" uri="http://www.springframework.org/tags" %>    ◁

<spring:message var="pageTitle" code="newUserRegistration.pageTitle" />    ◁
<spring:message var="msgAllFieldsRequired"
    code="newUserRegistration.message.allFieldsRequired" />       Stores messages
                                                                  in variables ❷
<html>
    <head><title>${pageTitle}</title></head>                  ◁    Displays
    <body>                                                    ❸   variable
        <form:form action="." modelAttribute="account">
<h1>${pageTitle}</h1>                                         ❹  Displays other
<div>${msgAllFieldsRequired}</div>                        ◁      variable
<div>
    <spring:message code="newUserRegistration.label.username" />    ◁
    <form:input path="username" />
</div>
                                                            Displays message
... snip ...                                                directly ❺

        </form:form>
    </body>
</html>
```

We've suppressed a good chunk of the code in listing 4.6, but it should be obvious given what we've included how to convert the rest of listing 4.3. First you declare the spring tag library ❶.[3] Then you use the <spring:message> tag to set a couple of variables to messages in the resource bundle ❷ so you can use them later. You use the pageTitle variable at ❸ and also inside the following <h1>, and you use the msgAllFieldsRequired variable at ❹. At ❺ you use <spring:message> in a slightly different fashion; this time, you dump the message right into the template. This occurs because you haven't specified a var attribute.

That's it for the changes. Run the app the same way you ran it in recipe 4.1. Under the hood, you've externalized the strings, but you shouldn't see any behavioral changes.

Discussion

It's a good practice to externalize application strings. Besides paving the way for internationalization, it gives you a central place to manage text. This helps with quality control, and it helps when you decide you want to change, for example, "Technical Support Representative" to "Customer Care Specialist" across the board.

So far your form is very permissive. You can enter whatever you like into the form—including nothing—and the result is always success. In the following recipe, you'll fix that with form validation.

4.3 Validating form data

PREREQUISITE
Recipe 4.2 Externalizing strings in the view

KEY TECHNOLOGIES
Spring Web MVC, Spring binding and validation APIs, JSR 303 Bean Validation, JSR 223 Java Scripting, Hibernate Validator, Spring form tag library

Background

No matter how intuitive your registration form, people will accidentally or even intentionally fill it out with invalid information. You treat such errors as user errors rather than system or application exceptions, meaning you usually want to explain the error to the user in nontechnical language and help them overcome it.

Problem

When users submit form data, validate it before performing further processing. If there are errors, help the user understand what went wrong and how to address the issue.

Solution

At the highest level, this recipe addresses two types of validation:

---

[3] The spring and form tag libraries come from the org.springframework.web.servlet artifact, and the corresponding tag library descriptors are spring.tld and spring-form.tld, respectively. You can find these inside the JAR's META-INF directory.

- *Field filtering*—Ensure that all submitted field names are permissible. In general, clients shouldn't be allowed to submit fields that don't appear on the form.
- *Field validation*—Ensure that all submitted field values follow validation rules.

We'll set the stage with an architectural overview. Spring Web MVC supports both types of validation just described using three key APIs: Spring's form-binding API, Spring's validation API, and JSR 303 Bean Validation. See figure 4.4.

Here's how it works. When users submit HTML form data, Spring Web MVC uses the form-binding API to bind the HTTP parameters to form bean properties in an automated fashion. In certain cases—for example, when a form bean is performing double duty as a persistent entity—the form bean may have properties that aren't intended binding targets. The form-binding API allows you to filter out unwanted HTTP parameters by silently ignoring them during binding.

When Spring Web MVC invokes a form-submission request-handler method, such as `postRegistrationForm()`, it passes in the form data. In general, the form data is encapsulated within a form bean, and you want to validate it. This is the domain of JSR 303 Bean Validation. Spring Web MVC uses JSR 303 to validate form data encapsulated in this fashion, and developers use the Spring validation API (specifically, the `BindingResult` interface) from within a controller to determine whether the bean is valid.

Sometimes you need to perform a bit of custom validation logic. You'll see an example. Spring's validation API provides a programmatic interface for implementing such logic.

That will do for an overview. Let's add field filtering to the `AccountController`.

FIELD FILTERING VIA @INITBINDER AND WEBDATABINDER
Recall that Spring Web MVC automatically binds HTML forms to an underlying form bean. Although this is a major convenience to application developers, it raises a security

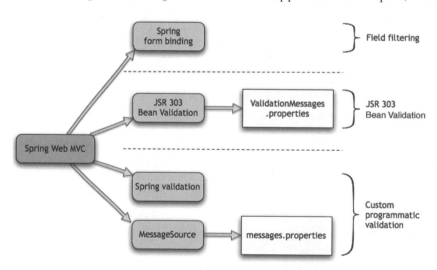

Figure 4.4   Validation in Spring Web MVC. The form-binding API handles field filtering, JSR 303 handles bean validation, and there's a Spring validation API for custom logic.

concern because it allows attackers to inject data into form bean properties that aren't intended to be accessed via the HTML form. You're not in that situation here, but it's a common state of affairs in cases where a single model object performs double duty as both a form bean and a persistent entity. In such cases you need a way to guard against data injection.[4]

Spring Web MVC supports this using `@InitBinder` methods. Add the following method to `AccountController`:

```
@InitBinder
public void initBinder(WebDataBinder binder) {
    binder.setAllowedFields(new String[] {
        "username", "password", "confirmPassword", "firstName",
        "lastName", "email", "marketingOk", "acceptTerms" });
}
```

The `@InitBinder` annotation tells Spring Web MVC to call this method when initializing the `WebDataBinder` responsible for binding HTTP parameters to form beans. The `setAllowedFields()` method defines a whitelist of bindable form bean fields. The binder silently ignores unlisted fields.

Whitelisting vs. blacklisting

The list of allowed fields is an example of a *whitelist*. The idea is that nothing gets through unless it's on the whitelist.

There is an alternative approach called a blacklist. With a blacklist, everything gets through unless it's on the blacklist.

Whitelists are generally more secure, because they start with an assumption of distrust rather than trust. But blacklists have their place as well. For example, you might filter out comment spammers using an IP blacklist, because it wouldn't be practical to use a whitelist for web traffic.

Now let's examine field validation.

VALIDATING THE FORM DATA

Several steps are involved in adding form validation to your app:

1 Add a JSR 303 implementation to the classpath.
2 Add validation annotations to `AccountForm`.
3 Add `@ModelAttribute`, `@Valid`, `BindingResult`, and validation logic to `Account-Controller`.
4 Create a `ValidationMessages.properties` resource bundle, and update the `messages.properties` resource bundle.

---

[4] Consider the case where you use a single `Account` POJO to serve as both an entity and a form bean. The entity might have an `enabled` field that indicates whether the account is enabled. You wouldn't want clients to be able to manipulate that field by sending a value for the field to the form processor.

118   CHAPTER 4   *Basic web forms*

5 Update registrationForm.jsp to display error messages.
6 Confirm that beans-web.xml has `<mvc:annotation-driven>` (for validation) and a message source (for certain custom error messages).

There's a lot to cover. Let's start at the top of the list and work our way down.

STEP 1. PLACING A JSR 303 IMPLEMENTATION ON THE CLASSPATH

Your Maven build takes care of placing Hibernate Validator 4, a JSR 303 implementation, on the classpath. Spring Web MVC will automatically pick it up. You can therefore move on to the next step, which is marking up AccountForm with validation annotations.

STEP 2. ADDING BEAN-VALIDATION ANNOTATIONS TO THE FORM BEAN

The following listing updates the AccountForm from listing 4.1 by adding validation annotations.

Listing 4.7   AccountForm.java, with validation annotations (updates listing 4.1)

```
package com.springinpractice.ch04.web;

import javax.validation.constraints.AssertTrue;
import javax.validation.constraints.NotNull;
import javax.validation.constraints.Size;
import org.apache.commons.lang3.builder.ToStringBuilder;
import org.apache.commons.lang3.builder.ToStringStyle;
import org.hibernate.validator.constraints.Email;
import org.hibernate.validator.constraints.ScriptAssert;

@ScriptAssert(                                                      ❶ @ScriptAssert for
    lang = "javascript",                                             password check
    script = "_this.confirmPassword.equals(_this.password)",
    message = "account.password.mismatch.message")
public class AccountForm {

    ... fields same as before ...

    @NotNull
    @Size(min = 1, max = 50)                                        ❷ @NotNull
    public String getUsername() { return username; }                  and @Size

    @NotNull
    @Size(min = 6, max = 50)
    public String getPassword() { return password; }

    @NotNull
    @Size(min = 6, max = 50)
    @Email
    public String getEmail() { return email; }                     ❸ @Email

    @AssertTrue(message = "{account.acceptTerms.assertTrue.message}")
    public boolean getAcceptTerms() { return acceptTerms; }

    ... other methods same as before ...                           @AssertTrue for
}                                                                  accepting terms ❹
```

The previous listing uses the Bean Validation (JSR 303) standard and Hibernate Validator to specify validation constraints. You attach the annotations either to the fields or to the getters. At ❷ you indicate that the username property can't be null, and its size must be 1–50 characters in length. At ❸ you use the Hibernate-specific @Email annotation to ensure that the email property represents a valid e-mail address. At ❹ you require that the acceptTerms property be true for validation to succeed, and you specify a message code to use when the validation fails. (More on that shortly.)

Finally, you declare a class-level @ScriptAssert annotation at ❶. This Hibernate annotation, which was introduced with Hibernate Validator 4.1, allows you to use a script to express validation constraints involving multiple fields. Here you use JavaScript to assert that the password and confirmation must be equal. (The Rhino JavaScript engine is automatically available if you're using Java 6; otherwise you'll need to place a JSR 223–compliant [Scripting for the Java Platform] script engine JAR on the classpath.) In addition to JavaScript, there are many other language options, including Groovy, Ruby, Python, FreeMarker, and Velocity.

Next you update AccountController to validate the account bean.

STEP 3. UPDATING THE CONTROLLER TO VALIDATE THE FORM DATA

The next listing shows how to update the AccountController from listing 4.2 to support both Bean Validation via JSR 303 and custom password validation.

> Listing 4.8 **AccountController.java, updated to validate form data (updates listing 4.2)**

```java
package com.springinpractice.ch04.web;

import javax.validation.Valid;
import org.springframework.stereotype.Controller;
import org.springframework.ui.Model;
import org.springframework.validation.BindingResult;
import org.springframework.validation.ObjectError;
import org.springframework.web.bind.WebDataBinder;
import org.springframework.web.bind.annotation.InitBinder;
import org.springframework.web.bind.annotation.ModelAttribute;
import org.springframework.web.bind.annotation.RequestMapping;
import org.springframework.web.bind.annotation.RequestMethod;

@Controller
@RequestMapping("/users")
public class AccountController {
    private static final String VN_REG_FORM = "users/registrationForm";
    private static final String VN_REG_OK = "redirect:registration_ok";

    @InitBinder
    public void initBinder(WebDataBinder binder) {
        binder.setAllowedFields(new String[] {
            "username", "password", "confirmPassword", "firstName",
            "lastName", "email", "marketingOk", "acceptTerms" });
    }

    @RequestMapping(value = "new", method = RequestMethod.GET)
    public String getRegistrationForm(Model model) {
        model.addAttribute("account", new AccountForm());
        return VN_REG_FORM;
    }
```

```
@RequestMapping(value = "", method = RequestMethod.POST)
public String postRegistrationForm(
        @ModelAttribute("account") @Valid AccountForm form,
        BindingResult result) {
    convertPasswordError(result);
    return (result.hasErrors() ? VN_REG_FORM : VN_REG_OK);
}

private static void convertPasswordError(BindingResult result) {
    for (ObjectError error : result.getGlobalErrors()) {
        String msg = error.getDefaultMessage();
        if ("account.password.mismatch.message".equals(msg)) {
            if (!result.hasFieldErrors("password")) {
                result.rejectValue("password", "error.mismatch");
            }
        }
    }
}
```

❶ @ModelAttribute and @Valid

BindingResult to record errors ❷

❸ Converts password errors

❹ Routing logic

You add `@ModelAttribute` and `@Valid` annotations to the `AccountForm` parameter ❶. The `@ModelAttribute` annotation causes the account bean to be placed automatically on the `Model` object for display by the view, using the key `"account"`. The `@Valid` annotation causes the bean to be validated on its way into the method.

Spring exposes the validation result via the `BindingResult` object ❷. This is how you can tell whether bean validation turned up any errors. You can also programmatically add new errors to the `BindingResult` by using its various `reject()` and `reject-Value()` methods. The `BindingResult` method parameter must immediately follow the form bean in the method parameter list.

The logic of the `postRegistrationForm()` method itself is straightforward. You call `convertPasswordError()` ❸, which converts the global error that `@ScriptAssert` generates into an error on the `password` field. You use the `rejectValue()` method to do this, as mentioned, passing in an error code `"error.mismatch"`. This *error code* resolves to one of the following *message codes*, depending on which message codes appear in the resource bundle:

- `error.mismatch.account.password` (error code + . + object name + . + field name)
- `error.mismatch.password` (error code + . + field name)
- `error.mismatch.java.lang.String` (error code + . + field type)
- `error.mismatch` (error code)

These message codes are listed in priority order: if the resource bundle contains the first message code, then that's the resolution, and so forth.[5] The first message code does in fact appear in `messages.properties`. See the Javadoc for Spring's

---

[5] It's probably worth emphasizing the fact that despite superficial similarities, error codes and message codes aren't the same thing. Validation errors have associated codes, and these generally map to a set of resource bundle message codes, which in turn map to error messages. It's pretty easy to get these mixed up.

`DefaultMessageCodesResolver` for more information on the rules for converting error codes to message codes.

Finally, once you've processed any password errors, you check to see whether there were any validation errors, and route to a success or failure page accordingly **④**. Notice that you're using the view name constants defined at the top of the file.

Let's take a more detailed look at the error messages here.

STEP 4. CONFIGURING ERROR MESSAGES

First let's talk about the default JSR 303 and Hibernate Validator messages. Strictly speaking, you don't have to override them at all. But the defaults aren't particularly user-centric (one of the defaults, for example, references regular expressions), so you'll change the messages for the constraints you're using. JSR 303 supports this by allowing you to place a `ValidationMessages.properties` resource bundle at the top of the classpath. You'll use this resource bundle not only to override the JSR 303 and Hibernate Validator defaults, but also to define an error message specific to the `acceptTerms` property.

Listing 4.9   ValidationMessages.properties, for JSR 303 error messages

```
javax.validation.constraints.Size.message=        ◁──① Overrides default @Size message
     Please enter {min}-{max} characters.
org.hibernate.validator.constraints.Email.message=  ◁──② Overrides default @Email message
     Please enter a valid e-mail address.
account.acceptTerms.assertTrue.message=            ◁──③ Defines message for acceptTerms
     You must accept the terms of use to register.
```

You override the default JSR 303 `@Size` **①** and default Hibernate Validator `@Email` **②** error messages as shown. The message for `@Size` is effectively a template that generates messages with the minimum and maximum sizes substituted in. You aren't overriding the default JSR 303 error message for `@NotNull` because that error shouldn't occur if you don't forget to implement any form fields. (And if you do, the default error message is OK because this is a programming error rather than an end user error.) Finally, you define an error message for the `acceptTerms` property at **③**.

In addition to the JSR 303 error messages, you need messages for the Spring-managed errors. You'll add these to `messages.properties` because `ValidationMessages.properties` is for JSR 303 error messages. Although it can be a little confusing to split the error messages into two resource bundles, it helps to do exactly this. The reason is that JSR 303 and Spring use different schemes for resolving error codes to message codes, and mixing error messages in a single resource bundle can make it harder to keep message codes straight.

Add the following two error messages to `messages.properties`:

```
error.global=Please fix the problems below.
error.mismatch.account.password=Your passwords do not match. Please try
     again.
```

Now you have an error message for the password-mismatch error code you used in the controller. You'll use the global error message in the form JSP.

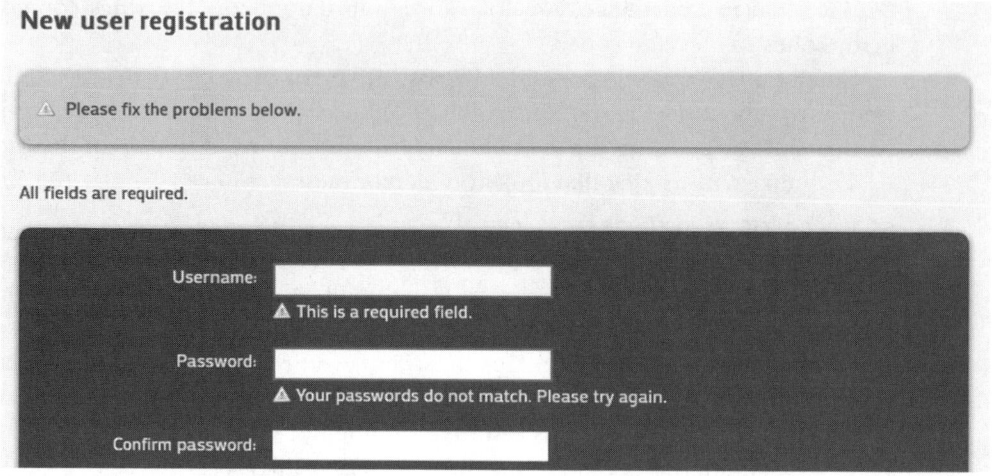

Figure 4.5   The revised registration form, with a global error message and field-level error messages

STEP 5. DISPLAYING VALIDATION ERRORS IN THE VIEW

You use the Spring `form` tag library to display both a global error message ("Please fix the problems below") and error messages on the form bean, as illustrated in figure 4.5.

The text fields for properties with errors are visually distinct (they have red borders), although it's hard to tell if you're viewing the figure in black and white. Also, fields are prepopulated with the user's submitted data so the user can fix mistakes instead of reentering all the data. The only exceptions are the two password fields, which for security reasons you don't prepopulate. The user has to reenter those values.

To accomplish this design, you'll need to revise registrationForm.jsp as shown next. (See the code download for the full version.)

Listing 4.10   registrationForm.jsp, updated with validation error messages

```
<%@ taglib prefix="form" uri="http://www.springframework.org/tags/form" %>
<%@ taglib prefix="spring" uri="http://www.springframework.org/tags" %>

<spring:message var="pageTitle" code="newUserRegistration.pageTitle" />
<spring:message var="msgAllFieldsRequired"
    code="newUserRegistration.message.allFieldsRequired" />

<html>
    <head><title>${pageTitle}</title></head>
    <body>
        <form:form cssClass="main" action="." modelAttribute="account">

<form:errors path="*">                                    ⬅   Displays global
    <div><spring:message code="error.global" /></div>       ❶   error message
</form:errors>

<h1>${pageTitle}</h1>
<div>${msgAllFieldsRequired}</div>

<div>
```

```
<div>
    <spring:message code="newUserRegistration.label.username" />
    <form:input path="username" cssClass="short"
        cssErrorClass="short error" />
</div>
<form:errors path="username">
    <div><form:errors path="username" htmlEscape="false" /></div>
</form:errors>
</div>

... other fields and submit button ...

        </form:form>
    </body>
</html>
```

At ❶ you display the global error message. The tag logic here is to look for the existence of any error whatsoever—a global error or a field error—and if there is one, display the global error message. The path="*" piece is your error wildcard.

You display the username field at ❷. By using the <form:input> tag, you get data prepopulation for free. This time around you include the CSS attributes because there's something interesting to show off. The cssClass attribute specifies the <input> element's CSS class when there's no error. (The short class just sets the text-field width in the sample code.) The cssErrorClass attribute specifies the class when there is an error. This allows you to change the visual appearance of the text field when there's an error.

In addition to the text field, you want to display the error message, and that's what's going on at ❸. You select the specific form bean property with the path attribute and use htmlEscape="false" so you can include HTML in the error message if desired.

The other fields are essentially the same, so we've suppressed them. Again, please see the code download for the full version of the code.

The last step in the process is to configure the application for validation.

STEP 6. CONFIGURING THE APP FOR VALIDATION
Surprise—you've already done what you need to do here. In recipe 4.1 you included the <mvc:annotation-driven> configuration inside beans-web.xml, which among several other things activates JSR 303 Bean Validation, causing Spring Web MVC to recognize the @Valid annotation. In recipe 4.2 you added a MessageSource.

Start up your browser and give the code a spin.

Discussion

The preceding recipe handles validation in the web tier. There's nothing wrong with that, because the constraints you've used so far make sense as web tier constraints. But it's important to bear in mind that modern validation frameworks like Spring validation and JSR 303 validation abandon the traditional assumption that bean validation occurs exclusively in the web tier. In the following recipe, you'll see what validation looks like in the service tier.

4.4   *Saving form data*

PREREQUISITES
Recipe 4.1 Displaying a web form
Recipe 4.3 Validating form data

KEY TECHNOLOGIES
Spring, JPA, Hibernate 3, Spring JdbcTemplate, MySQL, or other RDBMS

Background

So far you're accepting and validating user registrations, but you aren't saving the data to a persistent store. In this recipe, you'll persist data using Spring, JPA, Hibernate, and JDBC. You'll also perform service-tier validation to avoid duplicate usernames.

Problem

Save form data to a persistent store.

Solution

Although you'll save your form data to a database, you're not going to save the `AccountForm` form bean directly. The main reason is that there's a mismatch between the form bean and what you'd want out of a domain object:

- For security purposes, you don't want your domain object to have a password property. (You don't want a bunch of in-memory passwords sitting around.)
- Your domain object will have an `enabled` field that the form bean doesn't have.

Instead, you'll create a separate `Account` domain object and then have the controller translate the `AccountForm` into an `Account` before saving the `Account`.

> ### Why not save the form bean directly?
>
> It's possible to have a single POJO serve as both a form bean and a domain object, but architecturally it's cleaner to separate the two, especially if there are material differences between them. Here the security difference seems important enough to warrant two separate classes.
>
> Note that if you were to use a single POJO, then the `@InitBinder` method from recipe 4.3 would allow you to prevent users from setting the `enabled` property.
>
> Having said all that, the choice is partly a matter of style. Especially with traditional designs based on anemic domain objects, it's common to see a single POJO supporting presentational, domain, and persistence concerns. This might change, though, if domain-driven design (DDD) catches on in the Spring community. (Spring Roo promotes a DDD approach.) As domain objects get richer, they become less suitable as form beans.

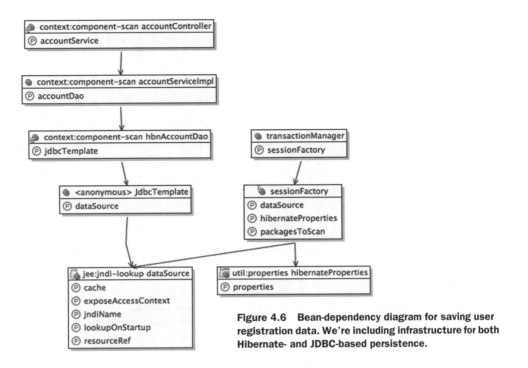

Figure 4.6 Bean-dependency diagram for saving user registration data. We're including infrastructure for both Hibernate- and JDBC-based persistence.

You'll use a combination of Hibernate, JPA annotations, and JDBC to persist the user registration data. Hibernate will work nicely for saving the Account domain object, but you need a way to save user passwords as well, and Hibernate won't help there because the password isn't part of Account. So, you'll use straight JDBC to save the password. The POJO and password data need to be saved as part of the same transaction, and we'll also show how to do that.

This recipe adds a lot of infrastructure to what you already have. See figure 4.6.

You'll start with the database schema, then build out the code and configuration on top of that.

CREATING A DATABASE SCHEMA FOR STORING USER ACCOUNTS

The following listing presents the database schema for MySQL, which involves a single table for storing user accounts.

Listing 4.11 User account table (MySQL)

```
create table account (
    id bigint unsigned not null auto_increment primary key,
    username varchar(50) unique not null,
    first_name varchar(50) not null,
    last_name varchar(50) not null,
    email varchar(50) not null,
    password varchar(64),
    marketing_ok boolean not null,
    accept_terms boolean not null,
```

```
    enabled boolean not null,
    date_created timestamp default 0,
    date_modified timestamp default current_timestamp
        on update current_timestamp,
    unique index account_idx1 (username),
    unique index account_idx2 (email)
) engine = InnoDb;
```

Notice that you coordinate the database constraints in listing 4.11 with the validation constraints in recipe 4.3. For example, the field-size maximums are generally 50 in both locations. (The exception is that the `password` column in the database allows 64 characters to accommodate SHA-256 hashes, as you'll see in recipe 6.7.) Also, you include a `password` column here even though the `Account` domain object won't have a corresponding property.

Speaking of `Account`, let's create it, because you'll need it for what follows.

ANNOTATING THE ACCOUNT MODEL FOR PERSISTENCE

The next listing presents the `Account` domain object, with JPA annotations for persistence.

Listing 4.12   Account.java with JPA annotations for persistence

```
package com.springinpractice.ch04.domain;

import java.util.Date;
import javax.persistence.Column;
import javax.persistence.Entity;
import javax.persistence.GeneratedValue;
import javax.persistence.GenerationType;
import javax.persistence.Id;
import javax.persistence.NamedQuery;
import javax.persistence.Table;
import javax.persistence.Transient;
import javax.validation.constraints.AssertTrue;
import javax.validation.constraints.NotNull;
import javax.validation.constraints.Size;
import org.hibernate.validator.constraints.Email;

@NamedQuery(                                                        ❶ Finder
    name = "findAccountByUsername",                                   query
    query = "from Account where username = :username")
@Entity                                                            ❷ Mark POJO
@Table(name = "account")                                            as persistent entity
public class Account {              ❸ Associate entity
    private Long id;                   with table
    private String username, firstName, lastName, email;
    private boolean marketingOk = true;
    private boolean acceptTerms = false;
    private boolean enabled = true;
    private Date dateCreated;

    @Id                                                       ❹ ID column
    @GeneratedValue(strategy = GenerationType.AUTO)
    @Column(name = "id")
```

```
public Long getId() { return id; }

@SuppressWarnings("unused")
private void setId(Long id) { this.id = id; }

@NotNull
@Size(min = 1, max = 50)
@Column(name = "username")                              ◄───⑤ Username column
public String getUsername() { return username; }

public void setUsername(String userName) { this.username = userName; }

@Transient                                                          ◄───┐
public String getFullName() { return firstName + " " + lastName; }     │

... other getters and setters ...                         Transient    │
}                                                  (nonpersistent) field ⑥
```

You use the JPA `@Entity` annotation ❷ to mark your domain object as a persistent entity, and `@Table` ❸ to associate the entity with a database table. At ❹ you use `@Id`, `@GeneratedValue`, and `@Column` on the `getId()` method to establish it as an ID property mapped to a database column called `id`, with `GenerationType.AUTO` indicating that the JPA provider (Hibernate in this case) is responsible for determining the right ID-generation strategy for the underlying database. (IDs might be generated by an autoincrement column, or perhaps by a sequence, and so on.)

For most properties, the column mapping is a matter of attaching an `@Column` annotation to the getter method or the field. You can see this with `getUsername()` ❺.

In the case of the `fullName` property, it's a convenience method rather than a persistent field, so you mark it with `@Transient` ❻ to prevent Hibernate from trying to persist it. You can also use JPA to define named queries supporting finder methods. At ❶ you define a named query to look up accounts by username. You'll use this query in your data access object.

CREATING THE ACCOUNT DATA ACCESS OBJECT

You need both an interface and an implementation for your DAO. The interface extends the `Dao` interface from chapter 1 by adding a password-aware `create()` method (recall that the `Account` doesn't have a `password` property) and a finder-by-username:

```
package com.springinpractice.ch04.dao;

import com.springinpractice.ch04.domain.Account;
import com.springinpractice.dao.Dao;

public interface AccountDao extends Dao<Account> {

    void create(Account account, String password);

    Account findByUsername(String username);
}
```

The DAO implementation in the following listing is more interesting. You derive it from `AbstractHbnDao` in chapter 1, but note that it isn't a pure Hibernate DAO.

Listing 4.13   HbnAccountDao.java, backed by both Hibernate and JDBC

```
package com.springinpractice.ch04.dao;

import javax.inject.Inject;
import org.hibernate.Query;
import org.springframework.jdbc.core.JdbcTemplate;
import org.springframework.stereotype.Repository;
import com.springinpractice.ch04.domain.Account;
import com.springinpractice.dao.hibernate.AbstractHbnDao;

@Repository                                              ◁── ❶ Mark as DAO
public class HbnAccountDao extends AbstractHbnDao<Account>
    implements AccountDao {

    private static final String UPDATE_PASSWORD_SQL =         ❷ JDBC update
        "update account set password = ? where username = ?";  ◁──┘    query

    @Inject private JdbcTemplate jdbcTemplate;          ◁── ❸ JDBC template

    public void create(Account account, String password) {   ◁─┐  Hibernate and JDBC
        create(account);                                      ❹ working together
        jdbcTemplate.update(
            UPDATE_PASSWORD_SQL, password, account.getUsername());
    }

    public Account findByUsername(String username) {
        Query q = getSession().getNamedQuery("findAccountByUsername"); ◁─┐
        q.setParameter("username", username);
        return (Account) q.uniqueResult();                        Invokes
    }                                                          named query ❺
}
```

You use @Repository ❶ to tag HbnAccountDao as a DAO. This allows Spring to discover the bean during component scanning.

Now we get to the interesting part. You're doing both Hibernate and JDBC inside this DAO. Hibernate handles everything on the Account POJO, but the password is a standalone field. So you need JDBC to update that. First you define a password-update statement at ❷. You also inject a JdbcTemplate at ❸ to execute the update. At ❹ you have Hibernate and JDBC working together to save the user account data, including the password. A Hibernate Session sits behind the call to create(). Then you run the JDBC password update using the JdbcTemplate.

Besides saving account information, you have a finder for looking up an account by username ❺. You'll use this to check for duplicate usernames when the user tries to register an account. The finder uses the JPA named query you created on the Account domain object in listing 4.12.

Now let's create an account service around the account DAO.

CREATING THE ACCOUNT SERVICE

You'll create a service with a single method for registering valid users. Here is the service interface:

```
package com.springinpractice.ch04.service;

import org.springframework.validation.Errors;
import com.springinpractice.ch04.domain.Account;

public interface AccountService {
    boolean registerAccount(
        Account account, String password, Errors errors);
}
```

Notice that the service interface accepts an Errors object. The idea here is that the registerAccount() method does a conditional registration—it registers the account if and only if there aren't any validation errors, either present in the Errors object, or discovered inside the registerAccount() implementation (such as a duplicate username). The controller will call registerAccount() with its BindingResult object, which works fine because BindingResult extends Errors. You use Errors in the AccountService interface, though, rather than BindingResult, because the service tier doesn't know anything about web binding.

> **Why call registerAccount() if there are already known errors?**
>
> It may seem odd to call the registerAccount() method if there are already errors in the Errors container. The reason: when doing form validation, you generally want to know about all validation errors, not just the first one. So you still check for duplicate usernames even if you already know, for example, that the passwords didn't match.

The following listing is the account service implementation.

Listing 4.14 AccountServiceImpl.java: service implementation

```
package com.springinpractice.ch04.service;

import javax.inject.Inject;
import org.springframework.stereotype.Service;
import org.springframework.transaction.annotation.Transactional;
import org.springframework.validation.Errors;
import com.springinpractice.ch04.dao.AccountDao;
import com.springinpractice.ch04.domain.Account;

@Service
@Transactional(readOnly = true)                              ← ① Default transaction
public class AccountServiceImpl implements AccountService {        definition
    @Inject private AccountDao accountDao;
                                                             ← ② Overrides
    @Transactional(readOnly = false)                              default
    public boolean registerAccount(
        Account account, String password, Errors errors) {
                                                             ← ③ Validates
        validateUsername(account.getUsername(), errors);          username
        boolean valid = !errors.hasErrors();
        if (valid) { accountDao.create(account, password); }  ← Creates
        return valid;                                         ④ account if valid
    }
```

```
    private void validateUsername(String username, Errors errors) {
        if (accountDao.findByUsername(username) != null) {
            errors.rejectValue("username", "error.duplicate",
                new String[] { username }, null);
        }
    }
}
```

**Checks for
duplicate
usernames** ⑤

A good practice when writing service beans is to associate a read-only transaction defi-nition at the class level ❶. This provides a basic layer of safety because individual methods have to override the definition explicitly ❷ in order to write to the persistent store. Here you have only one method, so it looks a little funny, but this way you won't forget if you decide to add more methods.

Inside `registerAccount()`, you validate the username ❸ and save the account to the database if the entire account is valid ❹. The username validation ❺ uses the finder you created to determine whether the username is a duplicate. If it is, then you use the `errors` object to reject the username, specifying the `errors.duplicate` error code (we'll define that momentarily) and the username for token substitution.

Let's quickly take care of that error message.

ADDING A NEW ERROR MESSAGE FOR DUPLICATE USERNAMES

All you need to do is add a single error message to `messages.properties`:

```
error.duplicate.account.username=The username {0} is already taken.
```

The `error.duplicate.account.username` message code will match the `error.dupli-cate` error code as explained in recipe 4.3. Spring will substitute the username for the `{0}` when displaying the error message, because the username is the 0th element of the `String[]` you passed into `rejectValue()`.

There isn't much you need to do to the controller to make it save accounts, as you'll see now.

UPDATING THE CONTROLLER TO SAVE ACCOUNTS USING THE SERVICE

To update the controller, you add a single line to the `postRegistrationForm()` method, and you add a helper method to convert the form bean into a domain object:

```
@RequestMapping(value = "", method = RequestMethod.POST)
public String postRegistrationForm(
        @ModelAttribute("account") @Valid AccountForm form,
        BindingResult result) {

    convertPasswordError(result);
    accountService.registerAccount(
        toAccount(form), form.getPassword(), result);
    return (result.hasErrors() ? VN_REG_FORM : VN_REG_OK);
}

private static Account toAccount(AccountForm form) {
    Account account = new Account();
    account.setUsername(form.getUsername());
    account.setFirstName(form.getFirstName());
    account.setLastName(form.getLastName());
```

```
account.setEmail(form.getEmail());
account.setMarketingOk(form.isMarketingOk());
account.setAcceptTerms(form.getAcceptTerms());
account.setEnabled(true);
return account;
}
```

You'll need to augment the existing configuration to support persistence. The main part of this effort involves adding a new Spring application context file. You'll need to modify web.xml slightly as well. First let's do the app context.

CREATING A NEW APPLICATION CONTEXT CONFIGURATION FOR PERSISTENCE

To add persistence to your registration form, you need to add several bits.

Listing 4.15 beans-service.xml: application context configuration

```
<?xml version="1.0" encoding="UTF-8"?>
<beans xmlns="http://www.springframework.org/schema/beans"
    xmlns:context="http://www.springframework.org/schema/context"
    xmlns:jee="http://www.springframework.org/schema/jee"
    xmlns:p="http://www.springframework.org/schema/p"
    xmlns:tx="http://www.springframework.org/schema/tx"
    xmlns:util="http://www.springframework.org/schema/util"
    xmlns:xsi="http://www.w3.org/2001/XMLSchema-instance"
    xsi:schemaLocation="http://www.springframework.org/schema/beans
        http://www.springframework.org/schema/beans/spring-beans-3.1.xsd
        http://www.springframework.org/schema/context
        http://www.springframework.org/schema/context/
                spring-context-3.1.xsd
        http://www.springframework.org/schema/jee
        http://www.springframework.org/schema/jee/spring-jee-3.1.xsd
        http://www.springframework.org/schema/tx
        http://www.springframework.org/schema/tx/spring-tx-3.1.xsd
        http://www.springframework.org/schema/util
        http://www.springframework.org/schema/util/spring-util-3.1.xsd">

    <jee:jndi-lookup id="dataSource" jndi-name="jdbc/Sip04DS"      ◁──── ❶ DataSource reference
        resource-ref="true"/>

    <bean class="org.springframework.jdbc.core.JdbcTemplate"       ◁──── ❷ JDBC template for JDBC calls
        p:dataSource-ref="dataSource" />

    <util:properties id="hibernateProperties">                     ◁──── ❸ Hibernate configuration
        <prop key="hibernate.dialect">
            org.hibernate.dialect.MySQL5InnoDBDialect
        </prop>
        <prop key="hibernate.show_sql">false</prop>
    </util:properties>
                                                                   ◁──── ❹ Hibernate SessionFactory
    <bean id="sessionFactory"
        class="org.springframework.orm.hibernate3.annotation.
                AnnotationSessionFactoryBean"
        p:dataSource-ref="dataSource"
        p:packagesToScan="com.springinpractice.ch04.domain"
        p:hibernateProperties-ref="hibernateProperties" />
```

```
<bean id="transactionManager"
    class="org.springframework.orm.hibernate3.
        HibernateTransactionManager"
    p:sessionFactory-ref="sessionFactory" />

<context:component-scan
    base-package="com.springinpractice.ch04.dao.hbn" />
<context:component-scan
    base-package="com.springinpractice.ch04.service" />

<tx:annotation-driven />
</beans>
```

⑤ Transaction manager

⑥ Discovers DAOs and services

⑦ Activates transactions

You declare a `DataSource` reference using a JNDI lookup at ❶. You'll need to consult the documentation for your servlet container to see what's involved with exposing a `DataSource` with JNDI using that container. The sample code includes a Jetty configuration.

At ❷ you declare the JDBC template you're using to set the user password. The Hibernate configuration is at ❸, and it's set up for MySQL 5 in listing 4.15. You'll need to modify that if you're using a different RDBMS; see the Javadoc for the `org.hibernate.dialect` package for more options.

You define a Hibernate `SessionFactory` at ❹, using the `DataSource` and configuration you just created. As its name suggests, the `SessionFactory` is a session source. Sometimes it creates brand-new sessions (for example, when starting a new transaction), and sometimes it returns sessions that have already been created (such as when executing DAO persistence operations).

The transaction manager ❺ provides (you guessed it) transaction management services. It knows, for example, how to start, suspend, and stop transactions. The `HibernateTransactionManager` implementation coordinates transaction management with Hibernate session management.

You use `<context:component-scan>` to discover DAOs and service beans ❻. Component scanning interprets classes annotated with `@Repository` as DAOs and classes annotated with `@Service` as service beans.

Finally, at ❼ you use `<tx:annotation-driven>` to activate transactions. The specific details of that process are fairly involved, and there's no need to dig into the details here, but the basic idea is that it causes Spring's IOC container to wrap transaction-aware Spring AOP proxies around components marked up with the `@Transactional` annotation.[6] It does this using Spring AOP's autoproxy facility.

Just one small tweak to go, and you'll be ready to run the app.

UPDATING WEB.XML TO POINT TO THE NEW APP CONTEXT CONFIGURATION

All you need to do here is add a single configuration element to web.xml. This tells the Spring Web MVC `DispatcherService` where to find your beans-service.xml configuration:

---

[6] In addition to Spring AOP proxies, AspectJ weaving is an option. See the reference documentation for `<tx:annotation-driven>` for more details.

```
<context-param>
    <param-name>contextConfigLocation</param-name>
    <param-value>classpath:/spring/beans-service.xml</param-value>
</context-param>
```

With that, you should be ready to go. Try it out.

Discussion

In this recipe we've shown how to save form data to a persistent store. That's of course a common requirement, and now you have a good feel for how to do it. You even saw how to use Hibernate and JDBC together in cases where the form data doesn't all fit nicely inside a single domain object.

Because our topic is web forms in general rather than user-registration forms in particular, we've neglected some persistence- and security-related topics that a real user form would take seriously. The good news is that we'll address them in chapter 6. They're the following:

- *Spring Security integration*—A key reason for user accounts is to support logins. Recipe 6.6 shows how to use the account data you've developed in chapter 4 as an authentication source.
- *Hashing and salting passwords*—It's a poor security practice to save passwords as plaintext in the database, because that makes it easier for a malicious person to see those passwords and use them on other websites. (Users often use the same password for multiple websites.) You can use password hashing and salting to mitigate this issue. We'll show how to hash and salt passwords in recipe 6.7.

4.5   Summary

In this chapter, you developed a basic registration form with several of the key features you'd expect such a form to have, including string externalization, validation, and persistence. Although we used user registration as an example, the topics we've treated are obviously general concerns when developing web-based forms.

In many cases, registration forms aren't as simple as the one you developed in this chapter. Instead they carry the user through a series of steps, implemented as a *web flow* spanning multiple pages. In chapter 5 you'll learn how to implement multistep flows using Spring Web Flow.

Enhancing Spring MVC
applications with Web Flow

This chapter covers

- An introduction to Spring Web Flow
- Building a Spring soccer demo application
- Using action classes
- Working with form data-binding and validation
- Understanding flow and state inheritance
- Securing web flows

Most enterprise Java developers have worked on web applications that have some sort of workflow component to them. Classic use cases consist of searching for products, booking a flight, and preparing your tax return. But without the right tools, determining how to manage this workflow can be a challenge.

Model-view-controller (MVC) frameworks work best in situations where the unit of work required to create or update the model can be implemented in a minimal number of views. By itself, though, the MVC pattern doesn't provide an efficient mechanism for managing a series of intermediate steps, their rules, and states that span multiple requests. As a result, page-flow logic typically seeps into both the view and controller tiers whereas the application state required to support the page-flow logic is often spread between a combination of session and request parameters. As a result, understanding, maintaining, and testing complex page flows in an MVC application can quickly become an arduous task.

In this chapter, we'll look at Spring Web Flow (SWF) and focus on how you can use this framework to complement your existing Spring MVC application. Before we dive in, let's go over some important background information.

5.1 Is Spring Web Flow right for you?

SWF is often confused with more general-purpose workflow engines. In general, workflow engines can route work through any number of sequenced tasks or activities. Processing in these engines takes place either synchronously or asynchronously using a number of predefined rules and other complex workflow patterns such as forks and joins.

In contrast, SWF provides only a subset of these capabilities. It's focused specifically on addressing the problem of navigation (page flows) in the web tier. Both the relationship and application of these tools should be viewed as complementary rather than competitive. But this narrow focus makes SWF intuitive to use and easy to learn.

SWF is best applied when you need to navigate a user through a series of predefined and/or dynamic steps (states) to achieve a desired outcome or complete a unit of work. Some examples of where SWF would be beneficial are as follows:

- Booking travel reservations
- Shopping carts
- Adaptive surveys or questionnaires
- Multistep product configuration

SWF greatly simplifies the work required to design, maintain, and understand complex page-navigation decisions. As you'll see in section 5.6, large flows can be broken down into reusable subflows with their own predefined contracts and lifecycle, making reusability and modularity straightforward.

5.2 An overview of Spring Web Flow

SWF is a framework that was introduced in 2005 and is focused on being the best solution for managing page flows in a web application. Over the next several sections, we'll introduce you to this framework and its core concepts. You'll build on this knowledge in section 5.3 by creating a brief demo application. The remainder of the chapter will focus on making you more productive by examining problems or tasks you're likely to encounter as you begin developing with SWF. Although SWF provides JSF and portlet support, we'll focus on complementing your existing Spring MVC configuration.

5.2.1   Defining a flow

As kids, we liked to read "choose your own adventure" books. Our favorite stories involved going on quests or exploring foreign lands. The format of these books was always the same. The first chapter introduced us as the main character and set up the initial story line. Subsequent chapters added to the story and presented several options that let us control what we as the main character did next. We were then routed back and forth through several parts of the book based on the actions we chose. It was common for these books to have varying endings depending on the choices made.

Flows are similar to these books in that they have a single place to start, followed by several intermediary steps. Each step can route the user to additional steps or different end points based on information captured in the flow.

In SWF, these flows are potentially reusable components that represent a unit of work and are defined using states, transitions, and flow data. Figure 5.1 represents a simple search flow.

A flow is defined using an XML-based flow definition language. Each flow is defined in its own file using the following root element.

Listing 5.1   Defining a flow

```
<flow xmlns="http://www.springframework.org/schema/webflow"
  xmlns:xsi="http://www.w3.org/2001/XMLSchema-instance"
  xsi:schemaLocation="
   http://www.springframework.org/schema/webflow
   http://www.springframework.org/schema/webflow/spring-webflow-2.0.xsd"
  start-state="enterSearchCriteria">                    ◁─┐
                                                    ❶  **Explicitly defines**
    . . .                                               **start state**

</flow>
```

In addition to defining a flow, at ❶ you explicitly define the `enterSearchCriteria` state as being the flow start state. Let's talk more about states next.

5.2.2   The five types of states

Each box in figure 5.1 represents an individual step in the flow called a *state*. This is where something is displayed to the user, a decision is made, and a flow ends or some other action is taken. Like the "choose your own adventure" books we talked about earlier, flows must have a single start state but can contain one or many end states. SWF defines five states, as shown in table 5.1.

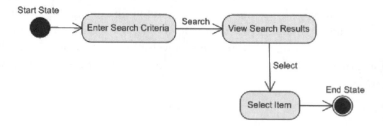

Figure 5.1   **In this simplified search flow, users start by entering search criteria and transition to a state where they can view their search results. The flow transitions to the end state after the user selects an item.**

Table 5.1   The five types of state in SWF

State type	What it does
View	The view state renders a view to the user and is used to either solicit information from or provide information to the user.
Action	An action state is used when you want to perform some type of work and transition to another state based on its outcome.
Decision	The decision state is similar to an action state but uses a convenient If...Then...Else statement to determine which state to transition to next.
End	The end state represents the end of a flow. There may be one or many flow end states.
Subflow	The subflow state starts another existing flow as a subflow and maps the subflow's end states to transitions in the current flow.

Missing from table 5.1 is the flow's start state. The start state is a marker state that designates another state (view, action, decision, end, subflow) defined in the flow as being the flow's starting point. You defined an explicit `start-state` at ❶ called `enterSearchCriteria` in listing 5.1. When `start-state` isn't explicitly defined, the first state defined in the flow is assumed to be the start state. Let's look at how each of these states is defined in SWF's XML-based flow definition language.

VIEW STATE

The view state is used to either display or solicit information from the user and is defined using the `view-state` element in the flow definition XML file. In the simplified search flow in figure 5.1, you use view states to interact with the end user by presenting a search form or viewing search results. In the following example, the logical view name is explicitly specified using the optional `view` attribute. If the `view` attribute isn't specified, the view is given the same name as the state's required `id` attribute along with a .jsp suffix. More on this later:

```
<view-state id="enterSearchCriteria" view="enterSearchCriteriaForm">
  <transition on="search" to="viewSearchResults"/>
</view-state>
```

Although our focus in this chapter is on enhancing your existing Spring MVC application, SWF supports a number of view technologies. In addition to JSF, SWF can use any of the view technologies that Spring MVC supports out of the box. As of this writing, these are JSP, JSTL, Velocity, and XSLT.

   When a view is rendered to the user, the flow pauses and waits for another event to occur. Users can continue flows by generating additional events by either clicking links or submitting forms containing event IDs. Event IDs can be specified as the value of the _eventId request parameter or directly in the request parameter's name itself using the prefix _eventId_. In the following code snippet, both lines are equivalent.

```
_eventId=enterSearchCriteria
_eventId_enterSearchCriteria
```

To specify an event ID in a link, you need to include the event ID using one of the conventions appended to `flowExecutionUrl`. `flowExecutionUrl` is a variable that SWF provides that contains the context-relative URI for the current execution of the flow and some information about the current view state. The two lines in the following example are equivalent and show how to specify event IDs using links:

```
<a href="${flowExecutionUrl}&_eventId=enterSearchCriteria">
New Search</a>

<a href="${flowExecutionUrl}&_eventId_enterSearchCriteria">
New Search</a>
```

When the view is rendered, `flowExecutionUrl` contains the context-relative URI for the current flow execution and a request variable called `execution`. The link specified on the first line in the example may be resolved as

```
<a href="/myWebApp/myFlowId?execution=e1s1&_eventId=enterSearchCriteria">
New Search</a>
```

In the example, the value of the `execution` request variable is specified in the format `eXsY` where `e` indicates the current instance of the flow `myFlowId`, which is denoted by `X`. The letter `s` indicates the current step that is being executed and is denoted by `Y`. Using the example you're executing the first instance and first step of the flow with `flowId` `myFlow`. We'll talk more about flow IDs and how they're specified and resolved later.

When using forms to capture user input, the event ID can be specified either in a hidden field or in the name of a submit button. The next code snippet provides an example of specifying the event ID using a hidden form field:

```
<form:form action="${flowExecutionUrl}" >
  <input type="hidden" name="_eventId"
    value="processSearchForm"/>
  <input type="submit" value="Search"/>
</form:form>
```

Similar to the previous code, the following snippet provides an example of how to specify an event ID using a form submit button:

```
<form:form action="${flowExecutionUrl}" >
  <input type="submit" name="_eventId_processSearchForm"
    value="Search"/>
</form:form>
```

Using a button
name to specify
❶ the event ID

Notice how this example provides both the event ID and its value together using the underscore character ❶. The view state is unique in that it's the only state where the currently executing flow pauses and waits for a user-generated event to occur. With the exception of the end state, other states continue the flow by evaluating events generated in the state. Let's look at the action state next.

ACTION STATE

As the name suggests, the action state is where the application does work. You express the work to be done using an expression in an `evaluate` statement. Look at the following example:

```
<action-state id="addVolunteer">
  <evaluate expression="volunteerAction.addVolunteer(volunteer)"/>          ◁──┐
  <transition on="success" to="successView" />           Using Spring Expression
  <transition on="failure" to="failureView" />        Language (SpEL) to do work  ❶
</action-state>
```

At ❶, your expression calls the `addVolunteer()` method of a Spring-managed bean named `volunteerAction`, passing it a flow-scoped variable named `volunteer`. When the expression is evaluated, the value that `volunteerAction` returns becomes the event ID to transition to.

If you need to execute additional code, you can add `evaluate` elements. SWF will execute each expression in order until the outcome of the code being called matches a local or globally defined transition. We'll discuss transitions in section 5.2.3.

DECISION STATE

A decision state provides a subset of the functionality of the action state mentioned earlier. Instead of checking the return value of one or more expressions to find a match to a local or global transition, the decision state evaluates a boolean expression and transitions to one of two states depending on the result. The `addVolunteer` code snippet is rewritten next as a decision state:

```
<decision-state id="addVolunteer">
  <if test="volunteerAction.addVolunteer(volunteer)"
    then="successView" else="failureView"/>
</decision-state>
```

Now that we've talked about how to start a flow, interact with users, and do work, let's see how you end the flow.

END STATE

Once the flow transitions to an end state, it's terminated:

```
<end-state id="myFlowEndState"/>
```
❶ Simplest form of flow's end-state

```
<end-state id="myFlowEndState" view="endOfFlowView"/>
```
❷ Renders endOfFlowView view and ends flow

In its simplest form, the flow ends at ❶. If a view is specified ❷, SWF renders the view in addition to ending the flow. As you'll see next, if you're ending a subflow, the end state's `id` is used as an event to transition to in the parent flow.

SUBFLOW STATE

In general, it's a good practice to break large, complex problems into smaller, more manageable pieces. Flows are no different. In SWF, the flow is a potentially reusable and self-contained component that is defined using states, transitions, flow data, inputs, and outputs. As shown in the following snippet, you use the subflow state in the top-level flow to call an existing flow as a subflow:

```
<subflow-state id="createdNewWidget" subflow="widget/createNew">
  <input name="widget" value="widget"/>
  <transition on="success" to "ourNextStateInParentFlow"/>
</subflow-state>
```

Here you are calling a subflow with the ID `widget/createNew`. You're using the `<input>` element to pass a widget object into the subflow for some type of configuration or modification. The example assumes that the subflow will transition to an end state with the ID `success`. As we mentioned earlier, the ID of the subflow's end state will be used as the event to transition to.

Now that we've discussed the five different types of states available in SWF, let's turn our attention to transitions and see how you can use them to move from state to state.

5.2.3   *Transitions between states*

In figure 5.1, the arrows represent transitions between states. Transitions can be defined in a given state or globally. A transition is defined using the `transition` element and maps an event occurring in the current state to the next state. Look at the following listing.

Listing 5.2   Defining transitions

```
<view-state id="displayFindExistingPlayerResult">
  <transition on="back" to="findExistingPlayerForm"/>
  <transition on="newSearch" to="newSearchEndState"/>
  <transition on="noneMatch" to="endState"/>           ❶ Catch-all
  <transition on="existingAccountFound"                  transition
    to="existingAccountFoundEndState"/>
  <transition to="newSearchEndState"/>                 ❷ Exception-based
  <transition on-exception=                               transition
    "com.springinpractice.exception.ServiceUnavailableException"
      to="systemUnavailable"/>
</view-state>
```

Each transition is evaluated in the order it's defined. At ❶, you implement a catch-all transition by omitting the event name. In this example, you transition to `newSearch-EndState` if an explicit match isn't found for the other transition events.

As seen at ❷, transitions aren't limited to events. Here, if a `ServiceUnavailable-Exception` is thrown, you can transition to a view state to provide the end user with a friendly message.

After writing a flow that contains many different states, you may find that you're defining certain transitions over and over again. Perhaps in a given flow, there are many points at which a user can choose to either quit and exit the flow or start over. Instead of specifying a transition from the `quit` event to an end state with the ID `quitEndState` in each location, you could define this transition globally. Let's look at an example:

```
<global-transitions>
  <transition on="quit" to="quitEndState"/>
  <transition on="startOver" to="newSearchEndState"/>
</global-transitions>
```

Here you use the `global-transitions` element to define two global transitions that can be used in any view or action state in the flow.

Up to this point, we've talked about events, the five types of states, and how to transition between them. The next section completes our overview by discussing how SWF manages its state. Then we'll put it all together in a brief example application in section 5.3.

5.2.4　Flow data

In most MVC applications that contain complex page flows, developers are left to figure out how they should maintain state for each individual step, rule, or entire workflow. Bugs are often introduced into these systems as a result of having multiple places and approaches to managing this state. Thinking about your past experience, was state managed using session variables, request variable, URL parameters, hidden form fields, or a combination of each? When a user restarted a given workflow or reused part of an existing flow, how were you sure you'd cleared out all the necessary state from the previous run?

This is where SWF shines. SWF provides facilities for creating, storing, and retrieving data as well as managing its lifecycle. Let's look at how you define variables in SWF and then at the approaches you can use to store and manage the lifecycle of this state in the flow.

DECLARING VARIABLES

There are several different ways to define variables in SWF. The `<var>` element is used at the flow level to define flow-scoped instance variables:

```
<var name="user" class="com.springinpractice.domain.User"/>
```

In the example, SWF instantiates an instance of the `User` class and assigns it to a variable named `user`. This variable is accessible from anywhere in the current flow.

As you saw in section 5.2.2, you can use the `<evaluate>` element in an action or view state to evaluate an expression and store its result:

```
<evaluate result="viewScope.userInfo"
  expression="userService.getUserInfo(currentUser.name)"/>
```

Here you're calling the `getUserInfo()` method of a Spring managed bean named `userService` and storing the result in a view-scoped variable named `userInfo`. When saving the result of an expression into a variable, you must explicitly specify the intended scope for the variable. We'll talk more about the scopes used in SWF in the next section.

Because the `<evaluate>` element determines the event it returns at runtime, it's ideally suited for driving transitions in an action state:

```
<action-state id="processSearchCriteria">
   <evaluate expression="searchService.getResults(searchCriteria)"/>
   <transition on="singleResult" to="detailView"/>
   <transition on="multipleOrNone" to="searchResultsView"/>
</action-state>
```

The `<set>` element is similar to `<evaluate>` but only provides a subset of its functionality. Like the `<evaluate>` element, it stores the result of an expression into a named variable using a slightly different syntax:

```
<set name="flowScope.widget"
   value="new com.springinpractice.domain.Widget()"/>
```

Here you're creating a new `Widget` instance and storing it in the `flowScope` under the name `widget`. The `<set>` element differs from the `<evaluate>` element in that it always returns the `success` event.

Up to this point, all the expressions you've seen use the Spring Expression Language (SpEL) which is new to Spring 3.0. Although other expression languages such as Unified EL, OGNL, and JBoss EL exist, SpEL was specifically created to provide developers with a single expression language that can be used throughout the entire Spring stack.

The expressions shown in both the `<evaluate>` and `<set>` elements are basic and use SpEL to invoke methods on Spring managed beans. SpEL is a powerful expression language and can be used to express many complex concepts both inside and outside of Spring. Because of its usefulness and application throughout the Spring stack, we strongly urge you to learn more about programming with SpEL. For more details about the expression language, its API, or its syntax, consult the documentation for the core Spring project available at www.springsource.org/documentation.

As you may have expected, defining variables in SWF is pretty straightforward. SWF has made managing the lifecycle of this data just as easy. We'll discuss this next.

THE FIVE VARIABLE SCOPES

The data you store as variables in a flow can have different lifecycles based on which of the following five scopes it belongs to:

- `requestScope`—Similar to an HTTP or portlet request, a variable in this scope is created when the flow is called for the current request and destroyed when it returns. The data will be available for the duration of the request, which may involve many states and transitions.

- `flashScope`—Variables in this scope are allocated when the flow starts and destroyed when the flow ends. They are cleared following a view rendering. Objects in this scope should be serializable.

- `viewScope`—Variables in this scope are created when you enter a view state and destroyed when the view state exists. They can only be referenced from the view state that created them. Objects in this scope should be serializable.

- flowScope—Variables in this scope are created when a flow starts and destroyed when the flow ends. They can only be referenced from the flow in which they were created. Objects in this scope should be serializable.

- conversationScope—Similar to flowScope, variables in this scope are created when a flow starts and destroyed when the flow ends. They can be referenced from the flow that defined them as well as all subflows. Objects in this scope should be serializable.

With the exception of the <var> element, when assigning variables, you need to be explicit about which scope the variable should be created in. When accessing a variable, specifying the scope is optional. In this case, SWF uses the scope-searching algorithm illustrated in figure 5.2 to determine which scope the variable is in. After searching each of the variable scopes, if no variable is found, an Evaluation-Exception is thrown.

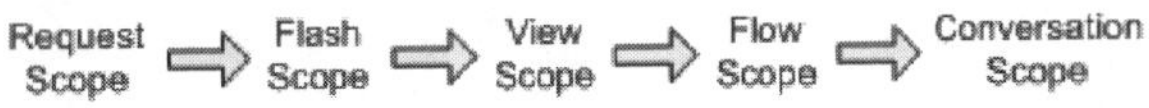

Request Scope ⟹ Flash Scope ⟹ View Scope ⟹ Flow Scope ⟹ Conversation Scope

Figure 5.2 If you don't explicitly identify which scope a variable is in, SWF starts looking in the request scope and continues looking in the flash, view, flow, and conversation scopes until the variable is found.

This algorithm is similar in concept to how the EL searches through scopes for a named object in a JSP page.

Now that we've provided a brief overview of all the major components of SWF, let's see how you can assemble them into a brief demo application that demonstrates the main features of SWF.

5.3 *The Spring Soccer Club demo application*

For the remainder of the chapter, you'll focus on building out a small demo application called Spring Soccer Club. Every spring and fall, hundreds of kids look forward to the start of a new youth soccer season. Their parents, on the other hand, dread the existing paper-based sign-up process. You're going to help them by defining an online registration process where they can create an account and register their kids for the upcoming season. Figure 5.3 illustrates this flow.

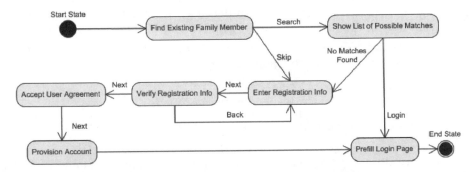

Figure 5.3 Before users are allowed to register, you first ask if they have registered in the past. If they haven't, users go directly to the registration page. If they have registered previously, the user is able to search for this registration. If they still are unable to find their existing registration, users can register again.

In the diagram, the boxes represent states in SWF and the arrows represent transitions between those states. Throughout the rest of this chapter, we use the word *state* and *step* interchangeably.

In the next several sections, you'll take an iterative approach to building this demo application, resulting in a working example of how all of SWF's main features work. After getting SWF installed and working, your first step will be to define views for each step in the flow. Second, you'll start to define the transitions between steps. Then you'll add dynamic transition logic with action states and decision-state constructs. Finally, you'll see how to bind data to forms and perform data validation. After working through the next several sections, you should have the knowledge necessary to start experimenting with SWF on your own. To keep the focus on SWF, we'll minimize extra coding by stubbing out the service code. Let's get started.

5.3.1   *Installing and configuring SWF*

PREREQUISITES
None

KEY TECHNOLOGIES
Spring MVC, SWF

Background

In chapter 3, you learned how to set up a basic Spring MVC application. This recipe builds on this knowledge and shows how to extend and validate this configuration to support SWF.

Problem

You would like to install SWF in a new application or extend an existing Spring MVC application.

Solution

As of this writing, the latest version of SWF is version 2.3.0. SWF requires at least Java 1.5 and Spring 3.0 or greater to run. If you're using Maven, there are two different dependencies you can define in your project object model (POM) depending on whether you'll be using JSF. As our focus is on extending an existing Spring MVC application, you'll use the following for the demo application:

```
<dependency>
    <groupId>org.springframework.webflow</groupId>
    <artifactId>spring-webflow</artifactId>
    <version>2.3.0.RELEASE</version>
</dependency>
```

If you were also using JSF, you could use the following Maven dependency instead. For clarity, the `spring-faces` artifact includes everything in the Maven dependency plus additional JARs to support JSF development. There is no need to include both:

```
<dependency>
    <groupId>org.springframework.webflow</groupId>
    <artifactId>spring-faces</artifactId>
    <version>2.3.0.RELEASE</version>
</dependency>
```

For those not using Maven, you can download the SWF JAR files from the project's site (www.springsource.org/webflow). Once you've unzipped the distribution, you'll find the following JAR files in the dist directory:

```
org.springframework.webflow-2.3.0.RELEASE.jar
org.springframework.binding-2.3.0.RELEASE.jar
org.springframework.js-2.3.0.RELEASE.jar
org.springframework.js.resources-2.3.0.RELEASE.jar
org.springframework.faces-2.3.0.RELEASE.jar
```

In addition to the Spring 3.x JAR files, you need the web flow and binding JARs for the demo application. The faces JAR file is only required if you'll be using JSF.

As of the 2.1 release of SWF, no additional dependencies are required. In the 2.0 release, the unified EL was the default expression language and users were given the choice to include either a unified EL implementation or Object Graph Navigation Language (OGNL). As of the 2.1 release, SpEL is the default and preferred expression language going forward. Although unified EL and OGNL are both supported, it's strongly recommended that users use or migrate to using SpEL as their expression language of choice. We'll talk more about this later.

BASIC SPRING MVC CONFIGURATION

To develop the Spring Soccer Club Demo application, you'll use Spring MVC. The next few steps are designed to quickly set up and validate the Spring MVC setup. Once you validate that Spring MVC is set up, you'll quickly extend that setup and get SWF working.

SWF uses several components from Spring MVC, the first of which is DispatchererServlet. Start by adding the following servlet and mapping to your web.xml file:

Listing 5.3 web.xml: `DispatcherServlet`

```
<!-- Source project: sip05, branch: 01 (Maven Project) -->
<servlet>
    <servlet-name>springSoccer</servlet-name>
    <servlet-class>
      org.springframework.web.servlet.DispatcherServlet
    </servlet-class>
    <init-param>
      <param-name>contextConfigLocation</param-name>
      <param-value>
        /WEB-INF/spring/web/dispatcherServlet-context.xml
      </param-value>
    </init-param>
    <load-on-startup>1</load-on-startup>
</servlet>
```

Later in the file, you also need to add the servlet mapping for the springSoccer serv-let. Starting in Spring 3.04, you can map DispatcherServlet to /. We'll discuss this more after listing 5.4:

```
<servlet-mapping>
  <servlet-name>springSoccer</servlet-name>
  <url-pattern>/</url-pattern>
</servlet-mapping>
```

Next, create a file named dispatcherServlet-context.xml in the WEB-INF/spring/web directory with the following contents.

Listing 5.4 dispatcherServlet-context.xml

```
<?xml version="1.0" encoding="UTF-8"?>
<!-- Source project: sip05, branch: 01 (Maven Project) -->

<beans xmlns="http://www.springframework.org/schema/beans"
  xmlns:xsi="http://www.w3.org/2001/XMLSchema-instance"
  xmlns:context="http://www.springframework.org/schema/context"
  xmlns:mvc="http://www.springframework.org/schema/mvc"
  xsi:schemaLocation="
  http://www.springframework.org/schema/context
  http://www.springframework.org/schema/context/spring-context.xsd
  http://www.springframework.org/schema/mvc
  http://www.springframework.org/schema/mvc/spring-mvc-3.0.xsd
  http://www.springframework.org/schema/beans
  http://www.springframework.org/schema/beans/spring-beans-3.0.xsd">

  <mvc:annotation-driven />

  <mvc:resources mapping="/resources/**" location="/resources/" />

  <bean class="org.springframework.web.servlet.
        view.InternalResourceViewResolver">
      <property
        name="viewClass"
        value="org.springframework.web.servlet.view.JstlView" />
    <property name="prefix" value="/WEB-INF/jsp/" />
    <property name="suffix" value=".jsp" />
  </bean>

  <context:component-scan base-package="com.springinpractice.ch05" />
</beans>
```

1 Enables @Controller programming model

2 Maps location of static resources

3 Configures view resolver

4 Location of annotated classes

The code should look familiar. At **1**, you enabled the @Controller programming model that enables Spring MVC's annotation-driven features. In Spring 3.04, a new <mvc:resources> element handles requests for static content. As you can see in list-ing 5.3, this allows you to configure DispatcherServlet to handle all requests **2**. At **3**, you configure InternalResourceViewResolver. Here you are prefixing your logical view names with /WEB-INF/jsp/ and adding a .jsp suffix. For more information on this, take another look at section 3.5.4. Finally, you add the <context:component-scan> element **4**. Our annotated controller test class is in the com.springinpractice.ch05 .mvc package.

Next, create the following controller and JSP page. You'll test to make sure the Spring MVC is working before moving on.

Listing 5.5   HelloWorldController

```
// Source project: sip05, branch: 01 (Maven Project)
package com.springinpractice.ch05.mvc;

import org.springframework.stereotype.Controller;
import org.springframework.web.bind.annotation.RequestMapping;

@Controller
public class HelloWorldController {

    @RequestMapping("/helloWorldControllerTest")
    public String showTestPage() {
        return "helloWorld";
    }
}
```

The controller is straightforward and returns the helloWorld view when called. Let's put together this view next.

Listing 5.6   /WEB-INF/jsp/helloWorld.jsp

```
<%-- Source project: sip05, branch: 01 (Maven Project) --%>
<!DOCTYPE html PUBLIC "-//W3C//DTD XHTML 1.0 Strict//EN"
    "http://www.w3.org/TR/xhtml1/DTD/xhtml1-strict.dtd">
<html>
    <head>
        <title>Hello World!</title>
    </head>
    <body>
    <h2>Hello World from Spring MVC!</h2>
    </body>
</html>
```

Start up your web server, and point your browser at the following address (adjusting for host name and port number): http://localhost:8080/sip/helloWorldControllerTest.

If everything is set up correctly, you should see a "Hello World" message from Spring MVC as shown in figure 5.4.

BASIC SWF CONFIGURATION

Now that you've validated that your Spring MVC configuration is working, let's extend this configuration to include SWF. To make things easier to keep track of, you're going to put the SWF configuration in a new file. Open the dispatcherServlet-context.xml file (see listing 5.4) and add the following line before the closing </beans> tag:

```
<import resource="webflowContext.xml"/>
```

Spring Soccer Club

Hello World from Spring MVC!

Copyright © 2011 Spring Soccer Club. All rights reserved.

Figure 5.4   If everything is working correctly, you should see "Hello World" from Spring MVC.

The next listing contains the contents of the webflowContext.xml file.

Listing 5.7   /WEB-INF/spring/web/webflowContext.xml

```xml
<?xml version="1.0" encoding="UTF-8"?>
<!-- Source project: sip05, branch: 02 (Maven Project) -->

<beans xmlns="http://www.springframework.org/schema/beans"
  xmlns:xsi="http://www.w3.org/2001/XMLSchema-instance"
  xmlns:flow="http://www.springframework.org/schema/webflow-config"
  xsi:schemaLocation="
    http://www.springframework.org/schema/beans
    http://www.springframework.org/schema/beans/spring-beans-3.1.xsd
    http://www.springframework.org/schema/webflow-config
    http://www.springframework.org/schema/webflow-config/
    spring-webflow-config-2.3.xsd">

  <flow:flow-builder-services id="flowBuilderServices"
    development="true"/>

  <flow:flow-executor id="flowExecutor" flow-registry="flowRegistry"/>

  <flow:flow-registry id="flowRegistry" base-path="/WEB-INF/flows">
    <flow:flow-location
      id="testWebFlow" path="/test/helloWorld-flow.xml"/>
  </flow:flow-registry>

  <bean
    class="org.springframework.webflow.mvc.servlet.FlowHandlerAdapter">
    <property name="flowExecutor" ref="flowExecutor"/>
  </bean>

  <bean
    class="org.springframework.webflow.mvc.servlet.FlowHandlerMapping">
    <property name="flowRegistry" ref="flowRegistry"/>
    <property name="order" value="0"/>
  </bean>

</beans>
```

① Flow definition files are hot-reloadable.

② Configures flow executor

③ References single flow

④ Custom HandlerAdapter

⑤ Implementation of HandlerMapping

We'll discuss the contents of this file in detail in the next several sections.

CUSTOMIZING FLOW BUILDER SERVICES

You use the `<flow:flow-builder-services>` element at **①** to customize how the flows are built in the flow registry. When defining this element, you only need to reference the settings that you want to change from the default. Here, you're setting `development="true"`. This enables hot-reloading of flow definition files.

CONFIGURING THE FLOW EXECUTOR

At **②**, you configure the flow executor using the `<flow:flow-executor>` element. The flow executor, as the name suggests, drives the execution of flow definitions. Here, you just need to make it aware of the flow registry. We'll talk about that in more detail next.

CONFIGURING THE FLOW REGISTRY

In SWF, each flow is configured in its own XML files. The flow registry maintains a catalogue of these files. At **③**, you make the flow registry aware of your helloWorld-flow.xml file using the `<flow:flow-location>` element. Notice that the optional `base-path` attribute is used to simplify the mapping.

`<flow:flow-location>` has an optional `id` attribute that is used to explicitly specify the flow ID for the flow. In the example, the flow ID is explicitly set to `testWebFlow`. Flow IDs are used to explicitly reference a particular flow. Without this optional attribute, the flow ID would have been determined to be `test`.

A more flexible configuration would be to configure the flow registry like this:

```
<flow:flow-registry id="flowRegistry" base-path="/WEB-INF/flows">
  <flow:flow-location-pattern value="/**/*-flow.xml" />
</flow:flow-registry>
```

Using the mapping, any directory after the base path, represented by the two asterisks, would represent the flow ID. If you were to use this configuration in the example in listing 5.7, the flow ID would be determined to be `test`.

You're almost finished. All that's left to do is make Spring MVC aware of SWF. We'll talk about this next.

INTEGRATING WITH SPRING MVC

The `FlowHandlerAdapter` created at ❹ in listing 5.7 joins the Spring MVC `DispatcherServlet` and the flow executor. As you'll recall from chapter 3, `DispatcherServlet` determines how best to dispatch a given request by looking at several handler mappings. The `FlowHandlerMapping` created at ❺ makes the `FlowHandlerAdapter` and hence the `DispatcherServlet` aware of all the flow IDs available in your registry.

To see this in action and to verify your setup, start your web server and point your browser at the following address (adjusting for host name and port number): http://localhost:8080/sip/testWebFlow.

If everything is set up correctly, you should see a "Hello World" message from SWF as shown in figure 5.5.

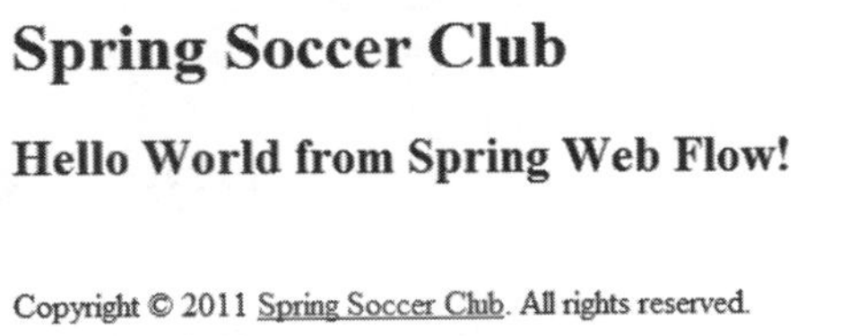

Now that you have SWF up and running, your next step is to create views for each state in the demo application.

Spring Soccer Club

Hello World from Spring Web Flow!

Copyright © 2011 Spring Soccer Club. All rights reserved.

Figure 5.5   If everything is working correctly, you should see "Hello World" from SWF.

5.3.2 Creating flows with different state types

PREREQUISITES
Installing and configuring SWF

KEY TECHNOLOGIES
SWF

Background

SWF is best applied when you need to navigate a user through a series of predefined and/or dynamic steps (states) to achieve a desired outcome or complete a unit of work. Now that you've installed SWF and validated that it's working properly, your next step is to use SWF to implement the different flows and states required by the Spring Soccer Club demo application introduced in section 5.3.

Problem

You would like to use SWF to manage a complex page flow representing a single unit of work.

Solution

Continuing with the Spring Soccer Club theme, your next step is to implement the different flows and states shown in figure 5.3. For a brief discussion of this demo application, refer back to section 5.3.

Because searching for an object is normally a reusable flow, you'll split the overall flow into a registration main flow and a `findExistingPlayer` subflow. Figure 5.6 illustrates this change.

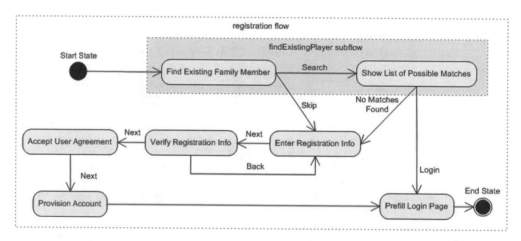

Figure 5.6   Being able to search for and select an existing player may be useful in several places in a larger application. As a result, you'll separate the `findExistingPlayer` functionality into its own subflow. It will be called from the main registration flow.

CREATING THE FINDEXISTINGPLAYER SUBFLOW

Let's get started putting together the `findExistingPlayer` subflow. The following listing contains the contents for the findExistingPlayer-flow.xml file. We'll discuss the contents of this file in detail in the next several sections.

Listing 5.8   /WEB-INF/flows/findExistingPlayer/findExistingPlayer-flow.xml

```xml
<?xml version="1.0" encoding="UTF-8"?>
<!-- Source project: sip05, branch: 03 (Maven Project) -->
<flow xmlns="http://www.springframework.org/schema/webflow"
  xmlns:xsi="http://www.w3.org/2001/XMLSchema-instance"
    xsi:schemaLocation="
    http://www.springframework.org/schema/webflow
    http://www.springframework.org/schema/webflow/spring-webflow-2.0.xsd"
```

Specifies explicit start state ❶

❷ First state in flow

Example of action class ❸

❹ Processes form submission

Alternative to ending the flow ❺

❻ Ends flow on new search

Restarts flow in place ❼

Example of returning a variable ❽

```
                          start-state="findExistingPlayerForm">

                            <view-state id="findExistingPlayerForm">
                              <on-render>
                                <!-- Prepares the form object for display on a form -->
                                <evaluate expression="findExistingPlayerAction.setupForm"/>
                              </on-render>
                              <transition on="find" to="findExistingPlayerActionState">
                                <evaluate
                                      expression="findExistingPlayerAction.bindAndValidate"/>
                              </transition>
                            </view-state>

                            <action-state id="findExistingPlayerActionState">
                              <evaluate expression="playerService.
                                findExistingPlayer(playerSearchCriteria)"
                                result="flowScope.player"/>
                              <transition on="success" to="displayFindExistingPlayerResult"/>
                            </action-state>

                        <!--
                          You can either end the subflow or reset the form and start over...
                        -->
                        <!--
                        <action-state id="newSearch">
                           <evaluate expression="findExistingPlayerFormAction.resetForm"/>
                           <transition on="success" to="findExistingPlayerForm"/>
                        </action-state>
                        -->

                        <view-state id="displayFindExistingPlayerResult">
                          <transition on="back" to="findExistingPlayerForm"/>
                          <transition on="newSearch" to="newSearchEndState"/>
                          <transition on="noneMatch" to="endState"/>
                          <transition on="existingAccountFound"
                            to="existingAccountFoundEndState"/>
                        </view-state>

                        <end-state id="newSearchEndState"/>

                        <end-state id="endState"/>

                        <end-state id="existingAccountFoundEndState" >
                          <output name="loginUsername" value="player.guardian.username"/>
                        </end-state>

                        <global-transitions>
                          <transition on="skip" to="endState"/>
                        </global-transitions>

                      </flow>
```

The previous listing contains many of the items we've talked about up to this point. Because this listing is large, let's start by focusing on the first several lines. At ❶, you explicitly set the starting state for the flow. At ❷ is your first view state, named find-ExistingPlayerForm. Recalling our discussion from section 5.2.2, if you don't explicitly specify a view name, the view name will be the same as the id attribute by convention. At ❸ you use an Action class to manage your form object. We'll discuss handling forms in more detail later.

The action state at ❹ processes the search criteria submitted from the view state at ❷. Here you pass the criteria object to your search service. Because you're focusing on SWF, this stub implementation always returns a single result.

On the search results view, the end user has an option to perform another search. Clicking the New Search link fires off a `newSearch` event that currently transitions to `newSearchEndState` at ❼. Looking at a snippet of code from the parent flow, you can see that `newSearchEndState` is mapped back to the `findExistingPlayer` subflow state:

```
<subflow-state id="findExistingPlayer" subflow="findExistingPlayer">
  <transition on="endState" to="newAccountForm"/>
  <transition on="newSearchEndState" to="findExistingPlayer"/>
  <transition on="existingAccountFoundEndState" to="sendToLoginEndState">
    <set name="flowScope.loginUsername"
      value="currentEvent.attributes.loginUsername"/>
  </transition>
</subflow-state>
```

What is happening here is that you're returning a `newSearchEndState` event from the subflow and mapping it back to another call to the `findExistingPlayer` subflow state. Your original subflow and its state are destroyed, and you repeat the subflow using a new instance. This approach is useful when you have a complex subflow that has several steps because it ensures that all of the intermediary state gets cleared out.

❺ in listing 5.8 provides another way to achieve the same behavior. Instead of destroying the current subflow and starting again, you can reset your form object and transition back to the `findExistingPlayerForm` to start your search again. All you have to do is change ❻ to transition to the `newSearch` action state. Because you're clearing out the state manually, this approach works best when there isn't a lot of intermediary state being captured. Both approaches are valid.

❽ demonstrates how a subflow can return information back to the parent flow. In this case, the user has identified that they have an existing account and have chosen to log in using that account. Figure 5.7 shows an unstyled snapshot of what the search results page looks like.

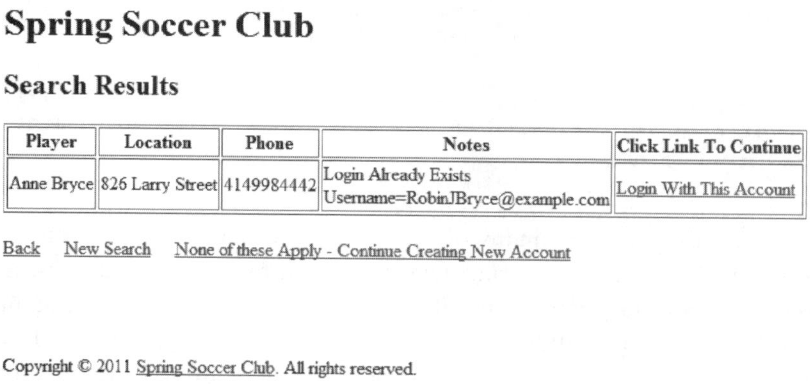

Spring Soccer Club

Search Results

Player	Location	Phone	Notes	Click Link To Continue
Anne Bryce	826 Larry Street	4149984442	Login Already Exists Username=RobinJBryce@example.com	Login With This Account

Back   New Search   None of these Apply - Continue Creating New Account

Copyright © 2011 Spring Soccer Club. All rights reserved.

Figure 5.7   Showing the result of the `displayFindExistingPlayerResult` view state

Here's a partial source listing for the displayFindExistingPlayerResult view.

Listing 5.9   /WEB-INF/flows/findExistingPlayer/displayFindExistingPlayerResult.jsp

```
<%-- Source project: sip05, branch: 03 (Maven Project) --%>
<%-- Partial code listing below --%>

  <c:set var="foundPlayer"
    scope="request" value="${!empty player}"/>

  <head><title>Search Results</title></head>

  <body>
    <h2>Search Results</h2>

    <c:choose>
      <c:when test="${foundPlayer}">
          <table border="1">
            <tr>
              <th>Player</th>
              <th>Location</th>
              <th>Phone</th>
              <th>Notes</th>
              <th>Click Link To Continue</th>
            </tr>
            <tr>
              <td>${player.firstName} ${player.lastName}</td>
              <td>${player.guardian.address1}</td>
              <td>${player.guardian.homePhone}</td>
              <td>
                Login Already Exists<br/>
                Username=${player.guardian.username}
              </td>
              <td>
                <a href="${flowExecutionUrl}&_eventId=existingAccountFound">    ◁
                  Login With This Account</a>
              </td>
            </tr>                                             **Log in with**
          </table>                                           **this account**  **❶**
      </c:when>
      <c:otherwise>
        No Player Found<br/>
      </c:otherwise>
    </c:choose>
```

...

The implementation is simple. If an existing account is found, the user can choose to log in with the account listed. A link is used at ❶ to fire the existingAccountFound event, which is later transitioned to existingAccountFoundEndState where the user name is returned to the parent flow.

Let's look at the findExistingPlayerForm.jsp file next.

Listing 5.10   /WEB-INF/flows/findExistingPlayer/findExistingPlayerForm.jsp

```
<%-- Source project: sip05, branch: 03 (Maven Project) --%>
<%@ include file="/WEB-INF/jsp/taglibs.jsp" %>
<!DOCTYPE html PUBLIC "-//W3C//DTD XHTML 1.0 Strict//EN"
```

```
         "http://www.w3.org/TR/xhtml1/DTD/xhtml1-strict.dtd">
<html
  xmlns:c="http://java.sun.com/jsp/jstl/core"
  xmlns:jsp="http://java.sun.com/JSP/Page"
  xmlns:spring="http://www.springframework.org/tags"
  xmlns:form="http://www.springframework.org/tags/form">

  <head><title>Find Existing Player(s)</title></head>

  <body>
    <h2>Find Existing Player(s)</h2>
    <p>
      Has anyone in your family registered with us in the
      past?  If so, enter your information below:
    </p>
                                                                ❶ Spring Form
    <form:form commandName="playerSearchCriteria"                 tag library
      action="${flowExecutionUrl}" >

      <label for="firstname">Player First Name</label>
      <form:input path="firstName" /><br/>

      <label for="lastName">Player Last Name</label>
      <form:input path="lastName" /><br/>

      <label for="birthDate">Birth Date</label>
      <form:input path="birthDate" /><br/>

      <label for="homePhone">Home Phone:</label>
      <form:input path="homePhone" /><br/>
                                                                ❷ Event ID and
      <input type="submit" name="_eventId_skip"                   value as name
        value="Skip"/>
      <input type="submit" name="_eventId_find"
        value="Find"/>
    </form:form>

  </body>
</html>
```

At ❶, you use the Spring Form tag library to generate your form tags. At ❷, you specify the name of the event you want to fire when the form is submitted. For more information, see the view-state discussion in section 5.2.2.

That about does it for the findExistingPlayer subflow. At this point, you should be able to test the flow by pointing your browser at the following address (adjusting for host name and port number): http://localhost:8080/sip/findExistingPlayer.

Keep in mind as you test the flow that because this subflow isn't getting called from a parent flow yet, when you transition to an end state, the flow ends and all the state for the flow is destroyed. As a result, you'll end up on the same URL that started the flow, causing a new instance of the flow to be created. Watch the value of the execution variable in the browser. You'll find that the execution represented by e is incremented every time the flow restarts. For more information about this variable, flip back to the view-state discussion in section 5.2.2.

CREATING THE REGISTRATION FLOW

With the `findExistingPlayer` subflow working, let's configure the other states that are left in the example application. The following listing details the flow definition for the registration flow.

Listing 5.11　/WEB-INF/flows/registration/registration-flow.xml

```xml
<?xml version="1.0" encoding="UTF-8"?>
<!-- Source project: sip05, branch: 03 (Maven Project) -->
<flow xmlns="http://www.springframework.org/schema/webflow"
  xmlns:xsi="http://www.w3.org/2001/XMLSchema-instance"
    xsi:schemaLocation="
    http://www.springframework.org/schema/webflow
    http://www.springframework.org/schema/webflow/spring-webflow-2.0.xsd"
    start-state="findExistingPlayer">

  <subflow-state id="findExistingPlayer" subflow="findExistingPlayer">
    <transition on="endState" to="newAccountForm"/>
    <transition on="newSearchEndState" to="findExistingPlayer"/>
    <transition on="existingAccountFoundEndState" to="sendToLoginEndState">
      <set name="flowScope.loginUsername"
        value="currentEvent.attributes.loginUsername"/>
    </transition>
  </subflow-state>

  <view-state id="newAccountForm">
    <on-render>
      <evaluate expression="newAccountFormAction.setupForm"/>
    </on-render>
    <transition on="next" to="confirmNewAccount">
      <evaluate expression="newAccountFormAction.bindAndValidate"/>
    </transition>
  </view-state>

  <view-state id="confirmNewAccount">
    <transition on="back" to="newAccountForm" />
    <transition on="next" to="processNewAccount" />
  </view-state>

  <action-state id="processNewAccount">
    <set name="flowScope.loginUsername"
      value="playerService.createNewAccount(newAccountForm)"/>
    <transition on="success" to="sendToLoginEndState"/>
  </action-state>

  <end-state
      id="sendToLoginEndState"
      view="externalRedirect:contextRelative:/login.jsp
              ?username=#{flowScope.loginUsername}"/>

</flow>
```

❶ Explicitly defines start state

❷ Retrieves value from subflow

❸ createNewAccount is only a stub.

At ❶, you explicitly define your start state as `findExistingPlayer`, which calls the `findExistingPlayer` subflow as its first step. At ❷, you see how to retrieve information from a subflow. `currentEvent` is a special EL variable that allows you to retrieve the attributes associated with the current `Event`. The attributes are returned in an `AttributeMap`, which is essentially an immutable interface that provides the read-only operations you would normally find on a map.

At ❸, you call a stub that pretends to create an account for the user. The service returns the username of the newly created account.

That wraps up the registration flow. We won't cover the last two views, `newAccountForm` and `confirmNewAccount`. They're available in the chapter's source. You can test the flow by pointing your browser at the following address (adjusting for host name and port number): http://localhost:8080/sip/registration.

In the "Declaring Variables" discussion in section 5.2.4, we spoke briefly about how the `<set>` element provides a subset of the functionality of the `<evaluate>` element. At ❸ in listing 5.11, you can see that the `<set>` element implicitly returns `success`. When creating a real system, you would more than likely be coordinating with multiple services and would want more control over error handling and the resulting views that are returned. To do that, you need to use the `<evaluate>` element and put your logic into an `Action` class. Let's talk about this next.

5.4   *Using action classes*

PREREQUISITES
Installing and configuring SWF

KEY TECHNOLOGIES
SWF

Background

You've learned that it's possible to call methods on POJOs to do work and drive transitions between states using the `<set>` or `<evaluate>` elements.

Problem

Although it's certainly easier to call POJOs directly, there are times when you would like to do more. Perhaps you want to read or set several variables in different flow scopes or invoke complex business logic that might be supported by multiple services. What happens when a business exception is thrown? How can you handle and map this exception to something meaningful to SWF?

Solution

Those who have experience with Spring MVC may immediately think about controllers. In Spring MVC, controllers provide a layer of indirection between the service layer and the view. Controllers typically delegate to application or business services to retrieve necessary data or invoke business operations. After completing its work, the controller selects a view to be rendered.

In SWF, the flow is considered to be the controller. Action classes provide a mechanism for you to provide a similar layer of indirection between the service layer and

SWF. Instead of selecting a view to be rendered directly, when an action is executed, it returns an Event providing an outcome that the flow can respond to.

You can create an action class by implementing the org.springframework.webflow.execution.Action interface. SWF provides several Action implementations out of the box. We'll focus our attention on the three implementations of the Action interface shown in figure 5.8.

An action is essentially a command that performs some work and returns an event. The Action interface contains a single method:

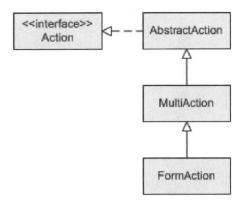

Figure 5.8 Although several classes implement the Action interface out of the box, we'll focus on AbstractAction, MultiAction, and FormAction.

```
public Event execute(RequestContext context) throws Exception;
```

The RequestContext, available as the flowRequestContext EL variable, gives information about the current flow execution and provides access to each of the variable scopes. Revisiting the Spring Soccer demo, you can create a simple action class that encapsulates the call to the playerService. The class in the following listing would be configured like any other Spring-managed bean, allowing you to inject any necessary resources.

Listing 5.12 FindExistingPlayerAction.java

```
// Source project: sip05, branch: 04 (Maven Project)
package com.springinpractice.ch05.mvc;

import com.springinpractice.ch05.service.PlayerService;
import com.springinpractice.ch05.domain.*;
import com.springinpractice.ch05.domain.search.PlayerSearchCriteria;
import org.springframework.webflow.execution.*;

public class FindExistingPlayerAction implements Action {
  private PlayerService playerService;

  public void setPlayerService(PlayerService playerService) {
    this.playerService = playerService;
  }

  @Override
  public Event execute(RequestContext context) {
    Event event = null;
    PlayerSearchCriteria criteria =
    (PlayerSearchCriteria)context.getFlowScope().get("playerSearchCriteria");
    if (criteria != null) {
      Player player = playerService.findExistingPlayer(criteria);
      context.getFlowScope().put("player",player);

      event = new Event(this, "success");
    }
```

```
    else {
      event = new Event(this, "error");
    }

    return event;
  }
}
```

With the `FindExistingPlayerAction` class in hand, the following line in the existing demo application

```
<evaluate expression="playerService.findExistingPlayer(playerSearchCriteria)"
  result="flowScope.player"/>
```

can now be replaced with the following line. When implementing the `Action` interface, it's no longer necessary to explicitly pass in the `flowRequestContext` EL variable:

```
<evaluate expression="findExistingPlayerAction" />
```

Although you can implement the `Action` interface directly, it's more convenient to take advantage of the convenience methods available in the `AbstractAction` class. We'll talk about this briefly next.

ABSTRACTACTION

SWF provides an `AbstractAction` class that provides a convenient base implementation for all of your action classes. Specifically, this class provides a default implementation of the `InitializingBean` interface, which provides a hook for you to do custom initialization or validation after your bean's properties have been set by the container. In addition, the `AbstractAction` class implements the `Action` interface's `execute()` method and provides a `doExecute()` method for you to place the code you would normally place in the `execute()` method, and two additional template methods, `doPreExecute()` and `doPostExecute()`, which you can override to do pre- and postprocessing. The class provides several factory methods that create common Events, such as `success` and `error`.

MULTIACTION

If you prefer to group all of your actions together, the `MultiAction` class builds on the functionality provided by the `AbstractAction` class and allows you to bundle two or more execution methods in the same class. As shown next, the signature of each method needs to be in the same format as the `execute()` method in the `Action` class. The only difference is that the name can be anything you like:

```
public Event ${method}(RequestContext context) throws Exception;
```

An example of a `MultiAction` class can be seen in the following listing.

Listing 5.13   PlayerActions.java

```
// Source project: sip05, branch: 04 (Maven Project)
package com.springinpractice.ch05.mvc;
import org.springframework.webflow.action.*;
```

```
import org.springframework.webflow.execution.*;
import com.springinpractice.ch05.service.PlayerService;
import com.springinpractice.ch05.domain.*;
import com.springinpractice.ch05.domain.search.PlayerSearchCriteria;

public class PlayerActions extends MultiAction {

  private PlayerService playerService;

  public void setPlayerService(PlayerService playerService) {
    this.playerService = playerService;
  }

  public Event findExistingPlayer(RequestContext context) {        ◁── Reimplemented in
    PlayerSearchCriteria criteria =                                    MultiAction class
      (PlayerSearchCriteria)context.getFlowScope().
            get("playerSearchCriteria");
    if (criteria != null) {
      Player player = playerService.findExistingPlayer(criteria);
      context.getFlowScope().put("player",player);

      return success();
    }
    else {
      return error();
    }
  }

  public Event doSomethingElse(RequestContext context) {...}

}
```

Here you reimplement the `setPlayerService` from listing 5.12 in a `MultiAction` class. This action can be invoked in two different ways. By default, the ID of the wrapping action state is treated as the method to execute. Look at the following example:

```
<action-state id="findExistingPlayer">
  <evaluate expression="playerActions/>
  ...
</action-state>
```

This code snippet would be functionally equivalent to the more explicit action state that follows, where the action-execution method, `findExistingPlayer()`, is explicitly identified:

```
<action-state id="findExistingPlayer">
  <evaluate expression="playerActions.findExistingPlayer"/>
  ...
</action-state>
```

Next let's look at a more configuration-based action, `FormAction`.

FORMACTION

The `FormAction` class helps simplify working with forms by providing several convenience methods that make it easy to set up, validate, and bind form data. Each method takes in an instance of `RequestContext`:

- setupForm()—Creates the form object as well as the errors object that accompanies it. Unless an exception occurs, this method returns success.
- bindAndValidate()—Binds all the available request parameters to the specified form object and validates the data. If a validation error occurs, an error event is returned. Otherwise, a success event is returned.
- bind()—Binds all the available request parameters to the specified form object without the additional validation step. This method returns a success event unless binding errors occur. In that case, an error event is returned.
- validate()—Only validates the data and assumes that the form data had already been bound. If a validation error occurs, an error event is returned. Otherwise, a success event is returned.
- resetForm()—Reloads the underlying form object, causing the form to reset. Unless an exception occurs, this method returns success.

There should be no reason to extend the FormAction class directly. Instead, you can configure the form action as a Spring bean, as show in the following listing.

Listing 5.14   FormAction: webflowContext.xml

```xml
<!-- Source project: sip05, branch: 04 (Maven Project) -->
<%-- Partial code listing below --%>
<bean id="findExistingPlayerFormAction"
      class="org.springframework.webflow.action.FormAction">
    <property name="formObjectClass"
     value="com.springinpractice.ch05.domain.search.PlayerSearchCriteria"/>
        <property name="propertyEditorRegistrar">
          <bean class="com.springinpractice.
    ch05.beans.CustomPropertyEditorRegistrar"/>
        </property>
</bean>
```

Three examples of using this bean were provided earlier, in listing 5.8, starting at ❸.

Each of the classes we talked about in this recipe is configured in webflowContext.xml in the chapter's source code (sip05, branch: 04). Look at the comments in the findExistingPlayer-flow.xml file for hints on how to use each. You can test the flow by pointing your browser at (adjusting for host name and port number) http://localhost:8080/sip/findExistingPlayer.

Now we'll take a deeper dive into form data binding in section 5.5 and validating form data using JSR-303 in section 5.6.

5.5   *Form data binding*

PREREQUISITES

Installing and configuring SWF

KEY TECHNOLOGIES

SWF, Spring form tag library

Background

Up to this point, we've talked about view states, but we haven't had a specific conversation about form data binding. In this recipe, you'll use the information you learned in section 4.1 to do data binding in SWF.

Problem

When a user submits a form, you would like to control how data is bound to your Java objects.

Solution

Data binding in SWF is pretty straightforward. In a view state, you use the `model` attribute to specify which object the view should bind to. Look at the view-state definition:

```
<view-state id="newAccountForm" model="accountForm">
  <transition on="next" to="confirmNewAccount"/>
</view-state>
```

The `newAccountForm` view state is bound to the `accountForm` object. Now that this association has been made, SWF will attempt to bind form data to this object by default.

At times, it may be desirable to skip the data-binding process. For example, look at the updated view-state definition:

```
<view-state id="newAccountForm" model="accountForm">
  <transition on="next" to="confirmNewAccount"/>
  <transition on="back" to="somePreviousState" bind="false" />
</view-state>
```

In the code (registration-flow.xml from project: sip05, branch: 05), when the view state transitions to `back`, the binding process is suppressed and the flow transitions to `somePreviousState` without binding data.

By default, SWF will attempt to bind data to every field in the target object. As we talked about in section 4.1, sometimes that behavior isn't desirable. To change the default behavior, you can create a whitelist by identifying each of the attributes you would like to bind using the `<binder>` element in the view state. Here's an example:

```
<binder>
  <binding property="guardian.firstName" required="true" />
  <binding property="guardian.lastName" required="true" />
</binder>
```

You're telling SWF that the `firstName` and `lastName` attributes of the `guardian` object are the only fields on the `guardian` object that should be bound. In addition, you're using the optional `required` attribute, telling SWF that each of these properties is required.

In the next section, we'll discuss how to take this one step further. You'll use the JSR-303 Bean Validation API to declaratively add additional validation constraints to your POJO.

5.6   *Form validation*

PREREQUISITES

Form Data Binding

KEY TECHNOLOGIES

SWF, Spring Validation, JSR-303 Bean Validation API

Background

Users interact with websites by clicking links and submitting forms. All but the simplest systems validate their form data to ensure that information is captured in the format that is expected and that any additional rules, such as required fields, are enforced.

Problem

When a user submits a form, you would like to validate the data that was submitted before doing additional processing. If validation errors occur, you would like to let the user know in a user-friendly way so they may make any necessary corrections before continuing.

Solution

JSR-303 defines a standardized metadata model and API for Java bean validation that allows you to define validation constraints without tying you to a specific application tier or programming model. The JSR-303 Bean Validation API became fully supported in Spring 3.0 and has been available to Spring MVC applications for quite some time. Information on how to configure JSR-303 validation with Spring MVC was covered in section 4.2. At the time of this writing, version 2.3.0 of SWF has been released and has added support for JSR-303–style validation.

If you've already configured JSR-303 support as part of your Spring MVC setup, you can skip the next section. If not, let's get started.

BOOTSTRAPPING A JSR-303 IMPLEMENTATION

As you've come to expect, Spring has made bootstrapping a JSR-303 implementation easy. All that is necessary is to create a single bean definition and have a JSR-303 provider on the classpath. You'll use Hibernate Validator, the JSR-303 reference implementation, here. Validate that you have the following dependency in your POM file:

```
<dependency>
  <groupId>org.hibernate</groupId>
  <artifactId>hibernate-validator</artifactId>
  <version>4.1.0.Beta1</version>
</dependency>
```

This Maven dependency adds the hibernate-validator-4.1.0.Beta1.jar file to your classpath. Once this is done, you can add the following bean definition to your Spring configuration. If you're following along with the source code from the project (sip05, branch: 06), this is already done for you:

```
<bean id="validator" class="org.springframework.validation.
        beanvalidation.LocalValidatorFactoryBean"/>
```

LocalValidatorFactoryBean implements three separate interfaces: javax.valida-tion.ValidatorFactory, javax.validation.Validator, and org.springframe-work.validation.Validator. Many applications use JSR-303 validation in addition to Spring validation. The added flexibility allows you to use the same bean definition for both.

CONFIGURING SWF TO USE JSR-303 VALIDATION

Now that your JSR-303 validator is configured, you need to make SWF aware of it. To do this, add a reference to your new validator to the flow-builder-services element in the webflowContext.xml file:

```
<flow:flow-builder-services id="flowBuilderServices"
  development="true"
  validator="validator"
/>
```

That's all there is to it. You've established the foundation; let's look next at adding JSR-303 annotations to a class. The following listing shows the code.

Listing 5.15   com.springinpractice.ch05.form.AccountForm

```
// Source project: sip05, branch: 06 (Maven Project)
package com.springinpractice.ch05.form;

import javax.validation.Valid;
import org.hibernate.validator.constraints.NotEmpty;
import com.springinpractice.ch05.domain.Guardian;
import com.springinpractice.ch05.domain.Player;
import java.io.Serializable;

public class AccountForm implements Serializable {
    private static final long serialVersionUID = 1L;

    protected Guardian guardian = new Guardian();
    protected Player child = new Player();
    protected String confirmPassword;
    protected String confirmEmail;

    public AccountForm() {}

    @Valid                                      ①  Validates constraints
    public Guardian getGuardian() {                 in the Guardian class
        return guardian;
    }

    public void setGuardian(Guardian guardian) {
        this.guardian = guardian;
    }
                                                ②  Validates constraints
    @Valid                                          in the Player class
    public Player getChild() {
        return child;
    }

    public void setChild(Player child) {
        this.child = child;
```

```
    }

    @NotEmpty
    public String getConfirmPassword() {
        return confirmPassword;
    }

    ...

}
```

3 **Provided by**
Hibernate Validator

You use two different annotations. The @Valid annotation at **1** tells the validator to validate the Guardian child class and aggregate any error messages with those from the AccountForm class as well. You see similar behavior at **2** with the Player class. Note that like JPA annotations, JSR-303 annotations can be placed on the attribute or on the getter method. For a more detailed discussion of the built-in JSR-303 constraints and the JSR 303 specification, see http://jcp.org/en/jsr/detail?id=303. Note that the annotation at **3** isn't part of the JSR-303 specification. Instead, it's a part of the Hibernate Validator framework that is the reference implementation for JSR 303. For more information on the Hibernate Validator, see the documentation at http://hibernate.org/subprojects/validator.

Now let's talk about how you can customize any resulting error messages.

MAPPING ERROR CODES TO MESSAGES IN A PROPERTIES FILE

When one or more validation rules fail, the validator generates a set of keys that Spring resolves to localized messages. Looking at example messages from the demo application's messages.properties file, you'll find that the naming convention is intuitive:

```
accountForm.confirmPassword.NotEmpty=The guardian's password confirmation
        is required
accountForm.confirmEmail.NotEmpty=The guardian's email confirmation is
        required

...

accountForm.child.firstName.NotEmpty=The child's first name is required
accountForm.child.lastName.NotEmpty=The child's last name is required
accountForm.child.birthDate.NotNull=The child's birth date is required
accountForm.child.birthDate.typeMismatch=The child's birth date must be in
        the format mm/dd/yyyy
```

In this example, the @NotEmpty annotation generates .NotEmpty, which is appended to the end of the full EL-like path of the property. To create a flow-specific message bundle, add a default message.properties file or a localized version of this file in the same directory as the flow-definition file. No additional configuration is necessary.

When a model is specified in a view state, validation follows the binding process. You can suppress this validation process by specifying validation="false" in the transition element. Look at the following example:

```
<view-state id="newAccountForm" model="accountForm">
  <transition on="next" to="confirmNewAccount"/>
  <transition on="back" to="somePreviousState" validate="false" />
</view-state>
```

When transitioning to next, information is bound to accountForm and validated. If an error occurs, the user is returned to the newAccountForm view where the errors are displayed. Because displaying form errors was covered in section 4.2, we won't discuss it again here. When transitioning to back, binding still occurs, but the data is no longer validated. Alternatively, you could specify bind="false" and omit the binding and validation process entirely.

You can test your handiwork by pointing your browser at http://localhost:8080/sip/registration (adjusting for host name and port number) and then navigating to the New Account Creation form.

5.7 *Flow and state inheritance*

PREREQUISITES
Installing and configuring SWF

KEY TECHNOLOGIES
SWF

Background

SWF has a couple of mechanisms to facilitate code modularity and reuse. Earlier in this chapter, we talked about how you can reuse individual flows by calling them as subflows. We also talked about defining common transitions globally in a flow so they can be reused in a given flow.

Problem

You want to reuse common states or transitions in several flows.

Solution

A flow definition can contain a lot of configuration information that might be useful for other flows. Similar to Spring's bean-definition inheritance, SWF has a built-in mechanism for inheritance at both the flow and state levels. Let's start by looking at flow-level inheritance.

FLOW INHERITANCE
Flow inheritance is similar to bean-definition inheritance but with a couple of key differences. Let's start by talking about what is similar. Like parent bean definitions, elements defined in a parent flow are exposed and available to a child flow. The following listing shows an abstract flow definition.

> Listing 5.16   \WEB-INF\flows\common\common-flow.xml

```xml
<?xml version="1.0" encoding="UTF-8"?>
<!-- Source project: sip05, branch: 07 (Maven Project) -->
<flow xmlns="http://www.springframework.org/schema/webflow"
  xmlns:xsi="http://www.w3.org/2001/XMLSchema-instance"
    xsi:schemaLocation="
    http://www.springframework.org/schema/webflow
```

```
      http://www.springframework.org/schema/webflow/spring-webflow-2.0.xsd"
      abstract="true">                              ◁━━  ❶  Marks flow
                                                             as abstract
  <view-state id="commonErrorView"
    view="/WEB-INF/flows/common/error.jsp"/>        ◁━━┐ Common error
                                                       └ view state
  <view-state id="commonView"
    view="/WEB-INF/flows/common/commonView.jsp"/>   ◁━━┐ Common
                                                       └ view state
  <global-transitions>
    <transition on="commonErrorView" to="commonErrorView"/>

    <transition                                     ◁━━┐ Example global
      on-exception="com.springinpractice.ch05.        └ transition
             webflow.action.DemoRuntimeException"
      to="commonErrorView"/>
  </global-transitions>

</flow>
```

As shown at ❶, a flow definition can be marked as being abstract. This prevents SWF from trying to use the flow directly.

The next listing defines a simple flow that inherits the elements in your abstract flow definition.

Listing 5.17   \WEB-INF\flows\inheritanceDemo\inheritance-demo-flow.xml

```
<?xml version="1.0" encoding="UTF-8"?>
<!-- Source project: sip05, branch: 07 (Maven Project) -->
<flow xmlns="http://www.springframework.org/schema/webflow"
  xmlns:xsi="http://www.w3.org/2001/XMLSchema-instance"
    xsi:schemaLocation="
    http://www.springframework.org/schema/webflow
    http://www.springframework.org/schema/webflow/spring-webflow-2.0.xsd"
    start-state="start"
    parent="common">                            ◁━━  ❶  Specifies
                                                         flow's parent
  <view-state id="start">                                        ❷  Inherited from
    <transition on="throwError" to="throwError"/>                   parent flow
    <transition on="commonViewDemo" to="commonView">   ◁━━━━━━━━━━┘
      <set name="flowScope.previousEventId" value="'start'" />
    </transition>
  </view-state>                                            Extends definition  ❸
                                                            of same type
  <view-state id="childOfInheritedView" parent="common#commonView"/>  ◁━━

  <action-state id="throwError">
    <evaluate expression="exceptionAction" />   ◁━━┐ Throws
  </action-state>                                ❹  DemoRuntimeException

  <end-state id="end" view="externalRedirect:contextRelative:/"/>

  <global-transitions>
    <transition on="start" to="start"/>
  </global-transitions>
</flow>
```

Unlike a bean definition, a flow can inherit from more than one flow. At ❶, you use the `parent` attribute of the `flow` element to indicate that the flow will inherit from the common flow. A comma-delimited list can be used to specify multiple flows to inherit from.

When inheriting view states, it's important to understand how flow inheritance works. If you've ever used static includes in a JSP file, you'll remember that the source of the included JSP file is copied into the main JSP file at compile time, creating a single composite file. This makes all relative links to resources (images or other documents) specified in that included JSP file relative to the resulting composite parent file, regardless of where the included JSP file originally was located.

Flow inheritance works the same way. Recall that a view state doesn't specify a `view` attribute; by convention the `view` attribute is assumed to be the value of the `id` attribute plus the `defaultViewSuffix`, which is .jsp by default. Using this convention, the view state at ❷ would have a view state of start.jsp. The default implementation of the `ViewResolver` would try to resolve this view in the same directory as the currently executing flow. Like statically included JSP files, this is always relative to the currently executing flow, not the inherited flow. For this reason, it's best to specify absolute paths to views in inherited view states. ❷ and ❸ in listing 5.17 provide an example.

The transition at ❷ transitions to a view state that appears in your parent flow (see listing 5.16). At ❹, you call an action that does nothing more than throw a `DemoRuntimeException`. This action is used to demonstrate how the transition at ❹ is inherited from the common flow.

STATE INHERITANCE

State inheritance behaves more like bean-definition inheritance, where a given state can only inherit from one parent of the same state type. As you can see at ❸ in listing 5.17, you specify the name of the parent state using the `parent` attribute in the form `flowId#stateId`. In the example, you're extending the `commonView` state of the `common` flow, which is identified as the flow's parent.

Although it certainly isn't pretty, you can click through this example by pointing your browser at the following address (adjusting for host name and port number): http://localhost:8080/sip/inheritanceDemo.

MORE INFORMATION

Through flow and state inheritance, you can obtain a much higher level of reuse than using subflows and global transitions alone. For details on the algorithm used to merge each and every element in the SWF definition language, consult the web-flow documentation located at www.springsource.org/spring-web-flow#documentation.

5.8 *Securing web flows*

PREREQUISITES

Understanding of Spring security (see chapter 6)

KEY TECHNOLOGIES

Spring Security, SWF

Background

In chapter 6 (recipes 6.1 and 6.2), you'll learn how to set up Spring Security to protect resources as well as provide a customized login page to authenticate users.

Problem

Now that you have a mechanism to authenticate users, you would like to secure specific web flows so that they can only be accessed by authorized users.

Solution

Once you've configured Spring Security for your application, authorizing individual flows is pretty straightforward. First we'll cover the three basic steps required to configure Spring Security. Then we'll look at how easy it is to secure individual flows, states, and transitions.

CONFIGURING SPRING SECURITY

Just as you'll do in recipe 6.1, you need to configure the `DelegatingFilterProxy` that will be used to load the Spring Security filter chain. The following listing focuses on the configuration relevant to Spring Security.

Listing 5.18   web.xml

```xml
<?xml version="1.0" encoding="UTF-8"?>
<!-- Source project: sip05, branch: 08 (Maven Project) -->

<web-app xmlns:xsi="http://www.w3.org/2001/XMLSchema-instance" xmlns="http://
    java.sun.com/xml/ns/javaee" xmlns:web="http://java.sun.com/xml/ns/
    javaee/web-app_2_5.xsd" xsi:schemaLocation="http://java.sun.com/xml/ns/
    javaee http://java.sun.com/xml/ns/javaee/web-app_2_5.xsd" version="2.5">
  <context-param>
    <param-name>contextConfigLocation</param-name>
    <param-value>
      /WEB-INF/spring/root-context.xml
      /WEB-INF/spring/applicationContext-security.xml
    </param-value>
  </context-param>
  <filter>
    <filter-name>springSecurityFilterChain</filter-name>
    <filter-class>org.springframework.web.filter.DelegatingFilterProxy</
    filter-class>
  </filter>
  <filter>
    <filter-name>sitemesh</filter-name>
    <filter-class>
        com.opensymphony.sitemesh.webapp.SiteMeshFilter
    </filter-class>
  </filter>
  <filter-mapping>
    <filter-name>springSecurityFilterChain</filter-name>
    <url-pattern>/*</url-pattern>
  </filter-mapping>
```

❶ **Spring Security configuration**

❷ **Required to intercept URL-based requests**

❸ **Intercepts all URL-based requests**

```
<filter-mapping>
  <filter-name>sitemesh</filter-name>
  <url-pattern>/*</url-pattern>
</filter-mapping>
<listener>
  <listener-class>
      org.springframework.web.context.ContextLoaderListener
  </listener-class>
</listener>
<servlet>
  <servlet-name>springSoccer</servlet-name>
  <servlet-class>org.springframework.
      web.servlet.DispatcherServlet</servlet-class>
  <init-param>
    <param-name>contextConfigLocation</param-name>
    <param-value>/WEB-INF/spring/web/
            dispatcherServlet-context.xml</param-value>
  </init-param>
  <load-on-startup>1</load-on-startup>
</servlet>
<servlet-mapping>
  <servlet-name>springSoccer</servlet-name>
  <url-pattern>/</url-pattern>
</servlet-mapping>
</web-app>
```

You load a file containing your Spring Security configuration at ❶. We'll look at this in a moment. At ❷, you configure the DelegatingFilterProxy, which will be used by Spring Security. At ❸, you configure the filter to be applied to all URLs.

Here are the contents of the applicationContext-security.xml file.

Listing 5.19 \WEB-INF\spring\applicationContext-security.xml

```
<?xml version="1.0" encoding="UTF-8"?>
<!-- Source project: sip05, branch: 08 (Maven Project) -->

<beans:beans
  xmlns="http://www.springframework.org/schema/security"
  xmlns:beans="http://www.springframework.org/schema/beans"
  xmlns:p="http://www.springframework.org/schema/p"
  xmlns:xsi="http://www.w3.org/2001/XMLSchema-instance"
  xsi:schemaLocation="
    http://www.springframework.org/schema/beans
    http://www.springframework.org/schema/beans/spring-beans-3.0.xsd
    http://www.springframework.org/schema/security
    http://www.springframework.org/schema/security/
            spring-security-3.0.xsd">                      ❶ Sets up several
                                                             defaults
  <http auto-config="true">
    <form-login                                          ❷ Custom
      login-page="/login.jsp"                              login page
      authentication-failure-url="/login.jsp?error=true"/>
    <intercept-url                                       ❸ URLs are processed
      pattern="/account/**" access="ROLE_USER"/>            in order.
    <intercept-url
      pattern="/**" access="IS_AUTHENTICATED_ANONYMOUSLY"/>
```

```
  </http>

  <authentication-manager alias="authenticationManager">
    <authentication-provider>
      <user-service>                                    ◁─┐  In-memory
        <user name="joshua"                            4  UserDetailService
          password="joshua"
          authorities="ROLE_USER"/>
        <user name="RobinJBryce@example.com"
          password="password"
          authorities="ROLE_USER"/>
      </user-service>
    </authentication-provider>
  </authentication-manager>

</beans:beans>
```

Here you're configuring Spring Security. Most of the items in this file will be covered by recipes 6.1 and 6.2, so we'll be brief here. Starting at ❶, you enable Spring Security's `auto-config`, which sets up Spring Security to use several defaults. At ❷, you customize your login page. See recipe 6.2 for more details.

At ❸, you protect a URL-based resource by creating an `intercept-url` definition. Remember that flows, specifically parent flows, are also URL-based resources. Although you could protect them here, we'll talk about a better solution to specifically secure a flow in a moment.

Starting at ❹, you create a simple in-memory `UserDetailService` with two accounts for testing.

CONFIGURING THE SECURITYFLOWEXECUTIONLISTENER

Now that you have Spring Security up and running, let's start plugging it into SWF. You do this by updating the webflowContext.xml file we discussed earlier with a new `flow-execution-listener`.

Listing 5.20   \WEB-INF\config\webflowContext.xml

```
  <flow:flow-executor id="flowExecutor">             ◁─┐  Spring Security is
    <flow:flow-execution-listeners>                  1  now flow aware
      <flow:listener ref="securityFlowExecutionListener" />
    </flow:flow-execution-listeners>
  </flow:flow-executor>
                                                       ◁─┐  Required for
<bean id="securityFlowExecutionListener"             2  Spring Security
 class="org.springframework.webflow.security.SecurityFlowExecutionListener" />
```

You add the `SecurityFlowExecutionListener` defined at ❷ to your collection of listeners defined at ❶. Spring Security is now aware of your SWF application. To secure an entire web flow or a specific state in a flow, you use the `<secured>` element; we'll talk more about this next.

SECURING FLOWS, TRANSITIONS, AND STATES

With SWF configured to use Spring Security, you can use the `<secured>` element to secure a flow, transition, or state. The `<secured>` element is placed in the element you want to secure. It should appear before any other elements. The following listing secures a view state.

Listing 5.21   \WEB-INF\flows\securityDemo\security-demo-flow.xml

```xml
<?xml version="1.0" encoding="UTF-8"?>
<!-- Source project: sip05, branch: 08 (Maven Project) -->

<flow xmlns="http://www.springframework.org/schema/webflow"
  xmlns:xsi="http://www.w3.org/2001/XMLSchema-instance"
    xsi:schemaLocation="
    http://www.springframework.org/schema/webflow
    http://www.springframework.org/schema/webflow/spring-webflow-2.0.xsd"
    start-state="unsecured">

  <view-state id="secured">                          ❶ Secures
    <secured attributes="ROLE_USER"/>                    specific state
    <transition on="next" to="end" />
  </view-state>

  <view-state id="unsecured">
    <secured attributes="ROLE_ANONYMOUS, ROLE_USER" match="any"/>
    <transition on="next" to="secured" />
  </view-state>                                      Valid values:
                                                      any, all ❷
  <end-state id="end"
    view="externalRedirect:contextRelative:/registration"/>
</flow>
```

❶ uses the `<secured>` element to secure the `secured` view state, whereas the unsecured view state at ❷ can be accessed by those with either a `ROLE_USER` or `ROLE_ANONYMOUS` role. Here you see that the `attributes` attribute can take a comma-separated list of roles. The `match` attribute specifies how they're interpreted. Valid values are `any` and `all`.

You can click through this example by pointing your browser at the following address (adjusting for host name and port number): http://localhost:8080/sip/securityDemo.

When you're asked for an email (username) and password, you can use the values we generated and hardcoded (see www.fakenamegenerator.com) in the applicationContext-security.xml file:

Email: RobinJBryce@example.com

Password: password

As you've seen, with an existing Spring Security configuration in place, adding a `SecurityFlowExecutionListener` to SWF's list of `flow-execution-listeners` is all that is required to make Spring Security aware of SWF. Securing entire flows, individual states, and transitions using the `<secured>` element is straightforward. Don't worry about the details of listing 5.19 just yet; we'll take a much deeper dive into Spring Security in the next few chapters.

5.9   *Summary*

SWF's narrow focus on addressing the problem of navigation in the web tier makes SWF intuitive to use and easy to learn. In this chapter, we introduced you to SWF and familiarized you with its features and functionality.

You started by learning about defining flows, states, how to use transitions, and managing flow data. Next you learned how to extend your existing Spring MVC application by installing and configuring SWF. Then we looked at using action classes, how to bind and validate form data, flow inheritance, and, finally, securing web flows. Our goal was to show how you can use this framework to complement your existing Spring MVC application and simplify the work required to design, maintain, and understand complex page flows in an application.

We touched briefly on using Spring Security to authorize individual states and flows in this chapter. Chapter 6 takes you much deeper into using Spring Security for authorizing user requests.

Authenticating users

6

This chapter covers

- Implementing user authentication with Spring Security
- Customizing a login page via Hibernate
- Using password hashing, salting, and auto-authentication

Many applications need a way to allow users to *authenticate*—that is, to say who they are and prove it. In this chapter, you'll learn how to support this common requirement using Spring Security 3. The first three recipes look at approaches to implementing a login form. The five remaining recipes look at sourcing user data from a persistent store.

6.1 *Implementing login and logout with remember-me authentication*

PREREQUISITES

None

KEY TECHNOLOGIES

Spring Security 3 (including tag libraries)

Background

Spring Security 3, although a large framework, makes it easy to get started with basic authentication. This recipe shows what you can do with a fairly minimal configuration.

Problem

Support basic logins and logouts, including remember-me authentication.

Solution

You'll use Spring Security 3 to add logins and logouts to a simple web app. You'll do this entirely through configuration; that is, you don't need to write any Java code to make it work.

The app is a simple university portal with nothing more than a home page and a login page (figure 6.1). To implement it, you'll need to configure Spring Security, configure web.xml, and add login and logout links to the app.

There's also a beans-web.xml configuration, but we won't address that here because it doesn't contain anything specific to this recipe. See the code download for more information.

Let's start by configuring Spring Security. You'll do the configuration itself first, and after that we'll dive into some of the behind-the-scenes details.

RECIPE 6.1 »

SiP University

Login with Username and Password

User:

Password:

☐ Remember me on this computer.

SUBMIT QUERY

RESET

Figure 6.1   The default login page, complete with Submit Query (or Submit, depending on the browser) button. The page is styled with CSS.

CONFIGURE SPRING SECURITY

The following listing shows a simple Spring Security 3 configuration that enables web-based authentication and creates an authentication source.

Listing 6.1   beans-security.xml, your Spring Security configuration

```
<?xml version="1.0" encoding="UTF-8"?>
<beans:beans xmlns="http://www.springframework.org/schema/security"
    xmlns:beans="http://www.springframework.org/schema/beans"
    xmlns:p="http://www.springframework.org/schema/p"
    xmlns:xsi="http://www.w3.org/2001/XMLSchema-instance"
    xsi:schemaLocation="http://www.springframework.org/schema/beans
        http://www.springframework.org/schema/beans/spring-beans-3.0.xsd
        http://www.springframework.org/schema/security
        http://www.springframework.org/schema/security/
            spring-security-3.0.xsd">
```

Spring Security namespace ❶

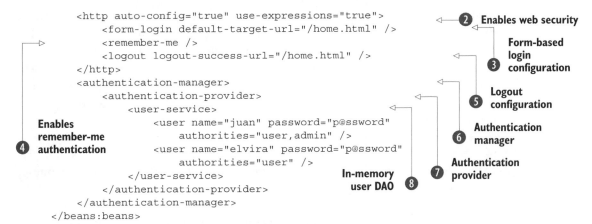

```
<http auto-config="true" use-expressions="true">
    <form-login default-target-url="/home.html" />
    <remember-me />
    <logout logout-success-url="/home.html" />
</http>
<authentication-manager>
    <authentication-provider>
        <user-service>
            <user name="juan" password="p@ssword"
                authorities="user,admin" />
            <user name="elvira" password="p@ssword"
                authorities="user" />
        </user-service>
    </authentication-provider>
</authentication-manager>
</beans:beans>
```

The first thing to notice is that beans-security.xml isolates your Spring Security configuration into its own configuration file. Because you've done this, it makes a lot of sense to declare the Spring Security namespace as the default namespace, which you do at ❶. That way you don't have to keep specifying a namespace prefix with each element.

At ❷ you enable web security using the <http> element. Although this element is responsible for web-based security generally (authentication, authorization, HTTPS, and so on), the focus in this chapter is authentication. (Chapter 7 covers web authorization in some detail.) The <http> element works by creating a chain of servlet filters to handle different aspects of web security.

By setting auto-config="true", you enable the filters for form-based logins (using the form from figure 6.1), HTTP basic authentication, and logouts. If you prefer, you can set auto-config="false" (that's the default) and specify the desired filters manually.

You also set use-expressions="true" to enable the SpEL, which you'll need when you create your JSPs.

You override the auto-config defaults by placing the desired configuration inside the <http> configuration. In the case of <form-login>, you choose your own value for default-target-url ❸ to indicate where you want the user to land after they successfully log in.[1]

At ❹ you enable remember-me authentication. Spring Security 2 automatically included remember-me authentication with its auto-config, but that's no longer the case with Spring Security 3. You must add it yourself.

The logout configuration at ❺ is similar to what you did with <form-login>, but this time you're specifying a target URL for successful logouts.

That takes care of your web authentication configuration. But you still need an authentication source, and that's what <authentication-manager> helps you

---

[1] Note that this is a default URL. When an unauthenticated user tries to access a protected resource, the login page intercepts the attempt, and the target URL is the originally requested page unless always-use-default-target="true" is set on the <form-login> element. See the Spring Security Reference Documentation for details.

establish ❻. This element allows you to identify a list of authentication providers that the manager will consult during authentication; authentication succeeds as long as at least one provider successfully authenticates the user. `<authentication-provider>` sets up a single `DaoAuthenticationProvider` backed by a DAO ❼. In general the DAO can be any `UserDetailsService` implementation; here `<user-service>` implicitly selects the `InMemoryDaoImpl` implementation ❽.[2] You use the in-memory DAO to create two users, one with username `juan`, password `p@ssword`, and roles called `user` and `admin`, and the other for username `elvira` with password `p@ssword` who only has the `user` role. (Note that the specific interfaces and classes are hidden by the namespace configuration, and that's the point of using namespace configuration in the first place.)

That's the Spring Security configuration. Even though it's small, it's pretty dense; it will help to examine some technical details before moving on to web.xml configuration, especially because you'll need them again in recipes 6.5 and 6.6.

AUTHENTICATION MANAGERS, PROVIDERS, AND USER DETAILS SERVICES

We stated that an authentication manager manages a list of providers. More exactly, `AuthenticationManager` is an interface with a single `authenticate()` method to process authentication requests. It doesn't care whether implementations use providers, although it's hard to imagine what else they would reasonably do. At any rate, from the `AuthenticationManager`'s point of view, providers are an implementation detail.

The default `AuthenticationManager` implementation is called `ProviderManager`. You're telling Spring Security to create a `ProviderManager` instance when you include the `<authentication-manager>` element. `ProviderManager` maintains a list of `Authentication-Providers` corresponding to the authentication sources you want to include. See figure 6.2.

Where things get interesting is with the providers themselves. Spring Security offers many provider options. You happen to be using the `DaoAuthentica-tionProvider`, but that's certainly not the only one there is—not by a long shot. See the class diagram in figure 6.3.

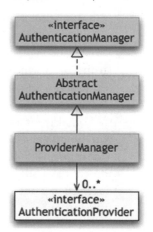

Figure 6.2   A class diagram for `AuthenticationManager` and `ProviderManager`

As figure 6.3 shows, Spring Security provides rich support for authentication. Besides the DAO provider, there are providers for CAS, JAAS, LDAP, OpenID, and more.

Let's drill down one more level. When you use a `DaoAuthenticationProvider`, you have to specify a DAO: that is, a `UserDetailsService` implementation. In essence,

---

[2]   Once again, we're glossing over many configuration options and details. Please consult the Spring Security Reference Documentation.

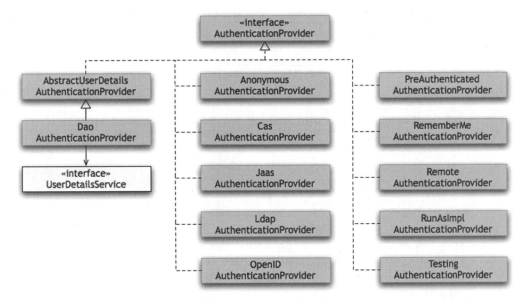

Figure 6.3 The `AuthenticationProvider` hierarchy, which includes tons of provider options

`DaoAuthenticationProvider` is an adapter that allows you to use any `User-DetailsService` implementation as an `AuthenticationProvider`. There are multiple `UserDetailsService` implementations; see figure 6.4.

UserDetailsService is a read-only interface with a single `loadUserByUsername()` method. This is how `DaoAuthenticationProvider` provides authentication services to `AuthenticationManager`. `UserDetailsManager` extends `UserDetailsService` to add write operations as well, although `AuthenticationManager` doesn't use that.

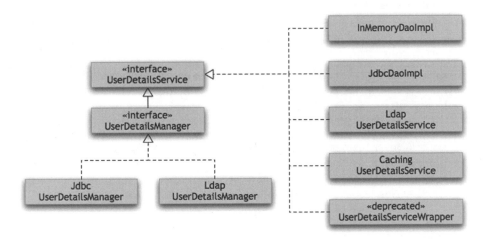

Figure 6.4 `UserDetailsService` hierarchy, containing DAOs used by the `DaoAuthenticationProvider`

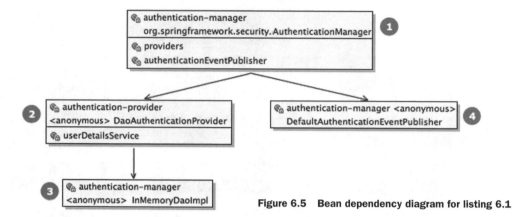

Figure 6.5   Bean dependency diagram for listing 6.1

Now you're in a better position to understand what's happening with listing 6.1. See the bean dependency diagram in figure 6.5. The `<authentication-manager>` element creates an `AuthenticationManager` bean—specifically, a `ProviderManager`—called `org.springframework.security.AuthenticationManager` at ❶.

At ❷, `<authentication-provider>` creates a single `AuthenticationProvider` bean—a `DaoAuthenticationProvider`—and adds it to the `ProviderManager`. It also creates an `InMemoryDaoImpl` at ❸. The net result is an in-memory authentication provider, which is fine for development purposes.

For the sake of completeness, `<authentication-manager>` also creates a `Default-AuthenticationEventPublisher` at ❹. The `ProviderManager` uses this to publish authentication events (successes and failures) so that listeners can respond as needed (for example, redirecting the user to the correct target URL).

That's enough behind-the-scenes for now. Let's configure web.xml.

CONFIGURING WEB.XML FOR WEB SECURITY

Spring Security uses a special servlet filter to secure web resources. We'll examine this in more detail momentarily, but first let's look at the following listing.

Listing 6.2   Configuring web.xml with the Spring Security filter

```
<?xml version="1.0" encoding="UTF-8"?>
<web-app xmlns="http://java.sun.com/xml/ns/javaee"
    xmlns:xsi="http://www.w3.org/2001/XMLSchema-instance"
    xsi:schemaLocation="http://java.sun.com/xml/ns/javaee
        http://java.sun.com/xml/ns/javaee/web-app_2_5.xsd"
    version="2.5">

    <context-param>
        <param-name>contextConfigLocation</param-name>
        <param-value>classpath:beans-security.xml</param-value>
    </context-param>
    <listener>
        <listener-class>
            org.springframework.web.context.ContextLoaderListener
        </listener-class>
```

❶ Specifies application context

```
    </listener>
    <filter>
        <filter-name>sitemesh</filter-name>
        <filter-class>
            com.opensymphony.sitemesh.webapp.SiteMeshFilter
        </filter-class>
    </filter>
    <filter>
        <filter-name>springSecurityFilterChain</filter-name>
        <filter-class>
            org.springframework.web.filter.DelegatingFilterProxy
        </filter-class>
    </filter>
    <filter-mapping>
        <filter-name>springSecurityFilterChain</filter-name>
        <url-pattern>/*</url-pattern>
    </filter-mapping>
    <filter-mapping>
        <filter-name>sitemesh</filter-name>
        <url-pattern>/*</url-pattern>
    </filter-mapping>

    ... DispatcherServlet configuration for main app functionality ...

</web-app>
```

Configures Spring Security filter chain ❷

Applies filter chain to all requests ❸

At ❶ you reference the beans-security.xml security configuration from listing 6.1. At ❷ you enable Spring Security web security by defining a `DelegatingFilterProxy` filter, which is part of the core Spring distribution rather than being part of Spring Security itself.[3] `DelegatingFilterProxy` is essentially a trick for injecting servlet filters. You can point it at any filter on the application context you like by giving the `DelegatingFilterProxy` a name that matches the target filter's bean ID. The target filter, being a bean, is injectable like any other bean.

Although it would certainly be possible to define one `DelegatingFilterProxy` for each filter you want to use, that would be a hassle. Instead you define a single `DelegatingFilterProxy` filter on the web.xml side and a single `FilterChainProxy` filter on the beans-security.xml side. Then you create the filters and filter chains you want to use entirely within the Spring Security configuration rather than in web.xml. Fortunately, using `<http auto-config="true" />` sets up the `FilterChainProxy`, filters, and filter chains for you, using the bean ID `springSecurityFilterChain`. See figure 6.6 for a visual overview of what we just described.

Figure 6.7 shows the same thing as a sequence diagram.

Finally, you indicate that you want all requests to pass through the filter ❸. This includes all requests, because login submissions and logouts aren't associated with any `DispatcherServlet`.

You're done with configuration. Now let's make sure your JSPs are equipped to display the login and logout links appropriately.

---

[3] `DelegatingFilterProxy` was inspired by the `FilterToBeanProxy` class, which originated with Acegi Security—the precursor to Spring Security.

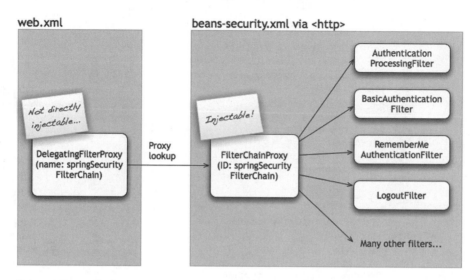

Figure 6.6   Filter proxying for injectable servlet filters

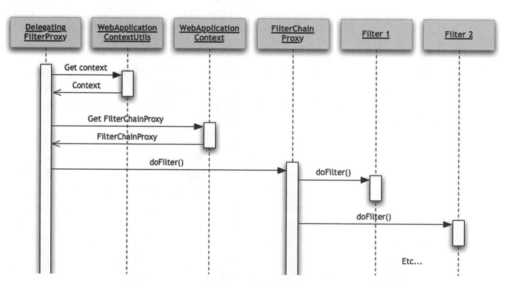

Figure 6.7 `DelegatingFilterProxy` **sequence diagram. This is a partial view; we've suppressed the full filter chain. Filter 1, Filter 2, and so on refer to filters in the chain.**

Quick tip: the filter mapping order matters

Note that you place the Spring Security filter mapping before the Sitemesh filter mapping for a reason: you want the request to pass through the Spring Security filter first so authentication information will be available on the request when the Sitemesh filter kicks in. This allows you to display, for example, the user's name as part of the template.

CREATING THE APPROPRIATE LINKS IN YOUR JSPS

So far your only special JSP is subhead.jspf.[4] The next listing shows a simplified (CSS suppressed) version of subhead.jspf. See the code download for the full version.

> **Listing 6.3   User information and shared navigation in subhead.jspf**

```
<%@ taglib prefix="c" uri="http://java.sun.com/jsp/jstl/core" %>
<%@ taglib prefix="security"
    uri="http://www.springframework.org/security/tags" %>          ❶ Spring Security
                                                                       tag library

<c:url var="homeUrl" value="/home.html" />
<c:url var="loginUrl" value="/spring_security_login" />            ❷ Login
<c:url var="logoutUrl" value="/j_spring_security_logout" />           page
                                                        Logout URL ❸   URL
<a href="${homeUrl}">Home</a>

<security:authorize access="isAnonymous()">                        ❹ Login link for
    Hi, guest. <a href="${loginUrl}">Log in</a>                       anonymous users
</security:authorize>
<security:authorize access="isAuthenticated()">
    Hi, <security:authentication property="principal.username" />.
    <a href="${logoutUrl}">Log out</a>                             ❻ Displays
</security:authorize>                                                 username
```
❺ **Tests for authentication**

You begin by declaring the Spring Security tag library ❶, because you're going to use it both to present/suppress links according to role and to display user information. Next you create a couple of variables to store the default login ❷ and logout ❸ URLs. The login URL here returns a login form, not the form submission URL.

At ❹ you display the login link to anonymous users using `<security:authorize>` and using SpEL for the access rule. This is why you had to set `use-expressions="true"` in listing 6.1. You'll learn more about `<security:authorize>` in recipe 7.1.

At ❺ you display a personalized welcome message and the logout link to authenticated users, once again using `<security:authorize>` and SpEL to perform the test. The personalized welcome message uses the `<security:authentication>` tag ❻, which exposes the user's authentication information to the JSP. The `property` attribute refers to a property on an underlying `org.springframework.security.core.Authentication` object; see the Javadoc for that class for more information on what's available.[5] By default, the principal is an `org.springframework.security.core.userdetails.User`, and its properties are available for use as well. You'll see how to use a custom principal object in recipe 6.5.

You now have fully functional login and logout capabilities. Try it at http://localhost:8080/sip/home.html.

---

[4] A .jspf file is a JSP fragment (or JSP segment in JSP 2.0). JSPF pages are JSPs that you want to include in other JSPs.

[5] Bear in mind that you're using Spring Security 3 here, not Spring Security 2. Some classes moved around in Spring Security 3, including `Authentication`.

Discussion

The main benefit of the default login form is that it's easy to set up. But it's merely serviceable; it's not necessarily what you'd want to use for a more polished app:

- The login button uses the awkward language Submit Query (or Submit on some browsers, which is somewhat better). We'd prefer something like Log in or Sign in.
- The form includes a reset button, which most users would consider superfluous.
- You may want a different page layout, form layout, or styling.

In the following recipe you'll learn how to customize the login form.

6.2   *Customizing the login page*

PREREQUISITE

Recipe 6.1 Implementing login and logout with remember-me authentication

KEY TECHNOLOGIES

Spring Security

Background

In recipe 6.1, you learned the mechanics of using Spring Security to set up form-based logins, but in most real-life applications you'll need (or at least want) to modify the form's appearance. This recipe shows how to replace the purely functional default login form with one that addresses not only the functional requirements but also those that are more visual or interactive in nature.

Problem

Create a custom login page.

Solution

To create a custom login page, you must

- Create a custom login JSP
- Add a `<mvc:view-controller>` element to beans-web.xml (part of the code download)
- Modify the `<form-login>` element in beans-security.xml
- Update subhead.jspf to use the new form

As in recipe 6.1, you don't have to write any Java language code to pull this off. You'll start with the JSP change.

CREATING THE LOGIN FORM JSP

Figure 6.8 shows a custom login page. It isn't hugely different in appearance than the default

Figure 6.8   A custom login page

form, but there is a key difference: you now control what's on the page. Notice that there's a nav bar at the top of the login form (although all we've put there is a Home link). That nav bar wasn't part of the default login form from figure 6.1. We've also changed the old Submit Query button to a new Log in button, and we've gotten rid of the unnecessary Reset button.

The following listing shows how to implement a custom form. For clarity, we've suppressed most of the actual layout and CSS because it's the form itself that matters.

Listing 6.4   Custom login form, login.jsp, whose appearance you control

```
<%@ taglib prefix="c" uri="http://java.sun.com/jsp/jstl/core" %>
<c:url var="postLoginUrl" value="/j_spring_security_check" />     ←┐ ❶ Form
                                                                        submission URL
<html>
    <head><title>Please log in</title></head>
    <body>                                                       ❷ Validation
                                                                    error message
        <c:if test="${param.failed == true}">                 ←┘
            <div>Your login attempt failed. Please try again.</div>
        </c:if>
                                                          Login form ❸
        <h1>Please log in</h1>

        <form class="main" action="${postLoginUrl}" method="post">  ←┘
            Username: <input type="text" name="j_username" /><br />
            Password: <input type="password" name="j_password" /><br />
            <input type="checkbox" name="_spring_security_remember_me" />
                Remember me<br />
            <input type="submit" value="Log in" />
        </form>
    </body>
</html>
```

You use `<c:url>` to store the form-submission URL at ❶. This allows you to avoid hard-coding the context path into the URL, because `<c:url>` provides it automatically. The specific URL you're using is the Spring Security default for login form submissions.

If there's a login failure, you need a way to say so. That's what ❷ is about. The JSP checks to see whether there is an HTTP parameter `failed=true`. If so, it displays the error message.

The form at ❸ uses the form-submission URL you created as its action. You also use specific parameter names for the username, password, and remember-me check box.

That's all there is to the login form. But you still need to make it reachable by updating beans-web.xml.

ADDING A VIEW CONTROLLER TO BEANS-WEB.XML

The beans-web.xml configuration (see the code download) already declares the `mvc` namespace, so all you need to do is add the following view controller:

```
<mvc:view-controller path="/login.html" />
```

This maps requests for /login.html to the logical view name `login`, thanks to the `DispatcherServlet`'s `DefaultRequestToViewNameTranslator`. (You can also pick a view name explicitly by using the `view-name` attribute on the `<mvc:view-controller>`.) Then of course the `InternalResourceViewResolver` carries the view name to an actual JSP. See figure 6.9.

Now that you have a login page, the next step is to tell Spring Security about it.

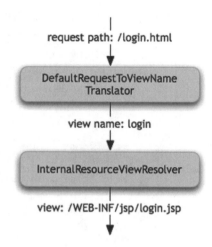

Figure 6.9   From request path to view with a view controller

MODIFYING THE <FORM-LOGIN> ELEMENT IN BEANS-SECURITY.XML

There isn't much to do to beans-security.xml. You need to tell Spring Security where to find your new login page, and you need to ensure that it uses the error-message capability you created in the JSP. Modify the `<form-login>` element as follows:

```
<form-login
    login-page="/login.html"
    authentication-failure-url="/login.html?failed=true"
    default-target-url="/home.html" />
```

The `login-page` attribute tells Spring Security where the custom login page is. It needs this so it can redirect unauthenticated users to the login page when they attempt to access a protected resource. You don't currently have any protected pages, so you can't yet see this in action, but you'll return to this in chapter 7.

The `authentication-failure-url` attribute, as you might guess, tells Spring Security where to direct the user if the login attempt fails. You send the user right back to your custom login page, but you include a `failed=true` HTTP parameter. That's how you tell the JSP to display the error message, as you saw in listing 6.4.

- Now that you've handled configuration, let's update the navigation JSP fragment.

UPDATING THE LOGIN LINK IN THE NAVIGATION

All you have to do in subhead.jspf is replace the /spring_security_login path with /login.html. Simple! Admire your handiwork at http://localhost:8080/sip/home.html.

Discussion

This recipe showed how to improve upon the default login page that Spring Security provides by creating a custom login page. In the next recipe, you'll consider a third way to handle login forms. This time, instead of using a login link that points to a separate login page, you'll build the login form right into the page navigation.

6.3 *Implementing an always-resident login form*

PREREQUISITES
Recipe 6.2 Customizing the login page

KEY TECHNOLOGIES
Spring Security, Spring Security tag library

Background

In recipes 6.1 and 6.2, you looked at two standard ways to present login forms: you can present a login link as part of the site navigation, or you can present a login form when an unauthenticated user attempts to access a protected resource.

Here we'll consider a third way: the always-resident login form. It allows the user to log in with one less click.

Problem

Display a login form that appears as part of the page template (and thus on every page) until the user logs in. See figure 6.10.

Figure 6.10   A login form that displays on every page until the user logs in

Solution

Normally an unauthenticated user either clicks a login link or attempts to access a protected resource, after which Spring Security redirects them to a login page. Here you don't have that; every page has a login form, and there isn't any login page.

Fortunately, Spring Security is sufficiently flexible that you can pull it off. The main thing you care about is having somewhere to post the form data, no matter where the form lives. You'll start by modifying the subhead.jspf navigation file.

MODIFYING SUBHEAD.JSPF TO INCLUDE THE LOGIN FORM
The next listing updates the subhead.jspf file from listing 6.3. As before, we've simplified the layout and CSS for clarity's sake; see the code download for the full version.

> **Listing 6.5   subhead.jspf updated to include an always-resident login form**

```
<%@ taglib prefix="c" uri="http://java.sun.com/jsp/jstl/core" %>
<%@ taglib prefix="security"
    uri="http://www.springframework.org/security/tags" %>

<c:url var="homeUrl" value="/main/home.html" />
```

```
<c:url var="postLoginUrl" value="/j_spring_security_check" />
<c:url var="logoutUrl" value="/j_spring_security_logout" />

<a href="${homeUrl}">Home</a>                          Login submission URL ❶

<security:authorize access="isAnonymous()">
    <form action="${postLoginUrl}">
        Username: <input type="text" name="j_username" />  
        Password: <input type="password" name="j_password" />  
        <input type="submit" value="Log in" />
    </form>
</security:authorize>                                    Always-resident login form ❷
<security:authorize access="isAuthenticated()">
    Hi, <security:authentication property="principal.username" />.
    <a href="${logoutUrl}">Log out</a>
</security:authorize>
```

You specify the login submission URL at ❶ and use it to create a login form at ❷. That's all there is to it. This is a special case of the custom login form from recipe 6.2.

You need two more JSPs. The first is a login-required page that you present to unauthenticated users when they attempt to access protected resources. The second is a login-failed page to display when (yup) a login attempt failed.

CREATING A LOGIN-REQUIRED PAGE

Normally, when an unauthenticated user attempts to access a protected page, you send the user to a login page, perhaps with some verbiage to the effect that they need to log in. Here you don't have a dedicated login page, so you need to do something different. You'll use loginRequired.jsp for this. It's simple:

```
<html>
    <head><title>Login required</title></head>
    <body>
        <%@ include file="includes/subhead.jspf" %>
        <h1>Login required</h1>
        <p>Please log in to access the requested page.</p>
    </body>
</html>
```

The subhead.jspf include has a built-in login form, so the user can log in from this page. Now let's create the login-failed page.

CREATING A LOGIN-FAILED PAGE

In recipes 6.1 and 6.2, the login pages displayed login-failed messages as appropriate; but now there's no login page, so you need some other way to communicate that message. Once again you'll create a simple page to do that, this time called login-Failed.jsp:

```
<html>
    <head><title>Login failed</title></head>
    <body>
        <%@ include file="includes/subhead.jspf" %>
        <h1>Login failed</h1>
        <div class="warning">
            Your login attempt failed. Please try again, or contact
```

```
                    technical support for further assistance.
            </div>
        </body>
</html>
```

Those are the JSPs you'll need. Let's add them to beans-web.xml because you'll need to reference them from beans-security.xml.

SPRING WEB MVC CONFIGURATION

Here all you need do is add a couple of view controllers to beans-web.xml, like so:

```
<mvc:view-controller
    path="/login-required.html" view-name="loginRequired" />
<mvc:view-controller
    path="/login-failed.html" view-name="loginFailed" />
```

Notice that this time around you're using the view-name attribute to specify view names explicitly, because, for example, /login-required.html wouldn't map to /WEB-INF/jsp/loginRequired.jsp under the implicit mapping. You could have named the JSPs login-required.jsp and login-failed.jsp, but you happened not to do that. Either way works.

With the JSPs and MVC configuration complete, let's update the Spring Security configuration.

SPRING SECURITY CONFIGURATION

All you need are a couple of tweaks to your existing beans-security.xml configuration. Once again it's the <form-login> element you need to change:

```
<form-login
    login-page="/login-required.html"
    authentication-failure-url="/login-failed.html"
    default-target-url="/home.html" />
```

Same attributes, different values. This time login-page points to the login-required page and authentication-failure points to the login-failed page.

There you have it: an always-resident login form. Spring Security makes it easy. You can give it a test drive using the same URL as before. Bear in mind that you don't yet have any way to exercise the login-required page, because the sample app doesn't include any access controls. We'll treat authorization in chapter 7.

Discussion

The always-resident login form described in this recipe is an alternative to the more typical login link. It works well if you have enough screen real estate to present it and if you want to avoid an unnecessary click. The Spring Community Forums (http://forum.springsource.org/), for example, use this login style. Always-resident login forms are good for highlighting the fact that a given website supports user registrations and logins. They're often located near links for registration and resetting forgotten passwords.

Once the user logs in, it's common to replace the login form with account settings information or links as well as a logout link. This helps to establish the piece of screen real estate as containing account/session information and options.

You now have a nice login front end. It's time to attend to back-end issues. Specifically you're ready to connect the login form to a backing database.

6.4   *Sourcing user data from a database*

PREREQUISITE
Recipe 6.1 Implementing login and logout with remember-me authentication

KEY TECHNOLOGIES
Spring Security, database

Background

In real applications, you want to source authentication data from a persistent store, and a database is a common choice. In this recipe you'll see how to replace your in-memory user service with one that's backed by a database.

Problem

Source user authentication data from a database.

Solution

We covered both the `DaoAuthenticationProvider` class and `UserDetailsService` interfaces in recipe 6.1, so we won't rehash that here. Instead we'll jump right into the changes you need to make. These recipes require that your Maven configuration be set up as described under "Building and Configuration" at http://springinpractice.com/code-and-setup to enable Jetty startup to find the jetty-env.xml configuration file.

The most straightforward approach to using a database back end is to replace the `InMemoryDaoImpl` user service with a `JdbcDaoImpl` user service. To do this, you'll need to perform the following steps:

1   Create user-related schema and tables in a database.
2   Grant appropriate permissions to whichever user you're using. (The sample scripts and configuration assume user sip/sip and database sip06. It's fine to grant all permissions to that user on the sip06 database.)
3   Expose the database through JNDI in your servlet container environment.
4   Use Spring to do a JNDI `DataSource` lookup.
5   Update the Spring Security authentication provider configuration.

When all is said and done, you're targeting the bean graph shown in figure 6.11.

You'll see more details as you work through the recipe. Let's get started by creating the database tables.

CREATING THE DATABASE TABLES

Although it's possible to use a custom database schema, in this recipe you'll use the default Spring Security user schema. In recipe 6.5, you'll customize the schema.

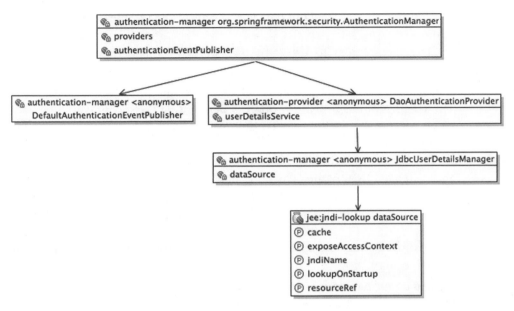

Figure 6.11 Bean dependency graph for a JDBC-backed authentication manager

The default user schema has only two tables: users and authorities, for user credentials and roles, respectively. Figure 6.12 shows the entity-relationship diagram (ERD) for the user schema.

Here's the MySQL DDL for the schema in figure 6.12:

```
create table users (
    username varchar(50) not null primary key,
    password varchar(50) not null,
    enabled boolean not null
) engine = InnoDb;

create table authorities (
    username varchar(50) not null,
    authority varchar(50) not null,
    foreign key (username) references users (username),
    unique index authorities_idx_1 (username, authority)
) engine = InnoDb;
```

Create the tables, and add users and authorities. You can use, for example, the following:

```
insert into users values ('juan', 'p@assword', 1);
insert into authorities values ('juan', 'user');
```

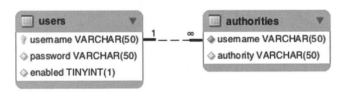

Figure 6.12 ERD for the default user schema. Each user has zero or more roles.

You can find the schema and data SQL scripts in the sample code in the src/main/sql folder.

The next step is to use JNDI to expose the database in the servlet container environment.

EXPOSING THE DATABASE USING JNDI

The specifics of this step are strongly dependent on the servlet container you're using. If you haven't already done so, consult your container documentation for instructions on how to do this.

For the sake of this exercise, assume that you've bound the `DataSource` to the `jdbc/Sip06DS` JNDI name. The code download contains a sample_conf/jetty-env.xml configuration for Jetty with the driver, URL, username, and password set to match some of the assumptions we've made (for example, database name is sip06, username is sip).

Next you'll make the `DataSource` available to Spring so you can use it as an authentication source.

LOOKING UP THE DATASOURCE FROM SPRING

For this step, you'll create a new application context configuration file. Although it would be possible to place the `DataSource` lookup directly in beans-security.xml, in general you'd expect to use the `DataSource` for general persistence needs and not merely security needs. Therefore the `DataSource` lookup doesn't belong in beans-security.xml.

Create a new configuration file called beans-data.xml. All it has is a lookup:

```xml
<?xml version="1.0" encoding="UTF-8"?>
<beans xmlns="http://www.springframework.org/schema/beans"
    xmlns:jee="http://www.springframework.org/schema/jee"
    xmlns:xsi="http://www.w3.org/2001/XMLSchema-instance"
    xsi:schemaLocation="http://www.springframework.org/schema/beans
        http://www.springframework.org/schema/beans/spring-beans-3.0.xsd
        http://www.springframework.org/schema/jee
        http://www.springframework.org/schema/jee/spring-jee-3.0.xsd">

    <jee:jndi-lookup id="dataSource"
        jndi-name="jdbc/Sip06DS" resource-ref="true"/>
</beans>
```

You also need to update web.xml to point to the new Spring configuration. Change the `contextConfigLocation` parameter definition to look like this:

```xml
<context-param>
    <param-name>contextConfigLocation</param-name>
    <param-value>
        classpath:/spring/beans-data.xml
        classpath:/spring/beans-security.xml
    </param-value>
</context-param>
```

Now you have a `DataSource`. Next you need to update the Spring Security configuration to use it to source authentication data.

WORKING WITH JDBCDAOIMPL

By now you may be noticing the common theme that you can make fairly major changes with minimal effort. Swapping a JDBC-backed user service for the in-memory user service is another case in point. Change the <authentication-manager> configuration so it looks like this:

```
<authentication-manager>
    <authentication-provider>
        <jdbc-user-service data-source-ref="dataSource" />
    </authentication-provider>
</authentication-manager>
```

Behind the scenes, the <jdbc-user-service> element creates a JdbcDaoImpl (implements UserDetailsService) to inject into the DaoAuthenticationProvider created by <authentication-provider>. Refer to recipe 6.1 for figures and details.

Table 6.1 shows the default SQL queries that JdbcDaoImpl uses for looking up users and roles. Note that these match the tables you created.

Table 6.1 Default SQL queries that JdbcDaoImpl uses to retrieve user data

Description	Query
Gets users by username	SELECT username, password, enabled FROM users WHERE username = ?
Gets roles by username	SELECT username, authority FROM authorities WHERE username = ?

That concludes the solution part of the recipe. Now you have a database back end for your authentication source. Try it at http://localhost:8080/sip/home.html.

Discussion

In this recipe, you saw how to source authentication data from a database. Although there was a little setup to do with respect to the database and DataSource configuration, presumably most of your apps have to do that anyway. The Spring Security part was trivial.

The default user schema that JdbcDaoImpl expects may or may not serve your needs in any given case. It's simple and minimalistic, so it won't be long before you're looking for ways to customize, expand, or replace it. We'll cover that topic in recipes 6.5 and 6.6.

6.5   *Customizing the user database schema*

PREREQUISITES

Recipe 6.4 Sourcing user data from a database

KEY TECHNOLOGIES

Spring Security, database

Background

In most instances, you'll want to use something a little more beefy than the default `JdbcDaoImpl` user schema. The good news is that it's easy to do.

Problem

Use a custom database schema for authentication.

Solution

As an example, suppose you want to use the schema from recipe 4.4—that is, the three-table schema shown in figure 6.13.

You can handle this by configuring `<jdbc-user-service>` to use custom queries, as follows:

```
<authentication-provider>
    <jdbc-user-service data-source-ref="dataSource"
        users-by-username-query=
            "select username, password, enabled
             from account where username = ?"
        authorities-by-username-query=
            "select a.username, r.name
             from account a, role r, account_role ar
             where ar.account_id = a.id and ar.role_id = r.id
             and a.username = ?" />
</authentication-provider>
```

This configuration uses the same `JdbcDaoImpl` user service you've been using, but you replace the two lookup queries with custom queries that reflect the underlying schema.

Be sure to run the SQL scripts in the src/main/sql directory of the sample code before starting up the app. Then point the browser at http://localhost:8080/sip/home.html, and you should be running successfully against the new database schema.

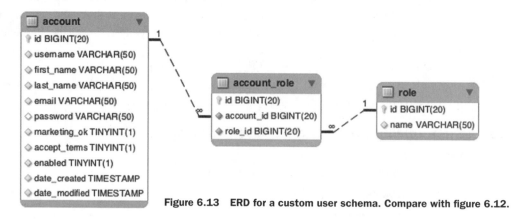

Figure 6.13   ERD for a custom user schema. Compare with figure 6.12.

Discussion

Being able to customize the database schema is certainly a useful thing to do, but sometimes the customizations you desire are more involved. Recall from the discussion following listing 6.3 that the default principal object for Spring Security user services is an org.springframework.security.core.userdetails.User. Even when you customize the database schema as just described, you're still stuck with the default User object, which is once again minimalistic. Ideally you'd like to be able to query the principal object for the user's first and last names, email, address, and so forth.

The next recipe shows how to overcome this limitation by sourcing your user data from the account service you implemented in recipe 4.4.

6.6 Using a custom user service and user principal

PREREQUISITES

Recipe 4.4 Saving form data
Recipe 6.5 Customizing the user database schema

KEY TECHNOLOGIES

Spring Security

Background

In general, user representations include important information beyond credentials and account flags. This might include demographic data (first name, last name, email address), preferences, and more. Because Spring Security makes the authenticated user principal available in the security context, it would be nice to use a more full-featured user instead of the default org.springframework.security.core.userdetails.User. In this recipe, you'll learn how to do that with a custom user service.

Problem

Enhance the user principal with first name, last name, email address, and so forth.

Solution

For this recipe, you'll connect the account service you created in recipe 4.4 with Spring Security. You did most of the heavy lifting in that recipe, but there's still a bit more work to do. Here are the steps you'll need to carry out:

1 Adapt the Account domain object from recipe 4.4 to the Spring Security UserDetails interface.
2 Create a DAO to get the password for the new UserDetails object, because neither Account nor AccountDao exposes the password.
3 Adapt the AccountService interface from recipe 4.4 to the Spring Security UserDetailsService interface.
4 Update the Spring configuration to use the new UserDetailsService. (You'll inject your custom UserDetailsService into the DaoAuthenticationProvider.)
5 Update subhead.jspf to take advantage of the new UserDetails object. You'll show the user's full name instead of only their username.

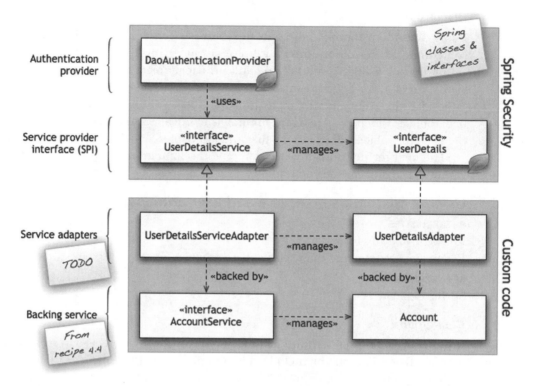

Figure 6.14   Class diagram for the `DaoAuthenticationProvider`**. In this recipe, you'll implement the adapters that allow you to use the account service from recipe 4.4 as a** `UserDetailsService`**.**

Figure 6.14 is a class diagram that shows several of the key pieces for this recipe.

You'll begin by implementing the `UserDetailsAdapter`.

ADAPTING THE ACCOUNT DOMAIN OBJECT TO THE USERDETAILS INTERFACE

To perform authentication, Spring Security needs your user principal to implement the `UserDetails` interface. Although you could add `implements UserDetails` to the `Account` object from recipe 4.4, this would be invasive. Instead you'll create an adapter to make the `Account` object conform to the `UserDetails` interface, as shown in the following listing.

Listing 6.6   UserDetailsAdapter.java, which adapts `Account` **to** `UserDetails`

```
package com.springinpractice.ch06.domain;

import java.util.Collection;
import java.util.HashSet;
import java.util.Set;
import org.springframework.security.core.GrantedAuthority;
import org.springframework.security.core.authority.GrantedAuthorityImpl;
import org.springframework.security.core.userdetails.UserDetails;

public class UserDetailsAdapter implements UserDetails {
```

Implements ❶
UserDetails

```
    private Account account;
    private String password;

    public UserDetailsAdapter(Account account) {
        this.account = account;
    }

    public Account getAccount() { return account; }

    public Long getId() { return account.getId(); }

    public String getFirstName() { return account.getFirstName(); }

    public String getLastName() { return account.getLastName(); }

    public String getFullName() { return account.getFullName(); }

    public String getEmail() { return account.getEmail(); }

    @Override
    public String getUsername() { return account.getUsername(); }

    @Override
    public String getPassword() { return password; }

    public void setPassword(String password) {
        this.password = password;
    }

    @Override
    public boolean isAccountNonExpired() { return true; }

    @Override
    public boolean isAccountNonLocked() { return true; }

    @Override
    public boolean isCredentialsNonExpired() { return true; }

    @Override
    public boolean isEnabled() { return account.isEnabled(); }

    @Override
    public Collection<GrantedAuthority> getAuthorities() {
        Set<GrantedAuthority> authorities =
            new HashSet<GrantedAuthority>();
        for (Role role : account.getRoles()) {
            authorities.add(new GrantedAuthorityImpl(role.getName()));
        }
        return authorities;
    }
}
```

2 Backed by Account

3 Exposes Account properties

4 Exposes UserDetails properties

5 Password setter

6 Handles extra properties

7 Roles to authorities

The listing is an adapter to make Account act like a UserDetails. Obviously that involves implementing the UserDetails interface **1** and accepting a backing Account **2**. You expose special Account properties like firstName **3**, lastName, fullName, and email because you want these to be available to the app for rendering or other purposes.

You must also implement the methods that UserDetails expects, such as username, password, various flag properties, and authorities. In the case of username, it's a pass-through ❹. The `password` property is different because `Account` doesn't include a `password` property (recall that you left it out for security reasons), so you implement it here and include a setter ❺ because the database has a password column. The flag properties other than `enabled`, on the other hand, have neither corresponding `Account` properties nor corresponding database columns, so you return `true` for all of them ❻. Finally, you support the `authorities` property by mapping roles to authorities ❼.

You now have a custom user principal class, but you still need a way to get the password out of the database. You'll create a DAO for that.

CREATING A DAO FOR RETRIEVING PASSWORDS

This DAO exists solely for the purpose of obtaining user passwords from the database. Although you could go back and modify the account service, that would again be invasive. We'll continue to show how to adapt the account service without changing it.

The interface for your DAO has a single method:

```
package com.springinpractice.ch06.dao;

public interface UserDetailsDao {
    String findPasswordByUsername(String username);
}
```

The next listing is a JDBC-based implementation of the `UserDetailsDao` interface.

Listing 6.7 JdbcUserDetailsDao.java for password lookups

```
package com.springinpractice.ch06.dao;

import javax.inject.Inject;
import org.springframework.jdbc.core.JdbcTemplate;
import org.springframework.stereotype.Repository;

@Repository
public class JdbcUserDetailsDao implements UserDetailsDao {    ❶ Injects
    @Inject private JdbcTemplate jdbcTemplate;                     JdbcTemplate

    private static final String FIND_PASSWORD_SQL =            ❷ Simple SQL
        "select password from account where username = ?";      query

    @Override
    public String findPasswordByUsername(String username) {   ❸ Runs
        return jdbcTemplate.queryForObject(                     query
            FIND_PASSWORD_SQL, new Object[] { username }, String.class);
    }
}
```

This DAO uses JDBC instead of Hibernate because you're not doing any ORM. You inject the `JdbcTemplate` at ❶ and define a simple query at ❷. You query for the password at ❸ by specifying the SQL, the username, and the `String` class.

With that, you have a user principal and a means to populate all of its properties. But what you don't have is an implementation of the `UserDetailsService` to inject into the `DaoAuthenticationProvider`. You'll take care of that in the next subsection.

ADAPTING THE ACCOUNTSERVICE INTERFACE TO THE USERDETAILSSERVICE INTERFACE

In the same way that you adapted the Account class to the UserDetails interface, you need to adapt the AccountService interface to the UserDetailsService interface. The following listing is an adapter to do this.

Listing 6.8   UserDetailsServiceAdapter.java, backed by `AccountService`

```java
package com.springinpractice.ch06.service;

import javax.inject.Inject;
import org.springframework.dao.DataAccessException;
import org.springframework.security.core.userdetails.UserDetails;
import org.springframework.security.core.userdetails.UserDetailsService;
import org.springframework.security.core.userdetails.
        UsernameNotFoundException;
import org.springframework.stereotype.Service;
import org.springframework.transaction.annotation.Transactional;
import com.springinpractice.ch06.dao.UserDetailsDao;
import com.springinpractice.ch06.domain.Account;
import com.springinpractice.ch06.domain.UserDetailsAdapter;

@Service("userDetailsService")              ←── ❶ Named service bean          ❷ Implements
@Transactional(readOnly = true)                                                  UserDetailsService
public class UserDetailsServiceAdapter implements UserDetailsService {  ←──
    @Inject AccountService accountService;
    @Inject UserDetailsDao userDetailsDao;          ←──
                                         ❹ UserDetailsDao for password
    @Override
    public UserDetails loadUserByUsername(String username)
        throws UsernameNotFoundException, DataAccessException {   ←── ❺ Method to
                                                                      implement
        Account account =
            accountService.getAccountByUsername(username);

        if (account == null) {                           ←── ❼ Validates
            throw new UsernameNotFoundException(              account
                "No such user: " + username);
        } else if (account.getRoles().isEmpty()) {
            throw new UsernameNotFoundException(
                "User " + username + " has no authorities");
        }                                                ❽ Creates
                                                             adapter
        UserDetailsAdapter user = new UserDetailsAdapter(account);  ←──
        user.setPassword(
            userDetailsDao.findPasswordByUsername(username));   ←── ❾ Sets
        return user;                                                 password
    }
}
```

❸ **Backing AccountService**

❻ **Gets account**

The adapter is a service bean. You give it a name ❶ so you can reference it from the Spring Security <authentication-provider> configuration. As an adapter, it implements UserDetailsService ❷ and accepts a backing AccountService ❸. It also accepts a UserDetailsDao ❹ so you have a way to look up the user's password.

The single method you need to implement is loadUserByUsername() ❺. To do this, you get the Account from the backing AccountService ❻ and then validate the account ❼, throwing UsernameNotFoundException as per the UserDetailsService contract. Then you create the UserDetailsAdapter ❽, inject the password ❾, and return the user principal.

The Java part of your effort is now complete, so let's look at the configuration changes you need to make.

UPDATING THE SPRING CONFIGURATION TO USE THE NEW USERDETAILSSERVICE

Now that you've added the custom user service from recipe 4.4, you need to update the configuration to support it. There's also some other configuration to handle, such as the configuration for the JdbcTemplate. Here's what you need to do for the data tier.

Listing 6.9 beans-data.xml, updated to support the custom user service

```xml
<?xml version="1.0" encoding="UTF-8"?>
<beans xmlns="http://www.springframework.org/schema/beans"
    xmlns:context="http://www.springframework.org/schema/context"
    xmlns:jee="http://www.springframework.org/schema/jee"
    xmlns:p="http://www.springframework.org/schema/p"
    xmlns:util="http://www.springframework.org/schema/util"
    xmlns:xsi="http://www.w3.org/2001/XMLSchema-instance"
    xsi:schemaLocation="http://www.springframework.org/schema/beans
        http://www.springframework.org/schema/beans/spring-beans-3.0.xsd
        http://www.springframework.org/schema/context
        http://www.springframework.org/schema/context/
            spring-context-3.0.xsd
        http://www.springframework.org/schema/jee
        http://www.springframework.org/schema/jee/spring-jee-3.0.xsd
        http://www.springframework.org/schema/util
        http://www.springframework.org/schema/util/spring-util-3.0.xsd">

    <jee:jndi-lookup id="dataSource" jndi-name="jdbc/Sip06DS"
        resource-ref="true"/>                                          ◁──❶ Still have a
                                                                            DataSource
    <bean class="org.springframework.jdbc.core.JdbcTemplate"
        p:dataSource-ref="dataSource" />                              ◁──❷ Adds JdbcTemplate

    <util:properties id="hibernateProperties">                        ◁──   Adds
        <prop key="hibernate.dialect">                                    ❸ Hibernate
            org.hibernate.dialect.MySQL5InnoDBDialect
        </prop>
        <prop key="hibernate.show_sql">false</prop>
    </util:properties>

    <bean id="sessionFactory"
        class="org.springframework.orm.hibernate3.annotation.
            AnnotationSessionFactoryBean"
        p:dataSource-ref="dataSource"
        p:packagesToScan="com.springinpractice.ch06.domain"
        p:hibernateProperties-ref="hibernateProperties" />

    <context:component-scan
        base-package="com.springinpractice.ch06.dao" />              ◁──❹ Finds DAOs
</beans>
```

As with recipes 6.4 and 6.5, you still have a `DataSource` ❶. But now you add a `JdbcTemplate` ❷ to help with the password lookup. You also add Hibernate ❸ and scan for DAOs ❹ because your user service will need those.

In addition to configuring your data tier, you must configure your service tier.

Listing 6.10   beans-service.xml for service configuration

```xml
<?xml version="1.0" encoding="UTF-8"?>
<beans xmlns="http://www.springframework.org/schema/beans"
    xmlns:context="http://www.springframework.org/schema/context"
    xmlns:p="http://www.springframework.org/schema/p"
    xmlns:tx="http://www.springframework.org/schema/tx"
    xmlns:util="http://www.springframework.org/schema/util"
    xmlns:xsi="http://www.w3.org/2001/XMLSchema-instance"
    xsi:schemaLocation="
        http://www.springframework.org/schema/beans
        http://www.springframework.org/schema/beans/spring-beans-3.0.xsd
        http://www.springframework.org/schema/context
        http://www.springframework.org/schema/context/
            spring-context-3.0.xsd
        http://www.springframework.org/schema/tx
        http://www.springframework.org/schema/tx/spring-tx-3.0.xsd">

    <bean id="transactionManager"
        class="org.springframework.orm.hibernate3.
            HibernateTransactionManager"
        p:sessionFactory-ref="sessionFactory" />

    <tx:annotation-driven />

    <context:component-scan
        base-package="com.springinpractice.ch06.service.impl" />
</beans>
```

The previous listing is of course entirely standard, and there's not much to say about it.

The third Spring configuration file you need to update is beans-security.xml. Here, the change is easy. Replace the old `<authentication-provider>` definition with a new one, as shown:

```xml
<authentication-provider user-service-ref="userDetailsService" />
```

You no longer need the `<jdbc-user-service>` from the previous recipe, because `UserDetailsServiceAdapter` (whose ID is `userDetailsService`; see listing 6.8) is your new user service.

Figure 6.15 shows the bean dependency graph for the `DaoAuthenticationProvider` bean and its supporting infrastructure. This is a visual summary of the work you've already done. The authentication provider at the top is something that Spring Security provides, and the account service at the bottom is what you did in recipe 4.4. The adapter layer, which you just implemented, is the glue that holds these two things together.

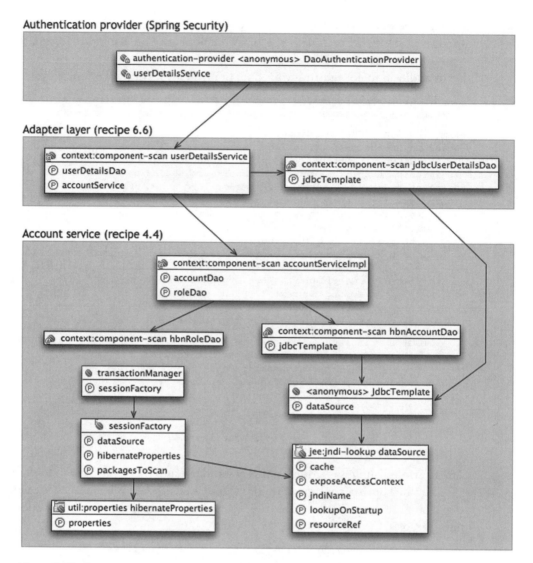

Figure 6.15   Bean dependency graph for `DaoAuthenticationProvider` and its dependencies

You don't need to change anything for beans-web.xml. But you do need to add the entry for beans-service.xml to web.xml:

```
<context-param>
    <param-name>contextConfigLocation</param-name>
    <param-value>
        classpath:/spring/beans-data.xml
        classpath:/spring/beans-service.xml
        classpath:/spring/beans-security.xml
    </param-value>
</context-param>
```

You also need to modify one of the JSPs slightly, so let's do that next.

UPDATING SUBHEAD.JSPF TO DISPLAY THE USER'S FULL NAME

In previous recipes, you displayed the user's username in the navigation area because you didn't have access to user properties beyond those provided by the default Spring Security `UserDetails` implementation. But now you're using the `UserDetails-Adapter` class from listing 6.6, which gives you access to nonstandard properties such as the user's first name, last name, full name, and email address. You can address the user by their full name by changing subhead.jspf as follows:

```
Hi, <security:authentication property="principal.fullName" />.
```

When you run this app, it will display "Hi, Juan Cazares" instead of "Hi, Juan." Go ahead and try it now: http://localhost:8080/sip/home.html.

Discussion

Recipe 6.6 ties together the custom authentication source you created in recipe 4.4 with Spring Security logins. This gives you a great deal of flexibility as regards your back-end authentication source, and it allows you to use rich user principals in your code and JSPs.

One issue we've neglected is storing passwords securely. All the examples so far have involved storing passwords as plain text. Recipe 6.7 remediates this issue.

6.7 Secure user passwords in the database

PREREQUISITES

Recipe 6.6 Using a custom user service and user principal (code dependency only)

KEY TECHNOLOGIES

Spring Security, cryptography

Background

When storing passwords, you need to take steps to ensure that nobody can see them, yourself included. This recipe shows how to use password salting and hashing to prevent anybody from viewing user passwords in the database. Although this recipe doesn't inherently depend on using a custom user service or user principal, you do build on the sample code from recipe 6.6.

Problem

Prevent people (including you) from viewing user passwords stored in the database.

Solution

You'll use cryptography to secure user passwords in the database, or at rest. The specific technique you'll use is hashing, which performs a one-way encryption of a user password; that is, hashing doesn't provide a corresponding decrypt operation. The way it works is as follows. When a user creates an account, you hash the user's password before

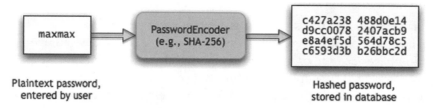

Figure 6.16 Hashing a plaintext password into a digest for improved security at rest

storing it in the database. That way, nobody except the user knows what it is, even if the database is compromised. When the same user wants to log in, you take the submitted password, hash it, and compare that hash to the one stored in the database. The authentication succeeds if and only if the hashes are the same. This works because different messages (here, passwords) are extremely unlikely to hash to the same value.

Figure 6.16 illustrates the process of hashing a plaintext message.

Spring Security makes it easy to add password hashing to your app, but to learn how, you need to treat both the initial password creation (as embodied, for example, in a user registration process) and subsequent authentications. The code download for this recipe combines the login work you've done in this chapter with the user registration code from recipe 4.4.

First you'll update the registration process to store password hashes instead of plain text.

HASHING PASSWORDS BEFORE STORING THEM IN THE DATABASE

The change here is fairly trivial. You need to inject the `HbnAccountDao` (from recipe 4.4, listing 4.13) with a Spring Security `PasswordEncoder` and then use the encoder to hash the password before saving it:

```
package com.springinpractice.ch06.dao;

import org.springframework.security.authentication.encoding.
        PasswordEncoder;

... other imports ...

@Repository
public class HbnAccountDao extends AbstractHbnDao<Account>
    implements AccountDao {

    @Inject private PasswordEncoder passwordEncoder;

    public void create(Account account, String password) {
        create(account);
        String encPassword =
            passwordEncoder.encodePassword(password, null);
        jdbcTemplate.update(UPDATE_PASSWORD_SQL,
            encPassword, account.getUsername());
    }

    ... other members ...
}
```

The encodePassword() method's second argument is an optional salt, which you're not using yet. You'll see that shortly. For now, you pass in null.

The only other thing to do is add a PasswordEncoder in the app context. You'll use it both for the initial password creation as well as for logins. To do this, you need to choose an appropriate hashing algorithm. MD5 and SHA-1, although popular choices, have known vulnerabilities. MD5 in particular is no longer considered a secure hash algorithm. Instead, you'll use SHA-256. Here's what you need to do to beans-security.xml:

```
<beans:bean id="passwordEncoder"
    class="org.springframework.security.authentication.encoding.
        ShaPasswordEncoder">
    <beans:constructor-arg value="256" />
</beans:bean>

<authentication-manager>
    <authentication-provider user-service-ref="userDetailsService">
        <password-encoder ref="passwordEncoder" />
    </authentication-provider>
</authentication-manager>
```

You use the ShaPasswordEncoder and its constructor to specify SHA-256. (Other choices include 1, 384, and 512.) Spring automatically injects this into the HbnAccountDao. This therefore takes care of the registration use case.

For logins, you use the <password-encoder> configuration to endow the DaoAuthenticationProvider with the ShaPasswordEncoder. The <password-encoder> element has an optional hash attribute that you can use to specify a hash algorithm (for example, hash="sha-256"), but you reference an external bean because you need to inject the bean into the HbnAccountDao as noted.

One other item is that the password column in the account database table supports 64 characters because that's how many characters SHA-256 requires. (Each hexadecimal digit represents 4 bits, and $256/4 = 64$.) Because any accounts you created in previous recipes will no longer work (the passwords aren't hashed), you may as well rebuild the database with the database scripts. (Be sure to run both the schema and the data script.) See the src/main/sql in the code download. If for whatever reason you don't want to do that, you can as an alternative use this:

```
ALTER TABLE account MODIFY COLUMN password varchar(64);
```

At this point, if you run the app, new registrations will create hashed passwords, and logins will hash tendered passwords before comparing with the database hashes. You'll need to create new accounts (with hashed passwords) through the registration process to log in.

The new password-storage scheme offers considerably better security than plain text, which is completely insecure. But it has some important weaknesses. The most significant is that despite the fact that hash algorithms don't support a decrypt operation, you (wearing your black hat) can do something that's almost as good: precompute hashes for all the words in a dictionary and use the result as a reverse-lookup table. Although this won't necessarily allow you to recover every password in the database, it will allow you to recover any password that's a dictionary word, and plenty of users use dictionary words for passwords. You need something to defend against so-called dictionary attacks, and that's where salt comes in.

DEFENDING AGAINST DICTIONARY ATTACKS USING SALT

The idea behind salt is to add extra bits to user passwords to ensure that they aren't dictionary words, thus making dictionary attacks harder to execute. There are various approaches to salt. One best practice is to associate a large, random set of bits with each user and append it to each password before hashing it. This makes it much more costly to precompute reverse-lookup tables because a table must be created for each possible combination of bits.

Here you'll do something that's weaker but still an improvement over simple hashing: you'll use the user's ID as a salt. We can best explain how Spring Security will use this by way of example. Suppose you have a user with ID 27 and password maxmax. Spring Security will incorporate the chosen salt (here, the ID) into a nondictionary password as follows: maxmax{27}. This is weaker because you can easily imagine somebody precomputing a catalog of reverse-lookup tables to attack apps that use Spring Security and this particular salt scheme. But it would require a table for each ID, which means more effort than a single table of dictionary word hashes. But if your security needs are more stringent, you would be well advised to consider a stronger salt scheme, such as the large random bitset we described.

Figure 6.17 shows how you'll encode passwords using salting and hashing.

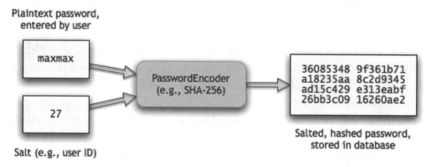

Figure 6.17 Improving security at rest by incorporating a variable salt

To add salt, once again you need to add it to both the password-creation and authentication processes. Here's what HbnAccountDao looks like with salt added:

```
package com.springinpractice.ch06.dao;

import org.springframework.security.authentication.dao.SaltSource;

... other imports ...

@Repository
public class HbnAccountDao extends AbstractHbnDao<Account>
    implements AccountDao {
```

```
@Inject private SaltSource saltSource;

public void create(Account account, String password) {
    create(account);
    Object salt = saltSource.getSalt(new UserDetailsAdapter(account));
    String encPassword =
        passwordEncoder.encodePassword(password, salt);
    jdbcTemplate.update(UPDATE_PASSWORD_SQL, encPassword,
        account.getUsername());
}

... other members ...
}
```

What you're doing is similar to what you did with the `PasswordEncoder`. You inject a `SaltSource` and then use it to generate a salt from the account in a way you'll see. Note though that you need to wrap the account with a `UserDetailsAdapter` because the `getSalt()` method expects a `UserDetails` argument. You update the call to `encodePassword()` by passing in the salt instead of `null`.

The new beans-security.xml configuration looks like this:

```
<beans:bean id="saltSource"
    class="org.springframework.security.authentication.dao.
           ReflectionSaltSource"
    p:userPropertyToUse="id" />

<authentication-manager>
    <authentication-provider user-service-ref="userDetailsService">
        <password-encoder ref="passwordEncoder">
            <salt-source ref="saltSource" />
        </password-encoder>
    </authentication-provider>
</authentication-manager>
```

You've added a `ReflectionSaltSource` bean to generate salts from the user's `id` property, and as with the PasswordEncoder, Spring automatically injects this into the `HbnAccountDao` so you can use it during account creation. You also configure the salt source into the `DaoAuthenticationProvider` so you can use it during logins.

Once again, this configuration effectively invalidates any existing accounts, because their passwords won't be recognizable anymore. But see the "Quick tip" sidebar.

Quick tip: preserving legacy passwords

If you want to upgrade a plaintext password-storage scheme to a hashed storage scheme, that's easy enough: you replace the plaintext passwords with hashed versions. But what if you want to upgrade a legacy hashed password-storage scheme to a salted, hashed scheme? Here you don't have the original passwords, so you can't recompute the passwords.

The answer is to use two authentication providers: the one with the salt source and the one without. Put them both inside the `<authentication-manager>` element, because it accepts a list of `<authentication-provider>` children. Problem solved!

Your password-storage scheme is now significantly more secure than the plaintext scheme you've been using up to this point.

Discussion

This recipe illustrated the link between the account-creation process and the authentication process. In general, the two processes need to be coordinated so that created accounts can serve in authentication contexts.

Something you'll notice if you run the sample code for this recipe is that you aren't automatically logged in after you register an account. That's an annoyance and another example of where it makes sense to coordinate account creation with authentication. The final recipe in this chapter shows how to fix that.

6.8   Auto-authenticating the user after a successful registration

PREREQUISITES
Recipe 4.4 Saving form data
Recipe 6.4 Sourcing user data from a database
Recipe 6.7 Securing user passwords in the database (code dependency only)

KEY TECHNOLOGIES
Spring Security

Background

Users expect applications to authenticate them automatically after creating an account. This recipe shows how to do this with Spring Security.

This recipe builds on the code from recipe 6.7, but it doesn't depend on hashing or salting. The sample code for recipe 6.7 is convenient in that it includes both the registration component and the login component.

Problem

Automatically authenticate the user after a successful new user registration.

Solution

This requires a couple of minor modifications to the sample code from recipe 6.7:

- Update the `AccountController` to perform the auto-authentication immediately following a successful user registration.
- Update beans-security.xml to support injecting your authentication manager into the controller.

Let's handle the controller first. You add an `AuthenticationManager` dependency to the `AccountController` class:

```
import org.springframework.beans.factory.annotation.Qualifier;
import org.springframework.security.authentication.AuthenticationManager;

...
```

```
public class AccountController {

    @Inject
    @Qualifier("authenticationManager")
    private AuthenticationManager authMgr;

    ...

}
```

You use Spring's @Qualifier annotation because it turns out there are two Authentication-
cationManager beans on the app context—one created as part of the <http> element
and one created as part of the <authentication-manager> element—and you need a
way to specify the one you want to inject. (Note that javax.inject also has an @Qual-
ifier annotation, but it has different semantics. You're using the Spring version.)

You also have to modify AccountController to use the authentication manager to
perform the auto-authentication:

```
import org.springframework.security.authentication.
        UsernamePasswordAuthenticationToken;
import org.springframework.security.core.Authentication;
import org.springframework.security.core.context.SecurityContextHolder;

...

public class AccountController {

    @RequestMapping(value = "", method = RequestMethod.POST)
    public String postRegistrationForm(
            @ModelAttribute("account") @Valid AccountForm form,
            BindingResult result) {

        convertPasswordError(result);
        String password = form.getPassword();
        accountService.registerAccount(toAccount(form), password, result);

        Authentication authRequest =
            new UsernamePasswordAuthenticationToken(
                form.getUsername(), password);
        Authentication authResult = authMgr.authenticate(authRequest);
        SecurityContextHolder.getContext().setAuthentication(authResult);

        return (result.hasErrors() ? VN_REG_FORM : VN_REG_OK);
    }

    ...

}
```

The part you care about starts where you create the authentication request. You feed it
the username and password. To authenticate the token, you need to pass it into the
authenticate() method on the AuthenticationManager. The authentication should
succeed because you've just created the associated account. After you have the authenticated token, you place it on the SecurityContext. The user is now authenticated.

There's one small detail you need to handle in the beans-security.xml configuration. Because there are (as we mentioned) two AuthenticationManagers, you can't
rely on type-based injection. You used @Qualifier to identify the bean you want to

inject, which is `authenticationManager`. The problem is that the bean's actual ID is `org.springframework.security.authenticationManager`, and that's an internal ID that Spring Security gives it rather than a published ID. To reference this bean, you need to give it an explicit alias. You do this as follows:

```
<authentication-manager alias="authenticationManager">
    ...
</authentication-manager>
```

With those changes, you now have a registration process that automatically authenticates the user after a successful registration.

Discussion

This final authentication recipe showed how to handle an important detail when integrating registration with authentication: auto-authenticating the user on a successful registration. You were able to accomplish this using the `AuthenticationManager` in a programmatic fashion.

6.9   *Summary*

You should now have a reasonable understanding of how to implement logins and logouts using Spring Security. We began by looking at different login UI options, then moved on to back-end options as well. Toward the end, you saw how to integrate different aspects of account creation with authentication, such as hashing, salting, and auto-authentication.

In chapter 7, we'll consider one of the major use cases for authentication: authorization. Authorization is the process of determining for a given user whether they're allowed to access a given resource. Once again, Spring Security provides a rich set of tools to handle the job.

Authorizing user requests

This chapter covers

- Implementing authorization using Spring Security
- Using authentication levels, roles, and permissions
- Establishing access control lists

Authorization is the area of security that deals with protecting resources from users or systems—generically, *principals*—which aren't allowed to view, modify, or otherwise access them. It generally builds on authentication. Authentication establishes the principal's identity, and authorization decides what the principal is allowed to do. This chapter continues the treatment of Spring Security we began in chapter 6, this time exploring its authorization features.

Figure 7.1 shows the relationship between the types of authorization in Spring Security 3. On the one hand we have authorization targets, which correspond to *what* is being protected: methods, views, and web resources. On the other we have authorization styles, or *how* we're protecting the targets: via authentication levels, roles, and access control lists (ACLs). Conceptually we'll break authorization into the grid in table 7.1.

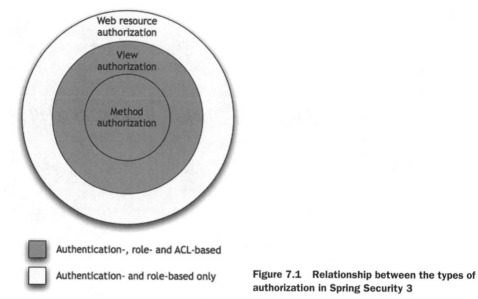

Figure 7.1 Relationship between the types of authorization in Spring Security 3

Table 7.1 Authorization combinations and their corresponding recipes

Authorization style	Authentication target		
	Methods	**Views**	**Web resources**
Authentication-, role- and permission-based	Recipe 7.1	Recipe 7.2	Recipe 7.3
ACL-based	Recipe 7.4	Recipe 7.5	Unsupported

Each recipe addresses one of the cells in the table.

Before tackling the recipes, let's discuss the authorization targets and styles.

AUTHORIZATION TARGETS

Spring Security allows you to authorize the three target types that appear as columns in table 7.1:

- *Methods*—We often need to protect Java methods from unauthorized access. We can define access rules on a per-method basis.
- *Views*—JSPs frequently contain navigation and content that we want to show or hide according to the user's permissions. For example, if the user doesn't have access to an admin console, it probably doesn't make sense to show the link to the admin console in the first place. We also need a way to suppress page content when the user isn't allowed to see it. Spring Security has tag libraries to help here.
- *Web resources*—We can grant or deny access to different HTTP requests based on the associated URLs and HTTP methods.

There are other targets—for example, databases and SMTP mailers—but security for such resources is typically handled by the resource itself. We won't discuss those here.

AUTHORIZATION STYLES

The two rows in table 7.1 deal with *how* access is determined. There are two complementary approaches:

- *Authentication-, role-, and permission-based authorization*—Authentication-based authorization uses authentication levels to determine access. Authentication levels range from anonymous (not authenticated) to remembered (authenticated via remember-me) to fully authenticated.

  Role-based authorization involves assigning roles to individual users and then using those roles to determine what users can see and do, ideally through associated permissions.

- *ACL-based authorization*—ACLs control access to an application's domain objects based on user permissions attaching to those domain objects. For example, I have access to my inbox but not yours. Because ACLs attach to domain objects, people often refer to this authorization style as *domain object authorization* or *domain object security.*

The following recipes center around a discussion forum sample application. The first three recipes cover authentication- and role-based authorization. The last two recipes deal with ACL-based authorization.

7.1 *Authorizing Java methods using authentication levels, roles, and permissions*

PREREQUISITE
Recipe 6.1 Implementing login and logout with remember-me authentication

KEY TECHNOLOGIES
Spring Security 3

Background

There are multiple reasons to protect Java methods from unauthorized access:

- To consolidate the definition of access rules so they can be managed in one place instead of being distributed and repeated across multiple clients
- To avoid having to rely on potentially untrusted clients to enforce access rules
- To provide for defense-in-depth, which is a security best practice

Spring Security allows you to define access rules, using either XML or annotations, that you can apply to Java service methods. We'll focus in this chapter on the annotation-based approach.

Problem

Secure service methods by defining authentication- and role-based access rules.

Solution

Approaches to securing Java methods involve defining rules that specify who has access to which methods. You'll define access rules using annotations, although XML-based rules are also an option. Consult the Spring Security reference documentation for information on using security pointcuts and AOP to secure Java methods. These recipes require that your Maven configuration be set up as described under "Building and Configuration" at http://springinpractice.com/code-and-setup to enable Jetty startup to find the jetty-env.xml configuration file.

The first thing to understand is how to define an access rule. Let's take the "who" part first. As of Spring 3, you can use the SpEL to define who has access to a target (whether a method or otherwise). Table 7.2 shows the predicates for defining authentication- and role-based access rules.

Table 7.2 SpEL predicates for defining authentication- and role-based access controls

Predicate	Truth condition
permitAll	Always true (truth constant).
denyAll	Always false (falsity constant).
isAnonymous()	Principal is anonymous.
isAuthenticated()	Principal isn't anonymous.
isRememberMe()	Principal authenticated via remember-me.
isFullyAuthenticated()	Principal authenticated by providing credentials explicitly.
hasRole(role)	Principal has the specified role.
hasAnyRole(role1, role2, ..., role n)	Principal has at least one of the specified roles.
hasIpAddress(ipAddr)	Client IP address matches a specified address. ipAddr can be either a single IP address or a range of IP addresses using IP/netmask notation. (Available only in web contexts.)

With the annotation-based approach, you add security annotations to your service beans, and then you add a single line to your beans-security.xml configuration.

Let's look at an example. You'll secure the ForumServiceImpl service bean in the sample app. This service allows clients to access forum-related functionality, like getting forums, updating messages in a forum, and so on. For now, your rules will be simple, although later you'll refine them. They will be things like these:

- The user must have a general, application-wide "read forums" permission to get a forum or forums from the service.
- The user must have a general, application-wide "create messages" permission to post a message to a forum.

You get the idea. Let's implement the rules using Spring Security annotations. List-ing 7.1 shows what ForumServiceImpl.java looks like with the annotations in place.

Listing 7.1   ForumServiceImpl.java with security annotations

```
package com.springinpractice.ch07.service.impl;

import java.util.List;
import javax.inject.Inject;
import org.springframework.security.access.prepost.PreAuthorize;
import org.springframework.stereotype.Service;
import org.springframework.transaction.annotation.Transactional;
import com.springinpractice.ch07.dao.ForumDao;
import com.springinpractice.ch07.dao.MessageDao;
import com.springinpractice.ch07.domain.Forum;
import com.springinpractice.ch07.domain.Message;
import com.springinpractice.ch07.service.ForumService;

@Service
@Transactional
@PreAuthorize("denyAll")                                              ❶ Whitelist
public class ForumServiceImpl implements ForumService {                 via denyAll
    @Inject private ForumDao forumDao;
    @Inject private MessageDao messageDao;                            ❷ Requires "read
                                                                        forums" permission
    @PreAuthorize("hasRole('PERM_READ_FORUMS')")
    public List<Forum> getForums() { return forumDao.getAll(); }

    @PreAuthorize("hasRole('PERM_CREATE_MESSAGES')")                  ❸ Requires "create
    public void createMessage(Message message) {                        messages" permission
        messageDao.create(message);
    }

    ... other methods ...
}
```

Despite its simplicity, this code snippet uses two key techniques that we need to discuss in a little detail. Let's cover the raw mechanics, then we'll look at the bigger picture.

The class-level @PreAuthorize annotation defines a default denyAll rule for the methods in the class ❶. The denyAll rule rejects access no matter what. That may seem like a strange thing to do, but it's one of the key techniques that we'll discuss momentarily.

@PreAuthorize means the denyAll check takes place before entering the method; there's also an @PostAuthorize annotation that's similar but performs a check after exiting the method. You'll see use cases for @PostAuthorize in recipe 7.4.

The default applies unless individual methods override it with method-level anno-tations. Of course, denying access to everybody doesn't make for a useful method. So at ❷ you override the default denyAll rule by specifying that having the PERM_READ_FORUMS permission is a necessary and sufficient condition for entering the getForums() method. Similarly, at ❸ you create a rule that says that having the PERM_CREATE_MESSAGES permission is necessary and sufficient for entering the createMessage() method.

You might wonder why you're using a `hasRole()` predicate to check for a permission, because roles and permissions aren't the same thing.[1] That gets to the second key technique we need to discuss. Without further ado, here are the two techniques.

KEY TECHNIQUE 1: WHITELISTING

Broadly speaking, there are two approaches to authorization: whitelisting and blacklisting. Whitelisting denies requests unless they're explicitly granted (on the whitelist), whereas blacklisting grants requests unless they're explicitly forbidden (on the blacklist). Whitelisting, as the more paranoid, generally makes for better security, and security professionals consider it a best practice. Use it whenever it's practical to do so.

Your default `denyAll` rule is effectively a whitelist implementation. If somebody adds a new method to `ForumServiceImpl` and forgets to attach an access rule, the default rule prevents anybody from using the method.

> **TIP** Whitelisting is a security best practice. Use class-level `@PreAuthorize` (`"denyAll"`) annotations to implement whitelists.

Now let's look at the second key technique.

KEY TECHNIQUE 2: SEPARATE ROLES AND PERMISSIONS

The goal behind this technique is to avoid embedding security policy decisions in the code. Such decisions should be set at runtime because they vary across customers, they vary over time, and sometimes they need to be changed immediately (for example, in response to a security breach).

Consider, for example, the difference between this rule

```
@PreAuthorize(
    "hasAnyRole('ROLE_STUDENT', 'ROLE_FACULTY_MEMBER', 'ROLE_ADMIN')")
public Forum getForum(long id){ ... }
```

and this one:

```
@PreAuthorize("hasRole('PERM_READ_FORUMS')")
public Forum getForum(long id) { ... }
```

The first rule breaks when somebody decides that teaching assistants, parents, faculty trainers, accreditors, or any number of other roles should gain access, or that one of the roles should lose access (for instance, faculty-only forums). The roles may be different for different customers using the software, and many of the roles may not make any sense for some customers.

The second rule is more resilient in the face of such changes, because in essence it says that a user can access a given forum if they have read access to forums generally. The rule isn't perfect—you may decide there isn't any such thing as read access to forums generally (that is, access exists on a forum-by-forum basis)—but clearly it's much more flexible, especially if you can establish the relationship between roles and permissions outside of the code itself. And you can certainly do that.

---

[1] A role typically entails a set of permissions. The "release engineer" role, for example, might have permission to deploy software packages to servers.

As a general rule, prefer permission-based rules to role-based rules. There are exceptions (you'll see an example in recipe 7.2), but it holds in general.

Spring Security 3 appears schizophrenic on the issue of separating roles and permissions. The interface underlying ROLE_STUDENT, PERM_READ_FORUMS, and so forth is called GrantedAuthority, and this sounds like a fancy way of saying permission rather than role. But the examples in the Spring Security reference documentation tend to treat granted authorities as roles; even the hasRole() and hasAnyRole() predicates steer you toward using roles directly, which is at best a questionable practice for the reasons already given.[2]

Apparent schizophrenia aside, Spring Security makes it easy to do the right thing. The sample code, for instance, uses a custom UserDetailsService backed by the user/role/permission schema shown in figure 7.2.[3] The src/main/sql/schema.sql script contains this schema, but it's just an example. Even if you're using JdbcDaoImpl instead of a custom UserDetailsService, you can take advantage of the Spring Security group schema to separate roles and permissions.[4]

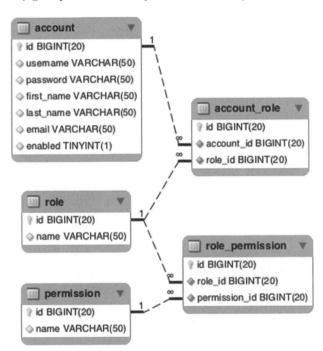

Figure 7.2 User schema that separates roles from permissions

---

[2] See Willie Wheeler, "Quick tip: Spring Security role-based authorization and permissions," October 27, 2010, http://mng.bz/010n, for a more extended treatment of this topic.

[3] The sample code uses BIGINTs but in real life you'll almost certainly want to use a smaller type, like INTs or even smaller. This will improve indexing and conserve storage. Of course, if you do need room for 18 quintillion accounts, then BIGINT is the data type for you.

[4] See Rich Freedman, "Spring Security Database Schema," August 19, 2008, http://mng.bz/NsB0, for more information. The basic idea is that groups are roles and granted authorities are permissions. The group schema itself is similar to figure 7.2.

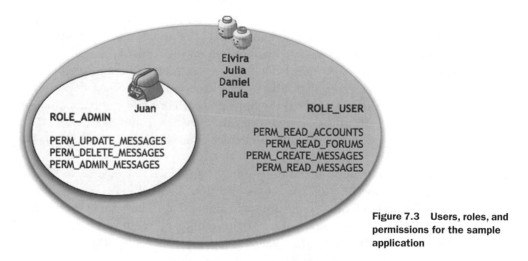

Figure 7.3   Users, roles, and permissions for the sample application

In addition to the schema, you also need sample data so you can test the security configuration. Figure 7.3 shows the roles and permissions that each sample user has, as contained in the `src/main/sql/data.sql` script.

That's it for source code changes. Now you need to activate the security annotations. To do that, you add a single line to the beans-security.xml configuration from recipe 6.1:

```
<global-method-security pre-post-annotations="enabled" />
```

You've enabled Spring Security's pre- and post-annotations, disabled by default, because they allow you to use SpEL to define access rules in an elegant fashion. This is the preferred approach in Spring Security 3. There are a couple of other options, which we'll list for completeness:

- `jsr250-annotations="enabled"`—Activates the standard JSR 250 security annotations. Although these are standard, they support only simple role-based rules and aren't nearly as powerful as Spring Security's pre/post annotations. These are disabled by default.
- `secured-annotations="enabled"`—Support for Spring's legacy `@Secured` annotation. Originally superseded by the JSR 250 `@RolesAllowed` annotation, and now by the Spring Security `@PreAuthorize` annotation. `@Secured` is disabled by default.

That's annotation-based configuration. To try the security annotations, try the following:

1 Start up the application, and click the Forums link. Spring Security forces a login because the call to `getForums()` requires the `PERM_READ_FORUMS` permission.

2 Log in as user `daniel/p@ssword`. He has just the student role.

3   Go into one of the forums, select a message, and try to block it (the link is available at the bottom of the message). You should get an error message in a dialog box because the `ForumServiceImpl.setMessageVisible()` method requires the `PERM_ADMIN_MESSAGES` permission, which the student role doesn't have.

4   Try the same thing with editing and deleting messages. You'll be able to access the edit page and the delete confirm box. But there will be an error message when you try to save the edit or confirm the deletion, because the student role doesn't have the required `PERM_UPDATE_MESSAGES` and `PERM_DELETE_MESSAGES` permissions.

5   Log out, and then log back in under `juan/p@ssword`. User `juan` has the admin role. Try the same operations. You should be able to execute all of them, because the admin role has the required permissions.

Discussion

The first authorization recipe showed how to create authorization rules and apply them to Java methods. You've focused on applying them to Java service beans, although it's also possible to use Spring Security with AspectJ to attach authorization rules to domain objects when implementing a domain-driven design.

    The next recipe shows how to secure views by applying authorization rules to code fragments inside a JSP.

7.2   Authorizing JSP views using authentication levels, roles, and permissions

PREREQUISITE
Recipe 6.1 Implementing login and logout with remember-me authentication

KEY TECHNOLOGIES
Spring Security 3 (including tag library), Spring Expression Language

Background

In many cases it's necessary to suppress JSP fragments.[5] One case would be where the fragment contains content the user isn't authorized to view. Another is where the fragment contains navigation pointing to pages the user isn't allowed to access.[6] This recipe shows how to use Spring Security 3 to implement this type of suppression.

    We'll use a basic forum application to illustrate the techniques involved.

Problem

Show or hide JSP page fragments based on the user's authentication level and role.

---

[5] Here we mean subsets of the content inside a JSP, rather than .jspf files per se.

[6] Note that there are also plenty of cases where it *does* make sense to show navigation that points to features or content the user can't access. One such example would involve trying to entice the user to purchase premium features or content.

Solution

Recipe 7.1 showed how to accomplish authorization based on authentication levels. We'll show how to add authorization based on roles and permissions. The main tool here is the Spring Security tag library.

Figure 7.4 presents the page navigation. The Home link appears for all users. The Forums link is present if the user has the read forums permission. The My Account and Logout (not displayed) links appear only if the user is authenticated; otherwise a Login link appears. Finally, the Admin link appears only if the user has the admin role.

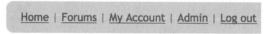

Home | Forums | My Account | Admin | Log out

Figure 7.4   Navigation display based on user authentication levels, roles, and permissions

To control the display, you use the `<spring:authorize access="[predicate]">` JSP tag along with SpEL predicates you saw in recipe 7.1. The tag displays its body if and only if the predicate evaluates `true` against the current principal.

Listing 7.2 shows how you use the predicates to implement the desired display controls.

Listing 7.2   subhead.jspf, containing the app's primary page navigation

```
<%@ taglib prefix="c" uri="http://java.sun.com/jsp/jstl/core" %>
<%@ taglib prefix="security"
    uri="http://www.springframework.org/security/tags" %>      ◁──┐  Security
                                                                ❶  tag library
<security:authentication var="myAccount" property="principal" />

<div id="topNav">
    <div id="welcomeUser">
        Hi,
        <security:authorize access="isAnonymous()">        ◁──┐  Checks for
            guest                                          ❷  anonymous
        </security:authorize>
        <security:authorize access="isAuthenticated()">    ◁──┐  Checks for
            <c:out value="${myAccount.firstName}" />       ❸  authenticated
        </security:authorize>
    </div>
    <div>
        <a href="${homeUrl}">Home</a>
        <security:authorize access="hasRole('PERM_READ_FORUMS')">  ◁──┐  Checks for
            | <a href="${forumsUrl}">Forums</a>                    ❹  permission
        </security:authorize>
        <security:authorize access="isAuthenticated()">
            <c:url var="myAccountUrl"
                value="${accountsPath}/${myAccount.username}.html" />
            | <a href="${myAccountUrl}">My Account</a>
        </security:authorize>
        <security:authorize access="hasRole('ROLE_ADMIN')">    ◁──┐  Checks for
            | <a href="${adminUrl}">Admin</a>                  ❺  admin role
        </security:authorize>
        <security:authorize access="isAnonymous()">
```

```
            |  <a href="${loginUrl}">Log in</a>
        </security:authorize>
        <security:authorize access="isAuthenticated()">
            |  <a href="${logoutUrl}">Log out</a>
        </security:authorize>
    </div>
    <div style="clear:both"></div>
</div>
```

As in recipe 6.1, you use the Spring Security tag library ❶ to implement page fragment shows and hides, and you use isAnonymous() ❷ and isAuthenticated() ❸ to decide whether to greet the user as a guest or by name. You use the same predicates to control the visibility of the My Account, Login, and Logout links.

The new piece is hasRole(). At ❹ you use it to show the Forums link according to whether the user has the PERM_READ_FORUMS permission, and at ❺ you use it to show the Admin link based on whether the user has the ROLE_ADMIN role. Keep in mind (as discussed in recipe 7.1) that the hasRole() predicate is a test for whether the specified granted authority exists; the granted authority doesn't strictly have to be a role.

Recall that recipe 7.1 mentioned that sometimes it does make sense to build access rules based on roles rather than permissions. Listing 7.2 provides a case in point. Here, it makes sense to tie the Admin page directly to the admin role, because that rule is unlikely to require revision: the page specifically targets the role. Similarly, it's fine to tie the Login link to isAnonymous(), and it's appropriate to tie the My Account and Logout links to isAuthenticated().

ANOTHER WAY TO SPECIFY A <SECURITY:AUTHORIZE> ACCESS CONDITION

There is a second way to specify access conditions for <security:authorize> tags. Instead of defining an access attribute, you can define a url attribute, along with an optional method attribute for HTTP methods, to establish an access condition. The idea is that the tag displays its body if and only if the user has access to the URL via the method in question. You'll see how to define access controls on a URL and method in the next recipe.

This approach is useful when rendering navigation, because it allows you to bind the visibility of a given navigation item to its access definition instead of duplicating what's essentially a single rule. You'll put this technique into use in recipe 7.3.

> ### What about the other <security:authorize> attributes?
> The <security:authorize> tag has other attributes we haven't covered: ifAnyGranted, ifAllGranted, and ifNotGranted. These are deprecated; use either access or url and method instead.

Discussion

This recipe showed how to hide links and content based on user authentication levels and roles. In the case of links, developers sometimes use the technique of hiding links as a substitute for proper access controls. This is known as *security by obscurity* and isn't generally considered real security, because users can still enter the target URL directly into the browser if they know or guess it.[7] Instead, the techniques in this recipe are more like user experience and usability techniques than security techniques where navigation and links are concerned. To defend the link targets against unauthorized access, it will help to have a way to selectively permit or deny HTTP requests, and that's what the next recipe shows how to do.

7.3 *Authorizing web resources using authentication levels, roles, and permissions*

PREREQUISITE
Recipe 6.1 Implementing login and logout with remember-me authentication

KEY TECHNOLOGIES
Spring Security 3

Background

In recipe 7.2, you saw how to display web-page content based on user authentication levels, roles, and permissions. This is often used as a way to keep the UI streamlined; in most cases it doesn't make sense to show users links that they aren't allowed to use.

But it's important not to mistake obscurity for security. Just because the link is hidden doesn't mean users can't get to it. To have real security, you must protect your web resources with access rules. This recipe shows how to do that.

Problem

Control users' access to web resources according to their authentication level, roles, and permissions.

Solution

You'll continue using Spring Security 3 to implement authentication-, role-, and permission-based authentication for the web URLs in your sample forum application. The relevant code is in the beans-security.xml file. You use the `intercept-url` element to define access rules for web URLs as shown in the following listing.

Listing 7.3 Defining access controls on URLs in beans-security.xml.

```
<?xml version="1.0" encoding="UTF-8"?>
<beans:beans xmlns="http://www.springframework.org/schema/security"
    xmlns:beans="http://www.springframework.org/schema/beans"
    xmlns:xsi="http://www.w3.org/2001/XMLSchema-instance"
    xsi:schemaLocation="http://www.springframework.org/schema/beans
        http://www.springframework.org/schema/beans/spring-beans-3.0.xsd
        http://www.springframework.org/schema/security
        http://www.springframework.org/schema/security/
```

---

[7] Try it using http://localhost:8080/sip/main/admin.html and some account other than `juan`. You'll find that you can still get to the admin page.

```
                    spring-security-3.0.xsd">
    <http auto-config="true" use-expressions="true">
        <intercept-url pattern="/skin/**" filters="none" />
        <intercept-url pattern="/styles/**" filters="none" />
        <intercept-url pattern="/scripts/**" filters="none" />
        <intercept-url pattern="/images/**" filters="none" />
        <intercept-url pattern="/home.html" method="GET"
            access="permitAll" />
        <intercept-url pattern="/admin.html" method="GET"
            access="hasRole('ROLE_ADMIN')" />
        <intercept-url pattern="/forums/*" method="GET"
            access="isAuthenticated()" />
        <intercept-url pattern="/forums/*/messages" method="POST"
            access="isAuthenticated()" />

        ... other rules ...

        <intercept-url pattern="/**" access="denyAll" />
        <form-login default-target-url="/home.html" />
        <logout logout-success-url="/home.html" />
        <access-denied-handler error-page="/accessdenied.html"/>
    </http>
    <authentication-manager>
        <authentication-provider user-service-ref="accountDao" />
    </authentication-manager>
</beans:beans>
```

1 Enables expressions

2 Disables filtering

3 Opens access to home page

4 Admins only

5 Forums require authentication

6 Posts message that requires authentication

7 Whitelists via denyAll

To define access rules, you once again take advantage of SpEL. You do that by setting use-expressions="true" at **1**. Prior to Spring Security 3, there was a non-SpEL method of defining rules. That approach is now legacy, so we won't cover it here.

Now you have the <intercept-url> rules. Before looking at the specific rules, let's discuss the high-level approach and some details about the mechanics of defining a rule.

As with recipe 7.1, you adopt the best practice of defining access on a whitelist model. To implement a whitelist, bear in mind that rules are evaluated on a first-match basis; that is, the first rule in the list with a pattern that matches the request URL is the rule that applies. Therefore you need to place more specific patterns before more general patterns. You make your list a whitelist by making the most general rule one that denies access to all resources using denyAll.

To specify rules, you use a URL pattern, an optional HTTP method (GET, POST, PUT, DELETE, and so on), and either filters="none" or access="[predicate]". The rule applies to all HTTP methods if the method is omitted. The first option, filters="none", indicates that the pattern and method don't require authentication, authorization, or any other security services. The second option allows you to use SpEL to define the conditions under which the user can use the URL/method pair in question.

The patterns have two possible syntaxes, which you choose by setting the path-type attribute on the containing <http> element. The default syntax is Ant, which uses either path-type="ant" or nothing because it's the default. The alternative is regular expression syntax via path-type="regex". You'll use the default Ant-style syntax.

Now let's look at the specific rules. The first four use `filters="none"` to indicate that neither the skin files nor the static assets (images, CSS, JavaScript) require security services ❷.

Next you have rules for specific URL and method combinations. Although the methods are optional, it's a good practice to specify them explicitly to avoid opening up access unnecessarily. (This is very much in line with the whitelist approach.) At ❸ you use `permitAll` to specify that `GET` requests for the home page are always to be granted. At ❹ you use `hasRole('ROLE_ADMIN')` to ensure that only administrators have access to the admin page. You define additional access rules for forums and messages at ❺ and ❻. Although it would have been possible to use Ant's `**` wildcard to shorten the list of rules, doing so would effectively create a blacklist inside of the whitelist, and from a security perspective it's safer to require grants to be explicit.

At ❼ you create the `denyAll` rule that makes your rule list a whitelist.

To test this:

- Try to access http://localhost:8080/sip/admin.html anonymously by manually entering it in the browser's address bar. You should be redirected to a login page. If you log in as `juan`, the request should succeed; otherwise, you should get the access-denied page.
- Log into the app as `elvira` using the normal login process. Once you've done so, manually enter the admin URL from the previous bullet. Unlike in recipe 7.2, you should now get the access-denied page.

There's one loose end to tie up before we move on to the next recipe.

UPDATING THE PAGE NAVIGATION TO ELIMINATE RULE DUPLICATION

In recipe 7.2, we pointed out that it's possible to specify `<security:authorize>` access rules in terms of URLs and HTTP methods instead of defining access conditions explicitly. Recall that the idea is to bind the display of a navigation item to the user's access to that item such that you can define the access rule in a single location (such as beans-security.xml) instead of defining it in two. Indeed, let's update subhead.jspf to take advantage of this feature (see listing 7.2 for the original listing):

```
<security:authorize url="${servletPath}/home.html" method="GET">
    <a href="${homeUrl}">Home</a>
</security:authorize>
<security:authorize url="${servletPath}/account/*" method="GET">
    <c:url var="accountUrl"
        value="${accountPath}/${myAccount.username}.html" />
    | <a href="${accountUrl}">My Account</a>
</security:authorize>
<security:authorize url="${servletPath}/admin.html" method="GET">
    | <a href="${adminUrl}">Admin</a>
</security:authorize>
<security:authorize access="isAnonymous()">
    | <a href="${loginUrl}">Log in</a>
</security:authorize>
<security:authorize access="isAuthenticated()">
    | <a href="${logoutUrl}">Log out</a>
</security:authorize>
```

Now, when you change the rules in beans-security.xml, the `<security:authorize>` tag's behavior automatically reflects the change. You can define rules authoritatively in the Spring Security configuration file instead of duplicating rule definitions in the JSPs.

Discussion

In the preceding three recipes, you've assumed fairly simple requirements around access, mostly around application-wide roles and permissions. For example, you've assumed that users either do or don't have permission to edit messages.

Real-world access requirements tend to be more nuanced. You might want each forum to have a moderator with administrative privileges over that forum, rather than having just a single site administrator. For any given message, you might want the site admin, the forum moderator, and the original author to have edit permissions, but no one else. You might want the site admin and forum moderator to be able to block, unblock, and delete messages, but nobody else.

The requirements just described require machinery more powerful than that offered so far, because they're based not on simple application-wide permissions but on relationships between a principal and a domain object being accessed. A given user either is or isn't the moderator for a given forum, and the answer makes a difference in terms of what the user is allowed to do with messages in that forum.

Recipes 7.4 and 7.5 show how to implement domain object security using Spring Security 3 access control lists.

7.4   Authorizing method invocations based on ACLs

PREREQUISITE
Recipe 6.1 Implementing login and logout with remember-me authentication
Recipe 7.1 Authorizing Java methods using authentication levels, roles, and permissions

KEY TECHNOLOGIES
Spring Security 3

Background

This is the first of two recipes that deal with authorizing access to and displaying specific domain objects that exist in your system. Keeping with the discussion forum example, imagine that you want to allow the author, the forum moderator, and the site admin to edit a message after it's been posted, and nobody else. Additionally, moderators must be able to block, unblock, and delete messages in forums they moderate.[8]

Enter access control lists (ACLs). The idea is that each domain object has an associated list of access rules specifying who is allowed to do what with the object. Each rule, more formally known as an access control entry (ACE), specifies an actor, an action, and either `grant` or `deny`, indicating whether the actor may perform the action on the

---

[8] You'll handle part of this requirement around blocking, unblocking, and deleting messages in this recipe. Recipe 7.5 completes the treatment of that requirement.

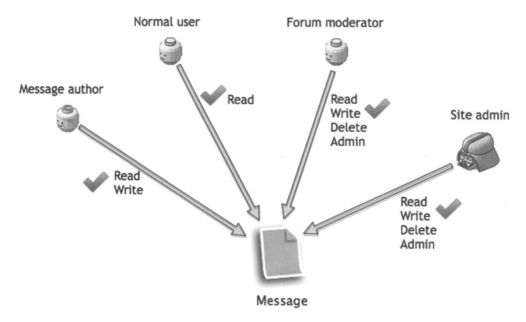

Figure 7.5   An ACL for a message. The author has one set of permissions with respect to the message, and other users have other permissions.

domain object. The end result is that you can resolve questions like, "Can Juan edit message 106?" This gives you the ability to define fine-grained access rules. See figure 7.5 for a visual explanation of access control lists.

Speaking more conceptually, you have actors, targets, and actions. Actors (like Daniel) want to perform actions (like editing) against domain object targets (like message 106). You need to decide in any given instance whether the desired action is permissible. This is where Spring Security's ACL module helps.

ACL-based authorization is more complex than role-based authorization. With role-based authorization, you manage predicates on principals without worrying about specific targets. You can use role-based authorization to answer questions like. "Can Daniel edit messages generally?" ACL-based authorization is finer-grained and involves managing relationships between actors and targets. Figure 7.6 shows the difference between role-based and ACL-based authorization.

With that background, you're ready to tackle the rest of the recipe.

Problem

Authorize service method invocations involving domain objects based on the relationship between the principal and the domain object(s) in question. Specifically, the author, the forum moderator, and the site admin must be able to edit existing posts. You also need to lay the groundwork allowing moderators to block, unblock, and delete posts, although that will require additional work in recipe 7.5.

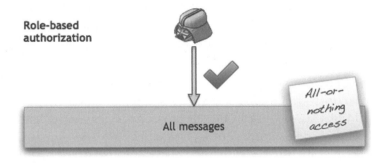

Role-based authorization

All messages

All-or-nothing access

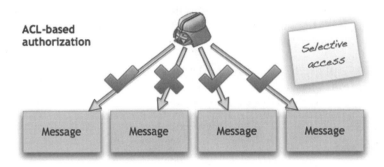

ACL-based authorization

Selective access

Message | Message | Message | Message

Figure 7.6 With role-based authorization, a user might have permission to (say) edit messages in general. With ACL-based authorization, you can set user edit permissions on a message-by-message basis.

Solution

You'll use the Spring Security ACL module to implement domain object authorization. Here's a roadmap of the recipe ahead:

- *Defining domain object ACLs*—First we'll cover the basics of granting (or, less commonly, denying) user permissions on domain objects using the ACL database schema to drive the discussion. (For example, "Daniel has permission to edit message 106.")
- *Defining ACL-based access rules for Java methods*—You'll see how to use annotations to define ACL-based access rules, specified in terms of user permissions, on Java methods. (For example, "Allow the method invocation if the current user has permission to edit the passed message.")
- *Configuring Spring Security for ACLs*—You need configuration to activate domain object security. You'll learn how to do that.
- *Optimizing ACL definition*—We'll look at ways to simplify and streamline ACL definitions.
- *Manipulating ACLs programmatically*—We'll look at programmatic manipulation of ACL data, which is often necessary in cases where the app creates new domain objects. (For example, give the author of a new message permission to edit the message even after it has already been posted.)

Because the ACL module is database-driven, you'll start there both to get a good grasp of the key concepts and details on the database schema. Note that the schema we're about to cover replaces the one from the earlier recipes, so you should rebuild the database using the scripts at src/main/sql at this time.

DEFINING DOMAIN OBJECT ACLS

To begin, you need to understand some key ACL concepts and how to define user permissions on domain objects so you can define access rules in terms of said permissions. The ACL database schema is the logical place to start both because it highlights the concepts and because it's where you define the user permissions.

The ACL module has four tables to store actors, actions, and targets (domain objects). Together they provide a framework for defining access rules for specific domain objects. Spring Security uses the access rules to make access decisions.

Figure 7.7 is the E/R diagram for the ACL module. Again, see the sample code for the MySQL scripts.[9]

> **TIP** In figure 7.7, all the IDs are MySQL BIGINTs. It's unlikely in the extreme that you'll require BIGINTs for your dataset, and using them consumes space unnecessarily. It pays to think about your expected data volumes and choose data widths accordingly.

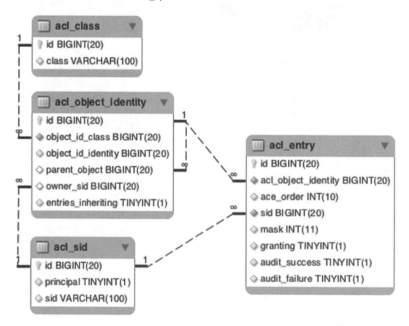

Figure 7.7   E/R diagram for the Spring Security ACL schema

9   Alternatively, see Willie Wheeler, "Spring Security 3 database schemas for MySQL," July 6, 2010, http:// mng.bz/Q3IZ.

Let's go over the tables in detail because it will help you better understand how ACL-based security works. As an example, you'll define a rule that grants user `daniel` permission to edit message 106.

You represent actors using the acl_sid table. A security identity (SID) can be a principal such as an end user or a system or a granted authority such as the admin role or even a system-wide permission as noted in recipe 7.1.

The principal column is a flag indicating whether the SID is a principal or a granted authority, and the sid column contains a username or granted authority name accordingly. Together the principal and sid columns allow Spring Security to associate SIDs in the ACL schema with app users and granted authorities, as figure 7.8 shows.

To be concrete, consider user `daniel` with a role called `ROLE_USER`. Table 7.3 shows how the sample app maps these to rows in the acl_sid table.

id	principal	sid
100	0	ROLE_USER
201	1	daniel

Table 7.3   Sample acl_sid rows (SIDs)

The IDs are arbitrary, but the other columns aren't. SID 100 is the granted authority (here, a role) called `ROLE_USER`. There is a corresponding row—that is, a row where the name is `ROLE_USER`—in your application's role table. SID 201 is the principal named `daniel`. Once again there is a corresponding row—a row where the username is `daniel`—in your application's account table. (See the sample code.)

You represent domain object targets using the acl_class and acl_object_identity tables, which model domain object types and instances, respectively. In the acl_class table, there are only two columns: id and class. The id column is an arbitrary ID. The

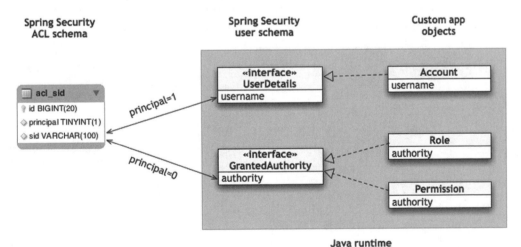

Figure 7.8   How Spring Security links its ACL schema to its user schema. This allows Spring Security to support custom app objects because the Spring Security user schema uses Java interfaces.

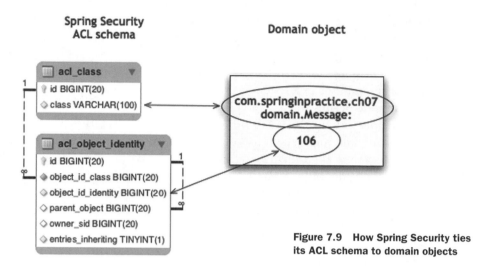

Figure 7.9   How Spring Security ties its ACL schema to domain objects

class column holds a fully qualified classname, such as `com.springinpractice.ch07`
`.domain.Message`.

There's a lot going on in acl_object_identity, whose rows are referred to as OIDs.
Each OID is Spring Security's representation of an application domain object. The
object_id_class column references the acl_class table and allows you to specify the
domain object's type. The object_id_identity column is for the domain object's native
ID, which Spring Security assumes to be numeric and exposed by an `id` property on
the domain object. Together these two columns pick out a domain object.

Continuing with the example, suppose you want to represent message ID 106. You
need to create a corresponding OID using the acl_class and acl_object_identity tables
in the ACL schema. (If the class already exists in `acl_class`, then you need create only
a row in acl_object_identity.) Figure 7.9 presents the situation schematically.

Tables 7.4 and 7.5 show the same thing in record form.

id	class
3	com.springinpractice.ch07.domain.Message

Table 7.4   Representing messages generally using acl_class

id	object_id_class	object_id_identity
112	3	106

Table 7.5   Representing message 106 using acl_object_identity (some columns suppressed)

In tables 7.4 and 7.5, the IDs in the `id` column (3 and 112 for class and OID, respectively) are arbitrary. But the ID in the object_id_identity column isn't. It contains the
message's native ID, which is 106.

We've focused on a subset of the OID columns, but there are a few other columns:
parent_object, entries_inheriting, and owner_id. These are more advanced in nature,
so we'll ignore them in this first pass and return to them shortly.

Actions are what SIDs want to do with OIDs, such as creating or editing them. Each row in the acl_entry table, or ACE, is essentially an assertion to the effect that such-and-such SID either does or doesn't have permission to perform such-and-such action on such-and-such OID. Each ACE involves a SID, an OID, a permission, and either grant or deny. The list of ACEs for a given OID is the OID's ACL.

Let's talk about permissions. The simplest way to think about permissions is that the BasePermission class defines five default permissions with associated codes (*masks*), as shown in table 7.6.

Table 7.6 ACL permissions and their numeric values

Permission	Mask	Notes
READ	1	
WRITE	2	
CREATE	4	
DELETE	8	
ADMINISTRATION	16	Principals with this permission can manipulate the object's ACL.

The precise interpretation of the specific permissions depends on the application, but they correspond to the standard CRUD (create, read, update and delete) operations plus an administrative operation. Principals with the administrative permission are able to manage the corresponding object's ACL (add or remove ACEs, change parent, change ownership, change audit information, and so on). There are other ways to be able to manage object ACLs, and you'll see those later in the recipe.

Up to 32 distinct permissions are possible, although the 5 just given should be sufficient for many use cases. If you create additional permissions, their masks must be powers of 2.[10]

Use only one ACE per permission

Spring Security supports up to 32 permissions: the 5 defaults from table 7.6 and up to 27 custom permissions. You can represent individual permissions using a bit index i (0-31) or, equivalently, as integers of the form 2^i, which explains why the default codes are all powers of 2. So far, so good.

---

[10] In some cases custom permissions are helpful. Our current project, for instance, is a software deployment automation system. Permission to deploy to environments like dev, test, and prod varies with role; for example, developers can deploy to the development environment but not to production. We distinguish the ability to update the environment domain object from the ability to update the real-world environment. We use the standard WRITE permission for the former and a custom DEPLOY permission for the latter, because the ability to update an environment's description (say) is distinct from the ability to deploy a change to it.

(continued)

Besides representing individual permissions, you might want to represent sets of permissions, as when granting such-and-such user both READ and WRITE permissions on some message. Bitmasks are a well-established and economical way to do that. The number 3, for instance, represents this combination because 3 = 1 (READ) + 2 (WRITE).

Unfortunately, despite the use of the mask terminology in the database table and in the API, the default ACL implementation, AclImpl, doesn't support arbitrary bitmasks. You can't grant READ and WRITE using a single ACE with the mask set to 3. Instead you need to create an ACE for the READ permission and a second ACE for the WRITE permission. The reason is somewhat difficult,[11] but suffice to say that many Spring Security beginners understandably but incorrectly assume that they can place bitmasks in the mask column.

It looks like Spring Security 3.1 will make it possible for AclImpl to treat the mask as a true bitmask using a strategy interface.[12]

There's also a granting flag. If it's 1, the ACE grants the permission. If it's 0, the ACE denies the permission.

Table 7.7 shows a sample ACE, one that grants the edit (a.k.a. write) permission to your hero daniel for message 106.

Table 7.7   Granting Daniel permission to edit message 106 (some columns suppressed)

id	acl_object_identity	ace_order	sid	mask	granting
42	112	0	201	2	1

SID 201 corresponds to daniel as per table 7.3, and OID 112 corresponds to message 106 as per table 7.5. The mask value 2 indicates the WRITE permission as per table 7.6, and granting value 1 means that you're granting the permission rather than denying it.

The ace_order column is the ACE's 0-indexed order in the domain object's ACL. The org.springframework.security.acls.model.Acl interface doesn't specify semantics for the ACE order. See the Javadoc for AclImpl.isGranted() for details on how the order matters for the default AclImpl implementation.[13]

Those are the basics. You're now ready to learn how to define access rules on Java methods in terms of user permissions like the one you've just defined.

---

[11] For a detailed explanation, see "ACE masks are not being compared as bitmasks," https://jira.springsource .org/browse/SEC-1140.

[12] "Provide strategy interface for AclImpl isGranted() method," https://jira.springsource.org/browse/SEC-1166.

[13] It's fairly complicated, but the basic idea is that the first matching ACE is the one that wins. But that's a simplification; again, consult the Javadoc for details.

DEFINING ACL-BASED ACCESS RULES FOR JAVA METHODS

You saw in recipe 7.1 that Spring Security provides an `@PreAuthorize` annotation that allows you to define access rules for Java methods using SpEL expressions. In recipe 7.1 you defined rules in terms of authentication status, roles, and system-wide permissions. But now you're going to define rules in terms of permissions on domain objects.

As it happens, Spring Security supports several access-control annotations, as shown in table 7.8.

Table 7.8 Annotations for controlling access to Java methods

Annotation	Description
`@PreAuthorize(expression)`	Checks the expression before allowing access to the annotated method
`@PostAuthorize(expression)`	Checks the expression after executing the method but before returning the return value to the caller
`@PreFilter(value=expression [, filterTarget=collection])`	Filters a collection of domain objects before passing it into the annotated method
`@PostFilter(expression)`	Filters a collection of domain objects returned from the annotated method before returning them to the caller

As we just mentioned, the expressions can reference domain objects. Table 7.9 introduces the SpEL expressions that support this.

Table 7.9 SpEL expressions for domain object security

Expression	Description
`#paramName`	Variable referring to a method argument by parameter name.
`filterObject`	Term referring to an arbitrary collection element in a filter annotation (either `@PreFilter` or `@PostFilter`).
`returnValue`	Term referring to the method's return value. Used in `@PostAuthorize`.
`hasPermission( domainObject, permission)`	Predicate indicating whether the current principal has a given permission on a given domain object. Legal values for `permission` are `read`, `write`, `create`, `delete`, and `admin` (no quotes).

Let's look at a few examples from the class `ForumServiceImpl` in the sample code.

First, here's `@PreAuthorize`:

```
@PreAuthorize("hasPermission(#message, delete)")
public void deleteMessage(Message message) { ... }
```

In the snippet, the rule is to allow entry into the method if and only if the current principal has the delete permission on the message being passed in. Spring Security checks this by matching on the `Message` class and domain object ID as previously described. You use the special variable syntax, #message, to reference the passed message.[14]

The @PostAuthorize annotation isn't as generally useful as @PreAuthorize, but it has its uses. Sometimes you want to drive access decisions based on something other than object IDs. For instance, the sample app allows forum moderators and site admins to block messages. Only users with the admin permission on a blocked message should be able to see it. The following code snippet shows how to use the @Post-Authorize annotation to accomplish this:

```
@PreAuthorize("permitAll")
@PostAuthorize(
    "(hasPermission(returnObject, read) and returnObject.visible) or
        hasPermission(returnObject, admin)")
public Message getMessage(long id) { ... }
```

In this example, you have no way of knowing whether the message is visible based on the message ID alone. You have to get the message (using the special returnObject term), check for the read permission (using the hasPermission predicate), and then check its visibility. @PostAuthorize is useful in such cases.

Notice that you're also using a @PreAuthorize("permitAll") annotation. The reason is that ForumServiceImpl has a type-level @PreAuthorize("denyAll") annotation whose purpose is to create a whitelist security model as we explained in recipe 7.1. You have to override that annotation so calls can enter the method.

The sample app doesn't use the @PreFilter annotation, and it's not commonly used, but for completeness we'll say something about it here. Prefiltering can be useful where bulk operations on domain objects are concerned. It allows you to remove a domain object from the bulk operation when the current principal doesn't have permission to perform the operation on that domain object. The domain objects need to be part of a java.util.Collection (an array won't work), and the Collection needs to support the remove() method. Null values in the collection aren't allowed.

Suppose, hypothetically, that you wanted to support a bulk delete on messages. The following code would allow you to do that:

```
@PreAuthorize("permitAll")
@PreFilter("hasPermission(filterObject, delete)")
public void deleteMessages(List<Message> messages) { ... }
```

You'd need to use @PreAuthorize("permitAll"). But after that, you'd use the @Pre-Filter annotation with the special filterObject (representing an arbitrary collection element) and hasPermission expressions to exclude messages for which the current principal lacks the delete permission.

In this case you have only one collection parameter, but if you had more than one, you'd use the filterTarget element to choose one.

---

[14] If you're wondering how Spring Security knows the parameter name, the answer is that it uses compiler debug information. You must compile the code with the debug local variable information turned on in order for this feature to work. There are other such examples in Spring, especially in Spring Web MVC.

When a method returns a collection of domain objects, sometimes you want to filter out individual elements before handing them over to the caller. That's what @PostFilter is for. The following snippet includes a given forum in the result set if—and only if—the principal has read permission on the forum:

```
@PreAuthorize("permitAll")
@PostFilter("hasPermission(filterObject, read)")
public List<Forum> getForums() { ... }
```

As with @PreFilter, you use filterObject and hasPermission to perform the desired filtering.

The annotations define the access rules, but you need to activate them to make them do anything. You'll need to add configuration to make that work.

CONFIGURING DOMAIN OBJECT SECURITY

There are a couple of different pieces to the configuration. First, you make a minor tweak to the <global-method-security> definition in beans-security.xml:

```
<global-method-security pre-post-annotations="enabled">
    <expression-handler ref="expressionHandler" />
</global-method-security>
```

Here you add an explicit expression handler definition to the <global-method-security> definition. Although <global-method-security> creates a default expression handler, it can't handle hasPermission() expressions because it doesn't come with a permission handler. You address that with a new beans-security-acl.xml configuration as shown next.

Listing 7.4   beans-security-acl.xml, supporting domain object security

```
<?xml version="1.0" encoding="UTF-8"?>
<beans xmlns="http://www.springframework.org/schema/beans"              Expression   ❶
    xmlns:p="http://www.springframework.org/schema/p"                    handler
    xmlns:xsi="http://www.w3.org/2001/XMLSchema-instance"
    xsi:schemaLocation="http://www.springframework.org/schema/beans
        http://www.springframework.org/schema/beans/spring-beans-3.0.xsd">

    <bean id="expressionHandler"
        class="org.springframework.security.access.expression.method.
            DefaultMethodSecurityExpressionHandler"               ACL permission   ❷
        p:permissionEvaluator-ref="permissionEvaluator" />            evaluator
    <bean id="permissionEvaluator"
        class="org.springframework.security.acls.AclPermissionEvaluator">
        <constructor-arg ref="aclService" />
    </bean>
    <bean id="aclService" class="org.springframework.security.acls.
        jdbc.JdbcMutableAclService">
        <constructor-arg ref="dataSource" />                         ACL service   ❸
        <constructor-arg ref="lookupStrategy" />
        <constructor-arg ref="aclCache" />                            JDBC ACL     ❹
    </bean>                                                       lookup strategy
    <bean id="lookupStrategy" class="org.springframework.security.
        acls.jdbc.BasicLookupStrategy">
```

```
        <constructor-arg ref="dataSource" />
        <constructor-arg ref="aclCache" />                    Audit logger  5
        <constructor-arg ref="aclAuthzStrategy" />
        <constructor-arg>
            <bean class="org.springframework.security.acls.domain.
                ConsoleAuditLogger" />
        </constructor-arg>
    </bean>                                                    ACL cache  6
    <bean id="aclCache" class="org.springframework.security.acls.
        domain.EhCacheBasedAclCache">
        <constructor-arg>
            <bean class="org.springframework.cache.ehcache.
                EhCacheFactoryBean" p:cacheName="aclCache">
                <property name="cacheManager">
                    <bean class="org.springframework.cache.ehcache.
                        EhCacheManagerFactoryBean"/>
                </property>
            </bean>
        </constructor-arg>
    </bean>                                              7  ACL authorization
    <bean id="aclAuthzStrategy"                             strategy
        class="org.springframework.security.acls.domain.
            AclAuthorizationStrategyImpl">
        <constructor-arg>
            <list>
                <ref local="adminRole" />
                <ref local="adminRole" />
                <ref local="adminRole" />
            </list>
        </constructor-arg>
    </bean>
    <bean id="adminRole" class="org.springframework.security.core.
        authority.GrantedAuthorityImpl">
        <constructor-arg value="admin" />
    </bean>
</beans>
```

Figure 7.10 is the same expression handler configuration as a bean dependency graph.

You use the beans namespace in listing 7.4 rather than the security namespace. The security namespace doesn't (at the time of this writing, anyway) directly support ACL configuration, so you need to do everything explicitly.

First you define the expression handler ❶. It's still the default expression handler, but you're giving it a nondefault configuration by injecting a permission evaluator that knows how to handle hasPermission() expressions, which is the whole point of the beans-security-acl.xml configuration. The specific permission evaluator you need is the AclPermissionEvaluator, so you create one at ❷.

The permission evaluator relies on an ACL service for ACL CRUD operations. You use a JdbcMutableAclService ❸ because your ACLs are in a database (that's the JDBC part) and you want to be able to create, update, and delete ACLs as you create, update, and delete the corresponding domain objects (that's the mutable part). Because it's a

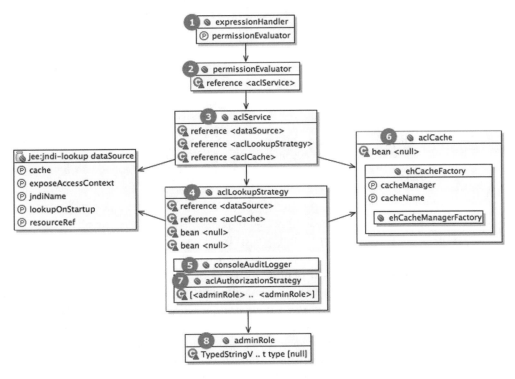

Figure 7.10   ACL configuration as a bean dependency graph

JDBC-based ACL service, you inject a data source. The service also uses caching for performance, so you inject an Ehcache-backed cache too ⑥.[15]

ACL lookups are the most common operation, so for performance the ACL service delegates them to a `LookupStrategy`. This allows you to adopt DBMS-specific optimizations as desired. For simplicity you use a `BasicLookupStrategy` ④, which is based on ANSI SQL. It doesn't have DBMS-specific optimizations, but it attempts to be performant within the confines of ANSI SQL. The `BasicLookupStrategy` uses the same data source and cache that the `JdbcMutableAclService` uses. You also inject a console logger ⑤ for logging purposes.

The `BasicLookupStrategy` also has an `AclAuthorizationStrategyImpl` ⑦, which it injects into the `AclImpls` that it returns from lookups. The `AclAuthorization-StrategyImpl` supports ACL administration by authorizing ACL modification attempts. Its constructor takes an array of three granted authorities as described in table 7.10.

You'll learn a little more about how these constructor arguments work when we discuss programmatic ACL management, but the idea is that not just anybody can

---

[15] Don't forget to configure your Ehcache, at least for production. See http://ehcache.org/documentation/configuration.html for information on how to do that.

Table 7.10 `AclAuthorizationStrategyImpl` **constructor arguments**

Index	Param name	Description
0	Change ownership	Authority able to change ACL ownership. That is, the specified authority has the special `AclAuthorizationStrategy.CHANGE_OWNERSHIP` permission.
1	Change auditing	Authority able to modify auditing details. That is, the specified authority has the special `AclAuthorizationStrategy.CHANGE_AUDITING` permission.
2	Change general	Authority able to change other ACL and ACE details (for example, inserting an ACE into an ACL or changing an ACL's parent). That is, the specified authority has the special `AclAuthorizationStrategy.CHANGE_GENERAL` permission.

manage (create, modify, and delete) ACLs. We already mentioned in connection with table 7.6 that one way to manage an object's ACL is to have the administrative permission on that object. Another way is to have the authority or authorities injected into the `AclAuthorizationStrategyImpl` constructor, because each entails a special ACL management permission. (These aren't to be confused with the normal permissions that appear inside the ACLs. You can think of the special permissions as metapermissions that sit outside the ACLs, determining who can change the ACLs.) In practice, the authority you pass into all three constructor slots is a system-wide administrative authority, and indeed that's what you've configured here.

That covers the ACL configuration. Now let's look at some optimizations you can make to your ACL definitions.

OPTIMIZING ACL DEFINITIONS

In the first pass, we skipped over the `parent_object` and `entries_inheriting` columns in the `acl_object_identity` table. These columns allow you to simplify the management of your ACLs and also to save what could potentially be a lot of storage space by creating OID hierarchies and then allowing OIDs to inherit ACEs from parent OIDs.

For example, in the sample app, you want the administrator to have the write permission (among others) for all messages in all forums, and you want forum moderators to have the write permission for all messages in forums they moderate. Although you could create one ACE for every <SID, OID> pair, this approach doesn't scale well. There are lots of users and lots of messages, and if you have to create a new set of ACEs for every new user or new message, things will get out of control in a hurry.

Instead you can do the following:

- Establish a parent-child relationship between forums and messages using the parent_object column on message OIDs.
- Set `entries_inheriting` true on the message OIDs so that messages automatically inherit ACEs from their parent forums.
- Give the site admin the write permission on the individual forums, and give forum moderators the write permission on the forums they moderate. The messages will inherit ACEs from the forum ACLs, allowing you to avoid creating lots of message ACEs.

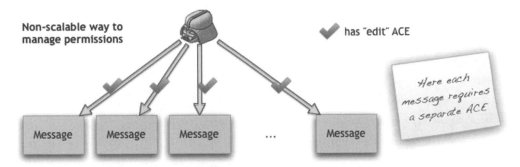

Figure 7.11 Creating separate ACEs for each message. Don't do this!

The preceding is easier to understand with a diagram. First see figure 7.11.

In figure 7.11, your user has the write (or edit) permission on each message, and you implement this using one ACE per message. Using this approach, if you want to give the user read permission on the messages, you need to create another set of ACEs granting the read permission. If you decide to revoke the write permission, you'll need to delete all the ACEs.

Compare the approach from figure 7.11 to the superior approach in figure 7.12.

In figure 7.12, you establish parent/child relationships between the forum and its messages using the `parent_object` column. Then you give the user the write permission on the forum. Finally you use inheritance to grant the user the write permission on the messages by setting `entries_inheriting` to true. Notice that this solves the issues we mentioned: you can add and revoke permissions on the messages by adding and revoking a single permission on the forum.

We need to cover one additional topic: manipulating ACLs programmatically.

MANIPULATING ACLS PROGRAMMATICALLY

Because applications create, update, and delete domain objects, you need to ensure that you keep the various ACL schema objects in sync. If you create a message, you need to create a corresponding OID and ACL. If you delete a message, you need to delete the corresponding OID and ACL as well.

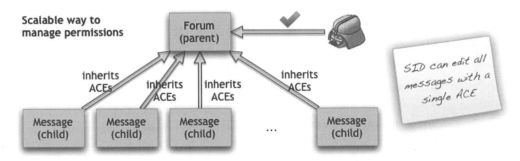

Figure 7.12 Best practice: establish parent/child relationships, then inherit permissions

Spring Security makes this possible via an ACL management API called Mutable-AclService. You included a JdbcMutableAclService in the configuration in listing 7.4. The following listing shows how you can use a MutableAclService to manage the creation, updating, and deletion of messages.

Listing 7.5 Using `MutableAclService` to manage message ACLs

```java
package com.springinpractice.ch07.service.impl;

import javax.inject.Inject;

import org.springframework.security.access.prepost.PreAuthorize;
import org.springframework.security.acls.domain.BasePermission;
import org.springframework.security.acls.domain.ObjectIdentityImpl;
import org.springframework.security.acls.domain.PrincipalSid;
import org.springframework.security.acls.model.MutableAcl;
import org.springframework.security.acls.model.MutableAclService;
import org.springframework.security.acls.model.ObjectIdentity;
import org.springframework.security.acls.model.Sid;
import org.springframework.stereotype.Service;
import org.springframework.transaction.annotation.Transactional;

import com.springinpractice.ch07.dao.MessageDao;
import com.springinpractice.ch07.domain.Forum;
import com.springinpractice.ch07.domain.Message;
import com.springinpractice.ch07.service.ForumService;

... other imports ...

@Service
@PreAuthorize("denyAll")                                    ❶ Declares
@Transactional                                                @Transactional
public class ForumServiceImpl implements ForumService {
    @Inject private MessageDao messageDao;
    @Inject private MutableAclService aclService;           ❷ Injects
                                                              MutableAclService
    ... other fields ...

    @PreAuthorize("hasRole('PERM_WRITE_MESSAGES')")
    public void createMessage(Message message) {
        messageDao.create(message);
        createAcl(message);                                 ❸ Calls
    }                                                         createAcl()

    @PreAuthorize("hasPermission(#message, admin)")
    public void setMessageVisible(Message message) {
        Message pMessage = messageDao.get(message.getId());
        pMessage.setVisible(message.isVisible());
        messageDao.update(pMessage);
        updateAcl(pMessage);                                ❹ Calls
    }                                                         updateAcl()

    @PreAuthorize("hasPermission(#message, delete)")
    public void deleteMessage(Message message) {
        messageDao.delete(message);
        deleteAcl(message);                                 ❺ Calls
    }                                                         deleteAcl()
```

```
    private void createAcl(Message message) {                          createAcl()
        Long forumId = message.getForum().getId();              6    implementation
        ObjectIdentity forumOid =
            new ObjectIdentityImpl(Forum.class, forumId);
        MutableAcl forumAcl =                                      7  Gets forum
            (MutableAcl) aclService.readAclById(forumOid);            ACL
        MutableAcl messageAcl =
            aclService.createAcl(getMessageOid(message));      8  Creates message ACL
        messageAcl.setParent(forumAcl);

        Sid author = new PrincipalSid(message.getAuthor().getUsername());
        if (message.isVisible()) {                                  Grants write
            messageAcl.insertAce(                               9   permission to author
                0, BasePermission.WRITE, author, true);
        }
                                                            10  Sets owner to author
        messageAcl.setOwner(author);
        aclService.updateAcl(messageAcl);                    11  Updates ACL
    }

    private void deleteAcl(Message message) {                        deleteAcl()
        aclService.deleteAcl(getMessageOid(message), true);    12  implementation
    }

    private void updateAcl(Message message) {                        updateAcl()
        deleteAcl(message);                                    13  implementation
        createAcl(message);
    }

    private ObjectIdentity getMessageOid(Message message) {
        return new ObjectIdentityImpl(Message.class, message.getId());
    }

    ... other methods ...
}
```

Listing 7.5 is `ForumServiceImpl`, which we referenced earlier when going over the security annotations. Like the other service beans, you declare it to be `@Transactional` ❶, which matters here in part because you want your domain modifications to execute in the same transactional context as your ACL modifications.

You inject a `MutableAclService` at ❷ because this is your API into the Spring Security ACL module.

You have different message modification methods that create, update, and delete messages. Each, in addition to modifying the domain model, makes a call as appropriate to `createAcl()` ❸, `updateAcl()` ❹, or `deleteAcl()` ❺ to keep the ACL model in sync with the domain model.

The `createAcl()` implementation ❻ is the most interesting. You create a forum OID, then use it to issue a forum ACL lookup against the ACL service ❼. Then you create a new message ACL and corresponding OID ❽. By default, the `JdbcMutableAclService` assigns OID ownership to the current principal, which may or may not be the author, as you'll see. Ownership is back-ended by the `owner_sid` column of the `acl_object_identity` table, which you saw in figure 7.9. Spring Security doesn't specify what it means to own a domain object, but by default the owner is allowed to perform administrative actions on the associated ACL in precisely the same way the admin ACL permission (see table 7.6) and the `AclAuthorizationStrategyImpl` constructor authorities (see table 7.10) can.

Now that you've created the message ACL, you make the forum ACL its parent. The current principal can do this because it owns the current OID, as noted. Any principal with the `AclAuthorizationStrategy.CHANGE_GENERAL` metapermission (see table 7.10) can change an OID's parent.

At ❾ you give the author write permission on the message if the message is visible. The idea is that the author can edit their own messages as long as an administrator hasn't put an administrative block on the message (that is, an administrator hasn't made it invisible). This change requires the `AclAuthorizationStrategy.CHANGE _GENERAL` metapermission.

You change the message ACL owner to the author at ❿. This requires the `AclAuthorizationStrategy.CHANGE_OWNERSHIP` metapermission, which the current principal has because it's the current owner. In most cases, the author will already be the owner, because in most cases it's the author who invokes the `createAcl()` method by posting a message. But you'll see momentarily that in some cases an administrator is creating the ACL, and in such cases you need the administrator to relinquish ownership to the author.

You update the ACL in the persistent store at ⓫. You now have a new message OID and ACL with the right parent, author write permission, and owner.

In addition to creating ACLs, you have to be able to delete them. At ⓬ you delete an ACL with a single `deleteAcl()` call against the ACL service.

You also have to be able to update ACLs ⓭. This can happen if the original author updates the message (not shown in listing 7.5, but it's in the code download), or it can happen if an administrator blocks the message. Either way, the most straightforward way to update the ACL is to delete the old ACL and create a new one. In the case of an administrative block, the current principal will be the administrator when you call the `createAcl()` method, which is why you have to make the author the owner as mentioned.

With that, you're able to manage ACLs alongside your domain objects.

Discussion

In this recipe, you learned how to add fine-grained authorization to your application. With the earlier recipes you had to be content with fairly crude rules, such as the rule that normal users can read and create messages in general and that the site admin can also edit, block, unblock, and delete messages in general. But now you can create more specific rules, such as the rule that relevant authors and forum moderators should also be allowed to edit specific messages.

But there's still a gap. You'd like forum moderators to be able to block, unblock, and delete messages in their forums, but the app doesn't yet support this. Under the hood you have the ACLs in place for it, but on the display side, the JSP doesn't yet know how to take the ACLs into account. The display of the block/unblock/delete options still hinges on coarse-grained permissions rather than on fine-grained ACLs. Also, the app always shows the Edit Message option, even if the user doesn't have that permission for that message. The final recipe in this chapter, recipe 7.5, addresses these issues.

7.5 *Displaying web navigation and content based on ACLs*

PREREQUISITE
Recipe 7.4 Authorizing method invocations based on ACLs

KEY TECHNOLOGIES
Spring Security, Spring Security tag library

Background

In addition to protecting URLs from being accessed and methods from being called, it's often useful to show or hide page navigation and content according to a user's authorization to view them. Spring Security's tag library allows you to display page navigation and content based on ACL data.

Problem

Show or hide web navigation and content based on domain object ACLs. Specifically, you need to show or hide the edit, block, unblock, and delete message options depending on whether the user has permission to perform those operations on the messages in question.

Solution

In previous recipes, the sample app always displays the Edit Message link, even if the user doesn't have permission to perform that operation. And it uses crude, general permissions to decide whether to display the block/unblock/delete options:

```
<li><a href="${editMessageUrl}">Edit message</a></li>
<security:authorize access="hasRole('PERM_UPDATE_MESSAGES')">
    <li><a href="#">Block message</a></li>
    <li><a href="#">Unblock message</a></li>
</security:authorize>
<security:authorize access="hasRole('PERM_DELETE_MESSAGES')">
    <li><a href="#">Delete message</a></li>
</security:authorize>
```

Instead, you want to show or hide those options based on the ACLs you created in recipe 7.4. The basic approach is to use the `<security:accesscontrollist>` JSP tag to decide whether to hide or show the edit link. The tag references the ACLs you created in the previous recipe.

Now that we've discussed the structure of the Spring Security ACL module, you're in a good place to understand the JSP that contains the ACL-based JSP tags. Let's look at that so you can keep the goal in mind.

THE MESSAGE JSP
The following listing shows the relevant part of the JSP that displays individual forum posts.

Listing 7.6   message.jsp, showing how you show or suppress privileged features

```
<%@ taglib prefix="security"
    uri="http://www.springframework.org/security/tags" %>      ←┐  Spring Security
                                                             ❶   tag library
... display message ...

<security:accesscontrollist hasPermission="2,8,16"           ←┐  Write, delete, and
    domainObject="${message}">                             ❷   admin permissions
    <ul>
        <security:accesscontrollist hasPermission="2"       ←❸  Write permission
            domainObject="${message}">
            <li><a href="${editMessageUrl}">Edit message</a></li>
        </security:accesscontrollist>
        <security:accesscontrollist hasPermission="16"      ←❹  Admin permission
            domainObject="${message}">
            <li><a href="#">Block message</a></li>
            <li><a href="#">Unblock message</a></li>
        </security:accesscontrollist>
        <security:accesscontrollist hasPermission="8"       ←❺  Delete permission
            domainObject="${message}">
            <li><a href="#">Delete message</a></li>
        </security:accesscontrollist>
    </ul>

    ... other stuff ...

</security:accesscontrollist>
```

The part shown is the list of options at the bottom of the message. Under normal circumstances, the only thing a user would see is the Reply link. But as you can see, there are other possibilities.

First you declare the Spring Security tag library ❶ because you're going to use the `<security:accesscontrollist>` tag. Next you have the tag itself ❷. It has exactly two attributes: `domainObject` and `hasPermission`. The idea behind the tag is simple. The `domainObject` attribute points to a domain object (no surprises there), and `hasPermission` describes individually sufficient permissions that the current user must have with respect to the domain object. In other words, you enter the body tag if and only if the current user has at least one of the listed permissions. Here you're basically displaying the `<ul>` only if there's at least one option to show.

The user role doesn't directly come into the picture here. Instead, it's all about having the right permissions on the specific message referenced by the `domainObject` attribute.[16] If you have them, that's it—you're in. Otherwise, you aren't.

At ❸, ❹, and ❺ are controls for specific permissions: write (2), admin (16), and delete (8). Note that in ❹, even though the JSP generates HTML for both the block and unblock options, JavaScript ensures that exactly one is visible.

---

[16] User roles are indirectly involved, though, because they factor into which general permissions are in place, and those in turn factor into specific permissions. In this specific case, the site admin role has all ACL permissions on the site object, and those propagate down to forums and messages through the ACL inheritance mechanism.

> ### How it works: AccessControlListTag
>
> The `<security:accesscontrollist>` tag is backed by the `AccessControlListTag` class. `AccessControlListTag` looks for an `AclService` on the application context, which it uses to find the ACL attaching to the domain object in question. Then `AccessControlListTag` delegates the access decision to `Acl.isGranted(...)` in much the same way that `AbstractSecurityInterceptor` delegates to an `AccessDecisionManager`.
>
> The `Acl` interface specifies the semantics that access is granted if—and only if—the user has at least one of the required permissions. This is different than how the `AccessDecisionManager` makes its decisions. We noted that `AccessDecisionManager`s (at least, the ones that ship with Spring Security) use a voting mechanism (in the form of `AccessDecisionVoter`) combined with a conflict-resolution mechanism (in the form of `AccessDecisionManager`) to yield access decisions. With `Acl` there is no such thing. If the user has at least one of the permissions, access is granted. Otherwise access is denied.

TRY IT OUT

Point your browser at http://localhost:8080/sip/home.html, and try it out. Log in to the application as user `julia`, and go to the Algebra I forum, which she moderates. Julia should be able to perform all operations on the messages in that forum. Then go into the Calculus II forum, which she doesn't moderate. She can edit messages that she wrote, but she can't do anything other than read messages that somebody else wrote.

Log out, and then log back in as user `juan`, the site admin. You should be able to perform all operations on all messages across all forums.

Discussion

As with role-based authorization, ACL-based authorization involves collaboration between an underlying authorization model and view-related controls based on that model. In this recipe, you learned how to use the `<security:accesscontrollist>` JSP tag to make display decisions based on an underlying ACL apparatus. All the hard work goes into the ACL model. Once that's in place, showing or hiding page content based on ACLs is a piece of cake.

7.6   Summary

With this chapter, we've completed our two-chapter tour of security-related problems. The issues we've examined are of a general nature and reappear in application after application. You've also seen that Spring Security provides a nice framework for solving such problems, providing services around authentication and authorization, including a rich ACL infrastructure.

In the next chapter, we switch gears and discuss how to build features for communicating with customers and end users.

Communicating
with users and customers

8

This chapter covers

- Creating customer feedback forms with email response
- Scheduling asynchronous background email tasks
- Enabling secure mailing list subscriptions
- Publishing RSS news feeds

The success of a website is often closely tied to your communication with users and customers. You need to understand their needs, desires, and concerns to provide the level of service required to acquire and retain them. By the same token, you need a way to communicate news and announcements, new products and services, marketing and PR information, operational issues, and so forth to people who need the information. It's clear that good communication is crucial to the success of many websites and businesses.

The ability to communicate depends of course on the existence of an appropriate technical infrastructure. Usually you want to have multiple channels available because users vary widely in how they prefer to contact you and to be contacted.

In this chapter, we'll look at how to use Spring to support some common communications requirements, including Contact Us forms, mailing lists, and news feeds.

8.1 Create a web-based Contact Us form

PREREQUISITES

None

KEY TECHNOLOGIES

Spring Web MVC, JSR-303 Bean Validation, Hibernate, database

Background

Most websites let users contact the organization behind the website. Users may need to ask questions, report issues, or leave general feedback.

One important avenue through which users will want to contact your organization is "through the computer." This can take various forms; it might be email-based, through a customer support forum, through instant messaging, and so on.

Although it's easy to put an email link on a web page, often this isn't the ideal way to collect user communications. Sometimes you need extra structure around the communication, such as asking whether it's a tech-support issue or a suggestion. This can be useful for routing the request and for analytic purposes. Sometimes users don't want to use their work email account to correspond with your business. Finally, if you post an email address, you have to worry about spammers having it.

In this recipe, we'll look at a common alternative to the `mailto` link: the web-based form. Web forms solve all the issues just mentioned. You can collect whatever information you like, users can provide whatever return email address they like, and you don't have to post an email address that spammers will spam.[1]

You'll need to update the Jetty configuration in this recipe for Maven, including specifying the username and password for the MySQL database (sip/sip).[2]

Problem

Create a web-based form so users can send you comments, questions, issues, and so forth.

Solution

You'll implement the form in figure 8.1 using Spring Web MVC for the controller, a POJO service bean, and a POJO data access object backed by Hibernate. For now, you'll save the user's message in the database. In the next recipe, you'll see how to automatically generate emails for the user and the site administrator.

---

[1] Note that spammers will probably still spam your contact form—it's just that they won't have an actual email address to spam. You can reduce the amount of email spam by using a CAPTCHA. See Willie Wheeler, "How to reCAPTCHA your Java application," March 13, 2008," http:// mng.bz/SiZ9, to learn how to add reCAPTCHA to your contact form.

[2] See Willie Wheeler, "Code & Setup," http://springinpractice.com/code-and-setup.

Figure 8.1   This is the simple contact form that you're creating.

The bean-dependency graph in figure 8.2 shows the main part of what you're doing in this recipe. It's only a controller, a service bean, and a DAO.

Let's begin with the web tier, where you'll build a controller and a JSP.

SPRING WEB MVC CONTROLLER AND FORM JSP
The following listing shows ContactController, which is responsible for serving the form and processing the user's submission.

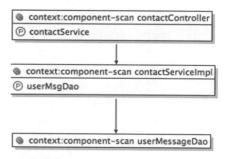

Figure 8.2   Key contact service dependencies: a standard controller/service/DAO stack

---

Listing 8.1   ContactController.java, a Spring web MVC controller

```java
package com.springinpractice.ch08.web;

import java.util.Date;
import javax.inject.Inject;
import javax.servlet.http.HttpServletRequest;
import javax.validation.Valid;
import org.springframework.beans.propertyeditors.StringTrimmerEditor;
import org.springframework.stereotype.Controller;
import org.springframework.ui.Model;
import org.springframework.validation.BindingResult;
import org.springframework.web.bind.WebDataBinder;
import org.springframework.web.bind.annotation.InitBinder;
import org.springframework.web.bind.annotation.ModelAttribute;
import org.springframework.web.bind.annotation.RequestMapping;
import org.springframework.web.bind.annotation.RequestMethod;
import com.springinpractice.ch08.model.UserMessage;
import com.springinpractice.ch08.service.ContactService;
```

```
@Controller
@RequestMapping("/contact")
public class ContactController {
    @Inject private ContactService contactService;

    @InitBinder                                              ❶  Defines whitelist
    public void initBinder(WebDataBinder binder) {              for security
        binder.setAllowedFields(new String[] {
            "name", "email", "text", "referer"
        });
        binder.registerCustomEditor(
            String.class, new StringTrimmerEditor(true));    Serves up    ❷
    }                                                         empty form

    @RequestMapping(value = "/new", method = RequestMethod.GET)
    public String getContactForm(HttpServletRequest req, Model model) {
        UserMessage userMsg = new UserMessage();
        userMsg.setReferer(req.getHeader("Referer"));
        model.addAttribute(userMsg);
        return getFullViewName("contactForm");
    }

    @RequestMapping(value = "", method = RequestMethod.POST)  ❸  Accepts form
    public String postContactForm(                              submissions
            HttpServletRequest req,
            @ModelAttribute @Valid UserMessage userMessage,      Validates
            BindingResult result) {                          ❹  submission

        if (result.hasErrors()) {
            result.reject("error.global");
            return getFullViewName("contactForm");
        }                                                    ❺  Sets message
        userMessage.setIpAddress(req.getRemoteAddr());          metadata
        userMessage.setAcceptLanguage(req.getHeader("Accept-Language"));
        userMessage.setUserAgent(req.getHeader("User-Agent"));
        userMessage.setDateCreated(new Date());
        contactService.saveUserMessage(userMessage);         ❻  Redirects
        return "redirect:/contact/thanks.html";                 after post
    }

    @RequestMapping(value = "/thanks", method = RequestMethod.GET)
    public String getThanksPage() {                             Shows
        return getFullViewName("thanks");                    ❼  a JSP
    }

    private String getFullViewName(String viewName) {
        return "contact/" + viewName;
    }
}
```

You implement ContactController as an annotated POJO controller. At ❶ you
define the form whitelist, which you definitely want in this case because the User-
Message bean includes properties that aren't part of the form. Spring binds only
whitelisted properties and silently ignores others. (See recipe 4.1 for a discussion
of initBinder().)

In the form-serving method ❷ you grab the *referer* (yes, that's the correct spelling—it's an HTTP header that gives the referring page, if any) of the request and insert it into the form bean. In the JSP (see listing 8.2), you'll expose the referer as a hidden field. The reason for storing the referer is that it's often useful to know which page the user was on just prior to asking a question or reporting a problem. You only get one chance to capture the referer, and this is it, so you grab it and store it. After that, you store the User-Message in the model. Because you didn't explicitly specify an attribute name, Spring applies a convention that stores the UserMessage bean under the name userMessage. But there is also an addAttribute(String name, Object value) method if you want to specify a different name.

In the form-processing method ❸ you attach the @Valid annotation to the User-Message ❹ to tell Spring to validate the form data on the way in. If there are any errors, you call reject(String) to signal a global error (something like "Please correct the errors") and return the logical view name contact/contactForm, which is mapped to the form's JSP. Otherwise, you set a bunch of other properties on the form bean ❺. Like the referer, these provide useful context when answering questions and troubleshooting. If somebody says "The site doesn't work," you can see it's because they're using an unsupported browser, for instance. You handle these in the form-processing method instead of in the form-serving method because you can—they don't change from request to request (or if they do, it doesn't matter), so you can avoid having to create hidden form fields by placing them in the form-processing method.

After processing the post, you redirect to a "thank you" page ❻. This redirect-after-post pattern allows you to minimize duplicate form submissions. You serve the "thank you" page by returning the appropriate logical view name ❼.

The "thanks" JSP isn't especially interesting (it just says "thanks"), so we won't look at it here, but we do want to check out the form which is shown in the next listing. We've suppressed most of the CSS, but it's in the code download if you're interested.

Listing 8.2   contactForm.jsp, a JSP to present the contact form

```
<?xml version="1.0" encoding="UTF-8"?>
<!DOCTYPE html PUBLIC "-//W3C//DTD XHTML 1.0 Strict//EN"
    "http://www.w3.org/TR/xhtml1/DTD/xhtml1-strict.dtd">

<%@ taglib prefix="c" uri="http://java.sun.com/jsp/jstl/core" %>
<%@ taglib prefix="form" uri="http://www.springframework.org/tags/form" %>
<%@ taglib prefix="spring" uri="http://www.springframework.org/tags" %>

<c:url var="contactUrl" value="/contact.html" />

...

<form:form cssClass="main" action="${contactUrl}"              ❶ Creates
    modelAttribute="userMessage">                                  HTML form

    <form:errors path="*">                                     ❷ Shows global
        <div class="warning alert">                               error, if any
            <spring:message code="error.global" />
        </div>
</form:form>
```

```
        </form:errors>
        <form:hidden path="referer"/>          ←┐   Hidden
                                                    referer field
        <div>Your name:</div>                                              Binds text field
        <div><form:input path="name" cssErrorClass=" error" /></div>        to property
        <form:errors path="name">
            <div><form:errors path="name" htmlEscape="false" /></div>   ←
        </form:errors>

        ... additional form fields for e-mail address and message text ...

        <div><input type="submit" value="Submit"></input></div>
    </form:form>                                              Shows property-specific
...                                                               error, if any
```

❸ Hidden referer field

❹ Binds text field to property

❺ Shows property-specific error, if any

Here you're using the Spring form tag library to generate the HTML form and to bind it to the userMessage form bean. First you declare a form with the model attribute set to userMessage ❶. This specifies the form bean, and the name is the one that Spring assigned by convention as discussed.

The next bit of code displays your global error, if any ❷. You use nested form:errors tags as described in chapter 3.

Next is the referer hidden field ❸. If you do a View Source in the browser, you should be able to see the field set to whatever referer brought you to the form page (it will be empty if you accessed the form directly).

At ❹ you bind a text field to the form bean's name property, and at ❺ you use nested form:errors tags to display any property-specific error messages.

That takes care of the web tier. Let's move on to the business tier.

A SIMPLE SERVICE BEAN

Take a peek at the magic behind the scenes. The following listing shows the service bean. (We've suppressed the interface, but it's exactly what you'd expect.)

Listing 8.3 ContactServiceImpl.java, the service bean

```
package com.springinpractice.ch08.service.impl;

import javax.inject.Inject;
import org.springframework.stereotype.Service;
import org.springframework.transaction.annotation.Isolation;
import org.springframework.transaction.annotation.Propagation;
import org.springframework.transaction.annotation.Transactional;
import com.springinpractice.ch08.dao.UserMessageDao;
import com.springinpractice.ch08.model.UserMessage;
import com.springinpractice.ch08.service.ContactService;

@Service
@Transactional(
    propagation = Propagation.REQUIRED,
    isolation = Isolation.DEFAULT,
    readOnly = true)
public class ContactServiceImpl implements ContactService {
    @Inject private UserMessageDao userMsgDao;
```

```
@Transactional(readOnly = false)
public void saveUserMessage(UserMessage userMsg) {
    userMsgDao.create(userMsg);
}
}
```

OK, there wasn't anything magical. In recipe 8.2, the service bean will become more interesting, but for now it's just a pass-through to the DAO.

Let's look at the UserMessage domain object and its persistence mapping.

USERMESSAGE AND PERSISTENCE

Like the service bean, the combined form bean/domain object is nondescript. Here it is.

Listing 8.4   UserMessage.java, a domain model for (surprise!) user messages

```
package com.springinpractice.ch08.model;

import java.util.Date;
import javax.persistence.*;
import javax.validation.constraints.NotNull;
import javax.validation.constraints.Size;
import org.apache.commons.lang.builder.ToStringBuilder;
import org.hibernate.validator.constraints.Email;
import org.hibernate.validator.constraints.Length;

@Entity
@Table(name = "user_message")
public final class UserMessage {
    private Long id;

    @NotNull
    @Length(min = 1, max = 80)
    private String name;

    @NotNull
    @Size(min = 1, max = 80)
    @Email
    private String email;

    @NotNull
    @Size(min = 1, max = 4000)
    private String text;

    private String ipAddr, acceptLanguage, referer, userAgent;
    private Date dateCreated;

    @Id
    @GeneratedValue(strategy = GenerationType.AUTO)
    @Column(name = "id")
    public Long getId() { return id; }

    @SuppressWarnings("unused")
    private void setId(Long id) { this.id = id; }

    @Column(name = "name")
    public String getName() { return name; }
```

```
        public void setName(String name) { this.name = name; }

        .... other getters and setters ...
}
```

UserMessage is a domain object, but you're using it as a form bean as well to avoid multiplying classes beyond necessity. (See chapter 3 for a discussion.) You're using JPA annotations for persistence and JSR-303 (including the Hibernate Validator implementation) for validation.

The UserMessageDao implementation, HbnUserMessageDao, extends AbstractHibernateDao<UserMessage> without adding anything extra. Therefore we won't show it here, but you can get it, as well as the user_message DDL, in the code download at the book's website.

You need the backing database schema too. As you might guess, it's very simple.

DATABASE SCHEMA

Here's the single MySQL table you need to support user messages:

```
create table user_message (
    id int unsigned not null auto_increment primary key,
    name varchar(80) not null,
    email varchar(80) not null,
    message_text text not null,
    ip_addr varchar(40) not null,
    accept_language varchar(255) not null,
    referer varchar(255) default null,
    user_agent varchar(255) not null,
    date_created timestamp default 0,
    date_modified timestamp default current_timestamp
        on update current_timestamp
) engine = InnoDB;
```

The only piece remaining is the application configuration. Because all you're doing is connecting a plain controller to a plain service bean and connecting that to a plain DAO, there's nothing to discuss. See the code download for the web.xml, beans-web.xml and beans-service.xml configurations.

With that, you're ready. Open your browser and try it out. You should be able to fill out the contact form, and the results should end up in the table you created.

Discussion

Creating a simple web-based Contact Us form is straightforward and isn't unlike other forms you've already seen. This recipe does show some useful techniques in action, such as using a domain object as a form bean (using @InitBinder to keep the domain data secure), prepopulating a form bean with metadata (in this case, referer data), and postpopulating the form bean with metadata before storing it in the database.

As mentioned previously, contact forms are useful for supporting multiple communications processes, including support and collecting suggestions and feedback. Although we didn't show it here, if users are contacting you in sufficient volume, you may want to add a type property to UserMessage and use it to route messages accordingly.

In the following recipe, you'll augment the contact form by creating emails from email templates and autogenerating email responses and notifications.

8.2   *Autogenerate an email response and email notification*

PREREQUISITES
Recipe 8.1 Creating a web-based Contact Us form

KEY TECHNOLOGIES
JavaMail, Velocity

Background

In recipe 8.1, you saw how to create a web-based contact form, which serves as an alternative to placing `mailto` links in a website. Despite the fact that sometimes email isn't the best communications medium, it's obvious that other times email is an entirely appropriate way to communicate with your users and customers.

In this recipe, you'll build on recipe 8.1 by adding autogenerated email messages, both to the user who completed the contact form and to an administrative mailbox. You'll generate the emails from Velocity templates, then you'll send them using JavaMail.

It's important to update the Maven configuration (sip08) for this second recipe because it contains additional Jetty configuration for JavaMail using a Gmail mail server, which wasn't included in the first recipe. Also, a username and password will need to be specified for the Gmail account to be used.[3]

Problem

When a user completes a web-based contact form, send two template-based emails: a confirmation to the user who completed the form and a notification to an administrative mailbox indicating that a user has submitted a contact form.

Solution

You'll use Velocity to define a couple of email templates and stamp out individual email messages. First let's create the templates. You'll create only one—the confirmation message template—here because the other template is entirely analogous. The next listing shows how to create a confirmation message template using the Velocity Template Language (VTL).[4]

> **Listing 8.5   src/main/resources/velocity/contactConfirm.vm**

```
<b>[This e-mail was automatically generated. Please do not reply.]</b>

Thank you for contacting Example.com. This is an auto-generated response to let
you know that we received your message. We typically respond within 24
hours.
```

[3]   See Willie Wheeler, "Configuring Jetty to use Gmail as an SMTP provider," April 29, 2012, http://mng.bz/ EALs.

[4]   For more information about Velocity, see http://velocity.apache.org/engine/devel/user-guide.html.

```
Thanks,
Example.com

<b>Your message:</b>

Name: ${userMessage.name}
E-mail: ${userMessage.email}
Date: ${userMessage.dateCreated}

${userMessage.text}
```

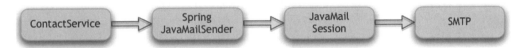

1 **Dynamic content via VTL reference**

As you would expect, most of this is static content, with some placeholders for dynamic content **1**. We won't get deep into VTL syntax here, but you can see that you can access bean properties using dot notation, just as with JSP EL. For more information about VTL, see the Velocity User Guide.

You have your template (or two templates if you've downloaded the code), so let's update the ContactServiceImpl bean to use it to create emails.

CONTACTSERVICEIMPL REVISITED

In recipe 8.1, ContactServiceImpl was boring, but we indicated that you'd be building it out. Figure 8.3 shows what you're aiming for.

```
ContactService  ⟹  Spring          ⟹  JavaMail   ⟹  SMTP
                    JavaMailSender      Session
```

Figure 8.3   Equipping the ContactService to send email

The following listing is an implementation of the design in figure 8.3.

Listing 8.6   New and improved ContactServiceImpl.java

```java
package com.springinpractice.ch08.service.impl;

import static org.springframework.util.Assert.notNull;

import java.io.UnsupportedEncodingException;
import java.util.HashMap;
import java.util.Map;
import javax.inject.Inject;
import javax.mail.MessagingException;
import javax.mail.internet.MimeMessage;
import org.apache.velocity.app.VelocityEngine;
import org.springframework.beans.factory.annotation.Value;
import org.springframework.mail.javamail.JavaMailSender;
import org.springframework.mail.javamail.MimeMessageHelper;
import org.springframework.stereotype.Service;
import org.springframework.transaction.annotation.Isolation;
import org.springframework.transaction.annotation.Propagation;
import org.springframework.transaction.annotation.Transactional;
import org.springframework.ui.velocity.VelocityEngineUtils;
import com.springinpractice.ch08.dao.UserMessageDao;
import com.springinpractice.ch08.model.UserMessage;
import com.springinpractice.ch08.service.ContactService;
```

```
@Service
@Transactional(
    propagation = Propagation.REQUIRED,
    isolation = Isolation.DEFAULT,
    readOnly = true)
public class ContactServiceImpl implements ContactService {
    private static final String CONFIRMATION_TEMPLATE_PATH =
        "contactConfirm.vm";
    private static final String USER_MSG_TEMPLATE_PATH =
        "contactUserMessage.vm";

    @Inject private UserMessageDao userMsgDao;
    @Inject private JavaMailSender mailSender;              ◄── ❶ JavaMailSender
    @Inject private VelocityEngine velocityEngine;              dependency
                                                           ◄──
    @Value("#{contactServiceProps.sendConfirmation}")      ◄──    ❷ VelocityEngine
    private boolean sendConfirmation;                                 dependency

    @Value("#{contactServiceProps.notifyAdmin}")
    private boolean notifyAdmin;                           ❸ Service
                                                              configuration
    @Value("#{contactServiceProps.noReplyEmailAddress}")
    private String noReplyEmailAddr;

    @Value("#{contactServiceProps.adminEmailAddress}")
    private String adminEmailAddr;

    @Transactional(readOnly = false)
    public void saveUserMessage(UserMessage userMsg) {
        notNull(userMsg, "userMsg can't be null");         ❹ Still saves
        userMsgDao.create(userMsg);                   ◄──     message
        if (sendConfirmation) {                            ◄──
            MimeMessage mimeMsg = createEmail(                ❺ Conditionally
                    userMsg, CONFIRMATION_TEMPLATE_PATH,         sends two emails
                    "Confirmation message", userMsg.getEmail(),
                    noReplyEmailAddr, null);
            sendEmail(mimeMsg);
        }
        if (notifyAdmin) {
            MimeMessage mimeMsg = createEmail(
                    userMsg, USER_MSG_TEMPLATE_PATH,
                    "User message", adminEmailAddr,
                    userMsg.getEmail(), userMsg.getName());
            sendEmail(mimeMsg);
        }
    }
                                                           ❻ Method to
    private MimeMessage createEmail(UserMessage userMsg,  ◄──  create email
            String templatePath, String subject, String toEmail,
            String fromEmail, String fromName) {          ❼ Creates
                                                              MimeMessage
        MimeMessage mimeMsg = mailSender.createMimeMessage();  ◄──
        Map<String, Object> model = new HashMap<String, Object>();
        model.put("userMessage", userMsg);
        String text = VelocityEngineUtils.mergeTemplateIntoString(  ◄──
            velocityEngine, templatePath, model);
        text = text.replaceAll("\n", "<br>");         ◄──
                                Format for HTML ❿        Instantiates
        try {                                           template ❾
```

❽ Model to instantiate template

```
        MimeMessageHelper helper = new MimeMessageHelper(mimeMsg);
        helper.setSubject(subject);
        helper.setTo(toEmail);

        if (fromName == null) {
            helper.setFrom(fromEmail);
        } else {
            try {
                helper.setFrom(fromEmail, fromName);
            } catch (UnsupportedEncodingException e) {
                helper.setFrom(fromEmail);
            }
        }

        helper.setSentDate(userMsg.getDateCreated());
        helper.setText(text, true);
    } catch (MessagingException e) {
        throw new RuntimeException(e);
    }

    return mimeMsg;
}

private void sendEmail(MimeMessage mimeMsg) {
    mailSender.send(mimeMsg);
}
}
```

⑪ Sets email subject and so on

⑫ Sets From name, if possible

⑬ Sets MIME type to "text/html"

There's a lot happening here, so let's take a look.

DEPENDENCIES

At ❶ you declare a JavaMailSender dependency. You'll use this to create and send email. At ❷ you declare a dependency on VelocityEngine, which you'll use to stamp out emails from a template. Next you define several configuration options ❸. Two of them are flags that indicate who (if anybody) should get an email when a user submits a contact form. You can choose whether or not to send the user a confirmation, and you can choose whether or not to send the site administrator an email notification. If you send these emails, you'll need to have a couple of email addresses handy: a nore-ply address and the administrator's address.

CREATING AND SENDING EMAIL

Now you get to the stage of saving the user message. You still have the call to UserMessageDao.save() that you had in recipe 8.1 ❹. But now you have a couple of extra things. If the sendConfirmation flag is true ❺, then you use the createEmail() method to create a MimeMessage (which supports HTML) that you then send via the JavaMailSender.send() method. You pass in all the parameters you need to create the email, including the name of the template you want to use. The process is similar for the notifyAdmin flag and notification emails to the admin.

Let's look at createEmail() ❻. It's designed to be fairly general so it can handle both the confirmation and notification requirements. It uses the JavaMailSender to create the MimeMessage ❼. You'll use Velocity to generate the email text, so you start by creating a simple model to resolve references in the email templates ❽. Then you run everything through the engine (using Spring's `VelocityEngineUtils`) to generate the result of applying the template to the model ❾. Because you'll send this as an HTML email, you replace newline characters with the `<br>` tag ❿.

That takes care of the text, but you have to set the other fields on the email as well. You do this using Spring's `MimeMessageHelper` class ⓫. Most of this is straightforward; the only exception is setting the sender's name, which can possibly generate an `UnsupportedEncodingException`. If the name is provided, you try to set it, but if you can't, you just set the sender's email address ⓬. Finally, by passing in `true` as the second argument to `setText()`, you set the message MIME type to `text/html` ⓭.

That's the guts of what you're doing in this recipe, but let's see what beans-service.xml looks like.

APPLICATION CONFIGURATION

You need to add definitions for the `JavaMailSender` and `VelocityEngine` dependencies to beans-service.xml. Configuration-wise, the target is the one in figure 8.4.

The next listing shows what you need to add to beans-service.xml to achieve this.

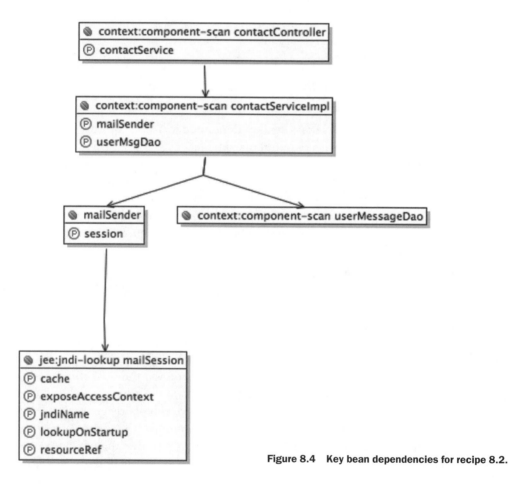

Figure 8.4   Key bean dependencies for recipe 8.2.

Listing 8.7   Additions to beans-service.xml

```
<beans ...
    xmlns:jee="http://www.springframework.org/schema/jee"
    xmlns:util="http://www.springframework.org/schema/util"
    xsi:schemaLocation="
        ...
        http://www.springframework.org/schema/jee
        http://www.springframework.org/schema/jee/spring-jee-3.0.xsd
        http://www.springframework.org/schema/util
        http://www.springframework.org/schema/util/spring-util-3.0.xsd">

    ...
    <jee:jndi-lookup id="mailSession"                          ◄─┐  ❶ Mail session
        jndi-name="mail/Session" resource-ref="true" />                lookup
    <bean id="mailSender"                                      ◄─┐  ❷ Spring mail
        class="org.springframework.mail.javamail.JavaMailSenderImpl"      sender
        p:session-ref="mailSession" />
    <bean id="velocityEngine"                                  ◄─┐  ❸ Email template
        class="org.springframework.ui.velocity.VelocityEngineFactoryBean"   engine
        p:resourceLoaderPath="classpath:/velocity/" />
    <util:properties id="contactServiceProps"                  ◄─┐
        location="classpath:/spring/contactService.properties" />
</beans>
                                                         Contact service
                                                         configuration ❹
```

For the JNDI lookup ❶, be sure to add the jee namespace. You'll also need to configure a JavaMail Session in your server. The code download includes a sample Jetty configuration at sample_conf/jetty-env.xml.[5] The mailSender bean ❷ references that session.

The VelocityEngineFactoryBean definition ❸ is a little interesting. If you're paying attention, you'll notice that the velocityEngine dependency in ContactServiceImpl is a VelocityEngine, but a quick look at the Javadocs for VelocityEngineFactoryBean reveal that it isn't a VelocityEngine, either directly or indirectly. What gives?

Here's what's going on. VelocityEngineFactoryBean implements Spring's FactoryBean interface. Because of this, it isn't itself injected into other beans (that's why it doesn't show up in figure 8.4); instead, the result of calling its getObject() method (which is declared by the FactoryBean interface) is injected into other beans.

Also, because you want to set a bunch of properties on the ContactServiceImpl bean, you add the util:properties definition ❹ and the corresponding util namespace. To supply values, you create a /spring/contactService.properties file:

---

[5] See also Willie Wheeler, "Configuring Jetty to use Gmail as an SMTP provider" April 29, 2012, http://mng.bz/mvG9. If you don't want to use JNDI to look up a mail session, you can configure the JavaMailSenderImpl directly. See Wheeler, "Send e-mail using Spring and JavaMail," May 15, 2008, http://mng.bz/5e84, for more information. The post also shows how to do JavaMail+JNDI using Tomcat 6. Finally, to troubleshoot PKIX certificate issues, see Wheeler, "Fixing PKIX path building issues when using JavaMail and SMTP," April 29, 2012, http://mng.bz/W4w8.

```
sendConfirmation=true
notifyAdmin=true
noReplyEmailAddress=noreply@example.com
adminEmailAddress=admin@example.com
```

That's it for this one. Configure the application context so the two `ContactService` flags are true, and set the admin email address to one of your own. Try it out, and see if it works. The service should generate two emails: one sent to whatever email address you provide in the form (again, use one of your own) and one to the admin email address.

Discussion

In this recipe you learned how to use JavaMail to send email and also how to use the Velocity template engine to create them. Clearly it's useful in a wide range of situations to be able to send email; you'll see more in this chapter (for example, in recipe 8.4), and even previous chapters offered opportunities to send email (for example, in chapter 4 where you did user registrations).

> **NOTE**   If you prefer the FreeMarker template engine (http://freemarker.org/) over Velocity, Spring provides support classes for integrating with FreeMarker.[6]

In the next recipe, we'll look at a simple but interesting enhancement to the email functionality you've just added.

8.3   *Speeding up autogenerated emails*

PREREQUISITES
Recipe 8.1 Creating a web-based Contact Us form
Recipe 8.2 Autogenerating an email response and email notification

KEY TECHNOLOGIES
Spring Task Execution API, JavaMail, threads

Background

When you complete the contact form from recipe 8.2, you may notice that there's a fairly significant delay between the time you submit the form and the time the "thank you" page appears. The reason is that it takes a while to send the confirmation and notification emails, which you're sending in a synchronous fashion on the calling thread. But there's no good reason to make the user wait, especially because email is an asynchronous form of communication. In this recipe, you'll see how to use the Spring Task Execution API to fork the calling thread when sending the emails.

Problem

Minimize the noticeable delay that the user experiences after submitting the contact form.

---

[6] Another interesting option is the Thymeleaf project at www.thymeleaf.org/. See for example José Miguel Samper, "Rich HTML email in Spring with Thymeleaf," www.thymeleaf.org/springmail.html.

Solution

Keep in mind that when the user submits the form, you do two things. First, you save the contact form data in the database. Second, you fire off a couple of emails. You want to leave the database call on the calling thread because you need to be able to alert the user when problems occur. (For now a stack trace will suffice, but obviously you'd have a proper error page in a production application.) You want to move the emails to a separate thread.

Spring 3 provides a Task Execution API that allows you to wrap beans with a proxy that calls @Async-annotated methods asynchronously. The easiest approach would be to annotate `ContactServiceImpl.saveUserMessage()` with @Async; but doing so would cause the database save to happen on the forked thread, which would mean the user would have no way to know if the save failed. So a little refactoring is in order: the `ContactServiceImpl` will call a dedicated `ContactMailSender` component that does the mail sending, and you'll wrap the `ContactMailSender` with the proxy. That way, your service bean can do the database call on the calling thread and then fork the email send. Figure 8.5 shows what this looks like.

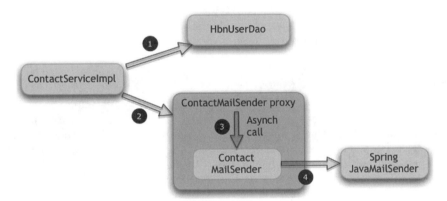

Figure 8.5   Refactored design to allow you to send email asynchronously: (1) save the form data, (2) invoke the mail-sender proxy, (3) call the mail sender asynchronously, and (4) send the email.

REFACTORING CONTACTSERVICEIMPL

You'll refactor `ContactServiceImpl` by splitting it into two pieces: a thin piece that saves to the database (by calling `HbnUserDao`) and a slightly larger piece that sends the email. The following listing shows the new `ContactServiceImpl`.

Listing 8.8   The newly refactored ContactServiceImpl

```
package com.springinpractice.ch08.service.impl;

import javax.inject.Inject;
import org.springframework.stereotype.Service;
import org.springframework.transaction.annotation.Isolation;
import org.springframework.transaction.annotation.Propagation;
import org.springframework.transaction.annotation.Transactional;
```

```
import com.springinpractice.ch08.dao.UserMessageDao;
import com.springinpractice.ch08.model.UserMessage;
import com.springinpractice.ch08.service.ContactService;

@Service
@Transactional(
    propagation = Propagation.REQUIRED,
    isolation = Isolation.DEFAULT,
    readOnly = true)
public class ContactServiceImpl implements ContactService {
    @Inject private UserMessageDao userMsgDao;
    @Inject private ContactMailSender contactMailSender;

    @Transactional(readOnly = false)
    public void saveUserMessage(UserMessage userMsg) {
        userMsgDao.create(userMsg);
        contactMailSender.sendEmail(userMsg);
    }
}
```

1 Injection point for proxy

2 Saves message on current thread

3 Sends email using proxy

Effectively, you've moved the former sendEmail() method to a separate class for proxying. At **1** you inject the ContactService, which for you is a proxy. At **2** you call the DAO on the calling thread, which means that if the call fails, the user will find out about it, as desired. At **3** you invoke sendEmail() on the proxy, which performs its job asynchronously as you'll see momentarily.

Why can't you annotate sendEmail() with @Async?

An alternative approach that turns out not to work would be to annotate the former ContactServiceImpl.sendEmail() method with @Async. This doesn't work because once the thread is inside saveUserMessage(), calls to sendEmail() go directly to the bean rather than jumping outside the proxy and coming back in. That's why you're creating a separate ContactMailSender class.

The next listing shows the ContactMailSender, which is the bean you want to proxy with forking behavior.

Listing 8.9   ContactMailSender, which you invoke asynchronously using @Async

```
package com.springinpractice.ch08.service.impl;

import java.io.UnsupportedEncodingException;
import java.util.HashMap;
import java.util.Map;
import javax.inject.Inject;
import javax.mail.MessagingException;
import javax.mail.internet.MimeMessage;
import org.apache.velocity.app.VelocityEngine;
import org.springframework.beans.factory.annotation.Value;
import org.springframework.mail.javamail.JavaMailSender;
import org.springframework.mail.javamail.MimeMessageHelper;
import org.springframework.scheduling.annotation.Async;
```

```
import org.springframework.stereotype.Component;
import org.springframework.ui.velocity.VelocityEngineUtils;
import com.springinpractice.ch08.model.UserMessage;

@Component
public class ContactMailSender {
    private static final String CONFIRMATION_TEMPLATE_PATH =
        "contactConfirm.vm";
    private static final String USER_MSG_TEMPLATE_PATH =
        "contactUserMessage.vm";

    @Inject private JavaMailSender mailSender;
    @Inject private VelocityEngine velocityEngine;

    @Value("#{contactServiceProps.sendConfirmation}")
    private boolean sendConfirmation;

    @Value("#{contactServiceProps.notifyAdmin}")
    private boolean notifyAdmin;

    @Value("#{contactServiceProps.noReplyEmailAddress}")
    private String noReplyEmailAddr;

    @Value("#{contactServiceProps.adminEmailAddress}")
    private String adminEmailAddr;

    @Async
    public void sendEmail(UserMessage userMsg) { ... same as before ... }

    ... createEmail() and sendEmail() methods same as before ...
}
```

① @Component for scanning

② @Async to indicate fork

As you can see, you haven't changed much as compared to when this code was in `ContactServiceImpl`. The only changes are a new `@Component` annotation **①** to support discovery via component scanning and a new `@Async` annotation **②** on the `sendEmail()` method, which is now public. This latter provides the desired behavior: it indicates that you want calls to `sendEmail()` to be asynchronous.

You're almost done, but you need to update beans-service.xml.

CONFIGURING THE APP FOR ASYNCHRONOUS TASKS

Just adding the `@Async` annotation isn't enough. You need to add some configuration to beans-service.xml. Fortunately the new configuration is easy, as we show next.

Listing 8.10   Additions to beans-services.xml to support @Async

```
<?xml version="1.0" encoding="UTF-8"?>
<beans ...
    xmlns:task="http://www.springframework.org/schema/task"
    xsi:schemaLocation="http://www.springframework.org/schema/task
        http://www.springframework.org/schema/task/spring-task-3.0.xsd
        ...">

    <task:annotation-driven />
    <task:executor id="userMessageExecutor"
        pool-size="5-10" queue-capacity="100" keep-alive="300" />
</beans>
```

① Task namespace

② Task namespace schema location

③ Activates @Async

④ Task executor for asynchronous calls

The configuration takes advantage of Spring 3's `task` namespace. You declare the namespace ❶ and its schema location ❷.

The `<task:annotation-driven/>` element ❸ tells Spring to activate the `@Async` annotation, which basically means to wrap any bean that uses the annotation with a proxy that calls down to the annotated method on a separate thread. The definition at ❹ creates a Spring `ThreadPoolTaskExecutor`, which is a convenient front end for a Java `ThreadPoolExecutor` that provides the threads. Table 8.1 presents the configuration options; see the Javadoc for `ThreadPoolExecutor` for details.

Table 8.1   `<task:executor>` configuration

Attribute	Description
`id`	Bean ID. Serves as a prefix for thread names.
`pool-size`	Number of threads in the pool. Either a single integer or a range such as "5-10." The lower end of the range is the *core pool size*: the size the pool tends toward as its steady state. The upper end is the maximum pool size.
`queue-capacity`	Task queue capacity.
`keep-alive`	Keep-alive time in seconds for threads in excess of the core pool size.
`rejection-policy`	Policy when threads are rejected (queue exhausted and pool size at maximum). Options are ABORT (default), CALLER_RUNS, DISCARD, and DISCARD_OLDEST.

Now you should be able to see the effect of the work you've done. Start the server, submit the contact form, and pay attention to how quickly you receive the response. Even after the response is complete, you should see in the server console output that the server is sending mail on a separate thread.

Discussion

The original version of this recipe showed how to create an aspect to handle thread forking in a generic fashion. With Spring 3, you have a native Spring API for performing this—one that uses the nice namespace configuration facility and avoids some of the complexities associated with AOP.

Note that you may need to adjust your server's security configuration in order to create threads for the thread pool. This is because thread creation is an expensive operation, and some server configurations disallow it.

That completes our treatment of contact forms. In the next recipe, we'll look at mailing lists and how to implement the subscription process, which turns out to be interesting due to some of the security-related elements we need to consider.

8.4   *Allowing users to subscribe to a mailing list*

PREREQUISITES

None

KEY TECHNOLOGIES
JavaMail, Hibernate, database, cryptography

Background

For marketing purposes, it's often beneficial to provide a way for users to sign up for an email mailing list. Because mailing lists are an opt-in communication, and because users generally understand that such lists serve marketing purposes, this can be an easy way to identify high-value customers and keep them up-to-date on company news, your products and services, helpful articles, and so forth. Although many users prefer to subscribe to a news feed (we'll discuss that in recipe 8.5), others are happy to provide their email address to a trusted site and receive email updates.

Another benefit of providing a mailing list is that it gives you a nice goal to track if you're using analytics tools such as Google Analytics. You can treat a confirmed subscription as a goal conversion, and that's a way to gauge interest over time in your organization, site, products, articles and blog posts, and so forth. This is similar to tracking feed subscriptions through a service like FeedBurner.

In this recipe, you'll create a mailing list using Spring. This recipe will handle only the subscription piece, but the sample code treats unsubscriptions as well. Also, we're not treating the topic of sending marketing emails to mailing list members. (We do cover confirmation emails, though, so you should have the tools you need.)

Problem

Create a mailing list for your website. Users also need a way to subscribe to and unsubscribe from the list. Subscriptions and unsubscriptions must require email confirmation to prevent attackers from falsely subscribing or unsubscribing people.

Solution

At first it might seem that mailing lists aren't very interesting from a technical perspective. But they're reasonably interesting after all, owing to the requirement that you avoid false subscriptions (signing up victims to a bunch of mailing lists to spam them) and unsubscriptions (unsubscribing victims from mailing lists they care about).

You'll create a `MailingListService` to handle subscriptions and unsubscriptions, although due to space limitations you'll focus on the subscription case. (The code download includes code for unsubscription as well.) It's a controller/service/DAO stack like the `ContactService`, but the implementation details are a little different. The user flow looks roughly like figure 8.6.

Figure 8.6 User flow when subscribing to the mailing list.

In the happy path flow, the user first clicks the site's Mailing List link, which presents a subscription form. The user completes the form, supplying their name and email address, and submits it. The response is a page that tells the user to go to their inbox and click the link in a confirmation email the site just sent. The user does that and receives a "subscription confirmed" success message. There are some sad path flows as well, such as when the user takes too long to confirm the subscription. You'll see those.

First up is the controller.

THE CONTROLLER

You'll begin at the top with the controller, which appears in the following listing.

Listing 8.11   Handling subscriptions with MailingListController.java

```java
package com.springinpractice.ch08.web;

import java.util.Date;
import javax.inject.Inject;
import javax.servlet.http.HttpServletRequest;
import javax.validation.Valid;
import org.springframework.beans.propertyeditors.StringTrimmerEditor;
import org.springframework.stereotype.Controller;
import org.springframework.ui.Model;
import org.springframework.validation.BindingResult;
import org.springframework.web.bind.WebDataBinder;
import org.springframework.web.bind.annotation.InitBinder;
import org.springframework.web.bind.annotation.ModelAttribute;
import org.springframework.web.bind.annotation.RequestMapping;
import org.springframework.web.bind.annotation.RequestMethod;
import org.springframework.web.bind.annotation.RequestParam;
import com.springinpractice.ch08.model.Subscriber;
import com.springinpractice.ch08.service.ConfirmationExpiredException;
import com.springinpractice.ch08.service.ConfirmationFailedException;
import com.springinpractice.ch08.service.MailingListService;

@Controller
@RequestMapping("/mailinglist")
public class MailingListController {
    private static final String SUBSCRIBER = "subscriber";

    @Inject private MailingListService mailingListService;

    @InitBinder(SUBSCRIBER)                                      ❶ Init
    public void initSubscriberBinder(WebDataBinder binder) {        binder
        binder.registerCustomEditor(
            String.class, new StringTrimmerEditor(true));
        binder.setAllowedFields(                                 ❷ Form field
            new String[] { "firstName", "lastName", "email" });     whitelist
    }

    @RequestMapping(value = "/subscribe", method = RequestMethod.GET)
    public String getSubscribeForm(Model model) {               ❸ Handles form
        model.addAttribute(new Subscriber());                      requests
        return getFullViewName("subscribeForm");
    }
}
```

```
@RequestMapping(value = "/subscribe", method = RequestMethod.POST)
public String postSubscribeForm(
        HttpServletRequest request,
        @ModelAttribute(SUBSCRIBER) @Valid Subscriber subscriber,
        BindingResult result) {                          Handles form
                                                         submissions      4
    if (result.hasErrors()) {
        result.reject("error.global");
        return getFullViewName("subscribeForm");
    }                                                  5  Populates form
    subscriber.setIpAddress(request.getRemoteAddr());     before adding
    subscriber.setDateCreated(new Date());
    mailingListService.addSubscriber(subscriber);
    return "redirect:/mailinglist/subscribe-preconfirm.html";
}

@RequestMapping(
    value = "/subscribe-preconfirm", method = RequestMethod.GET)
public String getConfirmSubscriptionPage() {           Preconfirmation
    return getFullViewName("subscribePreconfirm");   6  page
}

@RequestMapping(
    value = "/subscribe-confirm", method = RequestMethod.GET)
public String confirmSubscription(                     Confirms
        @RequestParam("s") Long subscriberId,        7  subscription
        @RequestParam("d") String digest,
        Model model) {

    try {
        mailingListService.confirmSubscriber(subscriberId, digest);
        return getFullViewName("subscribeSuccess");
    } catch (ConfirmationExpiredException e) {
        model.addAttribute("expired", true);
    } catch (ConfirmationFailedException e) {
        model.addAttribute("failed", true);
    }

    model.addAttribute(new Subscriber());
    return getFullViewName("subscribeForm");
}
private String getFullViewName(String viewName) {
    return "mailingList/" + viewName;
}
}
```

The controller handles three different requests: the initial subscription form, the form submission, and the confirmation. Let's see how it works.

- *Initial subscription form*—For the subscription form, you have a method to serve up the initial form ❸. There's nothing to do other than put an empty Subscriber form bean on the model and return the logical view name.
- *Form submission*—The form-submission process begins with an @InitBinder method for the subscriber form bean ❶. You specify an actual value because the code download supports an unsubscriber bean as well, and specifying a value

allows you to associate an @InitBinder method with a given form bean. Inside the method is a standard form field whitelist ❷. (See recipe 4.1 for a discussion.)

After that, Spring validates the request and calls the request handler method ❹. Assuming validation succeeds, you set a couple of fields on the subscription—the IP address and the creation date ❺—and save the unconfirmed subscription to the database. You're including the IP address mostly for your own information, but you'll use the date to assign an expiration date to your confirmation emails, so you need to set it before saving it to the database.

- After accepting the submission, you redirect to a preconfirmation page ❻ that offers the user instructions on how to confirm the subscription.

- *Confirmation*—At this point the user goes to their inbox, opens the confirmation email, and clicks the confirmation link. This brings them to the confirmation handler ❼. If the call to confirmSubscriber() succeeds, you return the success view. If the call fails because the subscription request has expired or for some other reason, you deliver an appropriate failure page. In the case of a failure, you set an appropriate model attribute to tell the JSP (and ultimately the user) what the problem was.

That's it for the controller. Now you'll see the subscription form, which serves two separate roles in your mailing-list module.

THE SUBSCRIPTION FORM

Your subscription form appears, of course, at the beginning of the subscription process. You also use it during the confirmation process when confirmations fail; for example, due to expiry. The next listing shows the form and how it supports both roles.

Listing 8.12   Subscription form, subscribeForm.jsp

```xml
<?xml version="1.0" encoding="UTF-8"?>
<!DOCTYPE html PUBLIC "-//W3C//DTD XHTML 1.0 Strict//EN" "http://www.w3.org/
    TR/xhtml1/DTD/xhtml1-strict.dtd">

<%@ taglib prefix="c" uri="http://java.sun.com/jsp/jstl/core" %>
<%@ taglib prefix="form" uri="http://www.springframework.org/tags/form" %>
<%@ taglib prefix="spring" uri="http://www.springframework.org/tags" %>

<c:url var="subscribeUrl" value="/mailinglist/subscribe.html" />

... html, head, body, etc. ...

<c:if test="${not empty expired}">          ◁──❶ Expiry test
    <div>
        Sorry, your previous subscription request has expired. To subscribe
        you will need to complete a new subscription request using the form

    </div>
</c:if>
<c:if test="${not empty failed}">                    ◁── Other
    <div>                                      ❷ failure test
```

```
        Sorry, we were unable to confirm your subscription. If you copied
        the URL from your confirmation e-mail into the browser, please make
        sure you copied the entire URL. Otherwise, you can complete a new
        subscription request using the form.
    </div>
</c:if>

<p>To subscribe, please provide your name and e-mail address.</p>

<form:form modelAttribute="subscriber" action="${subscribeUrl}">
    <form:errors path="*">
        <div><spring:message code="error.global" /></div>
    </form:errors>

    <div>Your first name:</div>
    <div><form:input path="firstName" cssErrorClass="error" /></div>
    <form:errors path="email">
        <div><form:errors path="firstName" htmlEscape="false" /></div>
    </form:errors>

    ... last name, e-mail address, submit button ...

</form:form>

...
```

This form is similar to forms you've seen in other recipes, so we'll go over only the two tests; if you want to see more, you can download the code from the book's website. The first test checks for the existence of an attribute called expired ❶. You saw in listing 8.11 that you set the corresponding `model` attribute. The second test checks for an attribute called failed ❷.

We'll talk about the conditions under which a confirmation might expire or fail in the next subsection, which covers the service bean.

THE SERVICE BEAN

Before we examine the service bean code, let's talk about a couple of security requirements:

- *Authentication*—You need to prevent people from maliciously subscribing other people to your mailing list, generating what the victim might consider to be spam. Essentially this is an authentication requirement: the subscriber must prove that he's the one being subscribed.
- *Privacy*—In cases where privacy is a concern, whether for regulatory or other reasons, it must be impossible for attackers to use the subscription process as a way to query the system for who's on the mailing list. The UI must respond to all subscription requests in exactly the same way (by telling the user to look for a confirmation email). It shouldn't say "You are already a subscriber"; there shouldn't be a difference in how long it takes to respond to new versus existing subscribers, and so on

We'll start with the authentication requirement; we'll worry about privacy later. Your tack is the standard one: you capture the subscriber's email address and send them a confirmation email containing a link that, when clicked, activates the subscription.

The challenge is that you need to know that the person clicking the link is the person who subscribed to the mailing list.

A naïve approach might be to include in the link the subscriber ID as an HTTP parameter. But this isn't a good approach. Clearly it's too susceptible to guessing, especially if the subscriber IDs are drawn from a sequence.

A much better way to do this would be to generate a large random string, save it with the rest of the subscriber information, and include both the ID and the random string as HTTP parameters in the email link. This approach makes it much more difficult for an attacker to guess the confirmation link.

But it turns out you can avoid the extra database column, which of course is better still. What you do is inject a secret key into the service bean (the key should be random-looking and not prone to dictionary attacks), then concatenate that with the subscriber ID before hashing it. The resulting string is called a *digest*, and you include the ID and digest in the email link. For any given ID, attackers can't compute the digest because they don't know the secret key. And from any given digest, attackers can't uncover the secret key because hashes are one-way and the key is sufficiently obscure that it wouldn't be found in a dictionary attack. Yet by passing the ID and digest to the server, the server can determine whether the digest is correct because it knows the secret key that was used in generating the digest. See figure 8.7.

Because email links aren't especially secure—once somebody sees it, they can use it—you should attach an expiration date to the link such that if somebody clicks it after the expiration, it won't work. This is easy: all you have to do is timestamp the subscription request and check the timestamp when processing confirmation requests.

We hope that explanation makes some sense; but if not, that's OK, because you have the code. The next listing shows MailingListServiceImpl.java, which contains the core mailing-list service logic, including the authentication feature described.

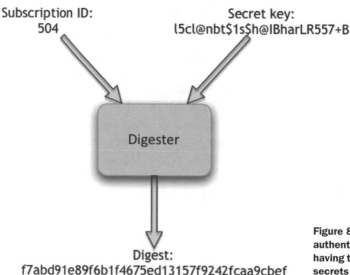

Subscription ID:
504

Secret key:
l5cl@nbt$1s$h@lBharLR557+B

Digester

Digest:
f7abd91e89f6b1f4675ed13157f9242fcaa9cbef

Figure 8.7   Using a digest to authenticate subscribers without having to store subscriber-specific secrets

Listing 8.13 MailingListServiceImpl.java, with secure subscriptions

```java
package com.springinpractice.ch08.service.impl;

import java.util.Date;
import java.util.HashMap;
import java.util.Map;
import javax.inject.Inject;
import javax.mail.MessagingException;
import javax.mail.internet.MimeMessage;
import org.apache.commons.codec.digest.DigestUtils;
import org.apache.velocity.app.VelocityEngine;
import org.springframework.beans.factory.annotation.Value;
import org.springframework.mail.javamail.JavaMailSender;
import org.springframework.mail.javamail.MimeMessageHelper;
import org.springframework.scheduling.annotation.Async;
import org.springframework.stereotype.Service;
import org.springframework.transaction.annotation.Isolation;
import org.springframework.transaction.annotation.Propagation;
import org.springframework.transaction.annotation.Transactional;
import org.springframework.ui.velocity.VelocityEngineUtils;
import com.springinpractice.ch08.dao.SubscriberDao;
import com.springinpractice.ch08.model.Subscriber;
import com.springinpractice.ch08.service.ConfirmationExpiredException;
import com.springinpractice.ch08.service.ConfirmationFailedException;
import com.springinpractice.ch08.service.MailingListService;

... @Service and @Transactional ...
public class MailingListServiceImpl implements MailingListService {
    private static final String SUBSCRIBE_TEMPLATE_PATH =
        "mailingListSubscribe.vm";
    private static final long ONE_DAY_IN_MS = 24 * 60 * 60 * 1000;

    @Inject private SubscriberDao subscriberDao;
    @Inject private JavaMailSender mailSender;
    @Inject private VelocityEngine velocityEngine;

    @Value("#{mailingListServiceProps.noReplyEmailAddress}")
    private String noReplyEmailAddress;

    @Value("#{mailingListServiceProps.confirmSubscriptionUrl}")
    private String confirmSubscriptionUrl;

    @Value("#{mailingListServiceProps.confirmationKey}")
    private String confirmationKey;

    public Subscriber getSubscriber(Long id) {
        return subscriberDao.load(id);
    }

    @Async
    @Transactional(readOnly = false)
    public void addSubscriber(Subscriber subscriber) {        // ❶ Adds unconfirmed subscriber
        subscriberDao.create(subscriber);
        sendConfirmSubscriptionEmail(subscriber);             // ❷ Sends confirmation email
    }

    private void sendConfirmSubscriptionEmail(Subscriber subscriber) {
        MimeMessage message = mailSender.createMimeMessage();
```

❶ Adds unconfirmed subscriber

❷ Sends confirmation email

```
        MimeMessageHelper helper = new MimeMessageHelper(message);

        String digest = generateSubscriptionDigest(subscriber);      ◁──     Generates
        String url = confirmSubscriptionUrl                              ❸    digest
            + "?s=" + subscriber.getId() + "&amp;d=" + digest;   ◁───

        Map<String, Object> model = new HashMap<String, Object>();
        model.put("subscriber", subscriber);                            Creates
        model.put("url", url);                                    confirmation URL  ❹

        String text = VelocityEngineUtils.mergeTemplateIntoString(
            velocityEngine, SUBSCRIBE_TEMPLATE_PATH, model);

        try {
            helper.setSubject("Please confirm your subscription");
            helper.setTo(subscriber.getEmail());
            helper.setFrom(noReplyEmailAddress);
            helper.setSentDate(subscriber.getDateCreated());
            helper.setText(text, true);
        } catch (MessagingException e) {
            throw new RuntimeException(e);
        }

        mailSender.send(message);                                     Confirms  ❺
    }                                                                 subscriber

    @Transactional(readOnly = false)
    public void confirmSubscriber(Long subscriberId, String digest)   ◁───
        throws ConfirmationFailedException {

        Subscriber subscriber = getSubscriber(subscriberId);          ❻   Checks
        checkTimestamp(subscriber.getDateCreated().getTime());   ◁──      for expiry
        String expectedDigest = generateSubscriptionDigest(subscriber);  ◁──
        if (!digest.equals(expectedDigest)) {
            throw new ConfirmationFailedException("Bad digest");        Compares
        }                                                              digests   ❼
        subscriber.setConfirmed(true);
        subscriberDao.update(subscriber);
    }

    private String generateSubscriptionDigest(Subscriber subscriber) {
        return DigestUtils.shaHex(subscriber.getId() + ":"
            + confirmationKey);                                    ◁──     Digest
    }                                                                ❽   details

    private static void checkTimestamp(long timestamp)
        throws ConfirmationExpiredException {

        long now = System.currentTimeMillis();
        if (now - timestamp > ONE_DAY_IN_MS) {                    ◁──    Expiry
            throw new ConfirmationExpiredException();                ❾   details
        }
    }
}
```

The service bean so far includes two high-level functions: the ability to accept a subscription request and the ability to confirm a subscriber. At ❶ you see the first of the two. Here you take the unconfirmed Subscriber and save it in the database, and then send a confirmation email. Note that you're using the @Async annotation you saw in recipe 8.3. In this case you're putting the annotation on the addSubscriber() method, the idea being that this helps you meet the privacy requirement described earlier in the recipe. (If the subscription already exists, a constraint violation occurs; but the user never sees it because it's on another thread.) It would be somewhat cleaner to emulate the approach from recipe 8.3 where the calling thread does the database access; in this case, you'd report any exception other than a duplicate subscription exception, which you'd suppress.

You build the email at ❷. We covered the mechanics of creating an email in recipe 8.2, so we won't rehash that here. But as indicated, you need to create a secure link that the user can click to confirm their subscription. To do this, you create a digest ❸ and include that as part of a URL you create ❹.

In addition to sending confirmation emails, you process the result when a user clicks the email link in confirmSubscriber() ❺. It checks the timestamp on the subscription to make sure it hasn't expired ❻ and then checks to see whether the submitted digest matches the expected digest ❼. The expected digest is the result of hashing the subscriber ID concatenated with a secret key (the key is arbitrary, and you inject it into the service bean) ❽, and the expiration period is set to one day ❾.

To save space, we won't look at code listings for Subscriber.java and mailingList-Subscribe.vm. Neither file is particularly interesting for the purposes of this recipe. It's easy enough to infer the fields available on the former by looking at listing 8.13, and the latter is only a Velocity template that asks the user to click the link within 24 hours. If you want to see these, download the code from the book's website.

Similarly, the database table mirrors the structure of the Subscriber class, so see the code download for that.

APPLICATION CONTEXT CONFIGURATION

The Spring configuration extends the beans-service.xml configuration used in recipe 8.3. There's little to add because you're using annotations for component scanning and dependency injection. Add the following configuration:

```
<util:properties id="mailingListServiceProps"
    location="classpath:/spring/mailingListService.properties" />
```

The corresponding mailingListService.properties file looks like this (but feel free to use your own property values):

```
noReplyEmailAddress=noreply@example.com
confirmSubscriptionUrl=http://localhost:8080/sip/mailinglist
➥       /subscribe-confirm.html
confirmUnsubscriptionUrl=http://localhost:8080/sip/mailinglist
➥       /unsubscribe-confirm.html
confirmationKey=15cl@nbt$1s$h@IBharLR557+B
```

At this point you should be able to run the app. Sign up for the mailing list, and work through the flow we described earlier. The end result (once you confirm) should be that you have a record in the database with the confirmed flag set to true.

Discussion

Mailing lists are a little more involved than they might initially seem, owing to the need to prevent malicious subscriptions and unsubscriptions. In this recipe, we covered the subscription side. The sample code shows how to do unsubscriptions as well.

> **NOTE**   Be aware that users may be reading your confirmation email with a non-HTML client. They may not be able to click the confirmation link. It helps to provide a non-hyperlinked version of the confirmation URL that the user can cut/paste into a browser. Note that because the URL is long, it's possible that it may line wrap, and the user may not copy/paste it correctly. You can handle this by including explicit instructions in the email and by advising the user about potential causes in the event of a failed confirmation.

8.5   Publishing a news feed

PREREQUISITES
None

KEY TECHNOLOGIES
Spring Web MVC, RSS, ROME

Background

In recipe 8.4, you saw how to create a mailing list for your website. Mailing lists are nice from the website operator's perspective, because they involve collecting certain useful bits of information from your customers, such as their name and email address. If you have actual user account information, you can even target the user based on demographics, behavior, stated preferences, and so forth. But many users want to be able to keep up to date on your site without having to give you any personal information.

Enter the news feed. Users can subscribe to news feeds (for example, RSS feeds and Atom feeds) without revealing personal information other than, say, their IP address, user agent information, and whatever else the browser sends in the request headers. This is yet another example of a growing trend in web-based business (and indeed business everywhere): the customer is king.

Problem

Publish a news feed from your website or web application.

Solution

Spring 3.0 introduces a set of `View` classes for publishing feeds. These have their origin in the `AbstractRssView` class from the defunct Spring Modules project (http://java.net/projects/springmodules/), but now the `View` classes have made their way into the framework proper. Like the Spring `Modules` class, the new `View` classes are based on Sun's open source ROME API (http://rometools.org/).

Here you'll publish an RSS feed, which means you'll be working with `Abstract-RssFeedView`. But note that there's also an `AbstractAtomFeedView` for (yep) Atom feeds, and they share a common subclass in `AbstractFeedView`.

The general approach is for the controller to grab the necessary data from the service bean, such as a list of news items, drop that on a Model, and return a logical view name that you map to an AbstractRssFeedView subclass. This allows you to keep the controller, service bean, and news items ignorant of the fact that you're going to render the news items as an RSS feed. Let's see the whole thing in action.

THE VIEW

We may as well start with the AbstractRssFeedView implementation, because that's the core piece.

Listing 8.14   RSS news feed view: RssNewsFeedView.java

```java
package com.springinpractice.ch08.web;

import java.util.ArrayList;
import java.util.List;
import java.util.Map;
import javax.servlet.http.HttpServletRequest;
import javax.servlet.http.HttpServletResponse;
import org.springframework.web.servlet.view.feed.AbstractRssFeedView;
import com.springinpractice.ch08.model.NewsItem;
import com.sun.syndication.feed.rss.Channel;
import com.sun.syndication.feed.rss.Description;
import com.sun.syndication.feed.rss.Item;

public class RssNewsFeedView extends AbstractRssFeedView {        ❶ Extends AbstractRssFeedView
    private String feedTitle;                                    ❷ Injects feed metadata
    private String feedDesc;
    private String feedLink;

    ... setters for dependency injection ...

    protected void buildFeedMetadata(                            ❸ Builds feed metadata
        Map model, Channel feed, HttpServletRequest request) {

        feed.setTitle(feedTitle);
        feed.setDescription(feedDesc);
        feed.setLink(feedLink);
    }

    protected List<Item> buildFeedItems(
            Map model,
            HttpServletRequest request,
            HttpServletResponse response)                        ❹ Builds feed items
        throws Exception {

        List<NewsItem> newsItems =
            (List<NewsItem>) model.get("newsItemList");          ❺ Gets news items from model
        List<Item> feedItems = new ArrayList<Item>();
        if (newsItems != null) {                                 ❻ Map to feed items
            for (NewsItem newsItem : newsItems) {
                Item feedItem = new Item();
                feedItem.setTitle(newsItem.getTitle());
                feedItem.setAuthor(newsItem.getAuthor());
                feedItem.setPubDate(newsItem.getDatePublished());
                feedItem.setLink(newsItem.getLink());
```

```
                    Description desc = new Description();
                    desc.setType("text/html");
                    desc.setValue(newsItem.getDescription());
                    feedItem.setDescription(desc);

                    feedItems.add(feedItem);
                }
            }

            return feedItems;
        }
    }
```

You implement the view, *sans* an @Component annotation (you want to configure this bean explicitly in beans-web.xml), by extending the AbstractRssFeedView class ❶. You include a few metadata properties ❷ so you can configure those externally when you build your feed ❸.

Besides building the metadata, you need to build the feed items themselves ❹. You first grab the domain objects (here, a List of NewsItem objects, which is your own class) off the model ❺. Then you iterate over the NewsItems, converting them to FeedItems that you add to a list ❻. Note that you do an explicit null check to handle the case where the list of items is empty (which, as it turns out, means Spring can't automatically discover the model key, which in turn means the corresponding attribute is null). AbstractRssFeedView takes care of building the RSS Channel and serializing it to the servlet output stream.

To use the view, you'll need a controller. Let's pay that a visit.

THE CONTROLLER

The controller is amazingly simple, as shown next.

Listing 8.15   Minimalistic NewsController.java

```
package com.springinpractice.ch08.web;

import javax.inject.Inject;
import org.springframework.stereotype.Controller;
import org.springframework.ui.Model;
import org.springframework.web.bind.annotation.RequestMapping;
import com.springinpractice.ch08.service.NewsService;

@Controller
public final class NewsController {
    @Inject private NewsService newsService;

    @RequestMapping("/news.rss")
    public String rss(Model model) {                              ❶ Drops news
        model.addAttribute(newsService.getRecentNews());             onto model
        return "news";                                            ❷ Returns
    }                                                                view name
}
```

As promised, the controller is entirely straightforward. You grab the List of News-Items from the service bean and add it as an attribute to the Model ❶. Because you didn't specify an explicit attribute name, `Model` applies a naming convention that generates the name `newsItemList` for this particular attribute. As we hinted, if the list of news items is empty, Spring can't autodiscover the model key, and so the news items won't be stored under the desired key. You handled this in listing 8.15 by doing an explicit null check.

You return the logical view name "news" at ❷. As you'll see in a moment, you'll map that view name to an actual bean using the `BeanNameViewResolver`.

There isn't any need to review the `NewsItem`, `NewsServiceImpl`, and other related classes because this shows how the RSS piece works. If you want to see the other classes, consult the sample code. We do need to look at the application context, though.

THE APPLICATION CONTEXT

You need to add two things to beans-web.xml. First, add the view you created in listing 8.15:

```
<bean id="news"
    class="com.springinpractice.ch08.web.RssNewsFeedView"
    p:feedTitle=" News"
    p:feedDescription="Recent updates"
    p:feedLink="http://example.com" />
```

Then map the "news" logical view name to this view. To do this, you'll use the `BeanNameViewResolver`, which maps the logical view name to the bean having the same name (or ID), which is why you called your view "news" in the snippet. Here's the definition:

```
<bean class="org.springframework.web.servlet.view.BeanNameViewResolver" />
```

That's all. Once you put the news back end in place, direct your browser to

```
http://localhost:8080/sip/news.rss
```

(or whatever URL you're using), and you should see your news items showing up as an RSS feed. Congratulations!

Discussion

In this recipe, we've explored Spring's support for feed publication. We hope you'll agree that Spring makes publishing feeds both easy and clean.

There are some useful websites you should know about if you're going to publish an RSS feed. One is www.feedvalidator.org, which will tell you whether your feed is valid. Another is www.feedicons.com, which has numerous icons you can use to make your feed look great.

Once your feed is in place, consider fronting it with FeedBurner or a similar service. FeedBurner acts as a proxy to your feed, serving at least two useful purposes.

- You don't have to worry about load issues, because subscribers hit FeedBurner, not you, and FeedBurner updates its cache of your feed or feeds only on a periodic basis (roughly every half hour, but we've observed quite a bit of variability in our server logs).

- FeedBurner captures statistics on how many subscribers you have and, optionally, how many people are clicking through to visit pages on your site. It's useful to have visibility into that kind of data without having to write it yourself, which is more involved than you might guess because you have to account for multiple subscribers coming out of the same aggregator (Netvibes, Google Reader, and so forth).

8.6   Summary

We've come to the end of what we hope has been an interesting chapter on ways to keep in touch with your users and customers. It's a tried and true way of being successful on the web and in business, so it helps to know some of the standard options available.

In chapter 9, we'll extend the present discussion to cover additional ways in which your users and customers can communicate not only with you, but also with one another. Many websites and organizations are finding that building and taking advantage of community is an important way to understand user characteristics, likes, and dislikes; to generate content and traffic; and in general to generate value.

Creating a rich-text comment engine

This chapter covers
- Enabling user comments
- Supporting article delivery
- Including rich-text editing

A striking characteristic of several successful modern websites and web applications is the way in which they support community, sometimes for its own sake and sometimes in the service of other goals. Examples include sites like Facebook (social networking), LinkedIn (career networking), Wikipedia (online encyclopedia), Digg (social bookmarking), DZone (tech-specific social bookmarking), Amazon (retail), Pinterest (photo sharing), and YouTube (video sharing).

One important way to create a sense of community is to allow users to submit comments. The comments might target articles, blog posts, user submissions, products, or anything else where it's useful to respond to items in a public fashion.

In this chapter, you'll implement a comment engine. It will be generic in that it won't care what kind of item serves as a target. You'll begin with a basic comment engine. Then you'll embed it in an article-delivery engine. Next you'll add support for rich-text editing, with real-time client-side previewing. Finally you'll write tests that deal with the security issues that rich-text editing raises.

9.1   *Creating a basic user comment engine*

PREREQUISITES

None

KEY TECHNOLOGIES

JPA, Hibernate Core and Validator, programmatic transaction management, JavaMail

Background

Allowing users to comment on articles, blog posts, products, other users, and so forth is useful in many ways. If you're trying to build a sense of community, there's nothing like seeing users out and about, speaking their minds. That can be helpful if you're trying to choose the topic of your next article, or if your users are trying to decide which laptop to buy. And giving your community a voice will keep your users coming back. Comments can also help generate traffic by improving search-engine rankings, tying your site into a larger community of related sites, and making your pages more attractive link targets by providing a well-balanced view of the subject under discussion.

In this recipe, you'll build a simple comment engine. You'll build it in a generic way that allows you to use it for arbitrary targets, whether articles, products, or something else. You'll start with recipes 9.1 and 9.2 and then elaborate the design in recipes 9.3 and 9.4.

Problem

Allow users to read and submit comments for articles, blog posts, products, and so on. For now the comment engine should support only plain text comments, not rich text (but see recipe 9.3). Once a user posts a comment, the engine must notify the site admin by email.

Solution

You'll build a comment engine as just described. Recipe 9.1 treats the engine, and recipe 9.2 shows how to integrate it with an article-delivery system. Figure 9.1 shows the result after you're done with recipes 9.1 and 9.2.

Figure 9.2 shows the beans you'll use and how you'll wire them all up.

Again, in this recipe you're building the comment engine, not integrating it with article delivery, product catalogs, and so on, so all you're seeing is the comment engine.

DATABASE SCHEMA

One key goal for the comment engine is that it be agnostic with respect to the sorts of targets (articles, products, and so on) that comments can attach to. You're building a generic comment engine, not one for any particular target type.

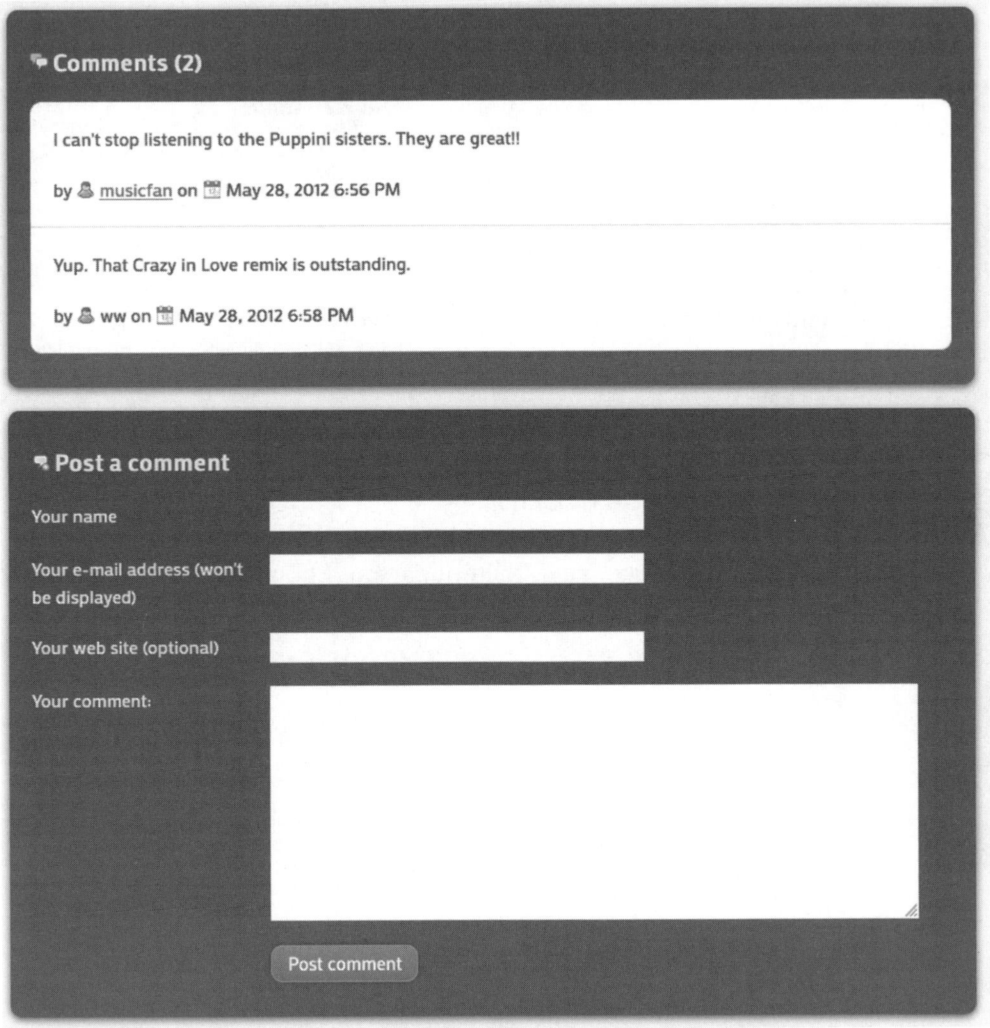

Comments (2)

I can't stop listening to the Puppini sisters. They are great!!

by 👤 musicfan on 🗓 May 28, 2012 6:56 PM

Yup. That Crazy in Love remix is outstanding.

by 👤 ww on 🗓 May 28, 2012 6:58 PM

Post a comment

Your name

Your e-mail address (won't be displayed)

Your web site (optional)

Your comment:

Post comment

Figure 9.1   The comment engine, with a comment list and a place to enter comments

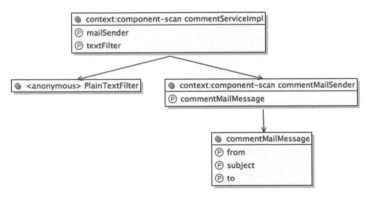

Figure 9.2   Comment engine bean-dependency graph. This shows what the comment service needs to filter comments and send notification emails.

Figure 9.3 shows a two-table E/R diagram for the database schema. You have a comment table for individual comments. You need a way to attach those to an arbitrary target, but you don't want to use a foreign key to something specific like an article; instead the generic comment_target table represents anything you might want to comment on. See schema.sql in the code download for the DDL for this pair of tables.

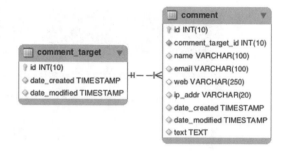

Figure 9.3   Comment engine E/R diagram. This simple schema allows you to attach comments to arbitrary targets.

Now let's see the Comment and CommentTarget domain objects that correspond to the two tables.

DOMAIN OBJECTS, ORM, AND VALIDATION

Listing 9.1 shows the Comment class. You're using it primarily as a domain object representing an individual comment, although you'll also use it as a form-backing bean when you get to the Spring Web MVC part in recipe 9.2.

Listing 9.1   Comment.java domain object

```
package com.springinpractice.ch09.comment.model;

import java.util.Date;
import javax.persistence.Column;
import javax.persistence.Entity;
import javax.persistence.GeneratedValue;
import javax.persistence.GenerationType;
import javax.persistence.Id;
import javax.persistence.Table;
import javax.validation.constraints.Size;
import org.hibernate.validator.constraints.Email;
import org.springframework.util.StringUtils;

@Entity
@Table(name = "comment")
public final class Comment implements Comparable<Comment> {        ①  Comparable for sorting

    ... various private fields ...

    @Id
    @GeneratedValue(strategy = GenerationType.AUTO)
    @Column(name = "id")
    public Long getId() { return id; }

    private void setId(Long id) { this.id = id; }

    @Size(min = 1, max = 100)
    @Column(name = "name")
    public String getName() { return name; }

    public void setName(String name) {
```

```
        this.name = StringUtils.trimWhitespace(name);
    }

    ... various getters and setters ...

    public int compareTo(Comment o) {
        return dateCreated.compareTo(o.dateCreated);
    }
}
```

2 Trims name

3 Sorts by date

As noted, Comment performs double-duty as a domain object and a form-backing bean. The various annotations reflect the dual roles: you have JPA annotations to store Comments in the database, and you have JSR 303 Bean Validation annotations to validate user-submitted form data.

At **1** you define Comment as implementing the Comparable interface. This is because you'll want to sort comments by date for display purposes.

At **2** you use Spring's convenient StringUtils.trimWhitespace() static method to trim any leading or trailing whitespace from the name. You use this instead of the standard JDK String.trim() method because the latter doesn't work when the name is null. Finally, you implement the compareTo() method **3** to sort by date.

The next listing contains CommentTarget.java, which represents an arbitrary target against which users can create comments.

Listing 9.2 CommentTarget.java, representing anything that can be commented on

```java
package com.springinpractice.ch09.comment.model;

import java.util.List;
import javax.persistence.CascadeType;
import javax.persistence.Column;
import javax.persistence.Entity;
import javax.persistence.GeneratedValue;
import javax.persistence.GenerationType;
import javax.persistence.Id;
import javax.persistence.JoinColumn;
import javax.persistence.OneToMany;
import javax.persistence.Table;

@Entity
@Table(name = "comment_target")
public final class CommentTarget {
    private Long id;
    private List<Comment> comments;

    @Id
    @GeneratedValue(strategy = GenerationType.AUTO)
    @Column(name = "id")
    public Long getId() { return id; }

    @SuppressWarnings("unused")
    private void setId(Long id) { this.id = id; }

    @OneToMany(cascade = CascadeType.ALL, orphanRemoval = true)
    @JoinColumn(name = "comment_target_id", nullable = false)
    public List<Comment> getComments() { return comments; }
```

Maintains comments **1**

```
public void setComments(List<Comment> comments) {
    this.comments = comments;
}
}
```

CommentTarget provides a way to group comments associated with a single target. Although in theory you could link comments to their articles, products, and other targets directly, the problem is that you want to keep the comment engine generic. You need some kind of generic grouping mechanism.

You have a list of comments ❶ with cascading persistence operations, meaning that if you save, update, or delete (there are some other operations as well) a CommentTarget, the same operation flows down to the Comment instances. orphanRemoval = true tells Hibernate to mark individual Comments for deletion when they're removed from their respective CommentTargets. You do this because individual Comments don't have their own lifecycle and don't have shared references.

Now it's time to check out the service bean for the comment engine.

THE COMMENTSERVICEIMPL SERVICE BEAN

The following listing presents the CommentServiceImpl service bean. (See the code download for the CommentService interface.)

Listing 9.3   CommentServiceImpl.java, a service bean

```
package com.springinpractice.ch09.comment.service.impl;

import java.util.Date;
import javax.inject.Inject;
import org.springframework.stereotype.Service;
import com.springinpractice.ch09.comment.model.Comment;
import com.springinpractice.ch09.comment.service.CommentService;
import com.springinpractice.ch09.comment.service.PostCommentCallback;
import com.springinpractice.ch09.comment.service.TextFilter;
import com.springinpractice.web.WebUtils;

@Service
public class CommentServiceImpl implements CommentService {
    @Inject private TextFilter textFilter;
    @Inject private CommentMailSender mailSender;

    public TextFilter getTextFilter() { return textFilter; }

    public void setTextFilter(TextFilter filter) {
        this.textFilter = filter;
    }

    public void postComment(                                        Posts comment ❶
        final Comment comment, final PostCommentCallback callback) {
        prepareComment(comment);                                    ❸ Saves
        callback.post(comment);                                        comment
        mailSender.sendNotificationEmail(comment);
    }                                                               Sends email
                                                                    ❹ notification

    private void prepareComment(final Comment comment) {
        comment.setWeb(WebUtils.cleanupWebUrl(comment.getWeb()));
```

Cleans up ❷
comment

```
        comment.setDateCreated(new Date());
        comment.setText(textFilter.filter(comment.getText()));
    }
}
```

The simple comment service is responsible primarily for saving user comments. It has a `postComment()` method ❶ that does a few things. First, it uses the `TextFilter` to clean up and format the comment ❷. The `TextFilter` abstraction hides the details, but this could be anything from converting newlines to `<br />` tags to processing a simplified markup language called Markdown.[1] (You'll see examples of both.) Second, it invokes the callback ❸, which is where you expect the associated application to link the comment to a domain object (such as an article) and save it. Finally, the method sends an email using the `CommentMailSender` ❹. We won't go into the details here because we did that in recipes 8.2 and 8.3. Those details are of course available in the code download.

Note that this service doesn't have an `@Transactional` annotation. You're assuming the client will already have a transactional context in place if one is necessary. In this case, it's important for the `sendNotificationEmail()` method to return quickly because you wouldn't want it unnecessarily extending the transaction's duration. In the `CommentMailSender` sample code, note that you use the `@Async` trick from recipe 8.3 to ensure a quick return.

You'll see more about `PostCommentCallback` in recipe 9.2, because that's where you'll link the comment engine to a simple article-delivery system. Now let's attend to the text filtering piece.

COMMENT TEXT FILTERING

Still referring to listing 9.3, in `prepareComment()` a bit of code does some text filtering. Because there are multiple strategies you might reasonably use to filter text, here we've created a `TextFilter` interface (see the code download) and made this property injectable. For now you'll use a simple text-filtering strategy, treating user input as plain text using the filter in the following listing. In recipe 9.3 you'll see more advanced text filtering.

Listing 9.4 PlainTextFilter.java: a simple strategy for filtering text

```java
package com.springinpractice.ch09.comment.service.impl;

import com.springinpractice.ch09.comment.service.TextFilter;

public final class PlainTextFilter implements TextFilter {

    public String filter(String text) {
        return text.replace("&", "&amp;")
            .replace("<", "&lt;")
            .replace(">", "&gt;")
            .replace("\n", "<br />");
    }
}
```

---

[1] See John Gruber, "Markdown: Basics," Daring Fireball, http://daringfireball.net/projects/markdown/basics for a good introduction.

This isn't the most time-efficient implementation of plain-text filtering, but it's simple and easy to speed up should you need to do that.

That does it for the comment service. You need to provide a couple of JSP fragments as well, to make it easier for client services to display comment lists and the form for posting new comments.

JSP FRAGMENT FOR DISPLAYING A COMMENT LIST

The next listing presents a JSP fragment for displaying a comment list. We've simplified the HTML to streamline the code; please see the code download for the full version.

> **Listing 9.5   /WEB-INF/jspf/comment/list.jspf**

```
<%@ taglib prefix="c" uri="http://java.sun.com/jsp/jstl/core" %>
<%@ taglib prefix="fmt" uri="http://java.sun.com/jsp/jstl/fmt" %>
<%@ taglib prefix="fn" uri="http://java.sun.com/jsp/jstl/functions" %>

<h2>Comments (${fn:length(commentList)})</h2>
<c:choose>
    <c:when test="${not empty commentList}">
        <c:forEach var="comment" items="${commentList}">
            <c:out value="${comment.text}" escapeXml="false" />
            by
            <c:choose>
                <c:when test="${empty comment.web}">
                    <c:out value="${comment.name}" />          ❶ c:out for output
                </c:when>                                          escaping
                <c:otherwise>
                    <a href="<c:out value="${comment.web}" />"
                       rel="nofollow"><c:out                   ❷ More output
                       value="${comment.name}" /></a>             escaping
                </c:otherwise>
            </c:choose>
            on
            <fmt:formatDate type="both" timeStyle="short"
                value="${comment.dateCreated}" />
        </c:forEach>
    </c:when>
    <c:otherwise>
        <p>No comments.</p>
    </c:otherwise>
</c:choose>
```

You loop over each of the comments, using `<c:out>` at ❶ and ❷ instead of JSP EL to ensure that you escape user-provided data appropriately for HTML. This helps prevent cross-site scripting (XSS) attacks.[2] Also, you include `rel="nofollow"` at ❷ to tell search engines not to follow the link. This makes comment spamming less attractive.

In addition to viewing a comment list, users need a way to post comments. We'll go over that next.

---

[2] See http://en.wikipedia.org/wiki/Cross-site_scripting for more information.

JSP FRAGMENT FOR POSTING A NEW COMMENT

The next listing contains the form for posting a new comment. We've suppressed parts of it here; see the code download for the full version.

> **Listing 9.6 /WEB-INF/jspf/comment/post.jspf**

```
<%@ taglib prefix="c" uri="http://java.sun.com/jsp/jstl/core" %>
<%@ taglib prefix="form" uri="http://www.springframework.org/tags/form" %>
<%@ taglib prefix="spring" uri="http://www.springframework.org/tags" %>

<spring:message var="postCommentLabel"
    code="commentForm.label.postComment" />

<h2>Post a comment</h2>
<form:form modelAttribute="comment" action="${postCommentUrl}">     ⟵   ❶ App-settable
    <form:errors>                                                          submit URL
        <div class="alert warning">
            <form:errors />
        </div>
    </form:errors>
    <div>
        <spring:message code="commentForm.label.yourName" />:
        <form:input path="name" />
        <form:errors path="name">
            <div class="formFieldError">
                <form:errors path="name" />
            </div>
        </form:errors>
    </div>

    ... other fields ...

    <div>
        <spring:message code="commentForm.label.yourComment" />:
        <form:textarea path="text" />
        <form:errors path="text">
            <div class="formFieldError">
                <form:errors path="text" />
            </div>
        </form:errors>
    </div>
    <input type="submit" value="${postCommentLabel}" />
</form:form>
```

We covered what you're doing here throughout chapter 4, so refer to that if anything looks confusing. At ❶ you set `action="${postCommentUrl}"`. You expect the client application to supply this URL so it can process posts as necessary.

It's time for the last piece: bean configuration.

BEAN CONFIGURATION

You need to do some bean configuration for the comment engine, as shown next.

> **Listing 9.7 /src/main/resources/spring/beans-service.xml**

```
<?xml version="1.0" encoding="UTF-8"?>
<beans xmlns="http://www.springframework.org/schema/beans"
    xmlns:context="http://www.springframework.org/schema/context"
```

```
xmlns:p="http://www.springframework.org/schema/p"
xmlns:task="http://www.springframework.org/schema/task"
xmlns:xsi="http://www.w3.org/2001/XMLSchema-instance"
xsi:schemaLocation="
    http://www.springframework.org/schema/beans
    http://www.springframework.org/schema/beans/spring-beans-3.1.xsd
    http://www.springframework.org/schema/context
    http://www.springframework.org/schema/context/
            spring-context-3.1.xsd
    http://www.springframework.org/schema/task
    http://www.springframework.org/schema/task/spring-task-3.1.xsd">

<context:property-placeholder
    location="classpath:/spring/environment.properties" />        ◀    ❶ Externalizes
                                                                       configuration
<bean id="commentMailMessage"                                   ◀
    class="org.springframework.mail.SimpleMailMessage"          Comment
    p:to="${comment.notification.to}"                           ❷ notification email
    p:from="${comment.notification.from}"
    p:subject="${comment.notification.subject}" />

<task:annotation-driven executor="executor" />        ◀──❸ For asynchronous email
<task:executor id="executor" pool-size="5" />

                                                Finds service and mail sender  ❹
<context:component-scan
    base-package="com.springinpractice.ch09.comment.service.impl" />  ◀

<bean class="com.springinpractice.ch09.comment.service.impl.    ◀
        PlainTextFilter" />                                         Creates
</beans>                                                           text
                                                                ❺ filter
```

This configuration should be easy to follow given what we've already discussed. First, you externalize your environment-specific properties into an environment.properties file ❶, and you use them to define a comment-notification email message ❷. You use the task namespace ❸ to activate the @Async annotation and define a thread pool to send email asynchronously. At ❹ you scan for the comment service and the mail sender, and at ❺ you create a plain-text comment filter for the comment service to use.

Let's discuss the comment engine briefly and then see how to use it.

Discussion

You've created a simple but effective comment engine. The design is such that you can use it for multiple purposes in a single application; it's not tied to articles, product reviews, or anything else. Having said that, the comment engine doesn't provide any value unless you integrate it with some other service. We'll address this issue in recipe 9.2.

By using the PlainTextFilter strategy for text filtering, you've taken the draconian step of preventing cross-site scripting and user-generated nuisance issues by disallowing HTML markup. But obviously there are plenty of situations in which you want to be more flexible. Can't you allow users to set font characteristics (bold, italics, subscripts and superscripts, and so on) without unduly exposing yourself to XSS attacks? What about hyperlinks and images? If you're running a technical software-development site, then you probably want a nice way for users to submit formatted code, and that probably involves `<pre>` tags. In short, although it's true that you want to minimize your exposure to security issues, you don't want to throw the baby out with the bath water. In many cases, you'd like to offer the end user the ability to enter rich text while simultaneously limiting security issues. We'll come back to that in recipe 9.3.

9.2 Integrating the comment engine with an article-delivery service

PREREQUISITES
Recipe 9.1 Creating a basic user comment engine

KEY TECHNOLOGIES
JPA, Hibernate Core, Spring Web MVC

Background

The comment engine you created in recipe 9.1 is generic, meaning you can use it to add comments to targets such as articles, blog posts, and products. But to use it, you have to integrate it with a relevant service.

In this recipe, you'll create a basic article-delivery engine and hook the comment engine up to it. We won't get into the details of the article-delivery engine because the point is to show how to use the comment engine, and the articles are incidental to that goal. If you're curious about those details, please look at the code download for the chapter. Also, chapter 12 revisits article delivery with a focus on different back-end strategies.

You'll need to update the Jetty configuration in this recipe for Maven, including specifying the username and password for the MySQL database.[3]

Problem

You have an article-delivery engine (or some other such service) that doesn't support user comments. You'd like to integrate it with the comment engine from recipe 9.1.

Solution

Because the purpose of this recipe is to show how to integrate the comment engine with a service you already have, you'll be minimalistic with respect to the service. That way we can keep the discussion focused on the integration, and we can minimize the number of assumptions we have to make about how the service works. For the sake of discussion, we'll assume you have an article-delivery service; but we intend this recipe to be more generally useful than that.

Let's begin by considering the bean-dependency graph in figure 9.4. This graph builds on figure 9.2 by adding article-specific context. Now you have a DAO, a service bean, and a controller to support article delivery. As the dependency graph shows, the

---

[3] See Willie Wheeler, "Code & Setup," http://springinpractice.com/code-and-setup.

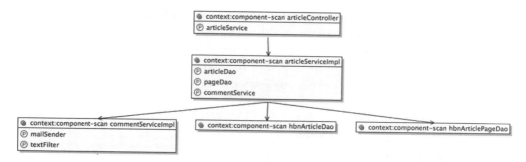

Figure 9.4   A bean-dependency graph showing the relationship between the comment service from recipe 9.1 and the article service from this recipe.

integration happens between the article and comment services. Specifically, you inject the comment service into the article service. You'll learn more about the collaboration shortly.

Next let's look at the slightly revised E/R diagram in figure 9.5. It's the same as figure 9.3, but it adds a couple of tables to support articles.

The schema is designed to support a 1-1 relationship between articles and comment targets in the domain model. If you look closely at the diagram, you'll see that you support this relationship by defining a foreign key from the article table to the comment_target table. Although you certainly could do that the other way around, that would make the comment engine aware of articles (the comment_target table would know about the article table), which would in turn undermine the goal of keeping the comment engine generic. So, the article table references the comment_target table instead of the reverse. You enforce a 1-1 relationship at the database level by including a unique constraint on the comment_target_id column in the article table. See schema.sql for the DDL.

You'll need to create an `Article` class and integrate it appropriately with `Comment-Target`. Let's do that next.

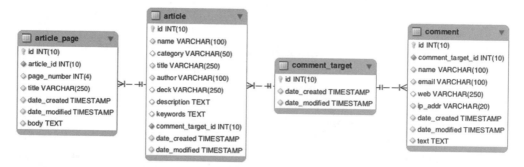

Figure 9.5   E/R diagram for the comment engine, with an article table added. You connect the tables using a foreign key in the article table that points at comment_target.

A SIMPLE ARTICLE CLASS, SHOWING HOW TO INTEGRATE WITH COMMENTTARGET

The following listing presents a simple `Article` class. We'll suppress the details (including the related `ArticlePage` class), focusing instead on the integration with `CommentTarget`, which is the real goal.

> **Listing 9.8   Article.java: an example of something that can be commented on**

```java
package com.springinpractice.ch09.article.model;

import java.util.*;
import javax.persistence.*;
import com.springinpractice.ch09.comment.model.Comment;
import com.springinpractice.ch09.comment.model.CommentTarget;

@Entity
@Table(name = "article")
... some named queries ...
public final class Article {
    private CommentTarget commentTarget;

    ... other fields ...

    @OneToOne(cascade = CascadeType.ALL, orphanRemoval = true)
    @JoinColumn(name = "comment_target_id")
    private CommentTarget getCommentTarget() {          ◁─┐  ❶ Private getter
        return commentTarget;                                  method
    }

    private void setCommentTarget(CommentTarget target) {
        this.commentTarget = target;
    }

    @Transient
    public List<Comment> getComments() {                ◁─┐  Transient
        return commentTarget.getComments();                ❷ property
    }

    ... other methods ...
}
```

The `Article` class has a getter ❶ and setter for the `commentTarget` property, but notice that you make them `private`. This doesn't prevent Spring from performing the dependency injection. You have this property to establish a 1-1 association between `Article` and `CommentTarget`, but you make it `private` because you don't want clients to have to code to it—that would be a nuisance. Instead, you want them to be able to work with comments directly. Therefore you expose a transient `getComments()` method ❷.

That does it for the article. For the details please see the code download. Let's build the corresponding DAO, which is very simple.

DATA ACCESS OBJECT FOR ARTICLES

This listing contains the DAO you use to save both articles and their comments.

Listing 9.9   HbnArticleDao.java

```java
package com.springinpractice.ch09.dao;

import org.springframework.stereotype.Repository;
import com.springinpractice.ch09.article.dao.ArticleDao;
import com.springinpractice.ch09.article.model.Article;
import com.springinpractice.dao.hibernate.AbstractHbnDao;

... other imports ...

@Repository
public class HbnArticleDao extends AbstractHibernateDao<Article>
    implements ArticleDao {

    ... a couple of finder methods, but nothing else ...
}
```

The only operations relevant to the current purpose are the ones defined in
`AbstractHibernateDao`. (The finders mentioned support article delivery and aren't
related to comments.) Also, because you've specified cascading persistence operations
on `Article.getCommentTarget()` and `CommentTarget.getComments()`, you don't
need separate DAOs for `CommentTarget` and `Comment`. Instead you add the comments
to the article and use the `ArticleDao` to save them.

Let's turn now to the article service bean.

THE ARTICLESERVICEIMPL SERVICE BEAN

The following listing shows the service bean for articles. (See the code download for
the interface.) It isn't part of the comment engine; it merely shows how to *use* the
comment engine.

Listing 9.10   ArticleServiceImpl.java service bean

```java
package com.springinpractice.ch09.article.service.impl;

import java.util.List;
import javax.inject.Inject;
import org.hibernate.Hibernate;
import org.springframework.stereotype.Service;
import org.springframework.transaction.annotation.Isolation;
import org.springframework.transaction.annotation.Propagation;
import org.springframework.transaction.annotation.Transactional;
import com.springinpractice.ch09.article.dao.ArticleDao;
import com.springinpractice.ch09.article.dao.ArticlePageDao;
import com.springinpractice.ch09.article.model.Article;
import com.springinpractice.ch09.article.model.ArticlePage;
import com.springinpractice.ch09.article.service.ArticleService;
import com.springinpractice.ch09.comment.model.Comment;
import com.springinpractice.ch09.comment.service.CommentService;
import com.springinpractice.ch09.comment.service.PostCommentCallback;

@Service
@Transactional(
    propagation = Propagation.REQUIRED,
    isolation = Isolation.DEFAULT,
```

```
    readOnly = true)
public class ArticleServiceImpl implements ArticleService {
    @Inject private ArticleDao articleDao;
    @Inject private ArticlePageDao pageDao;                       ❶ CommentService
    @Inject private CommentService commentService;                  dependency

    public List<Article> getAllArticles() { return articleDao.getAll(); }

    public ArticlePage getArticlePage(String articleName, int pageNumber) {
        ArticlePage page =
            pageDao.getByArticleNameAndPageNumber(articleName, pageNumber);
        Hibernate.initialize(page.getArticle().getComments());    ❷ Forces
        return page;                                                 eager load
    }

    @Transactional(
        propagation = Propagation.REQUIRED,
        isolation = Isolation.DEFAULT,
        readOnly = false)
    public void postComment(final String articleName, Comment comment) {
        commentService.postComment(comment, new PostCommentCallback() {
            public void post(Comment comment) {
                Article article = articleDao.getByName(articleName);
                article.getComments().add(comment);
                articleDao.update(article);             Article-aware
            }                                             callback ❸
        });
    }
}
```

`ArticleServiceImpl` is small but interesting. First, it has a dependency on `Com-mentService` ❶. This is entirely legitimate; `CommentService` is a lower-level service, and it often makes sense for higher-level services to call lower-level services. With respect to the comment engine, the expected use is for target-specific services (`Arti-cleService`, `BlogPostService`, `ProductService`, and so on) to delegate most of the work of posting comments to `CommentService`.

The next noteworthy item is a Hibernate tip. As you probably know, by default Hibernate loads collections lazily. Although it's possible to configure Hibernate to load any given collection eagerly, you mostly want the collection to be loaded lazily except in certain use cases. For example, when you load the master list of articles, you don't want to load all the comments, because you aren't displaying those with the article list. But when you load a single article, you do want to load the comments. There are different techniques to accomplish this with Hibernate, but one of the nicer ones is to call `Hibernate.initialize()` ❷. This call triggers an eager load.

Why we like Hibernate.initialize()

With Hibernate, there are various ways to specify whether a given association should be lazily or eagerly loaded. One way is to specify in the configuration that such-and-such association should always be lazily loaded, or else always eagerly loaded.

(continued)

But often that's not what you need. Take the relationship between articles and comments. When loading a master list of articles, you don't want to load the comments at all because you don't display them in that context. On the other hand, when you load a single article, you do want to load the comments. How do you handle that?

One approach is to use Spring's `OpenSessionInViewFilter` (or `OpenSessionInViewInterceptor`). This is a servlet filter that binds a Hibernate `Session` to the request-processing thread for the duration of the request. If the JSP needs to display something (say, a comment) that hasn't already been loaded, the `Session` is available and the data is loaded just-in-time.

We don't care for this approach, because it often triggers lots of database queries if you're not careful. Imagine, for instance, that you were to display comment counts with the master list of articles. The `OpenSessionInViewFilter` approach would generate a database query for each article.

Our preference is to define the association-loading behavior on a per-service-method basis. We might specify, for example, that calls to `getAllArticles()` (or whatever) don't necessarily load the comments, whereas a call to `getArticle(Long id)` definitely does load the associated comments. This approach, which involves using `Hibernate.initialize()` to trigger the eager load as illustrated in listing 9.10, offers flexibility in treating the association differently according to the use case. But some argue that it couples the service too tightly to the UI in that changes to the UI might necessitate changes to the service. This doesn't bother us because we don't find it surprising that adding new data elements to a UI might require support on the back end.

You delegate to `CommentService.postComment()` at ❸. With this call, you can see that the only thing `ArticleServiceImpl.postComment()` is doing is creating a callback and passing it to the `CommentService.postComment()` template method. The anonymous callback class implements the `PostCommentCallback` interface, which has a single `post()` method.

That takes care of the article service bean and the bulk of the integration. Let's move on to the web controller.

SPRING WEB MVC @CONTROLLER

The following listing shows the single controller, which handles article-related requests. We've suppressed code that isn't directly related to the comment engine, so if you want to see the whole thing you can check out the code download.

Listing 9.11   ArticleController.java

```
package com.springinpractice.ch09.article.web;

import javax.inject.Inject;
import javax.servlet.http.HttpServletRequest;
import javax.validation.Valid;
```

```
import org.springframework.beans.factory.annotation.Value;
import org.springframework.stereotype.Controller;
import org.springframework.ui.Model;
import org.springframework.validation.BindingResult;
import org.springframework.web.bind.WebDataBinder;
import org.springframework.web.bind.annotation.*;
import com.springinpractice.ch09.article.model.ArticlePage;
import com.springinpractice.ch09.article.service.ArticleService;
import com.springinpractice.ch09.comment.model.Comment;

@Controller
@RequestMapping("/articles")
public final class ArticleController {
    @Inject private ArticleService articleService;

    ... various fields and methods ...

    @RequestMapping(value = "", method = RequestMethod.GET)
    public String getArticles(Model model) {
        model.addAttribute(articleService.getAllArticles());
        return articleListViewName;
    }

    @RequestMapping(
        value = "/{articleName}/{pageNumber}", method = RequestMethod.GET)
    public String getArticlePage(
            @PathVariable String articleName,
            @PathVariable int pageNumber,
            Model model) {

        prepareModel(model, articleName, pageNumber);
        model.addAttribute(new Comment());
        return articlePageViewName;
    }
```

❶ Places comment on model

```
    @RequestMapping(
        value = "/{articleName}/comments", method = RequestMethod.POST)
    public String postComment(
            HttpServletRequest req,
            @PathVariable String articleName,
            @RequestParam("p") int pageNumber,
            Model model,
            @ModelAttribute @Valid Comment comment,
            BindingResult result) {

        if (result.hasErrors()) {
            result.reject("global.error");
            prepareModel(model, articleName, pageNumber);
            return postCommentFailedViewName;
        }
```

❷ Sets IP address before saving

```
        comment.setIpAddress(req.getRemoteAddr());
        articleService.postComment(articleName, comment);
        return "redirect:" + pageNumber + "#comment-" + comment.getId();
    }

    private void prepareModel(
        Model model, String articleName, int pageNumber) {
```

```
        ArticlePage page =
            articleService.getArticlePage(articleName, pageNumber);
        model.addAttribute(page);
        model.addAttribute(page.getArticle().getComments());
    }
}
```

❸ Gets page and comments

❹ Places comment list on model

In the `getArticlePage()` method, you create an empty comment and put it on the model **❶** so you can bind it to the comment form in the JSP. You require controllers to set the IP address before posting the comment **❷**.

In `prepareModel()`, you get the article page and the article's comments with a single service call **❸**. You place the comment list directly on the model **❹** so the generic comment JSP can find it, because that JSP doesn't know anything about articles or how to pull comments out of articles.

Let's pull together the comment list and comment form in a JSP.

AN ARTICLE JSP THAT USES THE TWO COMMENT JSP FRAGMENTS
The next listing shows a JSP that presents an individual article page. We've suppressed most of it, showing only the part that's relevant for displaying comments.

Listing 9.12   /WEB-INF/jsp/articles/articlePage.jsp

```
<!DOCTYPE HTML PUBLIC "-//W3C//DTD HTML 4.01//EN"
    "http://www.w3.org/TR/html4/strict.dtd">
...
<html xmlns="http://www.w3.org/1999/xhtml" xml:lang="en" lang="en">
...
<body>
...
<jsp:include page="/WEB-INF/jspf/comment/list.jspf" />
<jsp:include page="/WEB-INF/jspf/comment/post.jspf" />
...
</body>
</html>
```

❶ Comment list

❷ Posts comment form

At **❶** you show the list of comments, and immediately after that you show the form for posting a new comment **❷**.

To make it all work, you'll need a few Spring configuration files: beans-resources.xml, beans-service.xml, and beans-web.xml. Because none of those illustrates anything you haven't already seen, we won't cover them here; see the code download.

The comment-enhanced article engine is ready. Try it out!

Discussion

You learned here how to integrate the generic comment engine from recipe 9.1 with an arbitrary service, such as an article service. You did that using the template method pattern coupled with Spring's support for programmatic transaction management. Solid stuff, but not too much "wow" factor.

In recipe 9.3, you'll add pizzazz by introducing support for rich-text editing, courtesy of the RequireJS and PageDown JavaScript libraries. You'll see other goodies as well, including server-side JavaScript via Rhino and Spring's support for incorporating external resources (such as JavaScript files) into your apps.

9.3 *Adding rich-text support to the comment engine*

PREREQUISITES
Recipe 9.2 Integrating the comment engine with an article-delivery service

KEY TECHNOLOGIES
JavaScript, RequireJS, PageDown, Rhino, Spring resources

Background

In recipe 9.1, we looked at creating a simple comment engine. One basic requirement with comment engines is to prevent XSS attacks. The simplest way to do this is to prevent users from entering any markup, but in many cases that isn't an acceptable approach. A lot of times users need to be able to post links, images, code snippets, and so forth, and yet the requirement to prevent XSS doesn't go away.

> ### What is cross-site scripting (XSS)?
>
> XSS is a technique for attacking vulnerable web-based applications. Typically an attacker enters an HTML `<script>` tag into a web form, and the app redisplays it without filtering it. Users then download and execute potentially malicious code. Most of us are potential targets because we allow JavaScript to run in the browser.
>
> Despite the name, XSS also refers to attacks that inject malicious nonscript HTML. This could be anything from adding unmatched HTML tags (thus potentially messing up the page layout) to creating images with `width="1000000"` (again messing up the page) to creating malicious iFrames.
>
> Although web forms are the typical attack vector, they're by no means the only one. HTTP parameters in a URL are another possibility, as are web service inputs. Any user-provided input you display onscreen is a potential candidate for an XSS-based attack.

In this recipe we'll show how to support rich text in the comment engine while simultaneously guarding against XSS.

Problem

Support XSS-free rich text and content in the comment engine.

Solution

You'll do a number of fun and interesting things in this recipe. Principally you'll use the PageDown[4] rich-text editor from the folks at Attacklab and Stack Overflow to

---

[4] The PageDown project has a somewhat complicated history, including an original version called WMD by John Fraser (a.k.a. Attacklab), some forks, and most recently PageDown at http://code.google.com/p/pagedown/.

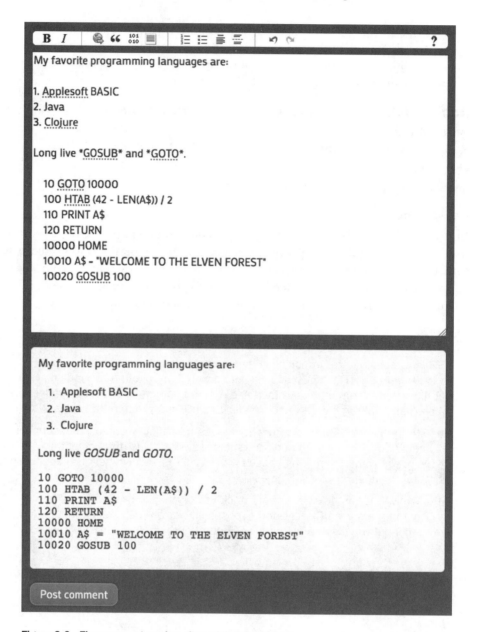

Figure 9.6   The comment engine after adding PageDown

endow the HTML <textarea> with rich-text capabilities, including a button bar for creating rich text, support for Markdown (also for creating rich text), and an impressive real-time, completely client-side HTML preview capability. See figure 9.6.

We won't go into the syntax of Markdown here because that's available on the web and because you can easily discover it by using the button bar interface. Instead let's preview the overall technical approach for this recipe:

- In the web browser, you're running a few PageDown scripts: `Markdown.Editor.js` (presents a rich-text editor), `Markdown.Converter.js` (converts Markdown to HTML), and `Markdown.Sanitizer.js` (cleans up the HTML and guards against XSS attacks). Users can create Markdown with the UI controls or enter it directly.
- When the user submits the form, you send Markdown to the server, not HTML. You do this for a couple of reasons. First, if there's any kind of validation error, you need to be able to prepopulate the `<textarea>` with the user's original Markdown, not with HTML. Second, if you wanted to support user edits after the comment had already been saved, you'd want the user to be able to edit the Markdown rather than the HTML.
- Once a valid form reaches the server, you use server-side JavaScript (via Rhino) to convert the Markdown to HTML. Specifically you use RequireJS (http://requirejs.org/) to set up a CommonJS (www.commonjs.org/) environment for PageDown, and then use PageDown (`Markdown.Converter.js` and `Markdown.Sanitizer.js`) to convert it to sanitized HTML.
- You save both the Markdown and the HTML to the database. Again, saving the Markdown makes it possible to support user edits, and saving the HTML allows you to avoid retranslating Markdown to HTML every time you display a comment.

That's the approach. Figure 9.7 presents the bean-dependency graph.

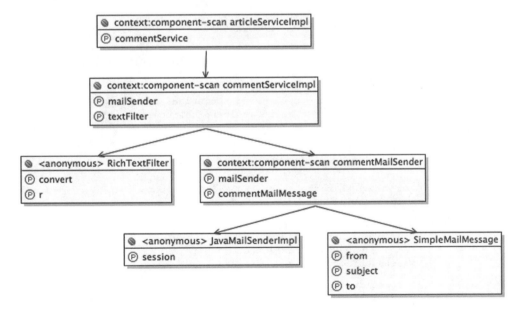

Figure 9.7 Bean-dependency graph for the version of the comment engine

Figure 9.7 is a lot like figure 9.2, but the text filter is a little more involved. Here the text filter supports rich text—specifically, Markdown (which allows embedded HTML). We'll discuss that shortly, but first let's see the updated application context configuration.

APPLICATION CONTEXT CONFIGURATION AND SPRING RESOURCES

The following listing shows the beans-service.xml configuration.

Listing 9.13   beans-service.xml configuration

```xml
<?xml version="1.0" encoding="UTF-8"?>
<beans xmlns="http://www.springframework.org/schema/beans"
    xmlns:context="http://www.springframework.org/schema/context"
    xmlns:p="http://www.springframework.org/schema/p"
    xmlns:task="http://www.springframework.org/schema/task"
    xmlns:tx="http://www.springframework.org/schema/tx"
    xmlns:util="http://www.springframework.org/schema/util"
    xmlns:xsi="http://www.w3.org/2001/XMLSchema-instance"
    xsi:schemaLocation="
        http://www.springframework.org/schema/beans
        http://www.springframework.org/schema/beans/spring-beans-3.1.xsd
        http://www.springframework.org/schema/context
        http://www.springframework.org/schema/context/
            spring-context-3.1.xsd
        http://www.springframework.org/schema/task
        http://www.springframework.org/schema/task/spring-task-3.1.xsd
        http://www.springframework.org/schema/tx
        http://www.springframework.org/schema/tx/spring-tx-3.1.xsd
        http://www.springframework.org/schema/util
        http://www.springframework.org/schema/util/spring-util-3.1.xsd">

    <context:property-placeholder
        location="classpath:/spring/environment.properties" />

    <bean id="sessionFactory"
        class="org.springframework.orm.hibernate3.annotation.
            AnnotationSessionFactoryBean"
        p:dataSource-ref="dataSource"
        p:packagesToScan="com.springinpractice.ch09.*.model"
        p:hibernateProperties-ref="hibernateProperties" />

    <util:properties id="hibernateProperties">
        <prop key="hibernate.dialect">
            org.hibernate.dialect.MySQL5InnoDBDialect
        </prop>
        <prop key="hibernate.show_sql">false</prop>
    </util:properties>

    <bean id="transactionManager"
        class="org.springframework.orm.hibernate3.
            HibernateTransactionManager"
        p:sessionFactory-ref="sessionFactory" />

    <tx:annotation-driven />

    <context:component-scan
        base-package="com.springinpractice.ch09.article.dao.hbn" />
```

```xml
<bean class="org.springframework.mail.javamail.JavaMailSenderImpl"
    p:session-ref="mailSession" />

<bean class="org.springframework.mail.SimpleMailMessage"
    p:to="${comment.notification.to}"
    p:from="${comment.notification.from}"
    p:subject="${comment.notification.subject}" />

<task:annotation-driven executor="executor" />
<task:executor id="executor" pool-size="5" />

<context:component-scan
    base-package="com.springinpractice.ch09.article.service.impl" />
<context:component-scan
    base-package="com.springinpractice.ch09.comment.service.impl" />

<bean class="com.springinpractice.ch09.comment.service.impl.
        RichTextFilter"
    p:r="classpath:/requirejs/r.js"
    p:convert="classpath:/convert.js" />
```

① **Injects classpath resource**

```xml
</beans>
```

In the listing you grab a couple of JavaScript resources off the classpath and inject them into the RichTextFilter **①**. The first one is r.js, which provides a RequireJS implementation that runs on Rhino.[5] The second one is convert.js, which is a custom script to launch a slightly modified version of Markdown.Sanitizer.js using RequireJS.[6] In both cases, Spring injects these into RichTextFilter as Resource objects so you can read and run them. Let's see how.

A RICH-TEXT FILTER FOR CONVERTING MARKDOWN TO HTML

The rich-text filter, RichTextFilter, converts user-entered Markdown to appropriately filtered HTML. You do this using Rhino, a helper object called JsRuntimeSupport (you'll see it in a bit) and a couple of scripts. See the following listing.

Listing 9.14 RichTextFilter.java: converts Markdown to sanitized HTML[7]

```java
package com.springinpractice.ch09.comment.service.impl;

import java.io.IOException;
import java.io.InputStreamReader;
import org.mozilla.javascript.Context;
import org.mozilla.javascript.Scriptable;
import org.mozilla.javascript.ScriptableObject;
import org.springframework.core.io.Resource;
import com.springinpractice.ch09.comment.service.TextFilter;
```

---

[5] See https://github.com/jrburke/r.js/. RequireJS is a CommonJS-compatible module system for loading JavaScript resources, and r.js adapts it to the Rhino JavaScript engine that ships with Java 6. You use RequireJS here because PageDown needs a CommonJS environment to run on the server side.

[6] The sample code contains the original and modified PageDown scripts at src/main/resources/pagedown. The modified scripts wrap the originals in a function to allow them to run correctly under RequireJS.

[7] Thanks to user sperumal on Stack Overflow for assistance in getting RequireJS to run on Rhino. See http://mng.bz/CC77.

```
public class RichTextFilter implements TextFilter {
    private Resource r;
    private Resource convert;

    public Resource getR() { return r; }

    public void setR(Resource r) { this.r = r; }

    public Resource getConvert() { return convert; }          Uses Rhino API directly ➊

    public void setConvert(Resource convert) { this.convert = convert; }

    public String filter(String text) {
        Context ctx = Context.enter();
        try {
            ScriptableObject scope =
                ctx.initStandardObjects(new JsRuntimeSupport(), true);

            String[] names = { "print", "load" };             Uses support object ➋
            scope.defineFunctionProperties(
                names, scope.getClass(), ScriptableObject.DONTENUM);
            Scriptable argsObj =
                ctx.newArray(scope, new Object[] { });
            scope.defineProperty(
                "arguments", argsObj, ScriptableObject.DONTENUM);
            ctx.evaluateReader(scope,
                new InputStreamReader(r.getInputStream()),      ➌ Reads r.js
                "r", 1, null

            scope.defineProperty(
                "markdown", text, ScriptableObject.DONTENUM);
            ctx.evaluateReader(scope,                           ➍ Reads
                new InputStreamReader(convert.getInputStream()),   convert.js
                "convert", 1, null);

            return (String) scope.get("html");                 ➎ Returns HTML
        } catch (IOException e) {
            throw new RuntimeException(e);
        } finally {
            Context.exit();
        }
    }
}
```

The filter() method ➊ uses the Rhino API directly instead of using the Java Scripting API because Rhino makes it easier to get RequireJS working. We won't get into all the details here—consult the Rhino API documentation for more information—but note that you initialize a top-level JavaScript scope at ➋ using a custom support object that provides load() and print() implementations for RequireJS. At ➌ you read and evaluate the r.js resource you injected in listing 9.13, which establishes RequireJS for loading JavaScript modules. At ➍ you do the same thing with a custom convert.js script, which loads the Markdown.Sanitizer.Modified module, converts the Markdown into sanitized HTML, and places the result in the global html variable so you can return it at ➎.

Here's convert.js:

```
require.config({
    baseUrl : "pagedown"
});

var html;

require([ "Markdown.Sanitizer.Modified" ], function(sanitizer) {
    html = sanitizer.getSanitizingConverter().makeHtml(markdown);
});
```

You don't have to load the Markdown.Converter.Modified module explicitly, because Markdown.Sanitizer.Modified loads it for you.

The next listing shows the JsRuntimeSupport class that we mentioned.

Listing 9.15 JsRuntimeSupport.java, providing load() and print() implementations

```
package com.springinpractice.ch09.comment.service.impl;

import java.io.IOException;
import java.io.InputStream;
import java.io.InputStreamReader;
import org.mozilla.javascript.Context;
import org.mozilla.javascript.Function;
import org.mozilla.javascript.Scriptable;
import org.mozilla.javascript.ScriptableObject;
import org.slf4j.Logger;
import org.slf4j.LoggerFactory;
import org.springframework.core.io.ClassPathResource;

public class JsRuntimeSupport extends ScriptableObject {
    private static final Logger log =
        LoggerFactory.getLogger(JsRuntimeSupport.class);

    public String getClassName() { return "test"; }

    public static void print(
        Context ctx, Scriptable thisObj, Object[] args, Function func) {

        for (int i = 0; i < args.length; i++) {
            log.info(Context.toString(args[i]));
        }
    }

    public static void load(
        Context ctx, Scriptable thisObj, Object[] args, Function func)
        throws IOException {

        JsRuntimeSupport support =
            (JsRuntimeSupport) getTopLevelScope(thisObj);
        for (int i = 0; i < args.length; i++) {
            String filename = Context.toString(args[i]);
            log.info("Loading file: {}", filename);
            support.processSource(ctx, filename);
        }
    }

    private void processSource(Context ctx, String filename)
        throws IOException {
```

❶ print() implementation

❷ load() implementation

```
        InputStream is = new ClassPathResource(filename).getInputStream();
        ctx.evaluateReader(
            this, new InputStreamReader(is), filename, 1, null);
    }
}
```

JsRuntimeSupport provides RequireJS with working print() ❶ and load() ❷ implementations, because the browser implementations aren't available on the server side. Note that the load() implementation grabs files from the classpath. This is how you load the Markdown.Sanitizer.Modified and Markdown.Converter.Modified modules.

Start the app, and point the browser at http://localhost:8080/sip to try the new editor. If you know Markdown, you can enter it directly. Otherwise, use the button bar on the editor to create Markdown.

Discussion

Recipe 9.3 enhanced the plain-text editor from recipe 9.2 into a rich-text editor. Rich text offers important features, such as the ability to style text, add images and links, and so forth. But such features carry their own risks, because they allow ill-intentioned parties to create XSS if you're not careful.

To that point, it's important from a security perspective that you test the filter. The next recipe shows how you can use JUnit and Spring's TestContext framework to get a handle on this task.

9.4   *Testing the HTML filter*

PREREQUISITES
Recipe 9.3 Adding rich-text support to the comment engine

KEY TECHNOLOGIES
JUnit, Spring TestContext framework

Background

Whether or not you're a proponent of test-driven development (TDD) or even unit and/or integration testing in general, there's no doubt that in some cases it makes a lot of sense to write such tests. One case is when you're writing code that's addressing security needs, such as the HTML filter.

Problem

Write tests to ensure that the comment engine filters out potential XSS attacks.

Solution

You'll get a slight jump on the content from chapter 10 and implement the first integration test here using JUnit and the Spring TestContext framework. The rich-text comment engine is exactly the sort of place where testing is critical, so we'll show how to do that here. It should be easy to follow, but if you have questions, continue on to chapter 10.

The next listing presents an example of what an integration test for RichTextFilter might look like. This isn't a full-blown test, but it gives you an idea of what would be involved in developing a more comprehensive test.

Listing 9.16 RichTextFilterTest.java: integration test based on JUnit

```java
package com.springinpractice.ch09.comment.service.impl;

import static org.junit.Assert.assertEquals;

import org.junit.After;
import org.junit.Before;
import org.junit.Test;
import org.springframework.test.context.ContextConfiguration;          Config file   ❶
import org.springframework.test.context.junit4.                        location
        AbstractJUnit4SpringContextTests;

@ContextConfiguration(locations = "/spring/beans-service-richtext.xml")  ◀─┘
public class RichTextFilterTests
        extends AbstractJUnit4SpringContextTests {      ◀─┐  Extends
                                                      ❷  support class
    private RichTextFilter filter;

    @Before
    public void setUp() throws Exception {
        this.filter = applicationContext.getBean(RichTextFilter.class);   ◀─┐
    }
                                                      Gets filter from
    @After                                            app context  ❸
    public void tearDown() throws Exception {
        this.filter = null;
    }
                                                      ❹  Verifies filtering
    @Test                                                behavior
    public void testAWithJavaScriptUrls() {     ◀─┘
        String in = "<a href=\"javascript:alert('hi')\">Hi</a>";
        String out = "<p>Hi</p>";
        assertEquals(out, filter.filter(in));
    }

    ... other tests ...
}
```

In the listing we've suppressed most of the test cases (even in the code download, the cover is thin), but we're focusing on how to conduct the test. The main issue for integration-testing beans is that you need access to the Spring application context so you can inject any necessary dependencies. Here you want to inject r.js and convert.js. Recall from recipe 9.3 that convert.js loads Markdown.Sanitizer.Modified, which in turn loads Markdown.Converter.Modified. Ultimately these latter two give you the conversion and sanitation that you want to see.

At ❶ you specify the locations for your Spring app context configuration files. You're using src/main/resources/spring/beans-service-richtext.xml, which is a simplified version of the beans-service.xml configuration from recipe 9.3:

```
<?xml version="1.0" encoding="UTF-8"?>
<beans xmlns="http://www.springframework.org/schema/beans"
    xmlns:p="http://www.springframework.org/schema/p"
    xmlns:xsi="http://www.w3.org/2001/XMLSchema-instance"
    xsi:schemaLocation="
        http://www.springframework.org/schema/beans
        http://www.springframework.org/schema/beans/spring-beans-3.1.xsd">

    <bean class="com.springinpractice.ch09.comment.service.impl.
                 RichTextFilter"
        p:r="classpath:/requirejs/r.js"
        p:convert="classpath:/convert.js" />
</beans>
```

Note that this involves moving the filter definition out of the existing beans-service.xml file into beans-service-richtext.xml and updating web.xml to reflect the new beans-service-richtext.xml file. See the code download.

At ❷ you extend `AbstractJUnit4SpringContextTests`, a support class for the `ApplicationContextAware` interface. Although you could implement the `ApplicationContextAware` interface directly and apply the type-level `@RunWith` (`SpringJUnit4ClassRunner.class`) annotation, that would require you to provide the setter for the `applicationContext` property yourself, and there's no reason to do that here. When you extend `AbstractJUnit4SpringContextTests`, you don't have to specify the `@RunWith` annotation because you inherit it from the abstract class.

At ❸ you get the filter bean under test from the application context. It comes with the resources already injected. Finally, at ❹ you verify that the filter converts and sanitizes Markdown input the way you expect.

Try running the tests using Maven: `mvn clean test`.

Discussion

The test in this recipe is an integration test because you're not testing the `RichTextFilter`: you're testing how it works in conjunction with several key external scripts. Usually you want to run unit tests and integration tests separately from one another. In a continuous integration context, you generally want to run unit tests (perhaps with a handful of strategically chosen integration tests) to get fast feedback about whether you broke the build. Integration tests, because they access external resources, are much slower than unit tests, and you should typically separate them.

Here you've added the test to the src/test folder, which is where you also place your unit tests. Also, you haven't used many of the features of the Spring TestContext framework, such as the ability to run any given test in a transaction that you roll back at the test's conclusion to maintain a known test data baseline. The following chapter explains how you can segregate integration tests from unit tests, and how you can take advantage of some of the more advanced features of the Spring TestContext framework.

9.5 *Summary*

In this chapter we've taken a detailed look at implementing a rich-text comment engine. In the course of doing that, we explored RequireJS, PageDown, Rhino, and Spring resources. You also learned how to use Spring's TestContext framework to remove XSS vulnerabilities from your rich-text filter.

In chapter 10, we'll build on recipe 9.4 and expand our coverage of integration testing with Spring.

10

This chapter covers

- Maven configuration for Spring integration testing
- Writing transactional happy-path tests
- Creating exception and performance tests

Ideally, testing is a core activity of the practicing software developer, and it so happens that the dependency-injection approach to software design is especially useful in the testing arena. Dependency injection is particularly useful in unit testing, where you desire to test small units of code in isolation from other code. With dependency injection you can inject *mock* dependencies with prescribed behavior into code units, which allows you to isolate faults to the code under test.

A step up from unit testing is integration testing. The idea here is to test collaborations between units of code. An integration test can be fairly narrow, perhaps involving a single collaboration between a web controller and a service bean (with DAO dependencies mocked out). At the other extreme it can involve deploying the code under test to a servlet container (or other container), sending HTTP requests and parsing HTTP responses for the expected output.

This chapter presents Spring's TestContext framework, which offers features useful for both unit and integration testing. Here we'll focus on integration testing because the features in this area are especially powerful.

Figure 10.1 A simple contact-management application for which you'll write integration tests

Maven and JUnit also play major roles. You typically want to be able to run the tests during project builds, so you'll see how to do that with Maven. Concerning the test framework itself, you have two options: JUnit and TestNG. Although Spring provides support for TestNG tests, you use JUnit here because the key Spring TestContext features don't depend on the underlying test framework, and JUnit is probably more familiar to most readers.

You'll build integration tests for the simple contact-management application that's available as part of the code download for this book; see figure 10.1. We won't present any of the code for the sample app because it's the test code we're interested in, but again you may download the code if you wish.

Your first task is Maven setup, mostly around declaring plug-ins and dependencies.

10.1 Configuring Maven for integration testing

PREREQUISITES
Basic familiarity with Maven 3

KEY TECHNOLOGIES
Maven 3, Failsafe Maven plug-in, Build Helper Maven plug-in

Background

Maven is one of the more popular build-automation tools in the Java world, and as you might expect, it supports integration testing. Unfortunately, its out-of-the-box configuration leaves a couple of things to be desired where integration testing is concerned:

- Although Maven's default lifecycle includes an `integration-test` phase, by default no goals bind to it.
- You could place integration tests and their associated resources in the src/test/java and src/test/resources folders, respectively, but it would be nice to separate integration tests from unit tests more cleanly.

This recipe shows how to remedy this situation. This is a Maven recipe rather than a Spring recipe, but you need it to set the stage for the recipes that follow.

Problem

Configure Maven to run integration tests, keeping integration tests separate from unit tests.

Solution

Before diving into the specifics of the Maven plug-in configuration, it will be helpful to review the phases of the default Maven lifecycle, which represents something like a standard build. Figure 10.2 shows these phases in graphical form. We've taken the liberty of collapsing closely related phases into a single box on the diagram to improve clarity. We don't need to peer too closely at the details (this is after all a Spring book), but suffice it to say that the phases provide hooks onto which you can hang additional goals related to integration testing. Let's start by creating new source and resource folders for your integration tests.

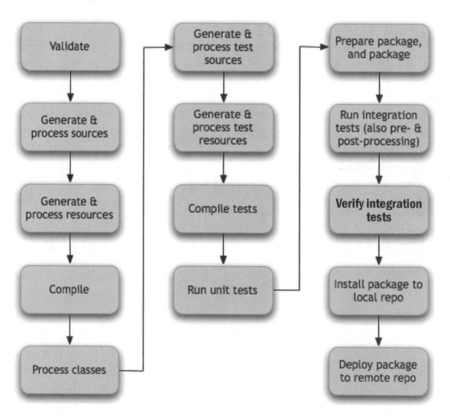

Figure 10.2   Overview of the default Maven lifecycle

BUILD HELPER MAVEN PLUG-IN

Your first task is to create dedicated source and resource directories for your integration tests to keep yourself from getting them mixed up with unit tests. To accomplish this, you'll use the Build Helper Maven plug-in as illustrated in the following listing. You're placing this in the top-level project object model (POM) because you want to enable integration testing across all projects.

> **Listing 10.1   Adding new source and resource directories to Maven**

```
<plugin>
    <groupId>org.codehaus.mojo</groupId>
    <artifactId>build-helper-maven-plugin</artifactId>
    <version>1.5</version>
    <executions>
        <execution>
            <id>add-it-source</id>
            <goals>
                <goal>add-test-source</goal>
            </goals>
            <configuration>
                <sources>
                    <source>src/it/java</source>          ❶ Adds test source
                </sources>                                    directory
            </configuration>
        </execution>
        <execution>
            <id>add-it-resource</id>
            <goals>
                <goal>add-test-resource</goal>
            </goals>
            <configuration>
                <resources>
                    <resource>                            ❷ Adds test
                        <directory>src/it/resources</directory>  resource
                    </resource>                               directory
                </resources>
            </configuration>
        </execution>
    </executions>
</plugin>
```

Normally there is a single test source directory (src/test/java) and a single test resource directory (src/test/resources). In effect what you're doing in the previous listing is adding a second test source directory and a second test resource directory. At ❶ you add the src/it/java ("it" stands for integration test) test source directory to the build. This is where you'll place the Java code for the integration tests. You accomplish this small feat using the plug-in's add-test-source goal. By default the plug-in binds this goal to the generate-test-sources lifecycle phase, and you don't have any reason to change that.

The configuration at ❷ is entirely analogous. This time you're adding the src/it/resources test resource directory to the build. You'll store things like bean configuration files and SQL scripts here. In this case you rely on the plug-in's `add-test-resource` goal, which this time is bound to the `generate-test-resources` phase.

Maven doesn't distinguish between unit-test, integration-test directories

The new test source and resource directories are nothing more than an attempt to make the project structure more developer-friendly. We happen to prefer keeping unit tests and integration tests separate, and that's what the Build Helper Maven plug-in is helping you do.

Note that from Maven's point of view, you've added new test source and resource directories. Maven has no idea that you intend to store unit-test goodies in one pair of directories and integration-test goodies in the other.

A couple of things follow from this. First, the `test-compile` phase compiles all the test code at once, whether it's unit-test code or integration-test code. It compiles any code in a test source directory. That shouldn't be a big deal.

Second, to run unit tests and integration tests separately (and that *is* a big deal, because you typically want to run unit tests with every build but not integration tests, because they're slower), you need some way to distinguish unit-test cases from integration-test cases. We'll get to that shortly.

Build Helper has indeed helped your build by allowing you to keep your project structure nice and tidy. The next concern is how to go about running your integration tests. Rather than using the standard Surefire Maven plug-in (which is designed for unit tests), we'll turn to the Failsafe Maven plug-in (designed specifically for integration tests).

FAILSAFE MAVEN PLUG-IN

Before going over the Failsafe configuration, it will help to understand the difference between Surefire and Failsafe. You might reasonably ask why you can't run your integration tests using Surefire. After all, it's designed to run tests.

The major difference between the two is that Surefire fails the build immediately when a unit test fails; Failsafe allows the build to proceed to a cleanup phase. With unit tests, there's no general environmental setup (there are only test fixtures specific to individual test cases, and these don't reference external resources), so there's nothing to tear down if a test fails. But with integration tests, there may very well be a general environmental setup, such as building a clean test database or perhaps deploying a package to a remote server. If an integration test were to fail, you'd want the build to perform the cleanup before ending the build.

That background should help you understand better how Failsafe works, so let's look more closely. In figure 10.2 we offered a high-level overview of the default Maven lifecycle, but we'll zero in on the specific phases we care about for integration testing. See figure 10.3.

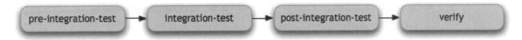

Figure 10.3   The key Maven lifecycle phases for integration testing

The Failsafe plug-in has two goals:

- An `integration-test` goal, binding by default to the `integration-test` phase, that runs the integration tests
- A `verify` goal, binding by default to the `verify` phase, that verifies that the integration tests passed

The Failsafe plug-in doesn't bind anything to either the `pre-integration-test` or the `post-integration-test` phase. You won't need to do anything during those phases for the purposes of this chapter because you'll handle environment setup and (as needed) teardown as part of the integration tests.

The following listing shows how to deploy the Failsafe plug-in.

Listing 10.2   Binding integration test goals to the default lifecycle

```
<plugin>
    <artifactId>maven-failsafe-plugin</artifactId>
    <version>2.5</version>
    <configuration>
        <junitArtifactName>
            org.junit:com.springsource.org.junit          Fix JUnit
        </junitArtifactName>                             ❶ artifact name
    </configuration>
    <executions>
        <execution>
            <id>integration-test</id>
            <goals>
                <goal>integration-test</goal>
            </goals>
        </execution>
        <execution>
            <id>verify</id>
            <goals>
                <goal>verify</goal>
            </goals>
        </execution>
    </executions>
</plugin>
```

There's not a lot to say here, but one thing to point out is that because you're using SpringSource's Enterprise Bundle Repository (EBR), you need to help the Failsafe plug-in deal with the fact that the EBR renames the JUnit artifact (or TestNG if you're using that). That's what you're doing at ❶.[1]

We mentioned in the earlier sidebar that Maven doesn't distinguish unit-test directories from integration-test directories. They're all test directories to Maven. Yet you

---

[1] See JIRA issue EBR-220 at https://issuetracker.springsource.com/browse/EBR-220.

need some way to ensure that only unit tests run during the test phase and only integration tests run during the integration-test phase. Here you rely on filename conventions that the Surefire and Failsafe plug-ins use. Basically, if a test case's filename matches a Surefire pattern, then Surefire will run it; and if it matches a Failsafe pattern, then Failsafe will run it. Table 10.1 lists the default patterns for Surefire and Failsafe.

Surefire patterns	Failsafe patterns
**/Test*.java	**/*Test.java
**/*TestCase.java	**/IT*.java
**/*IT.java	**/*ITCase.java

Table 10.1   Default Surefire and Failsafe filename pattern matching

You can change these patterns in your plug-in configuration, but here you'll go with these. For integration tests, you'll use the **/*IT.java pattern for no special reason.

You need to do only one more piece of setup: declare test dependencies.

MAVEN DEPENDENCIES

The plug-ins you just installed take care of the Maven integration-testing infrastructure, but you need to include integration testing dependencies as well.

Listing 10.3   Integration-testing dependencies

```
<dependency>
    <groupId>org.springframework</groupId>
    <artifactId>org.springframework.test</artifactId>       ◁──┐   Spring TestContext
    <version>${spring.version}</version>                       ❶   framework
    <scope>test</scope>
</dependency>
<dependency>
    <groupId>org.junit</groupId>
    <artifactId>com.springsource.org.junit</artifactId>     ◁──┐   JUnit for
    <version>${junit.version}</version>                        ❷   tests
    <scope>test</scope>
</dependency>
<dependency>
    <groupId>org.mockito</groupId>
    <artifactId>com.springsource.org.mockito</artifactId>   ◁──┐   Mockito for
    <version>${mockito.version}</version>                      ❸   mock objects
    <scope>test</scope>
</dependency>
```

You'll learn more about these dependencies in the upcoming recipes, but we can make a few high-level remarks here. The Spring TestContext framework dependency ❶ is Spring's integration-testing framework. JUnit ❷ is a unit-testing framework, but it's also useful for writing integration tests. Mockito ❸ allows you to mock out dependencies. Mock objects are especially useful for unit testing, but sometimes you need mocks in integration tests too.

That wraps up the first recipe. Now you can write your first integration test.

Discussion

In this recipe, you've prepared your Maven configuration for the integration-test recipes that follow. Although it's possible to run integration tests outside of a build context, in practice they're almost always included as part of a build, and that's what we've shown how to do.

Recipe 10.2 builds on this base to create simple but nontrivial happy-path integration tests involving transactional access to a live test database.

10.2 *Writing transactional happy-path integration tests*

PREREQUISITES
Recipe 10.1 Configuring Maven for integration testing

KEY TECHNOLOGIES
Spring TestContext framework, JUnit, DBMS

Background

Among the simplest sort of integration tests are those that test for routine, nonexceptional behavior, often called happy-path behavior in testing circles. This might involve, for instance, requesting an object from a web-based interface, having all the back-end transactional magic happen (for example, hitting a database), and then verifying that the returned result is what's expected. Because this type of test forms the basis for more sophisticated tests, it makes a good starting point, so we'll explore happy-path integration testing in this recipe.

Problem

Write happy-path integration tests to verify correct integration between web, service, DAO, and database components.

Solution

As a general statement, integration testing involves selecting large vertical slices of an application's architecture and testing such slices as collaborating integrated wholes. Ideally you're able to reuse as much of the app's native configuration as possible, partly to minimize code duplication, but more fundamentally to put the configuration to test. It is, after all, part of what makes the app work. In the normal situation, you fall short of that ideal because you don't want to run integration tests against live production databases. But you can get pretty close. If you can identify the relevant slices and make it easy to choose between the test and production databases, you have a winner.

We'll begin with details of how to implement the strategy just outlined using Spring. Spring's approach to configuration makes it easy and elegant to do this.

STRUCTURING APP CONFIGURATION TO FACILITATE INTEGRATION TESTING
In figure 10.4 we highlight the part of the stack we'll address with our approach to integration testing. Although you don't quite hit 100% of the stack (you're excluding the `DispatcherServlet` and JSPs from the scope), what you get represents a reasonable

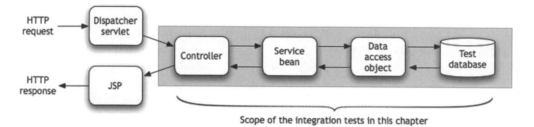

Figure 10.4 **You'll write integration tests for the stack that start from the controller and go all the way back to the database.**

balance between coverage on the one hand, and execution speed and ease of implementation on the other.

As illustrated, the stack starts from the controller and pushes all the way back to the database. It bears repeating that you can write integration tests that are more aggressive about coverage—tests that include the `DispatcherServlet` and JSPs, for example. And in the case of the `DispatcherServlet`, there are strong reasons for doing so, among them the desire to verify that controller annotations (`@InitBinder`, `@RequestMapping`, `@PathVariable`, `@Valid`, and so on)[2] do what they're supposed to do. But you'd take a hit for expanding that coverage, either by making the testing more complicated (you'd have to provide the `DispatcherServlet` configuration, which is more involved than controller configuration) or by slowing down the execution (for instance, by running the tests in-container). This chapter opts for the stack shown in figure 10.4, although it's useful to know that other options are available.

Now that you've identified the stack, you need to figure out how to implement the wiring only one time. You'll reuse that wiring across both normal app use and integration test contexts. You'll see that it's easy to do. First, figure 10.5 shows the application's bean-dependency diagram, using the normal data source.

In essence, two things differ between the app's normal configuration (the one shown in figure 10.5) and its integration-testing configuration:

- The database.
- How you get the `DataSource`. (JNDI lookups are available in Java EE container environments but require more work to establish outside such environments.)[3]

You want to carve off the `DataSource` definition from the rest of the configuration and select a definition based on the context. When all is said and done, you want the integration-test configuration to look like figure 10.6, and you want to factor out as much of what's common to the main and integration-test configurations as you can.

---

[2] The case for testing JSPs in this fashion is, in our opinion, somewhat weaker because view components change more often and are thus more prone to cause spurious test failures. Still, the right approach here can pay dividends.

[3] It can be done; it's just more work. See org.springframework.mock.jndi.SimpleNamingContextBuilder for details. In our opinion the approach we present here is more straightforward.

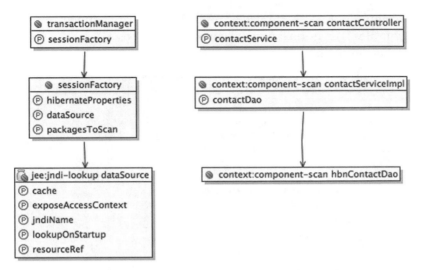

Figure 10.5 Bean-dependency diagram for a simple contact-management application. This is the normal app configuration, not the integration-test configuration.

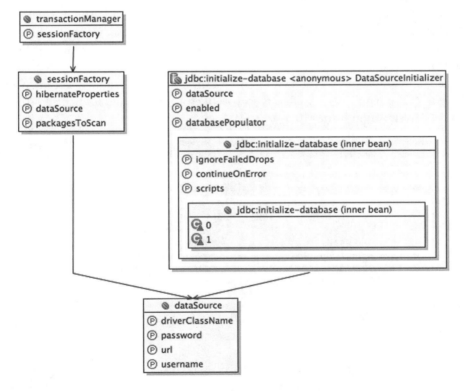

Figure 10.6 Spring app context configuration for integration tests. The `DataSourceInitializer` sets up the test database by running DDL and test data DML. The controller, service, and DAO are suppressed because they're exactly the same as in figure 10.5.

You can accomplish the desired refactoring by having two separate `DataSource` bean configuration files. For normal app execution, the app uses the bean configuration shown in the next listing.

Listing 10.4   beans-datasource.xml, for normal app usage

```xml
<?xml version="1.0" encoding="UTF-8"?>
<beans xmlns="http://www.springframework.org/schema/beans"
    xmlns:jee="http://www.springframework.org/schema/jee"
    xmlns:xsi="http://www.w3.org/2001/XMLSchema-instance"
    xsi:schemaLocation="http://www.springframework.org/schema/beans
        http://www.springframework.org/schema/beans/spring-beans-3.0.xsd
        http://www.springframework.org/schema/jee
        http://www.springframework.org/schema/jee/spring-jee-3.0.xsd">

    <jee:jndi-lookup id="dataSource" jndi-name="jdbc/sip10DS"
        resource-ref="true" />
</beans>
```

That's just the `DataSource` lookup; you configure the `DataSource` via whatever container-specific means the container makes available. The sample code uses /WEB-INF/jetty-env.xml to configure the `DataSource`.

The application pulls this configuration into the fold using the normal `context-ConfigLocation` means available through web.xml. You've seen that configuration so many times by now that we won't repeat it here, but look at web.xml in the sample code if you'd like to see it again.

For integration tests, the bean configuration is considerably different. You don't have a JNDI environment available, so you need to both build and configure a `Data-Source`, as shown in listing 10.5.

Listing 10.5   beans-datasource-it.xml, for integration testing

```xml
<?xml version="1.0" encoding="UTF-8"?>
<beans xmlns="http://www.springframework.org/schema/beans"
    xmlns:context="http://www.springframework.org/schema/context"
    xmlns:jdbc="http://www.springframework.org/schema/jdbc"
    xmlns:p="http://www.springframework.org/schema/p"
    xmlns:xsi="http://www.w3.org/2001/XMLSchema-instance"
    xsi:schemaLocation="http://www.springframework.org/schema/beans
        http://www.springframework.org/schema/beans/spring-beans-3.0.xsd
        http://www.springframework.org/schema/context
        http://www.springframework.org/schema/context/
            spring-context-3.0.xsd
        http://www.springframework.org/schema/jdbc
        http://www.springframework.org/schema/jdbc/spring-jdbc-3.0.xsd">

    <context:property-placeholder
        location="classpath:/spring/sip10-it.properties" />        ◁─┐ ❶ Externalizes
                                                                        DataSource config
    <bean id="dataSource"                                          ◁─┐
        class="org.apache.commons.dbcp.BasicDataSource"                │
        destroy-method="close"                                         ❷ Creates
        p:driverClassName="${dataSource.driverClassName}"              DataSource
```

```
            p:url="${dataSource.url}"
            p:username="${dataSource.username}"
            p:password="${dataSource.password}" />                    ③ Sets database
                                                                        to known state
        <jdbc:initialize-database data-source="dataSource"
            ignore-failures="DROPS">
            <jdbc:script location="classpath:/mysql/sip10-schema-mysql.sql" />
            <jdbc:script
                location="classpath:/mysql/sip10-test-data-mysql.sql" />
        </jdbc:initialize-database>
</beans>
```

At ① you observe the standard practice of externalizing volatile configuration such as username/password information. Next you build a `BasicDataSource` ② using that configuration, instead of performing a JNDI lookup, because you aren't in a Java EE container environment.

Next is something new for which there's no counterpart in listing 10.4. At a high level, this part of the configuration ③ resets the test database to a known state, which you obviously desire in order to have predictable and repeatable testing. The `<jdbc:initialize-database>` configuration (the `jdbc` namespace appeared in Spring 3) causes Spring to run the referenced SQL scripts in the given order against the referenced `DataSource` whenever you load this application context, typically just before running the integration test suite. The optional `ignore-failures="DROPS"` attribute says that if a script attempts to drop a table and fails (perhaps because the table doesn't yet exist), continue running the script.

You haven't yet seen the integration-testing counterpart to web.xml for specifying the configuration files you want; that comes when you write the integration test case (listing 10.8). But before you do that, let's look quickly at the SQL scripts you're using to reset the test database prior to running the integration tests.

SQL SCRIPTS FOR INTEGRATION TESTING

The following listing contains the database DDL—a single table—for the test database, based on MySQL's SQL dialect. The DDL file is located at src/it/resources/mysql/sip10-schema-mysql.sql.

Listing 10.6   sip10-schema-mysql.sql: integration test DDL

```
drop table if exists contact;

create table contact (
    id bigint unsigned not null auto_increment primary key,
    last_name varchar(40) not null,
    first_name varchar(40) not null,
    mi char(1),
    email varchar(80),
    date_created timestamp default 0,
    date_modified timestamp default current_timestamp
        on update current_timestamp,
    unique index contact_idx1 (last_name, first_name, mi)
) engine = InnoDB;
```

The next listing contains simple test data that you'll use to populate the contact table. This time the SQL script is located at src/it/resources/mysql/sip10-test-data-mysql.sql.

Listing 10.7   sip10-test-data-mysql.sql: test data

```
insert into contact values
    (1, 'Zimmerman', 'Robert', 'A', 'bobdylan@example.com', null, null),
    (2, 'Osbourne', 'John', 'M', 'ozzyosbourne@example.com', null, null),
    (3, 'Mapother', 'Tom', 'C', 'tomcruise@example.com', null, null),
    (4, 'Norris', 'Carlos', 'R', 'chucknorris@example.com', null, null),
    (5, 'Johnson', 'Caryn', 'E', 'whoppigoldberg@example.com', null, null),
    (6, 'Smith', 'John', null, 'johnsmith@example.com', null, null),
    (7, 'Smith', 'Jane', 'X', null, null, null);
```

There isn't much to say about these scripts. The DDL script drops the table and recreates it, which should provide a solid reset. The DML script feeds the table with test data that you can use for your integration testing.

In the following subsections, you'll write three separate happy-path integration tests, demonstrating different key capabilities of the Spring TestContext framework. The first is the simplest test, which involves asking for a specific contact and verifying that you got the information you expected to get.

HAPPY-PATH INTEGRATION TEST #1: GETTING A CONTACT

The bare-bones sample contact-management app is a master list of contacts with editable details pages corresponding to individual contacts. Each details page comes prepopulated with the contact's data. Figure 10.7 shows what a details page looks like.

When we said bare bones, we weren't kidding. All you have is a name and an email address. Your first integration test tests (the next listing) this contact details page feature.

Figure 10.7   A details page prepopulated with subterranean, homesick contact data

Listing 10.8   ContactControllerIT.java: integration test case

```java
package com.springinpractice.ch10.web;

import static org.junit.Assert.assertEquals;
import static org.junit.Assert.assertNotNull;
import javax.inject.Inject;
import org.junit.After;
import org.junit.Before;
import org.junit.Test;
import org.junit.runner.RunWith;
import org.springframework.beans.factory.annotation.Value;
import org.springframework.mock.web.MockHttpServletRequest;
import org.springframework.test.context.ContextConfiguration;
```

```
import org.springframework.test.context.junit4.SpringJUnit4ClassRunner;
import org.springframework.transaction.annotation.Transactional;
import org.springframework.ui.ExtendedModelMap;
import org.springframework.ui.Model;
import com.springinpractice.ch10.model.Contact;

@RunWith(SpringJUnit4ClassRunner.class)
@ContextConfiguration({
    "classpath:/spring/beans-datasource-it.xml",
    "classpath:/spring/beans-service.xml",
    "classpath:/spring/beans-web.xml" })
@Transactional
public class ContactControllerIT {
    @Inject private ContactController controller;

    @Value("#{viewNames.contactForm}")
    private String expectedContactFormViewName;

    private MockHttpServletRequest request;
    private Model model;

    @Before
    public void setUp() throws Exception {
        this.request = new MockHttpServletRequest();
        this.model = new ExtendedModelMap();
    }

    @After
    public void tearDown() throws Exception {
        this.request = null;
        this.model = null;
    }

    @Test
    public void testGetContactHappyPath() {
        String viewName = controller.getContact(request, 1L, model);
        assertEquals(expectedContactFormViewName, viewName);
        Contact contact = (Contact) model.asMap().get("contact");
        assertNotNull(contact);
        assertEquals((Long) 1L, contact.getId());
        assertEquals("Robert", contact.getFirstName());
        assertEquals("A", contact.getMiddleInitial());
        assertEquals("Zimmerman", contact.getLastName());
        assertEquals("bobdylan@example.com", contact.getEmail());
    }
}
```

1 Uses TestContext framework

2 Configures test context

3 Runs tests in transactions

8 POJO test case

5 Top of stack

6 EL works here

7 Uses Spring mock object

8 ExtendedModelMap works fine

9 Exercise code

10 Verifies view name

11 Verifies contact info

The first thing to notice in the listing is that the test case class is an annotated POJO **4**. It doesn't extend one of the now-deprecated (as of Spring 3) JUnit 3.8 base classes (for example, AbstractDependencyInjectionSpringContextTests). The annotated POJO approach is based on Spring's TestContext framework, and as of Spring 3 it's the standard approach to Spring-based integration testing, even though there are in fact optional, non-deprecated base classes for JUnit 4.5+.

@RunWith **1** is a JUnit annotation. It expects a JUnit Runner implementation class for a value. The test execution environment (Failsafe, for instance) uses this class to

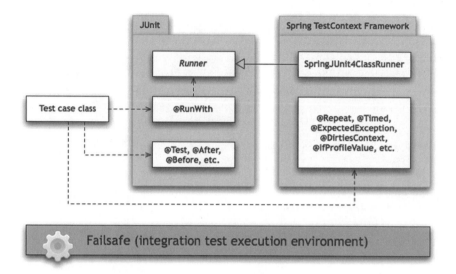

**Figure 10.8   Test cases use JUnit and Spring TestContext framework annotations.
The tests run in the Failsafe integration-test execution environment.**

create a `Runner` instance. We've chosen `SpringJUnit4ClassRunner`, which is effectively how you activate the Spring TestContext framework. Figure 10.8 shows how these elements fit together.

Figure 10.8 shows that Failsafe runs tests using the JUnit API and the Spring TestContext framework implementation of the JUnit `Runner`. The Spring TestContext framework performs the following services:

- Loads the test context (that is, bean definitions) from locations you'll specify, reusing most of the application context configuration files.
- Injects test fixture instances, and resolves any Spring EL expressions.
- Caches the test context between test executions unless otherwise directed.
- Wraps tests in transactions as directed, typically rolling back the transaction when the test completes.
- Honors not only standard JUnit test annotations like `@Test` and `@Ignore`, but also Spring TestContext framework annotations like `@ExpectedException`, `@Timed`, and `@Repeat`. (You'll see these and other framework annotations in upcoming recipes.)
- Provides a helpful utility API. `ReflectionTestUtils` allows test cases to inject dependencies into private fields, much as autowiring would do.

At ❷ you use the `@ContextConfiguration` annotation to tell the test-execution environment where to find the bean configuration files. Notice that you're getting the `DataSource` from beans-datasource-it.xml instead of beans-datasource.xml, thanks to the work you did earlier in separating the `DataSource` configuration. This is the test case counterpart to the `contextConfigLocation` parameter from web.xml.

The rules for specifying the `@ContextConfiguration` locations are explained by the Javadoc for `AbstractContextLoader#modifyLocations` as follows:

A plain path, e.g. `"context.xml"`, *will be treated as a classpath resource from the same package in which the specified class is defined. A path starting with a slash is treated as a fully qualified class path location, e.g.:* `"/org/springframework/whatever/foo.xml"`. *A path which references a URL (e.g., a path prefixed with* `classpath:, file:, http:,` *etc.) will be added to the results unchanged.*

At ❸, the `@Transaction` annotation indicates that you want to wrap each test with a transaction. That way you can roll back any database mischief you create at the end of each test. You'll reuse the transactional machinery from the application's bean-configuration files. (You might be seeing at this point why the TestContext framework is nice to have around.) If you wanted to specify a custom `PlatformTransactionManager` bean name (the default is `transactionManager`) or turn off the default rollback-on-test-completion behavior, you could add a `@TransactionConfiguration` annotation here, but you don't want to do either. You're happy.

We covered ❹, so let's start looking in the class. At ❺ you have an autowired controller-class-under-test (using the standardized Java EE `@Inject` annotation that Spring 3 supports), and the framework will in fact perform that dependency injection on your behalf. It's not just the controller under test, but rather the entire stack under the controller. The controller gives you something to poke and prod, and you can watch it to see what happens.

The framework resolves the EL at ❻ to give you an expected view name.

The test setup method creates a request and a model. The request object ❼ is a mock object and is part of Spring's wider offering around mock web objects for testing.[4] At ❽ you create a real `ExtendedModelMap` because there's no reason to prefer a mock to the real thing.

With all that test-case setup (whew!), you're finally ready to write your first happy-path test. You exercise the code by asking the controller to get the contact with ID 1, put it on the model, and return a view name ❾. At ❿ you verify that the expected view name matches the actual view name. At ⓫ you verify that the returned contact matches the SQL test data you saw in listing 10.7.

Before you can run the tests, you need a test database. Create one called sip10_it. After that you can run the tests from the command line as follows:

```
mvn -e verify
```

You launch the `verify` phase rather than the `integration-test` phase because you want to ensure that you run any cleanup goals bound to the `post-integration-test` phase. In this case nothing is bound to `post-integration-test`, but it's a good habit to launch integration tests using `verify` anyway just in case that phase happens to be performing cleanup.

---

[4] See org.springframework.mock.web for more examples.

This last subsection was a lot to digest, so please be sure to review as necessary before moving on. If you're ready, you'll do a slightly more interesting happy-path test, this time updating a contact.

HAPPY-PATH INTEGRATION TEST #2: UPDATING A CONTACT

Updating a contact is what you do when you click the Save button on the form in figure 10.7, so it's the logical next test. The following listing shows an updated version of ContactControllerIT.java, suppressing code you've already seen.

Listing 10.9   Testing contact updates

```
package com.springinpractice.ch10.web;

import javax.sql.DataSource;
import org.hibernate.SessionFactory;
import org.springframework.jdbc.core.simple.SimpleJdbcTemplate;
import org.springframework.validation.BeanPropertyBindingResult;
import org.springframework.validation.BindingResult;

... other imports as before ...

... @RunWith, @ContextConfiguration, @Transactional ...
public class ContactControllerIT {
    private static final String SELECT_FIRST_NAME_QUERY =
        "select first_name from contact where id = ?";

    @Inject private SessionFactory sessionFactory;
    @Inject private DataSource dataSource;

    @Value("#{viewNames.updateContactSuccess}")
    private String expectedUpdateContactSuccessViewName;

    private SimpleJdbcTemplate jdbcTemplate;

    ... other fields as before ...

    @Before
    public void setUp() throws Exception {                         ❶ Verifies
        this.jdbcTemplate = new SimpleJdbcTemplate(dataSource);       DB state
        ... other setup as before ...
    }

    @After
    public void tearDown() throws Exception {
        this.jdbcTemplate = null;
        ... other teardown as before ...
    }

    @Test
    public void testUpdateContactHappyPath() {                     ❷ Prepares updated
        Contact contact = new Contact();                             contact
        contact.setFirstName("Bob");
        contact.setLastName("Dylan");
        contact.setEmail("bobdylan@example.com");

        BindingResult result =                                     ❸ Creates test
            new BeanPropertyBindingResult(contact, "contact");        dummy
```

Exercises code ④

```
String viewName =
    controller.updateContact(request, 1L, contact, result);
assertEquals(expectedUpdateContactSuccessViewName, viewName);

Model anotherModel = new ExtendedModelMap();
controller.getContact(request, 1L, anotherModel);
Contact updatedContact =
    (Contact) anotherModel.asMap().get("contact");
assertEquals("Bob", updatedContact.getFirstName());

String firstName = jdbcTemplate.
    queryForObject(SELECT_FIRST_NAME_QUERY, String.class, 1);
assertEquals("Robert", firstName);

sessionFactory.getCurrentSession().flush();

String updatedFirstName = jdbcTemplate.
    queryForObject(SELECT_FIRST_NAME_QUERY, String.class, 1);
assertEquals("Bob", updatedFirstName);
    }
}
```

⑤ Verifies view name

⑥ Verifies first name in Hibernate

⑦ Shows update not flushed

⑧ Flushes update

Verifies first name in DB ⑨

The test for updating a contact looks a lot different than the test for getting a contact, and it is. One major difference is that updating a contact involves a database update that the test framework will roll back on test completion—whether or not the test is successful—to keep the test database in a known, clean state. But that's not the part that looks different, because you can't see that at all. The framework handles that transparently, which is one of its major selling points. See figure 10.9.

The part that looks different is that you have to deal with some complexity that Hibernate adds. The basic idea is that when you update the controller, this updates a service bean, which updates a DAO, which then updates a Hibernate session. For optimization purposes, Hibernate doesn't flush every change it receives immediately to the database. It collects changes and flushes them either automatically at appropriate points or manually on demand. The integration test deals with all of this, as you'll see. Let's walk through the steps.

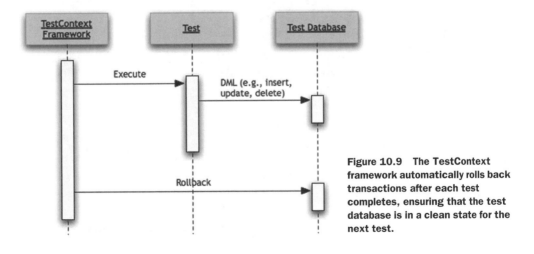

Figure 10.9 The TestContext framework automatically rolls back transactions after each test completes, ensuring that the test database is in a clean state for the next test.

In the setup, you create a new `SimpleJdbcTemplate` using an injected `DataSource` ❶. You'll use this to verify database changes directly instead of relying on Hibernate's report, because Hibernate session state is somewhat decoupled from database state.

Then you get to the test. You must simulate an update request from a web client. To do this, you create a `Contact` ❷ with the submitted update (here, the original first name Robert is being updated to Bob), create a dummy `BindingResult` to keep the controller's `updateContact()` method happy ❸, and finally exercise the method under test ❹.

Once you've exercised the method, it's time to verify the result. You verify the view name ❺, and then you want to determine whether you were successful in updating the first name. This is a slightly tricky question, as explained. Checking with the controller ❻, it will appear (on running the test) that the answer is yes. And that's true. But you can use `SimpleJdbcTemplate` to determine whether the change made its way all the way back to the database, and the answer will be no ❼. You're still in the middle of a transaction, and Hibernate hasn't flushed the change to the database yet. You can flush the change manually ❽ and check the database again ❾. This time, the change is in the database.

Normally you wouldn't write the first database check (the check to verify that the change didn't make it), although it doesn't hurt anything. You'd flush the session and *then* check the database. But we wanted to show how Hibernate works and how you'll need to flush the session and use the `SimpleJdbcTemplate` if you want to ensure that your code did what it was supposed to in the database.

We'll look at one more happy-path integration test. This time, let's delete the contact you've been working with.

HAPPY-PATH INTEGRATION TEST #3: DELETING A CONTACT
In the following listing, you test the deletion of the good Mr. Zimmerman.

Listing 10.10   Testing contact deletion

```
package com.springinpractice.ch10.web;

import static org.junit.Assert.fail;
import com.springinpractice.web.ResourceNotFoundException;

... other imports ...

... @RunWith, @ContextConfiguration, @Transactional ...
public class ContactControllerIT {

    ... various fields ...

    @Value("#{viewNames.deleteContactSuccess}")
    private String expectedDeleteContactSuccessViewName;

    ... setUp(), tearDown(), tests ...

    @Test
    public void testDeleteContactHappyPath() {
        controller.getContact(request, 1L, model);                    ❶ Verifies
        Contact contact = (Contact) model.asMap().get("contact");        existence
```

```
                assertNotNull(contact);

                String viewName = controller.deleteContact(1L);

                assertEquals(expectedDeleteContactSuccessViewName, viewName);

                try {
                    controller.getContact(request, 1L, new ExtendedModelMap());
                    fail("Expected ResourceNotFoundException");
                } catch (ResourceNotFoundException e) { /* OK */ }

                String firstName = jdbcTemplate.
                    queryForObject(SELECT_FIRST_NAME_QUERY, String.class, 1);
                assertEquals("Robert", firstName);

                sessionFactory.getCurrentSession().flush();

                try {
                    jdbcTemplate.queryForObject(
                        SELECT_FIRST_NAME_QUERY, String.class, 1);
                    fail("Expected DataAccessException");
                } catch (DataAccessException e) { /* OK */ }
            }
        }
```

Exercises code ➋

Verifies view name ➌

Verifies deletion ➍

Flushes to DB and verify ➎

By now you've seen this a couple of times, so we'll blast through it. You start with a quick check to make sure the contact you're about to delete (it's Bob Dylan again) exists ➊. Then you exercise the code ➋ and verify the view name ➌. Next you try to get the contact from the controller ➍. You expect a ResourceNotFoundException; you fail the test if you don't get one. Finally, you run through the same JDBC routine where you flush the session, then verify that the contact is removed from the database ➎. Once again, you didn't have to check the database twice; you did that in this case to demonstrate that the flush is required.

That's happy-path integration testing in Spring.

Discussion

This recipe covered a lot of ground. Even though we focused on the basic happy-path integration test, you learned how the Spring TestContext framework supports test database resets, configuration reuse, dependency injection of test fixtures, transactions and rollbacks, mocks, assertions against database state, and more. Fortunately, this basic training was the most grueling you'll see. In the following recipes, you'll be able to build in a more leisurely fashion on the knowledge you've just gained.

10.3 Verifying that code under test throws an exception

PREREQUISITES

Recipe 10.1 Configuring Maven for integration testing
Recipe 10.2 Writing transactional, happy-path integration tests

KEY TECHNOLOGIES

Spring TestContext framework, JUnit, Mockito

Background

Testing the happy path is only one part of what integration testing is all about. It's at least as important—and probably more important—to test how the code responds to exceptional and failure conditions:

- Happy-path integrations are exercised repeatedly in the normal course of development, which in many cases reduces the likelihood that a defect will make it out of dev. (You still want the testing because defects can easily go unnoticed.)
- Failures often occur at integration points. This can happen when different people with different assumptions write the code on either side of the integration point. It can also happen when the integration point involves communicating with a resource (like a database) that may be unavailable.

When exceptions occur, you want to ensure that you control the way the system responds, rather than letting the exception determine what happens.

Problem

Write an integration test that verifies the proper handling of an exceptional condition.

Solution

The following listing shows how to write a test to verify that an expected exception is thrown.

Listing 10.11   Elaborating ContactControllerIT.java

```
package com.springinpractice.ch10.web;

import static org.mockito.Mockito.mock;
import static org.mockito.Mockito.when;
import org.hibernate.HibernateException;
import org.springframework.test.annotation.DirtiesContext;
import org.springframework.test.annotation.ExpectedException;
import org.springframework.test.util.ReflectionTestUtils;
import com.springinpractice.ch10.dao.HbnContactDao;

... other static imports and normal imports ...

... @RunWith, @ContextConfiguration, @Transactional ...
public class ContactControllerIT {
    @Inject private HbnContactDao contactDao;
    private SessionFactory badSessionFactory;              ❶ Misbehaving
                                                              SessionFactory
    ... other fields ...

    @Before
    public void setUp() throws Exception {
        this.badSessionFactory = mock(SessionFactory.class);   ❷ Mocks
                                                                  SessionFactory
        when(badSessionFactory.getCurrentSession())
            .thenThrow(new HibernateException(             ❸ Defines mock
                "Problem getting current session"));          behavior

    ...
```

```
    }

    @After
    public void tearDown() throws Exception {
        this.badSessionFactory = null;
        ...
    }

    @Test
    @ExpectedException(HibernateException.class)
    @DirtiesContext
    public void testGetContactWithBadSessionFactory() {
        ReflectionTestUtils.setField(contactDao, "sessionFactory",
            badSessionFactory);
        controller.getContact(request, 1L, model);
    }

    ... other tests ...

}
```

④ Declares expectation

⑤ Marks context dirty

Wires private field ⑥

Exercises code ⑦

In the code, you want to verify that `HibernateExceptions` arising out of the `Session-Factory` pass through the DAO, service bean, and controller. The listing demonstrates several useful techniques. First, you need a way to induce a failure condition so you can test the system response. To do this you'll mock out a broken Hibernate `Session-Factory` ❶ to simulate a Hibernate failure when trying to get a session. At ❷ you create the mock object using the Mockito framework. You specify at ❸ that the mock is to throw a `HibernateException` when a client calls the `getCurrentSession()` method using Mockito's intuitive API.

With the setup complete, you can now write the test. You use Spring's `@Expected-Exception` annotation ❹ to declare the expectation that the test method will throw a `HibernateException`. The test fails if the exception isn't thrown. For instance, if the service bean were to catch the `HibernateException` and rethrow it as something else, the test would fail.

> ### @ExpectedException vs. @Test(Expected=. . .)
> JUnit supports the same expected-exception functionality by way of the `@Test(expected=...)` configuration. They do the same thing, but you can't use them together. If you're using JUnit 4, you'll need to choose one or the other.

You also annotate the test method with `@DirtiesContext` ❺. Normally the TestContext framework loads the application context one time at the beginning and caches it so it can be reused across all test methods in the test case. That speeds up the tests. The `@DirtiesContext` annotation tells the framework to mark the app context as being dirty so it will be automatically reloaded before running the next test. You use this annotation because you want to modify the contact DAO to use the mock `SessionFactory` instead of the real one, but you don't want that change to survive outside of this test. You mark the test method as one that dirties the app context, and the reload will follow when it's needed.

In the sample code, there is no setter for the `SessionFactory`; it's a private field. To work around this, you can use the `ReflectionTestUtils.setField()` method ❻. In this case, you're setting `contactDao.sessionFactory` to `badSessionFactory`.

Finally, you exercise the code ❼. Again, the test passes if and only if this call to the controller throws a `HibernateException`.

Discussion

At this point we've covered most of the basics: you've set up your integration-testing infrastructure, implemented happy-path tests, and implemented a test that demonstrates a desired response to an exceptional condition. In recipe 10.4, we'll examine a more advanced technique that allows you to create tests that run only in specific environments.

10.4   *Creating integration tests that verify performance*

PREREQUISITES
Recipe 10.1 Configuring Maven for integration testing
Recipe 10.2 Writing transactional, happy-path integration tests

KEY TECHNOLOGIES
Maven 3, Spring TestContext framework, JUnit

Background

You often want to be able to verify that code runs within specified time bounds. This can be challenging, because a given piece of code has different performance characteristics on different machines and in different environments, and so it may be unclear what response time to specify as the expected response time. You probably shouldn't expect production-level performance in a development environment, for example.

But you can pick a given machine—let's say a continuous-integration server—and build performance tests around the capabilities of that machine. Although that won't generally provide a good sense for performance in production, it can at least catch certain cases of performance drift and provide advance warning of issues.

Therefore you'd like to have performance tests that run during continuous-integration builds but not during private builds (that is, builds on an individual developer's machine).

This isn't a perfect technique, and it's certainly no substitute for proper performance testing in a system test environment. But it can flag issues and set a minimum bar.

Problem

Create time-bounded integration tests that run during continuous-integration builds but not during private builds.

Solution

There are two steps here. The first is to write the tests, as in the following listing.

Listing 10.12 Adding a time-bounded test to ContactControllerIT.java

```java
package com.springinpractice.ch10.web;

import org.springframework.test.annotation.IfProfileValue;
import org.springframework.test.annotation.Repeat;
import org.springframework.test.annotation.Timed;

... other imports ...

... @RunWith, @ContextConfiguration, @Transactional ...
public class ContactControllerIT {

    ...
    @IfProfileValue(name = "environment", value = "ci")        ❶ Runs only in CI environment
    @Repeat(20)
    @Test(timeout = 200L)                                      ❷ Repeats test 20 times
    public void testGetContactPerformanceSingleCall() {
        controller.getContact(request, 1L, new ExtendedModelMap());
    }
                                                              ❸ Each run ≤ 200 ms
    @IfProfileValue(name = "environment", value = "ci")
    @Repeat(20)
    @Timed(millis = 2000)                                     ❹ Run total ≤ 2000 ms
    @Test
    public void testGetContactPerformanceMultipleCalls() {
        controller.getContact(request, 1L, new ExtendedModelMap());
    }
}
```

You create two separate tests. Each tests the controller's `getContact()` method, albeit in slightly different ways to be described.

Each test uses the TestContext framework's `@IfProfileValue` annotation ❶ to make test execution dependent on having the system property `environment` set to the value `ci`, which stands for "continuous integration." Note that this system property isn't a standard, canned property—we made it up. You'll have to set `environment=ci` for continuous-integration builds and not elsewhere.

Each test also uses the TestContext framework's `@Repeat` annotation to repeat the test 20 times ❷, including the test-fixture setup and teardown for each test run. This repetition provides an extra level of assurance when tests pass because execution times can vary somewhat from run to run. But note that it's more likely that at least one test will fail, so your time bounds must be fairly conservative to avoid excessive failure rates.

The first test uses the JUnit `@Test` annotation to set a timeout ❸. This approach applies timeouts to individual test iterations: each iteration must complete within 200 ms. If the test fails on your machine under this setting, adjust the timeout upward so your test will pass. (It works on our laptop, and our laptop isn't particularly fast.)

The second test uses the TestContext framework's `@Timed` annotation ❹, which sets a timeout that applies to the overall set of iterations, including their respective setups and teardowns. Once again you may need to adjust the timeout for your machine.[5] Figure 10.10 offers a visual comparison of setting timeouts via `@Test` and `@Timed`.

---

[5] JUnit's `@RunWith` and `Runner` are nice. They allow custom test runners, like `SpringJUnit4ClassRunner`, that offer a way to support extension annotations such as Spring's `@IfProfileValue`, `@Repeat`, and `@Timed`.

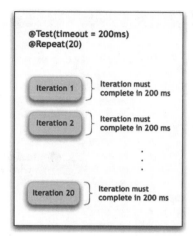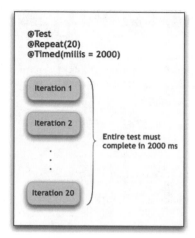

Figure 10.10   A visual comparison between setting timeouts using `@Test(timeout = ...)` **and** `@Timed`

In addition to writing the new tests, you need to pass system properties from the environment to the test runner. To do this, add the `<systemPropertyVariables>` section to the Failsafe configuration.

Listing 10.13   Updating Failsafe definition in pom.xml

```
<plugin>
    <artifactId>maven-failsafe-plugin</artifactId>
    <version>2.5</version>
    <configuration>
        <junitArtifactName>
            org.junit:com.springsource.org.junit
        </junitArtifactName>
        <systemPropertyVariables>
            <environment>${environment}</environment>
        </systemPropertyVariables>
    </configuration>
    <executions>
        <execution>
            <id>integration-test</id>
            <goals>
                <goal>integration-test</goal>
            </goals>
        </execution>
        <execution>
            <id>verify</id>
            <goals>
                <goal>verify</goal>
            </goals>
        </execution>
    </executions>
</plugin>
```

If you run this test the normal way using

```
mvn -e verify
```

then the test runner will skip the two
tests you just added, because you
haven't set the system property envi-
ronment=ci (see figure 10.11).

Figure 10.11   Without `environment=ci`**, the test runner skips two tests.**

To remedy this situation, type

```
mvn -e -Denvironment=ci verify
```

which sets the system property `environment=ci`. This time you won't skip any tests
(see figure 10.12).

Configure your CI server (Hudson
or Bamboo, for example) to run the
Maven build with `environment=ci`,
and you're ready to go.

Figure 10.12   No skipped tests

Discussion

Keep in mind that code runs faster or slower depending on the environment, so the
techniques described here are inappropriate for production performance testing.
Performance testing should generally be conducted under production-like loads, with
production-like data and data volumes (so the DBMS generates production-like execution plans) and so forth.

What these techniques do allow you to do is see that a test that once ran without
issue now exceeds the timeout period. That's a handy thing to know.

The next recipe presents a cleaner alternative to commenting out broken tests.

10.5   Ignoring a test

PREREQUISITES
Recipe 10.1 Configuring Maven for integration testing
Recipe 10.2 Writing transactional, happy-path integration tests

KEY TECHNOLOGIES
JUnit

Background

Ideally you would never have occasion to ignore a test. You might adopt test-driven
development (TDD) practices,[6] creating or changing tests before changing the corresponding code to make the lights turn from red to green. Code would never break a
test, and there wouldn't be cause to ignore tests.

Somewhat short of this ideal would be the situation in which you change some
code, you break a few tests, you fix the tests, and then you continue coding.

But in the real world (or at least in our real world), sometimes you change code, it
breaks stuff, and you aren't ready to go back and fix everything you just broke. So you

---

[6]   For more information about TDD or testing in general, consult *Effective Unit Testing: A Guide for Java Developers*
by Lasse Koskela (Manning, 2013) or *Test Driven: TDD and Acceptance TDD for Java Developers* by Lasse Koskela
(Manning, 2007). They present many techniques not discussed here.

comment out the test and rerun the tests. In the extreme case, this lack of discipline leads to way too many tests being commented out, but it's fair to say that sometimes you want to make a code change without fixing all the resulting broken tests at that moment. You'd prefer to do that in a clean way, rather than commenting everything out all over the place. This is where the @Ignore annotation comes in.

Problem

Ignore a test without commenting everything out.

Solution

This one is easy, and it uses a standard JUnit annotation. Apply the @Ignore annotation to the test method, as illustrated in the next listing.

Listing 10.14   Ignoring a test using `@Ignore`

```
package com.springinpractice.ch10.web;

import org.junit.Ignore;

... other imports ...

... @RunWith, @ContextConfiguration, @Transactional ...
public class ContactControllerIT {

    @Ignore
    ... other annotations ...
    public void testGetContactWithBadSessionFactory() { ... }

    ... other tests ...
}
```

There's nothing else to it. It's much cleaner than commenting out tests. The test runner will skip ignored tests.

Discussion

Even though applying the @Ignore annotation is cleaner than commenting out test code, it's still subject to abuse. Ignoring too many tests might be a sign that you weren't disciplined in preserving your tests. At some point you may pay the price through increased regression.

Setting up a code-coverage tool like Clover, EMMA, or Cobertura can be a big help with managing this issue. By ignoring a test, you prevent it from contributing to the coverage percentages that coverage tools typically provide as part of their reporting functionality. Having a code-coverage tool in place can help alert you to excessive ignoring, among many other things.

The final recipe shows how to run integration tests against an embedded database.

10.6   *Running integration tests against an embedded database*

PREREQUISITES
Recipe 10.1 Configuring Maven for integration testing
Recipe 10.2 Writing transactional, happy-path integration tests

KEY TECHNOLOGIES

Spring TestContext framework, embedded DBMS

Background

Recipe 10.2 introduced you to the `jdbc` namespace that appears in Spring 3. There you used it to initialize the test database to a known state because integration tests depend on that.

The `jdbc` namespace also provides a `<jdbc:embedded-database>` tag for creating an in-memory, embedded database that can be helpful for implementing a more lightweight testing capability—one that allows you to avoid having to set up one or more real test databases for the development team. This recipe shows how to take advantage of the `<jdbc:embedded-database>` tag.

Problem

Simplify the infrastructure needed to support integration testing by replacing real test databases with an embedded test database.

Solution

Spring 3 provides namespace support for embedded databases. Out of the box, Spring supports HSQL, H2, and Derby. It's also possible to implement support for other DBMSs, although here we'll stick with HSQL.

Figure 10.13 shows what you'll build in this recipe. Basically you use the `jdbc` namespace to create an embedded `DataSource` that the Hibernate `SessionFactory` can use.

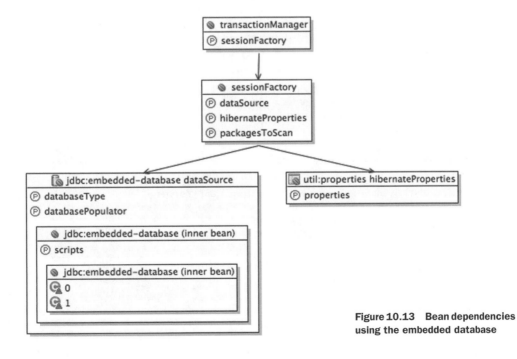

Figure 10.13 Bean dependencies using the embedded database

On to the changes. First add the following dependency to the Maven project object model (POM):

```
<dependency>
    <groupId>org.hsqldb</groupId>
    <artifactId>com.springsource.org.hsqldb</artifactId>
    <version>${hsqldb.version}</version>
    <scope>test</scope>
</dependency>
```

Next you need to add a new DDL script, because the existing MySQL script won't work with HSQL. The following listing shows the roughly equivalent DDL script for HSQL. This goes in src/it/resources/hsql.

Listing 10.15 sip10-schema-hsql.sql: integration test DDL for HSQLDB

```
create table contact (
    id bigint generated by default as identity
        (start with 1, increment by 1) not null primary key,
    last_name varchar(40) not null,
    first_name varchar(40) not null,
    mi char(1),
    email varchar(80),
    date_created timestamp default 0,
    date_modified timestamp default current_timestamp,
    unique (last_name, first_name, mi)
);
```

You'll also need a copy of the DML script in the hsql directory. Copy the MySQL version (the same DML works here) to sip10-test-data-hsql.sql.

Finally, you need to modify and even refactor your Spring configuration a bit. Until now, both the app and integration-test configurations have been using MySQL, so it hasn't been an issue that you're specifying the SQL dialect in beans-service.xml (which is shared across both configurations). But now the two configurations use distinct dialects, so you want to push the dialect selection out of beans-service.xml and into the two data-source configuration files.

First, the next listing shows the updated beans-service.xml file.

Listing 10.16 beans-service.xml, revisited

```
<?xml version="1.0" encoding="UTF-8"?>
<beans xmlns="http://www.springframework.org/schema/beans"
    xmlns:context="http://www.springframework.org/schema/context"
    xmlns:p="http://www.springframework.org/schema/p"
    xmlns:tx="http://www.springframework.org/schema/tx"
    xmlns:xsi="http://www.w3.org/2001/XMLSchema-instance"
    xsi:schemaLocation="http://www.springframework.org/schema/beans
        http://www.springframework.org/schema/beans/spring-beans-3.0.xsd
        http://www.springframework.org/schema/context
        http://www.springframework.org/schema/context/
            spring-context-3.0.xsd
        http://www.springframework.org/schema/tx
```

```
                http://www.springframework.org/schema/tx/spring-tx-3.0.xsd">

      <bean id="sessionFactory"
          class="org.springframework.orm.hibernate3.annotation.
                  AnnotationSessionFactoryBean"
          p:dataSource-ref="dataSource"
          p:packagesToScan="com.springinpractice.ch10.model"
          p:hibernateProperties-ref="hibernateProperties" />

      <bean id="transactionManager"
          class="org.springframework.orm.hibernate3.
                  HibernateTransactionManager"
          p:sessionFactory-ref="sessionFactory" />

      <tx:annotation-driven />

      <context:component-scan
          base-package="com.springinpractice.ch10.dao" />
      <context:component-scan
          base-package="com.springinpractice.ch10.service" />
  </beans>
```

All you've done here is replace the previous hibernateProperties configuration with
an external reference, which the individual data-source configurations will provide.

And here's the updated beans-datasource-it.xml configuration.

Listing 10.17   beans-datasource-it.xml, revisited

```
<?xml version="1.0" encoding="UTF-8"?>
<beans xmlns="http://www.springframework.org/schema/beans"
    xmlns:context="http://www.springframework.org/schema/context"
    xmlns:jdbc="http://www.springframework.org/schema/jdbc"
    xmlns:p="http://www.springframework.org/schema/p"
    xmlns:util="http://www.springframework.org/schema/util"
    xmlns:xsi="http://www.w3.org/2001/XMLSchema-instance"
    xsi:schemaLocation="http://www.springframework.org/schema/beans
        http://www.springframework.org/schema/beans/spring-beans-3.0.xsd
        http://www.springframework.org/schema/context
        http://www.springframework.org/schema/context/
                spring-context-3.0.xsd
        http://www.springframework.org/schema/jdbc
        http://www.springframework.org/schema/jdbc/spring-jdbc-3.0.xsd
        http://www.springframework.org/schema/util
        http://www.springframework.org/schema/util/spring-util-3.0.xsd">

    <jdbc:embedded-database id="dataSource">
        <jdbc:script location="classpath:hsql/sip10-schema-hsql.sql" />
        <jdbc:script
            location="classpath:hsql/sip10-test-data-hsql.sql" />
    </jdbc:embedded-database>

    <util:properties id="hibernateProperties">
        <prop key="hibernate.dialect">
                org.hibernate.dialect.HSQLDialect</prop>
        <prop key="hibernate.show_sql">true</prop>
    </util:properties>
</beans>
```

Annotations: **Creates database** ❶ · **Runs DDL** ❷ · **Runs DML** ❸ · **Updates dialect** ❹

At ❶ you replace the previous `BasicDataSource` definition with a new HSQL definition based on `<jdbc:embedded-database>`. (The tag accepts a `type` attribute with valid values `HSQL`, `H2`, and `DERBY`. The default is `HSQL` if the type isn't explicitly specified.)

You reference the DDL and DML scripts at ❷ and ❸ respectively to initialize the embedded database with the desired schema and test data. The external `hibernateProperties` definition appears at ❹. You're using the `util` namespace for this, so don't forget to add the corresponding namespace and schema location declarations to the top of the file.

You're almost done, but the change to beans-datasource-it.xml broke the app because there's no app-side target for the `hibernateProperties` reference yet. The next listing fixes this.

Listing 10.18   beans-datasource.xml, revisited

```xml
<?xml version="1.0" encoding="UTF-8"?>
<beans xmlns="http://www.springframework.org/schema/beans"
    xmlns:jee="http://www.springframework.org/schema/jee"
    xmlns:util="http://www.springframework.org/schema/util"
    xmlns:xsi="http://www.w3.org/2001/XMLSchema-instance"
    xsi:schemaLocation="http://www.springframework.org/schema/beans
        http://www.springframework.org/schema/beans/spring-beans-3.0.xsd
        http://www.springframework.org/schema/jee
        http://www.springframework.org/schema/jee/spring-jee-3.0.xsd
        http://www.springframework.org/schema/util
        http://www.springframework.org/schema/util/spring-util-3.0.xsd">

    <jee:jndi-lookup id="dataSource"
        jndi-name="jdbc/sip10DS" resource-ref="true"/>

    <util:properties id="hibernateProperties">
        <prop key="hibernate.dialect">
                org.hibernate.dialect.MySQL5InnoDBDialect</prop>
        <prop key="hibernate.show_sql">true</prop>
    </util:properties>
</beans>
```

You've added the necessary `hibernateProperties` configuration, along with the supporting `util` namespace declarations.

At this point, you should be able to run both the app and the integration tests. If everything is good, the app runs against the MySQL database, and the integration tests run against the embedded HSQL database.

Discussion

Using an embedded database is a useful technique for reducing the amount of setup necessary to get going with integration tests. The integration tests are more self-contained, and you don't have to worry about starting up a database, having a network connection to the database (if it's remote), and so forth. Also, in many cases working with an embedded database offers performance benefits over working with non-embedded databases.

Keep the following points in mind before using an embedded database:

- By using an embedded database, you're no longer including the database in the scope of your integration test. Yes, you're still using a database, but it's functioning essentially as a test double for the real database. You aren't testing the real database.

- You must keep the SQL for the real and embedded databases in sync. This can be painful if there are lots of database changes. One approach to dealing with this is to start off using only an embedded database (not only for the integration tests but also for the app) while the schema is still under heavy development. As schema changes slow down, introduce a real database on the app side.

- Embedded databases may not support all the features you'd expect to see from a non-embedded database. HSQL 1.8.x, for example, supports only READ UNCOMMITTED transaction isolation. (HSQL 2 supports the READ COMMITTED and SERIALIZABLE isolation levels as well.)

Our preference is to run integration tests against a local, nonembedded test database, mostly because we prefer to include the database in the scope of our integration testing, but you may find the embedded-database option useful.

10.7 Summary

That concludes our tour of the Spring TestContext framework. It's well-known that Spring's dependency injection lends to designs that are easy to unit-test. In this chapter, you've seen that Spring additionally provides several features to make integration testing simple and effective.

For more information about testing (including integration testing), check out *Effective Unit Testing: A Guide for Java Developers* by Lasse Koskela (Manning, 2013) or *Test Driven: TDD and Acceptance TDD for Java Developers* by Lasse Koskela (Manning, 2007).

Building a configuration management database

11

This chapter covers

- Creating a configuration database using Spring Data Neo4j
- Enabling REST web services using JSON and XML
- Invoking web services using the Maven deployment plug-in
- Accessing GitHub using Spring Social and OAuth 2 authorization
- Using Spring Security to encrypt GitHub access tokens

If you work with a technical infrastructure of any size, you may have run into a variety of common issues:

- *Poor visibility into system configuration*—It may be difficult to know exactly what's deployed, which apps live on which servers, who to call when apps fail, and so on. When multiple teams are involved (for example, multiple development and operations teams), they may not have the same way of referring to applications, making communication, planning, and incident response difficult.

338

- *Configuration drift*—Things aren't configured the way you expect them to be. This could include servers that are supposed to match but don't, firewall ports being closed when they should be open, and so forth.
- *Manual change processes*—Deploying software, for example, involves a large team performing manual releases late at night. Because they're manual, they take a long time, it's easy to miss steps (such as forgetting to update a configuration file on one of the servers), some team members may be absent, and so on. Manual change processes are a major contributor to configuration drift.
- *Rogue changes*—Another major cause of configuration drift, rogue changes are changes that somebody makes outside the official change process. Perhaps someone needs a firewall port opened and emails his networking buddy, who opens the port without logging the change, without making the corresponding change in other environments, without a proper security review, and so on.
- *Inability to reset to a known state*—It's important to be able to reset your environment, or elements of your environment, to a known good state. Examples include testing (tests should run against a known state), adding capacity to a farm (new servers should have the same configuration as existing servers), disaster recovery (DR environment requires standing up servers according to a known configuration), and more.
- *VM sprawl*—VM costs are running out of control because people create VMs as if they're free, without harvesting unused capacity.

These issues are a small sample of those that arise without proper configuration management in place. *Configuration management* is a set of practices around ensuring that you have good visibility into and control over the technology assets (infrastructure, middleware, apps, and so on) underlying your services. When the technology footprint is smaller, it's certainly possible (although arguably still not best practice) to use manual deployment and release processes, to make changes in the environment as they're needed, to document configuration information on a wiki, to build new servers from wiki documents, and so forth. But once there are hundreds or even thousands of servers in place, the approaches that work in smaller environments don't scale.

In sum, configuration management is useful for any organization wanting visibility and control over its technology, and it becomes more and more essential as your technology footprint scales up.

This chapter shows how Willie is using Spring to implement several features in an open source configuration management database (CMDB) called Zkybase[1] (http://zkybase.org/). A CMDB serves as the foundation for a more general configuration management capability by supporting data, tool, and process integration. In particular, it supports various sorts of automation, including build, test, deployment, and operations automation.

---

[1] The app is currently called Zkybase, but its former name was Skybase. It appears as "Skybase" in the various figures in this chapter.

Figure 11.1 is an architectural overview of a hypothetical configuration management system.[2] In this diagram, imagine that we want a code commit to result in an automatic deployment to a development environment. The architecture and use case are just one possibility among many; the point is to highlight the foundational role that a CMDB plays in such a system.

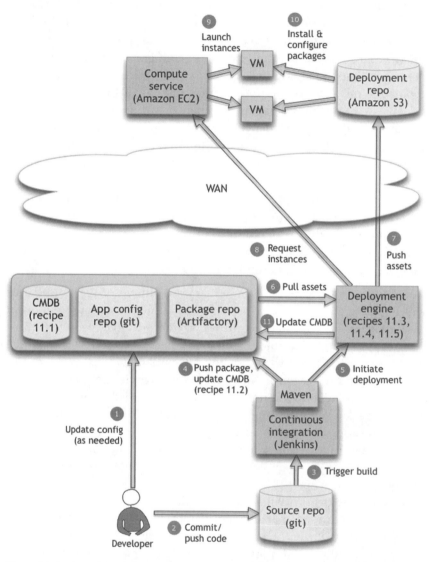

Figure 11.1 A hypothetical configuration management architecture built around a CMDB, supporting auto-deployment to dev servers on commit

---

[2] The Heliopolis team at the Apollo Group, of which Willie was delighted to be a member, established a configuration management architecture along these lines. Thus this is more than a purely hypothetical architecture.

Let's review the individual steps in the diagram:

1 The developer makes any necessary updates to the CMDB and to the app configuration. For the CMDB, this might include specifying instance IP addresses (in cases where instances already exist) or the desired number of instances (in cases where instances will be launched as part of the deployment). For app configuration, this could be anything you typically see in an app configuration, such as setting passwords, setting log levels, adding security rules, and so on. Usually the developer doesn't need to do anything here because the configuration is already in place from previous deployments.

2 The developer commits the code to a source control, such as Subversion or Git.

3 This triggers a build on the continuous-integration server, such as Jenkins or Bamboo.

4 Assuming the build succeeds (compiles, tests pass), Maven pushes the new snapshot build into the Maven package repository, such as Nexus or Artifactory. It also updates the CMDB with information about the new package.

5 With the build complete, Maven initiates the deployment.

6 The deployment engine grabs the package and configuration (both the app configuration and the general environmental configuration) from the relevant repositories.

7 The deployment engine pushes the assets across the WAN to a staging repository sitting at the target site.

8 The deployment engine requests instances from the compute provider, such as Amazon EC2.

9 The compute provider launches the instances.

10 As the instances come up, they grab the required assets from the staging repository and then perform the required installation and configuration.[3]

11 The deployment engine updates the CMDB with information about the deployment (for example, the IP addresses of any instances that were newly provisioned).

Again, this is just one use case. There are lots of others, such as self-service deployments to development and test environments, continuous delivery, and runbooks that source data from the CMDB.

Important: This chapter uses Spring 3.1

The other chapters in this book are based on Spring 3.0, but this one is based on Spring 3.1. Spring 3.1 was released as we were drawing the book to a close, and it includes new features that we wanted to present. This chapter presents several of those, including new MVC namespace configuration elements, producible and consumable media types, constructor injection, and profiles. We'll call out the new features as we use them.

---

[3] Alternatively, the deployment engine can push a bootstrapper onto the instance, which then takes care of getting the assets from the staging repo.

There's a ton to cover, so let's dive right into establishing the foundation for the entire system: the configuration management database.

11.1 *Creating a simple configuration item*

PREREQUISITES
None

KEY TECHNOLOGIES
Spring Framework 3.1, Neo4j, Spring Data Neo4j

Background

A CMDB centralizes system configuration, broadly conceived, in a way that enhances visibility, security, and management. Although there isn't a single, universally agreed-on definition, the general concept is that it manages the so-called configuration items (CIs) that allow you to keep your environments in an operational steady state, and also to manage changes to those environments. CIs can be anything you want to manage in this context: an entire data center can be a CI, as can an individual NIC on a physical server.

A CMDB isn't necessarily a single physical database, and there's nothing saying that it has to be a relational database or any other type of technology. It's more conceptual: it brings together the configuration necessary to stand up and maintain your technical environment. Strictly speaking, the app configuration repository in figure 11.1 is part of this logical CMDB concept because it contains configuration of the sort under discussion. But for present purposes we'll separate the environmental configuration from the app configuration, and we'll generally use the term CMDB to refer to the former.

Centralizing configuration is hugely useful. It's easiest to see this by contrasting it with in-place configuration "management" as shown in figure 11.2.

Because there's no gold copy of the configuration for a given set of server instances, the deployer has to go onto each server and update the configuration manually. In addition to being laborious (especially if you have farms that are many servers wide), it's also highly error prone. It's easy to make a single-character password mistake when you're slogging through a late-night release window with 10 more app releases to go.

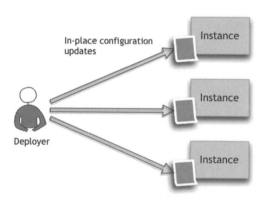

Figure 11.2 The deployer updates configuration in place on all target servers, requiring lots of manual, error-prone work. Not a best practice.

Instead, we prefer to adopt an approach more like the one in figure 11.3 where we have a different situation. The deployer updates a single configuration master in the CMDB (or app config repo; in this case we're using the term CMDB more generically), and then the automation deploys it. Although it's certainly possible for the deployer

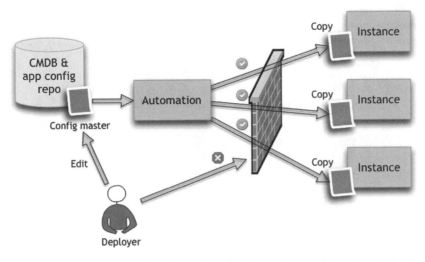

Figure 11.3   The deployer edits the configuration in one place, and then the automation pushes it through to the target servers.

to make a mistake, it's no longer possible for the configuration copies to be out of sync. If there's a mistake, all instances will have it, and a single fix will fix all instances. Centralization has therefore eliminated an important source of configuration drift.

Security is better here, too. Firewall rules (at least in environments where you need the control) prevent anybody other than the deployment automation from getting on the target servers. You can place appropriate access controls and auditing at the CMDB to ensure that only authorized activity takes place.[4]

Problem

Implement a simple CI for a CMDB.

Solution

In this solution, we'll show how to build some pieces of the Zkybase CMDB (http://github.com/williewheeler/zkybase), which is based on Neo4j and Spring Data Neo4j. Specifically, you'll build your first CI—a simple, relationship-free application CI—along with an associated data access object.

> **What is Neo4j?**
>
> Neo4j (http://neo4j.org/) is an open source graph database, which falls under the general rubric of NoSQL databases. Unlike many of the other NoSQL databases, Neo4j is fully transactional. Just as with relational databases, you want to represent entities and relationships, but instead of using tables, columns, foreign keys, and such, you use graph nodes and edges.

---

[4] We don't discuss CMDB security in this chapter, but see chapters 6 and 7 for information on adding access controls.

(continued)

Neo4j is schema-free. You can add nodes and edges to the database without worrying about database schema conflicts. (Alternatively, you have to worry about the schema in the app, because the database won't help.) This is particularly nice for a CMDB, which often has a rich set of entities and relationships that evolve over time to support maturing development and operational processes. It's easier to make the corresponding changes to the underlying data when there isn't an explicit schema in the way.

It's beyond our scope to get into a detailed discussion of Neo4j (there's just too much for us to cover here), but have a look at the Neo4j website for more information.

Because you'll build several CIs (one in this recipe and more in the next), you'll build out some framework code in this recipe to make subsequent CIs easier to implement. Let's begin with that groundwork.

CREATING A CI ABSTRACTION AND BASE CI

Even though we're only looking at the application CI here, your CMDB will have lots of different CI types, so it's sensible to define an appropriate abstraction. The following listing is the simple CI interface.

Listing 11.1   CI.java: the CI interface

```java
package com.springinpractice.ch11.model;

import java.util.Date;

public interface CI<T extends CI<T>> extends Comparable<T> {
    Long getId();

    void setId(Long id);

    Date getDateCreated();

    void setDateCreated(Date dateCreated);

    Date getDateModified();

    void setDateModified(Date dateModified);

    String getDisplayName();
}
```

You need a base class for implementation as well, as shown next.

Listing 11.2   AbstractCI: a base class for implementing CIs

```java
package com.springinpractice.ch11.model;

import java.util.Date;
import org.springframework.data.neo4j.annotation.GraphId;
import org.springframework.data.neo4j.annotation.NodeEntity;

@NodeEntity                                                          ① Marks CI as
public abstract class AbstractCI<T extends CI<T>> implements CI<T> {    node entity
```

① Marks CI as node entity

```
@GraphId private Long id;
private Date dateCreated;
private Date dateModified;

public Long getId() { return id; }

public void setId(Long id) { this.id = id; }

... accessors for dateCreated and dateModified ...

... equals(), hashCode(), compareTo() ...
}
```

Annotates
❷ **entity ID**

Your abstract CI uses annotations from the Spring Data Neo4j project to help perform the object/graph mapping. With Neo4j, you usually represent entities with nodes, and in such cases you use @NodeEntity ❶ to accomplish such a mapping.[5] You also need to tell Spring Data Neo4j which field you want to serve as an identifier, and you do that using @GraphId ❷.

What is Spring Data Neo4j?

In chapter 2 we glanced at Spring Data JPA.[6] Spring Data Neo4j is another Spring Data project, but this time for Neo4j databases. It offers a data-access API, the ability to generate dynamic DAO implementations, and annotations for mapping Java objects to Neo4j graphs. See www.springsource.org/spring-data/neo4j for more information.

Now that you have a simple interface and abstract base class, let's implement the application CI.

CREATING THE APPLICATION CI

The next listing shows how to create an application CI using the AbstractCI class you just created.

Listing 11.3 Application.java: the application CI

```
package com.springinpractice.ch11.model;

import javax.validation.constraints.NotNull;
import javax.validation.constraints.Size;
import org.springframework.data.neo4j.annotation.Indexed;

public class Application extends AbstractCI<Application> {
    @Indexed private String name;
    private String shortDescription;

    @NotNull
    @Size(max = 80)
    public String getName() { return name; }
```

❶ **Extends base class**

❷ **Indexed for lookups**

---

[5] In other cases, it's useful to represent an entity with an edge. An example might be a membership entity in a team roster, where you have a relationship between a person and a team, along with an additional role attribute attaching to the membership. Spring Data Neo4j provides @RelationshipEntity for that. You'll see this in recipe 11.2.

[6] You'll also see Spring Data MongoDB in chapter 12.

```
    public void setName(String name) { this.name = name; }

    @Size(max = 200)
    public String getShortDescription() { return shortDescription; }

    public void setShortDescription(String shortDescription) {
        this.shortDescription = shortDescription;
    }
    public String getDisplayName() {
        return "Application";
    }
}
```

Obviously this isn't an especially robust application model. You have only a couple of properties and no relationships at all. But that's OK, because you're just getting started. The main point is that you extend the `AbstractCI` base class ❶. This makes `Application` an `@NodeEntity` and endows it with an `@GraphId`.

You also index the name property using Spring Data Neo4j's `@Indexed` annotation ❷. This will allow you to perform name-based lookups.

Next you'll want a DAO for CRUD operations and queries. Spring Data Neo4j provides a way to generate DAOs dynamically using the `GraphRepository` abstraction.

CREATING THE APPLICATION DAO

The following listing creates `ApplicationRepository`, which is your DAO for persistence operations on applications.

Listing 11.4 ApplicationRepository.java: the DAO interface

```
package com.springinpractice.ch11.repository;                            Extends ❶
                                                          GraphRepository<Application>
import com.springinpractice.ch11.model.Application;
import org.springframework.data.neo4j.repository.GraphRepository;

public interface ApplicationRepository
    extends GraphRepository<Application> {
                                                              ❷ Custom
        Application findByName(String name);                    finder
}
```

This listing shows how simple it is to create a DAO using Spring Data Neo4j. All you have to do is create an interface extending `GraphRepository<Application>` ❶, which provides various CRUD methods and finders. You can even define a custom finder ❷ using method-naming conventions. Spring Data Neo4j generates a DAO implementation dynamically for you, including the custom finder.

There's only one more thing left to do, and that's the configuration.

SPRING CONFIGURATION

To make the magic work, you need some configuration.

Listing 11.5 beans-service.xml configuration

```
<?xml version="1.0" encoding="UTF-8"?>
<beans xmlns="http://www.springframework.org/schema/beans"
    xmlns:context="http://www.springframework.org/schema/context"
```

```
xmlns:neo4j="http://www.springframework.org/schema/data/neo4j"
xmlns:p="http://www.springframework.org/schema/p"
xmlns:xsi="http://www.w3.org/2001/XMLSchema-instance"
xsi:schemaLocation="
    http://www.springframework.org/schema/beans
    http://www.springframework.org/schema/beans/spring-beans-3.1.xsd
    http://www.springframework.org/schema/context
    http://www.springframework.org/schema/context/
            spring-context-3.1.xsd
    http://www.springframework.org/schema/data/neo4j
    http://www.springframework.org/schema/data/neo4j/
            spring-neo4j-2.0.xsd">

<context:property-placeholder
    location="classpath:/spring/environment.properties" />
<context:annotation-config />
```

❶ Points to database

```
<neo4j:config storeDirectory="${graphDb.dir}" />
<neo4j:repositories
    base-package="com.springinpractice.ch11.repository" />
</beans>
```

❷ Generates DAOs dynamically

At ❶ you tell Spring where to find the Neo4j database. This is a full file path to the database, such as /Users/williewheeler/dev/neo4j/zkybase/db.[7] Then you use ❷ to scan a base package for GraphRepository implementations, from which Spring Data Neo4j generates implementations dynamically.

With that, you've created your first Neo4j-backed CI and repository.

Discussion

In this recipe you got your feet wet with Spring Data Neo4j, creating a simple CI and a simple DAO for performing persistence operations. Although everything you've done has been straightforward, you have the basis for a powerful way of working with CMDB data.

Recipe 11.2 builds on the work you did here by elaborating both the data model and the application stack.

11.2 Creating related configuration items

PREREQUISITES
Recipe 11.1 Creating a simple configuration item

KEY TECHNOLOGIES
Spring Framework 3.1, Neo4j, Spring Data Neo4j

Background

In recipe 11.1 you created a simple application CI. But real CIs aren't *quite* so simple: they generally have relationships to other CIs. Applications, for example, can have

---

[7] It's also possible to run Neo4j as a standalone server, but we're not pursuing that deployment approach here.

modules, which in turn have associated packages. To do anything useful with your CMDB, you need to know how to create relationships between your CIs.

Problem

Create additional CIs, supporting relationships.

Solution

To illustrate a variety of techniques for creating relationships, you'll create CIs for modules, packages, and teams. In this recipe you'll lay down the code for the expanded domain model. After that, you'll create the DAOs as well, because you'll need them for subsequent recipes. Finally, with the persistence layer in place, you'll create a transactional service layer for your CIs.

ENHANCING THE APPLICATION CI TO SUPPORT RELATIONSHIPS

First, your application CI now has a one-many relationship to a new module CI and a many-many relationship to a new team CI. The following listing shows how you can establish the relationships in question. (You'll see the new CIs shortly.)

Listing 11.6   Expanding Application.java to support relationships

```java
package com.springinpractice.ch11.model;

import java.util.Set;
import javax.validation.Valid;
import javax.validation.constraints.NotNull;
import javax.validation.constraints.Size;
import org.neo4j.graphdb.Direction;
import com.springinpractice.ch11.model.relationship.ApplicationTeam;
import org.springframework.data.neo4j.annotation.Indexed;
import org.springframework.data.neo4j.annotation.RelatedTo;
import org.springframework.data.neo4j.annotation.RelatedToVia;

public class Application extends AbstractCI<Application> {
    @Indexed private String name;
    private String shortDescription;

    @RelatedTo(type = "APPLICATION_MODULE",          ❶ Relates app
        direction = Direction.OUTGOING)                 to modules
    private Set<Module> modules;

    @RelatedToVia(direction = Direction.OUTGOING)     ❷ Relates app
    private Set<ApplicationTeam> teams;                   to teams

    ... same name and shortDescription accessors as before ...

    public Set<Module> getModules() { return modules; }      ❸ Read/write Set

    public void setModules(Set<Module> modules) { this.modules = modules; }

    public Iterable<ApplicationTeam> getTeams() { return teams; }    ❹ Read-only Iterable

    public ApplicationTeam addTeam(Team team,          ❺ Method to add teams
        ApplicationTeam.TeamType type) {

        ApplicationTeam appTeam = new ApplicationTeam(this, team, type);
```

```
        teams.add(appTeam);
        return appTeam;
    }
    public String getDisplayName() { return name; }
}
```

You relate applications to modules using the Spring Data Neo4j `@RelatedTo` annotation ❶. This involves choosing a name for the relationship type; here you choose `APPLICATION_MODULE`.

In Neo4j, you model relationships between entities as directed edges in a graph.[8] Because the edges are directed, one end of the edge is the start node and the other end is the end node. The direction doesn't carry any inherent semantic significance. It's up to the app either to impose a meaning or to ignore the directionality, although all Neo4j edges are directed. The `direction = Direction.OUTGOING` indicates that applications appear as start nodes in this particular relationship; `direction = Direction.INCOMING` would indicate an end node. The default value is `Direction.OUTGOING` if you don't specify a direction, but here you've been explicit.

> ### Naming relationship types
> Note that relationship types need unique names. If, for example, you have a relationship called `CONTAINS` between an application and a module, you can't have another relationship called `CONTAINS` between a server farm and a server.

At ❷ you have another relationship, this time between applications and teams. But notice that the definition here looks slightly different than the definition in ❶. For one thing, you're using the Spring Data Neo4j `@RelatedToVia` annotation instead of `@RelatedTo`. For another, you haven't defined a relationship type. What's going on?

In this case you're dealing not with a simple relationship but with a relationship entity. A *relationship entity* is a relationship that exists as a first-class entity with an explicit class definition. In this case, what's happening is that you're relating the `Application` CI with a `Team` CI through a relationship entity called `ApplicationTeam`. The main use case for relationship entities is that you can attach properties to the relationship. You'll see in listing 11.7 that you can assign a team type to the relationship: a given app might have a development team, a test team, a release team, and an ops team. Another example might be a role property on the relationship between a team and a person.

A second use case for relationship entities would be wanting to have a way to connect two entities without either one knowing about the other. For example, you might want to constrain individual apps to be deployable to specific server farms, but you might not want apps to know about server farms and vice versa. Relationship entities are useful here even if you don't have any properties defined on the relationship.

---

[8] In fact, Neo4j refers to such edges as relationships, as opposed to saying that edges represent relationships.

When dealing with relationship entities, you still need a type. You can specify that either in the @RelatedToVia annotation (using @RelatedToVia(type = "SOME_TYPE")) or in the relationship entity class itself. In the present case, we've opted to specify the type in the relationship entity class; see listing 11.7.

At ❸ you have the getter for modules. Spring Data Neo4j allows you to use either a Set or an Iterable, depending on whether you want the collection to be read/write or read-only. (Unfortunately, Lists are unsupported.) You use a Set here so you can add modules directly.

For teams, you use the read-only Iterable instead ❹. You certainly could use a Set, but instead we opted to provide a convenient addTeam() method ❺ to avoid forcing your API users to create ApplicationTeam instances themselves. The addTeam() method creates the ApplicationTeam instance and returns it in case the caller wants to do anything with it.

The following CIs are more of the same, but with variants on how you establish relationships.

BUILDING OUT THE OTHER CIS AND THEIR RELATIONSHIPS

The next CI is a module. Modules provide a way to decompose an application into its package-producing parts. A given app might have, for instance, a web module (generates WARs containing web app/service combo), a client module (client for the web service, packaged as a JAR), and a domain module (domain classes shared by the web and client modules, once again packaged as a JAR). Again, these are just examples. Here's how your module looks.

Listing 11.7   Module.java, representing a module of code

```
package com.springinpractice.ch11.model;

import javax.validation.constraints.NotNull;
import javax.validation.constraints.Size;
import org.springframework.data.neo4j.annotation.Indexed;           ❶ Extends
                                                                        AbstractCI
public class Module extends AbstractCI<Module> {
    private String name;
    private String shortDescription;

    @Indexed private String groupId;                                ❷ Index supports
    @Indexed private String moduleId;                                   queries

    @NotNull
    @Size(max = 80)
    public String getName() { return name; }

    public void setName(String name) { this.name = name; }

    @Size(max = 200)
    public String getShortDescription() { return shortDescription; }

    public void setShortDescription(String shortDescription) {
        this.shortDescription = shortDescription;
    }
```

```java
    public String getGroupId() { return groupId; }

    public void setGroupId(String groupId) { this.groupId = groupId; }

    public String getModuleId() { return moduleId; }

    public void setModuleId(String moduleId) { this.moduleId = moduleId; }

    ... compareTo(), toString() ...

    public String getDisplayName() { return name; }
}
```

As with the application CI, you extend `AbstractCI` ❶ from listing 11.2. You also annotate the `groupId` and `moduleId` fields with `@Indexed` ❷, which will allow you to perform lookups against them later.

Notice that even though there's a relationship between applications and modules (you established it in your application CI), your module doesn't know anything about applications. The reason is that you might want to allow CIs beyond applications to have modules: you might define, for example, a `WebService` CI that has modules. If you were to do that, you wouldn't want the module to know directly about applications and web services. Spring Data Neo4j allows you to establish a relationship from a single side.[9]

The following listing shows the next CI: the package. A package is a JAR, a WAR, an EAR, and so forth, and it's the result of building a module. As such, it references a module, but it has a specific version too.

Listing 11.8 Package.java, representing a module package

```java
package com.springinpractice.ch11.model;

import javax.validation.constraints.NotNull;
import javax.validation.constraints.Size;
import org.neo4j.graphdb.Direction;
import org.springframework.data.neo4j.annotation.Fetch;
import org.springframework.data.neo4j.annotation.Indexed;
import org.springframework.data.neo4j.annotation.RelatedTo;

public class Package extends AbstractCI<Package> {             ❶ Eager-loads module

    @Fetch
    @RelatedTo(type = "FROM_MODULE", direction = Direction.OUTGOING)
    private Module module;

    @Indexed private String version;                           ❷ Indexes version

    @NotNull
    public Module getModule() { return module; }

    public void setModule(Module module) { this.module = module; }

    @NotNull
    @Size(min = 1, max = 80)
    public String getVersion() { return version; }
```

---

[9] It's not unlike other object persistence frameworks, such as Hibernate, in this respect.

```
    public void setVersion(String version) { this.version = version; }

    ... compareTo(), toString() ...

    public String getDisplayName() {
        return "Package";
    }
}
```

The previous listing demonstrates the use of the @Fetch annotation ❶, which eagerly loads the field so annotated. In this case, it makes sense to do so, because there aren't many (if any) contexts in which a module-free package would be useful. Once again, you use @Indexed ❷ to make the field available as a key for performing lookups.

Now that your apps have modules and packages, let's switch gears and create a team CI that you can attach to your apps. The intent is to establish a many-many relationship between applications and teams. The next listing is a basic team CI, having nothing more than a name (for example, Zkybase Development Team or Zkybase Operations Team). A real team CI would have team members, but we're suppressing those here because you don't need them for the current purpose.

Listing 11.9 Team.java, with team members suppressed

```
package com.springinpractice.ch11.model;

import javax.validation.constraints.Size;
import org.springframework.data.neo4j.annotation.Indexed;

public class Team extends AbstractCI<Team> {

    @Indexed(indexType = IndexType.FULLTEXT, indexName="findByName")
    private String name;

    @Size(max = 80)
    public String getName() { return name; }

    public void setName(String name) { this.name = name; }

    // compareTo and equals

    public String getDisplayName() { return name; }
}
```

Even though you want applications and teams to be related, notice that neither the application CI nor the team CI knows anything about the other. The reason is that whenever you relate an app to a team, you want to attach a team type to qualify the relationship. For this, you'll need a separate entity—a *relationship entity*—that allows you to represent not only the two related CIs, but also the type attribute.

Listing 11.10 ApplicationTeam.java relationship entity

```
package com.springinpractice.ch11.model.relationship;

import com.springinpractice.ch11.model.Application;
import com.springinpractice.ch11.model.Team;
import org.springframework.data.neo4j.annotation.EndNode;
```

```java
import org.springframework.data.neo4j.annotation.Fetch;
import org.springframework.data.neo4j.annotation.GraphId;
import org.springframework.data.neo4j.annotation.RelationshipEntity;
import org.springframework.data.neo4j.annotation.StartNode;

@RelationshipEntity(type = "APPLICATION_TEAM")          ①  Annotates as a
public class ApplicationTeam {                              relationship entity
    public enum TeamType {                    ②  Team type
        DEVELOPMENT(),                           enum
        OPERATIONS();

    }

        private String name;

        private TeamType(String name) { this.name = name; }

        public String toString() { return name; }

    @GraphId private Long id;                                 ③  Fetches
    @Fetch @StartNode private Application application;           start node
    @Fetch @EndNode private Team team;
    private TeamType type;                              ④  Fetches
                                                           end node
    public ApplicationTeam() { }

    public ApplicationTeam(
        Application application, Team team, TeamType type) {

        this.application = application;
        this.team = team;
        this.type = type;
    }

    public Application getApplication() { return application; }

    public void setApplication(Application application) {
        this.application = application;
    }

    public Team getTeam() { return team; }

    public void setTeam(Team team) { this.team = team; }

    public TeamType getType() { return type; }

    public void setType(TeamType type) { this.type = type; }

    ... equals(), hashCode(), toString() ...
}
```

This entity, unlike the previous ones, represents a relationship between CIs, so you use the `@RelationshipEntity` annotation to reflect that ①. In this case you're assuming that only two types of teams are available, so you create a typesafe enum for the team type ②.

Like all Neo4j relationships, this one is directed. It doesn't matter which CI is the start node and which is the end node. Here, you choose `Application` to be the `@StartNode` ③, and you eagerly fetch it. Similarly, `Team` is the `@EndNode` ④, and you eagerly fetch that as well.

TIP   The current example uses relationship entities to support attributes on the relationship. But relationship entities are useful in at least one other situation: when you want to decouple the two node entities in question. Suppose, for example, that you want a many-many relationship between packages and server farms, where a package and a farm are related if the package is deployed to the farm. It may be that you don't want packages to know about farms and vice versa. Here you could create a `PackageFarm` relationship entity to establish the relationship, even if `PackageFarm` doesn't have any additional attribute.

You've seen a variety of relationship scenarios with your small stable of CIs. Let's create some DAOs for the CIs.

CREATING DAOS FOR THE NEW CIS

You'll create DAOs for modules and packages, because you'll need those later in the chapter. Your first DAO is the `ModuleRepository`.

Listing 11.11   ModuleRepository.java

```
package com.springinpractice.ch11.repository;

import com.springinpractice.ch11.model.Module;                          Custom  ❶
import org.springframework.data.neo4j.annotation.Query;                  finder
import org.springframework.data.neo4j.repository.GraphRepository;

public interface ModuleRepository extends GraphRepository<Module> {

    @Query("start module=node:
            __types__('className=com.springinpractice.c11.model.Module')
            where module.groupId={0} and module.moduleId={1}
            return module")
    Module findByGroupIdAndModuleId(String groupId, String moduleId);    ◁
}
```

As with the `ApplicationRepository`, you have a custom finder ❶. This time you find a module based on two properties.

The next listing shows the DAO for packages.

Listing 11.12   PackageRepository.java

```
package com.springinpractice.ch11.repository;

import java.util.List;
import com.springinpractice.ch11.model.Module;
import com.springinpractice.ch11.model.Package;
import org.springframework.data.neo4j.annotation.Query;
import org.springframework.data.neo4j.repository.GraphRepository;

public interface PackageRepository extends GraphRepository<Package> {

    @Query("start module=node({0}) match package-[:FROM_MODULE]->module
      return package")
    List<Package> findByModule(Module module);                           ◁   Finds
                                                                      ❶  packages
                                                                          by module
```

```
@Query("start module=node({0}) match package-[:FROM_MODULE]->module where
  package.version = {1} return package")
Package findByModuleAndVersion(Module module, String version);
}
```

Finds package by module and version ❷

As with the DAOs, you have two custom finders: one to find a list of packages for a given module ❶ and one to find a specific package for a given module and version ❷.

It's time to create a service layer for your CIs. This will allow you to add transactions, and it will let you execute certain bits of business logic. As with your CIs, there are several service beans, so you'll want to have useful abstractions in place.

CREATE A SERVICE ABSTRACTION AND BASE SERVICE

The following listing shows the interface for your CI service beans.

Listing 11.13 CIService.java service interface

```
package com.springinpractice.ch11.service;

import java.util.List;
import com.springinpractice.ch11.model.CI;
import org.springframework.validation.Errors;

public interface CIService<T extends CI<T>> {

    void create(T ci);

    void create(T ci, Errors errors);

    List<T> findAll();

    T findOne(Long id);

    void update(T ci, Errors errors);

    void delete(T ci);

    void delete(Long id);
}
```

❶ Creates support validation

❷ Updates support validation

Your CI service interface exposes various CRUD operations, although individual services can, of course, add more specific methods. The GraphRepository interface exposes a save() method to handle creates and updates, but here you distinguish the two because you can more conveniently target RESTful POSTs and PUTs that way. We also include versions of create() ❶ and update() ❷ to support validation, such as flagging duplicate CIs for creates or nonexistent CIs for updates.

You'll want a base class for implementing CI service beans, and that's what the next listing provides.

Listing 11.14 AbstractCIService.java: base class for CI service beans

```
package com.springinpractice.ch11.service.impl;

import java.util.Date;
import java.util.List;
```

```
import javax.inject.Inject;
import com.springinpractice.ch11.exception.DuplicateCIException;
import com.springinpractice.ch11.exception.NoSuchCIException;
import com.springinpractice.ch11.model.CI;
import com.springinpractive.ch11.service.CIService;
import com.springinpractice.ch11.util.CollectionsUtil;
import org.springframework.data.neo4j.repository.GraphRepository;
import org.springframework.data.neo4j.support.Neo4jTemplate;
import org.springframework.transaction.annotation.Transactional;
import org.springframework.validation.Errors;
```
❶ Enables transaction
```
@Transactional
public abstract class AbstractCIService<T extends CI<T>>
    implements CIService<T>
```
❷ Template for subclasses
```
    @Inject protected Neo4jTemplate neo4jTemplate;

    protected abstract GraphRepository<T> getRepository();
```
❸ Subclasses provide repo
```
    public void create(T ci) { createAddDate(ci); }

    public void create(T ci, Errors errors) {
        if (!errors.hasErrors()) {
            try {
                createAddDate(ci);
            } catch (DuplicateCIException e) {
                errors.reject("error.duplicateCI");
            }
        }
    }

    private void createAddDate(T ci) {
        checkForDuplicate(ci);
        ci.setDateCreated(new Date());
        getRepository().save(ci);
    }
```
❹ Subclasses check for duplicates
```
    protected void checkForDuplicate(T ci) { }

    public List<T> findAll() {
        return CollectionsUtil.asSortedList(getRepository().findAll());
    }

    public T findOne(Long id) {
        T ci = getRepository().findOne(id);
        if (ci == null) { throw new NoSuchCIException(); }
        return ci;
    }

    public void update(T ci) { updateAddDate(ci); }

    public void update(T ci, Errors errors) {
        if (errors == null || !errors.hasErrors()) {
            updateAddDate(ci);
        }
    }

    private void updateAddDate(T ci) {
        ci.setDateModified(new Date());
        getRepository().save(ci);
```

```
    }
    public void delete(T ci) { getRepository().delete(ci); }
    public void delete(Long id) { getRepository().delete(id); }
}
```

You annotate the base class with @Transactional ❶ to ensure that you run your service methods in a transactional context. (Neo4j supports full ACID transactions.)

At ❷ you inject a Neo4jTemplate, which subclasses can use because it has protected visibility. This provides a programmatic interface for performing fine-grained persistence operations against the Neo4j database, which sometimes comes in handy.[10]

Subclasses must expose their backing repository through the getRepository() abstract method ❸. This allows the AbstractCIService to implement general CRUD operations against the repository, as the listing shows.[11]

Subclasses may optionally implement the checkForDuplicate() method ❹. The contract here is to throw a DuplicateCIException (see the code download) if the CI already exists in the database. The default implementation is a no-op.

You can see the service interface and base class in action by implementing a package service, which you'll use in some of the following recipes.

CREATING A PACKAGE SERVICE

You implement a package service interface in the following listing. It's little more than a wrapper interface around the package repository you created earlier.

Listing 11.15 PackageService.java

```
package com.springinpractice.ch11.service;

import java.util.List;
import com.springinpractice.ch11.model.Module;
import com.springinpractice.ch11.model.Package;

public interface PackageService extends CIService<Package> {

    List<Package> findByModule(Module module);

    Package findByModuleAndVersion(Module module, String version);
}
```

The implementation is more or less obvious.

Listing 11.16 PackageServiceImpl.java service bean

```
package com.springinpractice.ch11.service.impl;

import java.util.List;
import javax.inject.Inject;
import com.springinpractice.ch11.exception.DuplicateCIException;
import com.springinpractice.ch11.model.Module;
```

---

[10] The template has, for example, a fetch() method that helps when implementing programmatic eager loading.

[11] Due to type erasure, you can't inject a GraphRepository<T>.

```
import com.springinpractice.ch11.model.Package;
import com.springinpractice.ch11.repository.PackageRepository;
import com.springinpractice.ch11.service.PackageService;
import org.springframework.data.neo4j.repository.GraphRepository;
import org.springframework.stereotype.Service;

@Service
public class PackageServiceImpl extends AbstractCIService<Package>
    implements PackageService {

    @Inject private PackageRepository packageRepo;            ❶ Injects
                                                                  PackageRepository

    protected GraphRepository<Package> getRepository() {      ❷ Expose to
        return packageRepo;                                       base class
    }

    protected void checkForDuplicate(Package pkg) {
        Package duplicate = packageRepo.findByModuleAndVersion(
            pkg.getModule(), pkg.getVersion());
        if (duplicate != null) {                               Dupe check ❸
            throw new DuplicateCIException(pkg);
        }
    }

    public List<Package> findByModule(Module module) {
        return packageRepo.findByModule(module);
    }

    public Package findByModuleAndVersion(Module module, String version) {
        return packageRepo.findByModuleAndVersion(module, version);
    }
}
```

At ❶ you inject the `PackageRepository`. This gives the `PackageService` access to the custom finder methods you specified. You expose it as a `GraphRepository<Package>` ❷ so the base class can make calls against it.

You implement a custom duplicate-check method ❸, throwing an exception if a lookup by module and version yields an existing package.

Zkybase has other service beans, but this should be enough to give you a sense for what they do and how to implement them. Don't forget to add a `<context:component-scan>` to beans-service.xml to capture the new service bean.

Discussion

Recipe 11.2 continued our exploration of using Neo4j and Spring Data Neo4j to implement a CMDB domain model. In recipe 11.1 you created a basic CI and a corresponding repository. In the current recipe, you elaborated the model to include more CIs, relationships between them, more repositories, and transactional service beans. Although this treatment merely scratches the surface of what a fully fledged CMDB offers, it's enough to equip you to build your own domain models and services.

In the next recipe, you expose your package data through a RESTful web service.

11.3 Adding a RESTful web service

PREREQUISITES
Recipe 11.1 Creating a simple configuration item
Recipe 11.2 Creating related configuration items

KEY TECHNOLOGIES
Spring Framework 3.1, Spring Web MVC, XML, JAXB 2, JSON, Jackson

Background

One of the major points of a CMDB is to enable the process, tools, and data integration that support a mature operational capability. Web services are helpful for tying systems together. This recipe shows how you can expose configuration management data through a RESTful web service.

Problem

Expose configuration management data through a RESTful web service, supporting both XML and JSON.

Solution

In recipe 11.2 we showed how to create a simple package CI for your CMDB, with a focus on data modeling and persistence. What's missing is a web service view. This is important because you want to make it possible to create automation around packages:

- The continuous-integration build automation needs to be able to create package records in the CMDB following successful builds.
- The deployment automation needs to be able to see which packages are available for deployment.

You'll create both XML and JSON representations for your packages because both formats are popular and because it's easy to support them both. This will require a few steps. First, you need to annotate your package and module CIs with JAXB annotations. (Recall that packages reference modules, so you need to take care of the module mapping too.) Second, you want to create a package controller with appropriate endpoints. Finally, you need to update your Spring configuration to support your web service.

You'll begin by updating the package and module CIs.

> **Don't you need to include Jackson annotations for JSON mappings?**
>
> Nope. Although it's true that Jackson provides JSON-specific annotations for object/ JSON mapping, you can configure Jackson to understand JAXB annotations, and this allows you to avoid parallel sets of JAXB and Jackson annotations. XML and JSON are different, but they're close enough that JAXB annotations are good enough for most of what people need to do. You'll see the configuration later in the recipe.[12]

---

[12] See also Willie Wheeler, "Configuring Jackson to use JAXB2 annotations with Spring," Dec. 6, 2011, http:// mng.bz/vW7T.

AUGMENTING THE PACKAGE AND MODULE CIS

Among other things, you want a way to view individual packages and lists of packages as XML and as JSON. For the most part, this is a matter of adding JAXB annotations to the package and module CIs and letting some mapping frameworks (namely, JAXB and Jackson) do their thing. In the special case of mapping XML lists, JAXB needs a little help. First you'll create a `ListWrapper` interface that you can use for this purpose.

Listing 11.17 ListWrapper.java: supporting XML lists

```java
package com.springinpractice.ch11.model;

import java.util.List;

public interface ListWrapper<T extends CI<T>> {

    List<T> getList();

    void setList(List<T> list);
}
```

The idea is that if you want a root-level XML list, you have to create a wrapper object and map it. Unfortunately, with JAXB, unless you want every such list to have the same root element name (it would be something generic, like `<list>`), you have to create separate wrapper objects with separate root element names. The point of `ListWrapper` is to provide structure around these list wrapper objects.

Let's do one more bit of preparatory work. You have a bunch of CIs, and you want to support XML and JSON mappings for all of them. Therefore you need to update the `AbstractCI` accordingly.

Listing 11.18 AbstractCI.java, updated to support XML and JSON mappings

```java
package com.springinpractice.ch11.model;

import javax.xml.bind.annotation.XmlAccessType;
import javax.xml.bind.annotation.XmlAccessorType;
import javax.xml.bind.annotation.XmlAttribute;
import org.springframework.data.neo4j.annotation.GraphId;
import org.springframework.data.neo4j.annotation.NodeEntity;

@NodeEntity
@XmlAccessorType(XmlAccessType.NONE)                          ← ❶ Suppresses default mappings
public abstract class AbstractCI<T extends CI<T>> implements CI<T> {
    @GraphId private Long id;

    @XmlAttribute                                             ← ❷ Maps ID as attribute
    public Long getId() { return id; }

    public void setId(Long id) { this.id = id; }

    ... equals(), hashCode(), compareTo() ...
}
```

❶ Suppresses default mappings

❷ Maps ID as attribute

You add only a couple of things to the original class. You indicate that the mapper shouldn't automatically map either fields or JavaBean properties ❶; you'll specify all mappings explicitly. At ❷ you use `@XmlAttribute` to map the `id` property to an XML attribute, at least where XML is concerned. For JSON, there's no element/attribute distinction, and both `@XmlElement` and `@XmlAttribute` carry a Java property to a JSON property.

The next listing shows how you map the package CI, including how to use the `AbstractCI` base class and the `ListWrapper` to map package lists. For more information about the mapping annotations, please consult the JAXB 2 documentation.

Listing 11.19 Updating Package.java to support XML and JSON mappings

```java
package com.springinpractice.ch11.model;

import java.util.List;
import javax.validation.constraints.NotNull;
import javax.validation.constraints.Size;
import javax.xml.bind.annotation.XmlElement;
import javax.xml.bind.annotation.XmlRootElement;
import javax.xml.bind.annotation.XmlType;
import org.neo4j.graphdb.Direction;
import org.springframework.data.neo4j.annotation.Fetch;
import org.springframework.data.neo4j.annotation.Indexed;
import org.springframework.data.neo4j.annotation.RelatedTo;

@XmlRootElement                                                        ❶ Marks as root element
@XmlType(propOrder = { "module", "version" })                         ❷ Specifies property order
public class Package extends AbstractCI<Package> {

    @Fetch
    @RelatedTo(type = "FROM_MODULE", direction = Direction.OUTGOING)
    private Module module;

    @Indexed private String version;

    public Package() { }

    public Package(Module module, String version) {
        this.module = module;
        this.version = version;
    }

    @NotNull                                                          ❸ Marks as XML element
    @XmlElement
    public Module getModule() { return module; }

    public void setModule(Module module) { this.module = module; }

    @NotNull
    @Size(min = 1, max = 80)
    @XmlElement
    public String getVersion() { return version; }

    public void setVersion(String version) { this.version = version; }

    ... compareTo(), toString() ...

    @XmlRootElement(name = "packages")                               ❹ Marks as root element
    public static class PackageListWrapper
        implements ListWrapper<Package> {

        private List<Package> list;
```

```
        @XmlElement(name = "package")
        public List<Package> getList() { return list; }

        public void setList(List<Package> list) { this.list = list; }
    }
}
```

The updated package CI is mostly the same as before, except now it includes annotations and an inner class to support object/XML and object/JSON mapping.

You use @XmlRootElement to mark this class as one that can be so mapped ❶. You also use @XmlType ❷ to specify the order of the properties in the mapping output.

At ❸ you annotate the getModule() method with @XmlElement to indicate that you want to map this method to an element. As a last step, you create a root-level package list ❹ by implementing the ListWrapper interface.

The next listing shows the same thing for the module CI, which we include for completeness.

Listing 11.20   Updating Module.java to support XML and JSON mappings

```
package com.springinpractice.ch11.model;

import java.util.List;
import javax.validation.constraints.NotNull;
import javax.validation.constraints.Size;
import javax.xml.bind.annotation.XmlElement;
import javax.xml.bind.annotation.XmlRootElement;
import javax.xml.bind.annotation.XmlType;

import org.springframework.data.neo4j.annotation.Indexed;

@XmlRootElement
@XmlType(propOrder = { "name", "shortDescription", "groupId", "moduleId" })
public class Module extends AbstractCI<Module> {
    private String name;
    private String shortDescription;

    @Indexed private String groupId;
    @Indexed private String moduleId;

    @NotNull
    @Size(max = 80)
    @XmlElement
    public String getName() { return name; }

    public void setName(String name) { this.name = name; }

    @Size(max = 200)
    @XmlElement
    public String getShortDescription() { return shortDescription; }

    public void setShortDescription(String shortDescription) {
        this.shortDescription = shortDescription;
    }

    @XmlElement
    public String getGroupId() { return groupId; }
```

```
    public void setGroupId(String groupId) { this.groupId = groupId; }

    @XmlElement
    public String getModuleId() { return moduleId; }

    public void setModuleId(String moduleId) { this.moduleId = moduleId; }

    public String getDisplayName() { return name; }

    ... compareTo(), toString() ...

    @XmlRootElement(name = "modules")
    public static class ModuleListWrapper implements ListWrapper<Module> {
        private List<Module> list;

        @XmlElement(name = "module")
        public List<Module> getList() { return list; }

        public void setList(List<Module> list) { this.list = list; }
    }
}
```

Again, this is pretty much the same as what you saw with packages, so there's no need to study the details. Let's turn now to the task of creating web service endpoints for your packages.

CREATING WEB SERVICE ENDPOINTS

You could create a variety of endpoints, but for now you'll focus on the following read-only endpoints:

- JSON list
- JSON details
- XML list
- XML details

(In recipe 11.4 we'll look at an endpoint that creates a CI.) The following listing shows how to implement each of these endpoints using an abstract base controller class.

> **Listing 11.21 Generic read-only endpoints in AbstractCrudController.java**

```
package com.springinpractice.ch11.web.controller;

import java.util.List;
import com.springinpractice.ch11.model.CI;
import com.springinpractice.ch11.model.ListWrapper;
import com.springinpractice.ch11.service.CIService;
import org.springframework.web.bind.annotation.PathVariable;
import org.springframework.web.bind.annotation.RequestMapping;
import org.springframework.web.bind.annotation.RequestMethod;
import org.springframework.web.bind.annotation.ResponseBody;

... other imports ...

public abstract class AbstractCrudController<T extends CI<T>>      ❶ Generic
    extends AbstractController {                                       controller

    Class<T> ciClass;                                              ❷ CI class field
```

```
    ... other fields ...
    public AbstractCrudController() {                          ◄── ③ Sets CI class
        ParameterizedType paramType =
            (ParameterizedType) getClass().getGenericSuperclass();
        this.ciClass =
            (Class<T>) paramType.getActualTypeArguments()[0];
    }
                                                                    ④ Service
    protected abstract CIService<T> getService();          ◄──        accessor

    @RequestMapping(                                          ◄──      JSON list
        value = "",                                              ⑤    @RequestMapping
        method = RequestMethod.GET,
        params = "format=json")
    @ResponseBody                                            ◄──      JSON list
    public List<T> getListAsJson() { return getSortedList(); }  ⑥    @ResponseBody

    @RequestMapping(                                        ◄── ⑦ XML list
        value = "",
        method = RequestMethod.GET,
        params = "format=xml")
    @ResponseBody
    public ListWrapper<T> getListAsXml() throws Exception {
        String wrapperClassName = ciClass.getName() + "$"
            + ciClass.getSimpleName() + "ListWrapper";
        Class<ListWrapper<T>> wrapperClass =
            (Class<ListWrapper<T>>) Class.forName(wrapperClassName);
        ListWrapper<T> wrapper = wrapperClass.newInstance();
        wrapper.setList(getSortedList());
        return wrapper;
    }

    private List<T> getSortedList() { return getService().findAll(); }

    @RequestMapping(                                        ◄── ⑧ JSON details
        value = "/{id}",
        method = RequestMethod.GET,
        params = "format=json",
        produces = "application/json")
    public T getDetailsAsJson(@PathVariable Long id) {
        return getDetails(id);
    }

    @RequestMapping(                                        ◄── ⑨ XML details
        value = "/{id}",
        method = RequestMethod.GET,
        params = "format=xml",
        produces = "application/xml")
    @ResponseBody
    public T getDetailsAsXml(@PathVariable Long id) {
        return getDetails(id);
    }

    private T getDetails(Long id) { return getService().findOne(id); }

    ... other methods ...
}
```

Again, note that the controller in the listing is an abstract base-controller class. Each controller instance provides CRUD operations for a given type of CI ❶. Here we're focusing on the web service operations; we've suppressed the others. The code for those is available in the code download.

One of the things complicating the base controller is the fact that you're trying to handle operations in a general fashion. By putting the complexity in the base class, you help keep subclasses simple.

To that end, you want to autodiscover the CI class based on the type argument in the subclass, because this turns out to be useful. (You'll see an example shortly.) At ❷ you have a `ciClass` field, and the constructor uses reflection to set it at ❸. A subclass extending `AbstractCrudController<Package>`, say, would have the `Package` class object as its `ciClass`.

Another thing you need to be able to do is inject the right CI-specific service into your controller. You'd want to inject a `PackageService` into your `PackageController`, for instance. You handle this by leaving the injections up to the subclasses[13] and accessing the service through an abstract method ❹. This allows you to implement generic operations against the service in the `AbstractCrudController` while giving subclasses access to type-specific methods.

With that setup done, you can get to the real meat. You handle requests to list all CIs of the relevant type as JSON ❺. You assume that the subclass will provide a base path through a class-level `@RequestMapping`, so the method-level value is the empty string (meaning you won't append anything to the class-level path). But you need a way to route JSON requests to the `getListAsJson()` handler method. It would be nice if you could map paths like `/applications.json`, `/packages.json`, and so forth here, but there's currently no generic way to do that.[14] But you can do something that's almost as good, which is map paths like `/applications?format=json` and `/packages?format=json`, so that's what you do with `params = "format=json"`.

Notice also the `produces = "application/json"` definition. This is new with Spring 3.1. It does a couple of things. It filters out requests whose `Accept` header is incompatible with the specified media type (here, `application/json`). Second, it ensures that the generated output has the correct media type. In this case, it turns out that the method works without the `produces` definition, but there's no harm in being paranoid.[15]

The `@ResponseBody` annotation ❻ tells Spring to take the handler method's return value and directly map it to the response output, without involving either models or views. Normally, you put your objects on the model and return a logical view

---

[13] You can't inject `CIService<T>` in the base controller due to type erasure.

[14] Read Willie Wheeler, "Add extension element to Spring Web MVC @RequestMapping annotation," Feb. 22, 2012, https://jira.springsource.org/browse/SPR-9153 for an explanation and desired enhancement. Looks like Spring 3.2 will address the issue.

[15] Spring gets the mapping right because the `MappingJacksonHttpMessageConverter` happens to be the first match for the CI list, so the output is JSON. But that's a happy accident. We suggest being explicit about the expected output.

name. None of that here. We'll discuss the mapping when we look at configuration, because mapping is determined by that configuration.[16]

The XML list ❼ is similar to the JSON list, but this time you have to deal with the XML list wrapper issue we mentioned. Here the CI class comes to the rescue. You use it—along with a little reflection-based magic—to create an appropriately wrapped list that will yield the root element name you want. Once again, paranoia drives you toward an explicit `produces` definition, and you use `@ResponseBody` to effect a direct mapping of your list wrapper to XML.

With ❽ and ❾ you have JSON and XML details views, respectively. In the case of the JSON details view, here you need the `produces` definition to avoid having the XML converter preempt the JSON converter. (Spring won't use the XML converter when `produces = "application/json"`).[17]

Now let's build one of the CRUD controllers, `PackageCrudController`. CRUD controllers for other CIs follow the same general pattern, but you care about packages in particular because you need the `PackageCrudController` for recipe 11.4.

Listing 11.22 PackageCrudController.java: extending base CRUD controller

```java
package com.springinpractice.ch11.web.controller.pkg;

import javax.inject.Inject;
import com.springinpractice.ch11.model.Package;
import com.springinpractice.ch11.service.CIService;
import com.springinpractice.ch11.service.PackageService;
import com.springinpractice.ch11.web.controller.AbstractCrudController;
import org.springframework.beans.factory.annotation.Value;
import org.springframework.stereotype.Controller;
import org.springframework.web.bind.annotation.RequestMapping;

@Controller
@RequestMapping("/packages")                    ◁━❶ Maps package requests        ❷ Extends the
public class PackageCrudController                                                  abstract CRUD
    extends AbstractCrudController<Package> {                          ◁━          controller

    @Inject private PackageService packageService;  ◁━❸ Injects package service

    public CIService<Package> getService() { return packageService; }   ◁┐
}
                                                        Exposes package service ❹
```

Because you did most of the hard work in the `AbstractCrudController`, there's little to do here. You annotate the controller with `@Controller` and a class-level `@RequestMapping` ❶. You also extend the base controller, passing in the `Package` type argument ❷. At ❸ you inject your `PackageService` so the controller can use it in a typesafe way

---

[16] See also Willie Wheeler, "Supporting XML and JSON web service endpoints in Spring 3.1 using @Response-Body," Feb. 22, 2012, http://mng.bz/Qte0.

[17] As noted earlier, the `produces` element appeared in Spring 3.1. If you're using an earlier version of Spring, then `produces` isn't available. An alternative is to have the JSON `details` method call the Jackson `ObjectMapper` directly, writing its output to the response stream. That way you don't have to depend on Spring applying the correct HTTP message converter.

(although here you don't have any custom creators or queries), and at ❹ you expose the `PackageService` through `getService()` so the base controller can use it.

The CRUD controllers for other CIs are essentially the same, so we don't have to review them all here. Instead, let's see what the Spring configuration looks like.

CONFIGURING SPRING

The following listing shows how you configure your web application context for your nascent RESTful web service.

Listing 11.23 beans-web.xml configuration for RESTful web service

```xml
<?xml version="1.0" encoding="UTF-8"?>
<beans xmlns="http://www.springframework.org/schema/beans"
    xmlns:context="http://www.springframework.org/schema/context"
    xmlns:mvc="http://www.springframework.org/schema/mvc"
    xmlns:p="http://www.springframework.org/schema/p"
    xmlns:xsi="http://www.w3.org/2001/XMLSchema-instance"
    xmlns:oxm="http://www.springframework.org/schema/oxm"
    xmlns:util="http://www.springframework.org/schema/util"          ❶ Using
    xsi:schemaLocation="                                                Spring 3.1
        http://www.springframework.org/schema/beans
        http://www.springframework.org/schema/beans/spring-beans-3.1.xsd
        http://www.springframework.org/schema/context
        http://www.springframework.org/schema/context/
                spring-context-3.1.xsd
        http://www.springframework.org/schema/mvc
        http://www.springframework.org/schema/mvc/spring-mvc-3.1.xsd
        http://www.springframework.org/schema/oxm
        http://www.springframework.org/schema/oxm/spring-oxm-3.1.xsd
        http://www.springframework.org/schema/util
        http://www.springframework.org/schema/util/spring-util-3.1.xsd">

    <mvc:default-servlet-handler />
                                                            ❷ JAXB mapper
    <oxm:jaxb2-marshaller id="marshaller">
        <oxm:class-to-be-bound name="com.springinpractice.ch11.model.Module"
    />
        <oxm:class-to-be-bound name="com.springinpractice.ch11.model.Package"
    />
    </oxm:jaxb2-marshaller>                                  ❸ JAXB support
                                                               for Jackson
    <bean id="jaxbAnnIntrospector"
        class="org.codehaus.jackson.xc.JaxbAnnotationIntrospector" />
    <bean id="jacksonObjectMapper"                                       ❹ Jackson
        class="org.codehaus.jackson.map.ObjectMapper">                      mapper
        <property name="serializationConfig.annotationIntrospector"
            ref="jaxbAnnIntrospector" />
        <property name="deserializationConfig.annotationIntrospector"
            ref="jaxbAnnIntrospector" />
                                                    Activates HTTP  ❺
    </bean>                                         message converters
                          ❻
Allows    <mvc:annotation-driven conversion-service="conversionService">
overriding      <mvc:message-converters>
                    <bean class="org.springframework.http.converter.json.
                                    Custom-configured converter  ❼
```

```
⇒                     MappingJacksonHttpMessageConverter"
               p:objectMapper-ref="jacksonObjectMapper" />
          </mvc:message-converters>
     </mvc:annotation-driven>

     <context:component-scan
          base-package="com.springinpractice.ch11.web.controller" />

     ... converter/formatter stuff that we don't care about here ...

     ... view stuff that we don't care about here ...

</beans>
```

Component-scans controllers ⑧

For this recipe, you configure the app for Spring 3.1 ❶ because you're using some features that appeared in Spring 3.1. The web service needs a couple of mappers: an object/XML mapper and an object/JSON mapper. Ultimately you use the mappers to convert your CIs into JSON and XML. You define the object/XML mapper at ❷. You're using the `oxm` namespace to define a JAXB2 marshaller, which happens to be an unmarshaller too. (That is, it's a full object/XML mapper.) You enumerate the CIs that you want to map using `<oxm:class-to-be-bound>`.[18]

You also need an object/JSON mapper, but as we noted earlier, you need it to understand JAXB annotations. That's not a problem if you use the Jackson mapper. First you create a `JaxbAnnotationIntrospector` ❸, and then you feed it to your Jackson mapper ❹ on both the serializing side and the deserializing side.

> **TIP** Notice the use of compound property names where you inject the introspector into the mapper. It's not a common technique, but Spring supports it, and in certain situations it's helpful. The current one is a case in point. Creating new `SerializationConfig` and `DeserializationConfig` objects is nontrivial, and we'd much rather inject the introspector into the existing `SerializationConfig` and `DeserializationConfig` objects. With compound property names, you can do that.

To activate your mappers, you need to define what are known as *HTTP message converters*. Each such converter has a mapper that it uses for mapping objects to some format or other. Spring applies HTTP message converters to methods annotated with `@Response-Body` (and to method parameters annotated with `@RequestBody`, as you'll see in the next recipe).

You can define these implicitly using the `<mvc:annotation-driven>` annotation ❺, which places default HTTP message converters on the application context, among them one for XML and another for JSON. The problem with using the default JSON converter, though, is that it doesn't know anything about the JAXB-enabled object mapper you just created. You use the `<mvc:message-converters>` tag ❻ (new as of

---

[18] Jarno Walgemoed wrote an outstanding extension to the standard JAXB2 marshaller, which is his `ClasspathScanningJaxb2Marshaller`. It scans a base package for classes annotated with `@XmlRootElement` so you don't have to enumerate them explicitly. See Willie Wheeler, "ClasspathScanningJaxb2Marshaller," Dec, 29, 2011, http://mng.bz/vfX2.

Spring 3.1) to specify any HTTP message converters that you'd like to have override the default. In your case, you create a `MappingJacksonHttpMessageConverter`, injecting the JAXB-enabled object mapper **❼**.

> ### Converters vs. HTTP message converters
> Eagle-eyed readers will notice that the `<mvc:annotation-driven>` definition makes reference to a conversion service, which deals with converters and formatters such as you saw in recipe 11.3. The converters associated with the conversion service are *not* the same thing as the HTTP message converters. Converters are general, performing arbitrary type conversions. HTTP message converters, on the other hand, convert HTTP requests to objects and objects to HTTP responses. (Formatters convert objects to and from strings.)

Finally, you component-scan your controller **❽** the same way you generally do.

At this point you have a simple but functional web service that returns package list and details information, supporting both JSON and XML formats.

Discussion

Creating RESTful web services in Spring is similar to creating ordinary HTML-based services in the sense that you do it with controllers, `@RequestMappings`, and so on. There are differences: you can directly generate the HTTP response using `@ResponseBody` and HTTP message converters instead of doing it indirectly through views (although the latter option is available too), and you need to handle object mapping, even if that's a matter of including `<mvc:annotation-driven>` and going with the defaults. But by and large, if you're comfortable with Spring Web MVC for HTML pages, it shouldn't be a stretch to wrap your head around RESTful web services with Spring.

The current recipe intentionally started with the simplest web service endpoints. In the following recipe, you'll elaborate your web service to support package creation, and you'll build a Maven plug-in that uses a Spring REST client to invoke the new endpoint.

11.4   *Updating the CMDB after successful builds*

PREREQUISITES
Recipe 11.1 Creating a simple configuration item
Recipe 11.2 Creating related configuration items
Recipe 11.3 Adding a RESTful web service

KEY TECHNOLOGIES
Spring Framework 3.1, Maven 3, Spring `RestTemplate`

Background

In some organizations, when the test team wants a new build for testing, they have to coordinate with developers and, potentially, release engineers to get one. The tester asks for a build, the developer makes one available a few hours later, and the release engineer pushes it into the test environment a couple of hours after that. By the time the build appears in test, several hours may have passed.

A much better approach is for the tester to be able to deploy good builds on demand. Lean methodology calls this a *pull system*. Such systems eliminate needless delay by allowing workers to pull work instead of waiting for somebody else to push it.

To implement a pull system for deployments, it's useful to set up a CI server (such as Bamboo, Hudson, or Jenkins) that makes good builds available for deployment. One critical piece of this is to push good builds to a package repository (for example, Nexus, Artifactory, or even a simple fileshare) where the deployment process can find them.

In CMDB-based systems, another important step is to create a record for the package in the CMDB. This is useful if you want to join other data to the package. You might want, for instance, to associate development issues with the package, to track which packages are deployed to which servers in which environments, to schedule future automated deployments, and so forth.

In this recipe, you'll look at how to create a package record in the CMDB.

Problem

Following a successful CI server build, create a package record in the CMDB.

Solution

Assume here that the CI process involves running a Maven-based build. After Maven successfully compiles and tests the code, you want it to create a corresponding package record in the CMDB if one doesn't already exist. To do this, you'll implement a custom Maven plug-in that makes a web service call to the CMDB. You need to do two things: create an endpoint on the CMDB and create the Maven plug-in.

CREATING A "CREATE PACKAGE" ENDPOINT ON THE CMDB

Your first task is to create an endpoint capable of receiving web service requests to create new packages. The following listing shows how to add this to your `PackageCrudController`.

Listing 11.24   PackageCrudController.java with endpoint for creating packages

```
package com.springinpractice.ch11.web.controller.pkg;

import javax.inject.Inject;
import javax.servlet.http.HttpServletResponse;
import com.springinpractice.ch11.exception.DuplicateCIException;
import com.springinpractice.ch11.model.Module;
import com.springinpractice.ch11.model.Package;
import com.springinpractice.ch11.service.CIService;
import com.springinpractice.ch11.service.ModuleService;
import com.springinpractice.ch11.service.PackageService;
import com.springinpractice.ch11.web.controller.AbstractCrudController;
import org.springframework.beans.factory.annotation.Value;
import org.springframework.stereotype.Controller;
import org.springframework.web.bind.annotation.RequestBody;
```

```java
import org.springframework.web.bind.annotation.RequestMapping;
import org.springframework.web.bind.annotation.RequestMethod;

@Controller
@RequestMapping("/packages")
public class PackageCrudController
    extends AbstractCrudController<Package> {

    @Inject private ModuleService moduleService;
    @Inject private PackageService packageService;

    @Value("#{config['app.baseUrl']}")           ❶ Injects
    private String appBaseUrl;                        base URL

    public CIService<Package> getService() { return packageService; }

    // consumes : Spring 3.1
    @RequestMapping(
        value = "",
        method = RequestMethod.POST,               ❷ Matches XML
        consumes = "application/xml")                 payloads        ❸ Payload in
    public void postPackage(                                             request
        @RequestBody Package pkgData, HttpServletResponse res) {         body

        Module moduleData = pkgData.getModule();
        String groupId = moduleData.getGroupId();         Finds module CI ❹
        String moduleId = moduleData.getModuleId();
        Module module =
            moduleService.findByGroupIdAndModuleId(groupId, moduleId);
        pkgData.setModule(module);
        try {                                              ❺ Creates
            packageService.createPackage(pkgData);            package CI
            res.setHeader("Location",
                appBaseUrl + "/packages/" + pkgData.getId());    ❼ Ignores
        } catch (DuplicateCIException e) {                          duplicates
            res.setStatus(HttpServletResponse.SC_OK);
        }
    }
}
```

Sets ❻
header
for REST

At ❶ you inject a base URL using @Value. You need the base URL to create a Location header in response to create requests.

The consumes element ❷ tells Spring that you want to match requests having the application/xml content type (Content-Type header). You pair this with the @RequestBody annotation ❸, which indicates that the request's body will be XML that you can map to a Package instance.

When creating the package, you need to associate the package with a module having an ID. You use the group ID and module ID to look up the fully hydrated module ❹, then replace the module data transfer object with the result.

One issue you need to deal with is duplicate packages. You can either silently ignore attempts to create a duplicate package or throw an exception. Here we've chosen to ignore such attempts because the Maven plug-in won't know whether the package has been created. You try to create the package ❺, and if the attempt succeeds, you set the HTTP Location header as per the HTTP spec ❻. Otherwise, you ignore the attempt, responding with the OK status ❼.

That's the web service piece. Next is a client that calls the Zkybase web service.

Listing 11.25 ZkybaseClient.java: client for the Zkybase web service

```java
package com.springinpractice.ch11.client;

import java.net.URI;
import java.util.List;
import com.springinpractice.ch11.model.Package;
import org.slf4j.Logger;
import org.slf4j.LoggerFactory;
import org.springframework.web.client.RestTemplate;

public class ZkybaseClient {
    private static final Logger log =
        LoggerFactory.getLogger(ZkybaseClient.class);          ❶ Calls RESTful
                                                                  web services
    private RestTemplate template;
    private String skybaseUrl;

    public ZkybaseClient(RestTemplate template, String skybaseUrl) {
        this.template = template;
        if (!skybaseUrl.endsWith("/")) { skybaseUrl += "/"; }
        this.skybaseUrl = skybaseUrl;
    }

    public RestTemplate getRestTemplate() { return template; }

    public String getZkybaseUrl() { return skybaseUrl; }
                                                              Posts package ❷
    public void createPackage(Package pkg) {
        URI location = template.postForLocation(getPackagesUrl(), pkg);
        log.info("Created package: {}", location);
    }

    public List<Package> getPackages() {
        return template
            .getForObject(                                        Gets
                getPackagesUrl() + "?format=xml",             ❸ package list
                Package.PackageListWrapper.class)
            .getList();
    }

    private String getPackagesUrl() { return skybaseUrl + "packages"; }
}
```

The client is effectively a wrapper around Spring's RestTemplate ❶, which applies the template pattern to the task of calling web services. Your client supports two operations. First, a createPackage() method issues an HTTP POST request against the template ❷ and logs the resulting resource location. Second, a getPackages() method makes an HTTP GET request for the packages ❸. In a more robust implementation, you would include pagination (for example, get 30 packages at a time, and provide for navigation to get the previous and next 30), because the number of packages can grow large very quickly. But this implementation should make the basic approach clear.

Having a client allows you to build the Maven plug-in that you want to build. That's what you'll do next.

WRITING A MAVEN PLUG-IN THAT CALLS THE "CREATE PACKAGE" ENDPOINT
The next listing is a Maven plug-in `package` goal that calls the web service endpoint you just created. You'll configure it to record the existence of the new package in the CMDB as part of the Maven build lifecycle's `deploy` phase.

Listing 11.26   PackageMojo.java: Maven plug-in

```
package com.springinpractice.ch11.maven;

import org.apache.maven.plugin.AbstractMojo;
import org.apache.maven.plugin.MojoExecutionException;
import org.apache.maven.plugin.MojoFailureException;
import com.springinpractice.ch11.client.ZkybaseClient;
import com.springinpractice.ch11.model.Module;
import com.springinpractice.ch11.model.Package;
import org.springframework.web.client.RestTemplate;

/**
 * @goal package
 */
public class PackageMojo extends AbstractMojo {

    /**
     * @parameter expression="${zkybaseUrl}"
     */
    private String zkybaseUrl;

    /**
     * @parameter expression="${package.module}"
     */
    private Module module;

    /**
     * @parameter expression="${package.version}"
     */
    private String version;

    public void execute()
        throws MojoExecutionException, MojoFailureException {

        ZkybaseClient client =                                       ①  Creates
            new ZkybaseClient(new RestTemplate(), zkybaseUrl);          client
        client.createPackage(new Package(module, version));
    }                                                           Creates package ②
}
```

We won't go into the details of writing Maven plug-ins here, because this isn't a book on Maven, but do check the Maven reference if you're interested in learning more. In the `execute()` method, you instantiate your client ① and use it to create a new package ② against the web service.

To configure the plug-in for use in your project (presumably a project that you run as part of a continuous-integration build), include the following in your project's pom.xml file:

```
<plugin>
    <groupId>com.springinpractice.ch11</groupId>
    <artifactId>zkybase-maven-plugin</artifactId>
    <version>${zkybase.version}</version>
    <configuration>
        <zkybaseUrl>${skybase.url}</zkybaseUrl>
        <module>
            <groupId>${project.groupId}</groupId>
            <moduleId>${project.artifactId}</moduleId>
        </module>
        <version>${project.version}</version>
    </configuration>
    <executions>
        <execution>
            <phase>deploy</phase>
            <goals>
                <goal>package</goal>
            </goals>
        </execution>
    </executions>
</plugin>
```

You'll of course need to provide appropriate values for ${zkybase.version} and ${zkybase.url}. This causes Maven to run the plug-in during the deploy phase of the Maven build lifecycle.

Discussion

From a tools perspective, this recipe showed how to build a Maven plug-in that calls the Zkybase web service and creates a package. The larger process significance, though, is that you now have a way to make package information available to interested processes. Obvious examples are testing, deployment, and release management. Although Maven can deploy packages to artifact repositories such as Nexus or Artifactory, it's useful to be able to deploy to a CMDB so you can more readily associate packages with application modules, deployment definitions, server farms, and so on.

In the remaining recipes, you'll follow the social trend in application development and integrate the Zkybase CMDB with GitHub, a social software development web site.

11.5   Sourcing public GitHub data

PREREQUISITES

None

KEY TECHNOLOGIES

Spring Framework 3.1, GitHub API, Spring REST support, Spring Social, Spring Social GitHub

Background

When designing a CMDB, it's not necessary that all the data be in a single physical data store. In fact, in larger organizations, it makes a lot of sense to assume that the data *won't* be in a single store. In a federated design, data lives in multiple stores, and you bring it together in a unified UI.

This recipe considers GitHub integration.[19] This is useful in cases where you have applications whose source code repos live at GitHub. You can present repo data (such as the GitHub URLs, commits, repo collaborator, repo watchers, and so on), user data (such as followers or whom a user is following), and more, alongside other app-related data, such as build, deployment, and operational data. It's even possible (although we won't pursue this here) to create automation on the basis of this data, such as automation that provisions a continuous-integration server based in part on GitHub data.

Problem

Expose GitHub repository information through the CMDB user interface.

Solution

To be concrete, we'll show how to display a repository's watchers in your CMDB interface. We'll focus on the data-integration piece; the code for the UI isn't anything special. Figure 11.4 shows what it will look like when you're done.

Getting the watcher data from GitHub requires a web service call to the GitHub API (http://developer.github.com/v3/). It's a REST-based API that uses JSON for data transfer.

You'll use Spring Social to make the call to GitHub. Spring Social provides a programmatic, Java-based interface for making calls against social websites like Facebook, Twitter, LinkedIn, and GitHub. SpringSource and other providers create bindings for individual social sites, which makes it easy for Spring-based applications to interact with the site in question. See www.springsource.org/spring-social for more information about Spring Social.

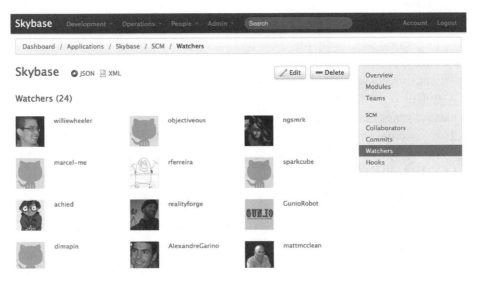

Figure 11.4 Displaying GitHub repo watchers from your UI

---

[19] It will help if you are familiar with Git and GitHub, although that may not be strictly required. GitHub is a socially oriented Git hosting website at https://github.com.

At the time of this writing, the Spring Social GitHub[20] binding is in its infancy and hasn't yet had a 1.0 release. We're going to use it here anyway to show how Spring Social works. (The more mature Facebook, LinkedIn, and Twitter bindings work in the same fashion.) We'll also look at the actual framework implementation, based on Spring's `RestTemplate`, just in case you decide you want to do the integration but you're not comfortable building your app on top of an unreleased piece of software. You'll see that it's easy to use the `RestTemplate` to accomplish your goals.

First you need to set up Maven.

SETTING UP MAVEN

By the time you read this, the situation may have changed, but at the moment Spring Social GitHub has only snapshots. To pull Spring snapshots, you need to add the Spring Maven Snapshot Repository to your POM:

```
<repository>
    <id>spring-snapshot</id>
    <name>Spring Maven Snapshot Repository</name>
    <url>http://maven.springframework.org/snapshot</url>
</repository>
```

With that repository defined, you can now declare your Spring Social and Spring Social GitHub dependencies:

```
<dependency>
    <groupId>org.springframework.social</groupId>
    <artifactId>spring-social-core</artifactId>
    <version>1.0.1.RELEASE</version>
</dependency>
<dependency>
    <groupId>org.springframework.social</groupId>
    <artifactId>spring-social-github</artifactId>
    <version>1.0.0.BUILD-SNAPSHOT</version>
</dependency>
```

The Spring Social GitHub dependency allows you to use the GitHub client. Let's build a controller that does just this.

CALLING SPRING SOCIAL GITHUB FROM A CONTROLLER

The following listing presents a controller that loads an app from the app repository, then uses the associated GitHub username and repo name to load the repo watchers from GitHub itself.

Listing 11.27   ApplicationScmController.java

```
package com.springinpractice.ch11.web.controller.application;

import java.util.List;
import javax.inject.Inject;
```

---

[20] The source repo is at https://github.com/SpringSource/spring-social-github. Willie contributed the watcher code under discussion to Spring Social GitHub.

```
import com.springinpractice.ch11.model.Application;
import com.springinpractice.ch11.repository.ApplicationRepository;
import org.springframework.social.github.api.GitHub;
import org.springframework.social.github.api.GitHubUser;
import org.springframework.stereotype.Controller;
import org.springframework.ui.Model;
import org.springframework.web.bind.annotation.PathVariable;
import org.springframework.web.bind.annotation.RequestMapping;
import org.springframework.web.bind.annotation.RequestMethod;

@Controller
@RequestMapping("/applications")
public class ApplicationScmController {                              ❶ Injects
    @Inject private ApplicationRepository applicationRepository;        app repo
    @Inject private GitHub gitHub;
                                                                    ❷ Injects GitHub client
    @RequestMapping(
        value = "/{id}/scm/watchers", method = RequestMethod.GET)
    public String getWatchers(@PathVariable Long id, Model model) {
        Application app = applicationRepository.findOne(id);        ❸ Gets
        String user = getScm().getUser();                             app
        String repo = getScm().getRepo();
        List<GitHubUser> watchers =
            gitHub.repoOperations().getWatchers(user, repo);       ❹ Gets
        model.addAttribute(app);                                      watchers
        model.addAttribute(watchers);
        return "applicationScmWatchers";
    }
}
```

You start with a couple of injections: the application repository ❶ from the previous recipe and the GitHub client ❷ from Spring Social GitHub. At ❸ you get the app from the repository, including the GitHub user and repo as we noted. Finally, you use the GitHub client to grab the watchers ❹.

Notice that the GitHub interface has a repoOperations() method. It also has user-Operations(), gistOperations(), and so forth. (See the GitHub API for more details.) The idea is to divide the client operations into groups so as to avoid having a monster GitHub interface.

You'll need a GitHub implementation.

CONFIGURING THE APP

This part is easy. All you need is the following:

```
<bean class="org.springframework.social.github.api.impl.
➡    GitHubTemplate" />
```

In Spring Social, the general pattern is to have interface names like Facebook, LinkedIn, Twitter, and GitHub, and to have implementation classes named FacebookTemplate, LinkedInTemplate, TwitterTemplate, and GitHubTemplate.

We noted that at the time of this writing, Spring Social GitHub hasn't yet been released. If you prefer not to use unreleased software, you can of course still call the GitHub API, but you'll need to use Spring's RestTemplate, as you'll see next.

GETTING GITHUB DATA USING SPRING'S RESTTEMPLATE

The Spring Social GitHub implementation, like most other Spring Social implementations, uses Spring's `RestTemplate` as a client for making RESTful web service calls. Here's the relevant code from Spring Social GitHub, edited to highlight the use of the `RestTemplate`.

Listing 11.28   RepoTemplate.java

```
package org.springframework.social.github.api.impl;

import static java.util.Arrays.asList;

import java.util.List;
import org.springframework.social.github.api.GitHubRepo;
import org.springframework.social.github.api.GitHubUser;
import org.springframework.social.github.api.RepoOperations;
import org.springframework.web.client.RestTemplate;

public class RepoTemplate implements RepoOperations {          ❶  RestTemplate
    private final RestTemplate restTemplate;          ◁───         REST client

    ... constructor (accepts RestTemplate) ...

    public List<GitHubUser> getWatchers(String user, String repo) {
        GitHubUser[] watchers = restTemplate.getForObject(          ◁──
            "https://api.github.com/repos/{user}/{repo}/watchers"),
            GitHubUser[].class,
            user,                                      Calls GitHub API  ❷
            repo);
        return asList(watchers);
    }

    ... other repo operations ...
}
```

The listing shows how to call the GitHub API using a `RestTemplate` ❶. As with other templates in the Spring Framework, it takes care of the boilerplate (for example, establishing and terminating the connection, performing the object mapping, and so on) so developers can focus on what's interesting.

Here, all you want to do is get the watchers for a given repository, which is specified by a username and a repo name. You call `getForObject()` ❷, which performs an HTTP GET against the provided URI (`RestTemplate` substitutes the actual username and repo name for the tokens) and returns an object of the specified type, which here is a `GitHubUser[]`. You convert the array to a `List` before returning it.

There are lots of other `RestTemplate` methods; see the Spring Javadoc for details.

Discussion

This recipe introduced the GitHub API as well as two different ways to call it: via Spring Social GitHub and using the Spring `RestTemplate` directly. We showed the latter approach because the Spring Social GitHub binding is currently (early 2012) in its infancy. Check on it from time to time, because it may have matured by the time you read this.

You used the `GitHubTemplate` to invoke public endpoints on the GitHub API. This is fine if all you need to do is call public endpoints. But if you want to use private endpoints, you need to introduce authorization. That's what recipe 11.6 shows how to do.

Keep in mind that even though Spring Social GitHub is in an early stage, other bindings under the Spring Social umbrella have production-ready releases. These include Facebook, LinkedIn, and Twitter. Craig Walls, the author of *Spring in Action* (Manning, 2011), is the Spring Social project lead.

11.6 *Sourcing private GitHub data*

PREREQUISITES
Recipe 11.5 Sourcing public GitHub data

KEY TECHNOLOGIES
Spring Framework 3.1, GitHub API, Spring REST support, Spring Social, Spring Social GitHub, Spring Security, OAuth 2, Spring JDBC

Background

In recipe 11.5, you learned how to call public endpoints on the GitHub API. But sometimes you want access to private endpoints. This might include sensitive read endpoints or perhaps endpoints that modify data. To accomplish this, you need to add authorization to the mix.

Problem

Allow individual end users to authorize Zkybase to perform sensitive GitHub operations on their behalf.

Solution

GitHub has a concept of service hooks, which are integration points between GitHub and other applications. You might create a hook, for instance, that posts a message to Twitter every time somebody commits code to a repository.

In this recipe we'll show how Zkybase retrieves hooks from a GitHub repository. Hooks are private information, so authorization is part of the story. We use OAuth 2 to support the need here. In the following subsection we'll take a high-level look at OAuth 2, and then we'll dive right into the code.

CONNECTING TO GITHUB VIA OAUTH 2
When we say we want to "connect to GitHub," what we mean is that we want any given user to be able to authorize Zkybase to perform potentially sensitive operations against the GitHub API on behalf of that user. In the case at hand, you want Zkybase to be able to read a GitHub repo's service hooks, which aren't normally public. That way you can display the hooks in the Zkybase UI, and maybe even use them for other purposes, such as provisioning continuous-integration servers with the hooks established. But there are other sensitive operations as well, such as editing repos, writing gists, and so on.

NOTE   The authorization holds only for the user in question. Zkybase doesn't have carte blanche to perform sensitive operations for arbitrary GitHub users. Also, the user can revoke the authorization at any time using the GitHub admin console.

A bit of a protocol is involved in establishing the desired authorization. It's sometimes known as the *OAuth 2 dance*. Figure 11.5 shows the overall process flow schematically.

The first thing is that you'll need to go to your GitHub account settings and register the Zkybase application. That allows Zkybase to get an access token as part of the OAuth process. This is a one-time action, but it's required.

Now for the dance itself. It will help to consider the flow in terms of screenshots. Figure 11.6 shows what the account page looks like at the beginning of the process, before you've connected Zkybase to GitHub.

After you click the Connect button, Spring Social redirects you to GitHub for authorization. If you aren't already authenticated into GitHub, you'll obviously need to log in first. But then you'll get a GitHub screen that looks like figure 11.7.

Here GitHub explains to the user exactly which capabilities it will grant to Zkybase, should the user allow the authorization. Assuming the user allows the authorization,

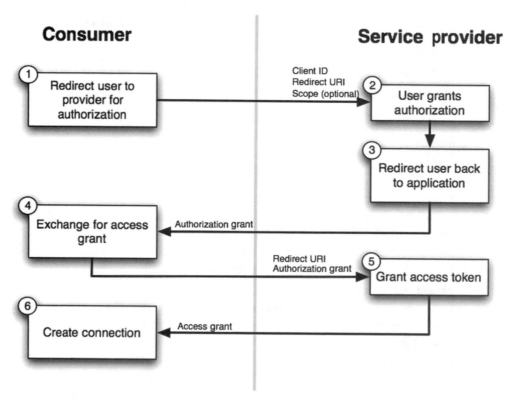

Figure 11.5   OAuth 2 flow, with Zkybase as the consumer and GitHub as the service provider

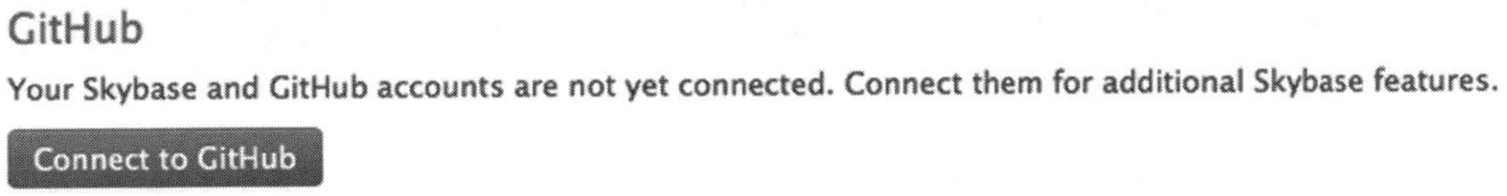

GitHub

Your Skybase and GitHub accounts are not yet connected. Connect them for additional Skybase features.

Connect to GitHub

Figure 11.6   The dance begins.

GitHub creates a record of that authorization in its own database. As noted, the user can revoke this at any time. GitHub then redirects the user back to the Zkybase app, passing the authorization along.

From here, Zkybase invokes GitHub again, exchanging the authorization for an access token. Conceptually, the token is the user's *connection*, and it's what allows Zkybase to make authorized calls against the GitHub API. Once Zkybase has the token, it stores it in its database. Among other things, this record associates the current Zkybase user with the access token that Zkybase uses to issue requests against the GitHub API. As long as the token remains valid (not revoked or expired), Zkybase can do what it needs to do for the user.

Figure 11.7   GitHub OAuth 2 authorization verification

The Zkybase user account page now has the GitHub information shown in figure 11.8.

Zkybase can use the access token to perform sensitive GitHub API operations on behalf of a user, such as getting repository hooks. See figure 11.9.

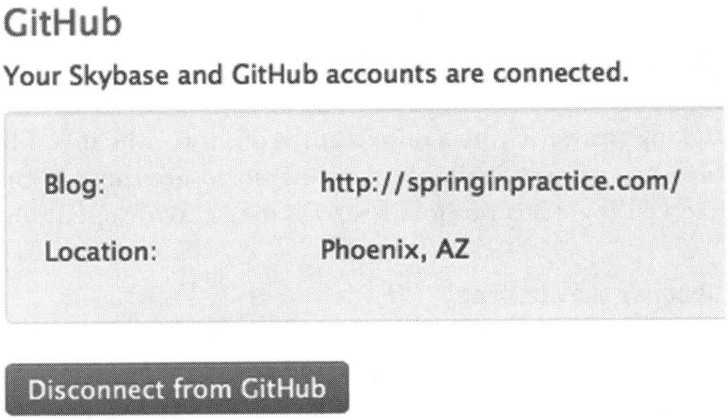

GitHub

Your Skybase and GitHub accounts are connected.

Blog:	http://springinpractice.com/
Location:	Phoenix, AZ

Disconnect from GitHub

Figure 11.8   The Zkybase user account page after establishing the current user's connection to GitHub

Figure 11.9   Zkybase displays the repository hooks it read from GitHub on behalf of the current Zkybase user.

Now that you've seen how the flow works, you're ready to look at some code.

CREATING A DATABASE TABLE FOR USER CONNECTIONS
As a preliminary, Zkybase needs a place to persist user connections once the user has established them. You use the default Spring Social DDL for this. The following listing shows the DDL for MySQL.

Listing 11.29   Creating the userconnection table

```
CREATE TABLE `userconnection` (
    `userId` varchar(255) NOT NULL,
    `providerId` varchar(255) NOT NULL,
    `providerUserId` varchar(255) NOT NULL DEFAULT '',
    `rank` int(11) NOT NULL,
    `displayName` varchar(255) DEFAULT NULL,
    `profileUrl` varchar(512) DEFAULT NULL,
    `imageUrl` varchar(512) DEFAULT NULL,
    `accessToken` varchar(255) NOT NULL,
    `secret` varchar(255) DEFAULT NULL,
    `refreshToken` varchar(255) DEFAULT NULL,
    `expireTime` bigint(20) DEFAULT NULL,
    PRIMARY KEY (`userId`,`providerId`,`providerUserId`),
    UNIQUE KEY `UserConnectionRank` (`userId`,`providerId`,`rank`)
) ENGINE=InnoDB;
```

This table is the backing store for your connection repository, which you'll see presently. First we'll show how to use Spring Social GitHub to get the currently authorized user. After that, you'll get a repository's service hooks. Both operations require authorization.

CREATING THE USER ACCOUNT SERVICE BEAN
Recall that the user account page displays either a Connect or a Disconnect button, depending on whether the user has established the connection between Zkybase and GitHub. The first thing you need then is a way to tell whether the connection exists.

Listing 11.30 UserAccountServiceImpl.java

```
package com.springinpractice.ch11.service.impl;

import javax.inject.Inject;
import com.springinpractice.ch11.model.UserAccount;
import com.springinpractice.ch11.repository.UserAccountRepository;
import com.springinpractice.ch11.service.UserAccountService;
import org.springframework.social.connect.Connection;
import org.springframework.social.connect.ConnectionRepository;
import org.springframework.social.github.api.GitHub;
import org.springframework.social.github.api.GitHubUserProfile;
import org.springframework.social.github.api.impl.GitHubTemplate;
import org.springframework.stereotype.Service;

@Service
public class UserAccountServiceImpl extends AbstractCIService
    implements UserAccountService {

    @Inject private ConnectionRepository connectionRepo;          ◄── ❶ Stores user
                                                                         connections

    public GitHubUserProfile getCurrentUserProfile() {            ◄┐   Gets current
        if (gitHub().isAuthorized()) {                            │    user if
            return gitHub().userOperations().getUserProfile();    ❷    authorized
        } else {
            return null;
        }
    }

    private GitHub gitHub() {                                     ◄── ❸ Gets API
        Connection conn =
            connectionRepo.findPrimaryConnection(GitHub.class);
        return (conn != null ? conn.getApi() : new GitHubTemplate());
    }

    ... various other fields and methods ...
}
```

Your first authorized service call grabs the current user's profile from GitHub. To do this, you need a connection repository ❶ and an authorized API client, which you acquire from the connection ❸. With these, getting the profile is a simple method call ❷ against the GitHub client.

Let's look at getting a repository's service hooks.

RETRIEVING REPOSITORY HOOKS

The next listing shows how to get hooks from a repository.

Listing 11.31 ApplicationServiceImpl.java

```
package com.springinpractice.ch11.service.impl;

import java.util.List;
import javax.inject.Inject;
import com.springinpractice.ch11.model.Application;
import com.springinpractice.ch11.service.ApplicationService;
import org.springframework.social.connect.Connection;
import org.springframework.social.connect.ConnectionRepository;
```

```
import org.springframework.social.github.api.GitHub;
import org.springframework.social.github.api.GitHubHook;
import org.springframework.social.github.api.impl.GitHubTemplate;
import org.springframework.stereotype.Service;

@Service
public class ApplicationServiceImpl extends AbstractCIService
    implements ApplicationService {

    @Inject private ConnectionRepository connectionRepo;

    public List findHooks(String user, String repo) {
        return gitHub().repoOperations().getHooks(user, repo);
    }

    private GitHub gitHub() {
        Connection conn =
            connectionRepo.findPrimaryConnection(GitHub.class);
        return (conn != null ? conn.getApi() : new GitHubTemplate());
    }

    ... various other fields and methods ...
}
```

As you can see, the process is essentially identical to that of getting the currently authenticated user.

Spring Social includes some web components, including a connection-management controller and a simple JSP tag library, to make it easier to build UIs for social apps. In the next section you'll see how this works.

DISPLAYING THE USER ACCOUNT PAGE

The following listing builds a user account details page.

Listing 11.32   userAccountDetails.jsp, for account details

```
<%@ taglib prefix="c" uri="http://java.sun.com/jsp/jstl/core" %>
<%@ taglib prefix="social"
    uri="http://www.springframework.org/spring-social/social/tags" %>

<c:url var="githubUrl" value="/connect/github" />                    ConnectController ❶
                                                                     endpoint
... various account details ...
                                                          ❷ When not connected ...
<social:notConnected provider="github">
    <p>Your Zkybase and GitHub accounts are not yet connected. Connect them
    for additional Zkybase features.</p>
    <form method="post" action="${githubUrl}">                  ❸ ... connect form
        <input type="hidden" name="scope" value="user, repo, gist" />
        <input type="submit" value="Connect to GitHub" />
    </form>
</social:notConnected>
                                                                   ❺ When
<social:connected provider="github">                               connected ...
    <p>Your Zkybase and GitHub accounts are connected.</p>
    <p>Blog: <c:out value="${gitHubUserProfile.blog}" /></p>
    <p>Location: <c:out value="${gitHubUserProfile.location}" /></p>

                                                  ... display profile info ❻
```

Specifies ❹ authorization scope

```
<form method="post" action="${githubUrl}">
        <input type="hidden" name="_method" value="delete" />
        <input type="submit" value="Disconnect from GitHub" />
    </form>
</social:connected>
```

⟵ **⑦ Disconnects form**

**Hidden field for
HTTP DELETE ⑧**

The Spring Social project provides a `ConnectController` that manages the flow of requests involved with the OAuth dance via a RESTful API. At ❶ you have the URL for interacting with the GitHub API service (Spring Social calls it a *provider*), which you'll use to connect to and disconnect from the service.

In generating the UI for the user account page, the user is either connected to GitHub or not. You use the Spring Social `<social:connected>` and `<social:notCon-nected>` JSP tags to control what we show in each case.

When the connection doesn't exist ❷, you present a button that allows the user to establish the connection ❸. The controller expects an HTTP `POST` here, so you use a form. GitHub also expects you to request a certain scope for authorization. The GitHub OAuth API describes the scopes in detail; here you want the user to grant Zky-base to perform arbitrary operations on GitHub users, repos, and gists on that user's behalf. You specify that scope to the `ConnectController` ❹, which in turn passes it along to GitHub.

In the case where the connection exists ❺, you want to show data from the user profile such as the user's blog URL ❻ and geographic location. You also want to display a button that allows the user to disconnect from GitHub. The controller expects an HTTP `DELETE`, so you use a form ❼ along with the hidden `_method=delete` parameter ❽ that tells the service that this is an HTTP `DELETE` rather than an HTTP `POST`.

There's one more piece to the puzzle, and that's the Spring configuration.

CONFIGURING SPRING

The last mile here is to make certain bits of the Spring Social infrastructure available to the application. You need a way for the app to acquire connections for any given user request, and this in turn involves having a connection repository (to store the user connections), as well as a way to establish new connections if they don't exist in the repository.

Listing 11.33   beans-social.xml: Spring Social configuration

```
<?xml version="1.0" encoding="UTF-8"?>
<beans xmlns="http://www.springframework.org/schema/beans"
    xmlns:aop="http://www.springframework.org/schema/aop"
    xmlns:c="http://www.springframework.org/schema/c"
    xmlns:context="http://www.springframework.org/schema/context"
    xmlns:jee="http://www.springframework.org/schema/jee"
    xmlns:p="http://www.springframework.org/schema/p"
    xmlns:xsi="http://www.w3.org/2001/XMLSchema-instance"
    xsi:schemaLocation="
        http://www.springframework.org/schema/aop
        http://www.springframework.org/schema/aop/spring-aop-3.1.xsd
        http://www.springframework.org/schema/beans
```

**❶ Constructor
injection
namespace**

```
            http://www.springframework.org/schema/beans/spring-beans-3.1.xsd
            http://www.springframework.org/schema/context
            http://www.springframework.org/schema/context/
                    spring-context-3.1.xsd
            http://www.springframework.org/schema/jee
            http://www.springframework.org/schema/jee/spring-jee-3.1.xsd">

    <context:property-placeholder
        location="classpath:/spring/environment.properties" />        JDBC data    ❷
    <context:annotation-config />                                       source

    <jee:jndi-lookup id="dataSource" jndi-name="jdbc/ZkybaseDS" />

    ... other config not directly relevant to social ...          ❸  Finds connection
                                                                      factories
    <bean id="connectionFactoryLocator"
        class="org.springframework.social.connect.support.
                ConnectionFactoryRegistry">
        <property name="connectionFactories">                      Connection factory  ❹
            <list>
                <bean class="org.springframework.social.github.connect.
                        GitHubConnectionFactory"
                    c:clientId="${gitHub.clientId}"
                    c:clientSecret="${gitHub.clientSecret}" />  ❺  Injects value
            </list>                                                  into constructor
        </property>
    </bean>
                                                                 ❻  User connection
    <bean id="usersConnectionRepository"                             repo
        class="org.springframework.social.connect.jdbc.
                JdbcUsersConnectionRepository"                   ❼  Injects reference
        c:dataSource-ref="dataSource"                               into constructor
        c:connectionFactoryLocator-ref="connectionFactoryLocator"
        c:textEncryptor-ref="textEncryptor" />

    <bean id="connectionRepository"                                 Request-scoped,
        factory-bean="usersConnectionRepository"              ❽    user-specific
        factory-method="createConnectionRepository"
        scope="request"
        c:userId="#{request.userPrincipal.name}">           ❾  SpEL injection

        <aop:scoped-proxy proxy-target-class="false" />         ❿  No-op
    </bean>                                                         encryptor

    <bean id="textEncryptor"
        class="org.springframework.security.crypto.encrypt.Encryptors"
        factory-method="noOpText" />
</beans>
```

There is a lot happening in this configuration. To begin, you declare the c namespace
❶, which is new with Spring 3.1. This namespace allows you to perform constructor
injection in the same way the p namespace allows you to perform property injection.
You'll see some examples.

At ❷ you define a JDBC data source, which you'll need for storing GitHub user
connections. You have a connection factory registry ❸, and you register a lone
GitHub connection factory ❹. If you needed connections for other Spring Social providers, such as Facebook, Twitter, or LinkedIn, you'd register them here as well.

Notice that you're using the c namespace to perform constructor injection into the GitHubConnectionFactory ❺. The names you use must match the parameter name; in this case they're clientId and clientSecret.

At ❻ is your user-connection repository. This grabs user-specific connections from the database, creating them if necessary. Again you're using constructor injection, this time with a reference ❼.

The connection repository ❽ is a little different than the user-connection repository. Here it's a request-scoped factory bean. The reason it's request-scoped is that different requests will have different Spring Security user principals, and you want to get the user connection for the user making the request. Once again you're using constructor injection at ❾, but this time the injection is into the createConnectionRepository() factory method. Note also that you can use the Spring Expression Language (SpEL) to perform the injection.

You have a no-op text encryptor ❿ to use for encrypting access tokens that Zkybase gets from GitHub. Spring Social applies this encryptor before storing the access tokens in the database. A no-op encryptor is fine for development but not for production. Recipe 11.7 shows how to handle the production scenario.

Figure 11.10 shows a bean-dependency diagram for the configuration. Recapping, you have a request-scoped connection repository that grabs user-specific connections from a user-connection repository, which in turn has references to a connection factory and a persistent connection store.

You also need to add a Spring Social ConnectController to the beans-web.xml configuration file. This is what handles the OAuth 2 web flow:

```
<bean class="org.springframework.social.connect.web.
        ConnectController" />
```

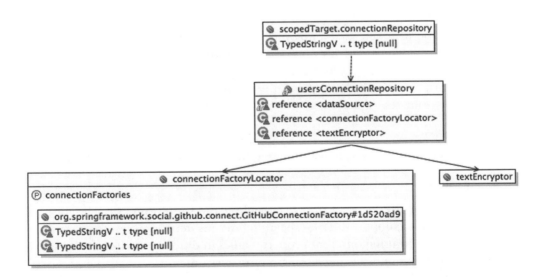

Figure 11.10   Spring Social GitHub bean dependency diagram

This reasonably modest configuration takes care of the OAuth 2 dance. Start the application, and try it.

Discussion

In this recipe and the previous one, we showed how to use Spring Social to make calls against GitHub's public and private API. In the first case, all you need to do is make a `GitHubTemplate` available to the app, and you can use it without having to configure it. For making private API calls, the process is considerably more involved because it requires OAuth 2, but Spring Social does a nice job of making this as simple as possible.

Spring Social GitHub is still a work in progress at the time of this writing (no 1.0 release yet), and the number of apps that want to interact with GitHub is probably relatively small compared to those that want to talk with Facebook, Twitter, or LinkedIn. Fortunately, the Spring Social projects for those providers are much more mature. You can easily apply what you've learned about Spring Social GitHub to the other Spring Socials, because they all use the same general approach.

The next recipe addresses a security issue with your work so far: you aren't protecting the access tokens in the database. In production, you definitely want to encrypt them.

11.7   Encrypting access tokens for production use

PREREQUISITES

Recipe 11.5 Sourcing public GitHub data
Recipe 11.6 Sourcing private GitHub data

KEY TECHNOLOGIES

Spring Framework 3.1, Spring Security

Background

In recipe 11.6, you used a no-op text encryptor for GitHub access tokens. That's fine for development, but it's no good for production-deployment scenarios where you don't want prying eyes to see user access tokens. An attacker with an access token can perform sensitive actions against the victim's GitHub account. In this recipe, we look at repairing that situation.

Problem

Encrypt access tokens for production, but leave them unencrypted for development.

Solution

You'll take advantage of the new profile feature in Spring 3.1. The idea behind this feature is to support different bean definitions depending on the environment. This goes beyond using different property values in different environments; here you want to use different beans depending on the environment.

Recall from recipe 11.6 that you used a no-op text encryptor:

```
<bean id="textEncryptor"
    class="org.springframework.security.crypto.encrypt.Encryptors"
    factory-method="noOpText" />
```

Here you'll continue using that for development, but you want to use the following for production instead:

```
<bean id="textEncryptor"
    class="org.springframework.security.crypto.encrypt.Encryptors"
    factory-method="text"
    c:password="${security.encryptPassword}"
    c:salt="${security.encryptSalt}" />
```

The following listing has the new Spring Social configuration.

Listing 11.34   Updated beans-social.xml with development and production profiles

```
<?xml version="1.0" encoding="UTF-8"?>
<beans xmlns="http://www.springframework.org/schema/beans"
    xmlns:aop="http://www.springframework.org/schema/aop"
    xmlns:c="http://www.springframework.org/schema/c"
    xmlns:p="http://www.springframework.org/schema/p"
    xmlns:xsi="http://www.w3.org/2001/XMLSchema-instance"
    xsi:schemaLocation="
        http://www.springframework.org/schema/aop
        http://www.springframework.org/schema/aop/spring-aop-3.1.xsd
        http://www.springframework.org/schema/beans
        http://www.springframework.org/schema/beans/spring-beans-3.1.xsd">

    <bean id="connectionFactoryLocator"
        class="org.springframework.social.connect.support.
                ConnectionFactoryRegistry">
        <property name="connectionFactories">
            <list>
                <bean class="org.springframework.social.github.connect.
                        GitHubConnectionFactory"
                    c:clientId="${gitHub.clientId}"
                    c:clientSecret="${gitHub.clientSecret}" />
            </list>
        </property>
    </bean>

    <bean id="usersConnectionRepository"
        class="org.springframework.social.connect.jdbc.
                JdbcUsersConnectionRepository"
        c:dataSource-ref="dataSource"
        c:connectionFactoryLocator-ref="connectionFactoryLocator"
        c:textEncryptor-ref="textEncryptor" />

    <bean id="connectionRepository"
        factory-bean="usersConnectionRepository"
        factory-method="createConnectionRepository"
        scope="request"
        c:userId="#{request.userPrincipal.name}">

        <aop:scoped-proxy proxy-target-class="false" />
    </bean>
```

```
<beans profile="dev">                                    ① Development profile
    <bean id="textEncryptor"
        class="org.springframework.security.crypto.encrypt.Encryptors"
        factory-method="noOpText" />
</beans>

<beans profile="prod">                                   ② Production profile
    <bean id="textEncryptor"
        class="org.springframework.security.crypto.encrypt.Encryptors"
        factory-method="text"
        c:password="${security.encryptPassword}"
        c:salt="${security.encryptSalt}" />
</beans>
</beans>
```

In listing 11.33, the text encryptor was defined alongside the other beans. In listing 11.34 that's not true: it's defined instead inside the development profile ①, which you indicate using a nested <beans profile="dev"> element. You define the production encryptor in the production profile ②. The values for security.encryptPassword and security.encryptSalt come from your environment.properties file. Note that the text encryptor expects the salt to be a valid hex-encoded value (for example, CAFED00D3141— but choose your own for actual production use).

You need a way to tell Spring which profile you want to use when you're running the app. There are different ways to do this, but in this case you want to pass the profile in as a command-line argument when starting up the server because you obviously don't want to bake it into the configuration. You can do that with a JVM system property as follows:

```
mvn -Dspring.profiles.active=prod -e clean jetty:run
```

Other alternatives are system environment variables (generally useful because most systems target a specific profile), web.xml servlet context parameters (not as useful because you don't want to hardcode the profile in the configuration), and JNDI entries. In each case the variable name remains spring.profiles.active. Note that you can specify multiple profiles with a comma-delimited list.

Discussion

This recipe showed how to secure access tokens by encrypting them. Doing so involves using different encryptor beans in the development and production profiles. There are other examples where this sort of thing happens. For instance, an app may use database-based authentication on the local machine but CAS-based authentication for dev, test, staging, and production.

Note that in a great many cases, the only things that change from environment to environment are property values, such as passwords or web service URLs. In such cases, there's no need to use profiles: just use different properties files for different environments.

11.8 Summary

This chapter concludes one of our favorite topics: configuration management. In it you learned how to create a CMDB with CIs backed by Neo4j. You also saw how to create a web service for your CMDB, as well as how to integrate tools like Maven with your CMDB via the web service. Finally, you learned how to make outbound calls to social apps like GitHub. These integrations are key to establishing an effective configuration management infrastructure.

The next chapter turns to the topic of content delivery in the form of an article-delivery engine. In it, we continue our exploration of NoSQL data stores, this time involving the Java Content Repository (JCR) and MongoDB/Spring Data MongoDB.

Building
an article-delivery engine

This chapter covers

- Building an article repository
- Enabling web upload and article display
- Using a MongoDB database

Among the tasks a content-management system (CMS) must support are the authoring, editing, and deploying of content by nontechnical users. Examples include articles (news, reviews, and so on), announcements, press releases, product descriptions, and course materials.

In this chapter, you'll create an article-delivery engine following three recipes.

- Recipe 12.1 builds an article repository using Jackrabbit, Java Content Repository (JCR), and Spring Modules JCR.
- Recipe 12.2 builds a web front end to upload and display the articles.
- Recipe 12.3 replaces the JCR repository with a MongoDB-based implementation using Spring Data MongoDB.

Figure 12.1 is the roadmap in graphical form. It shows how the various pieces fit together architecturally.

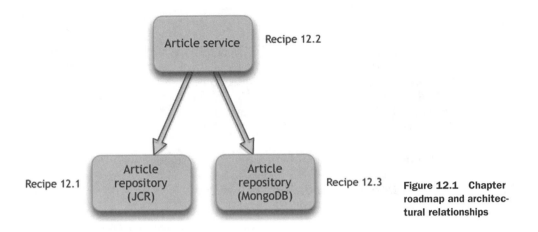

Recipe 12.2

Recipe 12.1

Recipe 12.3

Figure 12.1 Chapter roadmap and architectural relationships

Although it's not strictly required, to get the best value from this chapter you'll find it helpful to have experience with JCR, Jackrabbit, and MongoDB. If those are new areas for you, be prepared to do some self-study because we won't be covering them in detail. But we do provide sample code—be sure to make use of it, especially as regards the nontrivial Maven setup. The following resources are also available:

- For JCR and Jackrabbit, see the Jackrabbit website at http://jackrabbit.apache.org/.
- For MongoDB, see *MongoDB in Action* by Kyle Banker (Manning, 2011).

Before we continue, let's pause to discuss Spring Modules JCR.

A word about how we're using Spring Modules JCR

Spring Modules is a defunct project that includes several useful Spring-style libraries for integrating with various noncore APIs and codebases, including Ehcache, OS-Cache, Lucene, and JCR. Unfortunately, various promising attempts to revive Spring Modules, either in whole or in part, appear to have stalled.[1]

It's unclear whether Spring will ever directly support JCR,[2] but there's a lot of good Spring/JCR code in the Spring Modules project, and we wanted to take advantage of it instead of starting from scratch. Toward that end, we forked an existing Spring Modules JCR effort on GitHub to serve as a stable-ish basis for the book's code.[3] We've made some minor enhancements (mostly around cleaning up the POM and elaborating support for namespace-based configuration) to make Spring/JCR integration easier. But note that we don't plan to elaborate this fork beyond merging any useful pull requests that people might want to submit.

---

[1] See, for example, java.net/projects/springmodules and http://se-jcr.sourceforge.net/.

[2] Personally, we'd be excited to see a Spring Data JCR project emerge, but Spring Data seems to focus more on newer data technologies. There is a Spring Data JPA project, though, so you never know…

[3] See https://github.com/williewheeler/spring-modules-jcr. It's not a bad idea for you to search out other forks that may be further along and then create your own fork to ensure its availability for your project.

> *(continued)*
>
> To be perfectly clear, recipe 12.1 isn't about Spring Modules JCR. It's about Spring/JCR integration, and we use Spring Modules JCR because it's helpful and it's currently a sensible approach to take if you need to perform Spring/JCR integration. The reality is that integrating Spring and JCR requires extra effort because there isn't to date an established project for doing that.

You'll begin your explorations by setting up the article repository.

12.1 *Storing articles in a content repository*

PREREQUISITIES

None. Previous experience with JCR and Jackrabbit will be helpful.

KEY TECHNOLOGIES

JCR 2.0 (JSR 283), Jackrabbit 2.x, Spring Modules JCR

Background

Your first order of business is to establish a place to store your content, so let's start with that. In subsequent recipes, we'll build on this early foundation.

Problem

Build an article repository supporting article import and retrieval. Future plans[4] are to support more advanced capabilities such as article authoring, versioning, and workflows involving fine-grained access control.

Solution

Although it's often fine to use files or databases for content storage, sometimes you must support advanced content-related operations such as fine-grained access control, author-based versioning, content observation (for example, watches), advanced querying, and locking. A content repository builds on a persistent store by adding direct support for such operations.

You'll use a JSR 283 content repository to store and deliver the articles. JSR 283, better known as the JCR 2.0 specification,[5] defines a standard architecture and API for accessing content repositories. You'll use the open source Apache Jackrabbit 2.x JCR reference implementation at http://jackrabbit.apache.org/.

This isn't a book on JCR, so we'll limit our treatment of JCR to an overview. For more information, please see the Jackrabbit website or check out the JSR 283 home page at http://jcp.org/en/jsr/detail?id=283.

---

[4] We don't pursue them in this chapter. The future plans merely motivate the choice of JCR as opposed to a simpler approach.

[5] The specification for JCR 1.0 is JSR 170. See http://jcp.org/en/jsr/detail?id=170.

Do you need JCR just to import and retrieve articles?

No. If all you need is the ability to import and deliver articles, JCR is overkill. But we're assuming for the sake of discussion that you're treating the minimal delivery capability you establish in this chapter as a basis on which to build more advanced features. Given that assumption, it makes sense to build JCR in from the beginning because it's not especially difficult to do.

If you know you don't need anything advanced, you might consider using a traditional relational database back end or even a NoSQL document repository such as CouchDB or MongoDB. Either of those options is more straightforward than JCR. We don't pursue the relational approach here (the rest of the book equips you to pursue that yourself), but recipe 12.3 shows how to use a MongoDB document repo instead of JCR.

JCR BASICS

The JCR specification aims to provide a standard API for accessing content repositories. According to the JSR 283 home page:

> *A content repository is a high-level information management system that is a superset of traditional data repositories. A content repository implements "content services" such as: author-based versioning, full textual searching, fine-grained access control, content categorization and content-event monitoring. It's these "content services" that differentiate a content repository from a Data Repository.*

Architecturally, so-called *content applications* (such as a content authoring system, a CMS, and so on) involve the three layers shown figure 12.2.

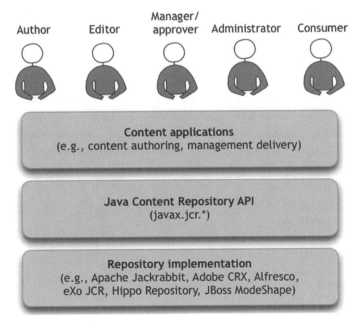

Figure 12.2 JCR application architecture. Content apps make calls against the standardized JCR API, and repository vendors provide compliant implementations.

The uppermost layer contains the content applications. These might be CMS apps that content developers use to create and manage content, or they might be content-delivery apps that content consumers use. This app layer interacts with the content repository[6] (for example, Jackrabbit) through the JCR API, which offers some key benefits:

- The API specifies capabilities that repository vendors either must or should provide.[7]
- It allows content apps to insulate themselves from implementation specifics by coding against a standard JCR API instead of a proprietary repository-specific API.

Apps can of course take advantage of vendor-specific features, but to the extent that apps limit such excursions, it will be easier to avoid vendor lock-in.

The content repository is organized as a tree of nodes. Each node can have any number of associated properties. You can represent individual articles and pages as nodes, for instance, and article and page metadata as properties.

That's a quick JCR overview, but it describes the basic idea. Let's take a fast look at the article repository, and after that you'll start on the code.

ARTICLE REPOSITORY OVERVIEW

At the highest level, you can distinguish article development (for example, authoring, version control, editing, and packaging) from article delivery. Our focus in this recipe is article delivery, specifically the ability to import an *article package* (assets plus metadata) into a runtime repository and deliver it to readers. Obviously there has to be a way to do the development too, but here you'll assume the author uses their favorite text editor, version-control system, and zip tool. In other words, development is outside the scope of this chapter.

See figure 12.3 for an overview of this simple article-management architecture.

That's the repository overview. Now it's time for specifics. As a first step you'll set up a Jackrabbit repository to serve as the foundation for the article-delivery engine.

SETTING UP THE JACKRABBIT CONTENT REPOSITORY

If you're knowledgeable about Jackrabbit, feel free to configure it as you wish. Otherwise, the chapter's code download has a sample repository.xml Jackrabbit configuration file. (It's in the sample_conf folder.) Create a fresh directory somewhere on your filesystem, and drop the repository.xml configuration file there. You shouldn't need to change anything in the configuration if you're trying to get something quick and dirty to work.

There isn't anything you need to start up. Eventually you'll point the app at the directory you just created. The app, on startup, will create an embedded Jackrabbit instance against your directory.

---

[6] Be sure to distinguish *content-management systems* from *content repositories*. A content repository is a back-end system that provides a content storage abstraction and also various services around that, such as read/write, querying, transactions, and versioning. A CMS provides a UI for working with a content repository.

[7] The JCR spec defines three levels of compliance, and providers target one of those levels.

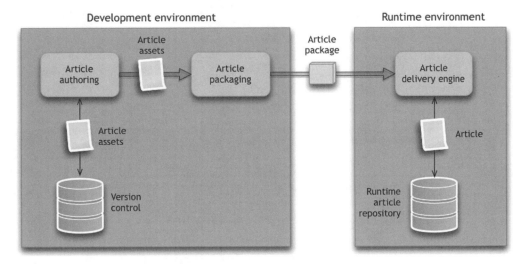

Figure 12.3 **An article CMS architecture with the bare essentials. The development environment has authoring, version control, and a packager. The runtime environment supports importing article packages (for example, article content, assets, and metadata) and delivering it to users. In this recipe, JCR is the runtime article repository.**

To model the articles, you'll need a couple of domain objects: articles and pages. That's the topic of our next discussion.

BUILDING THE DOMAIN OBJECTS

The articles include metadata and pages. The following listing shows an abbreviated version of the basic article domain object covering the key parts; please see the code download for the full class.

Listing 12.1   Article.java: simple domain object for articles

```java
package com.springinpractice.ch12.model;

import java.util.ArrayList;
import java.util.Date;
import java.util.List;

public class Article {
    private String id;
    private String title;
    private String author;
    private Date publishDate;
    private String description;
    private String keywords;
    private List<Page> pages = new ArrayList<Page>();

    public String getId() { return id; }

    public void setId(String id) { this.id = id; }

    public String getTitle() { return title; }
```

```
    public void setTitle(String title) { this.title = title; }
    ... other getters and setters ...
}
```

There shouldn't be anything too surprising about the article. You don't need any annotations for now. It's a pure POJO.

You'll need a page domain object as well. It's even simpler, as you can see.

Listing 12.2   Page.java: page domain object

```
package com.springinpractice.ch12.model;

public class Page {
    private String content;

    public String getContent() { return content; }

    public void setContent(String content) { this.content = content; }
}
```

It would probably be a nice addition to add a title to the page domain object, but this is good enough for your current purpose.

Next we want to look at the data access layer, which provides a domain-friendly API into the repository.

BUILDING THE DATA ACCESS LAYER

Even though you're using Jackrabbit instead of using the Hibernate back end from other chapters, you can continue to use the `Dao` abstraction. Figure 12.4 is a class diagram for the DAO interfaces and class.

The Hibernate DAOs had an `AbstractHbnDao` to factor out some of the code common to all Hibernate-backed DAOs. In the current case you haven't created the analogous `AbstractJcrDao` because you have only a single JCR DAO. But if you had more, it would make sense to do the same thing.

You'll want a couple of extra operations on the `ArticleDao`, as the next listing shows.

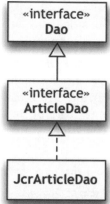

Figure 12.4   DAO class diagram

Listing 12.3   ArticleDao.java: data access object interface for articles

```
package com.springinpractice.ch12.dao;

import com.springinpractice.ch12.model.Article;
import com.springinpractice.dao.Dao;

public interface ArticleDao extends Dao<Article> {

    void createOrUpdate(Article article);

    Article getPage(String articleId, int pageNumber);
}
```

❶ Saves using a known ID

❷ Gets article with page hydrated

The articles have preset IDs (as opposed to being autogenerated following a save), so the createOrUpdate() method ❶ makes it convenient to save an article using a known article ID. The getPage() method ❷ supports displaying a single page (1-indexed). It returns an article with the page in question eagerly loaded so you can display it. The other pages have placeholder objects to ensure that the page count is correct.

Next, here's the JCR-based implementation of the ArticleDao.

Listing 12.4   JcrArticleDao.java: JCR-based DAO implementation

```
package com.springinpractice.ch12.dao.jcr;

import static org.springframework.util.Assert.notNull;

import java.io.IOException;
import java.io.Serializable;
import java.util.ArrayList;
import java.util.List;
import javax.inject.Inject;
import javax.jcr.Node;
import javax.jcr.NodeIterator;
import javax.jcr.PathNotFoundException;
import javax.jcr.RepositoryException;
import javax.jcr.Session;
import org.springframework.dao.DataIntegrityViolationException;
import org.springframework.dao.DataRetrievalFailureException;
import org.springframework.stereotype.Repository;
import org.springframework.transaction.annotation.Transactional;
import org.springmodules.jcr.JcrCallback;
import org.springmodules.jcr.SessionFactory;
import org.springmodules.jcr.support.JcrDaoSupport;
import com.springinpractice.ch12.dao.ArticleDao;
import com.springinpractice.ch12.model.Article;
import com.springinpractice.ch12.model.Page;

@Repository                                          ◄─── Class definition ❶
@Transactional(readOnly = true)
public class JcrArticleDao extends JcrDaoSupport implements ArticleDao {  ◄─┘
    @Inject private ArticleMapper articleMapper;     ◄─── Maps between
                                                     ❷ articles and nodes
    @Inject
    public void setSessionFactory(SessionFactory sessionFactory) {  ◄─┐
        super.setSessionFactory(sessionFactory);
    }                                               Creates JCR sessions ❸

    @Transactional(readOnly = false)
    public void create(final Article article) {      ◄───❹ Write method
        notNull(article);
        getTemplate().execute(new JcrCallback() {     ◄─── Uses
            public Object doInJcr(Session session)    ❺ JcrTemplate
                    throws IOException, RepositoryException {
                if (exists(article.getId())) {
                    throw new DataIntegrityViolationException(
                        "Article already exists");   ◄─── Throws
                }                                    ❻ DataAccessException
                articleMapper.addArticleNode(
```

```
                article, getArticlesNode(session));
            session.save();
            return null;
        }
    }, true);
}

... various other DAO methods ...

private String getArticlesNodeName() { return "articles"; }

private String getArticlesPath() { return "/" + getArticlesNodeName(); }

private String getArticlePath(String articleId) {
    return getArticlesPath() + "/" + articleId;
}

private Node getArticlesNode(Session session)
    throws RepositoryException {
    try {
        return session.getNode(getArticlesPath());
    } catch (PathNotFoundException e) {
        return session.getRootNode().addNode(getArticlesNodeName());
    }
}
}
```

The `JcrArticleDao` class illustrates ways in which you can use Spring to augment JCR. The first part is the high-level class definition **1**. You implement the `ArticleDao` interface from listing 12.3 and also extend `JcrDaoSupport`, which is part of Spring Modules JCR. `JcrDaoSupport` gives you access to JCR `Sessions`, a `JcrTemplate`, and a `convertJcrAccessException(RepositoryException)` method that converts JCR `RepositoryExceptions` to exceptions in the Spring `DataAccessException` hierarchy. You also declare the `@Repository` annotation to support component scanning and the `@Transactional` annotation to support transactions.

Transactions on the DAO?

It might surprise you that you're annotating a DAO with `@Transactional`. After all, you usually define transactions on service beans because any given service method might make multiple DAO calls that need to happen in the scope of a single atomic transaction.

But in this chapter, you don't have service beans—you'll wire the `ArticleDao` right into the controller. The reason is that the service methods would pass through to `ArticleDao`, and in that sort of situation there's no benefit to going through the ceremony of defining an explicit service layer. If you were to extend this simple app to something with real service methods (as opposed to data access methods), you'd build a transactional service layer.

At **2** you inject an `ArticleMapper`, which is a custom class that converts back and forth between articles and JCR nodes. You'll see that in listing 12.5.

You override `JcrDaoSupport.setSessionFactory()` at ❸. You do this to make the property injectable through the component-scanning mechanism, because `JcrDao-Support` doesn't support that.

The `create()` method ❹ is one of the CRUD methods. We've suppressed the others because we're more interested in covering Spring than in covering the details of using JCR, but the code download has the other methods. You annotate it with `@Transactional(readOnly = false)` to override the class-level `@Transactional(readOnly = true)` annotation. See the code download for the rest of the methods.

You implement the DAO methods using the template method pattern common throughout Spring (`JpaTemplate`, `HibernateTemplate`, `JdbcTemplate`, `RestTemplate`, and so on). In this case, you're using the Spring Modules JCR `JcrTemplate` (via `JcrDaoSupport.getTemplate()`) and its corresponding `JcrCallback` interface ❺. This template is helpful because it automatically handles concerns such as opening and closing JCR sessions, managing the relationship between sessions and transactions, and translating `RepositoryExceptions` and `IOExceptions` into the Spring `DataAccessException` hierarchy.

Finally, to maintain consistency with `JcrDaoSupport`'s exception-translation mechanism, you throw a `DataIntegrityViolationException` ❻ (part of the aforementioned `DataAccessException` hierarchy) in the event of a duplicate article.

In our discussion of the `JcrArticleDao`, we mentioned an `ArticleMapper` component to convert between articles and JCR nodes. The following listing presents the `ArticleMapper`.

Listing 12.5 ArticleMapper.java: converts between articles and JCR nodes

```
package com.springinpractice.ch12.dao.jcr;

import java.util.Calendar;
import java.util.Date;
import javax.jcr.Node;
import javax.jcr.RepositoryException;
import org.springframework.stereotype.Component;
import com.springinpractice.ch12.model.Article;
import com.springinpractice.ch12.model.Page;

@Component                                             Maps Node  ❶
public class ArticleMapper {                           to Article

    public Article toArticle(Node node) throws RepositoryException {
        Article article = new Article();
        article.setId(node.getName());
        article.setTitle(node.getProperty("title").getString());
        article.setAuthor(node.getProperty("author").getString());

        if (node.hasProperty("publishDate")) {
            article.setPublishDate(
                node.getProperty("publishDate").getDate().getTime());
        }

        if (node.hasProperty("description")) {
```

```
        article.setDescription(
            node.getProperty("description").getString());
    }

    if (node.hasProperty("keywords")) {
        article.setKeywords(node.getProperty("keywords").getString());
    }

    return article;
}

public Node addArticleNode(Article article, Node parent)
        throws RepositoryException {

    Node node = parent.addNode(article.getId());
    node.setProperty("title", article.getTitle());
    node.setProperty("author", article.getAuthor());

    Date publishDate = article.getPublishDate();
    if (publishDate != null) {
        Calendar cal = Calendar.getInstance();
        cal.setTime(publishDate);
        node.setProperty("publishDate", cal);
    }

    String description = article.getDescription();
    if (description != null) {
        node.setProperty("description", description);
    }

    String keywords = article.getKeywords();
    if (keywords != null) {
        node.setProperty("keywords", keywords);
    }

    Node pagesNode = node.addNode("pages", "nt:folder");
    int numPages = article.getPages().size();
    for (int i = 0; i < numPages; i++) {
        Page page = article.getPages().get(i);
        addPageNode(pagesNode, page, i + 1);
    }

    return node;
}

private void addPageNode(Node pagesNode, Page page, int pageNumber)
        throws RepositoryException {

    Node pageNode = pagesNode.addNode(
        String.valueOf(pageNumber), "nt:file");
    Node contentNode = pageNode.addNode(
        Node.JCR_CONTENT, "nt:resource");
    contentNode.setProperty("jcr:data", page.getContent());
    }
}
```

❷ Maps Article to Node

Maps Page ❸ to Node

The listing is more concerned with mapping code than with Spring techniques, but we're including it to give you a sense for what coding against JCR looks like in case you're unfamiliar with it. You use toArticle() ❶ to map a JCR node to an article.

Then you have `addArticleNode()` ❷ and `addPageNode()` ❸ to convert `Articles` and `Pages` to `Nodes`, respectively.

The next listing brings everything together with the Spring configuration.

Listing 12.6 beans-jcr.xml: Spring beans configuration for the JCR repository

```xml
<?xml version="1.0" encoding="UTF-8"?>
<beans xmlns="http://www.springframework.org/schema/beans"          JCR namespace ❶
    xmlns:context="http://www.springframework.org/schema/context"
    xmlns:jcr="http://springmodules.dev.java.net/schema/jcr"
    xmlns:jackrabbit=
        "http://springmodules.dev.java.net/schema/jcr/jackrabbit"
    xmlns:p="http://www.springframework.org/schema/p"
    xmlns:tx="http://www.springframework.org/schema/tx"              Jackrabbit
    xmlns:xsi="http://www.w3.org/2001/XMLSchema-instance"            namespace ❷
    xsi:schemaLocation="
        http://www.springframework.org/schema/beans
        http://www.springframework.org/schema/beans/spring-beans-3.0.xsd
        http://www.springframework.org/schema/context
        http://www.springframework.org/schema/context/spring-context-3.0.xsd
        http://www.springframework.org/schema/tx
        http://www.springframework.org/schema/tx/spring-tx-3.0.xsd
        http://springmodules.dev.java.net/schema/jcr
        http://springmodules.dev.java.net/schema/jcr/springmodules-jcr.xsd
http://springmodules.dev.java.net/schema/jcr/jackrabbit
http://springmodules.dev.java.net/schema/jcr/springmodules-jackrabbit.xsd">

    <context:property-placeholder                                   Repository
        location="classpath:/spring/environment.properties" />      configuration
                                                                     properties ❸
    <jackrabbit:repository id="repository"
        homeDir="${repository.dir}"
        configuration="${repository.conf}" />       ❹ Creates Jackrabbit repository

    <bean id="credentials" class="javax.jcr.SimpleCredentials">     Repository
        <constructor-arg value="dummy" />                           credentials ❺
        <constructor-arg value="dummy" />
    </bean>
                                                          JCR session factory ❻
    <jcr:sessionFactory id="sessionFactory"
        repository="repository" credentials="credentials" />

    <context:component-scan                                  ❼ Scans for
        base-package="com.springinpractice.ch12.dao.jcr" />     DAOs

    <jackrabbit:transaction-manager sessionFactory="sessionFactory" />

    <tx:annotation-driven />          Activates               Jackrabbit
</beans>                           ❾  transactions            transaction
                                                              manager ❽
```

As always, you begin by declaring the relevant namespaces and schema locations. In this case you need to declare (among others) the Spring Modules `jcr` ❶ and `jackrabbit` ❷ namespaces so you can use the custom namespace configuration they provide.

You need to pull in a couple of externalized properties so you can configure a Jack-rabbit repository without resorting to hardcoding. You do that at ❸. The environment.properties file has only two properties:

```
repository.conf=file:/path/to/repository.xml
repository.dir=file:/path/to/repository
```

(Of course, you'll need to adjust the values according to your own environment.) Note that the property values here are Spring resources, and they don't necessarily have to be file resources. You can, for instance, create classpath resources, network resources, and so forth.

Now you can create the Jackrabbit repository. You use the `<jackrabbit:repository>` element to do that ❹, along with the `repository.conf` and `repository.dir` properties you grabbed from `environment.properties`. Behind the scenes, this reads the Jackrabbit repository.xml configuration file we mentioned earlier and then builds a repository at whatever home directory you specify.

The DAOs need a way to get JCR sessions, and for that you need a Spring Modules `SessionFactory`. The `SessionFactory` gets sessions from the repository using credentials. You define the credentials at ❺. For the repository.xml configuration it's fine to use dummy credentials, so that's what you do. If you want to use real credentials, update repository.xml and beans-jcr.xml appropriately. Pass the repository and credentials into the `SessionFactory` ❻, and then component-scan `ArticleDao` ❼, which automatically injects the `SessionFactory`.

For transactions, you define a Jackrabbit `LocalTransactionManager` (courtesy of Spring Modules) ❽ and use `<tx:annotation-driven/>` ❾ to activate declarative transaction management.

Figure 12.5 shows the bean-dependency diagram for the configuration we just reviewed. You now have a JCR-backed DAO for the article-delivery engine.

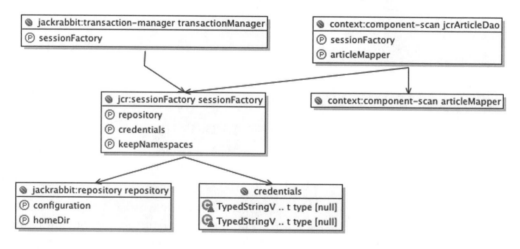

Figure 12.5   Bean-dependency diagram for the JCR-based article repository

Discussion

This recipe showed how to use Spring Modules JCR to integrate Spring and Jackrabbit, the JCR reference implementation. You followed this book's usual practice of defining a DAO interface and then implementing the DAO using a specific persistence technology.

The DAO is, of course, only the first piece of what you need to build. It doesn't do anything yet. In the next recipe, you'll create a simple, web-based article-delivery engine that uses the DAO you just created.

12.2   Creating a web-based article-delivery engine

PREREQUISITES

Recipe 12.1 Storing articles in a content repository

KEY TECHNOLOGIES

Spring Web MVC, file upload, REST

Background

In the previous recipe you created a repository for storing articles. To make the repository useful, however, you need a front end to present the articles to users. That's what this recipe covers.

Problem

Create an article-delivery engine supporting article importing, a master list view, and a details view.

Solution

Of the three required features, the master list and the details views are both straightforward. They aren't much more than calls straight to the DAO. The importer is a little more involved, though. Let's start by looking at the controller so you can get the master list and details views out of the way. After that, we'll go over the article importer.

BUILDING THE CONTROLLER

The following listing shows the `ArticleController` class.

> **Listing 12.7   ArticleController.java: web controller for articles**

```
package com.springinpractice.ch12.web;

import java.io.IOException;
import javax.inject.Inject;
import org.springframework.stereotype.Controller;
import org.springframework.ui.Model;
import org.springframework.web.bind.annotation.PathVariable;
import org.springframework.web.bind.annotation.RequestMapping;
import org.springframework.web.bind.annotation.RequestMethod;
import org.springframework.web.bind.annotation.RequestParam;
import org.springframework.web.multipart.MultipartFile;
import com.springinpractice.ch12.dao.ArticleDao;
```

```
import com.springinpractice.ch12.model.Article;
import com.springinpractice.ch12.model.Page;

@Controller
@RequestMapping("/articles")
public class ArticleController {
    @Inject private ArticleConverter articleConverter;
    @Inject private ArticleDao articleDao;

    @RequestMapping(value = "", method = RequestMethod.POST)
    public String createArticle(
        @RequestParam("file") MultipartFile file) {
        if (file.isEmpty()) {
            return "redirect:/articles.html?upload=fail"; }
        Article article = articleConverter.convert(file);
        articleDao.createOrUpdate(article);
        return "redirect:/articles.html?upload=ok";
    }

    @RequestMapping(value = "", method = RequestMethod.GET)
    public String getArticleList(Model model) {
        model.addAttribute(articleDao.getAll());
        return getFullViewName("articleList");
    }

    @RequestMapping(value = "/{id}/{page}", method = RequestMethod.GET)
    public String getArticlePage(
            @PathVariable String id,
            @PathVariable("page") Integer pageNumber,
            Model model) {

        Article article = articleDao.getPage(id, pageNumber);
        Page page = article.getPages().get(pageNumber - 1);
        model.addAttribute(article);
        model.addAttribute("articlePage", page);
        model.addAttribute("pageNumber", pageNumber);
        return getFullViewName("articlePage");
    }

    private String getFullViewName(String viewName) {
        return "article/" + viewName;
    }
}
```

① Inject converter

② Injects DAO

③ Imports using MultipartFile

④ Generates master list

⑤ Generates details view

In the controller, you inject an `ArticleConverter` **①** for article importing (we'll get to that in a moment) and also the `ArticleDao` **②** you created in the previous recipe. Then you have simple handler methods for each of the required functions: `createArticle()` for importing articles **③**, `getArticleList()` for viewing the master list **④**, and `get-ArticlePage()` for viewing an article page **⑤**. That's the entire controller.

Next we'll look at the JSPs for viewing the article master list and the article details.

BUILDING THE MASTER LIST AND DETAILS VIEW JSPS

The article master list shows the articles in a simple list, with the title, author, publication date, and description. The titles are links to the first page of the individual articles. See figure 12.6.

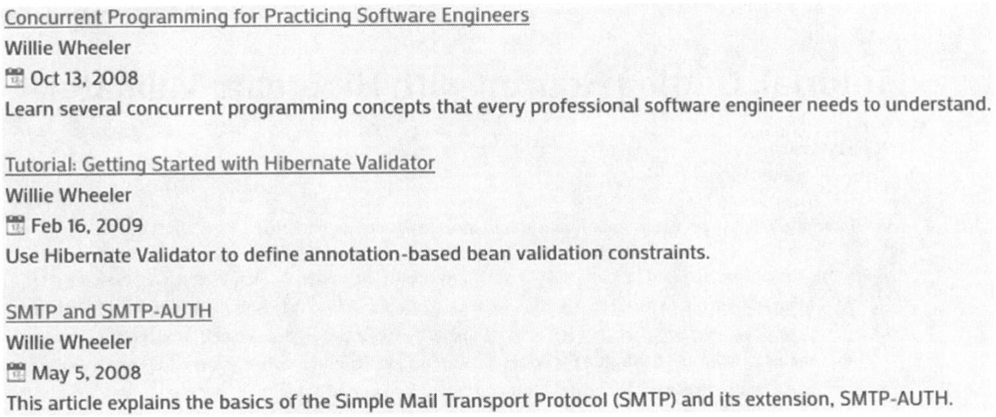

Concurrent Programming for Practicing Software Engineers

Willie Wheeler

📅 Oct 13, 2008

Learn several concurrent programming concepts that every professional software engineer needs to understand.

Tutorial: Getting Started with Hibernate Validator

Willie Wheeler

📅 Feb 16, 2009

Use Hibernate Validator to define annotation-based bean validation constraints.

SMTP and SMTP-AUTH

Willie Wheeler

📅 May 5, 2008

This article explains the basics of the Simple Mail Transport Protocol (SMTP) and its extension, SMTP-AUTH.

Figure 12.6   A screenshot of the article master list

The code for the article master list is in the next listing. We've simplified the HTML (by removing CSS stuff) to keep the listing short, but the full JSP is available in the code download.

Listing 12.8   articleList.jsp: displays the master list of articles

```
<?xml version="1.0" encoding="UTF-8"?>
<!DOCTYPE html PUBLIC "-//W3C//DTD XHTML 1.0 Strict//EN"
    "http://www.w3.org/TR/xhtml1/DTD/xhtml1-strict.dtd">

<%@ taglib prefix="c" uri="http://java.sun.com/jsp/jstl/core" %>
<%@ taglib prefix="fmt" uri="http://java.sun.com/jsp/jstl/fmt" %>

<html xmlns="http://www.w3.org/1999/xhtml">
<head><title>Articles</title></head>
<body>
<h1>Articles</h1>
<c:choose>
    <c:when test="${empty articleList}"><p>None</p></c:when>
    <c:otherwise>
        <c:forEach var="article" items="${articleList}">
            <c:url var="articleUrl"
                value="/articles/${article.id}/1.html" />
            <div><a href="${articleUrl}">
                <c:out value="${article.title}" /></a></div>
            <div><c:out value="${article.author}" /></div>
            <div><fmt:formatDate value="${article.publishDate}" /></div>
            <div><c:out value="${article.description}" /></div>
        </c:forEach>
    </c:otherwise>
</c:choose>
</body>
</html>
```

The article details page is somewhat more involved but still not too complicated. You need navigation, and the first page of the article should show the title, author, publication date, and description, as shown in figure 12.7.

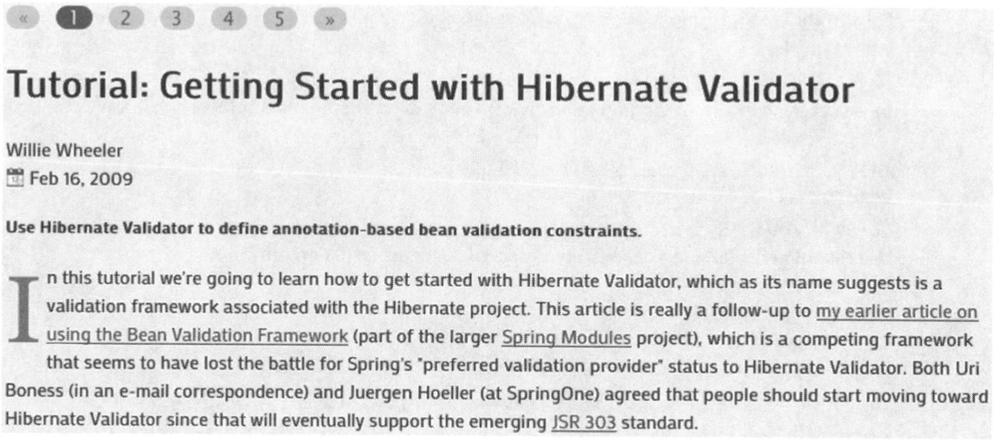

Tutorial: Getting Started with Hibernate Validator

Willie Wheeler
📅 Feb 16, 2009

Use Hibernate Validator to define annotation-based bean validation constraints.

I n this tutorial we're going to learn how to get started with Hibernate Validator, which as its name suggests is a validation framework associated with the Hibernate project. This article is really a follow-up to my earlier article on using the Bean Validation Framework (part of the larger Spring Modules project), which is a competing framework that seems to have lost the battle for Spring's "preferred validation provider" status to Hibernate Validator. Both Uri Boness (in an e-mail correspondence) and Juergen Hoeller (at SpringOne) agreed that people should start moving toward Hibernate Validator since that will eventually support the emerging JSR 303 standard.

Figure 12.7   The article details view must show page navigation, and the first page shows the title, author, publication date, and description.

The following listing shows the details view JSP. Again, we've taken some liberties with the actual code listing to highlight what's essential. See the code download for the full version.

Listing 12.9   articlePage.jsp: displays a single article page with page navigation

```
<?xml version="1.0" encoding="UTF-8"?>
<!DOCTYPE html PUBLIC "-//W3C//DTD XHTML 1.0 Strict//EN"
    "http://www.w3.org/TR/xhtml1/DTD/xhtml1-strict.dtd">

<%@ taglib prefix="c" uri="http://java.sun.com/jsp/jstl/core" %>
<%@ taglib prefix="fmt" uri="http://java.sun.com/jsp/jstl/fmt" %>

<html xmlns="http://www.w3.org/1999/xhtml">
<head>
<title>
    <c:out value="${article.title}" />
 - Page <c:out value="${pageNumber}" />
</title>
</head>
<body>
<div><jsp:include page="pageNav.jsp" /></div>
<c:choose>
    <c:when test="${pageNumber == 1}">
        <h1><c:out value="${article.title}" /></h1>
        <div><c:out value="${article.author}" /></div>
        <div><fmt:formatDate value="${article.publishDate}" /></div>
        <div><c:out value="${article.description}" /></div>
    </c:when>
    <c:otherwise>
        <h4><c:out value="${article.title}" /></h4>
    </c:otherwise>
</c:choose>
<c:out value="${articlePage.content}" escapeXml="false" />
```

```
<div><jsp:include page="pageNav.jsp" /></div>
</body>
</html>
```

As you can see, the page navigation appears at the top and bottom of the page. Next is the JSP `include` that generates the page navigation.

Listing 12.10   pageNav.jsp: page navigation

```
<%@ taglib prefix="c" uri="http://java.sun.com/jsp/jstl/core" %>
<%@ taglib prefix="fn" uri="http://java.sun.com/jsp/jstl/functions" %>

<c:if test="${fn:length(article.pages) > 1}">
    <div class="pageNavigation">
        <ul>
            <c:choose>
                <c:when test="${pageNumber == 1}">
                    <li><a class="disabled">&laquo;</a></li>
                </c:when>
                <c:otherwise>
                    <li><a href="${pageNumber - 1}.html">&laquo;</a></li>
                </c:otherwise>
            </c:choose>
            <c:forEach var="page"
                items="${article.pages}" varStatus="status">
                <c:set var="curr" value="${status.index + 1}" />
                <c:choose>
                    <c:when test="${curr == pageNumber}">
                        <li><a href="${curr}.html"
                            class="currentPage">${curr}</a></li>
                    </c:when>
                    <c:otherwise>
                        <li><a href="${curr}.html">${curr}</a></li>
                    </c:otherwise>
                </c:choose>
            </c:forEach>
            <c:choose>
                <c:when test="${pageNumber < fn:length(article.pages)}">
                    <li><a href="${pageNumber + 1}.html">&raquo;</a></li>
                </c:when>
                <c:otherwise>
                    <a class="disabled">&raquo;</a>
                </c:otherwise>
            </c:choose>
        </ul>
    </div>
</c:if>
```

With that, we've covered the article master list and details views. We still need to examine the topic of importing articles, so we'll do that next.

IMPORTING ARTICLES

Recall from figure 12.3 that the article-import functionality assumes you're importing an article package. In this case, an article package is a zip file whose contents are the following:

- A file article.xml that contains article metadata (ID, title, author, and so forth)
- Individual HTML files 1.html, 2.html, …, *n*.html, corresponding to the article's *n* pages

The sample code includes three sample article packages; unzip them to see their contents. For your convenience, here's an example of an article.xml file.

Listing 12.11   Example of an article.xml file for the article package

```xml
<?xml version="1.0" encoding="UTF-8"?>
<article id="spring-security-hash-salt-passwords">
    <category>Software Development</category>
    <title>Hashing and Salting Passwords with Spring Security 2</title>
    <author>Willie Wheeler</author>
    <publishDate>2008-10-11</publishDate>
    <description>
        Use Spring Security 2 to store your user passwords securely.
    </description>
    <keywords>
        spring,security,spring security,java,
        java security,hash,hashes,salt,
        crypto,storing passwords securely,md4,md5,sha-1,encryption,login,
        authentication
    </keywords>
    <thumbUrl>http://wheelersoftware.s3.amazonaws.com/articles/
        spring-security-hash-salt-passwords/ladybug-thumb2.jpg</thumbUrl>
</article>
```

The file should be fairly self-explanatory. The main advantage of this format is that you can use object/XML mapping to map between the `Article` class from listing 12.1 and the XML from listing 12.11. We'll get to that in a moment.

The HTML pages are normal HTML pages, although they use certain CSS classes to achieve various presentational effects. See the code download for those.

To understand how article importing works, you need to be familiar with the flow starting from an article package on the user's desktop to an article ending up in the article repository. Figure 12.8 explains how this flow works.

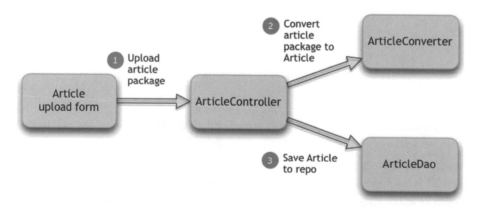

Figure 12.8   How an article package on the user's machine ends up as an article in the article repository

Figure 12.9 The article-upload form

You've already seen the controller and the DAO. Let's look at the article-upload form first and then the `ArticleConverter`.

From a UI perspective, you'll put the article-upload form at the top of the article master list. Figure 12.9 shows what the form looks like.

To implement this, you need to add a form to articleList.jsp. You'll add a couple of alert messages as well to indicate success or failure when uploading an article. Review the controller in listing 12.7 to see how you activate these alerts. Here's a slightly simplified version of what you need to add to articleList.jsp; see the code download for the full version:

```
<c:url var="uploadUrl" value="/articles" />

<c:if test="${param.upload == 'fail'}">
    <div class="error alert">The upload failed.</div>
</c:if>
<c:if test="${param.upload == 'ok'}">
    <div class="info alert">Uploaded.</div>
</c:if>
<form action="${uploadUrl}" method="post" enctype="multipart/form-data">
    <input name="file" type="file" />
    <input type="submit" value="Upload" />
</form>
```

That part isn't too bad. The important parts are the form's `enctype` attribute and the file-input field—these are what make this a file-upload form.

When the user uploads an article package, the browser sends the package to the `ArticleController`, whose `createArticle()` method picks it up as a `MultipartFile` object. The `createArticle()` method uses the `ArticleConverter` to convert the `MultipartFile` into an `Article`. See figure 12.10 to understand what's happening behind the scenes. The following listing offers the details of this process.

Figure 12.10 How `ArticleConverter` converts an article package to an `Article`

Listing 12.12 ArticleConverter.java: extracts an `Article` from the file upload

```
package com.springinpractice.ch12.web;

import java.io.*;
import java.util.*;
```

```
import javax.inject.Inject;
import javax.servlet.ServletContext;
import javax.xml.transform.stream.StreamSource;
import org.springframework.core.convert.converter.Converter;
import org.springframework.oxm.Unmarshaller;
import org.springframework.stereotype.Component;
import org.springframework.web.context.ServletContextAware;
import org.springframework.web.multipart.MultipartFile;
import com.springinpractice.ch12.model.Article;
import com.springinpractice.ch12.model.Page;

@Component
public class ArticleConverter
    implements Converter<MultipartFile, Article>, ServletContextAware {

    private static final int BUFFER_SIZE = 4096;

    @Inject private Unmarshaller unmarshaller;
    private ServletContext servletContext;
    private Random random = new Random();

    public void setServletContext(ServletContext servletContext) {
        this.servletContext = servletContext;
    }

    public Article convert(MultipartFile zipFile) {
        try {
            File tempDir = createTempDir();
            unzip(zipFile, tempDir);
            Article article = assembleArticle(tempDir);
            tempDir.delete();
            return article;
        } catch (IOException e) {
            throw new RuntimeException(e);
        }
    }

    private File createTempDir() {
        File tempDir = (File) servletContext.getAttribute(
            "javax.servlet.context.tempdir");
        File articleDir;
        int count = 0;
        while ((articleDir = new File(
            tempDir, "article-" +
                Math.abs(random.nextLong()))).exists()) {
            if (count++ > 5) {
                throw new RuntimeException(
                    "Can't create a temporary directory. " +
                    "Something is very wrong.");
            }
        }
        articleDir.mkdirs();
        return articleDir;
    }

    private void unzip(MultipartFile zipFile, File destDir)
        throws IOException {
        byte[] buffer = new byte[BUFFER_SIZE];
```

Interface declarations ❶

OXM Unmarshaller ❷

For ServletContextAware ❸

Primary conversion method ❹

Creates temporary directory ❺

Unzips file into temp directory ❻

```
            ZipInputStream zis = new ZipInputStream(
                new ByteArrayInputStream(zipFile.getBytes()));
            ZipEntry entry;
            while ((entry = zis.getNextEntry()) != null) {
                File entryFile = new File(destDir, entry.getName());
                BufferedOutputStream bos = new BufferedOutputStream(
                    new FileOutputStream(entryFile), BUFFER_SIZE);
                int len;
                while ((len = zis.read(buffer)) > 0) {
                    bos.write(buffer, 0, len); }
                bos.flush();
                bos.close();
            }
            zis.close();
        }

        private Article assembleArticle(File articleDir)          ⑦ Builds article from
            throws IOException {                                      zip contents
            File articleFile = new File(articleDir, "article.xml");
            StreamSource articleSrc = new StreamSource(articleFile);
            Article article = (Article) unmarshaller.unmarshal(articleSrc);

            List<Page> pages = article.getPages();           ⑨ Reads HTML
            File pageFile;                                       pages manually
            int pageNumber = 1;
            while ((pageFile = new File(articleDir, pageNumber +
                ".html")).exists()) {
                StringBuilder builder = new StringBuilder(4096);
                BufferedReader br = new BufferedReader(
                    new FileReader(pageFile));
                String line;
                while ((line = br.readLine()) != null) {
                    builder.append(line);
                    builder.append('\n');
                }

                String htmlPage = builder.toString();
                int startIndex = htmlPage.indexOf("<body>") + 6;
                int endIndex = htmlPage.indexOf("</body>");

                if (startIndex == -1 || endIndex == -1) {
                    throw new RuntimeException(
                        "Invalid HTML page: " + pageFile +
                        " must have <body> and </body> tags.");
                }

                String content = htmlPage.substring(startIndex, endIndex);
                Page page = new Page();
                page.setContent(content);
                pages.add(page);

                pageNumber++;
            }

            return article;
        }
    }
```

Unmarshals article.xml with OXM ⑧ (points to `Article article = (Article) unmarshaller.unmarshal(articleSrc);`)

The `ArticleConverter` class contains a fair bit of code, and we'll go over the key elements here. First, the interface declarations include the Spring `Converter` and `ServletContextAware` interfaces ❶. The `Converter` interface is for classes that convert objects from one type to another. You need `ServletContextAware` to get a reference to the `ServletContext`, which gives you a way to get the servlet context's temporary directory.

At ❷ is an Object/XML mapping (OXM) `Unmarshaller`, which unmarshals XML into Java objects. You use it to convert article.xml to an `Article`.

The `setServletContext()` method at ❸ is required by `ServletContextAware`. Spring automatically injects the `ServletContext` using this method.

The primary conversion method is `convert()` ❹. It's the single method that the `Converter` interface declares. At a high level, its logic follows the logic presented in figure 12.10. It creates a temporary directory ❺, unzips the article package into the temporary directory ❻, and, finally, builds the `Article` from the article package contents ❼. Note that you use OXM to build the `Article` ❽, but you build the pages manually ❾. This is because you care about the XML structure in article.xml, but you don't care about anything other than what's between the `<body>` tags in the HTML files.

You use Java Architecture for XML Binding (JAXB) to accomplish the OXM mapping. To make this work, you need to revisit the `Article` class and add some annotations. Because the structure of the XML matches the structure of the `Article` class almost exactly, you don't have to add many annotations. You add a class-level `@Xml-RootElement` annotation:

```
@XmlRootElement(name = "article")
public class Article { ... }
```

In article.xml, the ID is an attribute rather than an element, so you add the corresponding annotation:

```
@XmlAttribute
public String getId() { return id; }
```

Finally, you aren't OXM mapping the pages, so you add the following:

```
@XmlTransient
public List<Page> getPages() { return pages; }
```

You're almost done. To make everything work, you need to create a beans-web.xml configuration.

CONFIGURING THE APPLICATION

The following listing shows how to put everything together at the web tier.

Listing 12.13   beans-web.xml: Spring beans web configuration

```
<?xml version="1.0" encoding="UTF-8"?>
<beans xmlns="http://www.springframework.org/schema/beans"
    xmlns:context="http://www.springframework.org/schema/context"
```

```
xmlns:mvc="http://www.springframework.org/schema/mvc"
xmlns:oxm="http://www.springframework.org/schema/oxm"          ◁──── OXM
xmlns:p="http://www.springframework.org/schema/p"              ❶ namespace
xmlns:xsi="http://www.w3.org/2001/XMLSchema-instance"
xsi:schemaLocation="
   http://www.springframework.org/schema/beans
   http://www.springframework.org/schema/beans/spring-beans-3.0.xsd
   http://www.springframework.org/schema/context
   http://www.springframework.org/schema/context/spring-context-3.0.xsd
   http://www.springframework.org/schema/mvc
   http://www.springframework.org/schema/mvc/spring-mvc-3.0.xsd
   http://www.springframework.org/schema/oxm
   http://www.springframework.org/schema/oxm/spring-oxm-3.0.xsd">

<mvc:annotation-driven />
<mvc:default-servlet-handler />
<mvc:view-controller path="" view-name="redirect:/articles.html" />

<context:component-scan base-package="com.springinpractice.ch12.web" />

<bean id="multipartResolver"                                              ◁───────┐
 class="org.springframework.web.multipart.commons.CommonsMultipartResolver"        │
     p:maxUploadSize="4096000"                                                     │
     p:maxInMemorySize="4096" />                             ❸ JAXB        Multipart
                                                               (un)marshaller resolver
<oxm:jaxb2-marshaller id="marshaller">      ◁───┘                          for file
     <oxm:class-to-be-bound                                                upload ❷
         name="com.springinpractice.ch12.model.Article" />
</oxm:jaxb2-marshaller>

<bean class=
     "org.springframework.web.servlet.view.InternalResourceViewResolver"
     p:viewClass="org.springframework.web.servlet.view.JstlView"
     p:prefix="/WEB-INF/jsp/"
     p:suffix=".jsp" />

<bean id="messageSource"
     class="org.springframework.context.support.
               ReloadableResourceBundleMessageSource"
     p:basename="classpath:/spring/messages" />
</beans>
```

The previous listing is similar to other beans-web.xml configurations you've seen. There are a couple of noteworthy pieces here, though. You need to handle file uploads and OXM. You handle OXM by declaring the namespace ❶ and using it to declare a JAXB marshaller ❸, which happens to double as an unmarshaller. To enable file uploads, you place a CommonsMultipartResolver ❷ on the application context under the ID multipartResolver. You use some of the configuration options available; see the Javadoc for CommonsMultipartResolver for the full list of options. Figure 12.11 shows the combined beans-jcr.xml and beans-web.xml.

Congratulations—you've built a simple but useful article-delivery engine. Start up the app, and give it a try. You can find the article packages in the sample_articles directory in the code download. Import the article packages directly rather than unzip them.

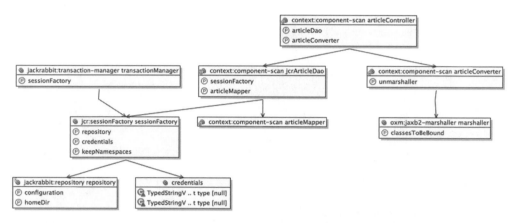

Figure 12.11   The combined beans-jcr.xml and beans-web.xml bean-dependency diagram

Discussion

Over the last two recipes, you've put together a basic article-delivery engine based on JCR, a powerful repository technology. The engine doesn't currently use any of the advanced features of JCR, but the idea behind using JCR is that it allows you to elaborate the article engine into a more full-blown article-management system, with authoring, versioning, fine-grained access controls, and more.

But it may be that all you want is an article-delivery engine of the sort you just built. It is, after all, a useful application as it stands, and technical users might prefer to edit content using a text editor, manage it using an existing source-control system, and package it with a zip utility. In such a situation, you might prefer to use a simpler approach on the back end. In the next recipe, you'll see how to replace the JCR repository with MongoDB using Spring Data MongoDB.

12.3   Storing articles in a document repository

PREREQUISITES

Recipe 2.6 Spring Data JPA overview
Recipe 12.2 Creating a web-based article-delivery engine

KEY TECHNOLOGIES

MongoDB, Spring Data MongoDB

Background

In recipes 12.1 and 12.2, you built a simple but useful article-delivery engine. The approach was to provide a basis for building a more sophisticated set of management capabilities, such as authoring, versioning, fine-grained access controls, and more. But if that's not required, then there are repository options that greatly simplify the data-access code. This recipe shows how to do that using MongoDB and Spring Data MongoDB. It's a short recipe, because Spring Data MongoDB does almost all of the work.

You'll find it helpful to review the Spring Data JPA overview in chapter 2 if you're unfamiliar with Spring Data.

Problem

All you need is article delivery, not advanced content-management functions. Choose a repository technology that allows you to simplify the data-access code.

Solution

You'll replace the JCR repository with MongoDB, a scalable document repository with much to recommend it. It has a nice query API and it's very easy to set up and administer. MongoDB is a good match for your needs because the articles are documents.

In chapter 2, we presented a brief overview of Spring Data JPA. You saw how the framework automatically generates DAO implementations for you, simplifying the creation of the data access layer. The Spring Data portfolio includes several other projects, including Spring Data MongoDB, which assists with the creation of a data access layer based on MongoDB.

As we mentioned in the background for this recipe, there isn't much to do here. We'll break it down into a handful of short, easy steps, a few of which are absolutely trivial.

STEP 1: SETTING UP A MONGODB INSTANCE

Go to the MongoDB website (www.mongodb.org/), download the MongoDB package, install it, and start up the instance. Even if you've never heard of MongoDB, you should be able to get the entire thing up and running in under 30 minutes using the MongoDB Quickstart guide.

STEP 2: REMOVING JCR CODE

If you completed recipe 12.1 before coming to this recipe, you'll want to get rid of the JCR-related code. You can take out `ArticleDao`, `JcrArticleDao`, `ArticleMapper`, and the beans-jcr.xml configuration. Between `JcrArticleDao` and `ArticleMapper`, that's a decent chunk of code you're eliminating. You can also remove JCR-related dependencies from the Maven POM.

STEP 3: CREATING A NEW ARTICLEDAO INTERFACE

The following listing is the new `ArticleDao` interface. It's similar to the one it replaces, but this time it uses Spring Data MongoDB.

> **Listing 12.14 ArticleDao.java, revised to work with Spring Data MongoDB**

```
package com.springinpractice.ch12.dao;

import org.springframework.data.mongodb.repository.MongoRepository;
import com.springinpractice.ch12.model.Article;

public interface ArticleDao extends MongoRepository<Article, String> { }
```

The `MongoRepository` interface already declares `save()`, `findAll()`, and `findOne()` methods, and these support your use cases, so you don't need to declare additional methods. All you have to do is parameterize the `MongoRepository` interface with the domain object type (`Article`) and the ID type (`String`).

Also, you don't have to implement the interface yourself because Spring Data MongoDB will generate an implementation for you automatically using Java's dynamic proxy machinery. Finally, you don't need to worry about mapping the Java `Article` object to MongoDB's native BSON format,[8] because Spring Data MongoDB also handles that for you. Bravo!

STEP 4: UPDATING ARTICLECONTROLLER

Because you've changed the method names on the `ArticleDao`, you need to make the corresponding changes in `ArticleController`, which calls the methods. Only three such changes are required, and they're straightforward, so we won't cover them here. See the code download.[9]

STEP 5: CREATING BEANS-MONGODB.XML

The next listing is effectively the replacement for beans-jcr.xml from recipe 12.1.

Listing 12.15   beans-mongodb.xml: Spring beans configuration for MongoDB

```
<?xml version="1.0" encoding="UTF-8"?>
<beans xmlns="http://www.springframework.org/schema/beans"
    xmlns:context="http://www.springframework.org/schema/context"
    xmlns:mongo="http://www.springframework.org/schema/data/mongo"
    xmlns:p="http://www.springframework.org/schema/p"
    xmlns:xsi="http://www.w3.org/2001/XMLSchema-instance"
    xsi:schemaLocation="
    http://www.springframework.org/schema/beans
    http://www.springframework.org/schema/beans/spring-beans-3.0.xsd
    http://www.springframework.org/schema/context
    http://www.springframework.org/schema/context/spring-context-3.0.xsd
    http://www.springframework.org/schema/data/mongo
    http://www.springframework.org/schema/data/mongo/spring-mongo-1.0.xsd">

    <mongo:mongo />

    <!-- More advanced configuration -->
    <!--
    <mongo:mongo host="localhost" port="27017">
        <mongo:options
            connections-per-host="10"
            threads-allowed-to-block-for-connection-multiplier="5"
            max-wait-time="12000"
            connect-timeout="0"
            socket-timeout="0"
            auto-connect-retry="false" />
    </mongo:mongo>
    -->
```

MongoDB namespace ❶

Defines MongoDB instance ❷

Advanced instance configuration ❸

---

[8] BSON is short for binary JSON. See www.mongodb.org/display/DOCS/BSON and http://bsonspec.org/ for more information.

[9] Note that we haven't pursued the `getPage()` optimization here, which eagerly loads a single page instead of loading the entire article. So, call `findOne()` (find one article with all pages eagerly loaded) instead of `getPage()` (find one article with one page eagerly loaded).

```
<bean id="mongoTemplate"
    class="org.springframework.data.mongodb.core.MongoTemplate"
    p:writeResultChecking="EXCEPTION">

    <constructor-arg ref="mongo" />
    <constructor-arg value="techsite" />
</bean>

<mongo:repositories base-package="com.springinpractice.ch12.dao" />

<context:annotation-config />
</beans>
```

MongoTemplate ❹

Generates DAO implementations ❺

Activates exception translation ❻

To use Spring Data MongoDB, it's useful to employ the namespace configuration, so you declare the namespace and the schema location ❶. Next you use `<mongo:mongo/>` to declare a Mongo instance with bean ID `mongo` running on the localhost, port 27017 (the defaults) ❷. Various instance configuration options are available; ❸ is a partial list. (Consult the Spring Data MongoDB documentation for more information.)

Once you have an instance, you need a `MongoTemplate` to access the instance ❹. This template is like other templates in Spring, such as `HibernateTemplate` and `RestTemplate`. You call the template `mongoTemplate` to support automatic discovery, which you'll see shortly. You pass the `mongo` instance into the constructor, and you choose `techsite` as the name of the database you want to use in the MongoDB instance.[10]

At ❺ you tell Spring Data MongoDB to scan `com.springinpractice.ch12.dao` for DAO interfaces (that is, interfaces that extend the `MongoRepository` interface) and to generate implementations dynamically. Finally, ❻ tells Spring to activate exception-translation in the generated DAO implementations. This will translate `MongoExceptions` into exceptions in the `DataAccessException` hierarchy.

Figure 12.12 is the bean-dependency diagram corresponding to the configuration.

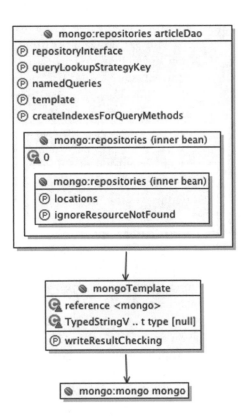

Figure 12.12　The bean-dependency diagram for the Spring Data MongoDB configuration

---

[10] Databases and collections are key MongoDB concepts. An instance hosts a set of databases, and each database has a set of collections. Consult the MongoDB documentation for more information.

STEP 6: UPDATING WEB.XML

Don't forget to update web.xml to reflect the new app context configuration file:

```
<context-param>
    <param-name>contextConfigLocation</param-name>
    <param-value>
        classpath:/spring/beans-mongodb.xml
    </param-value>
</context-param>
```

That's all there is to it. Restart the app, import the article packages, and be amazed. Other than `ArticleConverter` (the component that extracts an article from a file upload), the Java code in the app is close to trivial.

Discussion

This recipe showed how to simplify the data access layer using Spring Data MongoDB. You saw that the framework handles DAO implementation and persistence mapping for you. The result is a much streamlined codebase.

The Spring Data portfolio includes support for many of the new NoSQL offerings that have been appearing over the past few years. We looked at JPA in chapter 2 and MongoDB (an example of a document repository) here. Other database types include key/value stores, big data stores, graph databases, and several other general categories. See the Spring Data section of the SpringSource website for more information (www.springsource.org/spring-data).

Another popular document store is CouchDB. At the time of this writing, Spring Data CouchDB is planned, but it doesn't exist. Several comparisons between CouchDB and MongoDB are available on the web, so read those and choose the document store that makes the most sense for your project.

12.4   Summary

In this chapter, you learned how to use Spring to create an article-delivery engine. The work you did here falls under the more general category of content management, and you can apply the techniques you used here to building other CMS domains and functions.

JCR is a nice option if you have more advanced content-management needs that you don't want to build yourself. It's also useful if you need to offer support for different back-end stores, because JCR is a standard implemented by several vendors in the content-management space.

But be sure to explore the newer NoSQL document stores, including MongoDB and CouchDB. They're promising alternatives to some of the more traditional approaches to content management, including relational back ends and JCR. In addition, because NoSQL stores are especially well-suited to addressing issues of scale, there is a lot of industry excitement around their use. Thus you can expect over time that NoSQL stores will become even more capable.

In the next chapter, we'll look at implementing another important type of CMS: product catalogs. Product catalogs have some specialized needs relative to article-delivery engines, partly on the data modeling side and partly on the user interface side. We'll continue to consider content delivery, but we'll examine content authoring as well.

Enterprise integration 13

This chapter covers

- Shared database integration using Spring Data JPA
- Integrating web services with Spring Data REST
- Messaging via Spring Integration with RabbitMQ and JavaMail

An enterprise of any size might have hundreds of different software systems, such as monitoring tools, ticketing systems, collaboration platforms, and so forth. And if it appears that there isn't much rhyme or reason to the specific mix of tools, that's often because there isn't. In a perfect world, there might be a fixed set of business processes, and the systems chosen to support those processes would play nicely together. But this isn't a perfect world.

There are many reasons why the systems in an environment might be a jumbled mess. Among them:

- Business needs change. Those changes drive tool changes.
- Different teams in an organization have different tool preferences.
- A single vendor may offer a highly integrated tool suite, but the IT organization may prefer a best-of-breed tool strategy, or may prefer to keep multiple vendors in the game just to keep any one vendor from gaining too much leverage.

- Throw in some vendor-sponsored lunches, events, and outings, and suddenly the systems start to look as if they were deliberately chosen not to work together!

Those are some of the realities of enterprise IT. And despite the difficulty, the need for systems integration is very much alive and well.

In this chapter you'll imagine that you're building a Spring-based help desk system to support an external-facing, internally developed customer portal. On the inbound side, you have the following requirements:

- Customers must be able to create tickets in a self-service fashion.
- The help desk system must have an internal-facing UI that lets support reps create tickets on behalf of customers who call the help desk on the phone.
- You need to support self-service ticket creation through a legacy email address that some customers still use even though it is no longer published.

On the outbound side, you'll suppose that the help desk must send the customer a confirmation email regardless of whether the customer or a support rep creates the ticket. Figure 13.1 shows a conceptual overview of your eventual goal in this chapter.

A real help desk system has lots of other functionality, such as workflows, reporting, and so on. But we're more concerned with showing how to perform integrations than with creating an actual ticketing system, so we're sticking to a basic structure.

Although you'll use a variety of integration technologies—including Spring Data REST, Spring HATEOAS, Spring Integration, Spring AMQP, Spring Rabbit, and RabbitMQ—you're going to use Spring

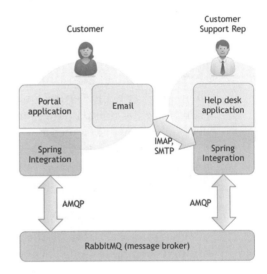

Figure 13.1   Overview of your help desk system and its integrations as they appear at the end of the chapter

Integration (SI) particularly heavily. That being the case, let's pause for a quick tour. Although it's outside the scope of this chapter to present SI comprehensively,[1] a better picture will emerge as you work through the recipes.

A whirlwind tour of Spring Integration

SI is an implementation of the patterns described in *Enterprise Integration Patterns* by Gregor Hohpe and Bobby Woolf (Addison-Wesley, 2003). EIP is a comprehensive catalog of patterns helpful in getting applications that weren't initially designed to work

---

[1] Please see *Spring Integration in Action* by Mark Fisher, et al., (Manning, 2012) for a more detailed treatment of Spring Integration.

together to do so. Note that we assume some familiarity with these patterns and the integration domain in general; see www.eaipatterns.com/ for more background if you require it.

Something interesting about SI is the way it uses dependency injection. The typical Spring application uses DI in what might be called a vertical fashion: the application is organized as a set of layers, and you inject beans at layer *n* into beans at layer *n*+1. For example, you inject DAOs into service beans and service beans into web controllers.

SI applies dependency injection primarily in a horizontal way. The idea is to build an integration layer just above an application's services and implement the integration layer in the pipes and filters architectural style.[2] In SI, the pipes are called *channels* and the filters are called *endpoints*, and the overall pipeline is a messaging system supporting the integration of connected services. Endpoints perform message routing and processing, whereas channels convey messages from endpoint to endpoint. You can build

an entire messaging system out of channels and endpoints by injecting channels into endpoints. Figure 13.2 shows how this works.

This horizontal use of DI is entirely compatible with the vertical use. Especially when you're integrating internally developed apps, it's sometimes helpful to have *service activators* in the integration layer invoke your Java service beans directly. You link service activators to service beans through DI.

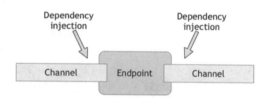

Figure 13.2   Two channels dependency-injected into an endpoint. The channels correspond to pipes in the pipes-and-filters architectural style, and the endpoint corresponds to a filter.

But in general, SI uses dependency injection as a way to build a horizontal layer of integration flows. Most of the communication with underlying services happens through the application's coarse-grained external interfaces (for example, web services and messaging endpoints) rather than through the fairly fine-grained mechanism of Java DI.

Note that although SI provides ready-made implementations of the various EIP patterns, there are architecturally different approaches to applying those patterns, and SI isn't prescriptive about it. You can use SI to implement a simple, in-process messaging

Integration and services: an architectural perspective

One of the things I (Willie) struggled with when I was first learning about integration was understanding just what it is that's being integrated. It can get confusing because there are multiple ways of talking about services, and they often come up in a single conversation.

---

[2]   For more information on the pipes-and-filters architectural style, see Pipes and Filters, Enterprise Integration Patterns, www.eaipatterns.com/PipesAndFilters.html.

> **(continued)**
>
> I won't attempt a definition here, but a loose characterization will help. *Services* in an integration context refers to the coarse-grained interfaces that different apps/systems happen to expose to the world and that provide integration hooks. This could be SOAP/REST web services, messaging endpoints, HTML forms, file-based, email-based, and so forth. Obviously this is a permissive conception, and not one you would use to prescribe for a green field, service-oriented architecture. But for integration it's appropriate because it's sometimes the case that the only way to talk to an app is to post data into an HTML form that it provides.[3]
>
> *Services* in this sense refers to something larger than the service beans we often find in Spring-based applications, because (for example) RESTful endpoints live above the service beans. There are certainly cases where the integration layer has direct access to an application's Java code, and so the integration layer might call that code directly, but this is a special instance. The more general case is an integration layer interacting with apps/systems through whatever interfaces they expose.
>
> You'll see in this chapter, for instance, how creating a ticket in the portal app causes the creation of a ticket in the help desk app, which in turn generates a confirmation email. These apps and systems were independently conceived, but you use integration to make them work together.

infrastructure that a given app uses to communicate with external resources. Alternatively, you can use it to communicate with an external message broker (ActiveMQ, RabbitMQ, SonicMQ, and so on), which usually provides better decoupling, flexibility, and resiliency. You'll see examples of both of those in the recipes ahead.[4]

The first recipe starts you off by illustrating a common form of application integration: a shared database.

13.1 *Integrating applications via a shared database*

PREREQUISITES
Recipe 2.6 Spring Data JPA overview

KEY TECHNOLOGIES
Database

Background

In many cases, multiple apps need to work with the same data. One app might capture leads, another might qualify the leads, and a third might present the leads to salespeople trying to close. Especially when the apps in question are developed internally, it's often easiest and most appropriate to have the apps all work with a shared database.

---

[3] Don't laugh. There are major, revenue-critical systems that work exactly this way.

[4] There are other possibilities as well. For instance, you could stand up a dedicated (that is, not directly attached to any existing app) integration bus based on Spring Integration. We won't explore that here, but by the end of this chapter it should be obvious how to do it.

Problem

Integrate applications by having them work against a shared database.

Solution

For your current purposes, assume that your help desk and portal applications need to work with common customer and ticket data. Customers need to be able to create tickets using the portal, and those tickets need to show up in the help desk app for processing by support representatives.

The approach here, as noted, will be to use a shared database. This approach generally requires that you control the apps in question because you have to be able to make them agree on the database schema. But where that's true, a shared database is an option to consider. At small scale, the coordination between apps on schema-related issues is generally manageable, and this allows you to avoid having to build out separate abstraction layers such as web services. See figure 13.3.

There isn't anything too special about having two different apps use the same database. You have to pay attention to transactions, but that's usually true for single apps. Point your apps at the same database, and you're in business.

Your real goal in this recipe is to establish a code baseline for subsequent recipes. To that end, you use Spring Data JPA as described in recipe 2.6, rather than working directly with the Hibernate API. (You still use Hibernate as a JPA provider.) The reason is that you want to set the stage for using Spring Data REST in recipe 13.2, and this depends on Spring Data JPA. Feel free to review recipe 2.6 or look at the sample code.

One special case comes up in the context of shared database integrations, and it's worth investigating.

GETTING A SINGLE APP TO WORK WITH MULTIPLE DATABASES

Even though this is a recipe about having multiple apps work with a shared database, sometimes that plays out via an app with a dedicated database, and the app needs data from another app's database as well. Now you have an app that has to work with two databases.

In this case, the portal app owns the customer database, and the help desk app owns the ticket database. But the help desk app needs customer data so it can resolve customer usernames in the tickets to the customer's full information (name, contact information,

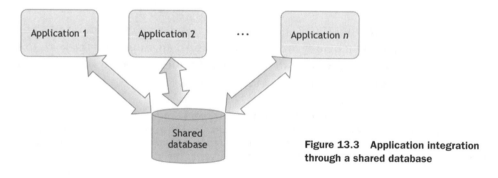

Figure 13.3   Application integration through a shared database

and so on). So the help desk app will use the customer database in addition to its own ticket database. See figure 13.4.

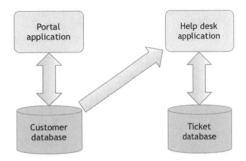

Figure 13.4 **The portal and help desk applications share customer data through direct access to a shared customer database. For small-scale integrations, this can be a clean and simple solution.**

Let's discuss the help desk for a moment. One possibility for working with multiple databases is to use distributed transactions. Even though you're only reading customer data, in theory transactions could be useful for proper isolation, setting lock modes, and setting timeouts. You might use them, for instance, to handle the case where the portal changes a customer username or deletes a customer entirely, either of which would break the soft association (based on usernames) between tickets and their customers.

But in fact there's no worry here, because the portal doesn't allow users to change their usernames, and it also doesn't delete customers. (With customer data, you'd probably want *soft deletes*, where you keep the customer record but use a flag to indicate whether the customer has been deleted.) And even if you were for whatever reason to allow these things, they would presumably be insufficiently common to warrant the performance overhead of distributed transactions.

Instead, your help desk will use two different transaction managers: one for working with tickets and the other for working with customers. You haven't seen that yet, so let's look at how the help desk app does it. First, the following listing shows the help desk's configuration for the ticket database.

Listing 13.1 beans-repo.xml: configuration for the ticket database

```xml
<?xml version="1.0" encoding="UTF-8"?>
<beans xmlns="http://www.springframework.org/schema/beans"
    xmlns:jee="http://www.springframework.org/schema/jee"
    xmlns:jpa="http://www.springframework.org/schema/data/jpa"
    xmlns:p="http://www.springframework.org/schema/p"
    xmlns:tx="http://www.springframework.org/schema/tx"
    xmlns:xsi="http://www.w3.org/2001/XMLSchema-instance"
    xsi:schemaLocation="
        http://www.springframework.org/schema/beans
        http://www.springframework.org/schema/beans/spring-beans-3.1.xsd
        http://www.springframework.org/schema/data/jpa
        http://www.springframework.org/schema/data/jpa/spring-jpa-1.2.xsd
        http://www.springframework.org/schema/jee
        http://www.springframework.org/schema/jee/spring-jee-3.1.xsd
        http://www.springframework.org/schema/tx
        http://www.springframework.org/schema/tx/spring-tx-3.1.xsd">

    <jee:jndi-lookup id="helpDeskDS"
        jndi-name="jdbc/Sip13HelpDeskDS" resource-ref="true" />

    <bean id="entityManagerFactory"
```

⬅ **❶ Using JPA**

```
        class="org.springframework.orm.jpa.
                LocalContainerEntityManagerFactoryBean"
        p:dataSource-ref="helpDeskDS">

        <property name="packagesToScan">
            <list>
                <value>com.springinpractice.ch13.helpdesk.model</value>
                <value>com.springinpractice.ch13.sitemap.model</value>
            </list>
        </property>
        <property name="persistenceProvider">
            <bean class="org.hibernate.ejb.HibernatePersistence" />
        </property>
        <property name="jpaProperties">
            <props>
                <prop key="hibernate.dialect">
                    org.hibernate.dialect.MySQL5Dialect
                </prop>
                <prop key="hibernate.show_sql">false</prop>
            </props>
        </property>
    </bean>

    <bean id="transactionManager"
        class="org.springframework.orm.jpa.JpaTransactionManager"
        p:entityManagerFactory-ref="entityManagerFactory" />
    <tx:annotation-driven transaction-manager="transactionManager" />

    <jpa:repositories
        base-package="com.springinpractice.ch13.helpdesk.repo"
        entity-manager-factory-ref="entityManagerFactory"
        transaction-manager-ref="transactionManager" />

    <jpa:repositories
        base-package="com.springinpractice.ch13.sitemap.repo"
        entity-manager-factory-ref="entityManagerFactory"
        transaction-manager-ref="transactionManager" />
</beans>
```

Explicit entity manager factory ❷

Explicit transaction manager ❸

Explicit entity manager factory ❹

Explicit transaction manager ❺

You're using Spring Data JPA, so you set up a factory for JPA entity managers at ❶. At ❷ you're explicit about the entity manager factory (EMF) because you want to avoid ambiguities with the EMF you're about to create in the next listing. Similarly for ❸. You're also explicit at ❹ and ❺ where you define the Spring Data JPA repositories. Spring Data JPA will apply the specified EMF and transaction manager to the repositories it generates. Your single transaction manager can handle multiple repositories just fine, because repositories correspond to tables, not to databases.[5]

The help desk app has a repository configuration file for the customer database as well.

---

[5] The `JtaTransactionManager` can handle multiple databases in support of distributed transactions, but you aren't using that here.

Listing 13.2   beans-repo-portal.xml: configuration for the customer database

```xml
<?xml version="1.0" encoding="UTF-8"?>
<beans xmlns="http://www.springframework.org/schema/beans"
    xmlns:jee="http://www.springframework.org/schema/jee"
    xmlns:jpa="http://www.springframework.org/schema/data/jpa"
    xmlns:p="http://www.springframework.org/schema/p"
    xmlns:tx="http://www.springframework.org/schema/tx"
    xmlns:xsi="http://www.w3.org/2001/XMLSchema-instance"
    xsi:schemaLocation="
        http://www.springframework.org/schema/beans
        http://www.springframework.org/schema/beans/spring-beans-3.1.xsd
        http://www.springframework.org/schema/data/jpa
        http://www.springframework.org/schema/data/jpa/spring-jpa-1.2.xsd
        http://www.springframework.org/schema/jee
        http://www.springframework.org/schema/jee/spring-jee-3.1.xsd
        http://www.springframework.org/schema/tx
        http://www.springframework.org/schema/tx/spring-tx-3.1.xsd">

    <jee:jndi-lookup id="portalDS"
        jndi-name="jdbc/Sip13PortalDS" resource-ref="true" />

    <bean id="portalEMF"
        class="org.springframework.orm.jpa.
                LocalContainerEntityManagerFactoryBean"
        p:dataSource-ref="portalDS"
        p:packagesToScan="com.springinpractice.ch13.helpdesk.portal.model">

        <property name="persistenceProvider">
            <bean class="org.hibernate.ejb.HibernatePersistence" />
        </property>
        <property name="jpaProperties">
            <props>
                <prop key="hibernate.dialect">
                    org.hibernate.dialect.MySQL5Dialect
                </prop>
                <prop key="hibernate.show_sql">false</prop>
            </props>
        </property>
    </bean>

    <bean id="portalTxManager"
        class="org.springframework.orm.jpa.JpaTransactionManager"
        p:entityManagerFactory-ref="portalEMF" />

    <tx:annotation-driven transaction-manager="portalTxManager" />
    <jpa:repositories
        base-package="com.springinpractice.ch13.helpdesk.portal.repo"
        entity-manager-factory-ref="portalEMF"
        transaction-manager-ref="portalxTxManager" />
</beans>
```

Explicit entity manager

Explicit transaction manager

In the previous listing you're explicit about the EMF and transaction manager, just as you were in listing 13.1.

Sometimes there's only one database, and all the apps use it, but the configurations show how to deal with multi-database scenarios where distributed transactions aren't a concern.

CONFIGURING AND RUNNING THE APPLICATIONS

You're dealing with two separate applications here, and each has its own configuration location and configuration files. The configuration approach is essentially the same as the one the other chapters use (the one from appendix A), but instead of a single sip13 folder, you'll need a sip13/helpdesk folder for the help desk configuration files and a sip13/folder for the portal configuration files.

Because you're dealing with two applications here, the URLs are different than other URLs in the book:

- *Help desk application*—http://localhost:8080/helpdesk/
- *Portal application*—http://localhost:8180/portal/

Run the apps, and try things out. You should see that they're both sharing the portal's customer data.

Discussion

In this recipe we looked at the common approach of using a shared database to integrate multiple applications. This didn't require any special technology beyond what the database natively provides with respect to transaction management.

Despite its simplicity, it's important to consider reasons why you might choose not to adopt this approach, even initially:

- A shared database works well enough at small scale, but as you add applications it becomes increasingly difficult to coordinate changes. One app may need a schema change that would break other apps, and so the change can't occur until all apps are ready for it.
- Depending on the database technology, it may be difficult to scale out as you add apps.
- The shared database quickly becomes a single point of failure.
- By the time you decide to pursue a different integration approach, the apps are generally tightly coupled to the database.
- If you don't control the apps in question, then a shared database probably isn't an option for you in the first place.
- Even if you do control the apps, there's a good chance that you have third-party apps that also need to work with the same data. So you may need to come up with an integration solution that doesn't require a shared database anyway.

Web services are a popular and effective solution for some of the challenges described. They make it possible to decouple the client view of the data from the details of the actual database implementation, which provides needed flexibility. The next recipe shows how to integrate applications using RESTful web services.

13.2 *Decoupling applications with RESTful web services*

PREREQUISITES

Integrating applications via a shared database

KEY TECHNOLOGIES
Spring Data JPA, Spring Data REST, Spring HATEOAS

Background

In recipe 13.1 you saw that although shared database integrations may be simple at small scale, the approach can quickly run into both development and operational issues with increasing scale. Web services are a battle-tested technique for decoupling clients from the data they use. Originally SOAP-based web services were the "official" approach, but over time the growing consensus was that SOAP was too heavyweight for many purposes, and so the REST-based approach to web services took the lead. But SOAP or REST, the idea is to create an abstraction layer in front of core capabilities and data so the owners of those capabilities and data can make back-end changes without breaking their clients and without being held hostage by those clients (that is, being prevented from making changes).

With the REST approach in particular, service designers try to minimize the amount of knowledge that clients must have to work with the service. For example, REST's Hypermedia as the Engine of Application State (HATEOAS) principle says that clients shouldn't require anything beyond a general knowledge of working with hyper-media-based systems.[6] This constraint, properly observed, further decouples clients from the services they use.

Problem

Integrate applications without the tight coupling entailed by shared database integrations.

Solution

This recipe takes a first step in the direction of decoupling your apps by eliminating their common dependency on the details of the shared customer database schema. You'll learn how to do the following:

- Use Spring Data REST to implement (as part of the portal app) a RESTful web service API in front of your customer data
- Use Spring HATEOAS to implement data transfer objects
- Use `RestTemplate` to implement (as part of the help desk app) a client for your web service

In the sample code we introduce a dependency in the other direction as well: the portal needs to get data (ticket statuses, ticket categories) from the help desk's ticket database to allow customers to create self-service tickets through the portal UI. See figure 13.5 for the updated, point-to-point integration architecture.

Because both directions are entirely symmetrical, we'll cover only one direction here: the one where the help desk calls the portal web service API to get customer data. Refer to the sample code if you want to see the other direction as well.

---

[6]   HATEOAS, Wikipedia, http://en.wikipedia.org/wiki/HATEOAS.

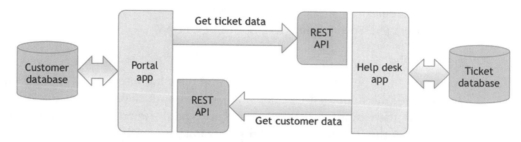

Figure 13.5   The point-to-point integration architecture for this recipe. The apps hide their databases from one another but expose RESTful web service APIs for data access.

You'll begin by implementing the web service on the portal app.

IMPLEMENTING A RESTFUL WEB SERVICE USING SPRING DATA REST

Spring Data REST (SDR) is a relatively recent addition to the Spring family.[7] It builds on Spring Data JPA (SDJ) to expose SDJ repositories through a RESTful, JSON-based web service API. SDR does this using an exporter servlet that knows how to interpret special REST annotations declared on the SDJ repository interfaces.

Let's look first at the portal app's single repository interface, `UserRepository`. This is the repo for customer data.

Listing 13.3   UserRepository: SDJ repository annotated for exporting by SDR

```
package com.springinpractice.ch13.portal.repo;

import java.util.Collection;
import java.util.List;
import org.springframework.data.jpa.repository.JpaRepository;          Path to ❶
import org.springframework.data.repository.query.Param;                resource
import org.springframework.data.rest.repository.annotation.RestResource;
import com.springinpractice.ch13.portal.model.User;

@RestResource(path = "users")
public interface UserRepository extends JpaRepository<User, Long> {

    @RestResource(path = "find-by-username")                      ❷ Query path
    User findByUsername(@Param("username") String username);

    @RestResource(path = "find-by-username-in")      ❹ Another query path
    List<User> findByUsernameIn(
        @Param("username") Collection<String> usernames);         Query
}                                                                 ❺ parameter
```

Query ❸
parameter

At ❶ you use the SDR `@RestResource` annotation to specify a path to the resource, relative to the servlet path. You're specifying `"users"` because otherwise SDR defaults to `"user"` (based on `UserRepository`), which you don't want. At ❷ you attach an SDR path to your custom SDJ finder query. You specify its HTTP parameter at ❸. You do the same thing at ❹ and ❺ for a collection-driven custom finder query.

---

[7] At the time of this writing, it's still a release candidate, so it may change a bit by the time you read this.

You're almost done. All that remains is to define the exporter servlet in web.xml.

Listing 13.4 Defining `RepositoryRestExporterServlet` in web.xml

```xml
<web-app ...>

    ...

    <servlet>
        <servlet-name>api</servlet-name>
        <servlet-class>org.springframework.data.rest.webmvc.
                RepositoryRestExporterServlet</servlet-class>
        <load-on-startup>1</load-on-startup>
    </servlet>
    <servlet-mapping>
        <servlet-name>api</servlet-name>
        <url-pattern>/api/*</url-pattern>
    </servlet-mapping>
</web-app>
```

That's all there is to it. Let's look at what it does. First, start up the portal app. Now go to http://localhost:8180/portal/api/users:

```json
{
  "links" : [ {
    "rel" : "users.search",
    "href" : "http://localhost:8180/portal/api/users/search"
  } ],
  "content" : [ {
    "links" : [ {
      "rel" : "self",
      "href" : "http://localhost:8180/portal/api/users/1"
    } ],
    "lastName" : "Jenson",
    "username" : "paul",
    "email" : "paul@example.com",
    "firstName" : "Paul"
  }, {
    "links" : [ {
      "rel" : "self",
      "href" : "http://localhost:8180/portal/api/users/2"
    } ],
    "lastName" : "Henshaw",
    "username" : "aimee",
    "email" : "aimee@example.com",
    "firstName" : "Aimee"
  } ],
  "page" : {
    "size" : 20,
    "totalElements" : 2,
    "totalPages" : 1,
    "number" : 1
  }
}
```

True to HATEOAS form, the resources specify links that you can follow to get further results. Let's see what happens when you hit the search endpoint:

```
{
  "links" : [ {
    "rel" : "users.find-by-username-in",
    "href" :
      "http://localhost:8180/portal/api/users/search/find-by-username-in"
  }, {
    "rel" : "users.find-by-username",
    "href" :
      "http://localhost:8180/portal/api/users/search/find-by-username"
  } ],
  "content" : [ ]
}
```

Let's try finding by a username in a collection. If you do http://localhost:8180/portal/api/users/search/find-by-username-in?username=aimee you get:

```
{
  "links" : [ ],
  "content" : [ {
    "links" : [ {
      "rel" : "self",
      "href" : "http://localhost:8180/portal/api/users/2"
    } ],
    "lastName" : "Henshaw",
    "username" : "aimee",
    "email" : "aimee@example.com",
    "firstName" : "Aimee"
  } ]
}
```

Try it with http://localhost:8180/portal/api/users/search/find-by-username-in?username=aimee&username=paul. You get the idea. For anybody who has ever implemented a RESTful web service, you can see that Spring Data REST is powerful, and that it saves a lot of effort.

To take advantage of the new web service, the help desk app will find it useful to have data transfer objects (DTOs) for data binding. You'll use Spring HATEOAS to create those.

IMPLEMENTING DATA TRANSFER OBJECTS USING SPRING HATEOAS

SDR uses Spring HATEOAS behind the scenes to generate the JSON representation for requested resources. Besides the actual payload, Spring HATEOAS supports links, which you would expect because that's a big part of the HATEOAS idea.

> **NOTE** At the time of this writing, Spring HATEOAS has not been officially released, so there may be material changes by the time you read this.

On the client side, you want those links because SDR uses URIs for resource identification (again, no surprise) rather than the database IDs.

You can use Spring HATEOAS to implement the desired DTOs on the client side. Because both individual users and collections of users have associated link information, you need separate DTOs for each. The next listing shows the resource for an individual user, which the help desk refers to as a *customer* rather than a user because the help desk's users are support representatives.

Listing 13.5   CustomerResource.java: HATEOAS-oriented DTO

```
package com.springinpractice.ch13.helpdesk.integration.resource;

import org.springframework.hateoas.ResourceSupport;

public class CustomerResource extends ResourceSupport {
    public String username;
    public String firstName;
    public String lastName;
    public String email;

    public String getUsername() { return username; }

    public String getFirstName() { return firstName; }

    public String getLastName() { return lastName; }

    public String getEmail() { return email; }

    public String getFirstNameLastName() {
        return firstName + " " + lastName;
    }
}
```

❶ Extends ResourceSupport

❷ Public fields

❸ Getters for JSPs

You extend the Spring HATEOAS `ResourceSupport` class at ❶, which does the heavy linking around generating links and such. The DTO's fields need to be public in order for data binding to work, so that's what you do at ❷. JSPs don't know how to deal with public fields, so you create getters at ❸.

Here's the same thing for a collection of customers.

Listing 13.6   CustomerResources.java: another HATEOAS-oriented DTO

```
package com.springinpractice.ch13.helpdesk.integration.resource;

import org.springframework.hateoas.Resources;

public class CustomerResources extends Resources<CustomerResource> { }
```

Here all you do is extend the `Resources` class, specifying `CustomerResource` as the type argument. The last step is to implement a client for the help desk app.

IMPLEMENTING A RESTFUL CLIENT USING RESTTEMPLATE

In integration parlance, a *gateway* provides an application with an interface to the underlying messaging infrastructure without the application realizing it. Because you want the help desk to be able to get customer data from the portal without realizing that it's making a web service call, you'll create a `PortalGateway` interface for the help desk to use, along with an implementation that makes the web service call using `RestTemplate` and your resource DTOs. Here's the interface.

Listing 13.7   `PortalGateway`: **hides messaging details from the help desk app**

```
package com.springinpractice.ch13.helpdesk.integration.gateway;

import java.util.Collection;
import com.springinpractice.ch13.helpdesk.integration.resource.
        CustomerResource;

public interface PortalGateway {

    CustomerResource findCustomerByUsername(String username);

    Collection<CustomerResource> findCustomersByUsernameIn(
        Collection<String> usernames);
}
```

The following listing contains the implementation.

Listing 13.8   `PortalGatewayImpl`: **uses** `RestTemplate` **to get customer data**

```
package com.springinpractice.ch13.helpdesk.integration.gateway.impl;

import java.util.Collection;
import org.springframework.web.client.RestTemplate;
import com.springinpractice.ch13.helpdesk.integration.gateway.
    PortalGateway;
import com.springinpractice.ch13.helpdesk.integration.resource.
    CustomerResource;
import com.springinpractice.ch13.helpdesk.integration.resource.
    CustomerResources;

public class PortalGatewayImpl implements PortalGateway {        ❶ RestTemplate
    private RestTemplate restTemplate;
    private String baseUrl;                              ❷ API base URL

    public PortalGatewayImpl(RestTemplate restTemplate, String baseUrl) {
        this.restTemplate = restTemplate;
        this.baseUrl = baseUrl;
    }

    @Override
    public CustomerResource findCustomerByUsername(String username) {
        String url = baseUrl +
            "/users/search/find-by-username?username={username}";
        CustomerResources customers = restTemplate
            .getForObject(url, CustomerResources.class, username);
        CustomerResource customer =
            customers.getContent().iterator().next();     ❹ Gets single
        return customer;                                         customer
    }

    @Override
    public Collection<CustomerResource> findCustomersByUsernameIn(
        Collection<String> usernames) {

        StringBuilder builder = new StringBuilder(
            baseUrl + "/users/search/find-by-username-in?");     ❺ Builds
        for (String username : usernames) {                         URL
            builder.append("username=");
```

❸ Gets customers

```
                    builder.append(username);
                    builder.append("&");                Removes trailing ? or &   6
          }
Gets   7  String url = builder.substring(0, builder.length() - 1);
customers CustomerResources customers =
resource     restTemplate.getForObject(url, CustomerResources.class);
          return customers.getContent();                Returns
      }                                                 customers
}                                                    8  collection
```

You use Spring's `RestTemplate` ❶ to invoke the portal's web service API, located at the `baseUrl` ❷. The gateway has two methods, corresponding to the two custom queries you implemented for the web service. The first one returns a single customer, which the help desk app uses to resolve a username to a customer record on a ticket details page. You use the `CustomerResources` ❸ you wrote earlier to get the wrapper container, because Spring Data REST doesn't know that customer usernames are unique. Then you get and return the desired `CustomerResource` ❹.

The second method returns a collection of customers corresponding to a collection of usernames. You use this one for the ticket summary page, because there are a bunch of tickets, each with its own username. You build out the URL from scratch at ❺ because there are arbitrarily many usernames (limited generally by paging the ticket summary). You drop the trailing ? or & at ❻ and then get the `CustomerResources` ❼. Finally you return the underlying collection of `CustomerResource` instances ❽ to match the API signature.

That does it for the help desk app's `PortalGatewayImpl`. Although we didn't cover it here, the portal app has an analogous `TicketGateway` and `TicketGatewayImpl` to handle calls against the ticket service's REST API. Take a look at the sample code for details.

One final note on gateways before we close the recipe. We mentioned earlier that gateways hide the details of the messaging approach from the app. Gateway implementations are part of the integration infrastructure, not part of the app. They allow you to change the integration approach with minimal disruption to the app. You'll do exactly this in the next recipe.

RUNNING THE APPLICATIONS

Again, the URLs are

- *Help desk application*—http://localhost:8080/helpdesk/
- *Portal application*—http://localhost:8180/portal/

Note that you have to run both apps at the same time in order for either to work, because they make web service calls against one another. We'll touch on this in the following discussion.

Discussion

The RESTful web service approach adopted in this recipe decouples the apps from the shared database from recipe 13.2. It also decouples the apps to some extent from one another because now it's possible for the apps to make back-end changes to their respective database schemas without impacting one another.

Unfortunately, the apps are still fairly tightly coupled to one another:

- From a development perspective, they need to coordinate with each other on changes to the web service API.
- From a configuration perspective, both apps have to know each other's location.
- From an operational perspective, both apps have to be up for either app to work properly. So instead of a single point of failure, you have two.

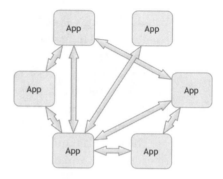

In addition to the coupling that remains, there's another problem. The point-to-point integration approach breaks down because it scales as $O(n^2)$ in the number of applications to be integrated. If you have more than a handful of applications to integrate, you'll need to manage a lot of development, configuration, and operational linkages, as you can see in figure 13.6.

Figure 13.6   The point-to-point integration strategy scales as $O(n^2)$. Managing all the integrations can become unwieldy over time.

Recipe 13.3 shows how you can use a centralized messaging infrastructure to alleviate much of the pain.

13.3   *Implementing a message bus using RabbitMQ and Spring Integration*

PREREQUISITES

Recipe 13.2 Decoupling applications with RESTful web services
Familiarity with the integration domain and Enterprise Integration Patterns in particular; see www.eaipatterns.com/ for background.

KEY TECHNOLOGIES

SI, RabbitMQ, Spring Rabbit, Advanced Message Queuing Protocol (AMQP), Spring AMQP

Background

Recipe 13.2 explored the use of RESTful web service APIs as a way to decouple applications from one another. Web service APIs provide a layer of abstraction over underlying capabilities and data, which makes it easier to change the implementations without impacting clients. In addition, the RESTful approach supports decoupling by reducing the knowledge that clients must have of the services they consume.

We noted in the discussion that improvements are possible in two major areas. First, the apps still have to know quite a bit about each other from development, configuration, and operational perspectives. Second, the point-to-point integration strategy scales poorly as you incorporate different apps. This recipe presents a broker-based approach that addresses both of these issues.

Problem

Further decouple your apps, and address scalability issues associated with the point-to-point integration strategy.

Solution

The solution is to use a centralized message broker to serve as the basis for your application integrations. Message brokers are specifically designed to address application integration, and they solve the previous issues as follows:

- Centralizing the integration infrastructure allows you to transform the $O(n^2)$ integration topology to an $O(n)$ topology. (Each app has a link to the central integration infrastructure.)
- The characteristics of message brokers promote decoupling through the use of asynchronous messaging with guaranteed delivery, well-known messaging endpoints, and so forth.
- Message brokers are generally reliable, runtime-configurable, and horizontally scalable, which helps with availability and performance. This largely mitigates the single-point-of-failure issues associated with being a central location in the architecture.

There are lots of options for message brokers, but you'll use RabbitMQ, which implements the AMQP messaging protocol. The advantage over the Java Message Service (JMS) API is that using a protocol decouples messaging clients from the broker. With JMS, the clients are Java clients (although any given broker has APIs for other platforms as well). With AMQP, any platform with an AMQP client can communicate with the broker, in much the same way that any web browser can communicate with any web server, regardless of the client and server platforms. Because most platforms have AMQP clients,[8] AMQP has outstanding interoperability.

We won't go into the details of RabbitMQ; fortunately it's fast and easy to set up a development instance.[9] You can also consult *RabbitMQ in Action* by Alvaro Videla and Jason J.W. Williams (Manning, 2012) for further information.

Recall from the previous recipe that you used gateways to hide the messaging system from the help desk and portal apps. In this recipe, you'll realize the advantage of that approach: you'll throw away the point-to-point REST implementations entirely and replace them with SI–generated proxies that use AMQP to speak to RabbitMQ.[10]

---

[8] Java, Ruby, Python, .NET, Perl, PHP, C/C++, Erlang, Lisp, Haskell . . .

[9] See www.rabbitmq.com/download.html for download and installation instructions.

[10] Although it would be possible to use Spring Integration to bridge web services to RabbitMQ, here there's no point. There are fewer moving parts if you remove the web services and connect the apps directly to the broker. In other situations it might be desirable to keep the web services around.

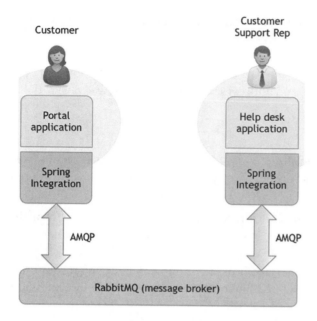

Figure 13.7   Integrating applications via a centralized RabbitMQ message broker. This improves scalability and enhances decoupling.

Figure 13.7 shows the goal for this recipe. Let's get started by looking at message buses and canonical data models.

MESSAGE BUSES AND CANONICAL DATA MODELS

You're going to use RabbitMQ to implement the *message bus* integration pattern. The idea behind this pattern is to provide a central medium through which applications can communicate with one another. Conceptually it's based on the hardware bus concept: plug in, and you're good to go. Hohpe and Woolf define a message bus as follows:

> *A Message Bus is a combination of a Canonical Data Model, a common command set, and a messaging infrastructure to allow different systems to communicate through a shared set of interfaces.*

> —*Enterprise Integration Patterns*, p. 139

You'll use message queues as the shared set of interfaces. But what's missing so far is the so-called canonical data model (CDM), which is the *lingua franca* that allows you to get away with $O(n)$—or even $O(1)$—message translations instead of $O(n^2)$. In the previous recipe, the two apps had their own data representations. Now you'll standardize those by creating a separate Maven module for the CDM.

In real life there are sometimes significant business, technical, and organizational challenges surrounding the creation of a CDM, but you can ignore those because you're lucky enough to have a simple data model. You'll use XML for your format because it's widely supported, although JSON would be another plausible option. Ideally you'd create XML schemas for the model, but you won't mess around with that here. Instead you'll create new DTOs (the Spring HATEOAS DTOs are more oriented around RESTful web services), define XML bindings, and treat the implied schema as constituting your CDM.

You have a handful of message types, but it will suffice to look at one. The following listing shows the DTO for tickets.

Listing 13.9 Ticket.java: DTO for tickets

```java
package com.springinpractice.ch13.cdm;

import java.util.Date;
import javax.xml.bind.annotation.XmlAccessType;
import javax.xml.bind.annotation.XmlAccessorType;
import javax.xml.bind.annotation.XmlRootElement;

@XmlRootElement
@XmlAccessorType(XmlAccessType.PROPERTY)
public class Ticket {
    private TicketCategory category;
    private TicketStatus status;
    private String description;
    private String createdBy;
    private Date dateCreated;

    public TicketCategory getCategory() { return category; }

    public void setCategory(TicketCategory category) {
        this.category = category;
    }

    public TicketStatus getStatus() { return status; }

    public void setStatus(TicketStatus status) { this.status = status; }

    public String getDescription() { return description; }

    public void setDescription(String description) {
        this.description = description;
    }

    public String getCreatedBy() { return createdBy; }

    public void setCreatedBy(String createdBy) {
        this.createdBy = createdBy;
    }

    public Date getDateCreated() { return dateCreated; }

    public void setDateCreated(Date dateCreated) {
        this.dateCreated = dateCreated;
    }
}
```

There isn't much to say here. It's a bare-bones DTO with some JAXB annotations to bind it to the CDM's XML representation.

You have DTOs for other message types as well, such as ticket categories, ticket statuses, customers, and so forth. Consult the sample code for details.

Now that you have a CDM in place along with a central set of DTOs, you need to make an interesting design decision. One possibility is for the existing apps to continue using their existing data models, and perform translations as messages enter and exit the bus. The other is for apps to adopt the central DTOs as their own data model, at least in cases where you have control over that (for example, internally developed apps).

In this case the choice is fairly clear because the Spring HATEOAS DTOs are more oriented to support RESTful web services.[11] The benefit is that you can avoid message translation between apps. You do need to modify the gateways to use the new DTOs, so let's do that now.

REVISITING THE GATEWAY INTERFACES

In recipe 13.3 you worked on the help desk side with the `PortalGateway`. For variety, this time you'll work on the portal side with the `TicketGateway`.

It happens that the gateway interfaces are slightly leaky: through the DTOs they use, they expose the fact that you're designing for Spring Data REST-based implementations with URIs instead of database IDs.[12]

Let's replace the Spring HATEOAS DTOs with the ones you created for the CDM. The next listing presents the new `TicketGateway`.

Listing 13.10   TicketGateway.java: using CDM DTOs

```java
package com.springinpractice.ch13.portal.integration.gateway;

import com.springinpractice.ch13.cdm.Ticket;
import com.springinpractice.ch13.cdm.TicketCategory;
import com.springinpractice.ch13.cdm.TicketCategory.TicketCategoryList;
import com.springinpractice.ch13.cdm.TicketStatus;

public interface TicketGateway {

    void createTicket(Ticket ticket);

    TicketStatus findOpenTicketStatus();

    TicketCategoryList findTicketCategories();

    TicketCategory findTicketCategory(Long id);
}
```

See the sample code for a similar treatment of the `PortalGateway`. Let's turn now to the gateway implementations.

REIMPLEMENTING THE PORTAL'S TICKETGATEWAY USING SPRING INTEGRATION

SI allows you to implement gateways dynamically. SI allows you to build integration logic that allows the portal app to send requests to other systems, and also to respond to requests from other systems. You can of course do the same thing for the help desk

---

[11] HATEOAS is a general architectural principle and might make sense outside the context of RESTful web services. But you don't have any use for links here, so you'll go with plain-vanilla DTOs. Spring HATEOAS may be useful for implementing message-bus CDMs in addition to REST APIs.

[12] See Joel Spolsky, "The Law of Leaky Abstractions," Nov. 11, 2002, http://www.joelonsoftware.com/articles/LeakyAbstractions.html.

app. In effect, you can use SI to create app-specific adapters to the RabbitMQ messaging infrastructure. Review figure 13.7 for a visual.

This section focuses on implementing the portal app's outbound messages; that is, you'll implement the `TicketGateway` interface. To complete the circuit, you also need to handle inbound messages into the help desk, so you'll do that as well.

We won't cover requests originating from the help desk app because the logic involved is more of the same. Refer to the sample code if you want to see it.

Let's start by implementing the integration logic for the portal's self-service ticket creation feature.

IMPLEMENTING SELF-SERVICE TICKET CREATION: PORTAL'S OUTBOUND MESSAGING

`TicketGateway` has a `createTicket(Ticket)` method that serves as a nice starting point because it's fairly straightforward. The idea is that the customer creates a ticket using the portal's web interface, and the portal passes it along to `TicketGateway`. Behind the scenes, the gateway does an asynchronous fire-and-forget at the messaging infrastructure, meaning that the call returns immediately. Later we'll look at the message-handling code on the help desk side, but to keep things simple let's focus on the portal's fire-and-forget code.

Figure 13.8 shows what this looks like using the EIP graphical language. Note that the Spring Tool Suite generates these diagrams automatically from the SI configuration files; click the Integration-Graph tab in the configuration file editor.

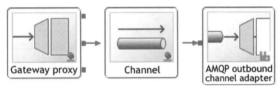

Figure 13.8 A portal-integration pipeline supporting fire-and-forget ticket creation. The channel adapter pushes ticket-creation messages onto the bus.

The pipeline is straightforward. At the front end is a `TicketGateway` proxy that accepts requests from the application through the `TicketGateway` interface. It passes ticket creation requests to the AMQP channel adapter by way of a channel, and the channel adapter in turn pushes the message to a RabbitMQ exchange.[13] In the case of ticket creation, all of this is completely asynchronous, so control returns to the portal immediately after invoking the `Ticket-Gateway`. The following listing shows how to implement the pipeline using SI, Spring Rabbit, and Spring AMQP.

> **Listing 13.11 beans-integration.xml: portal application**

```
<?xml version="1.0" encoding="UTF-8"?>
<beans xmlns="http://www.springframework.org/schema/beans"
    xmlns:context="http://www.springframework.org/schema/context"
    xmlns:int="http://www.springframework.org/schema/integration"
    xmlns:int-amqp="http://www.springframework.org/schema/integration/amqp"
```

---

[13] If the exchange concept is new to you, you might want to take a few minutes to read up on it. See www.rabbitmq.com/tutorials/tutorial-three-java.html for a quick overview.

```
    xmlns:oxm="http://www.springframework.org/schema/oxm"
    xmlns:p="http://www.springframework.org/schema/p"
    xmlns:rabbit="http://www.springframework.org/schema/rabbit"
    xmlns:xsi="http://www.w3.org/2001/XMLSchema-instance"
    xsi:schemaLocation="
        http://www.springframework.org/schema/beans
        http://www.springframework.org/schema/beans/spring-beans-3.1.xsd
        http://www.springframework.org/schema/context
        http://www.springframework.org/schema/context/
                spring-context-3.1.xsd
        http://www.springframework.org/schema/integration
        http://www.springframework.org/schema/integration/
                spring-integration-2.2.xsd
        http://www.springframework.org/schema/integration/amqp
        http://www.springframework.org/schema/integration/amqp/
                spring-integration-amqp-2.2.xsd
        http://www.springframework.org/schema/oxm
        http://www.springframework.org/schema/oxm/spring-oxm-3.1.xsd
        http://www.springframework.org/schema/rabbit
        http://www.springframework.org/schema/rabbit/spring-rabbit-1.1.xsd
        ">

    <context:property-placeholder
        location="classpath:/spring/environment.properties" />          ❶ RabbitMQ
                                                                            connection
                                                                            factory
    <rabbit:connection-factory id="rabbitConnectionFactory"
        username="${rabbitMq.username}"
        password="${rabbitMq.password}" />          Supports dynamic queue creation  ❷

    <rabbit:admin connection-factory="rabbitConnectionFactory" />

    <rabbit:queue name="createTicketRequest.queue" />            ❹ Template for
                                                                   Rabbit messaging
    <rabbit:template id="amqpTemplate"
        connection-factory="rabbitConnectionFactory"
        message-converter="marshallingMessageConverter" />

    <bean id="marshallingMessageConverter"                                  Message
        class="org.springframework.amqp.support.converter.                  converter,
                MarshallingMessageConverter"                             ❺  using OXM
        p:contentType="application/xml">

        <constructor-arg ref="marshaller" />
    </bean>

    <oxm:jaxb2-marshaller id="marshaller">          ❻ OXM configuration
        <oxm:class-to-be-bound
            name="com.springinpractice.ch13.cdm.Ticket" />
        <oxm:class-to-be-bound
            name="com.springinpractice.ch13.cdm.TicketCategory" />
        <oxm:class-to-be-bound
            name="com.springinpractice.ch13.cdm.TicketStatus" />
    </oxm:jaxb2-marshaller>

    <int:gateway
        service-interface="com.springinpractice.ch13.portal.integration.
                gateway.TicketGateway"
        default-request-timeout="2000">                 Gateway dynamic proxy  ❼
```

Queue ❸
for ticket
creation
requests

```
        <int:method name="createTicket"                    ⑧  Per-method routing
            request-channel="createTicketRequestChannel" />
    </int:gateway>
                                                           ⑨  Channel for ticket
    <int:channel id="createTicketRequestChannel" />             creation requests

    <int-amqp:outbound-channel-adapter                        AMQP outbound
        amqp-template="amqpTemplate"                       ⑩ channel adapter
        channel="createTicketRequestChannel"
        routing-key="createTicketRequest.queue" />
</beans>
```

Quite a bit is happening in this listing, but you can break the configuration into three sections: RabbitMQ, Object/XML mapping (OXM), and SI.

First, the RabbitMQ configuration begins with a connection factory ❶. (Note that the default credentials for a fresh RabbitMQ installation are guest/guest.)

You use `<rabbit:admin/>` at ❷ to create queues dynamically if they don't already exist. At ❸ you declare a single queue for ticket-creation requests.

At ❹ you create a template for sending messages to Rabbit. This follows Spring's general practice of template-based communication with external systems and resources. The template uses a `MarshallingMessageConverter` (part of Spring AMQP) at ❺ to perform OXM on message payloads. By default, the Rabbit template uses a `SimpleMessageConverter`, which handles strings, `Serializable` instances, and byte arrays. Because you want an XML-based CDM, you need a converter that performs OXM.

You configure a JAXB marshaller at ❻, declaring the `Ticket`, `TicketCategory`, and `TicketStatus` DTOs for OXM binding. The `MarshallingMessageConverter` uses this marshaller.

The rest of the configuration is for SI. At ❼ you define a dynamic proxy for the `TicketGateway` interface. The configuration at ❽ routes tickets coming in through the `createTicket()` method to the `createTicketRequestChannel` ❾, where the AMQP outbound channel adapter ❿ receives it and pushes it to Rabbit's default exchange, because you haven't specified an exchange explicitly. This channel adapter, like all channel adapters, is unidirectional. (Gateways support bidirectional, request/ reply messaging, but you don't require that here.) The channel adapter's routing key is set to `createTicketRequest.queue`, so the default exchange routes it to that queue. The message payload is ticket XML in the canonical format because the adapter uses the Rabbit template, which in turn uses the `MarshallingMessageConverter`.

That takes care of the fire-and-forget implementation of ticket creation on the portal side. Now there's a message with an XML ticket payload sitting in a request queue on your bus. The next step is to implement integration logic on the help desk side to receive and service the request.

IMPLEMENTING SELF-SERVICE TICKET CREATION: HELP DESK'S INBOUND MESSAGING

This section shows how to process inbound ticket-creation requests. See figure 13.9 for a diagram showing how this works.

Here's what's happening. An inbound channel adapter receives the request from Rabbit, maps the ticket XML to a ticket DTO, and passes it to a processing chain. The

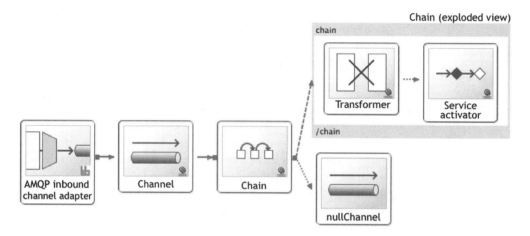

Figure 13.9   A help desk integration pipeline that receives ticket-creation messages from the bus and creates tickets in the help desk database

chain is a wrapper around a linear sequence of endpoints, obviating the need to define explicit channels connecting the chain's members. The chain's first endpoint is a transformer (SI's terminology for EIP's *message translator*) that maps the DTO to a ticket entity. Then a service activator invokes the `TicketRepository.save(TicketEntity)` method to save the ticket to the database. The repository's `save()` method returns the saved instance, but the chain discards that message by dropping it onto the global `nullChannel`, which is essentially a black hole like `/dev/null` in Unix. Here's the configuration for the integration logic just described.

Listing 13.12   beans-integration.xml: help desk application

```
<?xml version="1.0" encoding="UTF-8"?>
<beans xmlns="http://www.springframework.org/schema/beans"
    xmlns:context="http://www.springframework.org/schema/context"
    xmlns:int="http://www.springframework.org/schema/integration"
    xmlns:int-amqp="http://www.springframework.org/schema/integration/amqp"
    xmlns:int-xml="http://www.springframework.org/schema/integration/xml"
    xmlns:oxm="http://www.springframework.org/schema/oxm"
    xmlns:p="http://www.springframework.org/schema/p"
    xmlns:rabbit="http://www.springframework.org/schema/rabbit"
    xmlns:util="http://www.springframework.org/schema/util"
    xmlns:xsi="http://www.w3.org/2001/XMLSchema-instance"
    xsi:schemaLocation="
        http://www.springframework.org/schema/beans
        http://www.springframework.org/schema/beans/spring-beans-3.1.xsd
        http://www.springframework.org/schema/context
        http://www.springframework.org/schema/context/
            spring-context-3.1.xsd
        http://www.springframework.org/schema/integration
        http://www.springframework.org/schema/integration/
            spring-integration-2.2.xsd
```

```
          http://www.springframework.org/schema/integration/amqp
          http://www.springframework.org/schema/integration/amqp/
                  spring-integration-amqp-2.2.xsd
          http://www.springframework.org/schema/integration/xml
          http://www.springframework.org/schema/integration/xml/
                  spring-integration-xml-2.2.xsd
          http://www.springframework.org/schema/oxm
          http://www.springframework.org/schema/oxm/spring-oxm-3.1.xsd
          http://www.springframework.org/schema/rabbit
          http://www.springframework.org/schema/rabbit/spring-rabbit-1.1.xsd
          http://www.springframework.org/schema/util
          http://www.springframework.org/schema/util/spring-util-3.1.xsd
          ">

    <context:property-placeholder
        location="classpath:/spring/environment.properties" />          ❶ RabbitMQ
                                                                            configuration
    <rabbit:connection-factory id="rabbitConnectionFactory"       ◁
        username="${rabbitMq.username}"
        password="${rabbitMq.password}" />

    <rabbit:admin connection-factory="rabbitConnectionFactory" />

    <rabbit:queue name="createTicketRequest.queue" />

    <bean id="marshallingMessageConverter
        class="org.springframework.amqp.support.converter.
                MarshallingMessageConverter"
        p:contentType="application/xml">

        <constructor-arg ref="marshaller" />
    </bean>                                                          ❷ OXM
                                                                       configuration
    <oxm:jaxb2-marshaller id="marshaller">                    ◁
        <oxm:class-to-be-bound
            name="com.springinpractice.ch13.cdm.Ticket" />
        <oxm:class-to-be-bound
            name="com.springinpractice.ch13.cdm.TicketCategory" />
        <oxm:class-to-be-bound
            name="com.springinpractice.ch13.cdm.TicketStatus" />
    </oxm:jaxb2-marshaller>

    <context:component-scan base-package="com.springinpractice.ch13.
            helpdesk.integration.transformer" />

    <int-amqp:inbound-channel-adapter                      ◁        Receives ticket-
        queue-names="createTicketRequest.queue"            ❹       creation requests
        channel="createTicketRequestChannel"
        message-converter="marshallingMessageConverter" />         ❺ Channel for ticket-
                                                                      creation requests
    <int:channel id="createTicketRequestChannel" />        ◁

    <int:chain input-channel="createTicketRequestChannel"      ◁
        output-channel="nullChannel">
        <int:transformer ref="ticketTransformer" method="toEntity" />   Chain with
        <int:service-activator                             ◁            null output
                expression="@ticketRepository.save(payload)" />  ❻       channel
    </int:chain>
</beans>                                                            Service
                                                               ❽ activator
```

❸ Scans for transformers

Transformer ❼

As with the portal application, you have an initial RabbitMQ configuration ❶, although this time you don't need a template. You also have the OXM configuration ❷. This time around you have some transformers (more on that in a minute), so you scan for them at ❸.

In listing 13.11 you had an AMQP outbound channel adapter to send messages to the bus, so here you have the inbound counterpart ❹. The inbound channel adapter receives ticket-creation requests from `createTicketRequest.queue` and passes them via a channel ❺ to a chain ❻.

A *chain* is a linear sequence of endpoints connected by implicit channels. The first endpoint is a transformer ❼ that transforms the ticket DTO into a ticket entity, as you'll see. The second endpoint is a service activator ❽ that saves the ticket entity to the Spring Data JPA ticket repository using a Spring Expression Language (SpEL) expression. The variables `headers` and `payload` are available for use, although you're using only `payload` here. The `payload` is the ticket entity that the transformer generated. The call to `save()` returns the saved entity, but you don't want to return that to the original caller; you send it to the global `nullChannel` ❻, which sends the message to a black hole.

Next is the transformer that converts ticket DTOs into ticket entities.

Listing 13.13   TicketTransformer.java

```java
package com.springinpractice.ch13.helpdesk.integration.transformer;

import javax.inject.Inject;
import org.springframework.stereotype.Component;
import com.springinpractice.ch13.cdm.Ticket;
import com.springinpractice.ch13.helpdesk.model.TicketEntity;

@Component                                                    Transform method ❶
public class TicketTransformer {
    @Inject private TicketCategoryTransformer ticketCategoryTransformer;
    @Inject private TicketStatusTransformer ticketStatusTransformer;

    public TicketEntity toEntity(Ticket ticketDto) {
        TicketEntity ticketEntity = new TicketEntity();
        ticketEntity.setCategory(
            ticketCategoryTransformer.toEntity(ticketDto.getCategory()));

        Customer customerDto = ticketDto.getCreatedBy();
        String username = customerDto.getUsername();          Transformer
        if (username != null) {                               delegation ❷
            ticketEntity.setCustomerUsername(username);
        } else {
            ticketEntity.setCustomerEmail(customerDto.getEmail());
            ticketEntity.setCustomerFullName(getFullName(customerDto));
        }

        ticketEntity.setDateCreated(ticketDto.getDateCreated());
        ticketEntity.setDescription(ticketDto.getDescription());   ❸ Transformer
        ticketEntity.setStatus(                                       delegation
            ticketStatusTransformer.toEntity(ticketDto.getStatus()));
        return ticketEntity;
```

```
    }
    private String getFullName(Customer customerDto) {
        String firstName = customerDto.getFirstName();
        String lastName = customerDto.getLastName();
        if (firstName == null) {
            return (lastName == null ? "[Unknown]" : lastName).trim();
        } else {
            return (lastName == null ?
                firstName : firstName + " " + lastName).trim();
        }
    }
}
```

The transformer is a POJO. Although it's possible to use annotations to configure SI components, you're using XML because I (Willie) find it easier to understand when the SI configuration is in one place.

At ❶ you have a transformer method. This is the `toEntity()` method specified in listing 13.12. When there's a single public method, you don't have to specify the transformer method explicitly in the XML, but you do it anyway. Because the ticket DTO has references to category and status DTOs, you delegate the transformation to corresponding transformers ❷ and ❸.

With that, you have a full asynchronous flow from the portal application through the message bus and ending with the help desk. To be sure, there are some details we've neglected, such as error handling. But the basic integration is in place. The next section looks at a more complex case: implementing synchronous finder methods.

IMPLEMENTING THE FINDERS: PORTAL'S OUTBOUND MESSAGING

Finder methods involve a request/reply communication style, which takes more effort to implement in a messaging environment than the fire-and-forget style does. In this case you'll implement synchronous request/replies, meaning the caller will block until the reply arrives; but note that SI also supports asynchronous request/replies, which are based on a callback mechanism. We won't cover that here, though.

Integration and services: an architectural perspective

You might fairly ask why you would implement synchronous request/reply on top of a fundamentally asynchronous messaging infrastructure. Wouldn't it be simpler to have the caller invoke a web service on the target system?

In many cases it's indeed simpler to make a web service call. You can avoid implementing a bunch of integration patterns on the bus, as well as avoid forcing the request and reply messages to pass through the message bus.

But the arguments for using a bus for asynchronous communications mostly apply even for synchronous communications: (1) client systems can decouple themselves from service-specific locations, message formats, authentication schemes, and so on; and (2) you avoid the aforementioned $O(n^2)$ problem associated with point-to-point messaging.

> **(continued)**
>
> One pro-bus argument that doesn't apply in the case of synchronous messaging is the runtime decoupling argument. In the asynchronous case, it doesn't matter if a message receiver is offline when the sender sends the message, because the messaging system queues the message until the receiver is available. With synchronous communications, the receiver must be available when the sender sends it a request.
>
> We won't settle the issue here, but suffice it to say there's a design decision to consider. The rest of the recipe shows how to implement synchronous messaging without necessarily claiming that it's the right approach for all cases.

You'll add support for three finder methods. Figure 13.10 augments the portal-side pipeline you established in figure 13.8. Originally you had a single path to an AMQP outbound channel adapter. This time you add a couple of new paths to an AMQP outbound gateway.

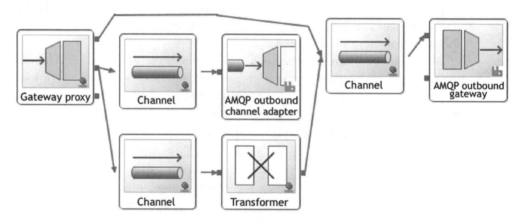

Figure 13.10   The portal's outbound pipeline with support for the `TicketGateway`'s finder methods

Channel adapters and gateways are alike in that they're both interfaces to external systems, but not alike in that channel adapters are unidirectional (fire-and-forget) while gateways support request/reply communications. In this case, the external system is the message bus. The following listing shows how to implement the pipeline in figure 13.10.

Listing 13.14   beans-integration.xml: portal application

```xml
<?xml version="1.0" encoding="UTF-8"?>
<beans ...>                                    Additional queues for finders  ❶

    ... RabbitMQ configuration from listing 13.11, plus the following ...

    <rabbit:queue name="findTicketStatusRequest.queue" />        ◁───┘
    <rabbit:queue name="findTicketCategoriesRequest.queue" />
    <rabbit:queue name="findTicketCategoryRequest.queue" />
```

```
... OXM configuration from listing 13.11, plus the following ...

<oxm:jaxb2-marshaller id="marshaller">                          ◁         Additional
    <oxm:class-to-be-bound                                                DTOs for
        name="com.springinpractice.ch13.cdm.DummyPayload" />    ❷        binding
    <oxm:class-to-be-bound
        name="com.springinpractice.ch13.cdm.Ticket" />
    <oxm:class-to-be-bound
        name="com.springinpractice.ch13.cdm.TicketCategory" />
    <oxm:class-to-be-bound
        name="com.springinpractice.ch13.cdm.
            TicketCategory$TicketCategoryList" />
    <oxm:class-to-be-bound
        name="com.springinpractice.ch13.cdm.TicketCategoryRequest" />
    <oxm:class-to-be-bound
        name="com.springinpractice.ch13.cdm.TicketStatus" />
    <oxm:class-to-be-bound
            name="com.springinpractice.ch13.cdm.TicketStatusRequest" />
</oxm:jaxb2-marshaller>

<int:gateway                                                          ◁
    service-interface="com.springinpractice.ch13.portal.integration.
            gateway.TicketGateway"
    default-request-channel="helpDeskRequestChannel"          Gateway dynamic
    default-request-timeout="2000"                                 proxy  ❸
    default-reply-timeout="2000">

    <int:method name="createTicket"                             ❹  Per-method
        request-channel="createTicketRequestChannel" />            enrichment
    <int:method name="findOpenTicketStatus"              ◁            and routing
        payload-expression="new com.springinpractice.ch13.cdm.
            TicketStatusRequest('open')">
        <int:header name="requestType"
            value="findTicketStatusRequest" />                 ❺  Per-method
    </int:method>                                                  enrichment
    <int:method name="findTicketCategories"              ◁        and routing
        payload-expression="new com.springinpractice.ch13.cdm.
            DummyPayload()">
        <int:header name="requestType"
            value="findTicketCategoriesRequest" />         ❻  Per-method
    </int:method>                                              enrichment
    <int:method name="findTicketCategory"            ◁            and routing
            request-channel="findTicketCategoryRequestChannel">
        <int:header name="requestType"
            value="findTicketCategoryRequest" />
    </int:method>
</int:gateway>

<int:channel id="createTicketRequestChannel" />

<int-amqp:outbound-channel-adapter
    amqp-template="amqpTemplate"
    channel="createTicketRequestChannel"
    routing-key="createTicketRequest.queue" />

<int:channel id="findTicketCategoryRequestChannel" />    ◁━❼  Channel

<int:transformer               ◁━❽  Expression-based transformer
```

```
              input-channel="findTicketCategoryRequestChannel"
              output-channel="helpDeskRequestChannel"
              expression="new com.springinpractice.ch13.cdm.
                     TicketCategoryRequest(payload)" />
      <int:channel id="helpDeskRequestChannel" />
      <int-amqp:outbound-gateway
          amqp-template="amqpTemplate"
          request-channel="helpDeskRequestChannel"
          routing-key-expression="headers['requestType'] + '.queue'"
          mapped-request-headers="requestType" />
</beans>
```

You add three new queues at ❶ to support your new finder methods. At ❷ you add more classes to be bound to the OXM configuration. You'll see why you're adding the dummy payload and special request objects in a moment.

You modify the gateway definition at ❸. You specify that by default all requests coming into the gateway will land on the `helpDeskRequestChannel`. You also set a default reply timeout, expressed in milliseconds, because now you're expecting replies.

On replies: unless you specify an explicit `default-reply-channel` (which you're not doing here), the gateway creates for any given request a temporary, anonymous reply channel, and adds the channel to the request message as a header called `replyChannel`. That way, reply-generating downstream endpoints know where to place the reply.

The first finder method is `findOpenTicketStatus()` ❹. You use a SpEL payload expression to create a `TicketStatusRequest` DTO for the open status. The reason you create a special request DTO is that you need the request to be XML. This is because the AMQP gateway expects an XML reply from the bus (recall your CDM), which it maps to an object via the AMQP template, which in turn uses the `MarshallingMessageConverter`. The template applies the converter to both the request and the reply, so the request needs to be a mappable DTO as opposed to a simple string.

In addition to the SpEL payload, the finder method definition includes a custom `requestType` header (custom in the sense that you invented it). Both SI and RabbitMQ support message headers, but here, the header is an SI header. You'll use this header to route finder requests to the right queue, as you'll see.

At ❺ is the second finder method. This time you get a list containing all ticket categories, which is useful for populating the category drop-down in the new ticket form. There is a small problem, though. By default, SI treats no-arg gateway methods as connecting to pollable (receive-only) channels, as opposed to no-arg request/reply (send-then-receive) channels. To implement a request/reply communication, you need to provide a dummy payload using `payload-expression`. Normally you can pass in a dummy string or a `Date`:

```
payload-expression="new java.util.Date()"
```

But here that doesn't work because you're using `MarshallingMessageConverter`, which expects payloads to be mappable XML. That's why you have the `DummyPayload` class, and you use `payload-expression` to create an instance here. Once again you enrich your message with a `requestType` header for routing purposes.

The third finder retrieves a specific ticket category by ID ⑥. Once again you need to represent the payload ID using XML rather than a `Long`. You'll need a transformer for this. You override the gateway's default request channel with a new channel called `findTicketCategoryRequestChannel` and then pass the message over that channel ⑦ to the transformer at ⑧. Here you take advantage of the transformer's `expression` attribute to wrap the `Long` ID in a mappable request DTO. Finally the message goes to the `helpDeskRequestChannel` ⑨ like the other help desk requests.

The next stop is an AMQP outbound gateway ⑩. You use the AMQP template to do the actual request and reply. Then there are a couple of header-related attributes. First you use `routing-key-expression` to specify a dynamic, message-driven routing key that allows Rabbit's default exchange to route messages to queues. In this case, the expression is a SpEL expression that appends `.queue` to the value of the `requestType` SI header you've been using.

You use `mapped-request-headers` to indicate that you want the SI `requestType` header to appear as an AQMP header as well once the message hits the bus. This is because you'll have further use for this header for routing on the help desk side.

As with the initial gateway, the AMQP outbound gateway generates a reply. Here's how this works behind the scenes. For any given request, the outbound gateway creates a temporary reply queue and sets the AMQP message's `reply_to` property to the queue's name. This tells downstream endpoints where to place the reply when it materializes. Once the reply appears in that queue, the AMQP outbound gateway grabs it and places it on the request message's reply channel. You'll recall from our discussion that the request message maintains a reference to the reply channel as the value of its `replyChannel` header.

IMPLEMENTING THE FINDERS: HELP DESK'S INBOUND MESSAGING

Now the portal sends finder requests to the bus, so the help desk needs to pick those up and service them. The supporting help desk pipeline appears in figure 13.11.

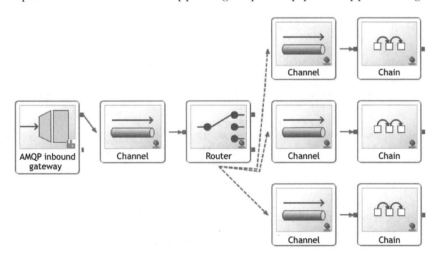

Figure 13.11   The help desk's inbound pipeline to support the `TicketGateway`'s finder methods. Although it's not shown here, each chain contains a service activator followed by a transformer.

This help desk pipeline receives finder requests at an AMQP inbound gateway and forwards them to a router, which uses the requestType header to pass the request to one of three chains. Each chain invokes a finder method on the TicketRepository and uses a transformer to convert the result into a DTO before returning it to the caller. Here's the configuration you use to implement the help desk pipeline.

Listing 13.15   beans-integration.xml: help desk application

```xml
<?xml version="1.0" encoding="UTF-8"?>
<beans ...>

    ... RabbitMQ configuration from listing 13.12, plus the following ...

    <rabbit:queue name="findTicketStatusRequest.queue" />          ◁─┐  Additional
    <rabbit:queue name="findTicketCategoriesRequest.queue" />        │  queues for
    <rabbit:queue name="findTicketCategoryRequest.queue" />        ❶ finders

    ... OXM configuration from listing 13.12, plus the following ...

    <oxm:jaxb2-marshaller id="marshaller">                         ◁─┐  Additional
        <oxm:class-to-be-bound                                       │  DTOs for
            name="com.springinpractice.ch13.cdm.DummyPayload" />   ❷ binding
        <oxm:class-to-be-bound
            name="com.springinpractice.ch13.cdm.Ticket" />
        <oxm:class-to-be-bound
            name="com.springinpractice.ch13.cdm.TicketCategory" />
        <oxm:class-to-be-bound
            name="com.springinpractice.ch13.cdm.
                  TicketCategory$TicketCategoryList" />
        <oxm:class-to-be-bound
            name="com.springinpractice.ch13.cdm.TicketCategoryRequest" />
        <oxm:class-to-be-bound
            name="com.springinpractice.ch13.cdm.TicketStatus" />
        <oxm:class-to-be-bound
            name="com.springinpractice.ch13.cdm.TicketStatusRequest" />
    </oxm:jaxb2-marshaller>

    <context:component-scan base-package="com.springinpractice.ch13.   ◁─┐
            helpdesk.integration.transformer" />
                                                                  Scans for
    ... inbound create ticket pipeline from listing 13.12 ...     transformers ❸

    <int-amqp:inbound-gateway                                    ◁─┐  AMQP inbound
        queue-names="findTicketStatusRequest.queue,               ❹ gateway
                findTicketCategoriesRequest.queue,
                findTicketCategoryRequest.queue"
        request-channel="helpDeskRequestChannel"
        mapped-request-headers="requestType"
        message-converter="marshallingMessageConverter" />
                                                            Routes by message ❺
    <int:channel id="helpDeskRequestChannel" />                header value

    <int:header-value-router input-channel="helpDeskRequestChannel"  ◁─
            header-name="requestType">
        <int:mapping value="findTicketStatusRequest"
            channel="findTicketStatusRequestChannel" />
        <int:mapping value="findTicketCategoriesRequest"
            channel="findTicketCategoriesRequestChannel" />
```

```
        <int:mapping value="findTicketCategoryRequest"
            channel="findTicketCategoryRequestChannel" />
    </int:header-value-router>

    <int:channel id="findTicketStatusRequestChannel" />

    <int:chain input-channel="findTicketStatusRequestChannel">
        <int:service-activator
            expression="@ticketStatusRepository.findByKey(payload.key)" />
        <int:transformer ref="ticketStatusTransformer" method="toDto" />
    </int:chain>

    <int:channel id="findTicketCategoriesRequestChannel" />

    <int:chain input-channel="findTicketCategoriesRequestChannel">
        <int:service-activator
            expression="@ticketCategoryRepository.findAll()" />
        <int:transformer ref="ticketCategoryListTransformer"
            method="toDto" />
    </int:chain>

    <int:channel id="findTicketCategoryRequestChannel" />

    <int:chain input-channel="findTicketCategoryRequestChannel">
        <int:service-activator
            expression="@ticketCategoryRepository.findOne(payload.id)" />
        <int:transformer ref="ticketCategoryTransformer" method="toDto" />
    </int:chain>
</beans>
```

6 Chain to find ticket status

7 Chain to find ticket categories

8 Chain to find single category

As was true with the portal SI configuration, you declare the three queues for finder requests at **1** to ensure that they exist. You also declare the same set of DTOs for OXM at **2** because you'll need to convert back and forth between the bus CDM and Java.

You need a few transformers to convert the entities you find into DTOs, so you scan for them at **3**. The entry point for synchronous messages into the pipeline is the AMQP inbound gateway at **4**. You specify its three feeder queues using the queue-names attribute. Just as you used mapped-request-headers in listing 13.14 to convert the custom SI requestType header into an AMQP header, you use it here to convert the AMQP header back into a custom SI requestType header.

The AMQP inbound gateway supports replies. When the gateway receives a message from a queue, it creates an anonymous reply channel and attaches it to the message using the replyChannel message header. Eventually some downstream component responsible for producing the reply will place the reply in that channel.

The gateway passes requests to a router that uses header values to drive routing **5**. As you've guessed, you're using the requestType header for that. The <mapping> elements provide the routing definitions.

Once the request leaves the router, it goes to one of three chains you've defined, corresponding to the three finder requests. First is a chain for the ticket status requests **6**. The chain has an expression-driven service activator that unpacks the key from the request object (recall that you wrapped the key with a TicketStatusRequest in listing 13.14) and calls the findByKey() method on the TicketStatusRepository. The result is an entity, so you use a transformer to convert the entity back to a DTO for subsequent mapping to the XML-based CDM on the return trip. See the sample code for the transformers, which are similar to the one from listing 13.13.

Because you haven't specified an explicit output channel for the chain, the chain sends the transformer's output to the channel you're storing under the `replyChannel` header. The circuit is now complete: the help desk AMQP inbound gateway receives the reply from the channel and sends it to the specified exchange and queue (as specified by the routing key). The portal AMQP outbound gateway receives the reply from the queue and places it on the `replyChannel`. Finally the initial portal gateway receives the reply and returns it to the caller. The chains at ❼ and ❽ are essentially similar to the one at ❻.

With that, you're done. You now have the plumbing on both the portal and the help desk sides to support both asynchronous and synchronous communications over Rabbit. Although we didn't cover it here, note that the help desk also requests customer information from the portal, using largely the same set of patterns, but in the opposite direction. See the sample code.

Discussion

Over the past three recipes we've shown how to integrate applications in a progressively more decoupled way. Though we've considered only two apps here, the architecture's power becomes more obvious as you place additional apps on the message bus. The number of potential integrations grows quadratically in the number of apps, but the integration complexity increases only linearly.

In this recipe you used RabbitMQ as the bus-implementation technology and SI as a way to implement app-specific bus adapters. But this isn't the only way to use SI. You can use SI itself to implement buses. In the recipes that follow, you'll reposition the help desk's SI pipeline as an application bus in its own right and then add both inbound and outbound email by attaching them to the application bus.

13.4 *Sourcing tickets from an IMAP store*

PREREQUISITES

Recipe 13.3 Implementing a message bus using RabbitMQ and Spring Integration (There's no conceptual dependency on RabbitMQ, but you use the code from recipe 13.3.)

KEY TECHNOLOGIES

SI, JavaMail, IMAP

Background

Email-based support is a common requirement. Although many sites offer a form-based option to better structure the ticket and to avoid email spam, email can be an attractive option because it's so easy to implement: all it requires is an inbox.

In this recipe, imagine that you only recently rolled out the form-based approach from recipe 13.1, but you still want to support a legacy support email address that was your primary ticket source prior to introducing the form. We'll show how to create help desk tickets based on incoming customer email.

Problem

Automatically create help desk tickets based on customer email.

Solution

Building on figure 13.7, figure 13.12 shows what you want to add to the integration landscape in this recipe.

One question you might be asking is why you wouldn't attach inbound email to the RabbitMQ bus instead of attaching it to the help desk's SI adapter. After all, the portal is a ticket source, and you've attached it to the RabbitMQ bus. And in the help desk, you're using SI as an adapter to the RabbitMQ bus, so accepting email from a source other than the bus seems to conflict with this design.

You could certainly do that, but one reason you're not is that you'd need a separate adapter to connect the inbound email channel to RabbitMQ, and that's a complexity you don't currently require. Only the help desk cares about inbound email, and if the help desk isn't available to receive email, then messages sit in the mailbox until the help desk is available again. (In effect, the mailbox functions as a persistent message queue.)

As to the design conflict, the conflict is only apparent. All the help desk sees are the gateway interfaces you happen to have in place; the app doesn't know anything about SI or RabbitMQ. Instead of thinking of the SI pipeline strictly as an adapter to the RabbitMQ bus, you can consider it to be an application bus in a federated bus

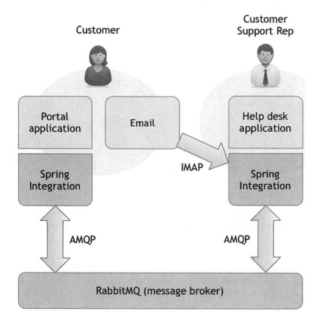

Figure 13.12 You'll add an email-based ticket channel using SI's support for inbound email.

architecture, one that connects the app to external buses and systems.[14] This includes RabbitMQ, but it can also include systems whose use is limited to specific applications, like inbound email in the current instance.

> ### Spring Integration supports multiple integration architectures
> The preceding discussion highlights the fact that SI is flexible; it doesn't prescribe a specific integration architecture. You can have a single central message broker with SI adapters if you like. You can have federated, hierarchical buses. Or you can even use SI itself as a central bus.

Figure 13.13 presents graphically the pipeline you're going to create. It builds on the pipeline from figure 13.9.

You're adding an IMAP inbound channel adapter to receive email messages from an IMAP mailbox. Then you pass the email messages to a transformer, which converts them into ticket DTOs. (The DTOs are the canonical data model for the help desk's application bus.) The transformer drops the DTOs onto the existing `createTicketRequestChannel`, which allows you to take advantage of the downstream chain for saving tickets you created in recipe 13.3, and also to use it as a single location for making changes to the integration logic. You'll see this benefit in action when you add confirmation emails in recipe 13.5.

As before, you use SI to implement the pipeline.

SPRING INTEGRATION CONFIGURATION

Listing 13.16 shows what you need to add to your help desk beans-integration.xml configuration to support the pipeline depicted. *But first, please read the following warning.*

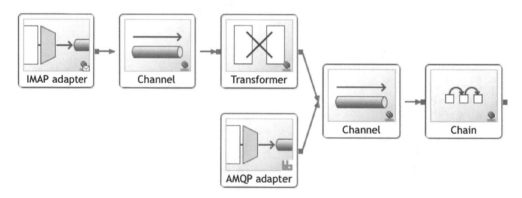

Figure 13.13   You'll augment the inbound pipeline to include support for IMAP messages.

---

[14] For an interesting discussion on bus federation, see Jack van Hoof, "A Federated Service Bus Infrastructure," March 27, 2009, http://mng.bz/Qfx7. Also, *Service Oriented Architecture Demystified: A Pragmatic Approach to SOA for the IT Executive* by Girish Juneja et al. (Intel Press, 2007) draws a related distinction between "big buses" and "little buses."

> **WARNING: listing 13.16 deletes all of your email!**
> The following configuration treats your IMAP mailbox as a message queue. The IMAP channel adapter treats every email in the mailbox as a message to be processed and *deleted*. ***Please use a test email account, not your personal or work account.*** I (Willie) learned this the hard way by stupidly deleting several years of Gmail messages from my personal inbox.

Now that you've read the warning and created a test account, please see the following listing to add support for inbound email.

Listing 13.16 Help desk's beans-integration.xml, with support for inbound email

```xml
<?xml version="1.0" encoding="UTF-8"?>
<beans
    xmlns:int-mail="http://www.springframework.org/schema/integration/mail"

    ... other namespaces ...

    xsi:schemaLocation="
        http://www.springframework.org/schema/integration/mail
        http://www.springframework.org/schema/integration/mail/
            spring-integration-mail-2.2.xsd
        ... other schema locations ... ">

    ... configuration from recipe 13.3 ...

    <int-mail:imap-idle-channel-adapter
        channel="newMailChannel"
        store-uri="${email.store.uri}"
        should-delete-messages="${email.shouldDeleteMessages}" />

    <int:channel id="newMailChannel" />

    <int:transformer input-channel="newMailChannel"
        output-channel="createTicketRequestChannel"
        expression="@ticketTransformer.toDto(payload)" />
</beans>
```

❶ IMAP IDLE channel adapter

❷ Transforms email to DTO

Little is involved here. You have the IMAP inbound channel adapter ❶. This is a special IMAP IDLE adapter, which supports the IMAP IDLE notification mechanism. If your provider doesn't support IMAP IDLE, then you can use a standard IMAP inbound channel adapter with a poller:

```xml
<int-mail:inbound-channel-adapter
    channel="newMailChannel"
    store-uri="${email.store.uri}"
    should-delete-messages="${email.shouldDeleteMessages}">

    <int:poller max-messages-per-poll="3" fixed-rate="30000" />
</int-mail:inbound-channel-adapter>
```

In any event, you specify the IMAP store (mailbox) URI and also tell the channel adapter to go ahead and delete messages from the mailbox after pulling them down.

(See the earlier warning.) Different services will have different URIs. For Gmail, it looks like this:

```
imaps://username:password@imap.gmail.com:993/Inbox
```

Notice the use of IMAPS, which is IMAP over SSL (standard port is 993).[15] Obviously you need to replace `username` and `password` with the actual credentials associated with the account.

After the channel adapter receives an email message, it sends it to a transformer ❷ so that it can be converted into a DTO. You're using the transformer's expression attribute to select the transformation. After that it goes to the `createTicket-RequestChannel`, where the chain from recipe 13.3 receives it and saves it to the `TicketRepository`.

The transformer code is important, so let's look at that.

UPDATING THE TICKETTRANSFORMER

The transformer is an updated version of `TicketTransformer` from listing 13.13. Here's the new version.

Listing 13.17   Updated version of TicketTransformer.java

```java
package com.springinpractice.ch13.helpdesk.integration.transformer;

import java.io.IOException;
import javax.annotation.PostConstruct;
import javax.inject.Inject;
import javax.mail.BodyPart;
import javax.mail.MessagingException;
import javax.mail.internet.InternetAddress;
import javax.mail.internet.MimeMessage;
import javax.mail.internet.MimeMultipart;
import org.springframework.stereotype.Component;
import com.springinpractice.ch13.cdm.Ticket;
import com.springinpractice.ch13.cdm.TicketCategory;
import com.springinpractice.ch13.cdm.TicketStatus;
import com.springinpractice.ch13.helpdesk.model.TicketCategoryEntity;
import com.springinpractice.ch13.helpdesk.model.TicketEntity;
import com.springinpractice.ch13.helpdesk.model.TicketStatusEntity;
import com.springinpractice.ch13.helpdesk.repo.TicketCategoryRepository;
import com.springinpractice.ch13.helpdesk.repo.TicketStatusRepository;

@Component
public class TicketTransformer {
    @Inject private TicketCategoryRepository ticketCategoryRepo;
    @Inject private TicketStatusRepository ticketStatusRepo;
    @Inject private TicketCategoryTransformer ticketCategoryTransformer;
    @Inject private TicketStatusTransformer ticketStatusTransformer;
```

---

[15] If you run into PKIX/certificate trust issues, you may need to import the Gmail IMAP certificate into your truststore. See Willie Wheeler, "Fixing PKIX path building issues when using JavaMail and SMTP," Spring in Practice, http://mng.bz/W4w8. This discussion involves SMTP, but with minor modifications it applies to IMAP as well.

```
    private TicketCategory generalCategoryDto;
    private TicketStatus openStatusDto;

    @PostConstruct                                     ❶ Post-construct
    public void postConstruct() {                         method
        TicketCategoryEntity generalCategoryEntity =
            ticketCategoryRepo.findByKey("general");
        this.generalCategoryDto =
            ticketCategoryTransformer.toDto(generalCategoryEntity);

        TicketStatusEntity openStatusEntity =
            ticketStatusRepo.findByKey("open");
        this.openStatusDto =
            ticketStatusTransformer.toDto(openStatusEntity);
    }

    public TicketEntity toEntity(Ticket ticketDto) {
        ... same as listing 13.13 ...
    }
                                                       ❷ Transforms
    public Ticket toDto(MimeMessage email)                email to DTO
        throws MessagingException, IOException {

        InternetAddress from = (InternetAddress) email.getFrom()[0];
        MimeMultipart content = (MimeMultipart) email.getContent();
        BodyPart body = content.getBodyPart(0);

        Ticket ticketDto = new Ticket();
        ticketDto.setCategory(generalCategoryDto);

        Customer customerDto = new Customer();
        customerDto.setEmail(from.getAddress());
        customerDto.setFirstName(null);
        customerDto.setLastName(from.getPersonal());
        ticketDto.setCreatedBy(customerDto);

        ticketDto.setDateCreated(email.getSentDate());
        ticketDto.setDescription(
            "[" + email.getSubject() + "] " + body.getContent());
        ticketDto.setStatus(openStatusDto);
        return ticketDto;
    }

    ... getFullName() same as listing 13.13 ...
}
```

You use the @PostConstruct annotation ❶ to declare a method for Spring to run after creating and injecting the bean. You use this to preload the General ticket category (the support rep can change it to something more appropriate) and the Open ticket status.

The actual transformation occurs at ❷. The IMAP channel adapter produces a MimeMessage, so you transform that into a DTO so the downstream chain can save it.

That's it for the code and configuration. It's time to try it out.

TRY THE CODE
Choose a test account for your IMAP store, and, if you're using GitHub code, change should-delete-messages from false to true on the IMAP inbound channel adapter.

Then start up the help desk app and send an email to the test account. The channel adapter should see the email, grab it, delete it from the mailbox, and then turn it into a ticket. You can see the ticket by viewing the ticket list in the help desk's UI.

Discussion

In this recipe, you learned that it's easy to add support for inbound email to a Spring-enabled application. This is useful because email is still a popular way to allow users to submit support requests and other communications.

In the following recipe, we'll revisit the topic of confirmation emails, which you saw in chapter 8. This time you'll use SI to send the confirmation email.

13.5   *Send confirmation messages over SMTP*

PREREQUISITES
Recipe 13.4 Sourcing tickets from an IMAP store

KEY TECHNOLOGIES
SI, JavaMail, SMTP

Background

Generally, when users submit support tickets, you want to send them a confirmation message thanking them for their ticket and letting them know when they can expect to hear back from you.

Problem

Send the user a confirmation email when they submit a ticket.

Solution

Figure 13.14 shows the last step in the evolution of your integration environment. This time you're adding support for confirmation emails, which you send by way of SMTP. This is the same as figure 13.1, but it's reproduced here for your convenience.

As it happens, you can add confirmation emails without changing any app code. Recall from recipe 13.4 that you connected the IMAP inbound channel adapter to a chain that your AMQP inbound channel adapter was already using for creating tickets. Because they're both using the same pipeline, you can modify that pipeline a bit to

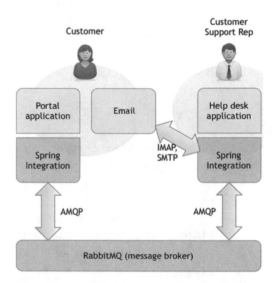

Figure 13.14   Adding outbound SMTP messaging to support confirmation emails

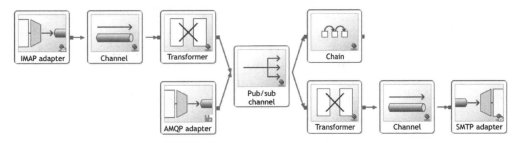

Figure 13.15 Modifying the pipeline to support confirmation emails whenever somebody creates a new ticket. No change to the app is required.

generate confirmation emails, regardless of whether the ticket came from the web form or an email. Figure 13.15 shows how. The following listing shows the required configuration updates.

Listing 13.18 Help desk's beans-integration.xml, with support for confirmation emails

```xml
<?xml version="1.0" encoding="UTF-8"?>
<beans xmlns:jee="http://www.springframework.org/schema/jee"

    ... other namespaces ...

    xsi:schemaLocation="
        http://www.springframework.org/schema/jee
        http://www.springframework.org/schema/jee/spring-jee-3.1.xsd
        ... other schema locations ... ">

    ... configuration from recipe 13.4 ...                            ❶ JavaMail
                                                                         configuration
    <jee:jndi-lookup id="mailSession"
        jndi-name="mail/Sip13HelpDeskMailSession"
        resource-ref="true" />
                                                                      Now a pub/sub ❷
    <bean id="mailSender"                                                   channel
        class="org.springframework.mail.javamail.JavaMailSenderImpl"
        p:session-ref="mailSession" />

    <int:publish-subscribe-channel id="createTicketRequestChannel" />

    <int:transformer input-channel="createTicketRequestChannel"
        output-channel="confirmationEmailChannel"
        expression="@ticketTransformer.toConfirmationEmail(payload)" />

    <int:channel id="confirmationEmailChannel" />            Transforms to
                                                         confirmation email ❸
    <int-mail:outbound-channel-adapter
        channel="confirmationEmailChannel" mail-sender="mailSender" />
</beans>
```

❹ **SMTP channel adapter**

First you have some JavaMail configuration ❶. This is the same as what you saw in recipe 8.2.[16]

---

[16] As before, if you run into PKIX issues, see "Fixing PKIX path building issues when using JavaMail and SMTP," http://mng.bz/W4w8.

You replace the original point-to-point channel ❷ with a publish/subscribe (pub/sub) channel. The difference between them is that a point-to-point channel can have at most one consumer, whereas a pub/sub channel broadcasts messages to any number of consumers. Here you want to continue broadcasting to the chain that saves the ticket, but you want to add a new consumer pipeline to generate confirmation emails.

The start of that new pipeline is the transformer at ❸. It converts ticket DTOs into outbound confirmation emails. Then you pass the emails along to an SMTP outbound channel adapter ❹, which sends the email.

Next you update `TicketTransformer` to support confirmation emails.

Listing 13.19 TicketTransformer.java with a transform method for confirmation emails

```
package com.springinpractice.ch13.helpdesk.integration.transformer;

... imports from listing 13.17 ...

import org.springframework.beans.factory.annotation.Value;
import org.springframework.mail.MailMessage;
import org.springframework.mail.SimpleMailMessage;

@Component
public class TicketTransformer {

    ... dependencies from listing 13.17 ...

    @Value("${confirmation.from}")                              ❶ Injects
    private String confirmationFrom;                               confirmation
                                                                   configuration
    @Value("${confirmation.subject}")
    private String confirmationSubject;

    ... methods from listing 13.17 ...

    public MailMessage toConfirmationEmail(Ticket ticketDto) {  ❷ Transform method
        MailMessage msg = new SimpleMailMessage();

        Customer customerDto = ticketDto.getCreatedBy();        ❹ Sets
        String customerFullName = getFullName(customerDto);        message
        String customerEmail = customerDto.getEmail();             fields
        String to = (customerFullName == null ? customerEmail :
            customerFullName + " <" + customerEmail + ">");
        msg.setTo(to);

        msg.setFrom(confirmationFrom);
        msg.setSubject(confirmationSubject);
        msg.setSentDate(new Date());
                                                                ❺ Sets
        String desc =                                             description
            "Thank you for reporting this issue. We will contact you " +
            "within one business day.\n\nYour message:\n\n" +
            ticketDto.getDescription();
        msg.setText(desc);

        return msg;
    }
}
```
❸ Creates message

You use `@Value` to inject a couple of confirmation email parameters into the transformer at ❶. The new transform method creates a confirmation email from a ticket DTO ❷. You create the email ❸ and then use the DTO to populate its fields ❹. With respect to the description ❺, you hardcode the confirmation message, but in a more realistic example you would use a template engine (Velocity, FreeMarker, and so on) as you did in recipe 8.2.

Start up the help desk and the portal, and try creating messages through the portal, help desk, and email interfaces. In each case you should see the help desk generating confirmation emails. Note that you'll need to change the email addresses of the sample portal users to your own email address if you want to receive confirmation emails when submitting tickets involving those users.

Discussion

This recipe demonstrated that it's possible to perform integrations without having to modify the apps. You added confirmation emails by replacing a point-to-point channel for ticket creation with a pub/sub channel and then attaching both the help desk service and the confirmation email pipeline to that channel.

Where you control the apps being integrated, it makes sense to consider combining integration logic with app modifications to eliminate redundancy and simplify integration. But this isn't always possible. In general, this means you'll want to create abstract representations of key actions on the bus. For example, before the integration, the "create ticket" action lived with the help desk. But to add a confirmation email, you had to represent that action in the bus and treat the actual ticket creation as just one flow out of the bus. Ultimately, the services become implementation details to the logical representations on the bus, which makes the architecture and services easier to evolve over time.

13.6 Summary

Integration is an important concern in enterprise environments, where there is generally a bewildering array of both complementary and competing tools in place, often with little hope of long-term harmonization. Integration *becomes* that harmonization— it provides a practical way to connect tools and their data to support higher-level process and workflow integration.

There are many approaches to integrating systems, and we've covered some of the important ones here. When custom, internally developed code is involved, shared databases can offer a simple and quick way to make data broadly available. But this approach scales poorly, and so the next step is often to use web services to enhance decoupling. Finally, domain- or even enterprise-level, broker-based messaging is a powerful way to increase decoupling even further, which becomes important as the number of collaborators in the integration grows.

Spring provides a number of APIs useful for integration styles, including Spring Data REST, Spring HATEOAS, Spring Integration, and Spring AMQP/Rabbit. Integration is such a large topic that it's impossible for a single chapter to do more than touch on the complexities and solutions involved, but we've tried to offer a starting point to support further exploration and study. *Spring Integration in Action* and *RabbitMQ in Action*, both published by Manning, are great places to start.

In the next and final chapter of the book, you'll learn how to use Spring to create your own framework, complete with annotations and namespace configuration.

Creating a Spring-based "site-up" framework

This final chapter covers the advanced topic of creating your own Spring-based "site-up" framework based on the circuit-breaker pattern, described by Michael Nygard in his book *Release It!* (Pragmatic, 2012). We'll begin a quick overview of the pattern, then jump right into the parts that build your framework. The code for this chapter is at https://github.com/springinpractice/sip14.[1]

---

[1] The code in this chapter is based on the open source Kite framework at https://github.com/springinpractice/kite.

467

Circuit-breaker overview

Integration points between systems are a common source of production issues. It's common for problems with a service to create performance and availability issues for clients. Similarly, it's common for misbehaving clients to create performance and availability issues for the services they use.

Here are possible scenarios:

- *Unavailable service makes client unavailable*—Service unavailability often propagates across an integration point to render the client unavailable.
- *Slow service depletes client resources*—When a service is merely slow rather than unavailable, client threads may spend a lot of time blocking on connections to the service, leaving fewer threads available for servicing new requests.
- *Client responds to slow service by hammering*—Sometimes clients include aggressive retry logic. When a service is having capacity issues, aggressive retrying only exacerbates the situation.

Figure 14.1 illustrates the second and third scenarios.

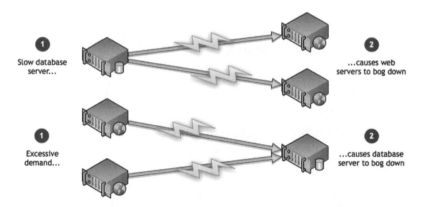

Figure 14.1   Fault propagation from service to client, and from client to service

You can use the circuit-breaker pattern to prevent failure from propagating across integration points. A software circuit breaker is like its counterpart in the physical world in that under normal conditions it's closed, and requests (analogous to current) flow freely across the breaker. But when the request failure rate crosses a given threshold, the breaker transitions into an open state for a period of time, during which client requests fail fast, protecting both the client and the service. See figure 14.2.

Figure 14.2   The breaker on the left is in the closed state, which is normal. Requests flow freely across a closed breaker. The breaker on the right is open. Requests can't flow across an open breaker.

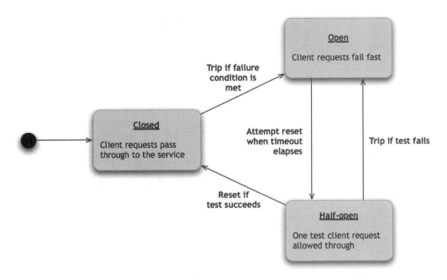

Figure 14.3   Circuit-breaker state diagram showing all three states and their transitions

Besides the closed and open state, circuit breakers have a third state: half-open. The breaker goes half-open after the open state's timeout has elapsed. A half-open breaker allows a single request to pass through. If the request succeeds, the breaker resets itself back to the normal and healthy closed state; otherwise, the breaker trips again (it goes open) and waits for the next timeout. See figure 14.3 for the state diagram.

You typically create multiple breakers, with any given breaker protecting all integrations against a specific resource. For instance, if you have an application that calls two web services and two databases, you might create four distinct breakers. All methods backended by a given resource go through a single breaker.

That's enough background to get you started. The first recipe shows how to implement a breaker using the template pattern.

14.1   Creating a circuit-breaker template and callback

PREREQUISITES
None

KEY TECHNOLOGIES
Template design pattern

Background
The template pattern is a well-known means for factoring out repetitive boilerplate code, especially in cases where repetitive pre- and post-execution code is involved. It works by placing the boilerplate code in a template class and the interesting code in a callback class. The template class has a so-called template method that accepts the callback as an argument and executes the pre-execution boilerplate, the callback,

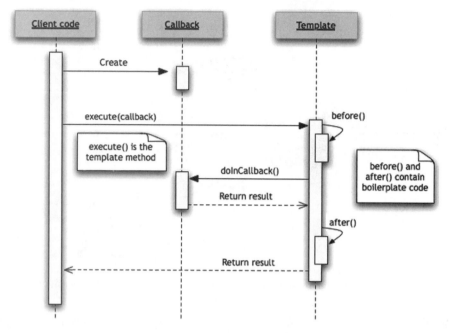

Figure 14.4   Sequence diagram illustrating the template pattern

and, finally, the post-execution boilerplate. Figure 14.4 is a sequence diagram showing how the template pattern works.

In this recipe we'll show how to implement a circuit breaker as a template.

Problem

Create a circuit breaker to protect against integration point faults.

Solution

From the background it should be clear that templates are ready-made for circuit breakers. You'll begin by creating a circuit-breaker template along the lines of `JdbcTemplate`, `HibernateTemplate`, and `TransactionTemplate`.

A LITTLE FRAMEWORK SETUP

Spring makes liberal use of the template pattern, and because it's a perfect fit for circuit breakers, you'll use it too. But first you'll do a little framework setup code. In this chapter all we're worried about is circuit breakers, but we want to make it easy to expand this to other similar components. We call such components *guards* because they guard integration points.[2] So you'll start by defining a simple interface for guards generally.

---

[2]   Other examples are rate-limiting throttles, concurrency throttles, and user blockers.

Listing 14.1 Guard.java: template interface for circuit breakers

```java
package com.springinpractice.ch14.kite;

public interface Guard {

    String getName();

    <T> T execute(GuardCallback<T> action) throws Exception;
}
```

Each guard has a name. That will be useful when you expose the guards through JMX in recipe 14.2. The execute() method reflects the fact that you're implementing a template here. You'll also require a callback interface.

Listing 14.2 GuardCallback.java: corresponding callback interface

```java
package com.springinpractice.ch14.kite;

public interface GuardCallback<T> {

    T doInGuard() throws Exception;
}
```

The next listing provides a simple base implementation.

Listing 14.3 AbstractGuard.java: simple base implementation

```java
package com.springinpractice.ch14.kite;

import org.springframework.beans.factory.BeanNameAware;

public abstract class AbstractGuard implements Guard, BeanNameAware {
    private String name;

    public String getName() { return name; }

    public void setBeanName(String beanName) { this.name = beanName; }
}
```

That's it for the framework code. Now let's use it to create a circuit breaker.

IMPLEMENTING A CIRCUIT BREAKER USING A TEMPLATE

It's time to write the circuit breaker. Because there's a fair amount of code, we'll break it into two pieces. The next listing presents what is mostly breaker configuration code. Listing 14.5 will treat state management.

Listing 14.4 CircuitBreakerTemplate.java, part 1: breaker configuration

```java
package com.springinpractice.ch14.kite.guard;

import java.util.ArrayList;
import java.util.List;
import java.util.concurrent.atomic.AtomicInteger;
import org.slf4j.Logger;
import org.slf4j.LoggerFactory;
import org.springframework.util.Assert;
import com.springinpractice.ch14.kite.AbstractGuard;
```

```
import com.springinpractice.ch14.kite.GuardCallback;
import com.springinpractice.ch14.kite.exception.CircuitOpenException;

public class CircuitBreakerTemplate extends AbstractGuard {          ◄──❶ Template
    private static final long NO_SCHEDULED_RETRY = Long.MAX_VALUE;
    private static Logger log =
        LoggerFactory.getLogger(CircuitBreakerTemplate.class);

    private int exceptionThreshold = 5;                             ◄──┐ Trips when
    private long timeout = 30000L;                                     ❷ threshold reached
    private List<Class<? extends Exception>> handledExceptions =   ◄──┐
        new ArrayList<Class<? extends Exception>>();                   ❹ Exceptions
                                                                         to process
    public CircuitBreakerTemplate() {
        handledExceptions.add(Exception.class);
    }

    public int getExceptionThreshold() {
        return exceptionThreshold;
    }

    public void setExceptionThreshold(int threshold) {
        Assert.isTrue(threshold >= 1, "threshold must be >= 1");
        this.exceptionThreshold = threshold;
    }

    public long getTimeout() { return timeout; }

    public void setTimeout(long timeout) {
        Assert.isTrue(timeout >= 0L, "timeout must be >= 0");
        this.timeout = timeout;
    }

    public List<Class<? extends Exception>> getHandledExceptions() {
        return handledExceptions;
    }

    public void setHandledExceptions(
        List<Class<? extends Exception>> exceptions) {

        Assert.notNull(exceptions, "handledExceptions can't be null");
        this.handledExceptions = exceptions;
    }

    private boolean isHandledException(
        Class<? extends Exception> exceptionClass) {

        for (Class<? extends Exception> handledExceptionClass :
            handledExceptions) {

            if (handledExceptionClass.isAssignableFrom(exceptionClass)) {
                return true;
            }
        }
        return false;
    }

    ... see listing 14.5 for state management ...
}
```

Retries after 30,000 ms ❸

There's a lot happening here. At ❶ you name the class `CircuitBreakerTemplate` to keep with Spring's template-naming convention. The reason you care about the bean name is that circuit breakers are state machines, and they ought to log all state transitions because that's important for monitoring and diagnostic purposes. The name allows you to indicate exactly which breaker underwent a state transition.

There are three important configuration parameters. One is the exception threshold ❷, which specifies how many consecutive exceptions it takes to trip the breaker. You've set the default to five. The next parameter is the timeout ❸, which you've set to 30 seconds. This is how much time must pass before an open breaker tries to reset itself. The list of handled exceptions ❹ indicates which exception classes cause the exception count to increment. This gives you a way to focus attention on exceptions that indicate a problem with the underlying resource.

That concludes the examination of breaker configuration, but you're not done with the breaker yet. The meat of the circuit breaker is the state-management and transition logic.

Listing 14.5 CircuitBreakerTemplate.java, part 2: breaker state

```
...                                                       ❶ Breaker
                                                             states          ❷ Volatile for
public enum State { CLOSED, OPEN, HALF_OPEN };    ←┘                           visibility and
                                                                              performance
private volatile State state = State.CLOSED;      ←
private final AtomicInteger exceptionCount = new AtomicInteger();
private volatile long retryTime = NO_SCHEDULED_RETRY;     ←┐  Volatile for visibility
                                                           ❹  and performance
public State getState() {
    if (state == State.OPEN) {
        if (System.currentTimeMillis() >= retryTime) {    ←❺ Go half-open?
            log.info("Setting circuit breaker half-open: {}",
                getName());
            this.state = State.HALF_OPEN;
        }
    }
    return state;
}

// For testing
void setState(State state) { this.state = state; }
                                                          ❻ Resets
public void reset() {                                        breaker
    log.info("Resetting circuit breaker: {}", getName());
    this.state = State.CLOSED;
    this.exceptionCount.set(0);
}
                                                          ❼ Trips
public void trip() { trip(true); }                           breaker

public void tripWithoutAutoReset() { trip(false); }

private void trip(boolean autoReset) {
    log.warn("Tripping breaker {}, autoReset={}", getName(),
        autoReset);
    this.state = State.OPEN;
```

❸ Supports atomic check/increment

```
        this.retryTime = (autoReset ?
            System.currentTimeMillis() + timeout : NO_SCHEDULED_RETRY);
    }

    public <T> T execute(GuardCallback<T> action) throws Exception {
        final State currState = getState();                           ◁── ⑧ Gets state
        switch (currState) {

        case CLOSED:                                          ◁──┐    Handle
            try {                                                ⑨  closed
                T value = action.doInGuard();
                this.exceptionCount.set(0);
                return value;
            } catch (Exception e) {
                if (isHandledException(e.getClass()) &&
                    exceptionCount.incrementAndGet() >=
                    exceptionThreshold) { trip(); }

                throw e;
            }                                              ⑩  Handle
        case OPEN:                                        ◁──┘  open
            throw new CircuitOpenException();

        case HALF_OPEN:                                ◁──┐   Handle
            try {                                         ⑪  half-open
                T value = action.doInGuard();
                reset();
                return value;
            } catch (Exception e) {
                if (isHandledException(e.getClass())) { trip(); }
                throw e;
            }

        default:
            throw new IllegalStateException("Unknown state: " + currState);
        }
    }

    public int getExceptionCount() { return exceptionCount.get(); }

    public long getRetryTime() { return retryTime; }

    void setExceptionCount(int exceptionCount) {
        this.exceptionCount.set(exceptionCount);
    }
...
```

You use a typesafe enum for the three circuit-breaker states ❶. You have three state variables. First you have the breaker state itself ❷, declared as volatile. Without going into all the gory concurrency details, the idea is that you want threads to see each others' state updates without creating a synchronization bottleneck, which would impact performance negatively. The volatile keyword accomplishes this: it forces reads and writes to the variable to go all the way out to main memory (where they're visible to all threads), but there's no mutex.

For exceptionCount ❸ you also want cross-thread visibility coupled with high performance, but you additionally need an atomic check/increment operation. Although the expression exceptionCount++ looks atomic, when translated down to machine code it actually isn't, and so volatile isn't enough. AtomicInteger provides an atomic, lock-free incrementAndGet() method (which you'll see) that you can use to get the job done.

attemptResetAfter ❹ contains a timestamp indicating when it's OK for the breaker to try to reset itself. Once again you need visibility and performance, but you don't need an atomic check/set operation, so volatile is fine. Note that even though this is a long (64 bits), reads and writes to volatile longs are always atomic.[3]

The getState() method ❺ is interesting because it doesn't return the state. Instead, it uses the opportunity to check whether the breaker needs to transition from the open state to the half-open state. Only after that's done does getState() return the state. Normally, getter methods shouldn't have side-effects like this, but this is arguably a case where it makes sense.

The reset() method ❻ forces the breaker into the closed state and clears out the exception count. The trip() method ❼ is similar, but it forces the breaker into the open state and sets a variable indicating when the breaker gets to attempt a reset.

The execute() method is the heart and soul of the circuit breaker. It starts by getting the current state ❽. Once you have the state, you handle each of the three possibilities in turn. If the breaker is in its closed state (the normal state) ❾, you attempt the action. A successful action clears the exception count and returns the result. Otherwise you increment the counter and trip if there are too many exceptions.

If the breaker is open ❿, you fail fast. This is how the breaker protects both the client and the service: it prevents them from communicating at all.

If the breaker is half-open ⓫, it gets one shot to perform the action. If the action succeeds, then the breaker resets back to its closed state. If the action fails, then the breaker trips again and must wait for the next timeout period to elapse before trying again. See figure 14.5 for a sequence diagram illustrating how it works.

For completeness, here's the CircuitOpenException class you reference from the template:

```
package com.springinpractice.ch14.kite.exception;

public class CircuitOpenException extends GuardException {
    public CircuitOpenException() { super("Circuit open"); }
}
```

And here's its superclass:

```
package com.springinpractice.ch14.kite.exception;

import org.springframework.core.NestedRuntimeException;

public class GuardException extends NestedRuntimeException {
    public GuardException(String msg) { super(msg); }
}
```

---

[3] See "Non-atomic Treatment of double and long," http://mng.bz/oaUo.

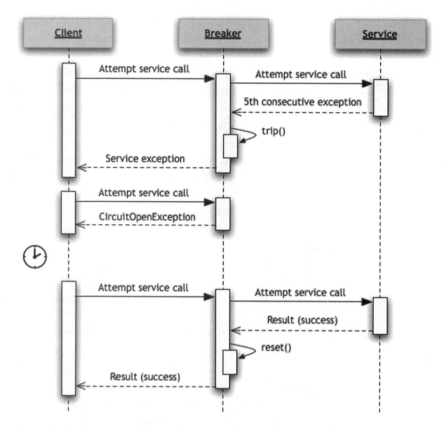

Figure 14.5   Sequence diagram illustrating tripping, timeouts, and resetting

With modest effort, you've created a component that promises to reduce the production support responsibilities. To accomplish that goal, you need to see how to apply the circuit breaker to the integration points.

CREATING A SAMPLE INTEGRATION POINT

To demo the circuit breaker, you'll need to create a toy transactional app with a client and a flaky service. The app will be a simple home page that calls a message service to get a couple of different kinds of messages: a message of the day (MotD) and a list of important messages. After the app gets the messages from the service, it displays them to the end user on the home page. Figure 14.6 shows the key elements of the app's bean-dependency diagram.

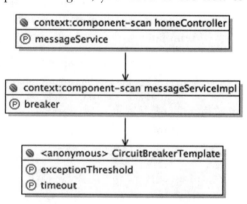

Figure 14.6   HomeController uses a circuit breaker to protect against problems with the MessageService.

Because you want to see the circuit breaker trip every now and then, you need a way to make the message service slightly flaky. The following listing is the component you'll use to do that.

Listing 14.6   Flakinator.java: component to make the service flaky

```java
package com.springinpractice.ch14.kite.sample.service.impl;

import org.springframework.stereotype.Component;

@Component
public class Flakinator {
    private volatile boolean up = true;

    public void simulateFlakiness() {
        if (up) {
            if (Math.random() < 0.05) {
                this.up = false;
            }
        } else {
            if (Math.random() < 0.2) {
                this.up = true;
            }
        }

        if (!up) {
            throw new RuntimeException("Oops, service down");
        }
    }
}
```

The idea is that if the service is up, there's a fairly low probability (0.05) that any given call to `simulateFlakiness()` will transition the service to a down state. If the service is down, the probability that it goes back up with any given call is somewhat low (0.2).

In the next listing you have the simple `Message` class that you'll use for the message of the day and the important messages.

Listing 14.7   Message.java: simple message object

```java
package com.springinpractice.ch14.kite.sample.model;

public class Message {
    private String htmlText;

    public String getHtmlText() { return htmlText; }

    public void setHtmlText(String htmlText) { this.htmlText = htmlText; }
}
```

Here's the interface for the message service.

Listing 14.8   MessageService.java: simple message service interface

```java
package com.springinpractice.ch14.kite.sample.service;

import java.util.List;
```

```
import com.springinpractice.ch14.kite.sample.model.Message;

public interface MessageService {

    Message getMotd();

    List<Message> getImportantMessages();
}
```

Now things get more interesting. This is the message service implementation: it shows how to use the CircuitBreakerTemplate class.

Listing 14.9   MessageServiceImpl.java: simple message service implementation

```
package com.springinpractice.ch14.kite.sample.service.impl;

import java.util.ArrayList;
import java.util.List;
import javax.inject.Inject;
import org.springframework.stereotype.Service;
import com.springinpractice.ch14.kite.GuardCallback;
import com.springinpractice.ch14.kite.guard.CircuitBreakerTemplate;
import com.springinpractice.ch14.kite.sample.model.Message;
import com.springinpractice.ch14.kite.sample.service.MessageService;

@Service
public class MessageServiceImpl implements MessageService {       ❶ Injects breaker
    @Inject private CircuitBreakerTemplate breaker;
    @Inject private Flakinator flakinator;                        ❷ Injects flakiness

    public Message getMotd() {
        try {
            return breaker.execute(new GuardCallback<Message>() {
                public Message doInGuard() throws Exception {
                    return doGetMotd();
                }
            });
        } catch (Exception e) {
            throw new RuntimeException(e);
        }
    }
                                                     ❹ Protects important messages
    private Message doGetMotd() {
        flakinator.simulateFlakiness();
        return createMessage("<p>Welcome to Aggro's Towne!</p>");
    }

    public List<Message> getImportantMessages() {
        try {
            return breaker.execute(new GuardCallback<List<Message>>() {
                public List<Message> doInGuard() throws Exception {
                    return doGetImportantMessages();
                }
            });
        } catch (Exception e) {
            throw new RuntimeException(e);
        }
    }
```

❸ **Protects MotD with breaker**

```
        private List<Message> doGetImportantMessages() {
            flakinator.simulateFlakiness();
            List<Message> messages = new ArrayList<Message>();
            messages.add(createMessage("<p>Important message 1</p>"));
            messages.add(createMessage("<p>Important message 2</p>"));
            messages.add(createMessage("<p>Important message 3</p>"));
            return messages;
        }

        private Message createMessage(String htmlText) {
            Message message = new Message();
            message.setHtmlText(htmlText);
            return message;
        }
    }
```

You inject the breaker ❶ and the flakiness-generator ❷. At ❸ you wrap the breaker around a method that gets the MotD. The breaker decides whether to invoke the callback based on the breaker's internal state. You apply the same approach at ❹ when getting the important messages.

Next is the controller that calls the message service.

Listing 14.10 HomeController.java: home-page controller

```
package com.springinpractice.ch14.kite.sample.web;

import javax.inject.Inject;
import org.slf4j.Logger;
import org.slf4j.LoggerFactory;
import org.springframework.stereotype.Controller;
import org.springframework.ui.Model;
import org.springframework.web.bind.annotation.RequestMapping;
import org.springframework.web.bind.annotation.RequestMethod;
import com.springinpractice.ch14.kite.sample.service.MessageService;

@Controller
public class HomeController {
    private static final Logger log =
        LoggerFactory.getLogger(HomeController.class);

    @Inject private MessageService messageService;

    @RequestMapping(value = "", method = RequestMethod.GET)
    public String getHome(Model model) {
        loadMotd(model);
        loadImportantMessages(model);
        return "home";
    }

    private void loadMotd(Model model) {
        try {                                                      ◄── ❶ Paranoia
            model.addAttribute("motd", messageService.getMotd());
        } catch (Exception e) {
            log.error("Unable to load MOTD");
        }
    }
```

```
    private void loadImportantMessages(Model model) {
        try {
            model.addAttribute("importantMessages",
                messageService.getImportantMessages());
        } catch (Exception e) {
            log.error("Unable to load important messages");
        }
    }
}
```

⊲── ❷ **More paranoia**

Because you want to be able to handle message-service failures gracefully, the Home-
Controller implementation is paranoid: it calls both getMotd() ❶ and getImpor-
tantMessages() ❷ in separate try/catch blocks. This avoids failure propagation.

You carry this paranoia over to home.jsp.

Listing 14.11   home.jsp: home-page view

```
<!DOCTYPE html>

<%@ taglib prefix="c" uri="http://java.sun.com/jsp/jstl/core" %>

<c:url var="loginUrl" value="/login" />
<c:url var="logoutUrl" value="/j_spring_security_logout" />

<html lang="en">
    <head>
        <title>Aggro's Towne BBS</title>
    </head>
    <body>
        <header>
            <h1>Aggro's Towne BBS</h1>
        </header>

        <section>
            <header>
                <h2>Message of the day</h2>
            </header>
            <c:choose>
                <c:when test="${not empty motd}">
                    <c:out value="${motd.htmlText}" escapeXml="false" />
                </c:when>
                <c:otherwise>
                    <p>[Message unavailable]</p>
                </c:otherwise>
            </c:choose>
        </section>
        <section>
            <header>
                <h2>Important messages</h2>
            </header>
            <c:choose>
                <%-- Empty means no messages; null means no service --%>
                <c:when test="${importantMessages != null}">
                    <c:forEach var="message" items="${importantMessages}">
                        <div style="margin:20px 0">
                            <c:out value="${message.htmlText}"
```

Still more paranoia

Paranoia is good

```
                    escapeXml="false" />
                </div>
            </c:forEach>
        </c:when>
        <c:otherwise>
            <p>[Important messages unavailable]</p>
        </c:otherwise>
        </c:choose>
    </section>
    </body>
</html>
```

As promised, home.jsp adopts defensive coding practices to ensure that the page remains available even if messages aren't.

The final step is to take care of the app configuration.

CONFIGURING THE CIRCUIT BREAKER

You have a handful of configuration files to create to make the app work. The beans-service.xml, beans-web.xml, and web.xml files are all fairly nondescript; they just set up the web app. They're in the code download if you want to see them. The beans-kite.xml file, however, contains the breaker definition.

Listing 14.12 beans-kite.xml: circuit-breaker configuration

```
<?xml version="1.0" encoding="UTF-8"?>
<beans xmlns="http://www.springframework.org/schema/beans"
    xmlns:p="http://www.springframework.org/schema/p"
    xmlns:xsi="http://www.w3.org/2001/XMLSchema-instance"
    xsi:schemaLocation="
        http://www.springframework.org/schema/beans
        http://www.springframework.org/schema/beans/spring-beans-3.1.xsd">

    <bean class="com.springinpractice.ch14.kite.guard.
            CircuitBreakerTemplate"
        p:exceptionThreshold="4"
        p:timeout="30000" />
</beans>
```

Notice that you've overridden the default exception threshold (5) with a new value (4).

Even though the app has only one breaker, an app that uses multiple resources might have a breaker for each one.

Let's run the app.

RUNNING THE APP

Go to the top-level project folder and type

```
mvn -e clean install
```

to install the project to your local repository, and then go to the `sample` module and type

```
mvn -e clean jetty:run
```

Once the server starts up, point your browser to http://localhost:8080/sip/.

You should see a simple Aggro's Towne BBS home page.[4] If you refresh the page several times, you should notice that periodically one or the other message is unavailable. This reflects the flakiness of the underlying service. Occasional flakiness won't cause the breaker to trip, but ongoing flakiness (four consecutive exceptions, per the configuration) will. It may take a little patience before you see a trip. If you like, hold down the reload/refresh key for your browser until the messages become unavailable. On the console you should see that the circuit goes open.

Discussion

Templates are a convenient way to avoid repeating boilerplate code everywhere, such as boilerplate code to apply circuit-breaker logic. Template methods have the additional benefit of being flexible, as you can place whatever code you like inside the callback method.

But a downside of templates is that they're invasive. Recipes 14.3 and 14.5 present declarative techniques (AOP and annotations, respectively) for installing circuit breakers, with the benefit that they're much less invasive.

Before we get to those, let's plug a gap in the current implementation: there isn't any way to control the breaker from a management console. That's the subject of recipe 14.2.

14.2   *Exposing the circuit breaker as a JMX MBean*

PREREQUISITES

Recipe 14.1 Creating a circuit-breaker template and callback

KEY TECHNOLOGIES

JMX, Spring JMX support, Java VisualVM

Background

For various reasons, it's sensible to provide a means by which your Network Operations Center or other operational staff can modify breaker timeouts and manually trip and reset circuit breakers through a management console. You might be trying to troubleshoot a production incident, or you might want to relieve pressure on a database. This recipe shows how to expose the circuit breaker as a JMX MBean so you can manage it through a JMX-enabled management console.

Problem

Expose `CircuitBreakerTemplate` as a JMX MBean.

Solution

Spring makes it easy to accomplish the goal. The first step is to add Spring JMX annotations to some of the classes. The following listing shows the modification required on the `AbstractGuard` class.

---

[4] Willie wrote a bulletin board system (BBS) called Aggro's Towne when he was a kid, and this is his way of honoring its memory.

Listing 14.13 Updating AbstractGuard.java for JMX

```
package com.springinpractice.ch14.kite;

import org.springframework.beans.factory.BeanNameAware;
import org.springframework.jmx.export.annotation.ManagedAttribute;

public abstract class AbstractGuard implements Guard, BeanNameAware {
    private String name;

    @ManagedAttribute(description = "Guard name")
    public String getName() { return name; }

    public void setBeanName(String beanName) { this.name = beanName; }
}
```

We'll consider the meaning of the @ManagedAttribute annotation momentarily. But first, here's the modification required for CircuitBreakerTemplate.

Listing 14.14 Updating CircuitBreakerTemplate.java for JMX

```
package com.springinpractice.ch14.kite.guard;

... various imports ...                                          Spring JMX imports ❶

import org.springframework.jmx.export.annotation.ManagedAttribute;
import org.springframework.jmx.export.annotation.ManagedOperation;
import org.springframework.jmx.export.annotation.ManagedResource;

@ManagedResource                                                 Managed ❷
public class CircuitBreakerTemplate extends AbstractGuard {       resource

    ... State enum, various fields, various methods ...

    @ManagedAttribute(                                           Managed ❸
        description = "Breaker trips when threshold is reached")  attribute
    public int getExceptionThreshold() { ... }

    @ManagedAttribute(
        description = "Breaker trips when threshold is reached",
        defaultValue = "5")
    public void setExceptionThreshold(int threshold) { ... }

    @ManagedAttribute(
        description = "Delay in ms before open breaker goes half-open")
    public long getTimeout() { ... }

    @ManagedAttribute(
        description = "Delay in ms before open breaker goes half-open",
        defaultValue = "30000")
    public void setTimeout(long timeout) { ... }

    @ManagedAttribute(
        description = "Breaker state (closed, open, half-open)")
    public State getState() { ... }

    @ManagedAttribute(
        description = "Number of exceptions since last reset")
    public int getExceptionCount() { ... }

    @ManagedAttribute(
```

```
                description = "Breaker will retry circuit at or after this time")
    public long getRetryTime() { ... }

    @ManagedOperation(description = "Resets the breaker")        ◄——  Managed
    public void reset() { ... }                                   ❹   operation

    @ManagedOperation(
        description = "Trips the breaker, auto-resetting after timeout")
    public void trip() { ... }

    @ManagedOperation(
        description = "Trips the breaker without auto-resetting")
    public void tripWithoutAutoReset() { ... }
```

At ❶ you import the various Spring JMX annotations you'll use. Then you annotate
the breaker with @ManagedResource ❷ to indicate that you want all breaker instances
to be MBeans. At ❸ and elsewhere you annotate various properties with @ManagedAt-
tribute, which allows you to view and set the property values through the JMX console. Annotating a getter allows you to view the values, and annotating a setter allows
you to edit the values. Finally, you annotate reset(), trip(), and tripWithoutAu-
toReset() ❹ with @ManagedOperation to indicate that you want to be able to call
them through the JMX console. You set descriptions on the managed attributes and
operations as well, to assist the console operator; the descriptions are typically displayed alongside the attributes and operations in the console.[5]

   You'll also need to update the beans-kite.xml configuration to include the context
namespace, along with a <context:mbean-export> tag.

Listing 14.15   Updating beans-kite.xml for JMX

```
<?xml version="1.0" encoding="UTF-8"?>
<beans xmlns="http://www.springframework.org/schema/beans"
    xmlns:p="http://www.springframework.org/schema/p"
    xmlns:xsi="http://www.w3.org/2001/XMLSchema-instance"
    xmlns:context="http://www.springframework.org/schema/context"
    xsi:schemaLocation="
        http://www.springframework.org/schema/beans
        http://www.springframework.org/schema/beans/spring-beans-3.1.xsd
        http://www.springframework.org/schema/context
        http://www.springframework.org/schema/context/
                spring-context-3.1.xsd">                              ❶  MBean
                                                                         exporter
    <context:mbean-export />
                                                  ❷  Breaker ID
    <bean id="messageServiceBreaker"
        class="com.springinpractice.ch14.kite.guard.CircuitBreakerTemplate"
        p:exceptionThreshold="4"
        p:timeout="30000" />
</beans>
```

---

[5] In addition to the annotations described here, there are @ManagedOperationParameter and
  @ManagedOperationParameters annotations. Moreover, the annotations support various elements that we
  aren't using here. Consult the Spring Framework Reference Documentation for more information.

The `<context:mbean-export>` tag ❶ tells Spring to register any MBeans with whatever MBean server happens to be running. In this case, the Maven POM includes the Jetty plug-in, so the configuration causes Spring to register the MBeans with Jetty's MBean server.[6] You add an ID to the breaker ❷ so that it appears with the same ID in the JMX console.

Those are the mods you need. Now let's start the app and use JMX to manage it.

RUNNING THE APP

Start the app in Jetty as follows:

```
mvn -Djava.rmi.server.hostname=127.0.0.1
        -Dcom.sun.management.jmxremote.authenticate=false
        -Dcom.sun.management.jmxremote.ssl=false
        jetty:run
```

You start it in this manner so you can connect a local JMX console (like JConsole or Java VisualVM) to it. For production use, you'd normally want a remote JMX console to avoid competing with the app for resources. (If you want to use the console that way, please consult the JMX documentation.[7]) For development, it's fine to use a local console with authentication and SSL disabled.

With the app started, you're ready to launch the JMX console.

USING A JMX CONSOLE TO CONNECT TO THE APP

The Java platform comes with a couple of JMX console options. One is JConsole, which is a no-frills console that gets the JMX job done.[8] Another option, available since JDK 6 update 7, is Java VisualVM. Although it isn't *primarily* a JMX console—indeed, the JMX console is a plug-in that you have to install yourself—it supports JMX just fine.[9]

To run Java VisualVM, do the following:

1 Make sure you have JDK 6 update 7 or higher.
2 Type `jvisualvm` on the command line. It should be on your path if your other JDK executables are.
3 If you haven't already done so, go to Tools > Plugins and install the VisualVM-MBeans plug-in. This will cause an MBeans tab to appear as an option, as shown in figure 14.7.
4 Start the sample app. It should appear in the Java VisualVM Applications pane.
5 Find your app's JMX connection, and double-click it. If you're running Java VisualVM on the same host where you're running your app, it should be under the Local node of the Applications hierarchy. If you're running the app using

---

[6] When running in a container without an MBean server, or when running in standalone mode, you'll need to create your own MBean server. Consult the Spring Framework Reference Documentation for details.
[7] See "Monitoring and Management Using JMX," http://mng.bz/Pgz6.
[8] See http://mng.bz/mFs0 for information on using JConsole, should you decide to use that.
[9] See Mick Knutson, "Java Profiling with VisualVM," DZone, http://mng.bz/iZFR, for more information on Java VisualVM.

the Maven Jetty plug-in, the correct child node should be `org.codehaus` `.classworlds.Launcher`.

6   Click the MBeans tab.

7   Drill down to `com.springinpractice.ch14.kite.guard > CircuitBreaker-` `Template > messageServiceBreaker`.

8   Click the Attributes, Operations, Notifications, and Metadata tabs, and explore. In particular, try tripping and resetting the breaker using the Operations tab, and notice how it impacts the service when the browser requests it.

Figure 14.7 shows the JMX attribute view in Java VisualVM. The attributes appearing here correspond to the properties annotated by `@ManagedAttribute` in listing 14.14.

In addition to the attribute view, there are views for exposing operations (like `trip()` and `reset()`) as well as notifications and management metadata. See figure 14.8.

JMX provides an important capability for your operations staff. We consider it critical because it's generally wise to support manual overrides. If, for example, some malicious user were to figure out how to induce exceptions on a service, then they could potentially create a denial of service using the breaker. With JMX, you could potentially increase the exception threshold or even (in an extended implementation) disable tripping altogether.

Discussion

JMX support is probably a must-have for any reasonable circuit-breaker implementation, and now you have it. And you can use the breaker as is to positive effect.

But we noted in the recipe 14.1 discussion that the template-based implementation is invasive. You had to inject a circuit breaker into `HomeController`, and you also

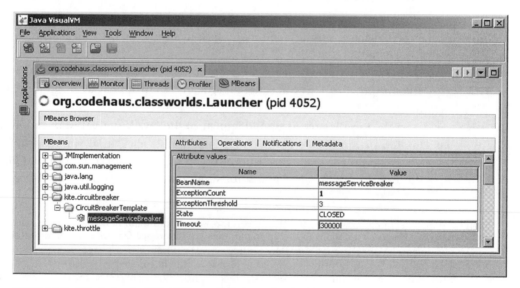

Figure 14.7   Viewing and editing MBean attributes using Java VisualVM

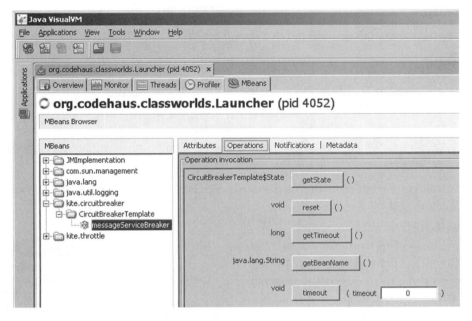

Figure 14.8   Management operations via Java VisualVM

had to directly modify `loadMotd()` and `loadImportantMessages()`. Although this
works, it's less than desirable, partly due to the invasiveness, and partly because it's
potentially a lot of work to modify every integration point in an application.

With Spring, other options are of course available. In recipe 14.3 we'll explore the
first such option, which is AOP-based configuration.

14.3   *Supporting AOP-based configuration*

PREREQUISITES
Recipe 14.1 Creating a circuit-breaker template and callback

KEY TECHNOLOGIES
Spring AOP

Background

One of the demerits of the template-based approach to circuit breakers is that you
have to change the client code to effect the protection. Although it's useful to have
the template option available, it's also highly desirable to have a means by which you
can install breakers without changing application code. This recipe shows how to do
that with Spring AOP.

Of necessity, we assume a basic working knowledge of Spring AOP. Please see chapter 4 of *Spring in Action*, 3rd ed. by Craig Walls (Manning, 2011) for more information.

Problem

Support declarative installation of circuit breakers.

Solution

As just discussed, you'll put together some code to support declarative, AOP-based configuration. You proceed in three steps:

  1 Implement AOP advice as an interceptor.
  2 Revert the client code to remove the programmatic template references.
  3 Update the Spring configuration.

You begin by building the circuit-breaker advice using the template you've already created.

IMPLEMENTING BREAKER ADVICE

In recipe 14.1 you created the CircuitBreakerTemplate class. Although the primary use case is the programmatic creation of circuit breakers by the library's users, you can use it to develop further framework code. Specifically, you'll use it to implement interceptor-based advice using Spring AOP. See figure 14.9.

That's the idea. The following listing shows how to do it.

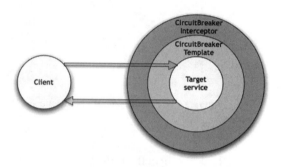

Figure 14.9   Interceptor-based advice using the breaker template

---

Listing 14.16   GuardListInterceptor.java advice implementation

```java
package com.springinpractice.ch14.kite.interceptor;

import java.lang.reflect.Method;
import java.util.Collections;
import java.util.LinkedList;
import java.util.List;
import org.aopalliance.intercept.MethodInterceptor;
import org.aopalliance.intercept.MethodInvocation;
import org.slf4j.Logger;
import org.slf4j.LoggerFactory;
import com.springinpractice.ch14.kite.Guard;
import com.springinpractice.ch14.kite.GuardCallback;

public class GuardListInterceptor implements MethodInterceptor {
    private static final Logger log =
        LoggerFactory.getLogger(GuardListInterceptor.class);

    private GuardListSource source;

    public GuardListSource getSource() { return source; }

    public void setSource(GuardListSource source) { this.source = source; }
```

Implements MethodInterceptor ❶

Guard list source ❷

```
public Object invoke(final MethodInvocation invocation)          Invokes
    throws Throwable {                                       ③ method

    List<Guard> guards = getGuards(invocation);

    if (guards == null || guards.isEmpty()) {                    No guards
        log.debug("Executing method {} without guards",     ⑤ case
            invocation.getMethod().getName());
        return invocation.proceed();                             Guards case ⑥
    }

    LinkedList<Guard> guardStack = new LinkedList<Guard>(guards);
    Collections.reverse(guardStack);

    Guard lastGuard = guardStack.pop();
    Interceptor interceptor =
        new LastInterceptor(lastGuard, invocation);

    while (!guardStack.isEmpty()) {
        Guard guard = guardStack.pop();
        interceptor = new NotLastInterceptor(guard, interceptor);
    }

    return interceptor.invoke();
}

private List<Guard> getGuards(MethodInvocation invocation) {     Class can  ⑦
    Method method = invocation.getMethod();                      be null
    Object thisObj = invocation.getThis();
    Class<?> clazz = (thisObj != null ? thisObj.getClass() : null);
    return source.getGuards(method, clazz);
}                                                                Gets guards
                                                            ⑧ from source
private static interface Interceptor {
    Object invoke() throws Throwable;
}

private static class NotLastInterceptor implements Interceptor {
    private Guard guard;
    private Interceptor interceptor;

    public NotLastInterceptor(Guard guard, Interceptor interceptor) {
        this.guard = guard;
        this.interceptor = interceptor;
    }

    public Object invoke() throws Throwable {
        return guard.execute(new GuardCallback<Object>() {

            public Object doInGuard() throws Exception {
                try {
                    log.debug("Entered guard: {}", guard.getName());
                    return interceptor.invoke();
                } catch (Exception e) {
                    throw e;
                } catch (Error e) {
                    throw e;
                } catch (Throwable t) {
                    throw new RuntimeException(t);
                } finally {
```

Gets guards ④

```
                            log.debug("Exiting guard: {}", guard.getName());
                        }
                    }
                });
            }
        }

        private static class LastInterceptor implements Interceptor {
            private Guard guard;
            private MethodInvocation invocation;

            public LastInterceptor(Guard guard, MethodInvocation invocation) {
                this.guard = guard;
                this.invocation = invocation;
            }

            public Object invoke() throws Throwable {
                return guard.execute(new GuardCallback<Object>() {

                    public Object doInGuard() throws Exception {
                        try {
                            log.debug("Entered guard: {}", guard.getName());
                            log.debug("Executing target method: {}",
                                invocation.getMethod().getName());
                            return invocation.proceed();
                        } catch (Exception e) {
                            throw e;
                        } catch (Error e) {
                            throw e;
                        } catch (Throwable t) {
                            throw new RuntimeException(t);
                        } finally {
                            log.debug("Exiting guard: {}", guard.getName());
                        }
                    }
                });
            }
        }
    }
}
```

Recall from recipe 14.1 that you're treating breakers more generically as guards. This makes it easier to extend the framework to handle other components, such as rate limiters.[10] Because it's possible to apply multiple guards to an integration point (for example, you might want a breaker and a rate limiter at some integration point), you deal with guard lists here instead of dealing with single breakers or even single guards.

In Spring AOP, you use interceptors to implement AOP advice ❶. You'll use Guard-ListInterceptor to apply guard lists at specified pointcuts.

You get guard lists from a GuardListSource ❷. You'll see more in a minute.

The invoke() method ❸ does the advising. The high-level logic is to get the relevant guard list ❹ and then process it according to two cases. First, if there aren't any guards ❺, proceed with the method invocation. Otherwise, there are guards ❻, so

---

[10] See https://github.com/springinpractice/kite for examples.

you have to apply them. You do that by wrapping the guards with individual interceptors and invoking them in reverse order.

Getting a little into the details, the GuardListSource interface requires that you
provide a method and an optional class so the GuardListSource can determine the
guard list. (The reason is that when you get to annotation-based configuration in recipe 14.5, you'll want to look up the guard list using an annotation on the method.)
You obtain the method and class from the MethodInvocation in the manner shown
❼. If the method is static, then thisObj will be null, and the source object will get the
guard list based on the method alone. At ❽ you get the breaker from the source, passing in the method and class you just derived.

The following listing presents the GuardListSource interface.

Listing 14.17 GuardListSource.java: interface for obtaining guard lists

```
package com.springinpractice.ch14.kite.interceptor;

import java.lang.reflect.Method;
import java.util.List;
import com.springinpractice.ch14.kite.Guard;

public interface GuardListSource {

    List<Guard> getGuards(Method method, Class<?> targetClass);
}
```

The initial implementation returns a specified guard list every time, independently of
the supplied method and class, as shown next.

Listing 14.18 DefaultGuardListSource.java: returns a configured guard list

```
package com.springinpractice.ch14.kite.interceptor;

import java.lang.reflect.Method;
import java.util.List;
import com.springinpractice.ch14.kite.Guard;

public class DefaultGuardListSource implements GuardListSource {
    private List<Guard> guards;

    public List<Guard> getGuards() { return guards; }

    public void setGuards(List<Guard> guards) { this.guards = guards; }

    public List<Guard> getGuards(Method method, Class<?> targetClass) {
        return guards;
    }
}
```

The new interceptor and its support classes allow you to forgo the programmatic circuit-breaker approach you adopted in recipe 14.1. You'll have to undo some of the
work you did earlier and update the configuration as well.

REVERTING THE CLIENT CODE

Recall from recipe 14.1 that you had to inject a circuit breaker into MessageServiceImpl
and also add template client code to getMotd() and getImportantMessages(). You

don't want that anymore because you're now using a noninvasive AOP-based approach. Here's the new `MessageServiceImpl` class.

Listing 14.19   MessageServiceImpl.java, revised to remove breaker code

```java
package com.springinpractice.ch14.kite.sample.service.impl;

import java.util.ArrayList;
import java.util.List;
import javax.inject.Inject;
import org.springframework.stereotype.Service;
import com.springinpractice.ch14.kite.sample.model.Message;
import com.springinpractice.ch14.kite.sample.service.MessageService;

@Service
public class MessageServiceImpl implements MessageService {
    @Inject private Flakinator flakinator;

    public Message getMotd() {
        flakinator.simulateFlakiness();
        return createMessage("<p>Welcome to Aggro's Towne!</p>");
    }

    public List<Message> getImportantMessages() {
        flakinator.simulateFlakiness();
        List<Message> messages = new ArrayList<Message>();
        messages.add(createMessage("<p>Important message 1</p>"));
        messages.add(createMessage("<p>Important message 2</p>"));
        messages.add(createMessage("<p>Important message 3</p>"));
        return messages;
    }

    private Message createMessage(String htmlText) {
        Message message = new Message();
        message.setHtmlText(htmlText);
        return message;
    }
}
```

As you can see by comparing listings 14.19 and 14.9, the new service is much cleaner. You've evicted the circuit-breaker code from the service.

Finally you need to update beans-kite.xml to include the AOP-namespace configuration.

UPDATING THE SPRING CONFIGURATION

In the next listing you supplement the breaker definition from recipe 14.1 with the Spring AOP interceptor bean (representing *advice* in general AOP parlance), a point-cut, and a Spring AOP advisor (representing an *aspect* in general AOP parlance).

Listing 14.20   beans-kite.xml, illustrating declarative configuration via AOP

```xml
<?xml version="1.0" encoding="UTF-8"?>
<beans xmlns="http://www.springframework.org/schema/beans"
    xmlns:aop="http://www.springframework.org/schema/aop"
    xmlns:context="http://www.springframework.org/schema/context"
```
❶ Declares AOP namespace

```
xmlns:p="http://www.springframework.org/schema/p"
xmlns:xsi="http://www.w3.org/2001/XMLSchema-instance"
xsi:schemaLocation="
    http://www.springframework.org/schema/aop
    http://www.springframework.org/schema/aop/spring-aop-3.1.xsd
    http://www.springframework.org/schema/beans
    http://www.springframework.org/schema/beans/spring-beans-3.1.xsd
    http://www.springframework.org/schema/context
    http://www.springframework.org/schema/context/
            spring-context-3.1.xsd">

<context:mbean-export />

<bean id="messageServiceBreaker"
    class="com.springinpractice.ch14.kite.guard.CircuitBreakerTemplate"
    p:exceptionThreshold="4"
    p:timeout="30000" />                                    ❷ Advice
                                                              definition
<bean id="messageServiceGuardListAdvice"
    class="com.springinpractice.ch14.kite.interceptor.
            GuardListInterceptor">
    <property name="source">
        <bean class="com.springinpractice.ch14.kite.interceptor.
                DefaultGuardListSource">
            <property name="guards">
                <list>
                    <ref bean="messageServiceBreaker" />
                </list>
            </property>
        </bean>
    </property>
</bean>
                                        ❸ AOP
                                          configuration    ❹ Pointcut
<aop:config>                                                 definition
    <aop:pointcut id="messageServicePointcut"
        expression="execution(* com.springinpractice.ch14.kite.sample.
            service.impl.MessageServiceImpl.*(..))" />
    <aop:advisor advice-ref="messageServiceGuardListAdvice"
            pointcut-ref="messageServicePointcut" />
                                                          Aspect
</aop:config>                                             definition ❺
</beans>
```

Because you're using AOP, you begin by declaring the AOP namespace ❶ and schema location. The breaker definition is the same as before, but now you add a definition for the associated AOP advice, implemented as an interceptor ❷. The interceptor definition includes a `DefaultGuardListSource` inner bean that makes the breaker available to the interceptor. The breaker is the guard list's single guard.

Next is the AOP configuration section ❸. You want to define an aspect, which requires both a pointcut and an advice. You already have the advice, so you need to create the pointcut and the aspect. You define the pointcut at ❹ using the AspectJ pointcut notation. Then you define the aspect at ❺, which in Spring AOP you implement as an advisor, using both the advice and pointcut you created earlier.

Using `<aop:config>` will trigger Spring AOP's powerful autoproxying mechanism. We won't get into all the details because you don't need them here, but essentially autoproxying automatically wraps beans with proxies as required by the aspects you define explicitly. In this case, autoproxying proxies the message service and applies the guard-list aspect to the `MessageServiceImpl` methods specified in the pointcut.

Discussion

AOP-based circuit breakers are much more convenient and noninvasive than the purely programmatic approach you saw in recipe 14.1. It's much easier to specify a pointcut than it is to go into a bunch of client methods and wrap then in callbacks and template methods.

In the next two recipes, you'll learn how you can simplify configuration even further. You'll do this in two phases. In recipe 14.4 you'll create a custom namespace that allows you to use a domain-specific language to simplify the circuit-breaker configuration. After that you'll learn in recipe 14.5 how to add support for annotation-driven configuration, which tidies up the Spring configuration considerably.

14.4   *Supporting custom namespaces*

PREREQUISITES
Recipe 14.1 Creating a circuit-breaker template and callback
Recipe 14.2 Support AOP-based configuration

KEY TECHNOLOGIES
Spring configuration infrastructure, XML Schema (XSD), Spring tool schema, Spring-Source Tool Suite

Background

Although Spring's bean-based configuration provides a general configuration mechanism, it doesn't always rank high on the usability front. Configuring DAOs, service beans, and web MVC controllers is intuitive enough, but when you start adding infrastructural beans to the mix, it can quickly become unclear exactly which beans you need to place on the context in order to get everything to work.

Spring 2 introduced custom namespaces, which essentially allow you to accomplish configuration tasks without having to know exactly which beans are required behind the scenes. Each custom namespace defines a domain-specific language (DSL) that simplifies configuration. Moreover, the custom namespace tags hide the details of what's going on, such as the fact that multiple beans were created, or that various post-processors were created, and so forth. This can make configuration easier.

Problem

Simplify configuration by supporting DSL-based configuration.

Solution

This recipe explains how to create your own custom namespace in Spring. For now we'll keep it simple: you'll create tags for the circuit breaker from recipe 14.1 and the interceptor (advice) from recipe 14.3. These new tags correspond almost exactly to the raw bean definitions, which may leave you wondering what the point is. Never fear; recipe 14.5 will expand the custom namespace in such a way that the benefit becomes clear.

Essentially, you need to do three things to implement a custom namespace:

- Create an XML schema for the DSL
- Create a `NamespaceHandler` and `BeanDefinitionParsers` to parse the custom tags
- Tell Spring where to find the schema and the `NamespaceHandler`

You'll begin with the third of those items.

CREATING THE POINTER FILES

To tell Spring where to find the XSD file, you create a properties file called spring.schemas inside the kite module's src/main/resources/META-INF:

```
http\://springinpractice.com/schema/kite/kite-1.0.xsd=
        com/springinpractice/ch14/kite/config/kite-1.0.xsd
http\://springinpractice.com/schema/kite/kite.xsd=
        com/springinpractice/ch14/kite/config/kite-1.0.xsd
```

This is mapping an XSD file to two different URIs. The file is a classpath resource and is thus relative to the kite module's src/main/resources. You have to escape the colon character because the colon is a permissible key/value separator in Java properties files, even though it seems as though everybody always uses the equals sign.

Besides the pointer to the XSD file, you also need a pointer to the `NamespaceHandler`. Once again you use a properties file. This time it's spring.handlers, also located in the src/main/resources/META-INF folder of the kite module:

```
http\://springinpractice.com/schema/kite=
        com.springinpractice.ch14.kite.config.xml.KiteNamespaceHandler
```

With the two properties files you just created, Spring knows where to find the schema and `NamespaceHandler` for the custom schema. You of course need to create those things, so let's do that now.

CREATING AN XML SCHEMA

For 13 chapters, you've managed to avoid creating an XML Schema, but the time has come. The following listing shows the first half of the XSD that specifies the DSL.

Listing 14.21   kite-1.0.xsd: DSL definition

```xml
<?xml version="1.0" encoding="UTF-8" standalone="no"?>
<xsd:schema xmlns="http://springinpractice.com/schema/kite"
    xmlns:xsd="http://www.w3.org/2001/XMLSchema"
    xmlns:beans="http://www.springframework.org/schema/beans"
    xmlns:tool="http://www.springframework.org/schema/tool"
    targetNamespace="http://springinpractice.com/schema/kite"
    elementFormDefault="qualified"
    attributeFormDefault="unqualified">
```

① Declares beans namespace

② Declares tool namespace

```
<xsd:import namespace="http://www.springframework.org/schema/beans"
    schemaLocation="http://www.springframework.org/schema/beans/
            spring-beans-3.1.xsd"/>
<xsd:import namespace="http://www.springframework.org/schema/tool"
    schemaLocation="http://www.springframework.org/schema/tool/
            spring-tool-3.1.xsd"/>
<xsd:element name="circuit-breaker">                         Circuit-breaker
    <xsd:annotation>                                      ③ definition
        <xsd:appinfo>
            <tool:annotation>
                <tool:exports type="com.springinpractice.ch14.kite.
                        guard.CircuitBreakerTemplate" />
            </tool:annotation>                           Spring IDE
        </xsd:appinfo>                                    integration  ④
    </xsd:annotation>
    <xsd:complexType>                                     ⑤ Sets base
        <xsd:complexContent>                                   type
            <xsd:extension base="beans:identifiedType">
                <xsd:attribute name="exceptionThreshold"
                    type="xsd:integer" />
                <xsd:attribute name="timeout" type="xsd:long" />
            </xsd:extension>
        </xsd:complexContent>                             Defines attributes  ⑥
    </xsd:complexType>
</xsd:element>

... guard list advice definition (see below) ...

</xsd:schema>
```

You're looking at some schema setup along with a circuit-breaker element definition. In the setup, two of the namespaces you declare are Spring's beans ❶ and tool ❷ namespaces. You import both. You'll see why in a moment.

At ❸ you begin the definition of the new circuit-breaker custom tag you want to create. You use an XSD annotation to embed a tool annotation ❹ that indicates to tools—like SpringSource Tool Suite—that this element creates a CircuitBreakerTemplate bean. Tools can do whatever they like with that information.[11]

You need to define attributes for the new tag. You don't have to define the id attribute explicitly because you declare the element to have the beans:identifiedType base type ❺, which automatically provides an id attribute of type xsd:ID.[12] After that, you define a couple of attributes ❻ corresponding to CircuitBreakerTemplate properties.

In addition to defining a custom tag for the circuit breaker, you want one for the guard list advice.

---

[11] Spring IDE, as of version 2.3.1, doesn't seem to do much with it other than display it as a tooltip when you hover over the circuit-breaker node in the bean-dependency graph. Note that to make the node show up at all, you'll need to go (in Eclipse 3.5) to Window > Preferences > Spring > Beans Support and select the Display Infrastructure Beans check box.

[12] You can see this in the beans XSD: www.springframework.org/schema/beans/spring-beans-3.1.xsd.

Listing 14.22   kite-1.0.xsd, continued, with guard list advice definition

```xml
<?xml version="1.0" encoding="UTF-8" standalone="no"?>
<xsd:schema ...>

    ...

    <xsd:element name="guard-list-advice">                      ❶ Advice
        <xsd:annotation>                                          definition
            <xsd:appinfo>
                <tool:annotation>                              Tool integration ❷
                    <tool:exports type="com.springinpractice.ch14.kite.
                            interceptor.GuardListInterceptor" />
                </tool:annotation>
            </xsd:appinfo>
        </xsd:annotation>
        <xsd:complexType>
            <xsd:complexContent>                               Guards reference ❸
                <xsd:extension base="beans:identifiedType">
                    <xsd:attribute name="guards" type="xsd:string"
                        use="required">
                        <xsd:annotation>                       ❹ Tool
                            <xsd:appinfo>                         annotation
                                <tool:annotation kind="ref">
                                    <tool:expected-type         Expected
                                        type="java.util.List" /> ❺ type
                                </tool:annotation>
                            </xsd:appinfo>
                        </xsd:annotation>
                    </xsd:attribute>
                </xsd:extension>
            </xsd:complexContent>
        </xsd:complexType>
    </xsd:element>
</xsd:schema>
```

Here you're defining the schema for guard list advice ❶, which behind the scenes you've implemented as a Spring AOP interceptor. As before, you use the tool namespace to indicate the bean class associated with this custom tag ❷.

The advice definition is fairly similar to the circuit-breaker definition, but notice at ❸ that you're defining a guards attribute even though the GuardListInterceptor doesn't itself have a guards property. (You may recall from the previous recipe that the interceptor has a GuardListSource that it uses to get a breaker. It's the Default-GuardListSource that has a guards property.) The idea is that when a user creates an advice using this custom tag, you want to wrap the referenced guards with a Default-GuardListSource automatically so the user doesn't have to do it. You'll learn how to pull that off in the next subsection, but for now it's enough to notice that you can define the element in whatever way you think will be most convenient for the user, which is the main point of a DSL.

In addition to telling tools about the beans that specific tags generate, you can also provide information about custom tag attributes. Here you have hints to provide about the guards attribute. One hint is <tool:annotation kind="ref">, which indicates that this attribute is a bean reference ❹. Another hint is that the expected type for this reference is `com.springinpractice.ch14.kite.interceptor.GuardListInterceptor` ❺. Taken together, SpringSource Tool Suite uses these to offer content assistance, hyperlink navigation, hover information, and validation.

You've now defined the DSL in XSD form. But you still need a way to parse the DSL into Spring beans. That's where the `NamespaceHandler` and `BeanDefinitionParsers` come into play.

CREATING A NAMESPACEHANDLER AND BEANDEFINITIONPARSERS

The entry point for custom namespaces is the namespace handler. This is where you register different bean-definition parsers that convert XML bean definitions into actual beans on the context. A namespace handler will include a registration for each custom tag you define. You create a `KiteNamespaceHandler` class that extends `NamespaceHandlerSupport`, which in turn implements `NamespaceHandler`.

Listing 14.23   KiteNamespaceHandler.java: entry point into the DSL

```
package com.springinpractice.ch14.kite.config.xml;
                                                              Extends        ❶
import org.slf4j.Logger;                             NamespaceHandlerSupport
import org.slf4j.LoggerFactory;
import org.springframework.beans.factory.xml.NamespaceHandlerSupport;

public class KiteNamespaceHandler extends NamespaceHandlerSupport {
    private static Logger log =
        LoggerFactory.getLogger(KiteNamespaceHandler.class);      ❷  Overrides
                                                                     init()
    public void init() {
        log.info("Initializing KiteNamespaceHandler");
        registerBeanDefinitionParser(
            "annotation-config", new AnnotationConfigParser());   ❸  Registers
        registerBeanDefinitionParser(                                advice
            "guard-list-advice", new GuardListAdviceParser());       parser
        registerBeanDefinitionParser(
            "circuit-breaker", new CircuitBreakerParser());   ❹  Registers
    }                                                            breaker parser
}
```

You extend `NamespaceHandlerSupport` to facilitate handler implementation ❶. To keep the superclass happy, you implement `init()` ❷. The support class gives you a means by which to register bean-definition parsers (for top-level tags) and bean-definition decorators (for custom nested tags). In this case you have only two registrations, both for parsers: one for `guard-list-advice` ❸ and one for `circuit-breaker` ❹. In a more full-fledged framework there could be many more, but here it's just two for the moment.

To finish the namespace handler, you'll need to create the two parsers you referenced from `KiteNamespaceHandler`. Spring provides some helpful base implementations for implementing parser classes. Table 14.1 offers high-level guidance on the best `BeanDefinitionParser` base class to use in a given situation.

The first parser will be `CircuitBreakerParser`, and it's a parser for the `circuit-breaker` tag. Because you're only creating a single `CircuitBreakerTemplate` bean,

Table 14.1 `BeanDefinitionParser` base implementations

Base class	Description
`AbstractSimpleBeanDefinitionParser`	Easiest implementation to extend. Appropriate when the tag's attribute names exactly match the bean's property names.
`AbstractSingleBeanDefinitionParser`	Appropriate when the tag corresponds to a single bean, but the tag's attribute names don't exactly match the bean's property names.
`AbstractBeanDefinitionParser`	Appropriate when the tag needs to create more than one bean. Takes more work to implement, but it's more flexible than the other implementations.

and because the tag attributes precisely match the bean properties, you can avail yourself of the `AbstractSimpleBeanDefinitionParser` base class.

Listing 14.24 CircuitBreakerParser.java: parses the breaker DSL into breakers

```
package com.springinpractice.ch14.kite.config.xml;

import org.springframework.beans.factory.xml.
        AbstractSimpleBeanDefinitionParser;
import org.w3c.dom.Element;
import com.springinpractice.ch14.kite.guard.CircuitBreakerTemplate;

class CircuitBreakerParser extends AbstractSimpleBeanDefinitionParser {

    protected Class<?> getBeanClass(Element elem) {
        return CircuitBreakerTemplate.class;
    }
}
```

All you have to do is tell Spring which class has the matching properties, so that's exactly what `getBeanClass()` does. Also note that you define the class as having package-private visibility. That's a best practice, because `KiteNamespaceHandler` is the façade into the custom namespace-handling capability, and nobody other than `KiteNamespaceHandler` needs to use or even see `CircuitBreakerParser`.

The second parser is `GuardListAdviceParser`. Again you're creating a single bean, this time a `GuardListInterceptor`. Here you'll need to get slightly more sophisticated (and we do mean *slightly*) because the XSD has a `guards` attribute whereas the actual interceptor class has a `source` property. The approach is similar to the `AbstractSimpleBeanDefinitionParser` approach, except that this time you need to build a `DefaultGuardListSource` around the guard list name in the DSL.

Listing 14.25 GuardListAdviceParser.java

```
package com.springinpractice.ch14.kite.config.xml;

import org.springframework.beans.factory.config.BeanDefinition;
import org.springframework.beans.factory.config.RuntimeBeanReference;
```

```
import org.springframework.beans.factory.support.BeanDefinitionBuilder;
import org.springframework.beans.factory.support.RootBeanDefinition;
import org.springframework.beans.factory.xml.
        AbstractSingleBeanDefinitionParser;
import org.w3c.dom.Element;
import com.springinpractice.ch14.kite.interceptor.DefaultGuardListSource;
import com.springinpractice.ch14.kite.interceptor.GuardListInterceptor;

class GuardListAdviceParser extends AbstractSingleBeanDefinitionParser {

    protected Class<?> getBeanClass(Element elem) {
        return GuardListInterceptor.class;
    }

    protected void doParse(Element elem, BeanDefinitionBuilder builder) {
        builder.setRole(BeanDefinition.ROLE_INFRASTRUCTURE);

        RootBeanDefinition srcDef =
            new RootBeanDefinition(DefaultGuardListSource.class);
        srcDef.setSource(elem);
        srcDef.setRole(BeanDefinition.ROLE_INFRASTRUCTURE);
        srcDef.getPropertyValues().add("guards",
            new RuntimeBeanReference(elem.getAttribute("guards")));
        builder.addPropertyValue("source", srcDef);
    }
}
```

Figure 14.10 presents a class diagram showing the relationship between the parsers you just implemented and the framework base classes that Spring provides.

Now you'll update the sample app to use the guard framework enhancements.

UPDATING THE SAMPLE APP

You'll update the sample app as follows. In beans-kite.xml, you need to declare the namespace and its schema location, and you'll replace the CircuitBreakerTemplate and GuardListInterceptor bean definitions with the custom tags you just created. While you're at it, let's make the new namespace the default namespace for this

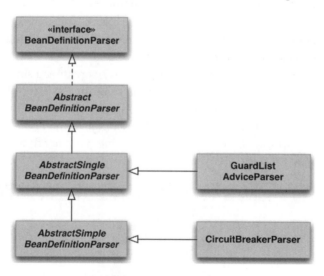

Figure 14.10 BeanDefinition-Parser **hierarchy and the parsers**

configuration file, because most of the configuration will eventually be custom namespace configuration. The following listing displays the result.

Listing 14.26   Namespace-based beans-kite.xml configuration

```
<?xml version="1.0" encoding="UTF-8"?>
<beans:beans xmlns=http://springinpractice.com/schema/kite          ⟵┐  Default
    xmlns:aop="http://www.springframework.org/schema/aop"              │  namespace
    xmlns:beans="http://www.springframework.org/schema/beans"       ❶  declaration
    xmlns:context="http://www.springframework.org/schema/context"
    xmlns:p="http://www.springframework.org/schema/p"
    xmlns:util="http://www.springframework.org/schema/util"
    xmlns:xsi="http://www.w3.org/2001/XMLSchema-instance"           ❷  Schema
    xsi:schemaLocation="                                          ⟵    location
        http://www.springframework.org/schema/aop
        http://www.springframework.org/schema/aop/spring-aop-3.1.xsd
        http://www.springframework.org/schema/beans
        http://www.springframework.org/schema/beans/spring-beans-3.1.xsd
        http://www.springframework.org/schema/context
        http://www.springframework.org/schema/context/
                spring-context-3.1.xsd
        http://www.springframework.org/schema/util
        http://www.springframework.org/schema/util/spring-util-3.1.xsd
        http://springinpractice.com/schema/kite
        http://springinpractice.com/schema/kite/kite-1.0.xsd">

    <context:mbean-export />

    <circuit-breaker id="messageServiceBreaker" exceptionThreshold="4"   ⟵┐
        timeout="30000" />
                                                CircuitBreakerTemplate
                                                      definition  ❸
    <util:list id="guardList">
        <beans:ref bean="messageServiceBreaker" />
    </util:list>
                                                   ❹  GuardListInterceptor
    <guard-list-advice id="messageServiceGuardListAdvice"   ⟵    definition
        guards="guardList" />
                                                   ❺  AOP config
    <aop:config>                                  ⟵    untouched
        <aop:pointcut id="messageServicePointcut"
            expression="execution(* com.springinpractice.ch14.kite.sample.
                    service.impl.MessageServiceImpl.*(..))" />
        <aop:advisor advice-ref="messageServiceGuardListAdvice"
            pointcut-ref="messageServicePointcut" />
    </aop:config>
</beans:beans>
```

You may find it interesting to compare listing 14.26 to listing 14.20. Listing 14.26 is significantly cleaner, owing to the new custom namespace.

You declare the namespace ❶ and schema location ❷ just like you have to do with any namespace. You make the `kite` namespace the default because this configuration file focuses specifically on Kite components. You define the `CircuitBreakerTemplate` ❸ and `GuardListInterceptor` ❹ using custom tags that roughly resemble the explicit bean definitions they replace, although the advice definition conveniently hides the `GuardListSource` configuration. The AOP configuration remains untouched ❺.

There you have it. Although custom namespaces can certainly get more complicated, the techniques you've just learned provide a solid foundation for further study.

Discussion

Custom namespaces are a useful mechanism for limiting the complexity of XML-based configuration, which addresses a common criticism that Spring Framework friends and foes alike have leveled against Spring over the years. But there is an even more powerful approach you can use to limit complexity, and that's annotation-based configuration. This is the topic of the next recipe.

14.5   *Supporting annotation-based configuration*

PREREQUISITES
Recipe 14.1 Creating a circuit-breaker template and callback
Recipe 14.3 Supporting AOP-based configuration
Recipe 14.4 Supporting custom namespaces

KEY TECHNOLOGIES
Spring configuration infrastructure, Spring custom namespaces, Java 5 annotations

Background

We generally prefer declarative configuration to programmatic configuration because it's simpler and less invasive. In recipe 14.3, you added support for declarative configuration based on AOP. In this recipe we'll explore the other major approach that Spring-based frameworks often support, which is declarative configuration based on annotations.

Problem

Configure circuit breakers using Java 5 annotations.

Solution

This recipe extends the infrastructure you've already created to add support for annotation-based configuration. Annotations are popular in both Java in general and Spring in particular, and many framework users have come to expect support for annotation-based configuration.

Design-wise, there are different approaches you might take. Spring's transaction support, for instance, uses annotations to specify transaction attributes such as isolation and rollback behavior. For the circuit breaker, the annotation will target methods (not types), and it will reference the associated breaker by name. The intent is that each separate resource has its own circuit breaker, and each method accessing that resource will use that breaker.

We'll need to cover several steps, but the overall process is in line with what you've already done. The first thing you'll need, of course, is an annotation.

CREATING THE ANNOTATION

You create an annotation called @GuardedBy as follows.

Listing 14.27   GuardedBy.java for annotation-based configuration

```java
package com.springinpractice.ch14.kite;

import java.lang.annotation.Documented;
import java.lang.annotation.ElementType;
import java.lang.annotation.Retention;
import java.lang.annotation.RetentionPolicy;
import java.lang.annotation.Target;

@Target({ ElementType.METHOD })
@Retention(RetentionPolicy.RUNTIME)
@Documented
public @interface GuardedBy {

    String[] value() default "";
}
```

The annotation takes a single value, which is the name of the guard list guarding the annotated method.

Next you'll create a new GuardListSource implementation to source guards from annotations, along with a corresponding pointcut and advisor.

IMPLEMENTING A NEW CIRCUITBREAKERSOURCE AND POINTCUT

In recipe 14.3 you created a GuardListInterceptor class whose job was in essence to wrap method calls with guard lists. You could have injected guards directly into interceptors, but you instead created a GuardListSource abstraction to give you flexibility in sourcing the guards. The original DefaultGuardListSource implementation held a guard list and returned it on demand, and so to use it you would need to create a separate interceptor for each guard list.

For annotations you'll do something different. You'll still use the GuardListSource abstraction, but the new implementation will use the @GuardedBy annotation to discover the guard list instead of directly referencing it. In addition to enabling annotation-based configuration, this allows you to use a single interceptor across all guard lists instead of creating separate interceptors for each one. Figure 14.11 shows the source hierarchy.

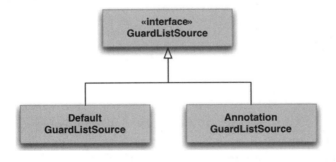

Figure 14.11   The GuardListSource **hierarchy, which includes two concrete implementations**

The following listing presents the new `AnnotationGuardListSource`.

Listing 14.28   AnnotationGuardListSource.java, for annotation-based sourcing

```java
package com.springinpractice.ch14.kite.interceptor;

import static org.springframework.util.Assert.notNull;

import java.io.Serializable;
import java.lang.reflect.AnnotatedElement;
import java.lang.reflect.Method;
import java.util.ArrayList;
import java.util.List;
import org.springframework.beans.BeansException;
import org.springframework.beans.factory.BeanFactory;
import org.springframework.beans.factory.BeanFactoryAware;
import org.springframework.core.BridgeMethodResolver;
import org.springframework.util.ClassUtils;
import com.springinpractice.ch14.kite.Guard;
import com.springinpractice.ch14.kite.GuardedBy;

public class AnnotationGuardListSource                              ❶ BeanFactory-
    implements GuardListSource, BeanFactoryAware, Serializable {       Aware

    private BeanFactory beanFactory;

    public void setBeanFactory(BeanFactory beanFactory)
        throws BeansException { this.beanFactory = beanFactory; }

    public List<Guard> getGuards(Method method, Class<?> targetClass) {
        notNull(method, "method can't be null");
        Method specificMethod =
            ClassUtils.getMostSpecificMethod(method, targetClass);   ❸ Handles
        specificMethod =                                                bridged
            BridgeMethodResolver.findBridgedMethod(specificMethod);     methods
        List<Guard> guards = parseAnnotation(specificMethod);
        return (guards != null ? guards : parseAnnotation(method));
    }

    private List<Guard> parseAnnotation(AnnotatedElement elem) {
        assert (elem != null);
        return parseAnnotation(elem.getAnnotation(GuardedBy.class));
    }

    private List<Guard> parseAnnotation(GuardedBy ann) {             ❺ Finds
        if (ann == null) { return null; }                              annotation
        List<Guard> guards = new ArrayList<Guard>();
        String[] guardNames = ann.value();
        for (String guardName : guardNames) {
            guards.add(beanFactory.getBean(guardName, Guard.class));
        }
        return guards;
    }
}
```

Finds most specific method ❷

Falls back to method ❹

This source is `BeanFactoryAware` ❶ so you can resolve the bean names embedded in the `@GuardedBy` value to actual guards. The `getGuards()` method finds the `@GuardedBy` annotation, if any, and returns the associated guards. First you use getMostSpecificMethod() ❷ to start the search with implementation methods; that is, you want to look for annotations on implementing methods before examining the corresponding interface methods.

The call to findBridgedMethod() ❸ deals with *bridge* and *bridged* methods. We won't go into the details of this advanced topic here, but suffice it to say that in certain situations (especially involving generics) the most specific method will be a bridge method, which won't have the annotation you're looking for. Instead you want to look for the annotation on the *bridged* method—that is, the method that the bridge method is bridging.

If the search for the annotation fails on the most specific method, you want to go back and check the passed method ❹. Usually this means looking at the interface method to see if the annotation is there.

The parseAnnotation() method ❺ is the one that looks up the guard list and returns it. If there's no annotation on the passed method, you return null.

The AnnotationGuardListSource gives the GuardListInterceptor a way to get a guard list according to the method being invoked. But you'll need to create a custom pointcut class as well. You didn't have to do that in recipe 14.3, but you have to do it here. The reason has to do with Spring's autoproxy mechanism, which you used implicitly in recipe 14.3 and which you'll use again here. In a nutshell, autoproxying figures out which advisors (aspects) apply to which beans by examining advisor pointcuts. In recipe 14.3 you used a pointcut expression to select the desired joinpoints, but here the placement of the @GuardedBy annotation determines the joinpoints. You have to give the autoproxying mechanism a pointcut that knows whether a given method has an associated guard list, indicating that a proxy must be created.

The GuardListSourcePointcut in listing 14.28 comes to the rescue. All you need is a pointcut with a reference to a GuardListSource. The next listing shows how to accomplish this.

Listing 14.29 GuardListSourcePointcut.java

```java
package com.springinpractice.ch14.kite.interceptor;

import java.io.Serializable;
import java.lang.reflect.Method;
import org.slf4j.Logger;
import org.slf4j.LoggerFactory;
import org.springframework.aop.support.StaticMethodMatcherPointcut;
import org.springframework.util.ObjectUtils;

public class GuardListSourcePointcut extends StaticMethodMatcherPointcut
    implements Serializable {

    private static final Logger log =
        LoggerFactory.getLogger(GuardListSourcePointcut.class);

    private GuardListSource source;                              Guard-list ❶ source

    public GuardListSource getSource() { return source; }

    public void setSource(GuardListSource source) { this.source = source; }
```

```
public boolean matches(Method method, Class<?> targetClass) {
    if (source == null) {
        throw new IllegalStateException("source can't be null");
    }
    boolean match = (source.getGuards(method, targetClass) != null);
    if (match) {
        log.debug("Found pointcut match for {}.{}",
            targetClass.getName(), method.getName());
    }
    return match;
}

public boolean equals(Object other) {
    if (this == other) { return true; }
    if (!(other instanceof GuardListSourcePointcut)) { return false; }
    GuardListSourcePointcut otherPc = (GuardListSourcePointcut) other;
    return ObjectUtils.nullSafeEquals(source, otherPc.source);
}

public int hashCode() {
    return GuardListSourcePointcut.class.hashCode();
}

public String toString() {
    return getClass().getName() + ": " + source;
}
}
```

❷ Tests for matches

The pointcut maintains a GuardListSource ❶ for getting a guard-list reference. The matches() method ❷ allows the autoproxy mechanism to determine whether a given method matches the pointcut, in which case a proxy would be created.

Following a general Spring convention, you'll create a new kite namespace element, <annotation-config>, to activate annotation-based configuration. Add the following element definition to kite-1.0.xsd:

```
<xsd:element name="annotation-config">
    <xsd:complexType>
        <xsd:attribute name="order" type="xsd:integer" />
    </xsd:complexType>
</xsd:element>
```

You'll also need a parser to parse that element. The parser, as you might expect, is much more involved than the element definition. This makes sense, of course, because the DSL aims to hide complex configurations from the app developer.

CREATING THE BEANDEFINITIONPARSER

The following listing shows the BeanDefinitionParser implementation responsible for parsing the new <annotation-config> element.

Listing 14.30   AnnotationConfigParser.java core

```
package com.springinpractice.ch14.kite.config.xml;

import org.slf4j.Logger;
import org.slf4j.LoggerFactory;
```

```
import org.springframework.aop.config.AopNamespaceUtils;
import org.springframework.aop.support.DefaultBeanFactoryPointcutAdvisor;
import org.springframework.beans.factory.config.BeanDefinition;
import org.springframework.beans.factory.config.RuntimeBeanReference;
import org.springframework.beans.factory.parsing.BeanComponentDefinition;
import org.springframework.beans.factory.parsing.
        CompositeComponentDefinition;
import org.springframework.beans.factory.support.BeanDefinitionRegistry;
import org.springframework.beans.factory.support.RootBeanDefinition;
import org.springframework.beans.factory.xml.BeanDefinitionParser;
import org.springframework.beans.factory.xml.ParserContext;
import org.w3c.dom.Element;
import com.springinpractice.ch14.kite.interceptor.
        AnnotationGuardListSource;
import com.springinpractice.ch14.kite.interceptor.GuardListInterceptor;
import com.springinpractice.ch14.kite.interceptor.GuardListSourcePointcut;

class AnnotationConfigParser implements BeanDefinitionParser {          Parser
    private static final String GUARD_LIST_ADV_BEAN_NAME =           ❶ implementation
        "com.springinpractice.ch14.kite.interceptor.
            internalGuardListAdvisor";
    private static final Logger log =
        LoggerFactory.getLogger(AnnotationConfigParser.class);

    public BeanDefinition parse(Element elem, ParserContext parserCtx) {
        new AopAutoProxyConfigurer(elem, parserCtx);
        return null;
    }
                                                                     ❷ Inner
    private static class AopAutoProxyConfigurer {                        class
        private final String tagName;
        private final ParserContext parserCtx;
        private final BeanDefinitionRegistry reg;                    ❸ For ordering
        private final Object src;                                       advisors
        private final int baseOrder;

        public AopAutoProxyConfigurer(Element elem,
            ParserContext parserCtx) {

            this.tagName = elem.getTagName();
            this.parserCtx = parserCtx;
            this.reg = parserCtx.getRegistry();                    Autoproxy  ❹
            this.src = parserCtx.extractSource(elem);              creator

            this.baseOrder = elem.hasAttribute("order") ?
                Integer.parseInt(elem.getAttribute("order")) : 0;
            AopNamespaceUtils
                .registerAutoProxyCreatorIfNecessary(parserCtx, elem);
            configureGuardList();
        }                                                          Test for guard- ❺
                                                                   list advisor
        private void configureGuardList() {
            if (reg.containsBeanDefinition(GUARD_LIST_ADV_BEAN_NAME)) {
                return;
            }                                                      ❻ Creates
                                                                      source
            RootBeanDefinition sdef =
                createDef(AnnotationGuardListSource.class);
```

```
       String sname = registerWithGeneratedName(sdef);

       RootBeanDefinition idef =                              Creates
           createDef(GuardListInterceptor.class);      7    interceptor
       addRuntimeProp(idef, "source", sname);
       String iname = registerWithGeneratedName(idef);

       RootBeanDefinition pdef =                              Creates
           createDef(GuardListSourcePointcut.class);   8    pointcut
       addRuntimeProp(pdef, "source", sname);
       String pname = registerWithGeneratedName(pdef);

       RootBeanDefinition adef =
           createDef(DefaultBeanFactoryPointcutAdvisor.class);
       addProp(adef, "adviceBeanName", iname);
       addRuntimeProp(adef, "pointcut", pname);        Creates advisor  9
       addOrderProp(adef, 0);
       reg.registerBeanDefinition(GUARD_LIST_ADV_BEAN_NAME, adef);

       doLogicalView(sdef, sname, idef, iname, adef,
           GUARD_LIST_ADV_BEAN_NAME);
   }

   ... helper methods in listing 14.31 ...
   }
}
```

The parser implements `BeanDefinitionParser` (figure 14.12) directly ❶ as opposed to using one of the base classes from table 14.1, just because the implementation is more complex than the base classes support. It's package-private because only `KiteNamespaceHandler` needs to access it, as you'll see. Basically, all the `parse()` method does is delegate to an autoproxy configurer (just its constructor really) and return a `null` bean definition.

You implement `AopAutoProxyConfigurer` as an inner class ❷. This is related to the distinction between class- and interface-based proxying. Class-based proxying doesn't use AOP, and so if you were to select class-based

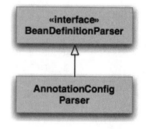

Figure 14.12   Complex parsers often implement **BeanDefinitionParser** directly.

proxying, you wouldn't want to load AOP-related classes. By isolating the AOP references to an inner class, the class-based approach can avoid loading the AOP classes by not using the inner class. As it happens, you aren't supporting the class-based approach here—you're supporting only interface-based proxies—but the implementation is set up to make it easy enough to add support for class-based proxying. See Spring's `AnnotationDrivenBeanDefinitionParser` class (part of Spring's transaction support) for an illustration showing how to do that.

Autoproxying needs to have some way to figure out how to order the different advisors it applies, whether those advisors are Kite advisors or some other type. For example, you'd generally want guard-list advisors to wrap transaction advisors rather than the other way around. To that end, the parser supports an `order` attribute that allows you to order Kite advisors relative to other advisors ❸. The value is a base order (default is 0), and each advisor is the base plus some offset determined by the component type; for example, circuit breakers have offset 0.

At ❹ you tell Spring to register the autoproxy creator if it hasn't already been registered by some other framework code, like the aforementioned transaction support. Then you launch into the guard-list configuration. If the guard-list advisor already exists, you return ❺. Otherwise, you create an annotation-based guard list source ❻, an interceptor ❼, a pointcut ❽, and an advisor ❾, using the following helper methods.

Listing 14.31 AopAutoProxyConfigurer.java helper methods

```java
private RootBeanDefinition createDef(Class<?> clazz) {
    RootBeanDefinition def = new RootBeanDefinition(clazz);      ❶ Sets definition
    def.setSource(src);                                               source
    def.setRole(BeanDefinition.ROLE_INFRASTRUCTURE);            ❷ Sets
    return def;                                                       bean role
}

private void addProp(RootBeanDefinition def, String name,      ❸ Sets bean
    Object value) {                                                 property

    def.getPropertyValues().add(name, value);
}

private void addRuntimeProp(RootBeanDefinition def, String name,  ❹ Sets bean
    String value) {                                                 reference

    addProp(def, name, new RuntimeBeanReference(value));
}

private void addOrderProp(RootBeanDefinition def, int offset) {  ❺ For ordering
    addProp(def, "order", baseOrder + offset);                       advisors
}

private String registerWithGeneratedName(RootBeanDefinition def) {
    return parserCtx.getReaderContext()
        .registerWithGeneratedName(def);            Autogenerates bean names ❻
}

private void doLogicalView(
        RootBeanDefinition sdef, String sname,
        RootBeanDefinition idef, String iname,
        RootBeanDefinition adef, String aname) {

    CompositeComponentDefinition ldef =
        new CompositeComponentDefinition(tagName, src);
    addComp(ldef, sdef, sname);
    addComp(ldef, idef, iname);
    addComp(ldef, adef, aname);
    parserCtx.registerComponent(ldef);
    log.info("Registered {} components", tagName);
}

private void addComp(CompositeComponentDefinition ldef,
    RootBeanDefinition def, String name) {

    ldef.addNestedComponent(
        new BeanComponentDefinition(def, name));
}
```

The `AopAutoProxyConfigurer` uses several helper methods to help keep the configurer's logic clear. The first helper creates a new definition, setting its source to the `<annotation-config>` element's source object ❶ and the role to mark it as an infrastructure bean ❷. (`BeanDefinition` also offers `ROLE_APPLICATION`, indicating a major application bean, and `ROLE_SUPPORT`, indicating a level of importance between a top-level application bean and a purely infrastructural bean that the user wouldn't care about.)

The `addProp()` helper method adds a name/value pair to the bean definition ❸. In the special case where the value is a bean reference, you can use `addRuntimeProp()`, which uses a `RuntimeBeanReference` to establish the link ❹. Also, at ❺ you provide a helper for setting an advisor's order, as explained.

In the cases of the source, interceptor, and pointcut beans, you don't care what the bean name is, so you use `registerWithGeneratedName()` to autogenerate names instead of having to provide them yourself ❻.

We're in the home stretch. Just a few more things to take care of to make the shiny new annotation-based configuration work. We'll take them one at a time.

UPDATING THE NAMESPACEHANDLER

Add the following registration to the `KiteNamespaceHandler.init()` method:

```
registerBeanDefinitionParser(
    "annotation-config", new AnnotationConfigParser());
```

That's it for the Kite part. Now you just need to update the client code and configuration.

UPDATING THE CLIENT CODE

For the client code, you add an annotation to the methods you want to protect.

Listing 14.32   MessageServiceImpl.java, with annotations

```java
package com.springinpractice.ch14.kite.sample.service.impl;

import java.util.ArrayList;
import java.util.List;
import javax.inject.Inject;
import org.springframework.stereotype.Service;
import com.springinpractice.ch14.kite.GuardedBy;
import com.springinpractice.ch14.kite.sample.model.Message;
import com.springinpractice.ch14.kite.sample.service.MessageService;

@Service
public class MessageServiceImpl implements MessageService {
    @Inject private Flakinator flakinator;

    @GuardedBy({ "messageServiceBreaker" })
    public Message getMotd() {
        flakinator.simulateFlakiness();
        return createMessage("<p>Welcome to Aggro's Towne!</p>");
    }

    @GuardedBy({ "messageServiceBreaker" })
    public List<Message> getImportantMessages() {
```

```
        flakinator.simulateFlakiness();
        List<Message> messages = new ArrayList<Message>();
        messages.add(createMessage("<p>Important message 1</p>"));
        messages.add(createMessage("<p>Important message 2</p>"));
        messages.add(createMessage("<p>Important message 3</p>"));
        return messages;
    }

    private Message createMessage(String htmlText) {
        Message message = new Message();
        message.setHtmlText(htmlText);
        return message;
    }
}
```

This configuration protects the getMotd() and getImportantMessages() methods
using the messageServiceBreaker breaker you've already defined. But you must
update the beans-kite.xml configuration to activate the annotations.

UPDATING THE CLIENT CONFIGURATION
In the next listing you replace the explicit AOP configuration with the new <annota-
tion-config> element you just created.

Listing 14.33   beans-kite.xml, updated for annotations

```
<?xml version="1.0" encoding="UTF-8"?>
<beans:beans xmlns="http://springinpractice.com/schema/kite"
    xmlns:beans="http://www.springframework.org/schema/beans"
    xmlns:context="http://www.springframework.org/schema/context"
    xmlns:p="http://www.springframework.org/schema/p"
    xmlns:xsi="http://www.w3.org/2001/XMLSchema-instance"
    xsi:schemaLocation="
        http://www.springframework.org/schema/beans
        http://www.springframework.org/schema/beans/spring-beans-3.1.xsd
        http://www.springframework.org/schema/context
        http://www.springframework.org/schema/context/
                spring-context-3.1.xsd
        http://springinpractice.com/schema/kite
        http://springinpractice.com/schema/kite/kite-1.0.xsd">

    <context:mbean-export />
    <annotation-config />
    <circuit-breaker id="messageServiceBreaker"
        exceptionThreshold="4"
        timeout="30000" />
</beans:beans>
```

This configuration style is very much along the lines offered by Spring transaction
support, Spring Integration, and so forth. The <annotation-config> element causes
the AnnotationConfigParser to kick in, thanks to the registration you added to Kite-
NamespaceHandler. Then the parser creates the source, interceptor, pointcut, and
advisor as you saw in listing 14.30.

Discussion

Annotation-based configuration is one of the key configuration styles in Spring, and now you know how to roll your own. Although annotation-based configuration doesn't have to involve a custom namespace, it typically does. You normally define one or more custom annotations, along with a custom namespace, a parser, and bean definitions to handle converting configuration into actual annotation-processing machinery.

You may have noticed that the more sophisticated (from a framework development perspective) configuration approaches build on the simpler ones. This is, of course, by design. You started with a template and then built an AOP-based approach off of that by using the template from an interceptor. Similarly, the annotation-based configuration uses annotations to decide where to apply interceptors. This is a common way of building Spring-based frameworks.

Whether you use annotation-based configuration is largely a matter of style, and your preference may vary depending on what's being configured. You might feel, for instance, that it's nice to be able to see your circuit-breaker annotations right where they're being used. Or you might instead prefer to manage such configuration centrally using the techniques from recipe 14.3. It's up to you.

14.6   *Summary*

We've completed our foray into the world of implementing Spring-based frameworks. We covered creating template methods, AOP- and annotation-based configuration, custom namespaces, and integration with SpringSource Tool Suite. We also looked at JMX and some interesting concurrent programming concepts along the way. Although creating a framework isn't necessarily the kind of thing a developer does every day, sometimes it's exactly what you want to do. Spring provides such powerful framework-building infrastructure and idioms that it pays to know how to use them. And even if you don't plan to roll your own framework anytime soon, it can help you as a user of the Spring Framework to understand how things work under the hood.

This chapter brings us almost to the end of the book. We hope you've enjoyed reading it as much as we've enjoyed writing it. We welcome any comments, questions or thoughts you may have for us:

- Manning author forum: www.manning.com/wheeler/
- Spring in Practice blog: http://springinpractice.com/

We look forward to hearing from you, and thanks for reading.

appendix
Working with the sample code

This appendix explains how this book's sample code is organized and how to configure it. These are areas where we had to come up with some kind of sensible scheme to support the needs of the book, and that scheme may not be completely transparent at first glance.

A.1   IDE and environment setup

As regards the IDE, we used the Spring Tool Suite for the development of this book, which is essentially a branded version of Eclipse with additional support for Spring-based development. You can of course use your preferred IDE. Although we can't speak to the details of what you'll need when using standard Eclipse, IntelliJ IDEA, NetBeans, or other IDEs, in general you'll need the following:

- Maven support
- Git support, if you plan to use Git to work with the code

Spring-specific support (such as bean-dependency graphs, Spring AOP, configuration files, custom configuration views for Spring Integration, Spring Web Flow, and so on) isn't strictly required, but you'll find it very helpful. The major Java IDEs all have Spring-specific support, either built in or as a plug-in. Consult your IDE documentation for details.

In terms of your broader system environment, you'll need to install Maven, and Git if you want to use it.

A.2   How the code is organized

The book's code is organized as a set of Git repositories managed at GitHub. The projects are all Maven projects conforming to Maven's conventions around internal project structure.

514 APPENDIX *Working with the sample code*

Most of the repositories are per-chapter repositories with names like sip01 and sip02. Each per-chapter repository has per-recipe branches with names like 01, 02, and so on. In addition, there are tags representing released versions of the recipe code. They have names like recipe_7.1-1.0 (recipe 7.1, version 1.0).

One of the repositories is a top-level project, called sip-top, that factors out what's common to the chapter repositories, such as dependencies and plug-ins. It's a multi-module project with support for Hibernate, JPA, DAOs, and web app development. There is also a Spring Modules JCR repository that we use in chapter 12.

From time to time we may release bug fixes or even enhancements. These may appear as new tags on existing branches, or they may appear as entirely new branches if the changes diverge from what's in the book. In the event of changes that conflict with what's in the book, we'll indicate this in the branch and tag names using *alt*. For example, an alternative version of recipe 4 will have a branch called 04-alt.

A.3 *Getting the code*

The source code is available at https://github.com/springinpractice. You have a couple of options for downloading the code.

OPTION 1: DOWNLOAD THE TARBALL OR ZIP

If you're not already familiar with Git, then the easiest option is to go to the GitHub site, download the tarball or ZIP file for a given tag, and import it into your IDE. The downloads are all Maven projects, so you should import your project as a Maven project.

OPTION 2: CLONE THE GIT REPOSITORY

If you're familiar with Git and GitHub, then perhaps a better option is to fork the various repositories and create local clones. This will give you more flexibility in working with the code.

Suppose your GitHub username is "felix" and you've forked the sip13 repo. Here's how you can create a local clone of that fork:

```
git clone
git@github.com:felix/sip13.git
```

This checks out the master branch, making it locally available.

If you want to switch to the branch for recipe 1, then go into the clone's directory and type the following:

```
git checkout 01
```

You can see a list of all the branches (local and remote) by typing

```
git branch -a
```

Information about using Git and GitHub is beyond the scope of this book, but a great deal of high-quality Git documentation is available both online and in book form.

Next we'll look at how to build the code.

A.4 *Building the code*

We use Maven for the projects in this book. If you aren't familiar with Maven, you'll find it useful (and probably necessary) to look for a quick online tutorial to get you up to speed on the basics.

Most of the projects in this book are small, single-module web applications. Here are the commands most useful for this book:

- `mvn clean`—Cleans the build
- `mvn compile`—Compiles the source code
- `mvn package`—Packages the compiled source code (executes the compile phase automatically)
- `mvn jetty:run`—Runs the app (discussed shortly)

Most of the chapters don't include unit tests, so even though `mvn test` is useful in general, we don't use it much in this book. The same is true for integration tests. Note however that we do have a recipe on unit tests and an entire chapter (chapter 10) on integration testing. In those special cases, the recipes explain how to run the relevant tests.

Chapters 11, 13, and 14 are multimodule projects, as is the top-level sip-top project. Here you'll need the following additional command:

- `mvn install`—Installs packages into the local Maven repo

For example, you'll need to run `mvn install` in the sip-top project to make the packages it generates visible to the other projects, which all depend upon the sip-top packages.

We use Maven to support configuration as well. The next section explains how this works.

A.5 *Configuring the app*

The projects are set up to work with externalized configuration files. That means you should be able to download the source code and place some configuration files in a location *outside* the project, and the app should run. This decoupling keeps environment-specific configuration out of source control and makes it easier to refresh your project without losing your configuration.

It works by adding an external file path to the Jetty plug-in's configuration. This allows the plug-in to find jetty-env.xml (JNDI resource configurations, among other things) as well as environment-specific app configuration files that need to be on the classpath. The sip-top project already handles this for you; see sip-top/pom.xml. But you'll need to provide a base path to allow the plug-in to find the various configuration files we just mentioned.

To do this, you'll need to create a Maven settings.xml file in your local .m2 Maven repo, if you don't already have one. The .m2 folder is typically in the user directory (it may be hidden). The settings.xml file appears directly underneath the .m2 folder. Here's a sample .m2/settings.xml file:

```
<?xml version="1.0" encoding="utf-8"?>
<settings>
    <profiles>
        <profile>
            <id>default</id>
            <properties>
                <sip.conf.dir>
                    /Users/williewheeler/projects/sip/conf
                </sip.conf.dir>
            </properties>
        </profile>
    </profiles>
    <activeProfiles>
        <activeProfile>default</activeProfile>
    </activeProfiles>
</settings>
```

(See the online Maven documentation for more information about settings.xml: http://maven.apache.org/settings.html.)

The /Users/williewheeler/projects/sip/conf directory is obviously specific to our example development environment; use whichever root folder you want to use.

Once you have this set up, the sample code will expect you to create chapter-specific folders in your root configuration folder. To give you an idea what this looks like, here's an example subset of configuration folders and files relative to the configuration root:

```
./sip08
./sip08/classes
./sip08/classes/log4j.xml
./sip08/classes/spring
./sip08/classes/spring/contactService.properties
./sip08/classes/spring/mailingListService.properties
./sip08/jetty-env.xml
./sip09
./sip09/classes
./sip09/classes/log4j.xml
./sip09/classes/spring
./sip09/classes/spring/environment.properties
./sip09/jetty-env.xml
```

You don't have to do them all up front. You can set up the folder for chapter 5 when you are working with chapter 5.

The Jetty plug-in configuration for any given project knows how to find the classpath resources (log4j.xml, various environment-specific properties files, and so on). In addition, projects that use jetty-env.xml know to find it at the top of the chapter-specific folders.

Most of the recipes have a top-level folder called sample_conf that shows you which files you need to put in the chapter configuration folders. Copy the contents of sample_conf into the chapter-specific folder before working through a chapter's first recipe, preserving its internal structure. Then modify the externalized configuration as needed. As you progress through the chapter's recipes, modify your configuration to reflect any additions to files in sample_conf. In general, these should be purely additive, meaning that if you decide to run something in recipe 1 against the configuration in recipe 5, it should still work.

You shouldn't need to modify the files in sample_conf, and you shouldn't need to copy them into the project.

A.6 *Running the app*

Use the Maven Jetty plug-in to run the app. All you have to do is type

```
mvn jetty:run
```

from the project or module whose WAR you want to run. If you want to clean the code before building and running it, you can type

```
mvn clean jetty:run
```

In most cases, you can then access the application by pointing your browser at http:// localhost:8080/sip/. There are some instances where that's not true; in those cases, the book gives explicit instruction on which URLs to use.

index

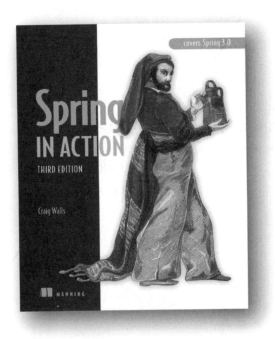

Spring in Action, Third Edition
by Craig Walls

ISBN: 978-1-935182-35-1
424 pages
$49.99
June 2011

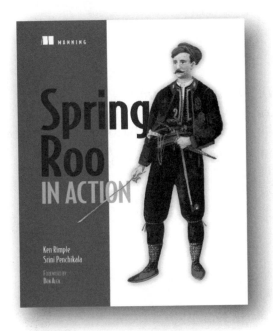

Spring Roo in Action
by Ken Rimple, Srini Penchikala

ISBN: 978-1-935182-96-2
408 pages
$49.99
April 2012

MORE TITLES FROM MANNING

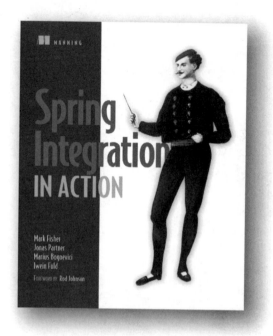

Spring Integration in Action
by Mark Fisher, Jonas Partner, Marius
   Bogoevici, and Iwein Fuld

   ISBN: 978-1-935182-43-6
   368 pages
   $49.99
   September 2012

Spring Batch in Action
by Arnaud Cogoluegnes, Thierry Templier,
   Gary Gregory, Olivier Bazoud

   ISBN: 978-1-935182-95-5
   504 pages
   $59.99
   October 2011

For ordering information go to www.manning.com